WITHDRAWN FROM
OHIO UNIVERSITY

PAPERS FROM THE 6th ICHL

AMSTERDAM STUDIES IN THE THEORY AND HISTORY OF LINGUISTIC SCIENCE

General Editor
E. F. KONRAD KOERNER
(University of Ottawa)

Series IV – CURRENT ISSUES IN LINGUISTIC THEORY

Advisory Editorial Board

Henning Andersen (Copenhagen); Raimo Anttila (Los Angeles) Tomaz V. Gamkrelidze (Tiflis); Hans-Heinrich Lieb (Berlin); J. Peter Maher (Chicago); Ernst Pulgram (Ann Arbor, Mich.); E. Wyn Roberts (Vancouver, B. C.); Danny Steinberg (Honolulu)

Volume 34

Jacek Fisiak, ed.

Papers from the 6th International Conference on Historical Linguistics

PAPERS
from the
6th International Conference
on
Historical Linguistics

edited by

JACEK FISIAK
Adam Mickiewicz University, Poznań

JOHN BENJAMINS PUBLISHING COMPANY
ADAM MICKIEWICZ UNIVERSITY PRESS

1985

TO
THE MEMORY OF
JERZY KURYŁOWICZ (1895 - 1978)
and
LUDWIK ZABROCKI (1907 - 1977)

Library of Congress Cataloging in Publication Data

International Conference on Historical Linguistics (6th: 1983: Poznań, Poland)
   Papers from the 6th International Conference on Historical Linguistics.

(Amsterdam studies in the theory and history of linguistic science. Series IV, Current issues in linguistic theory, ISSN 0304-0763; v. 34)
Bibliography: p.
Includes indexes.
1. Historical linguistics -- Congresses. I. Fisiak, Jacek. II. Title. III. Series.
P140.I5   1983   410   85-13465
ISBN 90-272-3528-7 (alk. paper)

© Copyright 1985 - John Benjamins B.V./Adam Mickiewicz University Press.
No part of this book may be reproduced in any form, by print, photoprint, microfilm, or any other means, without written permission from the publisher.

CONTENTS

Preface	IX
List of participants	XI
Conference programme	XVII
Henrik Birnbaum: Divergence and convergence in linguistic evolution	1
Lyle Campbell: Areal linguistics and its implications for historical linguistics	25
Andrew Carstairs: Paradigm economy in Latin nouns	57
C. J. Conradie: Ablaut: a Phoenix in the history of Afrikaans	71
Andrei Danchev: An analysis and synthesis in sound change	83
Wolfgang U. Dressler and Veneeta Acson: On the diachrony of subtractive operations: evidence for semiotically based models of Natural Phonology and Natural Morphology from Northern Anatolian Greek dialects	105
Thomas Fraser: Did Old English have a middle voice?	129
Hubert Gburek: The vowel /a:/ in English	139
Louis Goossens: Framing the linguistic actions scene in Old and Present-Day English: CWEþAN, SECGAN, SP(R)ECAN and Present-Day English SPEAK, TALK, SAY and TELL compared	149
Rita de Grandis: Lexical restructuring: rule loss versus rule intersection; evidence from Italian	171
Jadranka Gvozdanović: Theories of sound change fail if they try to predict too much	183
Hubert Haider: Chance and necessity in diachronic syntax — word order typologies and the position of Modern Persian relative clauses	199
Camiël Hamans: Umlaut as a harmony process	217
Martin Harris: Divergent patterns of word order in contemporary French	235
Robert K. Herbert: Articulatory modes and typological universals: the puzzle of Bantu ejectives and aspirates	251
Raymond Hickey: Velar segments in Old English and Old Irish	267

Eugene Holman: On the semasiologization of phonological rules: the semiotic evolution of Finnish consonant gradation 281
Ernst Håkon Jahr: Another explanation for the development of *s* before *l* in Norwegian 291
Kurt R. Jankowsky: Wilhelm Scherer's *Zur Geschichte der deutschen Sprache*: a milestone in 19th-century linguistics 301
Brian D. Joseph: Proto-Indo-European consonantism: methodological and further typological concerns 313
E. F. Konrad Koerner: The place of Saussurre's *Memoire* in the development of historical linguistics 323
Witold Mańczak: Indo-European numerals and the sexagesimal system 347
T. L. Markey: Absolute versus relative comparison: typology and development 353
Marianne Mithun: Diachronic morphologization: the circumstances surrounding the birth, growth and decline of noun incorporation 365
Ruta Nagucka: For a diachrony-in-synchrony analysis 394
Fred C. C. Peng: On the possible clusters of *mb*, *nd*, and *ŋg* in Proto-Japanese 409
Anna Giacolone Ramat: Are there dysfunctional changes? . . . 427
Jens E. Rasmussen: The Indo-European origin of the Balto-Slavic -ē- and -a- preterite 441
Suzanne Romaine: Variability in word formation patterns and productivity in the history of English 451
Edgar W. Schneider: Regional variation in 19th century Black English in the American South 467
Johan Taeldeman: Rule ordering and the dynamics of diatopic language variation 489
Moshé Taube: Le développement d'un auxiliaire modal en yiddish: *lozn* 'laiser' 499
Elizabeth Closs Traugott: Confrontation and association. . . . 515
Theo Vennemann: The bifurcation theory of the Germanic and German consonant shifts: synopsis and some further thoughts 527
S. Paul Verluyten: Prosodic structures and the development of French schwa 549
Wolfgang Viereck: On the origins and developments of American English 561
Bogdan Walczak: Quelques problèmes des recherches étymologiques sur les emprunts lexicaux 571

Wolfgang U. Wurzel: Morphologische Natürlichkeit und morphologischer Wandel. Zur Vorhersagbarkeit von Sprachveränderungen 587
Anders Ahlqvist: Summing up 601
Index of languages 607
Index of names 612

PREFACE

The 6th International Conference on Historical Linguistics took place in Poznań, Poland from August 22 to 26, 1983. The Conference was organized by the Department of English at Adam Mickiewicz University (Poznań) and was attended by 163 linguists from 26 countries. Unfortunately many colleagues who had already registered, cancelled their participation very late causing considerable inconvenience to the organizers, which can be easily inferred from the programme printed below.

Despite numerous cancellations enough papers were offered to require the organization of parallel sessions. The abstracts of papers presented at the conference were submitted for assessment to a committee (A. Ahlqvist, H. Andersen, L. Campbell, M. B. Harris, E. F. K. Koerner, A. G. Ramat, J. Fisiak) prior to the conference and the final decision as to which papers should be included in the programme was based on these recommendations.

The present volume contains a selection of papers read at the conference and two papers which were not presented but which had been sent earlier. (Their authors notified the organizers about their inability to participate and met all the financial obligations resulting from their decision.) The editor would here like to express his deep gratitude to all who have sent their comments on the papers included in the present volume, and in particular to E. F. K. Koerner for a prompt reaction in sending his own penetrating observations.

The Conference was preceded by a workshop on sociohistorical linguistics organized by S. Romaine and E. C. Traugott. Papers from this workshop will appear in a volume of *Folia Linguistica Historica*. The workshop was a great success and contributed meaningfully to promoting further this particular aspect of historical linguistics. The organizers of the 6th International Conference on Historical Linguistics are grateful to S. Romaine and E. C. Traugott for bringing the workshop to Poznań.

The 6th International Conference on Historical Linguistics could not have taken place without a substantial subsidy from Adam Mickiewicz

University. It is therefore our great pleasure to express our thanks to the Rector and the administration of the University for all the aid rendered to the conference organizers.

Last but not least our thanks go to all our colleagues from the Department of English for their invaluable help and personal involvement in the smooth running of the conference and in particular to Miss Barbara Płocińska and Mrs. Danuta Trawczyńska for their devotion to the cause of the conference running far above the call of duty.

Jacek Fisiak

Poznań, January 1984

LIST OF PARTICIPANTS

Adamska-Sałaciak, Arleta, A. Mickiewicz University, POZNAŃ, Poland
Ahlqvist, Anders, University College, GALWAY, Ireland
Ampel, Teresa, Pedagogical University, RZESZÓW, Poland
Awedyk, Wiesław, A. Mickiewicz University, POZNAŃ, Poland
Baghdikian, Sonia, Université Libre de Bruxelles, BRUXELLES, Belgium
Bańczerowski, Jerzy, A. Mickiewicz University, POZNAŃ, Poland
Beard, Robert E., Bucknell University, LEWISBURG, USA
Bednarczuk, Leszek, Pedagogical University, CRACOW, Poland
Birnbaum, Henrik, University of California, LOS ANGELES, USA
Bojarczak, Andrzej, University of Wrocław, WROCŁAW, Poland
Boij, G. E., Free University, AMSTERDAM, Holland
Breivik, Leiv Egil, University of Tromsø, TROMSØ, Norway
Bugarski, Ranko, University of Belgrade, BELGRADE, Yugoslavia
Campbell, Lyle, University of Mexico, MEXICO CITY, Mexico
Carstairs, Andrew D., University of Canterbury, CHRISTCHURCH, New Zealand
Chafe, Wallace, University of California, BERKELEY, USA
Charęzińska, Anna, M. Curie-Skłodowska University, LUBLIN, Poland
Christoffersen, Marit, Agder Distriktshøgskole, KRISTIANRAND, Norway
Conradie, C. J., Rand Afrikaans University, JOHANNESBURG, South Africa
Cygan, Jan, University of Wrocław, WROCŁAW, Poland
Danchev, Andrei, Institute for Foreign Students, SOFIA, Bulgaria
Danielsen, Niels, University of Odense, ODENSE, Denmark
Dressler, Wolfgang U., University of Vienna, VIENNA, Austria
Droździał, Krystyna, A. Mickiewicz University, POZNAŃ, Poland
Dziubalska, Katarzyna, A. Mickiewicz University, POZNAŃ, Poland
Eliasson, Stig, Uppsala University, UPPSALA, Sweden
Enkvist, Nils Erik, Åbo Akademi, ÅBO, Finland

Ezawa, Kennosuke, University of Tübingen, TÜBINGEN, Federal Republic of Germany
Fehling, Detlev, University of Kiel, KIEL, Federal Republic of Germany
Fisiak, Jacek, A. Mickiewicz University, POZNAŃ, Poland
Forbes, Isabel, The Queen's University, BELFAST, U.K.
Fraser, Thomas, University of Lille III, LILLE, France
Funk, Wolf-Peter, Humboldt University, BERLIN, German Democratic Republic
Gburek, Hubert, University of Erlangen-Nürnberg, ERLANGEN, Federal Republic of Germany
Göller, Karl Heinz, University of Regensburg, REGENSBURG, Federal Republic of Germany
Goossens, Louis, University of Antwerp, ANTWERP, Belgium
Górska, Elżbieta, A. Mickiewicz University, POZNAŃ, Poland
de Graaf, Tjeerd, University of Groningen, GRONINGEN, Holland
Grala, Maria, A. Mickiewicz University, POZNAŃ, Poland
de Grandis, Rita, Simon Fraser University, BURNABY, Canada
Gruchmanowa, Monika, A. Mickiewicz University, POZNAŃ, Poland
Grüner, Rolf Werner, University of the Orange Free State, BLOEMFONTEIN, South Africa
Gvozdanović, Jadranka, University of Amsterdam, AMSTERDAM, Holland
Hagland, Jan Ragnar, University of Trondheim, TRONDHEIM, Norway
Haider, Hubert, University of Vienna, VIENNA, Austria
Hamans, Camiel, University of Leiden, LEIDEN, Holland
Hamp, Eric P., University of Chicago, CHICAGO, USA
Hansen, Finn, University of Aarhus, AARHUS, Denmark
Harris, Martin, University of Salford, SALFORD, U.K.
Hasiuk, Michał, A. Mickiewicz University, POZNAŃ, Poland
Hentschel, Gerd, University of Cracow, CRACOW, Poland
Herbert-Nykiel, Barbara, POZNAŃ, Poland
Herbert, Robert K., SUNY at Binghamton, BINGHAMTON, USA
Hickey, Raymond, University of Bonn, BONN, Federal Republic of Germany
Holman, Eugene, University of Helsinki, HELSINKI, Finland
Horn, George, University of Newcastle, NEWCASTLE, Australia
Horne, Merle, A., University of Lund, LUND, Sweden
Jahr, Ernst Håkon, University of Tromsø, TROMSØ, Norway
Janicki, Karol, A. Mickiewicz University, POZNAŃ, Poland
Jankowska, Aleksandra, A. Mickiewicz University, POZNAŃ, Poland

Jankowski, Michał, A. Mickiewicz University, POZNAŃ, Poland
Jankowsky, Kurt R., Georgetown University, WASHINGTON, D. C., USA
Janssen, Anke, University of Regensburg, REGENSBURG, Federal Republic of Germany
Jaworski, Adam, A. Mickiewicz University, POZNAŃ, Poland
Job, Michael, Ruhr University, BOCHUM, Federal Republic of Germany
Kallen, Jeffrey, T., Trinity College, DUBLIN, Ireland
Karlsson, Fred, University of Helsinki, HELSINKI, Finland
Kastovsky, Dieter, University of Vienna, VIENNA, Austria
Kilani-Schoch, Marianne, University of Lausanne, LAUSANNE, Switzerland
Kleparski, Grzegorz, Catholic University, LUBLIN, Poland
Kniezsa, Veronika, University of Budapest, BUDAPEST, Hungary
Koerner, E. F. Konrad, University of Ottawa, OTTAWA, Canada
Kolbuszewski, Stanisław F., A. Mickiewicz University, POZNAŃ, Poland
Kopytko, Roman, A. Mickiewicz University, POZNAŃ, Poland
Kryk, Barbara, A. Mickiewicz University, POZNAŃ, Poland
Krzyżanowski, Henryk, A. Mickiewicz University, POZNAŃ, Poland
Krzyżyński, Janusz, A. Mickiewicz University, POZNAŃ, Poland
Kuczyński, Andrzej, A. Mickiewicz University, POZNAŃ, Poland
Kytö, Merja, University of Helsinki, HELSINKI, Finland
Larsen, Erik Vive, University of Aarhus, AARHUS, Denmark
Łęska, Iwona, A. Mickiewicz University, POZNAŃ, Poland
Lewandowska-Tomaszczyk, Barbara, Łódź University, ŁÓDŹ, Poland
Lubbe, H. J., University of the Orange Free State, BLOEMFONTEIN, South Africa
Lüdtke, Helmut, University of Kiel, KIEL, Federal Republic of Germany
Mackiewicz-Krassowska, Halina, University of Gdańsk, GDAŃSK, Poland
Malicka-Kleparska, Anna, Catholic University, LUBLIN, Poland
Mańczak, Witold, University of Cracow, CRACOW, Poland
Marcos-Míarn, Francisco, University of Madrid, MADRID, Spain
Marton, Waldemar, A. Mickiewicz University, POZNAŃ, Poland
Mausch, Hanna, A. Mickiewicz University, POZNAŃ, Poland
Mettinger, Arthur, University of Vienna, VIENNA, Austria
Miękisz, Maria, University of Wrocław, WROCŁAW, Poland
Miller, Michael I., Virginia Commonwealth University, RICHMOND, USA

LIST OF PARTICIPANTS

Mithun, Marianne, SUNY, ALBANY, USA
Moessner, Lilo, University of Freiburg, FREIBURG, Federal Republic of Germany
Mugdan, Joachim, University of Münster, MÜNSTER, Federal Republic of Germany
Nagucka, Ruta, University of Cracow, CRACOW, Poland
Nevanlinna, Saara, University of Helsinki, HELSINKI, Finland
Niedzielski, Henryk, University of Hawaii, HONOLULU, USA
Ó Buachalla, Brendan, University College, DUBLIN, Ireland
Ó Cléirigh, Conn, University College, DUBLIN, Ireland
Ó Gandhra, Nollaig, Galway Regional College, GALWAY, Ireland
Outakoski, Tesma, University of Helsinki, HELSINKI, Finland
Panzer, Baldur, Heidelberg University, HEIDELBERG, Federal Republic of Germany
Peng, Fred C. C., International Christian University, TOKYO, Japan
Płocińska, Barbara, A. Mickiewicz University, POZNAŃ, Poland
Przywarska, Wanda, A. Mickiewicz University, POZNAŃ, Poland
Puppel, Stanisław, A. Mickiewicz University, POZNAŃ, Poland
Ramat, Anna Giacolone, University of Pavia, PAVIA, Italy
Rasiński, Ryszard, A. Mickiewicz University, POZNAŃ, Poland
Rasmussen, Jens Elmegaard, University of Copenhagen, COPENHAGEN, Denmark
Rękawek, Monika, University of Warsaw, WARSAW, Poland
Rensch, Karl H., Australian National University, CANBERRA, Australia
Rindal, Magnus, University of Bergen, BERGEN, Norway
Rissanen, Matti, University of Helsinki, HELSINKI, Finland
Rockel, Martin, Humboldt University, BERLIN, German Democratic Republic
Romaine, Suzanne, University of Birmingham, BIRMINGHAM, U.K.
Róna-Tas, A., Jozsef Attila University, SZEGED, Hungary
Rubach, Jerzy, University of Warsaw, WARSAW, Poland
Ruszkiewicz, Piotr, University of Silesia, KATOWICE, Poland
Saari, Mirja, University of Turku, TURKU, Finland
Sadalska, Genowefa, University of Cracow, CRACOW, Poland
Sawala, Krzysztof, A. Mickiewicz University, POZNAŃ, Poland
Schaller, Helmut, University of Marburg, MARBURG, Federal Republic of Germany
Schaner-Woles, Ch., University of Vienna, VIENNA, Austria

Schendl, Herbert, University of Vienna, VIENNA, Austria
Schneider, Edgar W., University of Bamberg, BAMBERG, Federal Republic of Germany
Schrandt, Heinrich, Max Hueber Verlag, MUNICH, Federal Republic of Germany
Sobkowiak, Włodzimierz, A. Mickiewicz University, POZNAŃ, Poland
Sroka, Kazimierz, University of Gdańsk, GDAŃSK, Poland
Stefański, Witold, A. Mickiewicz University, POZNAŃ, Poland
Steffen-Batogowa, Maria, A. Mickiewicz University, POZNAŃ, Poland
Stein, Dieter, University of Giessen, GIESSEN, Federal Republic of Germany
Straková, Vlasta, Czech Academy of Sciences, PRAGUE, Czechoslovakia
Swan, Toril, University of Tromsø, TROMSØ, Norway
Szpyra, Jolanta, M. Curie-Skłodowska University, LUBLIN, Poland
Szwedek, Aleksander, Pedagogical University, BYDGOSZCZ, Poland
Szymanek, Bogdan, M. Curie-Skłodowska University, LUBLIN, Poland
Taeldeman, Johan, State University of Ghent, GHENT, Belgium
Tamuro, Kunihiko, SAGAMIHARA, Japan
Thrane, Torben, University of Copenhagen, COPENHAGEN, Denmark
Tiisala, Seija, University of Helsinki, HELSINKI, Finland
Tomaszczyk, Jerzy, Łódź University, ŁÓDŹ, Poland
Tomaszewicz, Ewa, University of Wrocław, WROCŁAW, Poland
Tomić-Mišeska, Olga, University of Skopje, SKOPJE, Yugoslavia
Traugott, Elizabeth Closs, Stanford University, STANFORD, USA
Trawczyńska, Danuta, A. Mickiewicz University, POZNAŃ, Poland
Veenker Wolfgang University of Hamburg, HAMBURG, Federal of Republic of Germany
Vennemann Theo, University of Munich, MUNICH, Federal Republic of Germany
Verluyten, Paul S., University of Antwerp, ANTWERP, Belgium
Viereck, Wolfgang, University of Bamberg, BAMBERG, Federal Republic of Germany
Walczak, Bogdan, A. Mickiewicz University, POZNAŃ, Poland
Wegner, Alicja, A. Mickiewicz University, POZNAŃ, Poland
Weichert, Adam, A. Mickiewicz University, POZNAŃ, Poland
Wierzchowski, Józef, University of Warsaw, WARSAW, Poland
Winter, Werner, University of Kiel, KIEL, Federal Republic of Germany
Wurzel, Wolfgang U., Academy of Sciences, BERLIN, German Democratic Republic
Wysocka, Hanna, A. Mickiewicz University, POZNAŃ, Poland

Zabrocki, Tadeusz, A. Mickiewicz University, POZNAŃ, Poland
Żarski, Waldemar, University of Wrocław, WROCŁAW, Poland
Zbierska, Anna, A. Mickiewicz University, POZNAŃ, Poland
Zimmermann, Rüdiger, University of Marburg, MARBURG, Federal Republic of Germany
Ziółkowska, Maria, A. Mickiewicz University, POZNAŃ, Poland

CONFERENCE PROGRAMME

SUNDAY, August 21
09.00 Registration

MONDAY, August 22
09.00 Opening of the conference by Pro-Rector of A. Mickiewicz University Professor Stefan Paszyc and Professor Jacek Fisiak, President of International Society for Historical Linguistics
09.30 Anna Giacolone Ramat (Pavia): Are there dysfunctional changes? (CHAIR: JACEK FISIAK)

SECTION I
CHAIR: KURT JANKOWSKY

10.15 Andrew Carstairs (Christchurch): Paradigm economy in Latin nouns
10.50 Henrik Birnbaum (Los Angeles): Divergence and convergence in linguistic evolution

SECTION II
CHAIR: LYLE CAMPBELL

10.15 Marianne Mithun (Albany): Diachronic morphologization: the circumstances surrounding the birth, growth and decline of noun incorporation

11.25 BREAK

SECTION I
CHAIR: SUZANNE ROMAINE

11.55 Thomas Fraser (Lille): Did Old English have a middle voice?
12.30 Elizabeth Closs Traugott (Stanford): Association and confrontation

SECTION II
CHAIR: E. G. BOOIJ

11.55 Jadranka Gvozdanović (Amsterdam): Theories of sound change fail if they try to predict too much

12.30 Dieter Stein (Giessen): Psycholinguistic determinants of linguistic change

13.15 BREAK

15.00 E. F. Konrad Koerner (Ottawa): The place of Saussure's *Mémoire* in the development of historical linguistics (CHAIR: ANNA GIACOLONE RAMAT)

SECTION I
CHAIR: HENRIK BIRNBAUM

15.45 Kurt Jankowsky (Georgetown): Wilhelm Scherer's *Zur Geschichte der deutschen Sprache*. A milestone in 19th century linguistics
16.20 Suzanne Romaine (Birmingham): Style and word formation in the history of English. Why *delicateness* hath very properly given way to *delicacy*?
16.55 C. J. Conradie (Johannesburg): Ablaut: a Phoenix in the history of Afrikaans

SECTION II
CHAIR: ANDREI DANCHEV

15.45 Ernst Håkon Jahr (Tromsø): Another explanation for the development of *s* before *l* in Norwegian
16.20 Ruta Nagucka (Cracow): For a diachrony-in-synchrony analysis
16.55 Eric P. Hamp (Chicago): Historical reconstruction cannot respect levels

TUESDAY, August 23

09.00 Lyle Campbell (Mexico City): Areal linguistics and its implications for historical linguistics (CHAIR: E. F. KONRAD KOERNER)

SECTION I
CHAIR: WOLFGANG U. DRESSLER

09.45 Robert E. Beard (Lewisburg): PIE case functions and IE lexical derivations
10.20 Hubert Haider (Vienna): Chance and necessity in diachronic syntax — word order typologies and the position of Modern Persian relative clauses

SECTION II
Chair: Andrei Danchev

09.45 Eugene Holman (Helsinki): On the semasiologization of phonological rules: the communicative function of Finnish consonant gradation

10.20 Fred C. C. Peng (Tokyo): On the possible clusters of *mb, nd, ŋg* in Proto-Japanese

10.55 BREAK

SECTION I
Chair: Elizabeth Closs Traugott

11.30 W. U. Dressler and V. Z. Acson (Vienna): On the diachrony of subtractive operations. Evidence for natural phonology and morphology from Northern and Anatolian Greek dialects

12.05 Robert K. Herbert (Binghamton): Articulatory modes as contact phenomena

SECTION II
Chair: Thomas Fraser

11.30 Mirja Saari (Turku): Zur Stabilisierung der Wortfolge im Neuschwedischen

12.05 Henryk Niedzielski (Honolulu): Le neutre en français du treizième siècle au vingtième siècle

13.15 BREAK

SECTION I
Chair: Aleksander Szwedek

15.00 Andrei Danchev (Sofia): On analysis and synthesis in sound change

15.35 Hubert Gburek (Erlangen): The vowel /a:/ in English

SECTION II
Chair: Wolfgang Viereck

15.00 G. E. Booij (Amsterdam): Morphological change as evidence for the structure of the lexicon

15.35 Michael Job (Bochum): On reconstruction

16.10 Michał Hasiuk (Poznań): Some linguistic evidence on the Sudovian language

WEDNESDAY, August 24
09.00 EXCURSION

THURSDAY, August 25
09.00 Martin Harris (Salford): Divergent patterns of word order change in contemporary French (CHAIR: DIETER KASTOVSKY)

SECTION I
CHAIR: THEO VENNEMANN

09.45 Aleksander Szwedek (Bydgoszcz): Towards a reconstruction of sentence stress

10.20 Louis Goossens (Antwerp): The linguistic action scene in English: a historical perspective

SECTION II
CHAIR: STIG ELIASSON

09.45 Jens E. Rasmussen (Copenhagen): The Indo-European origin of the Baltic -ē- and -ā- preterite

10.55 BREAK

CHAIR: MARTIN HARRIS

11.30 Theo Vennemann (Munich): High Germanic and Low Germanic. A new theory of the Germanic and High German consonant shift

12.05 Stanisław F. Kolbuszewski (Poznań): Notes on the *je-/ja*-isogloss in the languages of the Baltic area

12.40 Raymond Hickey (Bonn): Velar segments in Old English and Old Irish

13.15 BREAK

CHAIR: ERIC P. HAMP

15.00 Robert W. Murray (Munich): Syllable structure changes in early Germanic

FRIDAY, August 26

SECTION I
CHAIR: WERNER WINTER

09.45 Stig Eliasson (Uppsala): Is sound change teleological? The case of the central Scandinavian vowel shift

SECTION II
Chair: Anders Ahlqvist

09.45 Witold Mańczak (Cracow): Indo-European numerals and the sexagesimal system
10.20 Camiël Hamans (Leiden): Umlaut as a harmony process
10.55 BREAK

SECTION I
Chair: Wiesław Awedyk

11.30 Werner Winter (Kiel): Developments in the order of parts of the sentence in Proto-Indo-European
12.05 Johan Taeldeman (Ghent): Rule ordering, language change and spatial language variation
12.40 Paul Verluyten (Antwerp): Prosodic structure and the development of French schwa

SECTION II
Chair: Louis Goossens

11.30 Wolfgang Viereck (Bamberg): On the origins and the development of American English — sense and nonsense
12.05 Bogdan Walczak (Poznań): Quelques problèmes des recherches étymologiques sur les emprunts lexicaux
13.15 BREAK

SECTION I
Chair: Karol Janicki

15.00 Edgar W. Schneider (Bamberg): Regional variation in 19th c. Black English in the American South

SECTION II
Chair: Leiv Egil Breivik

15.00 Wolfgang U. Wurzel (Berlin): Morphologische Natürlichkeit und morphologischer Wandel zur Vorherssagbarkeit von Sprachveränderungen

15.30 BREAK
15.35 Anders Ahlqvist (Galway): Summing up (Chair: Jacek Fisiak)
16.00 Business meeting

DIVERGENCE AND CONVERGENCE IN LINGUISTIC EVOLUTION

HENRIK BIRNBAUM

1. Ever since the metaphor of the genealogical tree (*Stammbaum*) and what was conceived as a remedy or substitute for it, namely, the image conveyed by the wave theory (*Wellentheorie*), were found to be inadequate means to capture the essence of linguistic evolution, particularly as regards cognate languages within certain geographic areas, no single viable new model has been devised to describe, let alone explain, the overall phenomenon of linguistic change. This holds true even if we consider some insightful approaches to language modification over time, such as H. Andersen's abductive model (Andersen 1973; for some qualifications, see Birnbaum 1979). Also the notion of innovation spreading, more or less consistently and forcefully, from the center of a linguistic area toward its periphery, or some part of it, is but a variant or further elaboration of the basic wave-theoretical model of language change.

What has been discussed instead in the past few decades with refocused attention are the complementary concepts of divergence and convergence. In particular, attempts have been made to show how these opposite evolutionary trends underlie differentiation of genetically related languages and integration of spatially defined, typologically kindred language unions. However, although useful as preliminary tools for describing and analyzing certain facets of linguistic evolution, these twin concepts have frequently been applied much too narrowly and mechanically to allow for a full and genuine understanding of the highly complex processes involved in change and innovation on the various levels of linguistic structure. The following remarks are intended, therefore, to contribute toward overcoming the imprecision and redressing the imbalance currently inherent in the notions of divergence and convergence as they are generally used with regard to linguistic evolution.

To begin with, the concept of divergence, taken in isolation and carried to its logical conclusion, is upon closer examination not altogether very different from the idea of the genealogical tree, even though it is not encumbered with the latter's association with Darwinist evolutionary doctrine. For divergence, too, assumes in effect a uniform source — here, a parent language — as the point of departure for the emergence and subsequent development of a set of derived entities, diversified to varying degrees — here, daughter languages as members of a language family with a certain number of shared, inherited features or correspondences — treelike branching out, as it were, from the common trunk and displaying a differently, often unevenly ramified diversification in each branch and subbranch essentially arrived at as a result of a rectilinear, continuous evolution. Conversely, though in a parallel fashion, the concept of language union (league), or *Sprachbund* — characteristically also referred to, at least in American linguistic parlance, as convergence area (Weinreich 1958; for a suggestion of a possible terminological distinction, reserving 'convergence area' for incipient, not fully crystallized *Sprachbund*, see Birnbaum 1983a: 19; forthcoming b; cf. further the discussion in Schaller 1983c: 213 - 14) — is based primarily on the assumption of a convergent evolution of a variety of previously more or less different, unrelated or only in part related contiguous languages whose general makeup has undergone some fundamental secondary modification, implying the addition of some new, acquired characteristics, particularly in their grammatical (morphosyntactic) structure, but in addition usually also as regards the overall patterning of their sound system as well as their semantically informed lexicon. The languages concerned have thus been adapted to each other by a process of leveling and by integrating a number of their prior characteristics so as not only to increase the mutual comprehensibility, or rather, immediate translatability among the members of such an areally determined linguistic constellation but also to streamline, in a manner of speaking, and thus render uniform to a considerable degree their overall shared typological profile.

Even from these few remarks on divergence and convergence it can be gathered that any conception or method that takes into account and operates exclusively with one of these processes, that is, without considering also the simultaneous and/or consecutive effect of the opposite factor in the development of language, must be skewed and hence unrealistic. It is thus bound to distort rather than to elucidate the actual diachronic process of language change. This is true regardless of whether such change is viewed in the context of genetic relationship or typological affinity. As I have argued elsewhere (Birnbaum 1975; 1982; and

1983a, with reference to previous discussion), the former always implies a typological facet as well but not, obviously, vice versa: typological resemblance (or identity) does not need to presuppose descent from a common ancestral language, particularly if the criterion of contiguity is not applicable. In reality, linguistic change is characterized, of course, by a constant and subtle interplay of divergence and convergence, often with now one, now the other prevailing. In the bulk of this paper I shall attempt to illustrate with some concrete examples the intricate interaction of these two opposite yet mutually balancing and conditioning trends in linguistic evolution.

2. First, however, and prior to turning to such exemplification, a few more theoretical considerations seem called for. One of the more serious errors still sometimes committed in certain quarters concerned with genetic linguistics and, in particular, with the recovery of lost protolanguages is to view the underlying parent language as something purely abstract, static, itself not subject to change. Admittedly, it may be useful or even advisable, in a first approximation, to construct a theoretical system arrived at by projecting it, as it were, onto a single time plane from the evidence available — that is, from early attestation as well as from the subsequent documented full spatial (including dialectal) diversification, the latter owing to regional differences in pace and in the effect of retention vs. innovation. Such an abstract, synchronic model can therefore serve as a common starting point for the recorded evolution within a specific language family. But it would be a grave mistake not to recognize that this theoretical ultimate phase of a particular ancestral language is itself merely the result, or end product, of a longer or shorter development of that same protolanguage. Put differently, the reconstructed parent language is descendant, along with its sister tongues (which themselves may be protolanguages underlying some other family of closely related languages), from an earlier pre-protolanguage; for some discussion of that last concept, see Birnbaum 1977:51 - 60; 1980a. Before disintegrating into several relatively separate branches or individual languages, a protolanguage was, as a rule, subject to its own inherent synchronic dynamics of change and renewal.

It should be noted, moreover, that it is of course frequently a matter of pure chance whether an ancestral language happens to be recorded or not. Thus, for example, Latin, the parent language of the Romance language family, is amply attested by a vast body of writing extending over many centuries. By the same token, Proto-Nordic, the common source of the Scandinavian languages, is only very fragmentarily known from a few extant inscriptions in the older runic script (futhark). And it is largely a matter of perception and theoretical stance whether one chooses to consider Old Church Slavic the earliest written form of a Common Slavic dialect or the first recorded separate Slavic literary language (only in part reflecting a regional variety of actually once spoken Slavic, however, since it owes much to its Greek model, notably in syntax, phraseology, and lexicon); cf. Birnbaum 1971:20 - 35. In other instances, when a protolanguage is not attested, it may be recoverable only incompletely, by means of ever more improved and refined techniques of the comparative method, where necessary supplemented by devices taken from what has become known as internal reconstruction. Though this term is sometimes used rather loosely, I would suggest that it always imply deduction from sets of functional alternations operative within a given synchronic linguistic system; thus, "internal" in this context ought not to be understood as merely synonymous with linguistic proper as contrasted with extralinguistic reconstruction (cf. Kuryłowicz 1964; Birnbaum 1970a:92 - 122; 1977: esp. 10 - 17). Moreover, and largely as a consequence of external linguistic history — that is to say, as determined by extraneous (political, cultural, and/or societal) factors — it is often a matter of subjective judgment or relative assessment whether the linguistic branches emerging from a common ancestral language be considered independent, full-fledged languages or no more than dialects bound to evolve into fully crystallized languages at some later point in time. A fine line separates the notions (and terms) 'dialect' and 'language;' cf. as a case in point the dual status of Old Church Slavic just referred to.

Finally, while projecting some of the differences peculiar to a set of closely related languages (and dialects) into their common prehistory may indeed allow us to assume certain local isoglosses as having existed and taken on increased prominence in the final phase of what was still essentially a uniform parent language, there is nothing to suggest that other characteristics may not have set apart some region of that protolanguage in an earlier stage of its development. For just because such previous features may have subsequently disappeared without a trace (and thus become irretrievable), or, on the contrary, ultimately could embrace all of the ancestral language and its entire territory (so that its original, more limited diffusion can no longer be ascertained) — thus losing their significance as a criterion of prehistoric spatial differentiation and as a means of establishing hypothetic regional divisions

— that does not mean that such more restricted features could not once have existed. To take two telling examples: The sound change known as the Germanic Consonant Shift ($p>f$, $t>þ$, $k>x$; $b>p$, $d>t$, $g>k$; $bh>b$, $dh>ð$, $gh>g$, the latter also rendered $ʒ$ or $γ$), while probably not the very first process to set apart Proto-Germanic from Late Proto-Indo-European, was nonetheless among the earliest modifications peculiar to the Germanic sound system (the fixing of word-initial stress and some changes in the vowel system being equally significant and, in part at least, chronologically even prior to the consonant shift). Yet, although the Germanic Consonant Shift was to extend to all of Germanic, we can by no means be certain that it did not initially affect only some limited area within the overall Germanic linguistic territory, comparable to what subsequently occurred when the High German Shift took place (which thus did not reach beyond the area of High German). Similarly, it can be shown that in Slavic the (regressive) First Palatalization of Velars (k, g, $x>č$, $ǯ/ž$, $š$ before primary front vowel), paralleled by the genetically unrelated, much earlier process operational in Indo-Iranian ($kĕ$, $gĕ$, $khĕ$, $ghĕ$, $>că$, $jă$, $chă$, $jhă$), applied throughout the entire Slavic language area. However, again, we do not know whether in an earlier stage of Proto-Slavic (Early Common Slavic) this change was not perhaps restricted to only a limited region of Slavic, or carried out inconsistently, comparable to the inconsistent and incomplete spread of the outcome of the (regressive) Second Palatalization of Velars ($kĕ_2>cĕ$, etc.) or that of the (progressive) Third (but possibly earlier, also known as Baudouin de Courtenay) Palatalization ($ĭk>$ $>ic/ьc$, etc.); cf. further Žuravlev 1968: 173 - 5; 1970: 89; Birnbaum 1973: 43 - 4.

3. Leaving aside for now the issue of a possible Nostratic macrofamily of distantly related languages and the methodology tentatively employed to recover a hypothetic Nostratic pre-protolanguage or some segment of it — a set of techniques used for reconstruction referred to as external comparison (combining genetic and typological considerations) — let us first take a brief look at Indo-European and its prehistoric stages retrievable with some degree of certainty. As for the Nostratic problem it should perhaps only be mentioned here in passing that, while Proto-Nostratic was earlier thought to underlie, at considerable time depth, in addition to Indo-European, also Uralic, Altaic, Caucasian (or Kartvelian, to be precise), Dravidian (or more broadly, Elamo-Dravidian), Semitic, and Hamitic (cf. the progress report on Soviet relevant work

contained in *Konferencija* 1977), Nostratic is, according to a recent study (Bomhard 1983), believed to encompass a much larger group of southern languages of Asia and Africa, with their ancestral language labeled Proto-Afroasiatic, comprising Semitic, Egyptian, Berber, Cushitic, Omotic, and Chadic.

The idea that all the Indo-European languages are ultimately derived from one largely homogeneous parent language, Proto-Indo-European, established in the days of F. Bopp and A. Schleicher, upheld and elaborated by the neogrammarians, and adhered to by comparative linguists also long after the heyday of the Leipzig School, was seriously challenged by N. S. Trubeckoj in a famous, if controversial paper sketching his relevant thoughts, regarded by many as quite heretic (Trubetzkoy 1939/68). First presented in 1936 at a meeting of the Prague Linguistic Circle, Trubeckoj's essay discussed the possibility that rather than viewing Proto-Indo-European as the basically uniform and only gradually differentiated and disintegrating ancestral language underlying the various Indo-European linguistic subfamilies, the system lying at the root of all the Indo-European daughter languages could itself be ought of as the outcome of secondary convergence, although not a total merger, of a number of previously less closely connected linguistic entities. In terms of typological characterization, Trubeckoj was inclined to assume that the Indo-European structure had emerged in the course of overcoming a primitive inflecting type of language without however fully attaining the more advanced stage of an agglutinating language. Particularly unorthodox was, in the view of many, his claim that the existence of a language family did not necessarily imply common descent from one single protolanguage. Instead, Trubeckoj argued, the notion of a language family, or genetic class, merely suggested a group of languages which, in addition to exhibiting structural similarities and conformities, would also display a sizable number of material agreements in terms of lexical and morphological elements expressed by regular phonological correspondences (cf. L. Hjelmslev's analagous conception, by him labeled '[expression] element function,' as the basis for establishing genetic relationship). In other words, Trubeckoj considered it a conceivable, indeed a more likely alternative to assume that the predecessors, or rather prefigurations, of the various Indo-European language branches originally differed considerably but that they, as a result of continuous contact, mutual interference, and borrowing, had subsequently become more closely linked without ever merging completely and turning fully identical. In Trubeckoj's opinion, after this phase of convergence a period of divergence set in which led to the subsequent differentiation of the various branches of Indo-European. Here, the line separating language families from language unions, first established by Trubeckoj himself (Trubetzkoy 1928/30), suddenly seemed to have become a bit fuzzy.

While the view that the several branches of Indo-European can be directly related to or derived from some prehistoric linguistic subgroupings of Pre-Indo-European on a one-to-one basis may perhaps not be acceptable in this straightforward form today, the idea that Late Proto-Indo-European as such could well be the result of an evolution which included convergent processes, along with divergent developments, is certainly not far-fetched and thus deserving of further consideration. And although we nowadays tend to reject the Indo-Hittite hypothesis in its extreme formulation (as in the end embraced and propounded, in particular, by E. H. Sturtevant; cf. Sturtevant 1942: 23 - 30; 1962; see also Cowgill 1975), that is to say, the assumption of an initial major split between Proto-Anatolian and the rest of Indo-European (or Proto-Indo-European proper), an early branching-off or separate evolution of the Anatolian group, best attested by Hittite, is now nonetheless rather widely accepted and has produced a number of specific explanations and explorations well worth contemplating; cf., e.g., Schmid 1979 (for an overall reinterpretation) or Ivanov 1981a (contrasting the hypothetic Proto-Indo-European verbal system as reconstructable on the basis of the Hittite evidence with the archaic systems of Slavic, Baltic, and Early Balkan, represented by Phrygian and Albanian; on the conservative nature specifically of Slavic with regard to the verb even by comparison to Baltic, see also Trubačev 1982a:16). For some more discussion of the archaic structure of Hittite (said to have retained monothematic inflection both in the verb and the adjective), cf. Adrados 1982. Generally, on some of the pitfalls of a predominantly typological view of Indo-European, with some criticism of Trubeckoj's position, though explicitly not of the essence of his thinking, see, in particular, Benveniste 1971:esp. 91 - 4.

4. Moving on now to a specific problem of Late Proto-Indo-European, or Disintegrating Indo-European (to use Bomhard's term), and viewing it in the light of the conflicting forces of divergence (spelling disintegration) and convergence (frequently resulting in reintegration), let us briefly consider the issue of Balto-Slavic. Summing up my own recent thinking on this matter, I stated my position as follows on a different occasion

(Birnbaum 1982:12 - 13, here slightly abridged and adapted to American usage, omitting all references):

> Specific language types, whether they are at the same time genetically definable language families or not, owe their existence to a combination and succession of divergence and convergence, the two opposite kinds of evolution occasionally being so intertwined as to be difficult to disentangle. — Applying this realization to the earliest prehistoric development fo Slavic, or to be exact, to its very emergence from what must be regarded as a particularly closely connected group of Late Proto-Indo-European dialects, it is obvious that even the ultimate separation of Slavic from its nearest cognate. Baltic (or rather perhaps, a portion of it), did not occur until after an extended period during which divergent tendencies — at times pulling West Baltic (or at any rate the precursor of Old Prussian) into the orbit of what otherwise would seem as a Proto-Slavic evolutionary phase — alternated with convergent trends of development bringing the presumed predecessors of separate Slavic and Baltic closer together again. As for chronology, the disintegration of Common Baltic, if indeed there ever was such a uniform linguistic entity, must have set in quite early, and certainly much before the dissolution of Common Slavic in the second half of the first millennium AD. Also, given the strikingly late attestation of Baltic (not before c. 1400 for Old Prussian, Old Lithuanian and Early Latvian even later), it is certainly conceivable that at least some of the lexical parallels and syntactic agreements between Old Prussian and Lithuanian, on the one hand, and Slavic (esp. Polish and Belorussian), on the other, are owing not to any early Balto-Slavic ethnolinguistic community but rather can be explained in terms of a secondary convergence and even coterritorial existence or, in any event, close contiguity both in prehistoric and early historical times (but prior to the appearance of any Baltic linguistic evidence). Moreover, in contemplating the nature and origin of the Balto-Slavic linguistic ties, even so knowledgeable and circumspect a scholar as C. Stang did at one point not rule out *Sprachbund*-type phenomena, linking Slavic not only to Baltic but possibly also to prehistoric Germanic. While, as I have suggested elsewhere, I would not think that the Balto-Slavic problem can be viewed exclusively in these terms, considering several other approaches to it previously explored, the possibility of convergent developments as underlying certain conformities is undoubtedly one that must always be reckoned with.

And, only a few months ago, in the context of assessing the significance of "Winter's Law" (specifying the conditions required for certain instances of vowel lengthening in Baltic as well as Slavic) as that "sound law" pertains to the ongoing debate about the nature of the Balto-Slavic linguistic relationship and the hypothesis of a possible former Balto-Slavic protolanguage, I had this to say, commenting also briefly on the more recent *histoire de la question* (Birnbaum forthcoming a, again cut and adapted here, retaining references only where not previously mentioned):

> Over a decade ago, I tried to sum up the then prevailing situation by pointing to the at least four competing (but partly compatible and thus to some degree combinable) approaches to the Balto-Slavic problem (Birnbaum 1970b:69 - - 76):(a) the assumption of an intermediary phase of Balto-Slavic linguistic unity subsequent to PIE and preceding a separate Baltic and Slavic evolution; (b) the hypothesis of a separate, parallel evolution beginning with the disintegration of Late PIE; (c) the "modelling" approach, essentially viewing an abstract Proto-Baltic model as serving as the point of departure (or prototype) also for Common Slavic; and (d) the *Sprachbund*, or rather, convergence theory, maintaining that the many Balto-Slavic agreements are largely due to secondary contacts and symbiosis, to the extent they are not separately inherited from PIE. At the time, I indicated my own qualified preference for viewing shared exclusive Balto-Slavic characteristics primarily in the light of approaches (c) and (d); cf. similarly also Birnbaum 1967. In my subsequent thinking I have adopted a dynamic conception of simultaneous and/or consecutive divergence and convergence. Since my overview, one of my critics (Mayer 1978:52), an advocate of a separate development of Baltic and Slavic directly from PIE, has argued that it would have been sufficient to distinguish between only two viable approaches (namely, separate, parallel vs. convergent evolution) while in a previous paper (Mayer 1977), though insisting on his theoretical premise, he in effect provided an illustration of the advantage of the "modelling" approach. More recently, another advocate of a separate development of the two IE groups (while accepting the supplementary notion of secondary convergence) has forcefully argued (Trubačev 1982a:13) against conceiving of Common Slavic as a "noncontradictory model" rather than a living language. Other scholars have rehashed old arguments or introduced some new ones in support of either Balto-Slavic unity or separate development (assuming subsequent partial convergence). An initial Balto-Slavic "community" (within the framework of disintegrating Late PIE) was recently advocated, with some important qualifications, by Gołąb (1977 and 1983). Close to this view is also the conception set forth by Stang (1966:13 - 21), while a subtly differentiated but not entirely unequivocal stand was taken more recently by Ivanov (1981b:6 - 10). On the side of those who clearly oppose the idea of any early Balto-Slavic ethnolinguistic unity are, in addition to Trubačev (1981; 1982a; 1982b) and Mayer, Filin (1980:38 - 9) and Udolph (1979: 637 - 9, based on hydronymic data but adopting a view combining separate, parallel divergement with subsequent convergence and assimilation).

Adding to these recent statements of mine, I would today only make the following clarifying and qualifying points to indicate my present position regarding the issue of Balto-Slavic: Earlier I was inclined to think in terms of some combination of the "modelling" approach and an explanation assuming secondary convergence. The former was introduced by Ivanov and Toporov (1961), while the latter would imply a linguistic "intercommunity" (*soobščnost'*), *Verkehrsgemeinschaft*) along lines proposed by Bernštejn (1958; cf now also Schaller 1983a and 1983c: 214 - 17, 219 - 20). Now however, I would suggest that the genetic relationship between Baltic and Slavic be viewed as resulting basically from three factors: (1) an early Balto-Slavic unity, in effect amounting to a Balto-Slavic parent language which can best be regarded as a Late Proto-Indo-European dialect; (2) a subsequent divergence and separation of the two branches of Indo-European, concomitant with or followed by secondary convergent tendencies bringing Baltic and, especially, Slavic separately closer together with other linguistic branches of Indo-European (notably with Indo-Iranian, Germanic, Italic, and Celtic, though not necessarily, in this order); and (3) a later, secondary convergence between Baltic and Slavic, closing the gap, as it were, definable as coterritorial symbiosis, or coexistence, and implying massive interference, borrowing, and reciprocal influence taking place between the two linguistic groups, primarily going from advancing Slavic to receding Baltic. This latter process must have coincided timewise with the expansion of the Slavs from their earlier area of settlement (or presumed original homeland, controversial though this latter remains) deep into what heretofore had been Baltic territory. Antedating the appearance of any Baltic written records (i.e., completed before c. 1400 AD), this development lasted in all likelihood well into the period of Early Slavic literacy (9th through 14th cc.). Of the four conceivable approaches to Balto-Slavic mentioned, I would thus now favor considering some combination of approaches (a) and (d) over (c) combined with (d), that is to say, a conception comprising both (early) divergence and (later) convergence — the latter obviously preceding the subsequent complete split between Baltic and Slavic.

5. Remaining for a while with Slavic, it has long been established that the evolution of preliterate Common Slavic and its eventual breakup into separate subgroups and individual languages did not proceed in a consistent rectilinear fashion of unperturbed divergence and continuous ramification (cf. for details esp. Birnbaum 1965a; 1966; 1971: 20 - 35; 1974; 1982:13 - 14, with further references; see now particularly also Ivanov 1982). Thus, to take just one telling example, it is obvious from some striking phonological developments (most notably the treatment of the liquid groups) that the Common Slavic dialects underlying Czech and Slovak, though on the whole belonging to the West Slavic group, must have at some point shared in the evolution from which the South Slavic languages have emerged. In other instances, certain iso-

glosses or even isogloss bundles can cut across the lines dividing the basic subgroups of Slavic. Thus, for example, the isogloss reflecting the treatment of CS *CĺC* and *CelC* yields *ColC*(> *ColoC*) in all of East Slavic but also in a small northern segment of Lekhitic (Kashubian). Or, in the threefold treatment of the clusters *tl, dl* a portion of northwestern South Slavic (namely, a part of the Slovene dialects) shows retention of the cluster, as in West Slavic, rather than simplification (>*l*) as elsewhere in South Slavic and most of East Slavic (the change >*kl, gl* being the third, regionally restricted option). In this context it should also be noted that Mareš (1980) some years ago proposed to replace the traditional tripartite division of Slavic, arrived at on the basis of genetic — primarily phonological — criteria, by, according to him, a more adequate tetrachotomic (or, to be precise, double dichotomic: N/S vs. W/E) classification of the current Slavic standard languages on genetic as well as typological grounds. And, as a further illustration of the difficulties inherent in any unequivocal, noncomplex classification in the Slavic language area, I have in a recent study (Birnbaum 1983) attempted to demonstrate that the Rusin microlanguage spoken in northern Yugoslavia (primarily in some parts of the Vojvodina), though genetically classifiable as predominantly, but not exclusively, West Slavic (being closely related to dialectal East Slovak), from a typological point of view cannot easily be assigned to any of the traditional Slavic groups as it exhibits characteristics of all three of them — some owing to recent and, in part, deliberate convergent trends in the evolution of Rusin (involving adaptation to Serbo-Croatian and some rapprochement with standard Ukrainian). For some further thoughts on the genetic, typological, and areal classification of Slavic and attendant problems and complexities, see also Lötzsch 1982.

Continuing with some phenomena of contemporary Slavic, only a few more instances of recent or ongoing divergent and convergent evolutionary tendencies, counteracting and balancing each other, shall be touched upon here; for more details and additional exemplification, see Birnbaum 1982:14 - 24.

A particularly graphic example of how a language or dialect that itself was the outcome of a series of branching and subdividing processes can, subsequently, be reintegrated with a larger linguistic entity from which it originally split off, or rather, from whose precursor it, too, had developed, is provided by modern Kashubian, a Lekhitic idiom which never attained the status of a full-fledged Slavic standard language but which evolved into what may be termed an independent cultural dialect, with its own folkloric literature and everyday publications. Earlier threatened in its existence by forced Germanization, Kashubian is, as is generally known, the only extant representative of the West Lekhitic, or Pomeranian-Polabian, subbranch of West Slavic after Slovincian, considered by some to have been merely a dialect variant of Kashubian, became extinct about 1900. Polish, alone representing East or, more correctly, Southeast Lekhitic, is therefore the closest present cognate of Kashubian. Given its status of an isolated microlanguage (for discussion of the Slavic microlanguages, see Duličenko 1981), which, contrary to Rusin, lacks the cultural and moral support of any prestigeous Slavic standard language other than that prevalent in the sovereign territory of the state where it is spoken, Kashubian is currently in the process of being integrated into Polish, though of course not into its literary standard form but rather the northern dialect group of Polish. Usually referred to in recent years by Polish specialists as "dialectal Polish" or "the Kashubian dialect(s) of Polish" (see Stieber 1973: 9, 132, 137 - 41; Topolińska 1974; cf. however Popowska-Taborska 1980: 67 - 8), the East Pomeranian idiom, while often still accorded semi-autonomous status of sorts, is thus nowadays increasingly regarded as merely a — to be sure, highly distinct — Polish dialect even by those who presumably recognize its archaic characteristics (mobile and initial stress in the north and south, respectively, of the Kashubian area, retention of *CarC* groups, etc.) as once having set it off from the northern dialects of Old Polish. Needless to say, the emergence of post-World-War-II Poland as a virtual mononational state and, in particular, the impact of the Polish mass media have further contributed to speed up this process of convergence and assimilation.

There is currently some indication, but not yet any real evidence, suggesting that, within the East Slavic group, the status of Belorussian — but certainly not that of Ukrainian — might show some first signs of being in jeopardy of eventually being overtaken by far more prestigeous and influential Russian on its own home territory of the Belorussian Soviet Socialist Republic. If such a trend does indeed exist and should gain momentum, so that Belorussian would one day yield or even succumb to its close cognate, this would constitute another example of what may be termed the crossover phenomenon in linguistic evolution. In this particular case, it would mean that Belorussian would converge with, if not be fully absorbed by, Russian — a close cognate, no doubt, but at least in strictly genetic terms somewhat more removed than Ukrainian. For it should be remembered that Russian historically occupies a more peripheral position in the overall Slavic linguistic orbit, not to mention the fact that Ukrainian and Belorussian began to crystallize jointly in the territory of what in a slightly inadequate terminology is occasionally referred to as "Lithuanian Russia (Rus')" or *Jugozapadnaja Rus'*. Yet we should also keep in mind that all prediction in linguistic matters remains highly speculative, not to say hazardous, some attempts to prove otherwise notwithstanding, if only because of the unpredictability of extralinguistic factors and events.

Turning now to the South Slavic area, it should be noted that the number of irregular, combined divergent-convergent developments not following a rectilinear course, and of crossover phenomena, is there even greater than in the Slavic North and that not only because a portion of the South Slavic linguistic branch by the same token forms part of the typologically defined Balkan *Sprachbund* (briefly to be considered below). In this context we also disregard such complex but exceptional instances as the previously mentioned controversial position of the "mixed" Rusin language set in a South Slavic region.

First, let us briefly discuss the issue of Macedonian. As I have stated elsewhere (Birnbaum 1980b:170−4; 1982:18−20), I am of the opinion that, while there can of course be no doubt whatsoever as to the independent status of contemporary Macedonian as a standard language, it is equally clear that there is no reason to assume the existence of any Old (or, for that matter, Middle) Macedonian language in the medieval or early modern period. In other words, present-day Macedonian is a descendant of Old Bulgarian (in its literary form also known as Old Church Slavic) just as much as modern Bulgarian, albeit with a different − namely, western − dialectal basis. In this respect, therefore, the prehistory of Macedonian is roughly analogous to that of Slovak except that the latter was firmly established as a literary language by the mid-nineteenth century whereas the same applies to Macedonian only as of the 1940s. Yet nobody questions, of course, that some isoglosses characteristic of the two languages are of ancient, indeed Late Common Slavic date. However, such isolated features − e.g., *dz* (<CS *dj*, shared by Slovak and Polish) or *o* as a reflex of CS ъ (which Macedonian has in common not only with much of Old Church Slavic but also with all of East Slavic) − do not by themselves constitute a sufficient basis for the identification of separate, independent languages. And, as Auty (1979:73) has rightly pointed out, "it is arguable that if the provisions of the Treaty of San Stefano in 1878 had been carried out and a greater Bulgaria had come into existence, embracing wide areas of the central

Balkans including Macedonia, Bulgarian would have been accepted by the Macedonians as their literary language." Since Macedonia, following the decisions of the Berlin Congress, instead remained under Turkish rule until 1912, the linguistic evolution in the area took a different course, and it is precisely the period between 1878 and 1912 that proved decisive for the formation of a separate Macedonian language.

Even more interesting in light of the present discussion is the case of Serbo-Croatian today; for some elaboration of my pertinent views, see Birnbaum 1980b: 161—70. Clearly, what so far still can be considered essentially a single language, to be sure, with two standard variants of equal rank (Serbian and Croatian), is the end result of a lengthy and complex historical process which involved instances of convergence as well as divergence, particularly at the dialectal level. Thus, it is rather generally held that the Kajkavian dialect of Serbo-Croatian was initially closer to, if not a part of, early Slovene, or rather a pre-Slovene linguistic entity. Its integration with Serbo-Croatian is therefore a consequence of a secondary development involving both divergence (from the bulk of Slovene) and convergence (with the Croatian component of Serbo-Croatian). Similarly, Torlak, now unanimously acknowledged as the fourth dialectal subgroup of Serbo-Croatian, along with Štokavian (with which it has previously been lumped together), Čakavian, and Kajkavian, and, at the same time, a fullfledged member of the Balkan *Sprachbund*, though historically closer to Serbian than to Bulgarian, has subsequently drifted away from the mainstream of the Serbo-Croatian linguistic evolution taking on a number of striking characteristics shared with Bulgarian (and Macedonian). Moreover, there is much that speaks for the assumption that even the core dialects of Serbo-Croatian, Štokavian (underlying primarily Serbian and only secondarily, in its Jekavian variety and at the level of the literary language enhanced by Vuk's unifying language reform, also Croatian) and Čakavian (underlying Croatian in Dalmatia and its immediate hinterland), are not so much twigs of one and the same branch as separate branches — possibly reflecting different migratory routes in the past — that only later approached each other, that is, converged, without ever fully merging.

Given this history and prehistory of Serbo-Croatian, with some degree of probability traceable to the pre-landtaking phase, a recent development carrying the seed of potential far-reaching consequences is of particular interest. I am referring to the targeted policy of language planning implemented some time ago in the Socialist Republic of Croatia and aiming at the constitution of what amounts to a separate

Croatian standard language (anticipated in the current notion of *hrvatski književni jezik*). Quite aside from the desirability of such a course of development, obviously perceived differently by different people and accompanied by emotionally charged comments, if completed it would have major repercussions for the language situation in Yugoslavia. For one thing, it would require a sorting out of (and taking sides in) the linguistic entanglement currently existing in Bosnia and Hercegovina where part of the population claims Croatian, another part Serbian, and yet another part "Moslem" ethnicity. Moreover, the establishment of a separate Croatian literary language would almost certainly increase the weight and prestige of specifically Serbian linguistic (and ethnic) identity outside Croatia. In some ways, the Croatian linguistic evolution recently begun can be compared to the politically motivated creation of a Moldavian literary language in Soviet Moldavia, separate from standard Romanian. However, there is also a profound difference, namely the long-standing Croatian cultural tradition which has no counterpart in Moldavia.

6. Leaving now the Slavic area and moving on to another branch of Indo-European, let us consider some relevant aspects of Germanic. As is well known, the Germanic languages, too, are traditionally viewed as genetically divided into three subbranches, West Germanic, North Germanic (or Scandinavian, also called Nordic), and East Germanic. Again, as in the case of Slavic, other divisions — for example, positing a first breakup into only two groups, West Germanic and North Germanic (from which latter subsequently East Germanic, chiefly represented by Gothic, would have branched off, in connection with the presumed departure of the Goths and other East Germanic tribes from Scandinavia) — have also been considered.

As for the position specifically of Gothic within Germanic, while its precise relationship to North as well as West Germanic has long been a matter of some controversy and various scholars have placed the emphasis differently on particular isoglosses linking Gothic with one part of the Germanic ethnolinguistic community or another, Gothic's being the main, and only recorded, representative of the East Germanic subbranch (whether this subbranch was one of the original groups emerging from the disintegration of Proto-Germanic or rather resulted from a secondary divergence of North Germanic into Proto-Nordic proper and East Germanic) has so far not been in doubt. It was only quite recently that an attempt was made by Mańczak (1983) to suggest that the earliest place of Gothic within the Germanic language family was not at all in the North or the East but in the extreme South, in the close vicinity of Latin (or some area of the Latin-speaking world) from which a few early Gothic loanwords — notably, *wein* 'wine' and *aket/akeit* 'vinegar' — are said to have traveled the relatively short distance to the region of the Old Germanic language. As I have argued in some detail against Mańczak's whole line of reasoning (Birnbaum 1983b), his extraordinary classification of Gothic, whose speakers, however, also according to his hypothesis later appeared in the Oder-Vistula region and presumably subsequently migrated farther to the northern shores of the Black Sea and on to the Balkans, is untenable and cannot be corroborated by any incontrovertible evidence.

Regarding the North Germanic (Scandinavian) language group, though it appears to be fairly well defined in terms of both its localization and identity, it should be noted that its specific linguistic ties with East Germanic (Gothic) and, for that matter, also with West Germanic — heterogeneous from the very beginning of that subgroup's separate existence — are rather complex and not yet fully elucidated in all respects. Consequently, the details of the particular relationship between North Germanic and the two other branches of Germanic remain controversial as well; see further Haugen 1976:107—13.

As concerns the subgrouping of the Scandinavian languages, some illuminating examples of the divergence/covergence syndrome of linguistic evolution can be cited from their particular genetic classification and recorded history. Thus, as is well known, the Old Scandinavian languages and dialects are usually subdivided into two main branches — West Nordic (or Norse proper, *norrøn*), comprising Old Icelandic and Old Norwegian (including Faroese-tinted Old Norwegian, Faroese as a more or less developed literary language dating only to the late eighteenth century), and East Nordic, made up of Old Danish, Old Swedish, and, at first as a separate idiom, Old Gotlandic, or Gutnish (spoken and written on the island of Gotland; cf. the texts of the *Guta Saga* and the *Guta Law*). Now, to begin with, Gutnish was in due course — still in the medieval period — integrated with Old Swedish, with the Gotlandic dialect of Swedish remaining highly distinct and archaic to this very day. Thus, the fate of the speech of the indigenous population of Gotland in the Middle Ages, early affected and interfered with by speakers of Middle Low German, settling as merchants in the town of Visby, and by such of Old Danish, temporarily occupying the island (beginning with the conquest by King Valdemar Atterdag in 1361), was somewhat similar to that of the speakers of Kashubian in our own time. For further discussion of the Old Scandinavian dialects and their isoglosses, see Haugen 1976:198—214.

More importantly, though, as a result of the century-long Danish rule in Norway, the by far more widespread of the two Norwegian standard languages, *bokmål* ('book language', renamed from earlier *riksmål* 'official language,' the other, dialect-based one being *nynorsk* 'New Norwegian,' formerly known as *landsmål* 'country language'), is in fact a veritable blend, definable as Dano-Norwegian, with its phonology to a large extent adapted to the local norms of pronunciation but its grammatical structure in many respects closer to that of literary Danish. Moreover, Danish itself, exposed to Low German and other influences, has drifted away, as it were, from its close relationship to standard Swedish (while the South Swedish dialect of the province of Scania, long under Danish rule, continues to exhibit many agreements and similarities in sound pattern, morphosyntax, and lexicon with Danish, particularly with the speech of the island of Sjaelland). Also, modern Norwegian has some characteristics shared with Swedish, substitutive softening of velars ($k > \acute{c}$, $g > j$, before front vowels) and phonemic pitch ("accent 1" vs. "accent 2") most striking among them (the latter in Danish having its historical and functional counterpart in the *stød*, or 'glottal catch,' peculiar to that language). As a consequence, the once marked bifurcation into West vs. East Scandinavian is today all but obliterated, or rather perhaps eclipsed by a number of features rendering the former distinction virtually immaterial.

7. Turning, finally, to a language group defined typologically and not primarily genetically — as the latter was applicable to Indo-European, Balto-Slavic, Slavic, Germanic, and Scandinavian, surveyed so far — let us now briefly consider the languages usually referred to as Balkan and constituting what is frequently cited as the textbook example of an areally confined language union, or *Sprachbund*. As is well known, the member languages of the Balkan *Sprachbund* include Bulgarian, Macedonian, the Torlak dialect of Serbo-Croatian (other parts of Serbo-Croatian being only peripherally involved in the Balkan linguistic type; for details, see Birnbaum 1965b: 39—57; and now also esp. Simić 1982), Albanian, Romanian, and Modern Greek. Of these languages, Romanian and Modern Greek are sometimes considered somewhat more peripheral by comparison to the core Balkan languages — Bulgarian, Macedonian, Torlak (together also referred to as Balkan Slavic),

and Albanian. Turkish, although it has played a considerable role as an integrative force in the Balkans (notably by its penetration of the lexicon), and as such is comparable to Late (Vulgar) Latin in earlier centuries (see esp. Solta 1980: 64—170; cf. also Birnbaum 1981), is structurally not a Balkan language, not even its Gagauz dialect encountered in Bulgaria (and recently accorded standard status in Soviet Moldavia). It is not even certain that the verbal category of Bulgarian, Macedonian, and Torlak known as the narrative, as well as similar grammatical means of the verb system in Romanian (presumptive) and Albanian (resultative, admirative), frequently attributed to Osmanli influence (cf., e.g., Solta 1980: 173—4), actually have their source in Turkish.

Viewing the Balkan languages in terms of divergent and convergent evolutionary trends, it should be noted that, while divergence by and large is the predominant tendency in the development of genetically related languages, with convergence acting as the irregular, complicating, and obliterating factor, this relationship and balance is reversed when it comes to the emergence and formation of a *Sprachbund* such as that in the Balkans; this, incidentally, is of course implicit also in the term 'convergence area,' used as a synonym or near-synonym of *Sprachbund* (cf. above). For obviously, convergence is the very prerequisite of leveling, integration, and accomodation. Yet it is worth pointing out here that, although convergence is indeed the primary force in the crystallization of the Balkan language union, its member languages, by the same token continuing to represent various branches and subbranches of specific language families and, moreover, each having their own spatial continuum of dialectal variation, are also subject to contrary, i.e., divergent tendencies of evolution (cf. also Reiter 1981: esp. 178—83). This applies both to those languages which are the only extant representatives of a particular branch of Indo-European (as is the case with Greek and Albanian) and to those language families the majority of which does not form part of the Balkan linguistic group — Romanian, as the easternmost subbranch of Romance (in this context we disregard Moldavian), and Balkan Slavic, as the southernmost portion of Slavic. In other words, in all these languages we can observe a simultaneous — or better perhaps, concomitant — evolution toward a closer structural (typological) affinity with the other Balkan languages and toward greater diversity (unless counteracted by other convergent trends within the same language family; cf. above) by comparison to their sister idioms outside the Balkan area as well as at the level of dialectal differentiation. As regards, particularly, Balkan Slavic with its several member languages and dialects, such divergence has occurred in part even within the Balkan region, given the need or desire felt in the Macedonian-speaking community not to coincide, or be identified, with Bulgarian and, for that matter, by the speakers of Torlak Serbian to remain distinct from both Macedonian and Bulgarian. Thus, not all features characteristic of, say, Romanian vis-à-vis the other Romance languages, or of Bulgarian in relation to the rest of Slavic can simply be equated with Balkanisms. On the specific complexities of Bulgarian as a Balkan language, see now, e.g., Schaller 1983b. For an exemplary in-depth study of a particular phenomenon — the use of clitic pronoun forms — in Bulgarian viewed in light of the tension (and competition) between the Balkan and the Slavic linguistic types, see Orzechowska 1976. To be sure, it can be argued that in this age of language standardization and mass media impact, both the continued development and expansion of specific Balkan features and dialectal innovation have virtually come to a standstill or have to a large extent even been reversed (but cf. the spread of finite constructions replacing the infinitive in Serbo-Croatian beyond the Balkan area proper referred to below).

Finally, it should be mentioned in this context that, as I have tried to show in some recent studies (Birnbaum 1983c and forthcoming b), the characteristics of the Balkan *Sprachbund*, in addition to being manifest at the readily perceivable surface of linguistic structure, also have a "deep" dimension of their own, that is to say, are anchored, as it were, at the level of typologically defined semantic deep structure, with much of the change taking place there, rather than at the overt level. The following phenomena exemplify this: (1) the substitution of synthetic by analytic means in the declension — a breakdown and eventual complete disintegration of the case system (ultimately inherited from Indo-European) and, specifically, the early genitive/dative syncretism; (2) the postpositive article (though it is not encountered in Modern Greek, presumably because of the firm position of the definite article in that language, with its roots in Ancient Greek); (3) the periphrastic future tense with auxiliaries — partly reflected in the form of ossified particles — with an original volitional (as well as possessive) meaning, i.e., *volo* and *habeo* type constructions, going back to vernacular, post-classical Greek and Latin; (4) the loss of the infinitive and its substitution by subordinate phrases with a finite verb form — a phenomenon continuing to spread beyond the Balkan linguistic area proper, notably in Serbo-Croatian where it increasingly embraces also the Croatian standard variant; (5) so-called object reduplication, implying the seemingly pleonastic, but in fact not entirely redundant, use of the clitic form of the personal pronoun with an animate object. For some additional discussion of the mechanics of syntactic change, applicable in some points also to the Balkan linguistic type, see Birnbaum 1984, and, with particular reference to the Balkan languages, Civ'jan 1979.

8. In conclusion, it may be said that the notions of divergence and convergence are of course not new in historical linguistics. Implicitly or explicitly they have been assumed and recognized as driving forces in much of linguistic change and evolution. But the precise role that these two contrasting tendencies have played in the development of cognate, genetically related and kindred, typologically more or less analogously structured languages sharing a common destiny in a clearly defined area, and particularly the intricate interplay determining their relationship and often precarious balance, their concurrent or consecutive operation, are still in need of further elucidation and genuine understanding. By commenting on a number of telling instances of divergence and convergence in a variety of languages and language groups, I have attempted in the preceding remarks to contribute, in a modest measure, toward such improved knowledge and a better grasp of the nature and function of these factors in linguistic evolution. These factors, as must now be clear, are not merely handy labels or graphic metaphors for what actually is going on when languages undergo modification and change, but go to the heart of the matter when it comes to the constant, incessant dynamics inherent in the synchrony and diachrony of language.

REFERENCES

Adrados, F. R. 1982. The archaic structure of Hittite: the crux of the problem. *JIES* 10/1 & 2. 1 - 35.

Andersen, H. 1973. Abductive and deductive change. *Lg* 49. 765 - 93.

Auty, R. 1979. Language and nationality in East-Central Europe 1750 - 1950. *OxSlP*, N. S. 12. 52 - 83.

Benveniste, É. 1971. The classification of languages. *Problems in general linguistics*, tr. M. E. Meek, 85 - 100. Coral Gables, Florida: University of Miami Press (= *Miami Linguistics Series* 8).

Bernštejn, S. B. 1958. Balto-slavjanskaja jazykovaja soobščnost'. *Slavjanskaja filologija. Sbornik statej 1. IV Meždunarodnyj s'ezd slavistov*, ed. by S. B. Bernštejn, 45 - 67. Moscow: Izd-vo AN SSSR.

Birnbaum, H. 1965a. On some problems of Common Slavic dialectology. *IJSLP* 9. 1 - 19.

―――― 1965b. Balkanslavisch und Südslavisch. Zur Reichweite der Balkanismen im südslavischen Sprachraum. *ZfBalk* 3. 12 - 63.

1966. The dialects of Common Slavic. *Ancient Indo-European dialects*, ed. by H. Birnbaum and J. Puhvel, 153 - 97. Berkeley and Los Angeles: University of California Press.

1967. On the reconstruction and predictability of linguistic models: Balto-Slavic revisited. *ScSl* 13. 105 - 14.

1970a. *Problems of typological and genetic linguistics viewed in a generative framework*. The Hague and Paris: Mouton (= *Janua Linguarum*, Series Minor, 106).

1970b. Four approaches to Balto-Slavic. *Dionum Balticum: To Professor Christian S. Stang on the occasion of his seventieth birthday*, ed. by V. Rūke--Dravina, 69 - 76. Stockholm: Almqvist and Wiksell.

1971. Zur Problematik der zeitlichen Abgrenzung des Urslavischen. Über die Relativität der Begriffe Baltoslavisch/Frühurslavisch und Spätgemeinslavischer Dialekt/Ureinzelslavine. *ZfslPh* 35. 1 - 62.

1973. O możliwości odtworzenia pierwotnego stanu języka prasłowiańskiego za pomocą rekonstrukcji wewnętrznej i metody porównawczej. Kilka uwag o stosunku różnych podejść. *American contributions to the Seventh International Congress of Slavists, Warsaw, August 21 - 27, 1973*. Vol. I: *Linguistics and poetics*, ed. by L. Matejka, 33 - 58. The Hague and Paris: Mouton (= *Slavistic printings and Reprintings 295*).

1974. Über unterschiedliche Konzeptionen der slavischen Ursprache und ihrer mundartlichen Gliederung. Entgegnung zum Diskussionsbeitrag E. Weihers. *AnzfslPh* 7. 146 - 52.

1975. Typology, genealogy and linguistic universals. *Linguistics* 144. 5 - 26.

1977. *Linguistic reconstruction: its potentials and limitations in new perspective.* Washington, D. C.: Institute for the Study of Man (= *JIES*, Monograph 2).

1979. Ongoing sound change and the abductive model: some social constraints and implications. *Proceedings of the Ninth Congress of Phonetic Sciences, Copenhagen, 6 - 11 August 1979*. Copenhagen: Institute of Phonetics, University of Copenhagen, Vol. 2, 189 - 95.

1980a. On protolanguages, diachrony and 'preprotolanguages'. Toward a typology of linguistic reconstruction. *Ezikovedski proučvanija v čest na akad. V.I. Georgiev*. Sofia: BAN, 121 - 9.

1980b. Language, ethnicity, and nationalism: On the linguistic foundations of a unified Yugoslavia. *The creation of Yougoslavia 1914 - 1918*, ed. by D. Djordjevic, 157 - 83 Santa Barbara, Ca. and Oxford: Clio Books.

1981. Review of Solta 1980. *Studies in language* 5. 399 - 406.

1982. The Slavonic language community as a genetic and typological class. *WdSl* 27. 5 - 43.

1983a. Language families, linguistic types, and the position of the Rusin microlanguage within Slavic. *WdSl* 28. 1 - 23.

1983b. W sprawie prasłowiańskich zapożyczeń z wczesnogermańskiego, zwłaszcza z gockiego (Na marginesie artykułu Witolda Mańczaka). *IJSLP* 27. 25 - 44.

1983c. Tiefen- und Oberflächenstrukturen balkanlinguistischer Erscheinungen. *Ziele und Wege der Balkanlinguistik. Beiträge zur Tagung vom 2. - 6. März 1981 in Berlin*, ed. by N. Reiter, 40-58. Berlin/Wiesbaden: Harrassowitz (= Osteuropa Institut an der Freien Universität Berlin, *Balkanologische Veröffentlichungen* 8).

1984. Notes on syntactic change: Cooccurrence vs. substitution, stability vs. permeability. *Historical syntax*, ed. by J. Fisiak, 25 - 46. Berlin, New York and Amsterdam: Mouton.

forthcoming a Winter's Law and the issue of Balto-Slavic. *Synchronic and diachronic linguistics* (FS W. Winter), ed. by G. Stickel and U. Pieper. Berlin, The Hague and New York: Mouton.

forthcoming. New approaches to Balkan linguistics. *Mélanges Petar Skok*, ed. by R. Filipović, P. Guberina et al. Zagreb: JAZU.

Bomhard, A. R. 1983. *Toward Proto-Nostratic: A speculative reconstruction of the parent language of Proto-Indo-European and Proto-Afroasiatic*. Amsterdam and Philadelphia: Benjamins.

Civ'jan, T. V. 1979. *Sintaksičeskaja struktura balkanskogo jazykovogo sojuza*. Moscow: Nauka.

Cowgill, W. 1975. More evidence for Indo-Hittite: the tense-aspect systems, *Proceedings of the Eleventh International Congress of Linguists*, ed. by L. Heilmann, vol. II, 557 - 70. Bologna: Il Mulino.

Duličenko, A. D. 1981. *Slavjanskie literaturnye mikrojazyki. Voprosy formirovanija i razvitija*. Tallinn: Vaigus.

Filin, F. P. 1980. O proisxoždenii praslavjanskogo jazyka i vostočnoslavjanskix jazykov. *VJa* 1980/4. 36 - 50.

Gołąb, Z. 1977. Stratyfikacja słownictwa prasłowiańskiego a zagadnienie etnogenezy Słowian. *RS* 38. 15 - 30.

1983. The ethnogenesis of the Slavs in the light of linguistics. *American contributions to the Ninth International Congress of Slavists*. Vol. I: *Linguistics*, ed. by M. S. Flier, 131 - 46. Columbus, Ohio: Slavica.

Gornung, B. V. 1963. Iz prehystorii obrazovanija obščeslavjanskogo jazykovogo edinstva (*Doklady sovetskoj delegacii*). *V Meždunarodnyj s"ezd slavistov* (*Sofija, sentjabr' 1963*). Moscow: Izd-vo AN SSSR.

Haugen, E. 1976. *The Scandinavian languages: An introduction to their history*. Cambridge, Mass.: Harvard University Press.

Ivanov, V. V. 1981a. *Slavjanskij, baltijskij i rannebalkanskij glagol. Indoevropejskie istoki*. Moscow: Nauka.

1981b. K prostranstvenno-vremennoj interpretacii balto-slavjanskogo dialektnogo kontinuuma. *Balto-slavjanskie issledovanija 1980*. Moscow: Nauka, 6 - 10.

1982. Dialektnye členenija slavjanskoj jazykovoj obščnosti i edinstvo drevnego slavjanskogo jazykovogo mira (v svjazi s problemoj ėtničeskogo samosoznanija). *Razvitie ėtničeskogo slavjanskix narodov v ėpoxu rannego srednedekov'ja*. Moscow: Nauka, 212 - 36.

Ivanov, V. V. and V. N. Toporov. 1961. K postanovke voprosa o drevnejšix otnošenijax baltijskix i slavjanskix jazykov. *Issledovanija po slavjanskomu jazykoznaniju*, ed. by N. I. Tolstoj, 273 - 305. Moscow: Izd-vo AN SSSR.

Konferencija 1977. *Nostratičeskie jazyki i nostratičeskoe jazykoznanie. Tezisy dokladov*. Moscow: Institut slavjanovedenija i balkanistiki AN SSSR.

Kuryłowicz, J. 1964. On the methods of internal reconstruction. *Proceedings of the Ninth International Congress of Linguists, Cambridge, Mass., August 27 - 31, 1962*, ed. by H. G. Lunt, 9 - 36. The Hague: Mouton.

Lötzsch, R. 1982. Zum Verhältnis zwischen der genetischen, typologischen und arealen Klassifizierung der slawischen Sprachen und Dialekte. *ZfSl* 27. 356 - 63.

Mańczak, W. 1983. Czas i miejsce zapożyczeń germańskich w prasłowiańskim. *IJSLP* 27. 15 - 23.
Mayer, H. E. 1977. Kann das Baltische als das Muster für das Slavische gelten? *ZfslPh* 39. 32 - 42.
1978. Die Divergenz des Baltischen und des Slavischen. *ZfslPh* 40. 52 - 62.
Mareš, F. V. 1980. Die Tetrachotomie und doppelte Dichotomie der slavischen Sprachen. *WSlJb* 26. 33 - 45.
Orzechowska, H. 1976. *Procesy bałkanizacji i slawizacji bułgarskiego języka literackiego XVII - XIX w. w świetle użycia klitycznych form zaimków*. Warsaw: PWN.
Popowska-Taborska, H. 1980. *Kaszubszczyzna*. Warsaw: PWN.
Reiter, N. 1981. Balcanologia Quo Vadis? *ZfBalk* 17. 177 - 224.
Schaller, H. 1983a. Sprachbund — Sprachgemeinschaft — Sprachfamilie. Eine vergleichende Betrachtung. *Ling. balk.* 26/1. 11 - 16.
1983b. Das Bulgarische und seine Bedeutung für die Balkanphilologie. *Ling. balk.* 26/2. 9 - 17.
1983c. Neue Überlegungen zum Begriff des Sprachbundes und seiner Anwendung auf die Balkansprachen. *Ziele und Wege der Balkanlinguistik* (see Birnbaum 1983c). 210 - 220.
Schmid, W. P. 1979. Das Hethitische in einem neuen Verwandtschaftsmodell. *Hethitisch und Indogermanisch. Vergleichende Studien zur historischen Grammatik und zur dialektgeographischen Stellung der indogermanischen Sprachgruppe Altkleinasiens*, ed. by E. Neu and W. Meid, 231 - 5. Innsbruck: Institut für Sprachwissenschaft der Universität Innsbruck (= *Innsbrucker Beiträge zur Sprachwissenschaft* 25).
Simić, R. 1982. Das Serbokroatische zwischen den balkanslavischen Sprachen und den übrigen Slavinen. *ZfBalk* 18. 70 - 7.
Solta, G. R. 1980. *Einführung in die Balkanlinguistik mit besonderer Berücksichtigung des Substrats und des Balkanlateinischen*. Darmstadt: Wissenschaftliche Buchgesellschaft.
Stang, C. S. 1966. *Vergleichende Grammatik der Baltischen Sprachen*. Oslo, Bergen and Tromsø: Universitetsforlaget.
1972. *Lexikalische Sonderübereinstimmungen zwischen dem Slavischen, Baltischen und Germanischen*. Oslo, Bergen and Tromsø: Universitetsforlaget.
Stieber, Z. 1973. *A historical phonology of the Polish language*. Heidelberg: Winter (= *Historical Phonology of the Slavic Languages* 5).
Sturtevant, E. H. 1942. *The Indo-Hittite laryngeals*. Baltimore: LSA.
1942. The Indo-Hittite hypothesis. *Lg* 38. 105 - 10.
Topolińska, Z. 1974. *A historical phonology of the Kashubian dialects of Polish*. The Hague and Paris: Mouton.
Trautmann, R. 1923. *Baltisch-Slavisches Wörterbuch*. Göttingen: Vandenhoeck and Ruprecht.
Trubačev, O. N. 1981. Replika po balto-slavjanskomu voprosu. *Balto-slavjanskie issledovanija 1980*. Moscow: Nauka, 3 - 6.
1982a, b. Jazykoznanie i etnogenez slavjan. Drevnie slavjane po dannym etimologii i onomastiki. *VJa* 1982/4. 9 - 26; 1982/5. 3 - 17.
Trubetzkoy, N. S. 1928/30. Proposition 16. *Actes du Premier congres international de linguistes a la Haye, du 10 - 15 avril 1928*. Leiden: Sijthoff, 18.
1939/68. Gedanken über das Indogermanenproblem. *Acta linguistica* 1. 81 - 9.

[Reprint: *Die Urheimat der Indogermanen*. Darmstadt: Wissenschaftliche Buchgesellschaft, 214 - 23.]

Udolph, J. 1979. *Studien zu den slavischen Gewässernamen und Gewässerbezeichnungen. Ein Beitrag zur Frage nach der Urheimat der Slaven.* Heidelberg: Winter (=*Beiträge zur Namenforschung*, N. F., Beiheft 17).

Weinreich, U. 1958. On the compatibility of genetic relationship and convergent development. *Word* 14. 374 - 9.

Žuravlev, V. K. 1968. K probleme balto-slavjanskix jazykovyx otnošenij. *Baltistica* 4. 167 - 77.

—— 1970. Ešče raz o predmete, metode, celjax i zadačax nauki o praslavjanskom jazyke. *Jazyk i čelovek* (Commem. vol. P. S. Kuznecov). Moscow: Izd-vo Moskovskogo Universiteta, 86 - 92.

ABBREVIATIONS

AnzfslPh = Anzeiger für slavische Philologie.
BAN = Bǎlgarska Akademija na Naukite.
IJSLP = International Journal of Slavic Linguistics and Poetics.
JAZU = Jugoslavenska Akademija Znanosti i Umjetnosti.
JIES = The Journal of Indo-European Studies.
Lg = Language.
Ling. balk. = Linguistique balkanique.
LSA = Linguistic Society of America.
OxSlP = Oxford Slavonic Papers.
PWN = Państwowe Wydawnictwo Naukowe.
RS = Rocznik slawistyczny.
ScSl = Scando-Slavica.
VJa = Voprosy jazykoznanija.
WdSl = Die Welt der Slaven.
WSlJb = Wiener Slavistisches Jahrbuch.
ZfBalk = Zeitschrift für Balkanologie.
ZfSl = Zeitschrift für Slawistik.
ZfslPh = Zeitschrift für slavische Philologie.

AREAL LINGUISTICS AND ITS IMPLICATIONS FOR HISTORICAL LINGUISTICS

LYLE CAMPBELL

0. Introduction. Areal linguistics, as broadly conceived, deals with the results of the diffusion of structural features across linguistic boundaries. As commonly viewed, linguistic areas are characterized by a number of linguistic features shared by various languages (some of which are unrelated or are from different subgroups within a family) in a geographically contiguous area. The phenomena of the linguistic area (henceforth LA) are also at times referred to by such terms as convergence area, Sprachbund, affinité linguistique, diffusion area, adstratum, etc.[1] However, when it comes to more precise definitions, there is considerable controversy concerning just what areal linguistics (henceforth AL) is, what structural diffusion is, and what the relationship between the two is. Moreover, attempts at definition have occupied much of the attention in areal studies. My purposes in this paper are to refine the notion of LA

---

[1] Areal phenomena are, to a greater or lesser degree, also involved in such other well-defined linguistic enterprises as multilingualism, substrata, superstrata, dialectology, pidgins and creoles, borrowing, sociolinguistics, etc. I readily recognize the relationship and the utility of dealing with these in consideration of areal linguistics. However, in this paper attention is restricted more immediately to areal linguistics; this is sufficient for attaining its goals.

In this context perhaps some seemingly relevant but less important studies should be mentioned. Some use the term "areal linguistics" in the sense of dialect geography within a single language (see for example, Kurath 1972, Goossens 1973, etc.) This usage is not relevant to the concerns of this paper. Also, the Italian "neolinguistic" school has declared itself a champion of areal linguistics. However, as far as I can determine, they have contributed nothing new to the concept. Their dedication to linguistic geography seems motivated by an extremist reaction against neogrammarian sound laws, where they follow Schuchardt (see Spitzer 1928) and Gilliéron (see Gilliéron and Roques 1912). (See Bertoni 1909, 1923, 1925 [192 8]; Bàrtoli 1925a [1928], 1925b, 1929, 1933a, 1933b, 1939; and Bonfante 1945, 1947; cf. also Hall 1946).

and, having done this, to demonstrate some of the implications of AL for historical linguistic method and theory. Crucial to the presentation is my claim that, in general, linguistic diffusion or structural borrowing and AL are to be equated and cannot profitably be separated; i.e. I will argue that there is no sharp boundary between the two, that all areal linguistic phenomena involve diffusion and all structural diffusion involving more than two languages is areal. Having clarified the nature of AL and its relationship to diffusion, I then turn to a consideration of what can be diffused in language contact, i.e. in LAs, and to an examination of the theoretical and methodological implications of AL. In the interest of space, primarily phonological examples are considered, though morphological and syntactic cases are to be understood as also pertaining to this study.

1. The LA defined. It is important to consider how the linguistic area (LA) has been defined in the literature in order to arrive at a fuller understanding of the concept. We may begin by noting that there appear to be two fundamental notions of what a LA is, one which deals with a simple recognition of shared similarities among neighboring languages not necessarily related, and the other which requires historical evidence that proposed areal features are indeed diffused. I consider these in turn.

For some examples of the first, see Becker 1948, Birnbaum 1965, Emeneau 1978 [1980], Henderson 1965, Jakobson 1931a, Sebeok 1950: 101, Sherzer 1973, 1976, Trubetzkoy 1931, Wagner 1959, 1964, etc. Some of these definitions may profitably be cited in the interest of clarifying the concept. Many attribute the formal birth of AL to Trubetzkoy's (1928) famous proposition 16, presented at the First International Congress of Linguistics:

> Gruppen, bestehend aus Sprachen, die eine gross Ähnlichkeit in syntaktischer Hinsicht, eine Ähnlichkeit in den Grundsätzen des morphologischen Baus aufweisen, und eine grosse Anzahl gemeinsamer Kulturwörter bieten, manchmal auch äussere Ähnlichkeit im Bestande der Lautsysteme, — dabei aber keine gemeinsamen Elementarwörter besitzen, — *solche Sprachgruppen nennen wir Sprachbünde.* (Trubetzkoy 1928: 17 - 18, emphasis in original)

Trubetzkoy's term *Sprachbund*, roughly a "union of languages", came to be used as a technical term in English. The name "linguistic area" (LA) corresponds to a translation of *Sprachbund*, first employed by Velten (1943) and made known by Emeneau (1956). Trubetzkoy (1970 [1931]: 233—4) compared AL to traditional dialect geography, but with "isoglosses" which extend beyond the boundaries of a single language.

This view of LAs as akin to cross-language linguistic geography is common in later literature.

Perhaps even more influential than Trubetzkoy was the work of Jakobson (see especially 1931a, also 1931b, 1938 [1970] and 1944). His definition was not particularly precise:

> les "alliances" (Sprachbünde) possédant des ressemblances remarquables dans leur structure syntaxique, morphologique ou phonologique et les "families" (Sprachfamilien) caractérisées avant tout par un fond commun de morphèmes grammaticaux et de mots usuels. (Jakobson 1970 [1938]: 353)

This characterization reflects Trubetzkoy's definition closely.

Perhaps the most influential definition of this sort has been Emeneau's:

> Linguistic areas, i.e. areas in which 'languages belonging to more than one family show traits in common which do not belong to the other members of (at least) one of the families', have been recognized for a very long time. (Emeneau 1980 [1978]: 1, cf. 1980 [1956]: 127)

A very clear statement of this kind of AL is Sherzer's definition:

> A *linguistic area* is defined here as an area in which *several* linguistic traits are shared by the languages of the area and furthermore, there is evidence (linguistic and non-linguistic) that contact between speakers of the languages contributed to the spread and/or retention of these traits and thereby to a certain degree of linguistic uniformity within the area. It is important to remember that languages which are unrelated or distantly related may very well and probably do disagree with regard to many traits and yet still [sic] in the same linguistic area according to the above definition, since they share *several* traits (which one might want to call diagnostic traits). What is significant, then, is that linguistic structure, usually impervious to influences coming from outside its own internal mechanism, has been affected by linguistic contact. (Sherzer 1973: 132)

(For other similar definitions, see Bright and Sherzer 1978: 228, Décsy 1973: 29, Holt and Bright 1976, Haas 1978, Hill 1978: 4, Seidel 1965, Thomason and Kaufman 1975: 26, cf. also Aoki 1975, Voegelin 1945, 1961, Wolff 1959, Zeps 1962, Darnell and Sherzer 1971, etc.

Issues over which opinion has been divided are: the number of isoglosses required to define a LA, whether they must bundle, and whether a single isogloss is sufficient. Some have defined a LA based on isogloss bundling, the bundling considered diagnostic. For example, Emeneau had been of this opinion:

> The first necessity is to establish a typological feature as pan-Indic and at the same time not extra-Indic. Once several features have been established as having the same boundaries, so that there is an approximation to a 'bunching

of isoglosses', the linguistic area can be considered to be typologically established. (Emeneau 1980 [1978]: 2)

(Cf. also Trubetzkoy 1931: 345, Sherzer 1973: 132−3, Masica 1976: 179, Katz 1975: 12, 16, Holt and Bright 1976, etc.)

Nevertheless, few have insisted on the bundling criterion in their definitions of LAs, Many view AL as akin to traditional dialectology where isoglosses frequently fail to group at the boundaries, but are found more concentrated around some core, with vaguer peripheries and without abrupt boundaries, where the extension of individual isoglosses from the center varies greatly. The failure of areal features to bundle has been pointed out by Emeneau 1980 [1965]: 128, 136, Ramanujan and Masica 1969: 550, Winter 1973: 140, Masica 1976: 6, 170, 179, and Henderson 1965: 431.

Moreover, following the analogy of dialectology, some linguists have commented on the overlapping of areal isoglosses, some features from one LA crossing others from some other LA (see, for example, Jakobson 1944: 193, Becker 1948: 23, Weinreich 1958: 378−9, Winter 1973: 140, and Haarmann 1976: 24).

Given that it is difficult to find isogloss bundling at the boundaries of LA_s, some scholars came to define a LA as any group of neighboring languages which share any diffused or convergent structural features, even a single trait. For example, Weinreich (1958: 378−9) spoke of the logical difficulty of distinguishing LAs defined by but a single isogloss from others:

> Yet although the phenomenon is familiar, the term "Sprachbund" is admittedly unsatisfactory. Its fundamental fault is that it implies a unit, as if a language either were or were not a member of a given Sprachbund. But of course a grouping of this sort has no specific *a priori* criteria; a group of geographically continous languages may be classified as a Sprachbund ad hoc, with respect to any structural isogloss.

Katz (1975) makes a single, synchronic isogloss the basis of his definition:

> Von einem Sprachbund kann man sprechen, wenn:
> a) zu einer gegebenen Zeit
> b) ein zusammenhängendes geographisches Gebiet, das
> c) von mindestens einer Sprachgrenze durchzogen ist,
> d) von mindestens einer Isogloss umspannt wird.
> (Katz 1975: 16)

Masica (1976: 172) also came to understand a single areal isogloss as the minimum defining feature for LAs:

> Linguistic areas are apparently phenomena of differing magnitudes, starting from the limiting case, the area defined by a single trait.

(Cf. also Bright and Sherzer 1978: 236, Trubetzkoy 1931: 345, and Jakobson 1931a: 139.)

What can we conclude from these attempts at definition? First, most investigators view AL as being like traditional dialectology, only with isoglosses that extend beyond language boundaries. Second, since areal isoglosses rarely bundle, (and often overlap) it is of little use to attempt to define LAs based on the coincidence of structural traits at some boundary. Third, borrowed features are typically called "areal phenomena". Finally, it is to be recognized that no sharp boundary can be drawn between LAs which share a single diffused trait and those which share many. We can easily understand the issue by considering such analogies as, how many grains of sand does it take to make a heap?, how many birds are needed to constititute a flock, how many students are required to make a class?, and so on. However, given that borrowed features are called "areal phenomena" and given that in principle a single shared trait may be considered sufficient to define a LA, it is warranted to equate structural diffusion and AL — they cannot and should not be rigidly distinguished. That is, while some borrowing (e.g. those involving a single trait from one language to one other) may not necessarily be areal, all areal traits are the results of structural diffusion.

The conclusion that a LA might adequately be defined on the basis of a single shared feature may prove unsettling to some, and therefore I attempt to anticipate reactions. One possible reaction is, if a single isogloss is sufficient to define a LA, then either there are no worthwhile LAs or they are so poorly defined that they are of little value. Another is that there must be something to the popular notion that LAs share various traits. I answer these reactions by reiterating that in principle there is no meaningful way of distinguishing LAs defined on the basis of several features from those based on but a single shared trait. Nevertheless, the question can be posed, not in the form, does or does not some entity qualify as a LA?, but rather as, how strong or weak is a particular LA? That is, we can think of a continuum of LAs from those weakly defined on the basis of but a single shared feature to markedly strong ones based on many diffused elements. Given such a continuum, the popular notion corresponds to the clearly stronger LAs. This approach to defining LAs also implies a means of evaluating the strength of LAs, to which I now turn.

2. Evaluation metrics. One strategy for improving the definition of LAs has been to propose criteria of evaluation. For some this amounts to mere counting of the number of shared traits. For others it involves ranking them in some evaluative scale according to the varying social, cultural, or historical circumstances which gave rise to the areas. It is worth looking into some of these in order to understand AL better.

Melville Jacobs was aware of the problem of distinguishing truly diffused areal traits from the residue of unknown genetic unity. As a means of evaluation he proposed "the more the merrier":

> It would appear, other things being equal, that the larger the number of languages that share a phonetic feature, the less probable the deduction that this feature is a residue from an ancient oneness of such languages; and the more likely the deduction that the process of diffusion... can be applied... (Jacobs 1954: 50)

It is possible, all else being equal, that a greater number of languages with a shared trait indicates a higher probability of diffusion of that feature. Nevertheless, there are usually additional considerations, so that the probability suggested by Jacobs should be restricted, for example, by taking the kind of trait involved into account. Some traits easily develop independently, others are universal or nearly universal, and some may even be due to an undetected genetic relationship, in spite of the large number of languages involved.

Katz (1975) was aware of the problem of universals and near-universals in the selection of areal features. He proposed an evaluation scale to account for this:

> Es ist zwar klar, dass durch "near-universals" konstituierte Sprachbünde als solche nicht sehr interressant sind, dieser Mangel lässt sich aber ausleichen, wenn wir eine "Wertskala" aufstellen, die besagen soll: Ein Sprachgebiet, das von mehr Sprachbundisoglossen umschlossen ist, ist auf dieser Skala höher zu bewerten als eines innerhalb von weniger solchen Isoglossen. (Katz 1975: 16)

This also amounts to a "the more the merrier" proposal, where more isoglosses is taken as more highly valued.

These attempts to establish means of evaluating LAs make us realize that indeed different types of LAs exist. These differences depend on the circumstances that gave rise to them and contributed to their development, as indicated by Thomason and Kaufman (1975: 27):

> The various areas so identifiable, however, are not of a uniform type. In some of the areas in question, there is current institutionalized multilingualism, either multilateral or unilateral. In others there has been massive shift in the

past, with, however, some speakers of the languages shifted from still around. In still others there has been gradual diffusion of features over long centuries, without high degrees of multilingualism or massive shift. It might be profitable to try to separate these types, but at present we have no foolproof method of doing so.

(Cf. Masica 1976: 173, Martinet 1952: 123.) If the distinct types of LAs have historical backgrounds so varied, then it follows that their composition and their nature vary greatly in character and in the intensity with which their shared traits interrelate. Given this variation in the kinds of LAs and in the circumstances that produce them, the conclusion is greatly strengthened that AL and structural diffusion are not and should not be separated. This brings me to the second major approach to defining LA, which requires historical evidence.

3. The historicist approach. Perhaps the most important evaluative attempts have been based on the realization of the different historical factors which go into the creation of LAs. Masica's (1976: 173) distinction becomes very significant between those LAs which are the relics of past contacts which are no longer active and others which are in the process of formation and extension due to on-going interaction and change. Let us consider some of the history-sensitive proposals.

Jacobsen (1980) has proposed the criterion of "installation" to provide information about the antiquity and direction of areal diffusion; he says:

> I would like to refer to the... category as being more or less installed in a given language. This is a purely heuristic concept, which nevertheless seems to be helpful in approaching the data; it is intended to relate to historical depth... (Jacobsen 1980: 4)

The basic idea, then, is "the more deeply installed, the better", where a diffused trait is "installed" by having an integrated interrelation with a higher number of categories and structures of the language, with the belief that more time is required to produce a good or deep "installation". In this way, the relative installation of a feature in the languages of a LA is taken as an indication of its age and of the direction of diffusion.

Initially the "installation" criterion may appear plausible, but historical evidence from some languages, where the historical facts are clear, shows that the "installation" concept proves unreliable for determining the direction of areal borrowing. For example, Gair (1980) documented that Sinhala (an Indo-Aryan language) has borrowed a focus construction (similar to cleft sentences in English) from its Dravidian neighbors, but has integrated it very deeply into the grammar of Sinhala such that it turns out to be better installed in Sinhala than in the Dravidian source languages. Gair says:

> The Sinhala borrowing of the focusing construction and its subsequent history goes beyond mere adaptation, however, to illustrate a process for which I have suggested the term, "naturalization" (on the analogy of immigration and naturalization) by which a borrowed form enters into the grammar of the borrowing language in an intimate way, participating in its rule structures and even as in this case, serving as a model for further internal change. The Sinhala instance of naturalization we have examined has important implications for linguistic area studies. If we were to look only at the relevant linguistic characteristics of Sinhala and other Dravidian languages, without considering the known cultural-historical facts and the evidence of the northern Indo-Aryan languages, we might erroneously assume that the greater elaboration of the focusing construction in Sinhala and its centrality in the grammar points to borrowing from Sinhala into the other languages, a conclusion that is of course obviously contravened by the other evidence alluded to. In short, we should remember the lesson — that greater frequency or complexity, and in this case integration in the grammar, does not necessarily mean greater age or source of borrowing, but that it may be the result of naturalization or its cultural analogues... (Gair 1980:39)

Gair's "naturalization" corresponds closely to Jacobsen's "installation"; the Sinhala case shows that installation or naturalization should not be used as a definitive criterion for indicating the relative age or direction of areal borrowing.

The real lesson of "installation" and "naturalization" is that precise historical information is invaluable. Nevertheless, linguists have been divided in their opinions about the need for or value of historical facts in areal investigations. One group's approach has been merely to catalogue the similarities found in some particular area, allowing these similarities to suggest diffusion, but without carrying out the research necessary to demonstrate the actual borrowing. This is basically an approach of "guilt by association", which is judged on the basis of "circumstantial evidence". The "circumstantialist" approach, as I will call it, could be useful, particularly in the preliminary stages of investigation or in those LAs where reliable historical facts are difficult to obtain. Even so, ultimately we would like to be able to separate real areal features, those due to diffusion, from historical accidents, which may be due to such factors as undiscovered genetic relationships, universals, onomatopoeia, parallel or independent development, sheer chance, etc. Unfortunately, the "circumstantialists" do not see the need for carrying out the historical program. (For some examples, cf. Haas 1969a, 1976, Sherzer 1973, 1976, Sherzer and Bauman 1972, Campbell 1977, Sapir 1949 [1921]: 198, Trubetzkoy 1928, 1931, Bright and Sherzer 1978, Holt and Bright 1976, Kaufman 1973, etc.)

The sharpest criticism against this kind of AL concerns the selection of features to be considered areal. Since almost everybody considers LAs to be the products of diffusion, features designated as evidence for some LA should be due to borrowing or convergence, stemming from mutual influence (contact). As already seen a LA may be defined by any similarity that happens to be shared among contiguous languages, but if the selected shared features might be explained equally well as being due to accident, universals, genetic factors, or whatever, then the LA makes no sense as the product of diffusion and begins to seem like any linguistic typology whatever which might involve neighbouring languages, with no historical significance at all.

The other main group of arealists link their definition, or at least their research practice, more directly with historical proofs such that the features designated as real are demonstrably diffused. I call this the "historical" approach, exerzized by the "historicists". It is instructive to see why the "historicists" insist on historical evidence and to consider their criticisms of the "circumstantialists".

In this respect, Jacobsen (1980:2), speaking of Sherzer, calls for the historical program:

> The obvious way of making further progress in these matters... is to go beyond a mere cataloging of the presence or absence of a category in a language to a study of the actual means used for its expression and to a reliance upon the findings of historical linguistics as applied to the several languages and families.

Eric Hamp (1977) also sharply criticizes Sherzer (1976) and the "circumstantialist" approach. His comments on the relation of AL to genetic classification are directly to the point:

> while the comparative method is unquestionably an historical study, the field of areal linguistics is no less so; for it too is occupied with analyzing the result of specific, if multiple, linguistic events of the past. Both the comparative method and areal linguistics are historical disciplines — twin faces of diachronic linguistics, if you will. (Hamp 1977: 279)
> his [Sherzer's] methodology seems to make far too little provision for these distinctions [AL and comparative linguistics] that I consider essential... his study would lie properly within the realm of typology... for areal, i.e. ultimately specific historical, questions it may be damaging in two main ways. The conclusions may result in a listing of a catalogue of trivia; and the starting

> parameters may well have missed the most interesting and crucially tell-tale characteristics. (Hamp 1977:281)
>
> Such areal questions can be approached meaningfully and fruitfully only if they are treated in specific terms for what they are — the results of developments with historical depth and specificity. (Hamp 1977:282)

(See also Winter 1973:147 for a similar treatment and Silverstein's 1978 similar criticism of Sherzer for lack of historical validity.)

On the other hand, Murray Emeneau (1956, 1978, etc.) always had a historical component in his areal methodology. For example, he said:

> ... part of the methodology is then the historical one. It is an investigation into the language of origin of the feature in question, its direction of diffusion throughout the languages of the linguistic area... (Emeneau 1980 [1978]:2)

Even in his original definition of LAs, Emeneau had the "historicist" perspective (cf. Emeneau 1956:16). Some others who have proven to be "historicists", either in their theoretical discussions or in the way they document their studies, are Jacobs 1954, Gorbet 1977, Gair 1980, Pray 1980, Weinreich 1953, 1958, Thomason 1980, Gumperz and Wilson 1971, Nadkarni 1975, Silverstein 1974, Tai 1976, etc.

Beyond doubt, most linguists would say that it is always better to have historical documentation in areal consideration, whenever possible. This attitude shows once again that in the best of circumstances AL is not really different from structural diffusion in general, given that in the best cases of LAs the areal diffusion is documented with historical evidence. I conclude with Hamp (1977) and Winter (1973), then, that our goal should be to determine the historical facts which explain similarities among languages, be they due to common heritage from some proto language or to diffusion.

Acceptance of this "historicist" goal implies approaching our subject matter without prejudicial preconceptions. This being the case, and in light of the considerable attention given Sherzer's approach in the recent literature, it is important to point out some additional limitations of his "circumstantialist" approach which stem from methodological preconceptions about which I have serious reservations. Two of these, the "areal" and the "genetic" preconceptions, are revealed in the following:

> The linguistic traits investigated in this study are presented within the framework of the culture areas of North America... this manner of presentation enables the determination of the degeree of linguistic homogeneity with geographic areas that have been shown to be homogeneous or relatively homogeneous with regard to non-linguistic cultural traits. The distribution of each

trait will be stated in a way that reflects both its location(s) with the culture area in question and the genetic affiliations of the languages in which it is found. The genetic affiliations largely follow Sapir's 'intermediate classification' ... to provide the reader with both an areal and a genetic perspective from which to consider the distribution of each trait. (Sherzer 1976:10)

A study actually to determine the extent to which the anthropologists' culture areas (cf. Kroeber 1939, Driver 1961) correspond to LAs would have been valuable, but Sherzer's work simply presupposed a significant correlation. Of course, there is no a priori reason to suppose such a correlation, since it is well known that cultural diffusion may proceed at a much more rapid rate than structural borrowing among languages. Sherzer (1973) himself comments that the linguistic correlation in the Great Plains is perhaps so weak because that culture area is of recent formation.

Perhaps the presupposition of ready-made LAs corresponding to culture areas would not be so misleading if Sherzer had been able to show that the structural features found shared among the languages of these pre-existing areas were indeed due to borrowing as demonstrated by independent historical evidence. Nevertheless, Sherzer, as a circumstantialist, simply presented lists of linguistic similarities in the predetermined areas. With no indications of these similarities as historical products, the "selection" problem makes these LAs seem no more valid than any arbitrary grouping or typology of languages selected randomly and called an area based on whatever features they might happen to share for whatever reasons. For example, state boundaries might be considered to determine LAs composed of the languages within each state.

Perhaps one might think this criticism somewhat stark, since Sherzer indicates that he took genetic classifications into account. If the shared similarities in these predetermined areas extend beyond genetic boundaries, would that not be evidence of areal diffusion and therefore partial vindication of Sherzer's method? Aside from the fact that similarities may be due to factors other than common heritage and diffusion, this would be the case only if the presupposed genetic classifications could be confirmed on the basis of historical facts. However, if we accept the goal seriously of seeking to understand the past, whether from common heritage or borrowing, then linguistic similarities must be studied objectively. Unfortunately, Sherzer merely presupposed Sapir's ('intermediate') classification, but Sapir's scheme was presented as a hypothesis to be tested in subsequent research, not as established genetic relationships (Sapir 1925 :526); subsequent research has rejected and revised many aspects of this classification (see Campbell and Mithun 1979). Sherzer's imposition of Sapir's classification amounts to an unwarranted genetic preconception, a prejudiced treatment of many otherwise unanalyzed similarities as genetic. Starting with doubtful genetic presuppositions, one cannot easily determine the real nature of features, some of which may in fact be due to borrowing or other factors, but which are forcibly attributed to common ancestry. In fact, a realization of the existence of LAs is causing a reassessment of the many proposed but unconfirmed distant genetic relationships in recent research (cf. Campbell and Mithun 1979).

In sum, Sherzer's preconceived areas and predetermined but unconfirmed genetic classification virtually guarantee the impossibility of taking the historicist goal seriously of finding out in fact to what shared linguistic similarities are due. Sherzer's lists of similarities seem more to be artifacts of these constraining conditions rather than to be evidence of their usefulness. Certainly LAs established in this way are at best very doubtful.[2]

4. Methodological issues. With this consideration of Sherzer as a prologue, let us take up other methodological issues in the investigation of LAs.

Frequently in the areal literature questions about the value or usefulness of the data are repeated. Some ask, for example, how can information from incommensurate descriptions of distinct languages be compared, and what is to be done in cases deficient or totally lacking in relevant information about key traits in a particular language or languages, or in the case of the total absence of data on languages which are probably important members of some LA? That is, how can one be certain that attributes of one language are equivalent or comparable to those of the other languages? How are cases to be treated in which the compared phenomenon is allophonic in one language but

---

[2] This strong conclusion relative to the procedure of establishing LAs is indeed warranted. Still, in Sherzer's defense in a more general sense, it should be pointed out that his work has been beneficial in stimulating recent attention to AL. Furthermore, as initial hypotheses, such LAs may provide direction for future testing. Indeed it is worthwhile to investigate the extent to which known social or cultural history as reflected in culture areas may be reflected linguistically — to look for linguistic diffusion is one thing, but to assume it as Sherzer did in defining his LAs is methodologically unfortunate.

distinctive in another?; that is, how is the separation of levels to be dealt with in areal comparisons? A concrete and non-trivial example of this kind involves retroflexion in Lushai, a language of the eastern frontier of the Indian LA. The difficulty is, how are the /t^r/ and /d^r/ of Lushai to be interpreted, as consonant clusters and therefore not part of the area of retroflexion, or as retroflexes and therefore as evidence of Lushai's membership in the area? (See Henderson 1965.)

There are many ways in which one's theoretical persuasion may influence his or her areal decisions. To take just one example, Leslau (1945, 1952) showed extensive areal diffusion among the Ethiopian Semitic languages from Chusitic languages. But many of the individual examples presented by Leslau amount to what many today take as the borrowing of SOV basic word order from Cushitic into the formerly non-verb-final Semitic languages, e.g. postpositions, SOV, Verb-Auxiliary, relative clause-noun phrase, adjective-noun, etc. The question is, does this count as the diffusion of but a single feature, SOV basic word order, or as several? Leslau's pre-word-order-typology theory could see it only as many. More importantly, if it counts as only one feature, then clearly it requires stronger areal pressure to produce its borrowing than that needed for some other kinds of structural borrowings. This raises the question, how are different areal features to be evaluated, particularly in the proposed evaluation schemes aimed at determining the strength of a LA?

Many methodological difficulties involve multiple causation, where different kinds or sources of data come together. A simple example is the change of *f* to *h* (ultimately to ø) in Spanish, which is often attributed to Basque influence (cf., e.g., Menéndez Pidal 1926), but some attribute it to systematic pressure within Spanish to eliminate *f* for the sake of pattern congruity or symmetry (since it lacked a counterpart in *v* to support its position within the system; cf., e.g. Malmberg 1973). Regardless of the ultimate strengths and weaknesses of these competing explanations, they serve to illustrate what I mean by multiple causation. It is quite possible that both the areal explanation (Basque influence) and the internal account (systemic coherency) interacted to facilitate the Spanish change via a convergence of motivating factors.

One frequently controversial kind of multiple causation involves the confluence of diffusional phenomena with inherent, native factors. A famous example has to do with the origin of retroflexed consonants in Sanskrit and the Indo-Aryan languages. Arealists claim that retroflexion is an areal trait, which owes its presence in Indo-Aryan to Dravidian influence, where the phenomenon is native, present in Proto-Dravidian (Emeneau 1956, 1965, 1971, Henderson 1965, Masica 1976, Ramanujan and Masica 1969, Bhat 1973, Kuiper 1967, etc.). On the other hand, Indo-European purists insist that Sanskrit could have (or did) develop retroflexion on its own solely from native properties. They refer to such processes as the famous "ruki" rule, due to which Sanskrit's s exhibits an allophone $ṣ$ after i, u, r, and k. Another rule gives $ṣ$ before t, and yet another retroflexes t after $ṣ$ and in final position. Finally, n obtained a retroflexed allophone, $ṇ$, after r and $ṣ$. (Cf., e.g., Hock 1975.) So who is right? Are the Indo-Aryan retroflexes due to purely native developments or to diffusion? It appears that both explanations are involved in convergent fashion. Although the "ruki" rule is native, its retroflexed variants are very probably due to Dravidian influence. This is suggested by the fact that the Iranian and Slavic languages also have their own version of this rule, but its output is not necessarily retroflexed, but rather only a backed variety of s. The final result in Slavic, after other changes, is x (a velar fricative) (Andersen 1968). I conclude with Kuiper (1967: 98) that retroflexion owes its origins to a convergence of native and areal factors:

> these changes may be considered the results of a subtle interplay between internal factors inherent in the system and external factors of foreign influence; they may contribute to our insight into the ever-fascinating problem of change in language.

Another related kind of multiple causation involving native and foreign factors, also at times disputed, results in the preservation of native material in a language due to AL, where the same material is lost outside the area. A tractable example is the preservation of l^y in Andean Spanish, where this /l^y/ has merged with /y/ in most of the rest of Latin American Spanish. The preservation of the contrast in Andean Spanish has been attributed to contact with Quechua and Aymara, native languages which also contain /l^y/ (Lapesa 1981: 571).[3] In spite of the obvious reasonableness of this proposed areal explanation, certain tenacious scholars of Spanish maintain that the only relevant

---

[3] Central and southern Chile, except for packets, lack the (l^y) in spite of the contact with Araucanian which has it, but this is no problem in this context, since the Spanish interaction with Araucanian was very different from the influence of Quechua and Aymara. Thus in northern Chile, with its Quechua and Aymara population, the Spanish does have (l^y). (I assume the (l^y) of Paraguayan Spanish to be unrelated to these considerations.)

factor in the explanation of the Andean /lʸ/ is its arrival with the Spanish colonizers, where it has not changed as it did in other parts of America. Nevertheless, it is strange indeed that the contrast's maintenance coincides precisely with the zone in which other languages with the same contrast are spoken. This alone seems sufficient to negate pure chance. Some similar, but less clear cases of this sort are, for example, the assibilited *r* (phonetic [š]) of Guatemalan Spanish, shared by certain Peninsular dialects of Spanish (cf. Zamora Vicente 1970 :389) and the Quichean languages of Guatemala. Another case is that of the pleonastic possessive shared by Mayan languages and Guatemalan, Chiapan, and Yucatecan Spanish, as well as older varieties of Peninsular Spanish, e.g. "tengo un mi caballo" (literally, "I have one my horse"), Quiche *k'o xun nu-kye:x* (identical). In spite of controversies, the pleonastic possessive has proven to be the result of convergence between areal influence and the reinforcement of native Spanish material (cf. Keniston 1937: 242 - 7, Martin 1978, Sandoval 1941: 87, 458, 550, Francis 1960: 85, etc.).

Another kind of complicated multiple causation involves the interaction of contact phenomena with universal tendencies. To take a simple example, there is a natural, universal propensity not to express noun plurals with numbers, since the overt specification of the number covers the semantic terrain of the plural and therefore plural markers with quantified nouns are redundant. This is a pattern found in many languages throughout the world (e.g. Finnish). It is also found in Mayan languages and with a certain frequency in the Spanish of Chiapas, for example *tres manzana* for *tres manzanas*, literally "three apple". The question is, does Chiapan Spanish owe this fact to Mayan influence or to universal tendencies? It is quite reasonable to imagine that it is due to a convergence of both factors, contact and universal tendencies.

Finally, areal investigation is complicated by another kind of apparent multiple causation, somewhat similar to the last considered, where are al accounts compete with or converge with sheer chance as explanations. The best known examples involve changes which can easily take place independently, leaving us with the question in many cases of whether some shared similarity among languages of an area is to be explained by contact or by the parallel development that tends to happen easily in languages generally. For example, languages of the Baltic LA share contrastive vowel length. Given that length contrasts are apparently readily acquired due to segmental changes, particularly when compensatory lengthening is involved, one wonders to what extent Baltic areal lengthening is due to areal pressure and to what degree to accident. Perhaps a more revealing example is Sherzer's (1973: 160) Great Basin, said to share the areal features:

1) a single series of fricatives (voiceless)
2) suffixation of the nominal diminutive marker
3) pronominal plural
4) suffixation of the tense-aspect markers of verbs
5) distinct verb roots for nouns with distinct number.

If these are the only features defining the Great Basin LA, we must ask if it may not actually be the result of just accident. For example, Spanish shares the first four of these features. The fifth is not really typical of Spanish, but one might consider as strained examples from Spanish such verbs as *asesinar* "assassinate", with its preference for singular objects, and *masacar* "massacre", with plural objects.

Such cases as these make us realize more acutely the value of historical evidence of diffusion in order to deal adequately with features shared trivially by accident, parallel development, and the like.

5. Implications. To this point I have considered problems of definition and of methods in AL. I now turn to the theoretical and methodological implications of AL for historical linguistics. Today it is clear that structural features of all levels and components of grammar can be borrowed. I will consider specifically the implications of diffused phonological segments (or distinctive features), borrowed phonological rules, some morphological and syntactic changes due to contact, and exceptions to certain universals which are motivated by areal factors.

It is very common for foreign sounds to enter the phonological system of a language with the importation of loanwords which contain such sounds. Less common, but more interesting, is the installation of foreign sounds in native vocabulary, in native etyma, not necessarily depending on the occurrence of foreign lexical items. Some examples may be in order for potential skeptics. Some Bantu languages borrowed clicks from neighbouring Bushman and Hottentot languages. Proto-Bantu had no clicks, but Xhosa, Zulu, Swati, Ndebele, Sutho, Kwangari, Goiriku and Mbukushu do have them. Of this Westphal (1963: 242) said:

> the occurrence of speech sounds — including clicks — in language areas and in speech-sound systems in which they do not otherwise occur may be an

indication of contact areas... The general absence of clicks in Common Bantu or Ur-Bantu systems permits us to state that Bantu languages in which they do occur have come under the influence of, or have had contact with, languages in which they regularly occur.

(Cf. also Louw 1962.)

A second case involves the glottalized consonants in Ossetic, Eastern Armenian, and a few other Indo-European languages of the area. Indo-European languages have no native glottalized consonants, but Ossetic and Eastern Armenian, among others, have borrowed them from other languages in the Caucasian LA (Bielmeier 1977 :43, Thomason and Kaufman 1975 :49, Trubetzkoy 1931 :233 [1970 :13], Vogt 1945, 1954 :371, etc.). A third case, that of retroflexed consonants in Indo-Aryan, has already been discussed. Now there is no doubt that they owe their origin in Indo-Aryan, at least in part, to Dravidian influence. (See Emeneau 1956, 1965, 1971, Burrow 1971, Kuiper 1967, Ramanujan and Masica 1969, Henderson 1965, Bhat 1973, Campbell 1976, etc.). A fourth example is similar to the last; it involves the retroflexed dentals of Lake Miwok, clearly borrowed within the Clear Lake LA, where Patwin, Wappo and Eastern Pomo also share the feature. There is no doubt of its borrowed origin in Lake Miwok, since other Miwokan languages lack it (see Callaghan 1965, Haas 1978 [1976]: 359, Hill 1978: 3).

The examples considered so far show the acquisition of segments or distinctive features through diffusion, but language contact can also lead to the elimination of segments or features. A particularly clear case of this is found in Nootkan, where Proto-Nootkan had nasal consonants, as does Nootka, but Nitinat and Makah lost nasality (former nasals become voiced stops, *b, d*) due to areal pressure. Nitinat and Makah belong to that area of the Northwest Coast where languages of several different families lack nasals. Of this Haas says:

> In the Vancouver Island-Washington Coast area, one or more languages belonging to three different linguistic families (Wakashan, Chemakuan, and Salishan) have no primary nasal consonants. In the Wakashan family this includes Nitinat and Makah; in Chemakuan, it includes Quileute; and in Salishan it includes Puget Sound Salish (Duwamish, Snoqualmie, Snohomish, etc.) and Twana... The languages which have been mentioned have b and d (sometimes b' and d') where other languages within the same family have m and n (and ṁ and ṅ). This is clearly an areal feature which has spread across genetic boundaries. The Northwest Coast area as a whole is one which is rich in examples of areal spread of phonological features across such boundaries. (Haas 1969b: 112)

A few other examples of lost segments or features due to language contact are 1) the merger of /l/ and /lʲ/ in Czech, attributed to German influence in the fashionable speech of the cities (Weinreich 1935: 25, Jakobson 1938: 54); 2) the merger of /ć, ś/ with /ƈ, s/ in urban Croatian, believed to be due to the influence of Venetian Italian (Weinreich 1953: 25); and 3) the loss of the emphatic consonants and vowel length in Cypriotic Arabic, the result of Cypriotic Greek influence (Newton 1964: 43).

One obvious implication of these examples is that indeed segments or distinctive features can be borrowed. Another implication is that sound change due to diffusion should be distinguished from native or internal change. The native or internal changes appear to obey the neogrammarian regularity of exceptionless sound changes, however it is clear that areally motivated sound changes need not be regular or predictable. This violation of the regularity hypothesis in areal diffusion has been noted by others, as well (cf. Burrows 1971, Emeneau 1980 [1974]: 198, Thomason and Kaufman 1975: 52). Of the irregular reflexes in Indo-Aryan created by the retroflexed consonants, Burrows (1971: 36) said:

> The characteristic of this development in Old and Middle Indo-Aryan is that it cannot be reduced to any rules. The doctrine that sound changes are regular and without exception breaks down completely in this case. In these examples the cerebralization [retroflexion] is not only spontaneous but also sporadic and unpredictable.

(For some attempts at explaining the differences between diffused [external] changes and native [internal] changes, and the factors which cause them and thus contribute to their different characters, see Campbell 1976, 1980, Campbell and Ringen 1981, and cf. Emeneau 1980 [1974]: 198.)

Correlated with the failure of many areal changes to obey the neogrammarian principle of regular change is their failure to be "natural" in the linguistically popular sense. This concept that changes tend to be "natural" may have many merits with respect to native or internally motivated changes, but there is nothing "natural" in this sense about the introduction of, for example, clicks, glottalized consonants, or retroflexes in the examples presented above — these sounds are highly marked, not expected. Moreover the areal elimination of nasality in the Nootkan example caused unnaturalness of two kinds. First, the languages of this area are nearly the only ones in the world which lack primary nasals: nasality would be almost an absolute linguistic universal if it were not for the lack of nasality here, due apparently to areal diffusion. The phonological inventories of these languages became less natural as a result of the change, since the presence of voiced stops with the absence of nasals is taken as more highly marked. Second, several Nootkan phonological rules were rendered less natural, as a result of the change (see Sapir and Swadesh 1939). The famous "hardening" and "softening" processes turned out more complicated after the change, since instead of dealing with a natural class of sonorants, they had to take into account sonorants and voiced stops. (Note that the feature "voiced" is not adequate, since /t/ of the rules is sonorant but voiceless.)

Finally, areally induced sound changes have methodological implications for subgroup classification. The only valid criterion for determining the branches (internal relationships) of family trees is "shared innovations" (cf. Dyen 1953, Hamp 1953, 1958, 1960, Hoeningswald 1960, 1966, Sherzer 1972b, Chretién 1962, Greenberg 1957, and Campbell 1977: 62 - 73). In the Nootkan case, Nitinat and Makah appear to share the common innovation of the change of nasals to voiced stops, which might be used to support a closer relationship between Nitinat and Makah than between either of these and Nootka, which did not undergo the change. In this case, however, we know that the loss of nasality is due to areal diffusion and therefore happened independently in the separate histories of both Nitinat and Makah. Ultimately other shared innovations show that in fact Nitinat and Nootka are more closely grouped as opposed to Makah, which separated a bit earlier (Haas 1969b:115, Jacobsen 1969:141). This example shows that undetected areal diffusion can complicate subgrouping considerations and should therefore be taken into account and allowances made.

The final implication I consider might more appropriately be called a hypothesis, which is suggested by the clear cases of diffused sounds which come to be found in native lexical items. In general, borrowed segments (or distinctive features) lack distributional restrictions in the borrowing language(s) which they obeyed in the donor(s). For example, the retroflexed consonants in Proto-Dravidian did not occur word-initially (Burrow 1971, Meenakshisundaran 1965: 20, Zvelebil 1970: 77), although they can occur initially in Indo-Aryan, where they owe their origin to Dravidian influence. Similarly, Northern Slavic languages apparently acquired consonant palatalization from Uralic languages, but the feature is contrastive in Uralic only for apicals, while in Russian it was generalized to most of the consonants (Jakobson 1931a, Thomason and Kaufman 1975: 13). So I propose the following hypothesis:

> Borrowed segments (or distinctive features) which come to occur in native etyma may typically lack distributional restrictions in the borrowing language(s) that they obeyed in the donor language(s).

This will have to be tested in subsequent research.

Not only may foreign sounds be borrowed, but also foreign phonological rules may be borrowed and they do not necessarily depend upon the simultaneous borrowing of lexical items. One revealing example of this involves the rule which palatalizes velars in western dialects of Quichean languages, which was borrowed from Mamean languages. The rule is:

$$\begin{bmatrix} k \\ k' \end{bmatrix} \rightarrow \begin{bmatrix} k^y \\ k'^y \end{bmatrix} / -V \begin{Bmatrix} q(') \\ x \end{Bmatrix} \quad \text{e.g. } kaq \rightarrow k^y aq \text{ "red"} \\ \text{ke:} x \rightarrow k^y e\text{:} x \text{ "deer"}$$

There is no doubt about the borrowing or the direction, since evidence from dialectology, philology, and comparative studies converges to ensure the interpretation (see Campbell 1974, 1977, Kaufman 1969). The isogloss is striking, since the rule cross-cuts several languages, but reaches only western dialects of the various Quichean languages (adjacent to the Mamean western neighbors). Colonial documents show that the rule first entered Quichean dialects on the west around 1700 (first attested in 1704), spreading gradually towards the east. Mamean documents and comparative Mamean evidence show a much early presence of the rule within Mamean (Campbell 1974).

Some other cases of borrowed rules are: 1) Livonian has two rules attributed to German and Scandinavian influence, one of "umlaut", the other of "breaking" (Korhonen 1969, Campbell 1976); 2) Eastern Finnish dialects have a rule of consonant palatalization due to Russian and neighboring Balto-Finnic influences (Itkonen 1969, Rapola 1969: 136, Turunen 1959: 192–5); 3) A number of Greek dialects spoken in Asia Minor have encorporated a vowel-harmony rule borrowed from Turkish (Dawkins 1916, Thomason and Kaufman 1976); 4) The Albanian of San Marzano has two rules due to Italian influence, one of consonant gemination, the other of schwa insertion (Hamp 1968); 5) The French of Quimper has borrowed a rule of final devoicing from Breton (Vendryes 1921: 339); 6) Cypriotic Arabic has the borrowed morphophonemic rule which changes *py* to *pc* in verb conjugations, taken from Cypriotic Greek (Newton 1964: 46); etc.

The first and obvious implication is that phonological rules can be borrowed. (For greater details and additional examples, see Campbell 1976.) There is also a theoretical conclusion. Borrowing is one possible source of new phonological rules in a language. This is not a trivial conclusion, since it has at times mistakenly been denied (for example, see Hooper 1976: 84—7).

Also, just as phonological segments can be eliminated areally, the loss of phonological rules may be caused by language contact. Since such phenomena are reasonably well attested and uncontroversial, I present only a few examples in brief form. 1) Some Finnish dialects have lost the rule of "final gemination" (where a final segment, often postulated as underlying /?/, becomes a complete copy of the initial consonant of the word or morpheme which follows it) due to Russian influence in some cases and Swedish in others (Kettunen 1930: 151, Turunen 1959: 126). 2) Some Pipil dialects lost the rule which devoices final sonorants under Spanish influence (Campbell 1976). 3) Total or partial loss of the spirantization, gemination, prenasalization and preaspiration processes in Shoshoni is due to English influence (Miller 1971: 119).

A phenomenon related to borrowed segments and rules is the diffusion of a sound change within a LA from one language to another. Examples of this abound. 1) The change of k to $č$ has diffused throughout a continuous area from the west coast of Vancouver Island to the mouth of the Columbia River, affecting languages of various families (Sapir 1926, Kinkade 1973, Kinkade and Powell 1976). 2) A similar change of k to c [sic] before front vowels diffused through Telugu, Tamil, Malayalam, and some dialects of Tulu (Bhat 1970). 3) A change which affricated palatals in central India includes Marathi, Southern Oriya, Telugu and Northern Kannada (Emeneau 1980).

Similar to these diffused changes are "shifts" in native sounds in order to match phonetic values in some other language of influence. Again, examples abound, so I present few. 1) Finnish ð (The result of consonant gradation) shifted to d under influence from Swedish, due in part to the Swedish reading model with d (Rapola 1965: 127, Hakulinen 1968: 53). 2) Some Finnish dialects changed their $ä$ (/æ/) to e under Swedish influence—Swedish has no /æ/ (Kettunen 1930: 15). 3) The Nattavaara dialect of Finnish shifted jj (/yy/) to $d^y d^y$, medial h to /?/, and the geminates kk, tt, and pp to hk, ht, and hp, respectively, under Lapp influence (Kettunen 1930: 97—8). 4) Creek shifted its ϕ (bilabial fricative) to f (labiodental) under English influence (Haas 1941: 42). 5) Teotepeque Pipil shifted its /š/ to /r̃/ under the influence of the Spanish stigmatization of $š$ as an undesirable variant of its /r̃/; that is, the negative social value of the stigmatized variant in Spanish caused the shift in Pipil of its native sound (Campbell 1976).

I conclude this section with a discussion of the implications of diffusion for linguistic universals. In spite of the popular sense of the word "universal", some proposed universals may be violated by changes which are due to diffusion. For example, the implicational universal that uvulars imply the presence of velars in a language (for example, $q \supset k$) appears valid, but is violated by some of the languages of the Northwest Coast where the diffused change of k to $č$ left languages with q and $č$, but no k, at least for a period of time before new velars were developed (Kinkade 1973, Kinkade and Powell 1976, Sapir 1926). A second case is the change of Proto-Algonquian *a: to a nasalized vowel in Eastern Algonquian due to Iroquoian influence (Goddard 1965, 1971, Sherzer 1972a), which violates Ferguson's universal that nasalized vowels may originate only in the context of nasal consonants (i.e. $VN > \tilde{V}N > \tilde{V}$) (Ferguson 1963).[4] Finally, the areal elimination of primary nasal consonants in an area of the Northwest Coast resulted in nearly the only exceptions to the universal that all languages have nasals. In each case, the exceptions to the universals are due to diffusion. Of course there is nothing very surprising about universals having exceptions, since they are simply converted from absolute universals to statistical or near-universals. The questions remain much the same: why do the phenomena occur universally (or with greater-than-chance frequency in the case of the near--universals) in the languages of the world? In answering this question, it will be very important to take into account the effects of diffusion, as well as the aspects of human physiology and psychology which contribute to the limits and hence the potentials of human language which go into determining what may or may not be universal. (For details, see Campbell 1980.)

In the interest of space I do not take up grammatical (morphological and syntactic) borrowing in any detail. If in the past the picture was not clear enough to deny doubts, today it is absolutely certain that "grammar" can be borrowed, that all levels of syntactic structure are subject to foreign influence and borrowing. Since I take this point to be established, I simply mention a few relevant studies here which have presented particularly fetching examples.

---

[4] Recent work has shown that spontaneous nasalization may occur also in the environments of low vowels and glottals, perhaps requiring a modification of Ferguson's universal (cf. Matisoff 1975).

1) Sapir, a self-confession doubter, said of Sahaptian:

> the neighboring Sahaptian dialects, quite similarly to the Klamath, make an extended use of such case-suffixes. We would then have here a good example of the *grammatic*, not merely lexical, influence that dialects of one linguistic stock may exert on geographically contiguous dialects of a fundamentally distinct stock. (Sapir 1907: 533 - 44)

2) Sapir on the Northwest Coast and California:

> Examples of important morphological resemblances in unrelated, but geographically contiguous languages are the sex gender of Coast Salish and Chinookan; the occurrence of numeral classifiers and distributive (or plural) reduplication both in Tsimshian and in Kwakiutl-Nootka, Chemakum and Salish (pointed out by Boas); the instrumental verb prefixes of Maidu, Shoshonean, Washo, and Shasta-Achomawi; and the local verb suffixes of Maidu, Washo, and of Shasta-Achomawi and Yana. (Sapir 1949 [1916]: 458 - 9)

3) Silverstein on tense and aspect in Chinookan:

> it turns out that corresponding to linear geographical extension from west to east, the 'tense' category shows increasing development into an articulated morphosyntactic paradigm. The end points of the geographical area both fit into local patterns, simple taxis and aspect distinctions on the Pacific coast, multitense distinctions in the southern Plateau. (Silverstein 1974: 4 9)

4) Rédei (1970) documented many cases of Russian influence and borrowing in Permian (Zyrian and Permic) syntax; 5) Vendryes (1921: 301) presented cases of Breton influence on French dialects and of Irish influence in Irish English. 6) Leslau (1945, 1952) documented heavy areal borrowing in Ethiopian Semitic languages from Cushitic. 7) Gorbet (1977) treated the diffusion of headless relative clauses in Indian languages of the Southwest. 8) Pray (1980) documents grammatical convergence of Dakhani Urdu (Indo-Aryan) with Telugu (Dravidian) patterns. 9) Weinreich (1953) cited many examples, particularly morphological, but also syntactic. 10) Oswalt (1976) treated the diffusion of "switch reference" areally in languages of the western United States. 11) Thomason and Kaufman (1975) presented many examples, particularly of Frankish (Germanic) influence on earlier French and of Uralic borrowings into Slavic. 12) Moravcsik (1978) surveyed many cases of borrowed basic word order (see also Hyman 1975, Tai 1976, Campbell 1978). 13) Newton (1964) catalogued the various changes in Cypriotic Arabic due to Cypriotic Greek influence. 14) Finally, there are some excellent case studies in the Indian LA (e.g. Emeneau 1980, Gumperz and Wilson 1971, Masica 1976, Nadkarni 1975, etc.). (See also Menges (1945)

"iranization" of Özbek [Turkic] in syntactic subordination and the rise of the subjunctive mood.)

6. Conclusions. The answer to the question, what is a LA?, is that there are various kinds of LAs depending on the number and kind of features which define them and on the varying social, cultural, and historical circumstances that give rise to them. A single shared trait is sufficient to define a LA, although the strength of an area is determined by the relative number (and kind) of features shared by the languages of the area. Of the two approaches, "circumstantialist" and "historicist", clearly the "historicist" is to be preferred, particularly since even the circumstantialists imply that their LAs are the historical products of diffusion. It follows that AL and structural diffusion are not rigidly distinct. Some of the reasons for this conclusion are: 1) a single isogloss of a diffused trait is sufficient to define a LA, albeit usually a weak one; 2) in general any structural borrowing is referred to as an areal phenomenon; and 3) historical evidence of diffusion is required for shared features to be taken as good indicators of LAs.

All aspects of linguistic structure can be subject to diffusion, including those not so frequently discussed: borrowed segments (distinctive features) in native etyma, borrowed phonological rules, sounds and rules lost due to language contact, and diffused shared sound changes, among others.

Such borrowings bear important implications for historical linguistics: 1) such things can be borrowed; 2) the regularity of sound change need not hold for borrowed sounds in native vocabulary; 3) borrowed sounds and changes need not be "natural"; 4) subgrouping considerations may be complicated by changes shared areally, complicating the count of shared innovations for related languages; and 5) some universals may be violated by areal borrowing—this does not weaken the notion of universals, but rather constitutes a call for an explanation of why certain phenomena should be found in all or nearly all languages and under what circumstances may some language fail to conform.

I wish to thank Raimo Anttila, William Bright, Dell Hymes, Thomas Smith-Stark, and Sarah Grey Thomason for helpful comments on versions of this paper, though perhaps none of them will be in full sympathy with this version.

REFERENCES

Andersen, Henning. 1968. IE *s after i, u, r, k in Baltic and Slavic. *Acta Linguistica Hafniensia* 11. 171 - 90.
Aoki, Haruo. 1975. East Plateau linguistic diffusion area. *International Journal of American Linguistics* 41. 183 - 299.
Bàrtoli, Matteo. 1925a[1928]. Brevario de neolinguistica, parte 2a: criteri tecnici. Modena: Società Tipografica Modenese.
    1925b. *Introduzione alla neolinguistica*. Biblioteca dell'Archivum Romanicum, serie II, Linguistica V. 12. Geneva: L. S. Olschki.
    1929. La norma neolinguistica dell'area maggiore. *Revista di filologia e di istruzione classica* 57. 333 - 45.
    1933a. Le norme neolinguistiche e la loro utilità per la storia del linguaggi e dei costumi. *Atti della Società italiana par il progresso delle scienze* 1933. 157 - 65. Roma.
    1933b. La norma delle aree laterali. *Bollettino dell'Atlante linguistico italiano* 1. 28 - 45.
    1939. Der italienische Sprachatlas und die Arealnormen. *Zeitschrift für Volkskunde*, fascicle I.
Becker, Henrik. 1948. *Der Sprachbund*. Leipzig: Die Humboldt-Bücherei Gerhard Mindt.
Bertoni, Giulio. 1909. Le denominazioni dell'imbuto nell-Italia del Nord. *Ricerca di geografia linguistica con una tavola a colori fuori testo*. Bolonia.
    1923. La geografia linguistica. *La Cultura* 3. 404 - 45.
    1925[1928]. *Brevario de neolinguistica*, parte 1: principi generali. Modena: Società Tipografica Modenese.
Bhat, D. N. S. 1970. Review of *Historical linguistics and generative grammar*, by Robert King. *Indian Linguistics* 31. 49 - 57.
    1973. Retroflexion: an areal feature. *Working papers on language universals* 13: 27 - 68. Stanford: Stanford University Press.
Bielmeier, Roland. 1977. *Historische Untersuchung zum Erb-und Lehnwortschatzanteil im ossetischen Grundwortschatz*. Europäische Hochschulschriften, Reihe 27, Asiatische und Afrikanische Studien. Frankfurt am Main: Peter Lang.
Birnbaum, Henrik. 1965. Balkanslawisch und Südslawisch. *Zeitschrift für Balkanologie* 3: 12 - 63.
Birnbaum, Henrik. 1966. On typology, affinity and Balkan linguistics. *Zbornik za filologiju i lingvistiku* 9. 17 - 30.
Bonfante, Giuliano. 1945. On reconstruction and linguistic method. *Word* 1. 83 - 94, 132 - 61.
    1947. The neolinguistic position (a reply to Hall's criticism of neolinguistics). *Language* 23. 344 - 75.
Bright, William and Joel Sherzer. 1978. Areal features in North American Indian languages. *Variation and Change in Language*: essays by William Bright, 228 - 68. Stanford: Stanford University Press.
Burrow, T. 1971. Spantaneous cerebrals in Sanskrit. *Bulletin of the School of Oriental and African Studies* 34. 538 - 59.
Callaghan, Catherine. 1964. Phonemic borrowing in Lake Miwok. *Studies in*

Californian linguistics, ed. by William Bright, 46 - 53. Berkeley: University of California Publications in Linguistics. 34.

Campbell, Lyle. 1974. Quichean palatized velars. *International Journal of American Linguistics* 40. 59 - 63.

— 1976. Language contact and sound change. *Proceedings of the 2nd International conference on historical linguistics*, ed. by William Christie, 181 - 94. Amsterdam: North Holland Publishing Company.

— 1977. *Quinchean linguistic prehistory*. Los Angeles: University of California Publications in Linguistics. 81.

— 1978. Distant genetic relationship and diffusion: a Mesoamerican perspective. *Proceedings of the International Congress of Americnists* 52: 595 - 605. Paris: Singer-Polignae.

— 1980. Explaining universals and their exceptions. *Papers from the Fourth International Conference on Historical Linguistics*, ed. by Elizabeth Closs Traugott, R. LaBrum, and S. Shepherd, 17 - 25. Amsterdam: John Benjamins.

Campbell, Lyle and Marianne Mithun. 1979. North American Indian historical linguistics in current perspective. *The language of native America: an historical and comparative assessment*, ed. by L. Campbell and M. Mithun, 3 - 69. Austin: University of Texas Press.

Campbell, Lyle and Jon Ringen. 1981. Teleology and the explanation of sound change. *Phonologica* 1980, ed. by Wolfgang U. Dressler, Oskar E. Pfeifer, and John R. Rennison, 57 - 68. Innsbruck: Innsbrucker Beiträge zur Sprachwissenschaft.

Chretién, C. D. 1962. Shared innovation and subgrouping. *International Journal of American Linguistics* 29. 66 - 8.

Darnell, Regna and Joel Sherzer. 1971. Areal linguistic studies in North America: a historical perspective. *International Journal of American Linguistics* 37. 20 - 8.

Dawkins, R. M. 1916. *Modern Greek in Asia Minor: a study of the dialects of Silli, Cappadocia, and Phárasa, with grammar, texts, translations and glossary*. Cambridge: Cambridge University Press.

Décsy, G. 1973. *Die linguistische Struktur Europas: Vergenanheit, Gegenwart, Zukunft*. Wiesbaden: Harasso

Dressler, Wolfgang. 1972. On the phonology of language death. *Chicago Linguistic Society* 8. 448 - 57.

Driver, Harold E. 1961. *Indians of North America*. Chicago: University of Chicago Press.

Emeneau, Murray B. 1956. India as a linguistic area. *Language* 32: 3 - 16. Reprinted: *Language in culture and society*, ed. by Dell Hymes, 624 - 35. New York: Harper & Row (1964). [Reprinted: in Emeneau (1980) 105 - 25.]

Emeneau, Murray B. 1956. India as a linguistic area. *Language 32*: 3 - 16. Reprinted:

— 1965. India and linguistic areas. *India and historical grammar*. Annamalai University, Department of Linguistics Publication 5. 25 - 75. India. [Reprinted: in Emeneau (1980) 126 - 66.]

— 1971. Dravidian and Indo-Aryan: the Indian linguistic area. *Symposium on Dravidian civilization*, ed. by Andrée F. Sjoberg, 167 - 96. New York: Jenkins Publishing Co., Pemberton Press. [Reprinted: in Emeneau (1980)]

— 1974. The Indian linguistic area revisted. *International Journal of Dravidian*

Linguistics 3. 92 - 132. [Reprinted: in Emeneau (1980) 197 - 249.]

1978. Review of *Defining a linguistic area*, by Colin P. Masica. *Language* 54. 201 - 10. [Reprinted in part: *Linguistic area: introduction and continuation*, (with new parts) in Emeneau (1980) 1 - 18.]

1980. *Language and linguistic area*, essays by Murray B. Emeneau, selected and introduced by Anwar S. Dil. Stanford; Stanford University Press.

Francis, Susana. 1960. *Habla y literatura popular de la antigua capital chiapeneca.* Instituto Nacional Indigenista: Biblioteca de Fólklore Indígena, 3. Mexico.

Gair, James W. 1980. Adaptation and naturalization in a linguistic area: Sinhala focused sentences. *Berkeley Linguistics Society* 6. 29 - 43.

Gilliéron, Jules and Mario Roques. 1912. *Études de géographie linguistique d'après Atlas linguistique de la France*. Paris: É. Champion.

Goddard, Ives. 1965. The Eastern Algonquian intrusive nasal. *International Journal of American Linguistics* 31. 206 - 20.

Goddard, Ives. 1971. More on the nasalization of PA *a· in Eastern Algonquian. *International Journal of American Linguistics* 37. 139 - 45.

Goossens, Jan. 1973. *Areal Aspekte der Sprache. Lexikon der germanistischen Linguistik*, ed. by Hans Peter Althaus, Helmut Henne, and Herbert Ernst Wiegand, 319 - 26. Tübingen: Max Niemeyer. (Second enlarged edition 1980, Areal Aspekte, 445 - 53.)

Gorbet, Larry. 1977. Headless relatives in the southwest: are they related? *Berkeley Linguistics Society* 3. 270 - 8.

Greenberg, Joseph H. 1957. *Essays in linguistics*. Chicago: University of Chicago Press.

Gumperz, John J. 1964. Hindi-Punjabi code-switching in Delhi. *Proceedings of the Ninth International Congress of Linguistics*, ed. by H. Lunt, 1115 - 24. The Hague: Mounton. [Reprinted: in Gumperz (1971) 205 - 19.]

1971. *Language in social groups, essays by John J. Gumperz*, selected and introduced by Anwar S. Dil. Stanford: Stanford University Press.

Gumperz, John J. and Robert Wilson. 1971. Convergence and creolization: a case from the Indo-Aryan/Dravidian border in India. *Pidginization and Creolization*, ed. by Dell Hymes, 151 - 67. London: Cambridge University Press. [Reprinted: in Gumperz (1971) 251 - 73.]

Haarmann, Harald. 1976. *Aspekte der Arealtypologie*: die Problematik der europäischen Sprachbünde. Tübingen: TBL Verlag Gunter Narr.

Haas, Mary R. 1941. The classification of the Muskogean languages. *Language, culture, and personality*: Essays in memory of Edward Sapir, ed. by L. Spier, A. Hallowell, and S. Newman, 41 - 56. Menasha, Wisconsin: Sapir Memorial Publication Fund.

1969a. *The prehistory of languages.* Janua Linguarum (series minor, 57). The Hague: Mouton.

1969b. Internal reconstruction of the Nootka-Nitinat pronominal suffixes. *International Journal of American Linguistics* 35. 108 - 29.

1970. Consonant symbolism in northwestern California: a problem in diffusion. *Languages and cultures of Western North America: essays in honor of Sven S. Liljeblad*, ed. by E. Swanson, 86 - 96. Pocatello: Idaho State University Press. [Reprinted: in Haas (1978) 339 - 52.]

1976. The Northern California linguistic area. *Hokan studies*, ed. by Margaret Langdon and Shirley Silver, 347 - 59. The Hague: Mouton. [Reprinted: in Haas (1978) 353 - 69.]

1978. *Language, culture, and history, essays by Mary R. Haas*, selected and introduced by Anwar S. Dil. Standford: Standford University Press.

Hakulinen, Lauri. 1968. *Suomen kielen rakenne ja kehitys*. Helsinki: Otava.

Hall, Robert A. 1946. Bàrtoli's "neolinguistica". *Language* 22. 273 - 83.

Hamp, Eric. 1953. Morphological correspondences in Cornish and Breton. *Journal of Celtic Studies* 2. 5024.

1958. Proto-Popolocan internal relationships. *International Journal of American Linguistics* 24. 150 - 3.

1960. Chocho-Popoloca innovations. *International Journal of American Linguistics* 26. 62.

1968. Acculturation as a late rule. *Chicago Linguistic Society* 4: 103 - 10.

1977. On some questions of areal linguistics. *Berkeley Linguistics Society* 3. 279 - 82.

Henderson, Eugénie J. A. 1965. The topography of certain phonetic and morphological characteristics of South East Asian languages. *Lingua* 15. 400 - 34.

Hill, Jane H. 1978. Language contact systems and human adaptations. *Journal of Anthropological Research* 34. 1 - 26.

Hock, Henrich, 1975. Substratum influence on (Rig-vedic) Sanskrit? *Studies in the linguistic Sciences* 5. 76 - 125.

Hoenigswald, Henry. 1960. *Language change and linguistic reconstruction*. Chicago: University of Chicago Press.

1966. Criteria for subgrouping of languages. *Ancient Indo-European dialects*, ed. by H. Birnbaum and J. Puhvel, 1 - 21. Los Angeles; University of California Press.

Holt, Dennis and William Bright. 1976. La lengua paya y las fronteras lingüísticas de mesoamérica. *Fronteras de Mesoamérica*, 14a Mesa Redonda, tomo 1: 149 - 56. Mexico: Sociedad Mexicana de Antropología.

Hooper. Joan. 1976. *An introduction to natural generative phonology*. New York: Academic Press.

Hyman, Larry 1975. On the change from SOV to SVO: evidence from Niger-Congo. *Word order and word order change*, ed. by Charles Li, 113 - 47. Austin: University of Texas Press.

Itkonen, Terho. 1969. Zur Synchronie und Diachronie der ostfinnischen Palatalisation. *Studia Fennica* 14 : 1 - 31.

Jacobs, Melville. 1954. The areal spread of sound features in the languages north of California. *Papers from the symposium on American Indian linguistics held at Berkeley*, July 7, 1951, pp. 47 - 56. Berkeley. University of California Publications in Linguistics 10.1 - 68.

Jacobsen, William H., Jr. 1969. Origin of the Nootka pharyngelas. *International Journal of American Linguistics* 35.125 - 53.

1980. Inclusive/exclusive: a diffused pronominal category in native western North America. *Papers from the parasession on pronouns and anaphora*. Chicago: Linguistic Society, 204 - 27.

Jakobson, Roman. 1931a. Über die phonologischen Sprachbünde. *Travaux du*

Cercle Linguistique de Prague 4.234 - 40. (Réunion phonologique internationale tenue a Prague 18 - 21/XII, 1930).

1962 [1931b]. K charakteristike jevrazijskogo yazykovogo sojuza. *Selected writings of Roman Jakobson*, Vol. 1: Phonological Studies, 144 - 201. The Hague: Mouton.

1938. Sur la théorie des affinités phonologiques entre les langues. *Actes du quatrième congrès international de linguistes tenu à Copenhague du 27 aout au 1er septembre, 1936*, 48 - 58. [Reprinted: appendix to *Principes de phonologie*, by N. S. Troubetzkoy, Paris: Editions Klincksieck (1949 [1970 reedition], 351 - 65)].

English translation: 1972. On the theory of phonological associations among languages. *A reader in historical and comparative linguistics*, ed. by Allan R. Keiler, 241 - 52. New York: Holt, Rinehart and Winston.

1944. Franz Boas' approach to language. *International Journal of American Linguistics* 10. 188 - 95.

Katz, Hartmut. 1975. *Generative Phonologie und phonologische Sprachbünde des Ostjakischen und Samojedischen*. Munich: Wilhelm Fink Verlag.

Kaufman, Terrence. 1969. Teco—a new Mayan language. *International Journal of American Linguistics* 35. 154 - 74.

1973. Areal linguistics and Middle America. *Current trends in linguistics* 11: 459 - 83, ed. by Thomas Sebeok. The Hague: Mouton.

Keniston, Hayward. 1937. *The syntax of Castillian prose: the sixteenth century*. Chicago: University of Chicago Press.

Kettunen, Lauri. 1930. *Suomen murteet II: murrealueet*. Helsinki: Suomalaisen Kirjallisuuden Seuran Toimituksia, 188.

Kinkade, Dale. 1973. The alveopalatal shift in Cowlitz Salish. *International Journal of American Linguistics* 39. 224 - 31.

Kinkade, Dale and Jay Powell. 1976. Language and the prehistory of North America. *World Archeology* 8. 83 - 100.

Korhonen, Mikko. 1969. Pääpainottoman tavun vokaalin ja j:n regressiivisestä vaikutuksesta Liivissä. *Publications of the Phonetics Department of the University of Turku*, No. 6.

Kroeber, Alfred L. 1939. *Cultural and native areas of native North America*. Berkeley: University of California Press.

Kuiper, F. B. J. 1967. The genesis of a linguistic area. *Indo-Iranian Journal* 10. 81 - 102.

Kurath, Hans. 1972. *Studies in area linguistics*. Bloomington: Indiana University Press.

Lapesa, Rafael. 1981. *Historia de la lengua española*. (9th edition.) (Biblioteca Románica Hispánica, Manuales, 45.) Madrid: Gredos.

Leslau, Wolf. 1945. The influence of Cushitic on the Semitic languages of Ethiopia: a problem of substratum. *Word* 1. 59 - 82.

1952. The influence of Sidamo on the Ethiopic languages of Gurage. *Language* 28. 63 - 81.

Louw, J. 1962. The segmental phonemes of Zulu. *Afrika und Übersee* 46. 43 - 93.

Malmberg, Bertil. 1973. L'Extension du Castillan et le problème des substrats. *Linguistique générale et Romane: Études en allemand, anglais, espagnole et français*, 335 - 43. The Hague: Mouton.

Martin, Laura. 1978. Mayan influence in Guatemalan Spanish: a research outline and test case. *Papers in Mayan linguistics*, ed. by Nora England, 106 - 26. Columbia: University of Missouri.

Martinet, André. 1952. Diffusion of languages and structural linguistics. *Romance Philology* 6. 5 - 13.

Masica, Colin P. 1976. *Defining a linguistic area*: South Asia. Chicago: University of Chicago Press.

Matisoff, James. 1975. Rhinoglottophilia: the mysterious connection between nasality and glottality. *Nasalfest*, ed. by C. Ferguson et al. 265 - 87. Standford: Stanford University Press.

Meenakshisundaran, T. 1965. *A history of Tamil language.* Poona: Deccan College.

Menéndez Pidal, Ramón. 1926. *Orígenes del español: estado lingüístico de la península ibérica hasta el siglo XI.* Madrid: Espasa-Calpe, S. A. (Sixth edition, 1968).

Menges, Karl H. 1945. Indo-European influences on Ural-Altaic languages. *Word* 1. 188 - 93.

Miller, Wick. 1971. The death of a language, or: serendipity among the Shoshoni. *Anthropological Linguistics* 18. 114 - 120.

Moravcsik, Edith A. 1978. Universals of language contact. *Universals of Human Language*, ed. by Joseph H. Greenberg, 94 - 122. Standford: Standford University Press.

Nadkarni, M. 1975. Bilingualism and syntactic change in Konkani. *Language* 51. 672 - 83.

Newton, Brian. 1964. An Arabic-Greek dialect. *Papers in memory of George C. Pappageotes*, ed. by Robert Austerlitz, 43 - 52. Special publication 5, supplement to *Word* 20, No. 3.

Oswalt, Robert L. 1976. Switch reference in Maiduan: an areal and typological contribution. *International Journal of American Linguistics* 42. 297 - 304.

Pray, Bruce R. 1980. Evidence of grammatical convergence in Dakhini Urdu and Telegu. *Berkeley Linguistics Society* 6. 90 - 99.

Ramanujan, A. K., and Colin Masica. 1969. Toward a phonological typology of the Indian linguistic area. *Current trends in linguistics* 5. 543 - 77, Linguistics in South Asia, ed. by Thomas Sebeok. The Hague: Mouton.

Rapola, Martti. 1965. *Suomen kirjakielen historia I: vanhan kirjasuomen kirjoitus- ja äänneasun kehitys.* Helsinki: Suomalaisen Kirjallisuuden Seuran Toimituksia.

——— 1969. *Johdatus Suomen murteisiin.* Tietolipas 4. Helsinki: Suomalaisen Kirjallisuuden Seura.

Rédei, Károly. 1970. *Russische Einflüsse in der permjakischen Syntax. Symposium über Syntax der uralischen Sprachen.* Abhandlungen der Akademie der Wissenschaften in Göttingen, Philologisch-Historische Klasse dritte Folge, Nr. 76. Göttingen: Vandenhoeck und Ruprecht.

Sandoval, Lisandro. 1941. *Semántica guatemalense o diccionario de guatemaltequismos.* Guatemala: Tipografía Nacional.

Sapir, Edward. 1907. Preliminary report on the language and mythology of the Upper Chinook. *American Anthropologist* 9. 553 - 44.

——— 1916. *Time perspective in aborignal American culture: a study in method.* Canada Department of Mines, Geological Survey, Memoir 90, Anthropological

Series, 13. [Reprinted: Selected writings of Edward Sapir in language, culture, and personality, ed. by David Mandelbaum, 893 - 462. Berkeley: University of California Press (1949)].

 1925. The Hokan Affinity of Subtiaba of Nicaragua. *American Anthropologist* 27. 402. - 35.

Sapir, Edward. 1926. A Chinookan phonetic law. *International Journal of American Linguistics* 4. 105 - 10.

Sapir, Edward and Morrish Swadesh. 1939. *Nootka texts: tales and ethnological narratives, with grammatical notes and lexical materials.* William Dwight Whitney Linguistics Series. Philadelphia, Pennsylvania: Linguistica Societa of America.

Schuchardt, Hugo Ernst Mario. 1928. See Spitzer 1928.

Seidel, Eugen. 1965. Zur Problematik des Sprachbundes. *Beiträge zur Sprachwissenschaft. Volkskunde und Literaturforschung: Wolfgang Steinitz zum 60. Geburtstag am 28. Februar 1965 dargebracht*, ed. by A. V. Isačenko, W. Wissmann, and H. Strobach, 372 - 81. (Veröffentlichen der sprachwissenschtlichen Komission, 5.) Berlin: Akademie.

Sherzer, Joel. 1972a. Vowel nasalization in Eastern Algonquian: an areal-typological perspective on linguistic universals. *International Journal of American Linguistics* 38. 267 - 8.

 1972b. Review of the current status of anthropological research in the Great Basin. *International Journal of American Linguistics* 34. 384 - 6.

 1973. Areal linguistics in North America. *Current trends in linguistics* 10: 749 - 95, ed. by Thomas Sebeok. The Hague: Mouton.

 1976. *An areal-typological study of American Indian languages North of Mexico.* North-Holland Linguistic series, 20. Amsterdam: North Holland Publishing Company.

Sherzer, Joel, and Richard Bauman. 1972. Areal studies and culture contact. *Southwestern Journal of Anthropology* 28. 131 - 52.

Silverstein, Michael. 1974. Dialectal developments in Chinookan tense-aspect sytems: an areal-historical analysis. *International Journal of American Linguistics*, memoir 29.

 1978. Review of An areal-typological study of American Indian languages north of Mexico, by Joel Sherzer.

Spitzer, Leo (ed.). 1978. Hugo-Schuchardt-Brévier. Second edition, revised and enlarged. **Halle:** Max Niemeyer.

Suárez, Victor M. 1945. *El español que se habla en Yucatán.* Mérida: Díaz Massa. Second edition: Mérida: Ediciones de la Universidad de Yucatán (1979).

Tai, James. 1976. On the change from SVO to SOV in Chinese. *Papers from the parasession on diachronic syntax*, 291-304. Chicago: Linguistic Society.

Thomason, Sarah Grey. 1980. Morphological instability, with and without language contact. *Historical Morphology*, ed. by Jacek Fisiak, 359-82. (Trends in linguistics, studies and monographs, 17.) The Hague: Mouton.

Thomason, Sarah Grey, and Terrence S. Kaufman. 1975. Toward an adequate definition of creolization. Paper presented at the 1975 International Conference on Pidgins and Creoles, Honolulu, Hawaii.

 1976. Contact-induced language change: loanwords and the borrowing language's pre-borrowing phonology. *Current progress in historical linguistics: proceedings of the Second International Conference on Historical Lin-*

guistics, ed. by William M. Christie, Jr., 167-79. Amsterdam: North-Holland Publishing Company.

Trubetzkoy, (Prince) N. S. 1928. ([Proposition 16]). *Acts of the First International Congress of Linguistics*, 17-18. Leiden.

——— 1931. Phonologie und Sprachgeographie. *Travaux de Circle Linguistique de Prague* 4: 228-34. [French translation: Phonologie et géographie linguistique. Appendix to Principes de Phonologie, 343-50. [1949] (reprinted 1970). Paris: Éditions Klincksieck.]

Turunen, A. 1959. *Itäisten Savolaismurteiden äännehistoria*. Helsinki: Suomalaisen Kirjallisuuden Seuran Toimituksia.

Velten, H. V. 1943. The Nez Perce verb. *Pacific Northwest Quarterly* 34. 271.

Vendryes, J. 1921. *Le language: Introduction linguistique à l'histoire*. Paris: La Renaissance du Livre.

Voegelin, Carl F. 1945. Influence of area in American Indian linguistics. *Word* 1.54-8.

——— 1961. Culture area: parallel with typlogical homogeneity and heterogeneity to North American language families. *Kroeber Anthropological Society Papers* 25.163-80.

Vogt, Hans. 1945. Substrat et convergence dans l'evolution linguistique; remarques sur l'évolution et la structure de l'arménien, du géorgien, de l'ossète, et du turc. *Studia Septentrionalia* 2.213-28.

——— 1954. Language contacts. *Word* 10.365-74.

Wagner, H. 1959. *Das Verbum in den Sprachen der brittischen Inseln: ein Beitrag zur geographischen Typologie des Verbums*. Buchreihe der *Zeitschrift für Celtische Philologie* 1. Tübingen: Niemeyer.

——— 1964. Nordeuropäische Lautegeographie. *Zeitschrift für Celtische Philologie* 29.225-98.

Weinreich, Uriel. 1953. *Languages in Contact: findings and problems*. Publications of the Linguistic Circle of New York, 1. [Reprinted: The Hague: Mouton (1968)].

——— 1958. On the compatibility of genetic relationship and convergent development. *Word* 14.374-9.

Westphal, E. O. J. 1963. The linguistic prehistory of Southern Africa: Bushman, Kwadi, Hottentot, and Bantu linguistic relationships. *Africa* 33.237-65.

Winter, Werner. 1973. Areal linguistics: some general considerations. *Current trends in linguistics* 11: 135-47, ed. by Thomas Sebeok. The Hague: Mouton.

Wolff, Hans. 1959. Subsystem typologies and areal linguistics. *Anthropological Linguistics* 1.7: 39-51. Bloomington: Indiana University.

Zamora Vincente, Alonso. 1967. *Dialectología española*. (Second edition). Biblioteca Románica Hispánica. Madrid: Gredos.

Zeps, V. 1962. *Latvian and Finnic linguistic convergences*. Uralic and Altaic series, 9. Bloomington: Indiana University Press.

Zvelebil, K. 1970. *Comparative Dravidian phonology*. The Hague: Mouton.

PARADIGM ECONOMY IN LATIN NOUNS

ANDREW CARSTAIRS

1. Introduction.[1] In this paper I want to do three things. First, I want to explain briefly a universal principle which, I believe, constrains the organisation of inflexions into paradigms; I call this the Paradigm Economy Principle. Second, I want to point out a set of facts about noun inflexion in Latin which at first sight conflicts with the Paradigm Economy Principle. Third, I want to try to demonstrate that, on closer examination, these facts do not seriously conflict with the Paradigm Economy Principle but rather tend to support it, inasmuch as the Principle can help to explain in quite precise detail a series of changes which affected the inflexion of certain Latin nouns during the historical period — between about 200 BC and about 50 AD.

2. The Paradigm Economy Principle. Anyone who has ever learnt a highly inflected language such as Latin knows very well that, for any one inflexionally relevant combination of morphosyntactic properties (in the sense of Matthews (1972)), there is often more than one inflexional realisation available. For example, in Latin the property-combination Genitive Singular may be realised -$\bar{\imath}$ (as in *dominī* 'of the lord') or -*is* (as in *rēgis* 'of the king'). This sort of situation is traditionally handled by arranging the relevant inflected words into paradigms (declensions or conjugations), each paradigm being defined by the set of inflexions chosen by words belonging to it. Thus in Latin the ending -$\bar{\imath}$ is appropriate to 'second declension' nouns; -*is* is appropriate to 'third declension' ones; and so on.

I now want to pose a question about the organisation of inflexions into paradigms. The question is: is there any constraint on the number

---

[1] A fuller version of sections 3 and 4 of this paper appears in Transactions of the Philological Society (Carstairs 1984). The material on the declension-type of *puppis* given in section 5 appears only here, however. This work was supported by a Leverhulme Trust Senior Studentship and by University of Canterbury Research Grant 573346.

of paradigms into which a given array of inflexional resources can be arranged? Let's imagine a language in which nouns are inflected for three Cases (Nominative, Accusative and Genitive) and two Numbers (Singular and Plural). Let's imagine also that in this language there are precisely two inflexions available for each of the six Case-Number combinations: two for Nominative Singular, two for Genitive Plural and so on. It is obvious that the minimum number of noun declensions in that language is two. One can also work out arithmetically a maximum number of noun declensions. This total will be got by multiplying together the number of inflexions available for each of the six property-combinations: 2^3 (for the Singular) times 2^3 (for the Plural) yielding 64. So, in connexion with this hypothetical language, my question is: is there any general linguistic principle (any general principle of morphological behaviour, or inflexional universal) which will enable one to predict that the actual total of nominal paradigms in the hypothetical language must be something less than 64 — say, 33, or 10, or 6?

I contend that there is such a general principle, and that the prediction that it will make in connexion with our hypothetical language is an extremely precise and restrictive one: the number of nominal paradigms must not exceed the mathematical minimum (namely two) except under precisely specifiable circumstances. This Principle, which I call the Paradigm Economy Principle, can be stated in its strong, unqualified form as follows:

> The inflexional resources of any word-class must be organised into as few paradigms as is mathematically possible (i.e. as few as is necessary to give each available inflexion a 'niche' in at least one paradigm).

I will not attempt to justify this principle here; I have suggested arguments in favour of it elsewhere (Carstairs 1983). There is no doubt that the strong version of the Principle just given is too strong; it certainly needs qualification and refinement. But the Principle as stated seems to me close enough to the truth to warrant further exploration; and what I want to do here is explore some of its consequences for Latin — more specifically, its consequences for certain subtypes of what is traditionally known as the third declension.

3. *Some problematic Latin facts*. The three third-declension sub-types that I will be concerned with initially are set out at table 1. This table illustrates the sort of attempt generally offered by conscientious pedagogical grammars of Latin to depict as part of a static état de langue

what is in fact a quite rapidly changing situation at around the beginning of the first century AD.[2] The fact that the situation is so rapidly changing is important to my argument. But first I need to show why the state of affairs represented at table 1 is incompatible with the Paradigm Economy Principle. This should become clear when we look at table 2, where I highlight those four Cases for which more than one inflexion is available. For each of these Cases, the total number of inflexions available is two. The minimum number of paradigms into which these inflexional resources could be arranged mathematically is therefore two. So, on the face of it, the Paradigm Economy Principle predicts that there should be only two subtypes of the 'third declension' using this particular set of inflexional resources. Yet there are in fact three subtypes; type A and type C each has at least one inflexion which is peculiar to that subtype, but there is also a third type, B, which 'goes like' type A in some Cases and like type C in others.

	A	B	C
Sg Nom	ignis 'fire'	dens 'tooth'	rēx [re:ks] 'king'
Acc	ignem	dentem	rēgem
Gen	ignis	dentis	rēgis
Dat	ignī	dentī	rēgī
Abl	ignī, igne	dente	rēge
Pl Nom	ignēs	dentēs	rēgēs
Acc	ignīs, ignēs	dentēs (or -īs in some nouns)	rēgēs
Gen	ignium	dentium	rēgum
Dat/Abl	ignibus	dentibus	rēgibus

Table 1. Three subtypes of the Latin third declension

	A	B	C
Sg Nom	-is	-s	-s
Abl	-ī or -e	-e	-e
Pl Acc	-īs or -ēs	-ēs or -īs	-ēs
Gen	-ium	-ium	-um

Table 2. Distribution of inflexional differences

---

[2] I have derived information on Latin from the handbooks of Latin historical morphology by Ernout (1953), Leumann (1977), and Sommer (1948), and also from the study of the third declension by Janson (1971). These are supplemented by the detailed information on the behaviour of individual nouns given by Neue and Wagener (1902), and for Lucretius's usage, by Ernout (1918).

One possible solution to this problem is phonological. It might be argued that there are not in fact two distinct inflexions for each of the four Cases listed in table 2, but only one; and that the superficial, or phonetic, differences that we observe between the three subtypes are indeed merely superficial, and attributable to phonological interaction between the inflexional endings and the stems. In my view, however, both synchronic and diachronic facts militate against any phonological solution of this kind. I have not space to argue this in detail here. But notice that, in rejecting a phonological solution, I am making my task of defending the Paradigm Economy Principle more difficult, not easier. The phonological solution would represent an 'easy way out' for me. What I want to do here is explore whether, even without that 'easy way out', the facts can somehow be reconciled with paradigm economy.

4. The Paradigm Economy Principle as an explanation for the Latin facts. The first stage in the reconciliation involves a phonological process of syncope, affecting certain original Nominative Singular forms in *-is*. We know that the type B noun *mens* 'mind' originally had a Nominative Singular *mentis*, because that form is attested in the third-century-BC poet Ennius as well as being confirmed by cognates such as the Sanskrit *matih* 'intellect'. Similarly, *sors* 'fate' occasionally had a Nominative Singular *sortis* in the early dramatists Plautus and Terence, writing between the middle of the third and the middle of the second century BC. In fact, it is usual in the handbooks to regard type B as a Latin innovation, not a preservation of an inherited Indo-European declension-type, and furthermore to associate its origin with the phonological process of syncope which affected certain Nominative Singuars, yielding *mens*, *frons* 'leaf' etc. from an earlier *mentis*, *frondis* etc. (e. g. Ernout 1953:55-6; Niedermann 1953:54-5). According to the usual view, therefore, before syncope occurred there were only the two types, A and C; the 'mixed' type B is a later development, somehow triggered off by syncope. I share this usual view.

Consider now what the third declension would have looked like before syncope had occurred — i. e. in the proto-Latin stage of which only traces remain in the earliest texts. What it would have looked like is set out in table 3, on the left (where the endings of the four Cases in question have been normalised to their first-century-AD shapes for the sake of clarity, in a manner which does not affect the argument). This pre-syncope situation complies perfectly with the Paradigm Economy Principle: there are two distinct endings for each of the four crucial Cases, yielding a mathematical upper limit of sixteen for the number of possible declensions; yet the actual number of declensions coincides with the mathematical minimum, namely two. What we find as the immediate result of syncope, however, as set out on the right in table 3, is a situation which conflicts with paradigm economy, in that there are still no more than two distinct inflexions for each of the four Cases concerned, but the number of distinct paradigms has risen to three, through the creation of a new one (B') containing just those nouns formerly of type A which underwent syncope. A phonological innovation has, by accident, led to a situation which is morphologically intolerable — intolerable, that is, if the Paradigm Economy Principle is close to being correct. So, if we are to maintain the Principle, we must predict that some therapeutic measures will be taken to repair the breach in paradigm economy that syncope has created — measures involving further changes in the inflexional behaviour of types A, B' and C.

Further changes did indeed take place. I will briefly describe what these changes were, and then discuss whether they are the sort of changes that the Paradigm Economy Principle would lead us to expect.

The further changes are as follows:

(a) -$\bar{\imath}$ to -e in the Ablative Singular of type B'; general in all texts.
(b) -um to -ium in some Genitive Plurals; everywhere except in Varro (116-27 BC), *De lingua latina* viii 67.
(c) -$\bar{\imath}s$ to -$\bar{e}s$ in the Accusative Plural of types A and B; not usual in Plautus and Terence (around 200 BC), but increasingly common thereafter.
(d) -$\bar{\imath}$ to -e in the Ablative Singular of type A; not usual in Lucretius (early first century BC) but mentioned by Varro and prevalent by the first century AD, overtaking change (c).

Some of the complications underlying this rather simplified presentation are nicely illustrated by the passage from the Roman grammarian Varro mentioned at (b) (my translation): 'What could be more similar than *gens*, *mens* and *dens*, although their Genitive and Accusative Plurals are different? For the first has *gentium* and *gentīs*, with i in both; the second has *mentium* and *mentēs*, with i in only the first of the two forms; and the third has *dentum* and *dentēs*, with i in neither.'

At this stage I want to emphasise two points. First, I have counted as separate changes the shift from -$\bar{\imath}$ to -e in the Ablative Singular of type B and the similar shift in type A. This separation is justified by the clear evidence that the change took place in two bursts. In type B nouns it was early and complete. In type A nouns, on the other hand, it began later and was not complete even by the first century AD; a small group of nouns of type A (*amnis* 'river', *orbis* 'ball', *ignis* 'fire', *vītis* 'vine') maintain a consistent preference for an Ablative in *-ī* even at this stage. Secondly, none of the four changes goes exactly in parallel with any of the others. A priori, we might expect change (c) to proceed in step with either (a) or (d), but it does not. Roughly speaking, (c) starts earlier than (d) but takes longer. There are a number of type A nouns in first-century-AD Latin which still preserve an Accusative Plural in *-īs* but have completely gone over to *-e* in the Ablative Singular (e. g. *auris* 'ear', *crīnis* 'hair', *vallis* 'valley'); and what Varro says about the contrast between *gens* and *mens* in the Accusative Plural is nicely confirmed by the usage of Lucretius, as researched by Ernout (1918:164).

		Before syncope		After syncope		
		A	C	A	B′	C
Sg	Nom	-is	-s	-is	-s	-s
	Abl	-ī	-e	-ī	-ī	-e
Pl	Acc	-īs	-ēs	-īs	-īs	-ēs
	Gen	-ium	-um	-ium	-ium	-um

Table 3. Effect of syncope on third-declension subtypes

		Step 1		Step 2		Step 3	
		A	B	A	BC	A	BC
Sg	Nom	-is	-s	-is	-s	-is	-s
	Abl	-ī	-e	-ī	-e	-ī	-e
Pl	Acc					-ēs (exceptionally -īs)	
	Gen			-um ~ -ium		-um ~ -ium	

Table 4. Restoration of paradigm economy

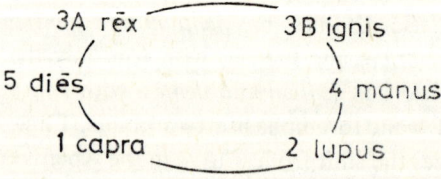

Table 5. Arrangement of Latin declensions by Risch (1977:233)

We now need to consider whether these changes are of a kind that the Paradigm Economy Principle would lead us to expect. Table 3, illustrating the immediate effects of syncope, certainly leads us to expect that something should be done about the Ablative Singular of type B', to repair the breach of paradigm economy in the Singular; specifically, that type B' will acquire the type C Ablative Singular ending -*e* so as to align itself with type C completely. And this is precisely what happens, in the guise of change (a). Notice that paradigm economy does not require that any change should take place at this stage in the Ablative Singular of type A; so it is no surprise to find that the change that does eventually take place in type A is not contemporaneous with the change in type B. (The question remains, of course, why the change in type A should take place at all; I will say something about that later.)

The Ablative Singular change which I have just described is represented in table 4 as Step 1 in the restoration of paradigm economy. Paradigm economy is still violated in the Plural, however. We might expect type B to be realigned completely with type C, so as to yield an economical two-paradigm arrangement in the Plural as well as the Singular. This would involve all syncopated nouns such as *gens, mens, sors, frons* acquiring C-type Genitive Plurals (*gentum, mentum* etc.) and C-type Accusative Plurals (*gentēs, mentēs* etc.). But this is not what happens. We will consider first what actually happens in the Genitive Plural. We find not that -*um* encroaches on -*ium* but rather the reverse: -*ium* (the ending originally proper to type A) encroaches on -*um*. How can this possibly be compatible with any prediction about the restoration of paradigm economy? It is compatible, I suggest, in that it points to the development in the Plural not of two paradigms but of a single paradigm. The endings -*um* and -*ium* acquire a distribution which is predictable partly phonologically and partly morphosyntactically (just as the second-declension Nominative Singular endings -*um* and -*us* correlate with the contrast between Neuter and non-Neuter Gender):

— after long vowel plus plosive:
    — not /t/:   -*um* (or -*ium* in Feminines)
    — /t/   -*um* Masculine (e.g. *nepōt-* 'grandson'), -*ium* Feminine (e.g. *dōt-* 'dowry')
— after other heavy syllables and /w/: -*ium*
— after light syllables: -*um*

The phonological element in this conditioning extends right across types A, B and C, and even beyond, as demonstrated by Janson (1971).

Indo-Europeanists will be aware that the noun which I chose in table 1 to illustrate the mixed type B, namely *dens* 'tooth', never underwent syncope at all, since it is an old consonant-stem noun, not an -*i*- stem one; so the Genitive Plural that Varro gives for it (*dentum*) is historically the ‚correct' one. But, despite Varro's testimony, the Genitive Plural of *dens* appears everywhere else as *dentium*, in accordance with the distribution principle just set out. So far as the Genitive Plural is concerned, then, we see a development which is perfectly compatible with the goal of restoring paradigm economy, provided that we can demonstrate that a single paradigm is established throughout the Plural of types A, B and C. This development is represented as Step 2 in table 4.

But what of the Accusative Plural? The account of the Plural in terms of a single paradigm can only be made to work if we can supply some suitable account of the alternation between -*īs* and -*ēs*. One might ask: if the alternation in the Genitive Plural between -*um* and -*ium* came to be phonologically and morphosyntactically conditioned, why did not the alternation between -*īs* and -*ēs* come to be conditioned in exactly the same way? Certainly it did not; and, at first sight, this fact seems a serious blow to any hope of reconciling the Paradigm Economy Principle with what happened in the Plural. But I suggest that there is an independent factor at work here, involving certain aspects of the Latin declension system pointed out by Risch (1977). Risch noted resemblances between various Latin declensions on the basis of six inflexional characteristics, such as whether or not the Nominative Singular ends in -*s*, whether the Dative-Ablative Plural ends in -*īs* or -*ibus*, and so on. The result of this comparison was an intriguing circular arrangement of declensions, set out at table 5. The arrangement in table 5 is such that all the declensions which share any one of Risch's characteristics form a continuous arc on the circumference of the circle. There are just two anomalies which interfere with Risch's arrangement:

(a) *ignis* and *lupus*, but not *manus*, share Dative-Ablative syncretism in the Singular;

(b) *ignis* and *lupus*, but not *manus*, fail to syncretise (i.e. have distinct forms for) Nominative and Accusative in the Plural (non-Neuter).

The most important of these anomalies for the moment is (b). The declension-type of *ignis* (our type A) differs from those on either side of it in having distinct Nominative and Accusative forms in the Plural. If, then, Risch's circular pattern represents something real in Latin, we will expect some sign of a tendency to remove the anomaly by introducing a syncretised inflexion for the Nominative and Accusative Plural in type A. Now, this expectation is directly relevant to our problem about the Accusative Plural of types A, B and C. If paradigm economy were to be restored throughout the Plural on the basis of the same phonological and morphosyntactic conditioning as governs the distribution of *-um* and *-ium* in the Genitive Plural, this would run directly counter to the expectation we have derived from Risch's circular pattern, in that it would increase the number of nouns displaying anomaly (b).

The right way to regard the Accusative Plural developments, I suggest, is as follows: a single paradigm was indeed established in the Plural, removing the infringement of paradigm economy, on the basis that one of the two competing Accusative Plural endings, namely *-ēs*, became the sole regular one, while the other, *-īs*, survived only as a lexically marked exception. Paradigm economy was therefore restored in the manner indicated at Step 3 in table 4. But this analysis is empirically empty unless we have some independent evidence for saying that, by about the first century BC, *-ēs* was regular and *-īs* was exceptional. Fortunately, we do have independent evidence of the necessary kind. Logically, it would be quite possible for the nouns displaying *-īs* to constitute a stable and clearly defined group, with no members either defecting to the *-ēs* type or vacillating in the Accusative Plural between *-īs* and *-ēs*. But this is not what we observe in the Latin data. Rather, we find evidence for word-by-word defection — Varro's statement already quoted shows that *mens* defects before *gens* does — and also evidence of widespread vacillation, in that (for example), out of the 18 type A nouns which appear in Lucretius with an Accusative Plural in *-īs*, ten vacillate, in that they also appear with *-ēs* (Ernout 1918: 162—3). So to call *-īs* exceptional and *-ēs* regular is not simply an ad hoc dodge to 'save' the Paradigm Economy Principle; it accurately reflects the synchronic and diachronic facts as we observe them over the period in question, between the second century BC and the first century AD.

Finally I turn to the fourth of the four inflexional changes mentioned earlier: the second burst of the change from *-ī* to *-e* in the Ablative Singular. In terms of paradigm economy, there seems to be no motivation for this. Even if all type A nouns remained faithful to the ending *-ī*, paradigm economy would be observed, as indicated at Step 3 in table 4. But this change does have a motivation in terms of Risch's anomaly (a). The switch from *-i* to *-e* in the declension of *ignis* renders the Dative Singular distinct from the Ablative Singular, bringing *ignis* into line with the declensions immediately flanking it in Risch's pattern. So it is no surprise to find that this change coincides with none of the others; for the first three changes represent stages in the restoration of paradigm economy after it has been disrupted by syncope, whereas this last change is quite independent of paradigm economy.

5. *Further problematic facts.* The declension-types of *ignis*, *dens* and *rēx*, presented in table 1, account for the great majority of those third-declension nouns whose behaviour seems to infringe paradigm economy. But there is a further third-declension subtype which is relevant here: that exemplified by *puppis* in table 6, which I have called type D. Type D differs from type A in having *-im* instead of *-em* in the Accusative Singular and in preferring more consistently the *-i-* endings in the Ablative Singular and the Accusative Plural. The problem is that, although there are still no more than two endings for any one Case in types A, B, C and D, we seem to have to recognise a fourth declension--type; type A now appears as a mixture of type D and type C. Type D has far fewer adherents than types A, B or C, and one might argue on that ground that it is not necessary to worry about the breach of paradigm economy that its existence entails. But this is a pessimistic argument; it seems better first to look closely at the actual behaviour of D-type nouns, in case this suggests a more illuminating way of reconciling them with the Paradigm Economy Principle.

	Singular	Plural
Nom	puppis 'stern'	puppēs
Acc	puppim	puppēs *or* puppīs
Gen	puppis	puppium
Dat/Abl	puppī	puppibus

Table 6. Third-declension subtype D

Here is a complete list of the nouns which at least sometimes 'go like' type D (with M and F indicating Masculine and Feminine Gender respectively):

(a) No alternative Accusative Singular in *-em* attested:

  (i) Agricultural terms:

   buris F 'plough-beam', *rumis* F 'teat, dug', *cucumis* F 'cucumber' (alternative Accusative Singular, with stem change, *cucumerem*)

(ii) Terms relating to the body or bodily states: *rāvis* F 'hoarseness', *sitis* F 'thirst', *tussis* F 'cough'
(iii) Rivers: *Tiberis* M 'Tiber'
(iv) Nautical terms: *prōris* (rare variant of *prōra*) F 'prow'
(v) Others: *futis* F 'pitcher'
(b) Alternative Accusative Singular in *-em* attested:
(i) Agricultural terms: *crātis* F 'hurdle', *sēmentis* F 'sowing', *messis* F 'harvest'
(ii) Terms relating to the body or bodily states: *febris* F 'fever', *cutis* F 'skin'
(iii) Rivers: *Albis* M 'Elbe', *Lĭris* M 'Garigliano' etc.
(iv) Nautical terms: *nāvis* F 'ship', *puppis* F 'stern', *restis* F 'rope, hawser'
(v) Others: *clāvis* F 'key', *neptis* F 'grand-daughter', *pelvis* F 'basin', *secūris* F 'axe', *strigilis* F 'scraper', *turris* F 'tower'

This is clearly not a simple list; the nouns are arranged in such a way as to bring out certain features. First, all except the river names are Feminine. Secondly, most of the nouns fall into one of four reasonably clear semantic groupings: rivers, agricultural or nautical terms, and terms to do with the body or bodily states. Thirdly, most of the nouns have *-im* consistently in the Accusative Singular, but at least sometimes appear with *-em*. I will suggest that these features relate to paradigm economy in such a way as to render type D innocuous to the Paradigm Economy Principle.

Consider first the Gender distribution. In section 4 above I suggested that the distribution of *-um* and *-ium* as Genitive Plural endings was determined partly on a morphosyntactic basis: for stems ending $-\bar{V}t-$, the ending is *-um* with Masculines and *-ium* with Feminines. A much clearer example of such morphosyntactic conditioning is provided by the second declension, in which the Nominative Singular endings *-us* and *-um* correlate exactly with non-Neuter and Neuter Genders respectively. That is essentially why we happily use the same label 'second declension' for nouns with different Nominative endings: we can regard them all as belonging to a single paradigm, within which we can predict the Nominative Singular ending on the basis of the Gender and, conversely, the Gender on the basis of the Nominative Singular ending (at least to the extent of whether a noun is Neuter or not). In type D, I suggest, we find a similar situation. If a noun has an Accusative Singular in *-im*, then, unless it is a river name, we can predict that it will be Feminine. The parallel with the second declension breaks down, admittedly, in that we cannot make the converse prediction; there is no set of Latin nouns — no subset of the third declension, say — within which we can predict that all Feminines will have -*im* as the Accusative Singular ending and all non-Feminines will have some other ending — say, -*em*. An attempt to combine type D with type A on this basis will fail, because there are numerous Feminine nouns which regularly have -*em* as their Accusative Singular ending, just like Masculines. But the fact that prediction is possible in one direction, from ending to Gender, can legitimately be regarded as at least mitigating the violation of paradigm economy that the existence of type D entails. To put it another way: if we call type D a subtype of type A identified by an 'exceptional' Accusative ending, we will not be merely taking refuge in an ad hoc solution to 'save' the Paradigm Economy Principle, because the Accusative in -*im* is not in fact wholly unpredictable within this putative AD type. Let us call this the AD analysis. Is there any further evidence for it?

Further evidence for the AD analysis can be derived from the second feature of type D, namely the semantic groupings. I have already mentioned that the Masculines of type D belonging to a precise semantic group, namely rivers; and one can in fact predict conversely that if a noun is a Masculine river name and belongs to type AD, then it will have an Accusative in -*im* (at least optionally). Coining a term, we can say that, for Masculines of type AD, the distribution of -*im* and -*em* as Accusative endings is 'morphosemantically' determined: river names will take -*im*, the rest -*em*. This may seem an odd suggestion. We are used to the notion that a category such as Gender, which has syntactic relevance, may be relevant to inflexional morphology too. But is it plausible to suggest that inflexion may be influenced also by properties which have no syntactic relevance whatever, such as the property of designating a river? In fact, this sort of thing happens quite often. In Russian, the properties Animate and Inanimate have no syntactic relevance, yet they play a big role in noun inflexion in that (for example) most Masculines have an Accusative which is like the Genitive if the noun is Animate and like the Nominative if it is Inanimate. One might argue that the distinction between Animates and Inanimates is semantically much more fundamental than that between Rivers and Non-Rivers. Yet it is not difficult to find other examples of semantic distinctions which are inflexionally relevant even though far from fundamental. In English, the class of count nouns with zero Plural marking (e.g. *deer, grouse, snipe, cod, trout*) coincides closely with the class of nouns denoting animals, birds or fish which are hunted or caught and eaten;[3] and in Latin the second- and fourth-declension nouns which are consistently Feminine in Gender (e.g. *quercus* 'oak', *fāgus* 'beech', *pīnus* 'pine') are all names of trees. Returning to the Latin type D, I suggest that 'morphosemantic' conditioning affects the Feminines too; if a Feminine noun declines like *puppis*, it is most likely to relate to agriculture, sea-faring or the body.

This morphosemantic conditioning is admittedly not watertight. There are some D-type Feminine nouns, such as *turris* 'tower' and *clāvis* 'key', which fit into no obvious semantic grouping; conversely, there is at least one AD-type noun relating to sea-faring for which no Accusative in *-im* is ever recorded, namely *ratis* 'raft'. So we do not find in type AD the clear correlation between semantics and inflexion that we find between Animateness and the Genitive-Accusative in Russian Masculines, for example. But at this point the third feature of type D becomes relevant, namely the fact that most of its members also decline like type A. If morphosemantics really does contribute to paradigm economy in the way I have suggested, we will expect to find that the type D nouns which are most prone to 'defect' to type A are those which fall outside any of the four relevant semantic groupings. And this is precisely what we do find; of the nouns in the 'Others' category, only the hapax legomenon *futis* (Varro *De lingua latina* v 119) has no attested Accusative Singular in *-em*, whereas six (*clāvis*, *neptis*, *pelvis*, *secūris*, *strigilis* and *turris*) do at least sometimes have *-em*.

At the beginning of this section I suggested that, rather than merely overlook type D because of the fewness of its adherents, we should explore whether its existence could be reconciled with paradigm economy, despite first appearances. It seems fair to claim that this exploration has been quite successful. Logically, type D might have been exemplified by a large and semantically diverse group of both Masculines and Feminines, showing no tendency to defect to any other type. If that had been the case, the existence of type D would have constituted a serious problem for paradigm economy. But the smallness of the type D group, its instability and its restrictedness in Gender and meaning all fall into

---

[3] This fact was pointed out to me by R. A. Hudson; it has also been noticed by Coates (1982: 124, 126). As Coates says, zero-marking for Plural is to some extent productive; *we bagged a brace of cat* is acceptable on the interpretation that the cats were hunted with a view to eating.

place quite neatly if, as the Paradigm Economy Principle suggests, we treat it as a subtype of a single AD paradigm; and to that extent the existence of type D actually tends to support the Principle.

6. Conclusion. There are no doubt other aspects of inflexional change in Latin which impinge on my proposal concerning paradigm economy — aspects concerning not only nouns but also adjectives, participles and verbs. And there are sure to be relevant facts about inflexional change in other languages too. But I hope I have succeeded in showing that some facts which at first sight look as if they present a serious difficulty for the Paradigm Economy Principle turn out on closer examination to support it, in that, using the Principle and Risch's observations in conjunction, we can account in quite precise detail for the nature and timing of certain inflexional changes in third-declension nouns — in greater detail, perhaps, than has previously been achieved in descriptions of Latin historical morphology.

REFERENCES

Carstairs, Andrew. 1983. Paradigm economy. *Journal of Linguistics* 19.115-28.
　　1984. Paradigm economy in the Latin third declension. *Transactions of the Philological Society.*
Coates, Richard. 1982. On inflection, variation and the paradigm. *Folia Linguistica* 16.119-36.
Ernout, Alfred. 1918. Cas en -*e*- et cas en -*i*- de la troisieme declinaison dans Lucrece. *Revue de philologie* 42.133-68.
　　1953. *Morphologie historique du latin* (3rd ed.). Paris: Klincksieck.
Janson, Tore. 1971. The Latin third declension. *Glotta* 49.111-42.
Leumann, Manu. 1977. *Lateinische Laut- und Formenlehre.* (Handbuch der Altertumswissenschaft Abt. 2, Teil 2, Band 1.) Munich: C. H. Beck'sche Verlagsbuchhandlung.
Matthews, P. H. 1972. *Inflectional morphology: a theoretical study based on aspects of Latin verb conjugation.* (Cambridge Studies in Linguistics 6.) Cambridge: Cambridge University Press.
Neue, F. and Wagener, C. 1902. *Formenlehre der lateinischen Sprache* I: Das Substantivum (3rd ed.). Leipzig: Reizland.
Niedermann, Max. 1953. *Historische Lautlehre des Lateinischen* (3rd ed.). Heidelberg: Carl Winter.
Risch, Ernst. 1977. Das System der lateinischen Deklinationen. *Cahiers Ferdinand de Saussure* 31.229-45.
Sommer, F. 1948. *Handbuch der lateinischen Laut- und Formenlehre* (2nd and 3rd ed.). Heidelberg: Carl Winter.

ABLAUT: A PHOENIX IN THE HISTORY OF AFRIKAANS

C. J. CONRADIE

1. Introduction. The presence of strong past participles with retained ablaut in a language characterised by thoroughgoing simplification of the verb system has been noted by linguists such as Hutterer 1975, comparing such forms as *geskryf* × *geskrewe* and *verbied* × *verbode* (p. 284), and Grayson 1970, pointing out that "the strong form tends to have a figurative meaning, while the weak conveys the literal meaning of the verb" (p. 47). After a brief sketch of the process of regularisation in p.p.'s in purely verbal function and the differentiation between these and the other p.p.'s which are mainly used adjectivally, I shall in more detail deal with the usage of and the morphological, semantic and syntactic factors involved in the differentiation. As more than 80% of the strong or irregular p.p.'s are characterised by an ablaut vowel differing from the stem vowel of the basic verb, the status of the "irregular p.p." often referred to below must be understood to be that of the amin vehicle of the ablaut system. The present paper is based on an empirical study of mainly Cape Dutch texts in the period from 1652 (date of Dutch settlement) to 1875 (beginning of Afrikaans language movement), and of Afrikaans texts in the period from 1875 to 1925 (official recognition of Afrikaans), and 1925 to 1978 as a final synchronic phase of the language.

The regularisation of the verbal p.p. was a gradual process which took place during the 18th and 19th centuries.[1] Although many intermediate forms occur in the texts, e.g. *gedronk, geholp, gekreegt, genoom, begon, vas gebond, ingetrok*, etc. without the /ə/-suffix, and *ontbieden, bedrijven, gekrijgen, bewijsen, gesenden, aangetreffen*, etc. without the ablaut vowel, it is stil possible that the normal process was one of direct replacement

---

[1] For more detail in connection with this and other sets of data mentioned in the paper, cf. Conradie 1979.

of the irregular form (e.g. *geholpen*) by the regular (*gehelp*). However, insofar as intermediate forms represent actual usage and loss of final /ə/ took place in a certain defined period, a closer scrutiny of the intermediate forms suggests that front ablaut vowels (as in *gekregen*) were regularised before back ablaut vowels (as in *gedronken*) since *gekrygen* and *gedronk* are the predominant intermediate types.

The ablaut vowel in the p.p. might be "supported" by the same vowel in another semantically similar word, e.g. that in *bedroë* (deceived) by that in the noun *bedrog* (deceit); that in *gedronken* (drunk) by that in the adj. *dronk* (drunk); and that in *gedwongen* (compelled) by that in the preterite *dwong* (compelled), and vice versa in all cases. While certain irreg. p.p.'s, such as *verbonde*, *geboë*, *gesnede*, *veelbesproke*, *gevonde*, *besope* and the above-mentioned *bedroë* still have nominal correlates, support from more than 20 preterites like *begon*, *bond*, *bleef*, etc. fell away with the virtual disappearance of the preterite as a verbal category during the first half of the 19th century. However, it is noteworthy that approximately 17 of the irreg. p.p.'s still extant today have ablaut vowels corresponding to that of the preterite, cf. *onbegonne*, *gebonde* and *agtergeblewe*, and that in two cases either the preterite or the p.p. gave rise to a new basic verb. form, viz. *verloor* (lose; Du. *verliezen*) and (*om-*)*dolwe* (dig up deeply; Du. *delven*) beside *delf* (dig, mine).

During the second half of the 19th century Afr. began to be consciously employed as a written language and was increasingly put to serious use, e.g. in newspapers, periodicals, history and grammar books and Bible translations. In a period in which regularisation of the verbal p.p. is known to have been virtually completed, we find large numbers of irreg. p.p.'s appearing in a form closely resembling the Dutch form — and not only in non-verbal usage but also often in verbal usage, cf. both, respectively, in: "Een *genome* besluit (a decision reached) kan nie weer verander worde nie of daar moet op die dag as dit *genome* word (when it is reached) …". *Gebede*, (*uit-/weg-*) *gesonde*, *geskolde*, *geskonke*, etc. were also found in verbal usage. This very artificiality is a clear indication of secondary Dutch influence, probably via the written word. Hints of a similar situation are found in a Bible translation into a Dutch creole by the Hernhutters. While the verb (including the p.p.) normally occurred only in one basic form, they employed purely Dutch forms like *gegeven*, *-genomen* and *gevonden* in passives, and *verborgenheid* as nominalisation. (In a parallel translation of St. Matthew Ch. 13 : 11 – 12 by the Danish, these forms are absent). Cf. Hesseling 1905: 217, 264, 268.

The 19th Century texts analysed have thus far yielded only one clear example of the differentiation which was to arise. A lengthy letter published in a newspaper of as far back as 1851 (cf. Nienaber 1971: 171—4) contains nine instances of p.p.'s of the verbs (*uit-/af-/weg-*)*neem* in verbal but also in a variety of non-verbal functions. Out of five instances of purely verbal usage, reg. *-geneem* occurs four times as in mod. Afr. As would also be the case in mod. Afr. the irreg. form is found pre-nominally in *de..genome(n) perde* (twice) while the remaining cases are compatible with mod. Afr.

In the following paragraphs I shall take the modern period of 1925—1978, in which the innovative system has become established, as point of departure, referring back to the period before 1925 occasionally.

2. Pattern of usage and age of acquisition. The usage of non-verbally used p.p.'s and — as a sub-group — irreg. p.p.'s in various registers of the spoken and written language is shown in Fig. 1 below, where the graphs represent the following:

A: the number of non-verbal p.p.'s as a percentage ($\times 100$, for graphic purposes) of all the words [2] in the corpus of the register in question;
B: the number of irreg. p.p.'s as a percentage of the total number of non-verbal p.p.'s; and
C: the number of irreg. non-verbal p.p.'s which may be considered on the basis of subjective judgement *not* to have been restructured to a new lexical item with no relationship with the basic verb, expressed as a percentage of the total number of irreg. p.p.'s.

The corpora (d), (e) and (f) are representative of the entire period 1925—1978; (a), (b), (c), (g) and (h) however, are from the latter part of this period. (a)-(d) are transcriptions [3] of spoken language: (a) of spontaneous conversations, (b) of conversations recorded during a nation-wide survey of the official languages, (c) of a series of interviews with well-known personalities on the radio and (d) of Afr. speeches in the House of Assembly (Hansard excerpts of equal length from 1925, 1950, and 1975). The written language is represented by (e) newspaper excerpts from 1925, 1950, and 1975, (f) belletristic prose from the entire period and

---

[2] The number of words in texts were estimated rather than counted; in the case of (a) — (c) the exact number is known.
[3] The transcriptions of (a) — (c) were provided by the language service of the Rand Afrikaans University; (c) represents a joint project with the Human Sciences Research Council.

texts of (g) a scientific and (h) a legal nature from the period 1960—5.[4] The spoken registers (a)-(d) may be said to represent increasing formality of style; the rise in the percentage of non-verbal p.p.'s (A), the increase in the percentage of irreg. forms (B) and the increase in base-related irreg. p.p.'s (C) clearly correlate with the differences in formality. The

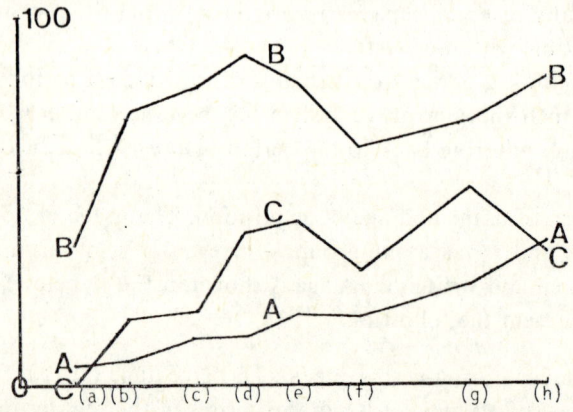

Fig. 1. Non-verbal p.p.'s in spoken and written language

percentage of non-verbal p.p.'s (A) rises further in the purely written texts (e)-(h), in particular in (g) and (h) which represent more technical texts. The percentage of irreg. p.p.'s (B) is comparable to that in more formal spoken language in general and the percentage of non-restructured p.p.'s (C) comparable to the most formal type of spoken language, indicating a relatively high level of semantic control of the irreg. p.p.'s by the users.

---

[4] The full set of data is the following, where numbers in brackets are the number of words on which each percentage is based:

Register	No. of words	A %	B %	C %
(a)	58 979	0,05(29)	38(11)	0(0)
(b)	313 015	0,07(231)	74(171)	18(31)
(c)	51 600	0,13(67)	81(54)	20(11)
(d)	62 500	0,13(82)	89(73)	41(30)
(e)	86 210	0,19(163)	82(133)	44(59)
(f)	71 500	0,18(129)	64(83)	31(26)
(g)	59 500	0,27(163)	71(116)	53(61)
(h)	29 800	0,38(114)	82(93)	35(33)

A limited test applied to students in primary and secondary school (Standards 2, 5, 7, 9 and 10) indicated that the acquisition of irreg. p.p.'s only gained momentum during the high school period and that some students had problems with acquiring these irreg. forms and with relating them to the basic verb right up to the end of their school careers. That the acquisition of irreg. p.p.'s takes place long after the period of basic language acquisition, is born witness to by lists of irreg. p.p.'s even in first language grammar books for the highest grades, cf. Du Toit *et al.* 1978: 156—7 — who head their list with the comment that the p.p.'s play an important part in the living language. While the fact that irreg. p.p.'s are part and parcel of the language is corroborated by the details given above, both the part played by irreg. p.p.'s in the more formal registers and the relatively late acquisition of these forms indicate that they are more typical of sophisticated rather than everyday language.

3. Phonological and morphological factors. In the period 1925—1978 virtually no intermediate forms (e.g. *gebrook, geblyven*) were found and very few in the preceding 50 years, in contrast to a substantial number in the regularisation period of the verbal p.p., suggesting secondary derivation from (written) Dutch rather than retention in the spoken language.

In combination with most prefixes — in some cases linked to the stem by means of *-ge-* — the p.p. is predominantly or exclusively irreg., cf. *ongeskonde, onverskrokke*; *bedroë, begrepe, bekrompe*; *onbegonne, onbekrompe, onbesproke*; *herrese, herwonne*; *onderbroke*; *oordrewe* (× *oordryf*), *oorwoë*. With *ver-* and *ont-* regularisation is often possible, cf. *verberg* × *verborge, verbied* × *verbode*; *ontbind* × *ontbonde*. Regularisation is even more consistently inhibited by suffixes, which (except in the case of the attributive suffix *-de/te* on reg. p.p.'s) cause functional change, cf. nominalisations like *afgestorwene, oorwonnene, uitgeworpenes*; *verborgenhede, gebondenheid*. When loosely linked to prepositions, the p.p. can be either reg. or irreg., cf. *uitgesluit* × *uitgeslote*. When adjectives and adverbs such as *vas, toe, saam, omhoog, vol, terug, ineen*, etc. combine with p.p.'s to form compounds, they often seem to make regularisation obligatory, cf. *vasgebind* (as against *vasgebonde, etc.), *krom-/teruggebuigde, dik-/leeggedrink, teruggedwing, vasgevries*. Types like *fasgebonde, kromgeboë* and *toegeslote* from the period before 1925 have become archaic. P.p.'s in compounds with a noun as first member were found to be irreg. in about 3/4 of the cases, cf. *tydgebonde* (× *oliegebinde*), *noodgewonge* and *spuitaangedrewe* (jet propelled). The lower degree of "transparency" which characterises irreg. forms seems to be in consonance with the more idiosyncratic relationship which may exist between members of the compound; e.g. the last example when paraphrased as "*deur uit*spuit*ing* aangedryf".

4. Semantic factors in ablaut retention. The fact that the form contrast between reg. and irreg. p.p.'s can be employed in expressing semantic differences, is perhaps the reason for its continued cultivation in the language. Hauptfleisch 1953 described at length its function in marking the distinction between "literal" and "figurative" meaning; contrasting pairs like *bederfde voedsel* (spoilt food) × *'n bedorwe kind* (a spoilt child), *n gebreekte bord* (a broken plate) × *n gebroke hart* (a broken heart), *n opgeswelde been* (a swollen leg) × *n geswolle hoof* (a swollen head) — the figurative sense often in fixed or semi-fixed expressions — abound in school textbooks. However, since all language is abstraction, the difference between "literal" and "figurative" may be only one of degree; certain p.p.'s express no contrast but nevertheless have a meaning on the same level of abstractness as the figurative meaning of others; other types of semantic differentiation, such as specialised meaning, exist. Examples of the latter — probably of more pragmatic value in communication — are: *'n bedorwe stembrief* (a spoilt vote), *gebonde koolstof* (combined carbon), *gegote yster* (cast iron), *'n gesplete verhemelte* (a cleft palate), *betrokke lug* (cloudy sky) and *'n oortrokke bankrekening* (an overdraft). A *geskrewe aansoek* (written application) differs subtlely from a *geskryfde aansoek* in that the former contrasts with a verbal application while the latter is specifically hand-written. Furthermore there is a tendency for p.p.'s expressing an emotionally non-neutral attitude or frame of mind to be irreg., cf. *aangedaan* (touched), *ingenome* (pleased), *opgewonde* (excited), *vasbeslote* (determined) and *teruggetrokke* (reticent); here in all probability the link between p.p. and basic verb has long been severed.

Table 1 may serve as an illustration of the complex of lexical, semantic and syntactic relationships in which a basic form such as BIND is involved. For the corpora mentioned in par. 2 above and a number of others, it was found that reg. and irreg. correlated with "literal" and "figurative/abstract" in the case of BERG, BIND, BREEK, BUIG, DRYF, HEF, HOU, SLAAN, SPAN, TREK and VANG, but not in the case of LEES and WYS. Nevertheless, this indicated that an implicational relationship may be assumed for the period 1925–1978, according to which non-regularisation in literal function generally implies

Table 1. Forms of BIND: semantic and syntactic factors

Basic form: BIND P.p.'s and associated contexts/entities	Syntactic context/function		Comments
	Post-nominal	Pre-nominal	
REGULARISED			L: literal sense
			F: figurative sense
gebind: tied up (of dog);	L × 6		
bound (of volume);	S		S: specialised meaning
limited (to);	F × 2		
obliged (to someone);	F		
bound (by Satan);	F		
vasgebind: attached (of label);	L × 3		
toegebind: bound up (of wound);	L × 2		
saamgebind: united;	F		
verbind: connected;	L × 9		
linked (of dams);	S		
pledged (to);	F		
ontbind: dissolved (of partnership);	F		
ingebinde: bound (of blueprints);		S	With *-de* attributive suffix
olie-gebinde: oil-based (of paint);		S	
doodgebinde: numbed (of finger);		L × 2	
verbinde: bandaged;		L	
ontbinde: dissolved (of group);		F	
UNREGULARISED			
gebonde: committed (to person, religion);	F	F	
captivated;	F × 3, L	S × 3	
bound (to oneself);	F × 2		
pledged (of seller);	F × 8		
ongebonde: unrestrained (of character);	F	F	
aardgebonde earthy (of approach);	F		
lotsgebonde: sharing similar fate;	F		
kortgebonde: short-tempered;		F	
verbonde: attached (to person);	F × 3		
related (to);	F × 25		
member (of institution);	F × 12		
ontbonde: decayed		S × 3	

non-regularisation in figurative function too, while regularisation in figurative function implies regularisation in literal function. The data for the period before 1925 — though much less clear — already hint at this implicational relationship.

5. **Syntactic factors and mechanisms.** The syntactic distribution of reg. and irreg. p.p.'s is likewise characterised by an implicational relationship. If the various syntactic contexts in which p.p.'s appear are divided into a post-nominal and a pre-nominal group, with noun+copula+p.p. as the main representative of the former and p.p.+noun as the main representative of the latter, we find the following distribution of reg. and irreg. forms:

Post-nominal contexts	Pre-nominal contexts	Basic forms
+reg.	−reg.	BEDERF, HOU, LOOP, SKRYF
±reg.	−reg.	BIED, BIND, DRYF, DWING, GEE, HEF, STRYK, WYS
+reg.	±reg.	KIES, LEES, NEEM
±reg.	±reg.	BREEK, BUIG, DUIK, SKEI, SLUIT, SPAN, TREK, VANG, WERP
−reg.	±reg.	no examples
±reg.	+reg.	no examples

Note that post-nominal regularisation is always comparable to or more far-reaching than pre-nominal regularisation. The smaller amount of data analysed for the period 1875–1925 indicates that, with few exceptions, the same kind of implicational relationship existed then (and cf. the 1851 letter mentioned in par. 1).

Abandoning for the moment the data from the corpora and the many syntactic contexts or functions involved, I would like to demonstrate the existence of an implicational relationship with reference to only three contexts, viz.

A: the p.p. in purely verbal usage in combination with *is*, commonly expressing the passive in the past;
B: the p.p. in adjectival function with the copula *is*, expressing present tense; and
C: the directly pre-nominal or attributive p.p.

Whoever regularises in C will have done so in B, and regularisation in B seems to depend to a large extent on the occurrence of a reg. p.p. in an A context. This situation — I shall deal mainly with the relationship B-C — is implicit in the following sets of sentences and noun phrases:

	Context A (passive, [+past])	Context B (complement, [−past])	Context C (pre-nominal)
1. Sy fiets is	gesteel;	...gesteel:	die gesteelde f.
2. Die vereniging is	ontbind;	...ontbind:	die ontbinde/ ontbonde v.

3. Die mate is	aangegee;	...aangegee:	die *aangegewe* m.	
4. Die rekening is	ingesluit;	...ingesluit/ ingeslote:	die ingesluite/ ingeslote r.	
5. Die klant is	gehelp;	...gehelp/ geholpe:	die ? gehelpte/ geholpe k.	
6. Hulle kinders is	aangeneem;	...aangeneem/ aangenome:	hulle *aangenome* k.	
7. Haar gedagtes is	?verberg;	...verborge:	haar *verborge* g.	
8. Die skip is	— — — —;	...?verdwene:	die *verdwene* s.	
9. Onderhandelings is	voortgesit;	— — — — — —:	*voortgesette* o.	
10. Die weduwee is	— — — —;	— — — — — —:	die *agtergeblewe* w.	

Jackendoff 1972 mentions the possibility that "we allow at least some adjectives to be generated in their surface position in noun phrases and not as reduced relative clauses" (p. 62). If we assume irreg. p.p.'s to be marked in the lexicon as [±prenominal], e.g. *verborge* as [−prenominal] and *aangegewe* as [+prenominal] and furthermore that a regularised form is blocked by an irreg. form already present in the context, the distribution of forms in Contexts B and C are specified quite adequately by the traditional transformational concept of an adjective preposing transformation, viz.

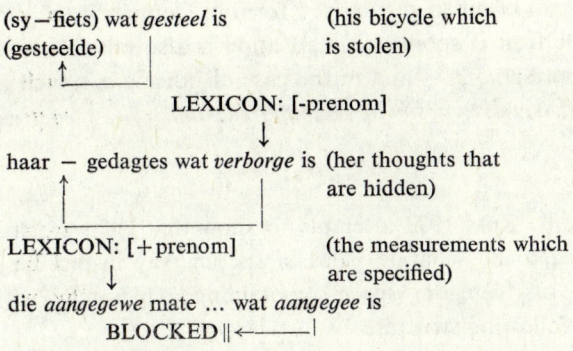

A few empirical observations may be made in support of the above: (a) When the "regularisation route" from B to C is blocked because the p.p. in question cannot occur in B at all, regularisation is excluded in C, cf.

Perfect(active):   Die bergklimmer het verdwyn.
                    (The mountaineer (has) disappeared.)
Context A: *Die bergklimmer is toe (then) verdwyn.
Context B: *Die bergklimmer is nou (now) verdwyn.
Context C: die verdwene (/*verdwynde) bergklimmer

and likewise: *die pas verskene boek* (the recently published book), *die uitgeweke anargis* (the exiled anarchist), *die gestorwe leier* (the deceased leader).

(b) A group of p.p.'s of transitive verbs are quite consistently irreg. in pre-nominal context despite the fact that Context A is always filled and Context B might contain a reg. p.p. However, the *is*+p.p. in Context B is in competition with the passive in the present, viz. *word*+p.p., because in the case of these verbs the two constructions can be synonymous: *Hierdie boeke is* (copula) *voorgeskryf* and *Hierdie boeke word* (aux. vb.) *voorgeskryf* are equivalent. Cf. also:

die verbode geskrif:	Die geskrif word verbied
	= Die geskrif is verbied/verbode
'n gebonde werknemer:	Die werknemer word gebind
	= Die werknemer is gebind/gebonde
'n bedorwe kind:	Die kind word bederf
	= Die kind is bederf/bedorwe
'n verborge uitgang	Die uitgang word verberg
	= Die uitgang is verberg/verborge

(c) Insofar as p.p.'s of intransitive verbs — which in Afr. are excluded from Context A — do occur in regularised form in Context B (cf. *Die vrugte is bederf*: The fruit is spoilt), regularisation is also possible in C (die *bederfde* × *bedorwe vrugte* — and in the case of other p.p.'s such as *verdrink, weggesink, verslyt, gesmelt, saamgetrek, ontsteek, toegetrek, gebreek*).

6. Conclusion. J. R. Ross 1972 attempts to show that what are traditionally considered to be separate parts of speech may in fact be a "quasi-continuum" or "category space" containing a hierarchy with something like the following structure:

Verb > Present participle > Perfect participle > Passive participle > Adjective > Preposition (?) > "adjectival noun" (e.g. *fun, snap*) > Noun (p. 316).

Without commenting further on the strength of Ross's arguments and theory, I would like to mention a number of developments in the Afr. verb system which follow the same lines, and from this hypothesise that these are governed by the general factor of "remoteness from the basic verb in its basic, literal meaning".

(a) Loss of final stem or inflexional /ə/ took place in the finite form of the verb (i.e. plural marker) well before it took place in the infinitive and strong p.p. Seemingly non-functional adjectival inflexion was maintained in the language to a certain extent, supported by a completely new system (cf. Raidt 1968), and nominal stem-final and plural /ə/ generally remained.
(b) Morphologically, the basic form of the verb, e.g. *uitsluit*, gives rise to the regular perfect/passive participle *uitgesluit*, which in adjectival use or as pre-/postposition can be either *uitgesluit* (reg.) or *uitgeslote* (irreg.), while there are no regularised versions of the nominalisations (*uit-*)*geslotene/geslotenheid*.
(c) Three degrees of syntactic remoteness from a simple underlying structure might be represented by (i) the adjective preposing transformation, (ii) direct derivation from the lexicon blocking the former and (iii) functional change into adverbs, prepositions and nouns, etc. In adverbs and prepositions the irreg. form is highly preferred and in nominalisations obligatory.
(d) In regard to the semantic factor it was pointed out above that the more "figurative" or "abstract" the meaning of the p.p. is — i.e. the further removed from the "basic" meaning of the verb — the greater the chances are of the p.p. being irregular. In addition, p.p.'s that have become idiomatically isolated (e.g. *'n gegewe perd in die bek kyk*: look a gift horse in the mouth) or have been restructured into separate lexical items as a result of semantic change (e.g. *onverskrokke*: undaunted × *skrik*: be frightened) are more often than not found to be irregular.

REFERENCES

Conradie, C. J. 1979. *Die diachronie van die Afrikaanse voltooide deelwoord.* Unpublished Ph.D. dissertation, University of the Witwatersrand.
Du Toit, H. A. et al. 1978. *Die lewende taal* (standerds 9 en 10), Kaapstad, etc.: Juta en Kie.
Grayson, J. D. 1970. The past participle in Afrikaans. In Lugton and Saltzer 1970. 47-8.
Hauptfleisch, D. C. 1953. *Vorm en gebruik van attributief-adjektiwiese voltooide deelwoorde in Afrikaans, met inbegrip van skynbare partisipia.* Unpublished M.A. thesis, University of Stellenbosch.
Hesseling, D. C. 1905. *Het Negerhollands der Deense Antillen.* Leiden: Sijthoff.
Hutterer, C. J. 1975. *Die germanischen Sprachen; ihre Geschichte in Grundzügen.* Budapest: Akadémiai Kiadó.

Jackendoff, R. S. 1972. *Semantic interpretation in Generative Grammar*. Cambridge, Mass.: MIT Press.

Lugton, R. C. and G. Salzer (eds.) 1970. *Studies in honor of J. Alexander Kerns*. The Hague: Mouton.

Nienaber, G. S. 1971. *Afrikaans in die vroeër jare*. Johannesburg: Voortrekkerpers.

Peranteau, P. M., J. N. Levi and G. C. Phares (eds.) 1972. *Papers from the Eighth Regional Meeting*. Chicago: CLS.

Raidt, E. H. 1958. *Geskiedenis van die byvoeglike verbuiging in Nederlands en Afrikaans*. Kaapstad: Nasou.

Ross, J. R. 1972. The category squish: endstation hauptwort. In Peranteau et al. 1972. 316-28.

ON ANALYSIS AND SYNTHESIS IN SOUND CHANGE

ANDREI DANCHEV

The purpose of this paper is (1) to present a fuller picture of linguistic data which make up a paradigm illustrating a certain type of reversible sound change and (2) to examine briefly some of the theoretical implications of the changes under consideration.

As used here, the term 'analytical' refers to changes in which the distinctive features that are articulated simultaneously in the input form are redistributed linearly in the output form, the number of structural elements in the receiving language thus exceeding the number of such elements in the source language forms (this partly in terms of Polivanov 1931: 80). Although analytical change is thus syntagmatic, syntagmatic change is not necessarily analytical, so that the two notions cannot be equated.[1]

More specifically, this paper considers the crosslanguage analytical perception and reproduction of the rounded front vowels /y/, /Y/ and /ø/, /œ/ (called 'interior' vowels in Crothers 1978), and of the low front vowel /æ/ in a number of languages. The copious evidence of loanword phonology shows that the phonological adaptation of the said vowels in the receiving languages often follows a Vf > /j/ + Vb pattern (where Vf = 'front vowel' and Vb = 'back vowel'), this resulting in a rising diphthong.[2] In order to avoid misunderstandings it must be stated at the very beginning that although there exist various alternative types of monophthongal substitution, this paper concentrates on the diphthongal adaptations.

As can be expected, the term 'synthetic' is used here for the opposite movement, that is, the synthesis into one output sound (rounded front

---

[1] It has been pointed out that syntagmatic identifications fall into two basic groups: /AB/→/A/ and /A/→/AB/ (cf. e.g. Fisiak 1968: 70). The analytical changes discussed in this paper belong to the second type.

[2] The problem of the phonological status (one or two phonemes?) of the resulting diphthongs has not been addressed here (for references and discussions of such cases see e.g. Andersen 1972 and Danchev 1975).

vowels and /æ/) of distinctive features which in the input form are in a linear sequence (/j/+/Vb/ or /Vb/+/j/).

For convenience and also to throw into relief the common features of the changes described here the /ü/ (for both /y/ and /Y/), /ö/ (for both /ø/ and /œ/) and /ä/ 'umlaut' notation has been used. So as to simplify the presentation slanting phonemic bracketing has been used everywhere. Vowel length is not marked consistently in all cases. Although most of the changes referred to are still living processes, the wedge rather than the arrow has been used so as to cover also the purely historical instances.

I. ANALYTICAL CHANGES

There is an abundance of examples resulting from both natural (historical) and artificial language contact, the latter in situations of foreign language teaching. Two corpora are thus available, this in accordance with the requirement in Polivanov 1931: 95. There are cases, of course, where it is difficult to decide whether the contact has been natural or artificial.[3]

Historical language contacts. Numerous instances of analytical change, or, to be more precise, of substitution,[4] can be seen in common and proper nouns that have passed from one language into another. There are hundreds of examples, a selection of which is offered below (cf. also the APPENDIX).

/ü(:)/ > /ju(:)/

This is probably the most frequently mentioned change of this type, mostly in connection with the adaptation of French loanwords in English (cf. Luick 1921, Brunner 1941, Andersen 1972, Lass 1976, Vachek 1976), the alternative monophthongal variants being mostly /i(:)/ and /u(:)/. To the generally well-known examples in English one can add numerous words that have passed from French, German, Turkish and other languages into Russian and Bulgarian.

---

[3] As in Danchev 1984, the distinction between 'subordinative' and 'co-ordinative' bilingualism is not kept up here.

[4] 'Substitution' is undoubtedly the more precise term, favoured by a number of authors. It must be recalled, however, that sound change in unilingual settings may also be due to substitution rather than to a gradual process of change. The difference between sound 'substitution' and 'change' thus being somewhat difficult to pinpoint, the latter and broader term has been used throughout this paper. In terms of Andersen 1972 these changes would be 'adaptive'. 'Processes' could be used as a cover term.

Table 1

SOURCE LANGUAGES	RECEIVING LANGUAGES		
French	*English*	*Russian*	*Bulgarian*
b*u*reau	b*u*reau	bj*u*ro	bj*u*ro
déb*u*t	déb*u*t[5]	debj*u*t	debj*u*t
rev*ue*	rev*iew*	revj*u*	revj*u*
t*u*lle/T*u*lle	t*u*lle	tj*u*l	tj*u*l
H*u*go	H*u*gh	Gj*u*go/J*u*go	J*u*go
German			
B*ü*rger		bj*u*rger	bj*u*rger
D*ü*se		dj*u*za	dj*u*za
F*ü*hrer	F*ue*hrer	fj*u*rer	fj*u*rer
M*ü*nchen	M*u*nich	Mj*u*nxen	Mj*u*nxen
N*ü*rnberg	N*ü*remberg	Nj*u*rnberg	Nj*u*rnberg
Turkish			
d*ü*z 'flat'			dj*u*s
g*ü*l 'rose'			gj*u*l
k*ü*p 'jar'			kj*u*p
m*ü*ft*ü* 'mufti'			mjuʃtija
t*ü*t*ü*n 'tobacco'		tj*u*tj*u*n	tj*u*tj*u*n
*ü*c 'three'			j*u*č
Finnish			
H*y*rylä (place name)		Xj*u*rjulja	Xj*u*rjul(j)a
*Y*rjö ,,		J*u*rjo	J*u*rjo
Swedish			
N*y*bro (place name)		Nj*u*bru	Nj*u*bru
R*ü*rik (pers. name)		Rj*u*rik	Rj*u*rik[6]

/ö(:)/ > /jo/

Though well attested, this type of change, more or less parallel to the preceding one, does not seem to have been noticed much.

Table 2

SOURCE LANGUAGES	RECEIVING LANGUAGES	
French	*Russian*	*Bulgarian*
fris*eur*		friz*jor*
grav*eur*	grav*jor*	grav*jor*
liqu*eur*	lik*jor*	lik*jor*
min*eur*		min*jor*
chef-d'*oevre*	šed*jovr*	šed*jovər*
Past*eur*		Past*jor*

---

[5] So as to avoid cluttering up the tables with too many words, the alternative phonetic variants of déb*u*t and some of the other examples have not been recorded.
[6] Rj*u*rik and some loanwords from the European languages have entered Bulgarian through Russian.

German		
Föhn	f*j*on	f*j*on
Goethe	G*j*ote	G*j*ote
Hölderlin		H*j*olderlin
Köln	K*j*oln	K*j*oln
Löss 'loess'	l*j*os	l*j*os
Turkish	English	
dönme 'renegade'		d*j*onme
göl 'lake', 'pond'		g*j*ol
gön 'leather'		g*j*on
kör 'blind'		k*j*or
kösk	ki*o*sk	k*j*ošk
lök 'putty'		l*j*ok
Hungarian	Russian	
Benkő (personal name)		Benkjo
Petöfi (personal name)	Pet*j*ofi	Pet*j*ofi
Swedish		
Göteborg	G*j*oteborg	G*j*oteborg
Malmö	Malm*j*o	Malm*j*o

/ä(:)/ > /ja/

This type of change does not seem to have attracted much attention, either.

Table 3

SOURCE LANGUAGES	RECEIVING LANGUAGES	
English	Russian	Bulgarian
catgut		k*j*atgut
slabbing	sl*j*abink	sl*j*abink
Blackpool	Bl*j*akpul	Bl*j*akpəl
Campbell	K*j*ambel	K*j*ambel
West Ham		West X*j*am
Finnish		
Hämenlinna	X*j*amenlina	X(*j*)amenlina
Jyväskylä	Juv*j*askjulja	Juv(*j*)askjul(*j*)a
Turkic languages[7] > *Russian*: e.g. bl*j*azik 'bracelet', dev*j*anuš 'ostrich', koben*j*ak 'coat', min*j*at 'mercy', sel*j*amlik 'men's room', sjur*j*aka 'headkerchief', tjuf*j*ak 'rifle', etc. For more examples and details see Šipova 1976.		
Old Common Slavic 'jat' > Various languages: *Albanian*: place names such as Dr*j*anovo, L*j*aska, R*j*axovo. *Greek*: astr*j*axa 'roof', gas*j*anica 'caterpillar', kol*j*anica 'breech'. *Romanian*: le*a*c 'medicine', hr*e*an 'horse-radish', v*e*ac 'age'. For more examples see Galabov 1962 and Samilov 1964.		

[7] In this paper this is a cover term for the various Turkic languages spoken in the Soviet Union.

Worth noting is the fact that such an adaptation pattern was also observed in early Modern English, presumably in the course of intra-lingual (dialectal, sociolectal, etc.) contacts. Variants with /ja/ have been attested e.g. in c*y*an 'can' (reported in Wallis 1653) during the Middle English /a/ > early MdE /æ/ transition period.

An intriguing case arises in connection with the /â/ > /ja/ change as reflected in various Turkish loanwords in Bulgarian, e.g. ajl*j*ak 'idle', ajr*j*an 'buttermilk', bel*j*a 'mischief', djuk*j*an 'shop', isl*j*am 'islam', k*j*ar 'profit', K*j*amilev (personal names) a.o. from Turkish aylâk, eyrân, belă, dükkân, islâm, kâr, kâmil (perfect) [8].

Since Turkish has the /ü/ and /ö/ vowels, which are substituted quite consistently by /ju/ and /jo/ in Bulgarian, one might be tempted to seek an /ä/ input vowel (as in other Turkic languages) in the Turkish loanwords that have /ja/ in Bulgarian. Moreover, the /ä/ vowel in other languages can be substituted by /ja/ in Russian and Bulgarian (cf. the foregoing table). However, the standard phonological descriptions of Modern Turkish (e.g. Kondratiev 1976, Lewis 1978[3]) do not contain such a front vowel. According to Lewis the Turkish /a/ is "a back, open, unrounded vowel like the *a* of French *a*voir or northern English m*a*n" (Lewis 1978:13) and in his textbook he indicates the palatal quality of the preceding consonant through a slight raised y (yod), inserted between the consonat and the following back vowel. It would seem thus that the diphthongal pronunciation was taken over from Turkish and further enhanced in Bulgarian. It should be noted, however, that the problem of whether to assign the 'palatality' feature to the vowel or the preceding consonat can receive a convenient compromise solution in terms of the Firthian 'prosodic analysis' notion, which in the opinion of Robins (1957)can be applied to palatalization in Slavic (and Turkish, one might add here). In such a case the palatality feature will be assigned to both segments and this would imply a front rather than a back (a) in the above mentioned examples.Worth noting in this connection is the reference by Lewis to "a front sound of (a), verging on that of (e), which can be heard in careful speakers' pronunciation of some Arabic borrowings" (Lewis 1978:13).

The problem as to the exact allophones of (a) in the Turkish dialects from which Bulgarian has borrowed words probably requires further research.

---

[8] For helpful consultations on various points relating to Turkish→Bulgarian language contacts I am grateful to Dr. M. Stajnova from the Institute of Balkan Studies in Sofia and to Dr. Koopmans, Dr. Hamans and Prof. Dr. Kortlandt from the University of Leiden in Holland.

Language Acquisition and Teaching. This corpus of data consists of the pronunciation errors of Bulgarian learners of French, German and English.

Concerning the adaptation of /ü/ and /ö/ in learners' interlanguages (in the sense this term is used in Selinker 1972 and generally in the extensive literature on error analysis today), every Bulgarian teacher of German (cf. here the remark in Trubetzkoy 1939/1969:64) and French is quite familiar with the 'incorrect' but frequently tolerated diphthongs /ju/ and /jo/ instead of the correct monophthongal pronunciations (for details see Krumova 1983 and Pərveva 1983). In fact, the diphthongal pronunciations are often fossilized in the interlanguages of Bulgarian learners. No examples need be given here, as these diphthongs occur in practically every German and French word containing the rounded front vowels /ü/ and /ö/ (including the loanwords in the preceding sections). Identical developments have been reported concerning the perception and reproduction of the rounded front vowels of French by Russian (Weinreich 1961), Romanian (oral communication of Prof. T. Christea from the University of Bucharest) and Italian learners (in the latter case learners with a Southern Italian dialectal background — oral communication of Prof. E. Arcaini from the University of Rome). This applies also to Russian learners of Chinese (Spešnev 1980:43). Similar observations in various situations have been reported by other authors as well.[9]

The diphthongal Bulgarian /ja/ adaptation of the English /ä/ vowel is somewhat less frequent and /ja/ cannot be regarded as the dominant functional equivalent.[10] The more typical interlingual indentification (in terms of Weinreich 1953) for Bulgarians is towards /e/ (for details see Danchev 1979a/1982), as seems to be actually the case with the speakers of most European languages (judging e.g. by the evidence in Fisiak 1968 and Filipović 1982).

Is is interesting to note that /ja/ occurs in the interlanguages of learners

---

[9] Prof. Malmberg heard once a Russian native speaker substitute /ju/ for /ü:/ when pronouncing the Finnish numeral *yksi* 'one' and Prof. Tengstrand noted the same substitution on the part of an English native speaker trying to pronounce a Swedish word (Both observations are reported with more details in Kristensson 1978: 26, f. 6).

[10] The notion of 'functional equivalent', which is borrowed from translation theory, can be applied conveniently also to the cases considered in this paper, as it helps to incorporate them into the broader context of cross-language communication. Together with the input form the paradigm of functional equivalents, headed by the 'dominant' (which is statistically most frequent) functional equivalent, can be said to form a 'fan' of correspondences. The terms 'dominant' functional equivalent and 'fan' have been used in this sense in Danchev 1979b.

from Eastern Bulgaria, whereas /e/ (or rather ε) dominates in the speech of learners, whose idiolects are influenced by the increasingly important Western Bulgarian interdialect of the capital Sofia. From the point of view of generative phonology this would imply that in the underlying representation of Modern Bulgarian there is still an /ä/ segment, and this assumption is actually to be found in Scatton 1975. There are certain deviations from that pattern, but this division nevertheless reenacts roughly the one time dialectal split of the early Slavic 'jat' vowel, which, according to a number of authors (cf. the references in Stojkov 1953 and Samilov 1964) was a monophthong more or less similar to the MdE /æ/ vowel. This shows once more how synchrony can overlap with diachrony (cf. also Danchev 1974).

The Common Element. The changes discussed so far can now be presented in the following more generalized manner:

/ü(:)/ > |/j/| + /u/ = /ju/
/ö(:)/ > |/j/| + /o/ = /jo/
/ä(:)/ > |/j/| + /a/ = /ja/

Whatever one may think of symmetry in language and language description, in this case it is quite conspicuous, with the palatal element as an independent yod segment in anticipatory position emerging as something like a common denominator of all three changes.

The fact that in conditions of language contact simultaneously articulated combinations of distinctive features in the source language can be redistributed into a linear sequence in the receptor language (the bilingual 'unwrapping', as it were, the bundle of simultaneous features — cf. Weinreich 1957:132), has been noted before (in addition to the references already mentioned earlier in this paper cf. also Trubetzkoy 1939/1969, Fisiak 1968, Householder 1971, Szulc 1973, Ternes 1976), but the phenomenon does not seem to have been fully described and theoretically appreciated yet. To be more precise, the whole paradigm of the change as presented above does not seem to have been reported and discussed yet. Several aspects of these processes call for comment.

To begin with, let us return briefly to the matter of their inner mechanism. The observations of a number of authors suggest that such instances of analytical perception (cf. also the denasalization of vowels described by various authors, e.g. Andersen 1972 and Stampe 1979) can be regarded as manifestations of a universal strategy of foreign language acquisition.

It ties in with what has also been termed the 'decomposition' of difficult elements in the structure of the foreign language (cf. Polivanov 1931 and more recently Wode 1981).

On a broader plane the tendency towards phonetic analyticity can be viewed as part of the general drift towards overall analytical structure[11] characteristic of interlanguages, including pidgins and creoles, that emerge in situations of language contact (cf. also Danchev 1983).

Next comes the difficulty of predicting the direction of the unconscious perception strategy of the speakers of various languages when they hear /ü(:)/, /ö(:)/ and /ä(:)/. If we accept now that substitutions are mental in occurrence and physical in teleology, their purpose being to maximise the perceptual characteristics of speech and to minimise its articulatory difficulties (Stampe 1979:9), we see that there exist various (or 'multiple') such teleologies. /ü(:)/, for example, can be replaced by several different functional equivalents, the basic ones being /ju/, /i(:)/ and /u(:)/, plus occasional other sounds. The interesting fact is that although all three (or more) basic functional equivalents are usually to be met with in most of the respective languages, there is nearly always a 'dominant' functional equivalent. Though varying from language to language, it is mostly shared by groups of languages, e.g. /ju/ for /ü(:)/ in English, Russian and Bulgarian, and /i(:)/ in Serbo-Croatian, Greek, Hebrew and some African languages (personal communication of Dr. Spaa from the University of Amsterdam). The assertion that "different languages have different ways of resolving phonological problems" (although ascribed to Dinnsen in Hooper 1980, statements to this effect have been formulated by a variety of authors) is thus at least partly true. And yet why, one may ask, does Bulgarian side with English, Russian, Romanian and some other languages, whereas Serbo-Croatian (in respect of the /ü(:)/ in German and French) sides with Greek, Czech, Hebrew, African and other languages? And why does Serbo-Croatian itself treat the /ü(:)/ in German and French words in one way (/i(:)/) and in many Turkish loanwords in another (/u(:)/)? Many further questions of this kind can obviously be asked.

---

[11] Albeit in a somewhat different context, essentially similar changes have been discussed by E. Nida, who points out that "the process of transfer may involve an *analytical redistribution* (emphasis provided). This means that what is carried by one lexical unit in the source language is distributed over several terms in the receptor language" (Nida: 1969: 493). It should, of course, also be recalled that the notion of 'phonological translation' has been used in a similar context (Catford 1965). The obvious common element in all such cases is that they take place in situations of language contact.

It has been claimed that the direction of such changes depends on distinctive feature patterning (Gvozdanovich 1983). This is probably true, although it is rather difficult to obtain psychologically valid information. A clue to feature hierarchy is provided by the observation that "the study of diphthongs can be expected to yield essential information that cannot be obtained from a study of phonetic monophthongs" (Andersen 1972 : 42 - 43). The circumstance that in all three cases of diphthongization the palatal feature is in prothetic position could tentatively be interpreted as indicating perceptual primacy. This would corroborate the claim that rounded palatal vowels are closer to the unrounded palatals than to the rounded back vowels (Crothers 1978: 98). If such an interpretation of the data is correct, the 'palatality' feature will be more relevant (or 'weightier') than the 'roundness' feature and will therefore rank higher in the respective feature hierarchies.[12] Things are complicated by the aforementioned fact that beside the dominant functional equivalent in most of the receiving languages one usually also finds the whole fan of functional equivalents. In a number of cases there are obviously additional factors such as phonetic environment and influence of the written forms (particularly in the case of more recent borrowings) to be reckoned with. This issue too evidently requires further study.

Thus, although in principle a change *can* be predicted in such cases, it is often difficult to predict its exact course. To use Wright's metaphor of the rabbit fleeing a pursuing dog, "given certain circumstances, we may be able to predict the rabbit will flee, but we may not be able to predict the escape route the rabbit will follow" (quoted from Campbell & Ringen 1980: 64). In the cases considered here it can be predicted with a fair degree of certainty that the /ü/, /ö/ and /ä/ vowels are not likely to survive language contact and that they will be replaced by more 'elementary' sounds. The claim of some authors that sound change is unpredictable and therefore cannot be accounted for 'scientifically' can thus be countered at least partly. The data considered here show that the 'unconscious rationality' on the part of language users determines a certain teleology of change, after all (cf. Campbell & Ringen 1980, and also Harris 1982 and Itkonen 1982).

---

[12] If the 'palatality' feature is accepted as the dominant one, it would be more appropriate to speak of 'rounded front vowels' (as in this paper) than of 'front rounded vowels'. Both word order patterns are to be met with in the literature, although the second seems to be more frequent.

II. SYNTHETIC CHANGES

Two types of data will be considered. In the first type the constituent elements — the yod and the respective back vowel — are in contiguous position and their linear order coincides with the output forms of the analytical changes. In the second type the constituent elements are in a noncontiguous position with an inverse linear order.

The first kind of evidence is illustrated by cases such as /ju/>/ü(:)/ in some Old High German and all the Low German dialects (for details and additionl references cf. Žirmunskij 1956: 212), in Old Danish- (cf. examples such as di*u*r>d*y*r 'animal' and li*u*d>l*y*d 'sound' in Andersen 1972 :23), Middle English (in certain dialects and words — cf Mincoff 1967 :210), and /e(j)o(:)/>/ö(:)/ in Middle English dialects[13] (the standard view that OE /eo(:)/>/ö(:)/ in Middle English has been challenged by some authors, cf. e.g. Reszkiewicz 1971). The general tendency in the Germanic languages for /ju/ to develop into /ü(:)/ seems to lend support to the claim of authors such as Smith and Wallis that there was an /ü(:)/ sound in early Modern English, not only in words borrowed from French, but also in native words such as n*e*w and br*e*w (Melchior 1972). For arguments in favour of an early Middle English /ew/>/i(j)w/ change cf. Kristensson 1978.

The second type of synthetic change is exemplified by i-umlaut in the Germanic languages, which can obviously be regarded as a synthesis of the distinctive features of the accented vowels and a following /j/ or /i/.

Although i-umlaut proceeded more or less independently in the various Germanic languages and dialects, the basic phonetic mechanism (regardless of the long standing dispute whether the umlaut was caused by the intervening consonant or the following vowel) appears to have been essentially the same everywhere. The evidence being well-known (for theoretical overviews and examples cf. e.g. Antonsen 1961, Steblin-Kamenskij 1962, Bennett 1969, Awedyk 1975, Voyles 1982, and all the standard textbooks), a few examples should suffice:

/u(:)/+C(C)+/j/>/ü(:)/, e.g. OE *s*u*nnja>s*y*nn
/o(:)/+C(C)+/j/>/ö(:)/, e.g. OSc. *d*o*mjan>d*ø*ma
/a(:)/+C(C)+/j/>/ä(:)/, e.g. OHG *z*a*ljan> *z*ä*len [14]

---

[13] The typological evidence displayed in this paper would seem to suggest that the /éo(:)/>/jó(:)/ accent shift in the ME dialects where OE /eo(:)/ became /ö(:)/ must have been more widespread than is usually assumed.

[14] Although the attested umlauted forms of early Germanic /a/ in Old High German are with /e/, an intermediate /ä/ stage has been assumed by most authors (cf. e.g. Twaddell 1938).

Similar changes having taken place in a number of other languages as well (cf. e.g. Anttila 1972, Awedyk 1975), they are obviously no less 'natural' (should one decide to use this notion) than the reverse analytical changes. As a matter of fact, according to Schane rules of assimilation, which also include umlaut, provide some of the clearest examples of natural rules (Schane 1972 :207).

III. THE COMPARISON OF ANALYTICAL AND SYNTHETIC CHANGES

The comparison of the generalized patterns of analytical and synthetic change:

ANALYTICAL CHANGE: $V(ü, ö, ä) > /j/ + V(u, o, a)$

SYNTHETIC CHANGE:
(1) $V(u, o, a) + /j/$
(2) $/j/ + V(u, o, a)$ $> V(ü, ö, ä)$

renders their reversible nature even more conspicuous. Indeed, in the analytical changes a rounded front vowel is decomposed into a yod followed by a back vowel, and in the synthetic changes we have the opposite movement — the same yod, followed by a back vowel, is changed into a rounded front vowel. In the second type of synthetic change the reversibility is of a double order.

In addition to some purely formal differences, there are also different underlying factors. Schane makes the plausible suggestion that "when segments become more alike, there is a physiological explanation; that is, assimilation phenomena are a consequence of inherent properties of the articulatory mechanism. On the other hand, it does not seem unlikely that when segments are made less like each other (...), the explanation to be sought would be a psychological one" (Schane 1972 :213).

Despite certain differences, the obvious similarities between the generalized patterns of analytical and synthetic change warrant further probing into that reversible relationship and generally into the directionality of such changes. Reversible (also called 'mutual', 'converse', 'reciprocal') changes have, of course, been discussed before, e.g. by Jakobson, Andersen, Ferguson, Stampe and some other authors,[15] but these

---

[15] Hooper questions the claim by Sanders that the directionality of rules is universal, so that if one language has a rule A→B, no language will contain the converse rule B→A in the same environment (Hooper 1980: 128). The evidence in the present paper tends to confirm the view that bidirectional converse changes are possible not only in the same environment, but even within the same language.

particular instances of reversible change, which suggest the possible existence of a common framework of cause and effect, do not seem to have been reported yet. It would be worthwhile, indeed, to find out if the reversibility relationship applies also to the causes of the respective changes. One can set out from the facts that are more or less certain, gradually moving onto more speculative ground.

What is certain so far is that analytical sound changes of the type considered in this paper occur in situations of natural or artificial bilingualism, that is, in the *presence* of language contact. The available evidence points towards the assumption that the opposite movement, that is, synthetic change, is more likely to occur in the *absence* of language contact. The question arises thus whether synthetic change in general is a predominantly internal phenomenon. Should this prove to be the case, it opens up interesting possibilities for speculation on the causes of changes that have so far defied any attempts at adequate causal explanations.

Although the phonetic mechanism of the synthetic changes is more or less clear, there is still no sufficiently satisfactory account of why umlaut and the other synthetic changes took place during the particular historical periods and not earlier or later, the same question naturally arising in connection with the actuation of practically every type of language change (cf. Weinreich et al 1968).

Concerning the assumption that the synthetic changes discussed here were internal developments, it is rather difficult, of course, to recover with any degree of precision the extralinguistic facts during the time of the respective changes. But since no serious suggestion that i-umlaut and the other synthetic changes are to be linked in any way with substratum, adstratum or superstratum phenomena seems to have been advanced so far, one can assume indeed that they were basically internal developments.

Rounded front vowels have naturally resulted also from 'simpler', that is, non-synthetic internal developments. There are various examples in a number of languages, e.g. the late OE rounding of /i(:)/ (and also of /ie(:)/, which would already be a synthetic development) after /w/ in certain dialects and words (cf. Mincoff 1967 : 64), the Northern Middle English raising and fronting of /o:/, the Old Scandinavian /o/ > /ö/ fronting (Heusler 1921: 13), the rounding of front vowels in Austrian dialects (Keller 1961), the /u(:)/ > /ü(:)/ change in Southern Yiddish, which, in the opinion of King 1969: 197 cannot be ascribed to any areal influence, /i/ > /ü/ in Hungarian (Kálmán 1972), etc.

Out of the possible counter-examples to the claim that rounded front vowels result chiefly from internal developments, one may point to the much discussed development of /ü(:)/ in Old French and Northern Italian dialects. The substratum theory, advanced by Wartburg and other scholars has not been convincingly disproved yet, although alternative solutions in terms of internal developments have been proposed as well (for French cf. Bichakijan 1974).

Perhaps one should also note the fact that in Turkish there is a constraint on the operation of vowel harmony in loanwords (for exceptions cf. Lewis 1978), this indicating again that language contact is not conducive to the establishment of the more ˙complex˙ vowels.

Although the available evidence is still insufficient for drawing any final conclusions, it seems to warrant the provisional assumption that the emergence of /ü/, /ö/ and /ä/ is characteristic above all of the *absence* of language contact, whereas their linear decomposition into rising diphthongs is demonstrably connected with the *presence* of language contact.[16]

The data reviewed so far lend support to the views that the vowels /ü/, /ö/ and /ä/, which are less frequent in the languages of the world[17], are more ˙complex˙, but less ˙stable˙. Despite various recent refinements of Chomsky & Halle's markedness theory (in this particular case one would expect roughly equal complexity indices for /ü/, /ö/ and /ä/, with at least one value higher than the indices for Skalicka's (1961) 'fundamental' vowels /e/ and /o/. Chomsky & Halle assign the same index (2) to /e/, /o/, /æ/, and /ü/ whereas /ö/ receives index 3 in their table — cf. Chomsky & Halle 1968: 409), the basic idea behind their approach, which has been challenged by some authors (e.g. Lass 1980: 25 and elsewhere), apparently receives confirmation, after all. Before proceeding, however, one may recall that "the generative model, in stopping with the mere statement of these facts, however elegantly expressed,

---

[16] The early Slavic /ü(:)/ > /ju(:)/ change may constitute a counterexample to the affirmation that analytical changes are typical of language contact. However, the presence of /ü(:)/ in early Slavic is not universally accepted (for some references and examples cf. e.g. Velčeva 1980: 88-91). What regards this hypothetical change in Bulgarian, the language contact factor cannot be ruled out, while the case with Slovak and other Slavic languages is rather unclear.

[17] According to Sedlac 1969, rounded front vowels occur only in about 15% of the languages in the world: the Germanic, some Romance, the Turkic, Uralo-Altaic and Sino-Tibetan languages, i.e. chiefly in Europe and Northern Asia (cf. also Crothers 1978).

fails to explain *why* (emphasis provided) these features or this marking convention, rather than different features or marking conventions, should be the ones which are actually true or appropriate for human languages" (Crothers 1978: 135).

The elements that turn out to be less stable in language contact are usually the ones that are typologically marked, at least in the cases considered here, this is in accordance with the Greenbergian principle that "what is more marked changes to what is less marked". In the course of language contacts it is above all the idiosyncratic elements of every language that are shorn away, the resulting interlanguages, pidgins and créoles being built up of typologically more elementary structures and units. Further elaborating on Trubetzkoy's well-known statement that "the sounds of a foreign language receive an incorrect phonological intepretation since they are strained through the "phonological sieve" of one's own mother tongue" (Trubetzkoy 1939/1969: 52) one can compare language contact to a "typological complexity filter" (or/sieve"). The 'simpler' (and 'easier') elements pass through, whereas the more 'complex' (and 'difficult') elements are processed in one way or another in the receiving language speaker's mind. The substitution of simpler elements, e.g. one of the 'fundamental' vowels (/i, e, u, o, a/: cf. Skalicka 1961) or the analytical linear combination of a yod and one of the fundamental vowels, is obviously one of the universal unconscious language perception and acquisition strategies.[18]

An interlanguage is thus less likely to have rounded front vowels, /æ/, nasalised vowels, velar /ŋ/, etc., than an ordinary language. This type of simplification pattern in interlanguages could provide a clue, for example, as to why /ü/, /ö/ and /ä/ were gradually eliminated in those areas of Middle English, where interlanguages seem to have developed (cf. Poussa 1982, and also Danchev 1983). On the other hand, there were Middle English dialects in which /ü/ and /ö/ emerged as internal developments, this showing how in different varieties of the same language both analytical and synthetic processes can proceed more or less simultaneously (D. Stampe finds it surprising that opposite substitu-

---

[18] The processes considered here show how language typology and error analysis yield useful information about each other. The errors in language acquisition obviously render certain typological characteristics of the target language more conspicuous. This is, of course, one of the most expedient ways of pinpointing the features that characterize a given language as 'foreign', which is so very important for the optimization of foreign language learning and teaching.

tions — assimilations and dissimilations (in his case nasalisation and denasalisation) — apply in most languages — Stampe 1979: 18).

These data appear to throw some new light on the causation of language change — the perennial problem of historical linguistics. In spite of the enormous amount of literature that has already piled up, the whole issue is obviously still wide open and has recently even been reviewed with marked scepticism (Lass 1980). Since it is obviously impossible to offer an exhaustive survey of the issue as it stands today, I shall mention several relatively more recent and well-known opinions which can serve as a convenient starting point for the brief final discussion of the issues raised in this paper.

From a more general point of view one is tempted to quote R. King, according to whom "many linguists, probably an easy majority, have long since given up inquiring into the *why* (emphasis provided) of phonological change" (King 1969: 189) and in the opinion of R. Lass "there are at present no intellectually respectable strategies for explaining linguistic change" (Lass 1980: xi). In a fairly recent (1981) survey of language change explanations J. Aitchison concludes that "language is developing in some mysterious fashion that linguists have not yet identified" (Aitchison 1981: 234).

More directly relatable to the evidence and line of argument in this paper is R. Lakoff's interesting essay on 'drift', which she defines as "historical fluctuation between syntheticity and analyticity, acting as a sort of linguistic pendulum", and posing the question as to why languages should have such a pendulum built in she admits that she has "no idea why this metacondition exists" (Lakoff 1972: 179).

Using different terminology, but commenting on essentially similar phenomena, Schane writes that "on the surface it looks as though there are two conflicting tendencies at play: things being made more like each other (assimilation), and things being made less like each other", and concerning the direction of assimilations Schane says that "one still wonders why they should work that way rather than conversely"[19] (Schane 1972: 216 - 226).

Other similar statements can be quoted adding up to an impressive consensus of scholarly opinion which admits the existence of unknown factors determining the direction of various reciprocal changes. A multi-

---

[19] The external explanations for the directions of conflicting assimilations and dissimilations considered by Schane are physiological and psychological.

factor approach is clearly indicated, and in what follows I would like to draw some attention to the speech tempo factor, which, though not unknown, does not seem to have received yet the full attention it probably deserves, especially in the light of the evidence adduced and discussed in this paper.

As in so many other cases, linguists do not always share the same definitions of 'fast speech' and 'normal speech'. Indeed, it has been pointed out that "tempo is an aspect of speech that is basic to its functioning and yet difficult, if not impossible to define" (Wieden 1979: 21). It has also been recognized that 'fast speech phenomena' occur in casual speech that is not necessarily rapid. In any case, a number of recent studies by various authors (e.g. Zwicky 1972, Dressler 1972, Bolozky 1977, Kuliš 1982) have shown that speech tempo is a highly complex idiolectal, situational, diatopic and diachronic variable.

In view of the complexity of the speech tempo notion the following arguments are obviously open to various criticism and doubts. Let us nevertheless consider the possible connection of the speech tempo factor with the causality of both analytical and synthetic sound change. One can begin again with what may be regarded as more or less certain.

First of all, it is an established fact that interlanguages originating from language contact are characterized by a slower speech tempo. For obvious reasons the non-native speakers of a language articulate it more slowly than the native speakers of that same language [20]. *Lento* speech can therefore be regarded as a conscious or unconscious communicative strategy of bilingual speakers in situations of language contact.

Whereas *lento* speech is thus typical of the *presence* of language contact, *allegro* speech will presumably be associated with the *absence* of language contact. At this point one will recall the observations of R. Jakobson that linguistic innovations may begin in the allegro or elliptic style (1949: 332) and of D. Jones that in rapid styles there may develop sounds that do not occur at all in the 'ordinary' style (Jones 1962; 197). The relevant point is that increases in the speech tempo usually lead to increases in various types of assimilations. Summarizing his observations S. Bolozky states that "the faster the tempo of speech, the greater the likelihood of variable assimilation processes..." (Bolozky 1977:235).

---

[20] It has been observed that "people for whom a pidgin is a second, subsidiary language speak it slowly (...). When Tok Pisin is learned as a first language, the rate of speech speeds up remarkably. This in turn has a dramatic effect on the phonology" (Aitchison 1981: 203).

. The data showing then that allegro speech conditions assimilations [21] and i-umlaut and the other type of synthetic change coming under the heading of one kind of assimilation or another, one will conceivably be led into considering them as allegro speech phenomena.[22]

There exists thus both substantive and argumentative evidence suggesting that some instances of analytical and synthetic language change can be accounted for in terms of ±LANGUAGE CONTACT and SPEECH TEMPO changes, the latter depending on extralinguistic circumstances. This makes it possible to offer some tentative answers to the vexed questions about the causality of some type of language change.

Setting out from some plain facts the argument in this paper has moved on to increasingly speculative matters, which may be confirmed or modified by further research. In any case, the present discussion tends to imply that, as has already been pointed out elsewhere (Danchev 1983), a broader interdisciplinary approach, which takes into account various aspects of language contact and is based on a larger body of relevant data, can sometimes offer new insights into old problems.

APPENDIX: ADDITIONAL DATA

/ü(:)/ > /ju(:)/

FRENCH > ENGLISH: cure, curious, fugitive, furious, future, human, humid, humour, mule, music, mutual, pupil, pure, tulip, union, unit. For more examples and details see Lenz 1913, Luick 1921, Brunner 1941, Lass 1976.

FRENCH > RUSSIAN: aljur, aljuminij, bjuleten, bjust, brjunet, brošjura, etjud, galjucinacija, gljukoza, gravjura, kokljuš, noktjurn,

---

[21] There are numerous cross-language instances of synthetic changes, that is, of 'simpler'/'fundamental'/'basic'/etc. elements turning into more 'complex'/ /'special'/'peripheral'/etc. ones, e.g. the /n/ > /ŋ/ change in Hebrew (Bolozky 1977: 219).

[22] It has been pointed out that vowel harmony can fulfil an integrative role and attention has been drawn to Baudouin's metaphor that it serves to "cement" all the syllables of words or of smaller grammatical units (Jakobson & Waugh 1979: 38). It can similarly be assumed that i-umlaut (and some of the other Old English combinative changes, which have puzzled generations of scholars) thus contributed to a more global, that is, *synthetic* perception of words and their component elements (cf. also Ilyish 1948), which in turn might have been due to increases in the speech tempo.

parven*ju*, pil*ju*lja, p*ju*pitr, p*ju*ré, pl*ju*maž, ševel*ju*ra, s*ju*rpris, s*ju*rtuk, s*ju*žet, t*ju*rban, tr*ju*mo, turn*ju*r(a). For details see Elenski 1980.

FRENCH > BULGARIAN: b*ju*letin, b*ju*st, br*ju*net, deb*ju*t, et*ju*d, grav*ju*ra, xal*ju*cinacija, *ju*zina, k*ju*loti, n*ju*ans, nokt*ju*rno, pardes*ju*, parven*ju*, p*ju*ré, s*ju*rpris, s*ju*zet. As has already been pointed out (cf. Note No 6), it is often unclear which of the French loanwords in Bulgarian have been borrowed directly from French and which indirectly through Russian. For more examples and details see Patev 1967 and Ilčev 1982.

GERMAN > BULGARIAN: b*ju*gelxorn, d*ju*bel, d*ju*na (originally from Dutch), tr*ju*fel, D*ju*seldorf, L*ju*neburg, V*ju*rtemberg. For more examples and details see Paraškevov 1981 and Ilčev 1982.

TURKISH > BULGARIAN: d*ju*beš, d*ju*djuk, d*ju*kjan, d*ju*lger, d*ju*šeš, g*ju*derija, g*ju*lé, g*ju*m, g*ju*mé, g*ju*ruk, g*ju*rultija, g*ju*več, g*ju*vendija, *ju*nak, *ju*tija, k*ju*lče, k*ju*ljaf, k*ju*nec, k*ju*skija, k*ju*tjuk, m*ju*djur, m*ju*ezin, m*ju*ftija, m*ju*ré, m*ju*sjulmanin, m*ju*šterija, s*ju*nger, s*ju*rija, s*ju*rme, s*ju*tljaš, t*ju*fek, t*ju*flek, t*ju*rlu (g*ju*več), x*ju*riet, z*ju*mbj*u*l, Gj*u*zelev, Lj*u*tvi, X*ju*sein. The /ju/ in k*ju*fte, k*ju*mjur and many other words is from Turkish /ö/ with the frequent Bulgarian /o/ > /u/ raising in unaccented positions. For more examples and details see Ilčev 1982.

TURKIC LANGUAGES > RUSSIAN: bir*ju*k, bir*ju*za, burd*ju*k, iz*ju*m, serd*ju*k, sevr*ju*ga, t*ju*fjak, t*ju*ja, t*ju*k, t*ju*lka, t*ju*men, t*ju*rik, ut*ju*k. For more examples and details see Šipova 1976.

/ö(:)/ > /jo/

FRENCH > BULGARIAN: asans*jo*r, f*jo*tjojl, f*jo*tər, plas*jo*r, poz*jo*r, rezis*jo*r, šof*jo*r, Kr*jo*zo, L*jo*bon, N*jo*i. For more examples and details see Patev 1967 and Ilčev 1982.

TURKISH > BULGARIAN: g*jo*bek, g*jo*ture, g*jo*z, *jo*rs, k*jo*ček, kjopek, kjopolu, kjose, kjoše, kjotek. For more examples and details see Ilčev 1982.

/ä/ > /ja/

ENGLISH > BULGARIAN: in proper names such as Bl*ja*k, Br*ja*dfort, Brodk*ja*stink, G*ja*ləri Xaus, Gl*ja*dis, K*ja*kstən, K*ja*mel, N*ja*šənəl, P*ja*tən, R*ja*zəl-D*ja*zəl, Sautx*ja*mptən, Stjandiš, Xjarolt, Xjazlit. These and many other similar examples are attested in various Bulgarian texts, especially older ones. For more examples and details see Danchev 1979a/1982. To the common nouns in table 3 one can add sl*ja*nk (slang).

REFERENCES

Aitchison, Jean. 1981. *Language change: progress or decay?* London: Fontana Paperbacks.
Andersen, Henning. 1972. Diphthongization. *Language* 48. 11-50.
Anttila, Raimo. 1972. *An introduction to historical and comparative linguistics.* New York: Collier-Macmillan.
Antonsen, Elmer H. 1961. Germanic umlaut anew. *Language* 37. 215-30.
Awedyk, Wiesław. 1975. *Palatal umlaut versus velar umlaut and breaking. A comparative study of the palatalization and velarization of vowels in Germanic languages.* Poznań: Wydawnictwo Naukowe Uniwersytetu im. Adama Mickiewicza.
Bennett, William H. 1969. Manifestations of i-umlaut in Old English. *Linguistics* 50. 5-26.
Bichakjian, Bernard H. 1974. The evolution of French [y:] An integrated change. *Historical linguistics*, II, ed. by John Anderson, 71 - 88. Amsterdam: John Benjamin.
Bolozky, Shmuel. 1977. Fast speech as a function of tempo in natural generative phonology. *Journal of Linguistics* 13. 217 - 38.
Brunner, Karl. 1941. Die Wiedergabe von franz. *ü (u)* im Englischen. *Beiblatt zur Anglia* 52. 219 - 27.
Campbell, Lyle and Jon Ringen. 1981. Teleology and the explanation of sound change. *Phonologica 1980*, ed. by Wolfgang U. Dressler, Oskar E. Pfeiffer, John R. Rennison, 57 - 68. Innsbruck: Universität.
Catford, John C. 1965. *A linguistic theory of translation.* London: Oxford University Press.
Chomsky, Noam and Morris Halle. 1968. *The sound pattern of* English. New York: Harper & Row.
Crothers, John. 1978. Typology and universals of vowel systems. *Universals of human language*, ed. by John Greenberg, 93 - 152. Stanford: University Press.
Danchev, Andrei. 1974. Za səotnošenieto na sinxronijata i diaxronijata. *Ruski i zapadni ezici* 2/3, 1 - 13.
    1975. On the phonemic and phonetic values of the short *ea* and *eo* digraphs in Old English. *Annuaire de l'Université de Sofia: Faculté des lettres* LXX, 1. 33 - 88.
    1979a/1982. *Bəlgarska transkripcija na anglijski imena.* Sofia: Narodna Prosveta.
    1979b. *Kontrastivna lingvistika, analiz na greškite i čuždoezikovo obučenie*, I. Veliko Tərnovo: University Press.
    1983. Translation and syntactic change. Historical syntax, ed. by Jacek Fisiak, The Hague: Mouton. Forthcoming. The Middle English lengthening in open syllables and the interlanguage hypothesis. *Sofia studies in English language and literature.*
Dressler, Wolfgang U. 1972. Methodisches zu Allegro-Regeln. *Phonologica* 1972, ed. by Wolfgang U. Dressler & F. Mareš, 219 - 34. München/Salzburg: Wilhelm Fink Verlag.
Elenski, Jordan. 1980. *Istoričeskaja leksikologija russkogo jazika.* Veliko Tərnovo: University Press.

Filipović, Rudolf. 1982. (ed.). *The English element in European languages*, 2. Zagreb: University Press.

Fisiak, Jacek. 1968. Phonemics of English loanwords in Polish. *Biuletyn Fonograficzny* IX. 69 - 79.

Gələbov, Ivan. 1962. Les données de l'onomastique byzantine et grecque touchant la prononciation du 0 vieux bulgare. *Byzantinobulgarica* I. 313 - 20. (Sofia: Izdatelstvo na Bəlgarskata Akademija na Naukite.)

Gvozdanovich, Jadranka. 1983. Theories of sound change fail if they try to predict too much. Paper presented at the 6th International Conference on Historical Linguistics, Poznan, 22 - 26 August, 1983.

Harris, Martin. 1982. On explaining language change. *Papers from the 5th International Conference on Historical Linguistics*, ed. by Anders Ahlqvist, 1 - 14. — Amsterdam/Philadelphia: John Benjamins.

Heusler, Andreas. 1921. *Altisländsiches Elementarbuch.* Heidelberg: Carl Winter.

Hooper, Joan B. 1980. Formal and substantive approaches to phonology. *Language and Speech* 23. 125 - 31.

Householder, Fred W. 1971. *Linguistic speculations.* Cambridge: University Press.

Ilčev, Stefan. 1982. (ed.). *Recnik na čuždite dumi v bəlgarskija ezik.* Sofia: Izdatelstvo na Bəlgarskata Akademija na Naukite.

Ilyish, Boris A. 1958. *Istorija anglijskogo jazika.* Moscow—Leningrad: Prosveščenie.

Itkonen, Esa. 1982. Short-term and long-term teleology in linguistic change. *Papers from the 3rd International Conference on Historical Linguistics*, ed. by John P. Maher et al, 85 - 118. Amsterdam/Philadelphia: John Benjamins.

Jakobson, Roman. 1949. Principes de phonologie historique. Appendix in *Principes de phonologie* by N. S. Trubetzkoy, 315 - 36. Paris: Editions Klincksieck.

Jakobson, Roman and Linda R. Waugh. 1979. *The sound shape of language.* Brighton: The Harvester Press.

Jones, Daniel. 1962. *The phoneme, its nature and use.* Cambridge: Uźiversity Press.

Kálmán, Béla. 1972. Hungarian historical phonology. *The Hungarian language*, ed. by Lóránd Benkö & Samu Imre, 49 - 83. The Hague: Mouton.

Keller, Rudolf E. 1961. *German dialects: phonology and morphology.* Manchester: University Press.

King, Robert D. 1969. *Historical linguistics and generative grammar.* Englewood Cliffs, New Jersey: Prentice-Hall.

Kondratjev, Vladimir G. 1976. *Vvodnij fonetičeskij kurs tureckogo jazika.* Leningrad: Izdatel'stvo Leningradskogo Universiteta.

Kristensson, Gillis. 1978. A note on OE (e : ow) and OFr (y) in Middle English *Studia Neophilologica* 50. 25 - 27.

Krumova, Jordanka. Forthcoming. Za njakoj greški, dopuskani ot belgari pri usvojavane proiznošenieto na frenskite glasni. *Səpostavitelno ezikoznanie i čuždoezikovo obučenie* V. Veliko Tərnovo: University Press.

Kuliš, Larisa J. 1982. *Psixolingvističeskie aspekti vosprijatija ustnoj inojazičnoj reči.* Kiev: Višča škola.

Lakoff, Robin. 1972. Another look at drift. Linguistic change and generative theory, ed. by Robert P. Stockwell & Ronald K. S. Macaulay, 172 - 98. Bloomington: Indiana University Press.

Lass, Roger. 1976. *English phonology and phonological theory*: *synchronic and diachronic studies*. Cambridge: University Press.
— 1980. *On explaining language change*. Cambridge: University Press.
Lenz, Karl. 1913. *Zur Lautlehre der französischen Elemente in den schottischen Dichtungen von 1500 - 1550*. Marburg: Karl Gleiser.
Lewis, Geoffrey L. 1978[3]. *Turkish grammar*. London: Oxford University Press.
Luick, Karl. 1921. *Historische Grammatik der englischen Sprache*, I. Leipzig: Tauchnitz.
Melchior, A. B. 1972. Sir Thomas Smith and John Wallis: The problem of early Modern English [y:] re-examined. *English Studies* 53. 210 - 23.
Mincoff, Marco. 1967. *English historical grammar*. Sofia: Naouka i Izkustvo.
Nida, Eugene A. 1969. Science of translation. *Language* 45. 483 - 98.
Paraškevov, Boris. 1981. Nemski, niderlandski i skandinavski zaemki v bəlgarskija ezik. *Contrastive linguistics* 3. 181 - 89.
Pərveva, Elka. Forthcoming. Njakoj osobenosti pri artikulacijata na nemskite glasni ot bəlgari, izučavašti nemski ezik. *Səpostavitelno ezikoznanie i čuždoezikovo obučenie* V. Veliko Tərnovo: University Press.
Patev, Pavel. 1967. Fonetična adaptacija na frenskite dumi v bəlgarskija ezik. *Annuaire de l'Université de Sofia*: *Faculté des lettres* LXI, 2. 267 - 316.
Polivanov, Evgenij. 1931. La perception des sons d'une langue étrangère. *Travaux du cercle linguistique de Prague* 4. 79 - 96. Prague:
Poussa, Patricia. 1982. The evolution of early Standard English: The creolization hypothesis. *Studia Anglica Posnaniensia* XIV. 69 - 85.
Reszkiewicz, Alfred. 1971. The elimination of the front rounded and back unrounded short vowel phonemes from medieval English: A reinterpretation. *Kwartalnik Neofilologiczny* XVIII. 279 - 96.
Robins, Robert H. 1970. Aspects of prosodic analysis. *Prosodic analysis*, ed. by Frank R. Palmer, 188 - 200. London: Oxford University Press.
Samilov, Michael. 1964. *The phoneme jat' in Slavic*. The Hague: Mouton.
Scatton, Ernest A. 1975. *Bulgarian phonology*. Cambridge (Mass.): Slavic Publishers.
Schane, Sanford A. 1972. Natural rules in phonology. Linguistic change and generative theory, ed. by Robert P. Stockwell & Ronald K. S. Macaulay, 199 - - 229. Bloomington: Indiana University Press.
Sedlak, P. 1969. Typological considerations of vowel quality systems. *Working Papers on Language Universals* I. Stanford: University Press.
Selinker, Larry. 1972. Interlanguage. *International Review of Applied Linguistics* X. 209 - 31.
Šipova, Elizaveta N. 1976. *Slovar' tjurkizmov v ruskom jazike*. Alma-Ata: Nauka.
Skalička, Vladimir. 1961. The fundamental and the special phonemes. *Universitas Carolina — Philologica* 2. 41 - 53.
Spešnev, Nikolaj A. 1980. *Fonetika kitajskogo jazika*. Leningrad: Izdatel'stvo Leningradskogo universiteta.
Stampe, David. 1979. *A dissertation on natural phonology*. Bloomington: Indiana University Linguistics Club.
Steblin-Kamenskij, Mixail I. 1962. Umlaut v germanskix jazikax. *Sravnitel'naja gramatika germanskix jazikov*, ed. by M. M. Guxman, Viktor M. Zirmunskij,

Enver A. Makaev, Viktorija N. Jarceva, 141 - 159. Moscow: Izdatel'stvo Akademii Nauk SSSR.
Stojkov, Stojko. 1953. Jatoviət vəpros v novobəlgarskija knižoven ezik. *Annuaire de l'Université de Sofia: Faculté des lettres* XLIV, 4. 1 - 145.
Szulc, Aleksander. 1973. Die Haupttypen der phonischen Interferenz. *Zeitschrift für Phonetik, Sprachwissenschaft und Kommunikationsforschun*γ 26. 11 - 119.
Ternes, Elmar. 1976. *Probleme der kontrastiven Phonetik.* Hamburg: Helmut Buske Verlag.
Trubetzkoy, Nikolaj S. 1939/1969. *Principles of phonology.* Translated by Christiane A. M. Baltaxe. Berkeley & Los Angeles: University of California Press.
Twaddell, W. Freeman. 1938. A note on Old High German umlaut. *Monatshefte für deutschen Unterricht, deutsche Sprache und Literatur* 30. 177 - 81.
Vachek, Joseph. 1976. Kratkoe zamečanie o nekotorix fonemnix substitucijax v procese razvitija anglijskogo jazika. *Teorija jazika, anglistika, kel'tologija*, ed. by M. P. Alekseev, 163 - 67. Moscow: Nauka.
Velčeva, Borjana. 1980. *Praslavjanski i starobalgarski fonologičeski izmenenija.* Sofia: Izdatelstvo na Balgarskata Akademija na Naukite.
Voyles, Joseph. 1982. Old Norse i-umlaut. *Linguistics* 20. 267 - 85.
Wallis, John. 1653. Quoted from Mincoff 1967.
Weinreich, Uriel. 1953. *Languages in contact. Findings and problems.* New York: Publications of the Linguistic Circle of New York.
    1957. On the description of phonic interference. *Word* 13. 1 - 11.
    1961. Unilingualism and multilingualism. *Le Langage*, ed. by André Martinet, 647 - 84. Paris: Encyclopedie de la Pléiade.
Weihreich, Uriel, Wlliam Labov and Marvin I. Herzog. 1968. Empirical foundations for a theory of language change. *Directions for historical linguistics*, ed. by Winfred P. Lehman and Yakov Malkiel, 95 - 195. Austin & London: University of Texas Press.
Wieden, Wilfried. 1979. On the psycho-physics of speech tempo. *Arbeiten aus Anglistik und Amerikanistik* 4. 21 - 36.
Wode, Henning. 1981. Language acquisitional universals: A unified view of language acquisition. *Arbeitspapiere zum Spracherwerb.* Englisches Seminar der Universität Kiel, No 26.
Žirmunskij, Viktor M. 1956. *Nemeckaja dialektologija.* Moscow & Leningrad Izdatel'stvo Akademii Nauk SSSR.
Zwicky, Arnold. 1972. Note on a phonological hierarchy in English. *Linguistic change and generative theory.*, ed. by Robert P. Stockwell & Ronald K. S. Macaulay, 275 — 301. Bloomington: Indiana University Press.

ON THE DIACHRONY OF SUBTRACTIVE OPERATIONS: EVIDENCE FOR SEMIOTICALLY BASED MODELS OF NATURAL PHONOLOGY AND NATURAL MORPHOLOGY FROM NORTHERN AND ANATOLIAN GREEK DIALECTS[1]

WOLFGANG U. DRESSLER, VENEETA ACSON

0. In this paper we will examine the case of unstressed high vowel deletion within a semiotically based model of Natural Phonology and Natural Morphology. A theory of Natural Phonology and Natural Morphology explains why certain linguistic phenomena are universally more natural than others. In following this aim it must also account for language specific unnatural phenomena. Many of them must be considered as historic accidents. We present data and argumentation to support the need of the diachronic dimension in Natural Morphology.

   1.0 Our theoretic orientation is a semiotically based polycentristic/ interactionist model of dialectic conflicts between phonology and morphology.[2]

In this paper we follow two basic principles: One of assuming a diachronic trend towards efficiency in the components of the language system (Jespersen 1949). This does not imply that a language as a whole becomes more efficient, due to the dialectic/conflictual nature of language, but rather that the trend is towards either more phonological or more morphological naturalness in specific parameters of Natural Phonology or Natural Morphology. "Efficiency" is equivalent to naturalness on various scales of phonological or morphological naturalness. Our second

---

[1] This paper came about through the interaction between the first author's respective one-minute stretch of the Collitz lecture in July 1982 at the University of Maryland and the second author's Northern Greek background.

[2] Cf. Dressler 1981, to appear a, b, c; Dressler, Mayerthaler Panagl, and Wurzel, in press. The semiotic theory used is Peirce's (1965).

assumption is that possible diachronic change is restricted both by semiotically based universals of Natural Phonology and Natural Morphology, and by typological properties of languages.[3]

1.1 It is relatively easy to find masses of data which fit both nicely to the models we espouse and contradict neither the concept of efficiency in language change nor the restrictions of universals and typology. In order to test our approach we find it crucial to analyze data which seem to contradict flatly any assumptions of semiotically based naturalness and of efficiency in language change.[4] E.g. data from the Northern Greek dialects seem to present contradictory materials for the theory. The high-vowel deletion in these dialects is a subtractive operation/technique (Seiler, 1978; Dressler to appear a, b, c) that has stayed in the language for many centuries, beginning in late antiquity or early Byzantine times. And subtraction is one of the worst operations conceivable in a theory of Natural Morphology.

From the standpoint of an extended semiotic basis of Natural Phonology and Natural Morphology,[5] any deletion process has 'undesirable' effects since it disturbs semiotic transparency.

1.2 After presenting our data from various Northern and Anatolian Greek dialects, we will discuss the process of rule formation and change, first of phonological rules (PR), then on to the intermediate stage of morphonological rules (MPR), and finally the development of morphological rules (MR).[6] We will illustrate how phonologically unnatural rules which disturb morphological naturalness reveal a typical scenario

---

[3] For elaboration on the typological approaches by Skalička (e.g. 1979) and Seiler (e.g. 1978), cf. Dressler, to appear a, b, c; Dressler, Mayerthaler, Panagl, and Wurzel, in press.

[4] For other experimenta crucis cf. Dressler, to appear b, c.

[5] Dressler 1977c, 1980, 1981, to appear a, b, c; Mayerthaler 1980, 1981; Wurzel 1980a, 1981, to appear; Dressler, Mayerthaler, Panagl, and Wurzel, in press.

[6] MRs are morphological rules of all sorts, including allomorphic ones; they correspond to derivational rules in Derivational Phonology. MPRs are morphonological rules which correspond roughly to phonological rules in Derivational Phonology, to cyclical rules in Cyclic Phonology, and to lexical rules in Lexical Phonology. PRs are phonological rules, which correspond roughly to phonetic rules in Derivational Phonology, to post-cyclic rules in Cyclic Phonology, and to postlexical rules in Lexical Phonology.

of diachronic change: They change from PRs to MPRs and then to allomorphic MRs.[7]

In the literature the diachronic change of PRs to MPRs and allomorphic MRs has often been described as dephonologization or decrease/loss of phonological naturalness.[8] On the contrary, Dressler (1977a, 1980, to appear a) has stressed the 'active' role of morphology, sc. that already less natural PRs are not further dephonologized, but morphologized to MPRs and MRs by increasing morphological naturalness at the expense of already diminished phonological naturalness. This concept of morphological naturalness repressing phonological naturalness is a direct consequence of, and follows deductively from, the semiotic priority of morphological over phonological signs.

The history of high-vowel deletion in Northern and Anatolian Greek dialects offers multiple evidence for the 'morphologization' concept and against the 'dephonologization' concept view that morphology, not phonology is the main driving force in changing PRs to MPRs and further to MRs.

1.3 At this point, a few words are in order about the geographic divisions of the linguistic areas. Modern Greek is divided into Northern and Southern dialect areas, based on the process of high-vowel deletion. Standard Greek is included in the Southern grouping. The Northern dialects are found in the northern part of the Greek mainland, the Northern Aegean islands, and in parts of Anatolia. In this paper we include language examples from the dialect of Germa in Macedonia and dialects from Anatolia: Pontus and Cappadocia.

Apparently the loss of unstressed high vowels spread in Byzantine times (that is, before the Turks invaved Anatolia and separated the dialect regions geographically) from the capital of Constantinople via the coastal regions of the Black Sea (the Pontic dialects being its most easterly remnant) to Central Anatolia (with the Cappadocian dialects still alive). In the process of this geographic diffusion our first phonological rule of unstressed high vowel deletion was successively dephonologized or, morphologized and lexicalized.

2.0 The following partial paradigms of nominal declension exemplify the basic pattern of phonological change. We cite first the Classical (Ancient) Greek (CG) form, then the Southern (including Standard)

---

[7] E. g., umlaut in Germanic languages, see e.g. Dressler 1977a, 1980, 1981, to appear a; Mayerthaler 1977; Wurzel 1980a, 1980b, 1981.

[8] E. g. Hyman 1977; Mayerthaler 1977; Wurzel 1980b, 1981 with references.

Modern Greek (SG) form, followed by the form Germa (Ge), in Northern Greece.

		'the man'	'the hare'
Nom Sg	CG	ho ánthrōpos	ho lagós
	SG	o ánθropos	o laγós
	Ge	u ánθrupus	u laγós
Gen Sg	CG	toũ anthrṓpou	toũ lagoũ
	SG	tu anθrópu	tu laγú
	Ge	t anθróp	t laγú
Nom Pl	CG	hoi ánthrōpoi	hoi lagoí
	SG	i ánθropi	i laγí
	Ge	i anθróp	i laγí

The pronunciation of the Southern Greek forms is presumably identical with underlying phonological representations.[9] The forms today are similar to those of the late Roman Empire.

These two nouns illustrate the historical difference between unstressed and stressed /u, i/. 'The hare' is stress final, hence unchanged and permitting no differences between the Northern and Southern dialects. On the other hand, 'the man' has varying stress, always non-final, and illustrates the loss of unstressed /u, i/ and the raising of unstressed /o/ to /u/ in the dialect of Germa.

The above cited Northern Greek forms show that a) these sound changes still persist as synchronic rules and b) at least some restructuring must have occurred. In other words the underlying phonological form of the masculine nominative plural article must have been restructured because otherwise it would be zero (/i/→[ø]).

The origin of these Northern Greek sound changes is traced back by Thavoris (1980: 420ff) to antiquity, according to attested words such as:

'I walk up&down'	'last year'	'Apollo'
CG peripatṓ	périsü	apóllōn
perpatṓ	pérsü	áplun [10]
(3 c. AD)	(20 AD)	(3 c. BC)

---

[9] Unless one adheres to a fairly abstract phonological analysis which keeps length distinctions in phonological representations in order to account for stress shift in SG *anθrópu* by postulating a long Gen. Sg. ending /u:/. Along this line, Malikuti (1970 : 129) postulates an underlying geminate /uu/.

[10] The loss of stressed *ó* in *apóllōn* is an ancient Thessalian matter.

Notice the loss of the medial unstressed high vowel /i/.

2.1 Based on these and other examples we posit a sporadic PR (Phonological Rule) of late Ancient Greek:

$$\text{i} \rightarrow \emptyset / \underline{\text{liquid}} \; [-\text{stress}]$$

This PR was then extended to /u/; in other words, to all high vowels. However, the extant forms with *u*-deletion are still more sporadic in modern Southern Greek dialects than those with *i*-deletion (Pernot 7; 157ff). Later this PR of unstressed high vowel deletion was generalized to all positions and to the whole lexicon in Northern Greek dialects:

$$\text{PR-1} \quad \begin{bmatrix} V \\ +\text{high} \end{bmatrix} \rightarrow \emptyset / \underline{[-\text{stress}]}$$

Within Natural Phonology, this rule is identified with a natural phonological process type of highest vowel deletion which belongs to the weakening processes, a subclass of backgrounding processes (G. Entdeutlichungsprozesse). (Compare the loss of unstressed *jer* and *jor* in Slavic languages.) Typically palatal vowels are more easily subjected to this process than labial vowels, as espoused in our variant[11] of Natural Phonology:[12]

$$\begin{matrix}\text{universal} \\ \text{phonological} \\ \text{process} \\ \text{type:}\end{matrix} \quad \begin{bmatrix} V \\ \text{high!} \\ \text{Palatal!} \end{bmatrix}^{13} \rightarrow \emptyset / \underline{\begin{bmatrix}-\text{long}\\-\text{stress}\end{bmatrix}}$$

Along with our rule of unstressed high-vowel deletion, we must posit a rule of unstressed mid-vowel raising, which is also identified as a natural phonological process of weakening or backgrounding:[14]

---

[11] Dressler 1973, 1975, 1977a, b, 1980, 1981, to appear a.

[12] Stampe 1969, 1980; Donegan 1978; Donegan and Stampe 1977, 1979a, b.

[13] '!' means 'especially or most, in the position of' i.e., the most palatal vowel is most subject to high vowel reduction. 'high 1, 2, and 3' are n-ary distinction features of vowel height (1 = a; 2 = e, o; 3 = i, u).

[14] Cf. Dressler 1975; Dressler and Hufgard 1980: 35ff.

PR-2   V
            [high 2]→[high 3]/ ―――――――
                              [− stress]

The generalization of PR-1 from a sporadic rule, presumably first of casual speech to an obligatory PR is an instance of backgrounding processes being generalized from casual speech (Dressler 1973, 1975) and/or of lexical diffusion (Wang 1977; Labov 1981). The generalization of PR-1 from the position in the neighborhood of all liquids to all positions is an instance of a generalization from a favoring environment to all contexts.

The raising of unstressed mid-vowels (PR-2) must have occurred later than PR-1, and can scarcely be traced back to pre-Hellenistic Greek dialects, since otherwise, at least in a certain number of words, unstressed /e, o/ would have ended everywhere via /i, u/ as zero, which is not the case.[15] Presumably the unstressed /e, o/ of PR-2 were first raised allophonically to intermediate high vowels as in a few modern dialects (Kretschmer 1905: 69f). But then in almost all Northern Greek dialects PR-2 became phonemic, insofar as unstressed [i, u] from /e, o/ could be identified with stressed ['i, 'u] from /i, u/. Therefore recoverability[16] of the inputs or signata of [i, u] decreased and opacity increased. Moreover semiotic transparency and iconicity of PR-2 suffered from the relatively bigger perceptual distance between /e, o/ and [i, u], respectively.

The resulting decrease of morphological transparency can be easily seen on the contrasting forms in the Germa dialect. In these forms stressed *e* alternates with unstressed *i* (é~i) and stressed *o* alternates with unstressed *u* (ó~u):

masc	'merchant'	'lightly armed'	'inspector'
N.Sg.	émburas	évzunas	éfuras
N.Pl.	imbór	ivzón	ifór

neut.	'tax'	'icon'	'tying, binding'
N.Sg.	δósmu	ikóndzma	δésmu
N.Pl.	δusímata	ikunísmata	δisímata

―――――――
[15] There are instances in some dialects elsewhere, though, see Kretschmer 1905: 90f. — Note that in the dialect of Skyros PR-1 is in effect, but not PR-2 (Kretschmer 1905: 69, 72, 86, 230, 236).
[16] Kaye 1974. The desirability of easy recoverability follows as well from the principle of semiotic transparency.

verbs	'I embroider'	'I loosen'	'I recall'	'I shorten'
pres.	budónu	bulkénu	mnimunévu	mkrénu
pret.	bóduna	bólkina	mnimóniva	míkrina

3.0 Earlier we mentioned that the two PRs we posit here have undesirable effects within the framework of an extended semiotic basis of Natural Phonology and Natural Morphology. By this we mean that any deletion process disturbs semiotic transparency. In semiotic terms, if we regard PRs as signs, then PR-1 has a high vowel as its signatum, but no overt signans (output). When this high vowel coincides with the exponent of a morphological category, then semiotic transparency is even more seriously disturbed. In all modern dialects of Greek /u/ and /i/ are the inflectional exponents of the Gen. Sg. and Nom. Pl., respectively, of the masculine -*o* paradigm. These exponents are present on the surface in *layú* and *layí* in all dialects because of their stress patterns. As we have seen in the preceeding examples, the signans of these same cases is absent in Northern Greek *anθróp* and in the Gen. Sg. article *t*.

3.1 However, to counterbalance this lack of semiotic transparency, the indexical functioning has been preserved in two ways. One by introducing an indexical trace, and secondly, by restructuring the definite article system.

One preservation of indexical functioning has taken place in the form of stress shift. The presence of the morphosemantic case in the Northern Greek Nom. Pl. *anθróp* can be induced indexically by the hearer from the shift in stress. This introduction of an indexical trace of a case form which is absent on the surface is a first symptom that the speakers have reacted to a lack of semiotic transparency.[17] In the Nom. Pl. the stress has shifted from initial stress in Classical Greek *ánthrōpoi* to final stress in Northern Greek *anθróp*.

The Nom. Pl. forms of the type *anθróp* would now be identical with the Gen. Sg. forms of the type *anθróp*, were it not for the fact that Greek nouns are generally accompanied by the definite article, creating a tight-knit noun phrase group. In this way, the Gen. Sg. is *t anθróp* and the Nom. Pl. is *i anθr óp*. The article *t* signals the Gen. Sg. as an index of the noun as well. The Nom. Pl. article *i* has also been restructured from Classical Greek *hoi* (instead of zero). In fact the article *i* appears

---

[17] Of course we may also think of analogical change, see Sec. 7.2.

not only in the Nom. case of the Masc. Pl., but also in the Fem. forms of both the Sing. (from *hē*) and Pl. (from *hai* > Middle Greek *e* > Northern Greek *i*). Thus we may speak of an analogical spread by means of restructuring the article *i*, resulting in the preservation of the indexical forms.[18]

4.0 We looked at examples from a Northern dialect in Macedonia. Now we would like to examine the dialects of Anatolia, specifically those in Pontos and Cappadocia.[19] Interestingly, nearly all Northern Greek dialects have been subjected to both PR-1 and PR-2, whereas Anatolian dialects only to PR-1. The interaction of PR-1 and PR-2 makes PR-1 opaque and less recoverable. The concept of dephonologization predicts that PR-1 should have been dephonologized more in Northern dialects than in Anatolian ones, but exactly the reverse has taken place. We will return to this interesting phenomenon after examining the processes of vowel deletion in the Anatolian dialects.

4.1.0 In the Pontic dialects of Trapezunt, Ofis, Xaldia, etc., PR-1 has been applied to a large part of the lexicon (Oeconomides 1908: 79ff; Papadopoulos 1955: 19f), although restructuring has taken place later on. High vowel deletion has thus become a MPR, i.e. MPR-1, which is now restricted to a few morphological categories as a synchronic rule. In the nominal system MPR-1 can best be exemplified in the following forms:

	ms. art.	'cowboy'	nt. art.	'wood'	'child'	'field'	'honey'	'milk'
NSg.	o	vukólos	to	ksílon	peδí	xoráf	mélin	γála
GSg.	tu	vukól	tu	ksilí	peδí	xorafí	melí	γalatí
NPl.	i	vukól	ta	ksíla	peδía	xoráfa	mélta /mélita/	γálta /γálita/

Of interest in these forms is the preservation of unstressed /i, u/ within the stem as in *vukólos* and in the case of stress alternation in *ksílon* and *ksilí*; *mélin* and *melí*. Also, notice the restoration of unstressed /u/ in the Gen. Sg. article *tu*.

---

[18] Classical Greek *hē* > *i* would have given ø by PR-1 as well.
[19] Adams 1977; Dawkins 1937; Newton 1972. Dialect descriptions available to us were Oeconomides 1908 and Papadopoulos 1955 for Pontic dialects; Andriotis 1948, Kesisoglou 1951, Mavroxalividis and Kesisoglou 1960, Fosteris and Kesisoglou 1960 and Dawkins 1916 for Cappadocian dialects.

4.1.1 There are minor traces of MPR-1 in the declension of adjectives, numerals, and pronouns, often in a rather idiosyncratic way. For example, in the masc. pl. of the word 'other' there is *u*-deletion in the accusative, but no *i*-deletion in the nominative:

NSg. állos
NPl. álli
APl. álls

4.1.2 The same Pontic dialects which show high vowel deletion in declension, have the same process in conjugations. In verb paradigms, /i/ is stressed in the present tense of *-izo* and *-io* verbs, but unstressed in the corresponding aorist /-isa/ (always 1 Sg.), as in the following alternations of í~ø:

	'exorcize (3 Sg.)'	'get drunk (1 Sg.)'
Pres.	eporkízi	meθío
Aor.	epórksen	emétsa

Rare alternations such as the first person singular forms of the verb 'hear': pres. *akúo*, aor. *éksa*, imperative *ákson* (Oeconomides 1908: 86) are best interpreted as suppletion.

4.1.3 Finally in the Pontic dialects, MPR-1 is at work in sentence phonology in noun phrases of article - noun - possessive pronoun. If an enclitic follows a final /i/, this /i/ is preserved, as in the phrase 'my foot' *to podári m* from *to podárion mu* where *podárion* has lost noun final *-n* (Acson 1979: 135ff), and further underwent high-vowel deletion (thus to *podár*), only to be restored when followed by the possessive pronoun enclitic. Moreover, due to rule inversion, the dialects now have epenthetic *i*, as in *o γambrós i m* 'my son-in-law' from earlier *ho gambrós mu* (Papadopoulos 1955: 22). This change signals that high vowel deletion has become a MPR.

4.2.0 In Cappadocia, we look at five dialects: Ulaγats (Kesisoglou 1951: 15ff, 41ff), Aksos (Mavroxalividis-Kesisoglou 1960: 11, 53ff), Aravani (Andriotis), Delmesó (Dawkins 1916:95, 115), and Farasa (Andriotis 1948: 22ff, 33ff). All these Cappadocian dialects have a MR of *i*-deletion in the aorist and a MR of *i*-epenthesis similar to that of Pontic.

4.2.1 In Ulaγats we find the following high vowel deletion in the aorist of the following forms:

	'harvest (1 Sg.)'		'appear (aor. imperative)'
Pres.	xerízo	2 Sg.	fánse
Aor.	xérsa	1 Pl.	fanís
		2 Pl.	fansét
		3 Pl.	faníson

(These are the only remnants of a synchronic $i \sim \emptyset$ alternation. This is one of the few classes without analogical leveling.)

4.2.2. In Farasa we find the same *i*-deletion in the aorist:

		'harvest'
Pres.	(1 Sg.)	θerízo
Aor.	(3 Pl.)	θértsan

Basically MPR-1 has been lost in declension, although vowel deletion has left a historical effect in the Nom. Sg. of the *-is* declension, an older category of nominals:

	'prophete'	'Arab'
Nom. Sg.	profít (<profítis)	aráp (<arápis)
Gen. Sg.	profíti	arápi
Acc. Sg.	profíti	arápi
Nom. Pl.	profíti	arápi

And finally, in Farasa there is a MR of sentence phonology which applies before the enclitic possessive pronouns, as in 'your door' *to* θ*ir tsu* from *to* θ*íri* 'the door'. Notice that this is the reverse of the situation in the Pontic dialects.

4.2.3 In other Cappadocian dialects some masculine nouns have vowel deletion in the genitive singular and nominative plural, creating identical forms. The following forms for 'man' are from Aksos and Delmesó, respectively:

Nom. Sg.	árxopos	áθropos
Gen. Sg.	arxóp	aθróp
Nom. Pl.	arxóp	aθróp

5.0 As we have seen, PR-1 has gone on to become MPR-1 in Northern Greek, whereas PR-2 has remained as such. Both phonological rules have phonologically unnatural properties and disturb morphological naturalness (PR-1 has no overt signans and PR-2 has a large perceptual distance between signatum and signans.). These PRs have taken the route of established diachronic change: the PRs become MPRs, and then to allomorphic MRs. PR-2 is much more natural than MPR-1 both from a semiotic point of view (PR-1 has no signans, PR-2 has one), and because no unstressed mid vowels are spared by this rule. As we shall see in the following examples from Germa, MPR-1 does not always apply where it should. This is a first step towards either a still more unnatural PR or already to a MPR.[20] Specifically, unstressed high vowels are preserved if difficult consonant clusters can be avoided and if loss of initial vowels can be avoided.

verbs	'I distribute'	'I sweat'	'I groan'	
Pret.	míraza	íðruna	múgrza	
Pres.	mirázu	iðrónu	mugrízu	
not:	*mrázu	*ðrónu	*mgrízu	

nouns	'Demetrios'	'dream'	'misdemeanor'	'income'
NSg.	ðmítrs	ínuru	énglima	isóðima
not:			*énglma	*isóðma
NPl.		inórata	inglímata	isuðímata
not:		*nórata		
Dim.	ðimitráks[21]			
not:	*ðimtráks			

These forms illustrate the non-application of MPR-1. Unstressed high vowels are preserved when difficult consonant clusters might occur, as in *mugrízu* (*mgr* is avoided), *ðimitráks* (*ðmtr* is avoided), and *énglima* (*glm* does not occur). However, notice the clusters in *múgrza* (*grz* occurs) and *ðmítrs* (*trs* occurs). Consonant clusters of this sort are not uncommon in Northern Greek dialects. Compare the cluster *θk* in the possessive *θkós* from *iðikós*, the cluster *ktx* in the word *ktxáravus* from *kutiáravos* 'box maker', and the cluster *psx* in *psxós* from *psixós*, 'cold'.

For other Northern dialects Newton (1972: 187ff), has noted that syllable final clusters are avoided much more than syllable initial ones. This is not an idiosyncratic phenomenon of high voweldel etion, but rather a universal characteristic of relative syllable strength.

The non-application of MPR-1 also seems to take place in order

---

[20] On the issue of how to distinguish these two classes, see the dispute between Wurzel 1981 and Dressler 1981, and cf. Dressler, to appear a.
[21] The first /i/ surfaces due to alternating/secondary stress.

to avoid the loss of initial vowels as in the following examples: *uranós* (and derivatives) 'sky', *usía* 'property', and from the preceeding set of examples, *iðrónu*, *inórata*, and *isóðima*. However, notice this very loss in the possessive *Okós* from *iðikós*, and the variant *kunumía* of *ikunumía* from *ikonomía* 'economy'.

5.1 Of course, some of these exceptions may be words loaned from Southern, including standard, dialects. The non-application of a PR to a loan-word may indicate that it has been already transformed into a MPR.[22] So we can state that MPR-1 has been restricted to a large set of morphological alternations, whereas PR-2 is still determining pronouncibility and the distribution of vowels.[23] Furthermore, PR-2 is productive in loan-words such as *Amirikí* 'America' and *Amirikánus* 'American' (for *Amerikanós* in southern dialects).

5.2 MPR-1 continues to have the two phonological conditions of PR-1: that only unstressed and high vowels are deleted. However, as a subtractive operation, that is, total deletion of the input, it has an inherently bad semiotic property. Even an otherwise very natural PR of vowel deletion has this unnatural phonological property. Since we know from the study of how PRs evolve in time that PRs which have unnatural properties tend to become even more unnatural and thus to develop into MPRs, we expect that the PRs of vowel deletion should turn into MPRs rather quickly. And indeed, PR-1 has turned into a MPR in all Greek dialects. The contrast is striking that PR-2, which does not have this inherent unnatural property of PR-1, has remained a PR to the present in most northern dialects.

6.0 At this point we would like to return to the concept of dephonologization *vs.* morphologization. These Northern and Anatolian Greek examples that we have presented here offer multiple evidence for the morphologization concept and against the dephonologization concept. This morphological restructuring in declension clearly fits the principles of Natural Morphology. According to diagrammaticity or constructional iconicity[24] it is the best solution if the least marked case form on the content level is also least marked on the expression level. This has been

---

[22] Cf. Dressler 1977a: 35ff, to appear a; Linell 1979: 195ff; Field 1981.
[23] See preceeding section (5.0) and Kretschmer 1905: 68ff, 72.
[24] Mayerthaler 1980, 1981; Wurzel 1980a; Dressler 1980, to appear a.

achieved by morphological restructuring, for example, in Farasa and Aksos. In Farasa, the class *profit* has been restructured from older *profítis*, and the Gen. Sg., Acc. Sg., and Nom. Pl. have been leveled into one form: *profíti*. In Aksos (Mavroxalividis-Kesisoglou 1960: 40ff), the Pontic type *vukólos* (Nom. Sg.) and *vukól* (Gen. Sg. and Nom. Pl.) have been replaced with the declension type 'sleep', where again the Nom. Sg. is most unmarked both in content and expression:

Nom. Sg.   jípnos
Gen. Sg.   jípnozju
Nom. Pl.   jípnozja

These changes toward a more diagrammatic expression are contradicted on the surface by the preservation of the type *ánθropos* (Nom. Sg.) and *anθróp* (Gen. Sg. and Nom. Pl.) in the aformentioned dialects of Pontos and in Aksos. Here the morphosemantic mark of either Gen. or Pl. has no segmental counterpart on the expression level. In other words, we find a "zero" or bare stem, a solution which can be classified as non-diagrammatic.

Moreover, we must compare whole word forms, since the relationship between whole word forms is also relevant for the native speaker.[25] The relationship between morphosematically unmarked *ánθropos* and marked *anθróp* is antidiagrammatic insofar as addition of meaning is contradicted by subtraction of form, a subject we will discuss shortly.

6.1 However, proponents of the 'dephonologization' concept might harken back to the apparent contradiction, stated earlier that PR-1 should have been dephonologized more in Northern dialects than in Anatolian ones, but the reverse is in fact what occurred. In order to explain this contradiction, the dephonologizationists might be tempted to introduce further intermediate variables which disturb the expected consequences: a) Rule morphologization/dephonologization in Anatolian dialects may be due to interdialectal borrowing, specifically the geographic spread of PR-1. However, spread must have taken place in the Greek mainland and on the Aegean islands as well. Furthermore, there has been the view in generative linguistics that spread leads to generalization rather than degeneralization. However, good arguments have been found for the opposite view (cf. references in Adams 1977). b) Turkish influence

---

[25] Not just in a word-and-paradigm model (Matthews 1972). The psychological reality is supported by diachronic and psycholinguistic evidence.

of massive loaning, typological factors, etc. may have inhibited high vowel loss. But the same factor should hold true for Northern dialects where the massive influence of Modern Standard Greek, which lacks vowel deletion, would also inhibit PR-1.

6.2 It is a constitutive feature of MPRs that they are restricted to certain morphological categories where they have the indexical function of cosignaling MRs and morphological categories (Dressler 1977a, 1980, 1981, to appear a). However, in spite of this morphological, indexical function, they still violate morphotactic transparency, which may be the basic reason why MPRs die out in the long run. Whereas it is often impossible to predict which MPRs will die out or which will change into MRs and at what time, it seems feasible to explain at least partially why certain applications of MPRs are more resistant in time than others.

6.3 In the Cappadocian dialects we find that the most resistant phenomenon of synchronic vowel deletion is in the verbal system. These holdouts occur in the alternations between the present and aorist tenses, such as in Farasa:

	'I harvest'	'I ask'
Pres.	θerízo	rotáo
Aor.	θértsa	rótsa (< rótisa < CG ērótēsa)

This opposition is characterized by the fact that it indexes a very important morphosemantic distinction. The Classical Greek distinction between present imperfect and aorist has been extended in Modern Greek to an opposition between imperfective and perfective verbal aspect. This modern innovation is expressed in nearly all tenses and modes outside the perfect (Seiler 1952; Babiniotis 1972). Thus a morphological subregularity, be it a MR or a suppletion, which expresses an important morphosemantic distinction has a more important indexical function and thence may be expected to be more resistant (cf. Anttila 1975).

7.0 The theory of Natural Morphology predicts three main properties about language: One, that non/anti-diagrammatic morphological phenomena should be very rare both cross-linguistically and within a given language. Second, that such phenomena be restricted typologically. Specifically, that non/anti-diagrammatic case forms be barred from agglutinative languages.[26] And thirdly, that the phenomena be limited by system-defining language specific properties.[27]

7.1 The first principle that non/anti-diagrammatic morphological phenomena be rare both cross-linguistically and within a given language is borne out by the preceding discussion about the extreme rarity of subtraction.

7.2 The second claim of Natural Morphology that non/antidiagrammatic morphological phenomena are restricted typologically, refers to the fact that these case forms are nonoccurring in agglutinative languages. A consequence of this second claim is the prediction that Greek dialects which are more agglutinative and less inflectional/fusional than others should show less non/anti-diagrammaticity. Of course, degree of agglutinativity must be measured by some independent indices, such as lack of fusion, of suppletion, etc. If we take the example of declension in Aksos (Mavroxalividis-Kesisoglou 1960: 40ff), then we find new agglutinative paradigms, which at the same time are more diagrammatic than their historic antecedents:

	'sleep' ms	"type of inst." ms	'herd' fm.	'girl' nt.	'rasp' nt.
Sg.N&A	jípnos	anajót	neɣél	korítš	kšístro
G	jípnoz-ju	anajot-jú	neɣel-jú	korítš-jú	kšístro-ju
Pl.N&A	jípnoz-ja	anajót-ja	neɣél-es	korítš	kšístro-ja
G	jípnoz-ju	anajot-jú	neɣél-ez-ju	korítš-jú	kšístro-ju

Special notice should be given to the G. PL. *neɣél-ez-ju*, where plurality and genitive are expressed by separate case-forms, that is in a typically agglutinative way. Compare also Nom. *jípnos* and Gen. *jípnoz-ju*, where apparently *jípnos* is not analyzed anymore as *jípno-s* or *jípn-os*. In general, Cappadocian dialects have been most exposed to the influence of Turkish, an agglutinative language. These examples support our claim that non//anti-diagrammatic phenomena are restricted typologically.

This second claim is further supported by the fact that MPRs have a function in fusional/inflectional languages, and Northern and Pontic Greek dialects are highly fusional/inflectional. Thus MPR-1 is most

---

[26] Dressler to appear b, c, based on Skalička 1979.
[27] See especially Wurzel, to appear; and Dressler, Mayerthaler, Panagl, and Wurzel, in press.

restricted, lexicalized, and morphologized in the Cappadocian dialects. These are the dialects which have evolved the most toward the agglutinative type.

This conclusion can be further corroborated by the observation of stress shift. The shift in stress in the Nom. Pl. from Classical Greek *ánthrōpoi* to *anθróp* in Germa, Pontic, and Delmesó, and *arxóp* in Aksos, etc. is clearly morphologically induced. Recall earlier discussions of the indexical trace of a case form which is absent on the surface and the alternating stress pattern in the present and aorist of some Pontic dialects.

The likeliest analogic influence on the stress shift comes from the Gen. Sg. form, not from other plural cases, since there is no homogeneity in plural stress placement. Compare Pontic Gen. Pl. *anθropíon*, Acc. Pl. *anθróps*, and Voc. *ánθropi*. The Nom Pl. and the Gen. Sg. have two factors in common: One, that they have one morphosemantic mark more than the unmarked Nom. Sg., sc. 'plural' and 'genitive', and second, that they are the only two forms with zero inflectional endings. Generally the more similar two forms are, the more easily they can influence one another analogically (cf. Schindler 1974). But why did the Gen. Sg. form influence the Nom. Pl. and not the other way around? It has been shown in studies on diagrammaticity (constructional iconicity) that morphosemantically marked forms which display any modification on the level of expression in relation to the morphosemantically unmarked forms are more natural/adequate than forms which show either no change at all or subtraction. With respect to unmarked N. Sg. *ánθropos*, the pre-stress shift form N. Pl. *ánθrop was antidiagrammatic without modification, whereas the G. Sg. *anθróp* displays modification in the form of stress shift. And as a way of decreasing diagrammatic unnaturalness this technique of modification has been carried over to the N. Pl [28].

The degree of non/anti-diagrammaticity of G. Sg. = N. Pl. *anθróp* is further diminished by the fact that it can still be derived by MPR-1 from an underlying /anθróp-u, anθróp-i/, because there still exists G. Sg. forms in [-ú] and N. Pl. forms in [-í] in the same dialects.

So far we have assumed the application of MPR-1 in case forms such as *anθróp*. For example, the underlying forms /anθróp-u, anθróp-i/ have been thought to surface as *anθróp* by application of MPR-1. Our justifications are threefold: One, the parallelism with surface case endings in

---

[28] Note that the G. Sg. is the only singular form with stress shift. Apparently paradigm homogeneity was less important than diagrammaticity.

laɣú, laɣí, etc.; Second, the applicability of MPR-1 in other inflectional forms. But this may be a spurious abstract generalization, as critics of generative phonology and morphology might say;[29] and Third, MPR-1 is a continuation of an earlier PR-1, for which we could not find any compelling reasons to believe that the rule had been lost. But this might be an anachronistic approach correctly criticized by the same antagonists of very abstract generative phonologies.

7.3 So we are left to deal with the suspicion that we may have misanalyzed simple subtractive or zero morphology as involving a spurious MPR. For this purpose we must consider the third aspect of Natural Morphology, the system-defining and similar language specific properties. Whereas typological properties (the second aspect of Natural Morphology) filter universal options and adjust them for a given language type, system defining properties filter these options even further in order to adapt them to the conventional or symbolic system of a specific language.[30]

7.3.1 Seiler (1958) has identified an important language specific paradigm structure condition of Modern Greek declension: If the N. Sg. ends in a consonant, then the G. Sg. ends in a vowel and vice-versa, as in the following examples from Standard Modern Greek:

	'human'	'man'	'thief'	'priest'	'grand-father'	'coffee'
masc. N.Sg.	áθropos	ańdras	kléftis	pappás	pappús	nt.: kafés
G.Sg.	aθrópu	ándra	klélti	pappá	pappú	kafé
fem.	'day'	'hope'	'bride'	'Samos'	'fox'	'error'
N.Sg.	méra	elpíδa	nífi	Sámo	alepú	láθos
G.Sg.	méras	elpíδas	nífis	Sámos	alepús	láθu

---

[29] Linell 1979 with references; Crothers 1973.
[30] These system defining properties must be of a certain generality, otherwise one could elevate any isolated idiosyncratic phenomenon of a language into such a property in order to protect one's hypotheses against falsification. Of course there are other legitimate classes of language specific properties in diachronic explanation, namely in the form of specific ‚historic accidents', e.g. a) that Greek having a particular morphological structure underwent particular prosodic changes, resulting in PR-1, which then made Greek morphology less natural; and b) that Anatolian dialects came under Turkish influence, which had certain lexical and structural consequences.

However, most common neuters do not follow this system. Compare the following sets:

neut.	'wood'	'child'	'mouth'
N.Sg.	ksílo	peδí	stóma
G.Sg.	ksílu	peδiú	stomátu

But notice that these forms are a recent development from earlier:
ksílon   peδí(o)n   stóma
ksílu   peδíu   stómatos

As we can see from these forms, the declension N. Sg. = V_is vs. G. Sg. = V_i (The vowel rarely changes from *o* to *u*.) indexes masculine and a few neuters, and the declension N. Sg. = V_j vs. G. Sg. = V_js indexes feminines. Seiler's principle elevates the non/anti-diagrammatic Masc. Gen. Sg. forms to a paradigm structure condition and thus explains the stability of this declensional phenomenon of Modern Greek. From a semiotic point of view this language specific property is an indexical device of expressing the combination of case and gender in an inflectional language type by a minimum of formal means. At the same time it is metaphorical,[31] because the grammatical relations on the content level are reflected by vaguely similar relations on the expression level.[32]

7.3.2 At first glance the effect of PR-1 in Northern Greek dialects seems to have impaired Seiler's principle, as in the following forms from Germa:

masc.	'human'	'Emanuel'	fem.	'bride'
N. Sg.	ánθrupus	Manól'ts		níf
G. Sg.	anθróp	Manól',		nífs

Seiler's principle would still hold true in these forms although in a more abstract manner, if we regard the underlying forms:

/ánθropos Manólis   nífi
 anθrópu Manóli   nífis/

---

[31] Metaphors are the weakest kinds of icons.
[32] This reflection is elevated to diagrammaticity, i.e. a stronger form of iconicity, in the feminine, because the marked genitive is reflected by the addition of the Gen. Sg. −*s* ending. Since diagrammaticity is semiotically better than metaphoricalness, we would expect that the relation N. Sg. = V_i vs. G.Sg. = V_is should be more resistant in time than the metaphorical, but antidiagrammatic relation N. Sg. = VC vs. G. Sg. = V. This expectation is realized in the neuter paradigm.

These underlying forms and the application of MPR-1 to them, are justified by the parallel surface forms with word final stress:

	'hare'	'coffee-shop keeper'	proper name
masc.			
N. Sg.	laɣós	kafidz'ís	Arití
G. Sg.	laɣú	kafidz'í	Aritís

7.3.3 Additional evidence comes from the diachronic development of exceptions to MPR-1. Compare the following proper names and the loan-word 'girl' from Albanian *cupë* which adhere to Seiler's principle:

N. Sg.	Aristídis	Lénku	ts'úpu
G. Sg.	Aristídi	Lénkus	ts'úpus

The obvious assumption is that in these forms the underlying /i, u/ were restored on the surface.

7.3.4 Seiler's principle also seems to hold in the dialects of Cappadocia.

In Farasa unstressed Gen. *-u* has been restored, and the new declension type Nom. *profít*, Gen. *profíti* follows the consonant-vowel principle. In fact it is even diagrammatic, in that more meaning equals more form.

7.3.5 In Aksos, the Genitive ending *-ju* has been expanded in an agglutinative way:[33]

	masc	'sleep'	'master'	fem.	'herds'
				N. Pl.	neɣél-es
N. Sg.		jípnos	aféndis		
G. Sg.		jípnoz-ju	aféndiz-ju	G. Pl.	neɣél-ez-ju

However, compare the following forms, in particular the N. Sg. of Aksos with that of Standard/Southern Greek:

	ms. "type of an inst"	nt. 'girl'	fm. 'herd'
N. Sg.	anajót	korítš	neɣél
(Stand. N. Sg.	anaδótis	korítsi	aɣéli)
G. Sg.	anajot-jú	koritš-jú	neɣél-ju

These forms seem to imply that the N. Sg. is identical to the underlying forms. If they are, then they fit Seiler's principle in a general way: N. Sg.

---

[33] Cf. Sec. 7.2. For Ulagats see Kesisoglou 1951: 31f, 34.

$=C_i$ vs. G. Sg. $=C_iXV$. They would not fit if we assume an underlying final -*i* in the M. Sg. However, if we assume an underlying morphological and phonological representation which differs from the phonetic surface, and if we assume Seiler's morphological principle, then it would be absurd to assume that this morphological principle would not hold for the underlying morphological/phonological representation, were it not for the deviating surface phonetic level. Note also the contrasting stress placement in the following feminine forms:

	'herd'	'trouble'
Nom. Sg.	neγél	norγí
Gen. Sg.	neγél-ju	norγís

There are different declension types in Greek, and this would be partially obliterated if we assumed identical underlying Nom. Sg. case forms. The putative underlying form for the genitive would hold if we assume a similar position for the underlying Nom. Sg.

In contrast to other G. Sg. $=$ N. Pl. paradigms, *arxóp* is a rather isolated form. Compare the following sets from Aksos:

masc.	'man'	'wolf'	'shepherd'
Sg. N.	árxopos	líkos	pištikós
G.	arxóp	likjú	pištikú
A.	árxopo	líko(s)	pištikó
Pl. N.	arxóp	lík	pištikí
G.	árxopozju	likjú	pištikú
A.	arxopjús	likjús	pištikjús

Only one form can be interpreted as an advanced agglutinative one. And that is the G. Pl. *árxopozju*, if indeed it is related to the N. Sg. The other forms with -*ju* seem to come from the root and -*ju* is not added to the N. Pl. Thus *arxóp* is more like a bare root/stem than morphologically subtractive. However it is difficult to argue about these paradigms which seem to indicate a transition period.

8.0 In this paper we have presented data from the Northern and Anatolian Greek dialects which support not only a semiotically based model of Natural Phonology and Natural Morphology, but also the strong need of diachrony to explain language specific unnatural phenomena. The unnatural MPRs come about due to the interaction of phonology and morphology. And the theory has specified ways how MPRs develop from PRs. In fact this major concern was one of the reasons why Natural Morphology originated alongside Natural Phonology.[34]

Generally typological constraints on universal options are best studied in a diachronic perspective. Since very few languages can come close to an ideal language type (cf. Skalička 1979), any purely synchronic account of typological mixes risks to comprise ad hoc statements, because the investigator may feel free to choose from basic language types whatever ingredients he needs for the given 'mix'. However if we investigate the diachronic evolution of languages in the direction towards one language type and move away from another, then we are more constrained in connecting changes of typological criteria.

Consideration of the relative stability of a phenomenon in time is an important safeguard against making spurious generalizations. Many language specific phenomena are due to 'historical accidents', e.g. the amount of Turkish influence. Any valid explanation of universal and typological phenomena needs a diachronic (i.e. genetic) explanation of these 'accidents' as a corollary.

REFERENCES

Acson, V. 1979. *A diachronic view of case-marking systems in Greek: a localistic-lexical analysis*. University of Hawaii dissertation. Ann Arbor: University Microfilms.
Adams, D. R. 1977. Interdialectal rule borrowing: some cases from Greek. *GL* 17. 141 - 151.
Andriotis, N. T. 1948. *To Glossiko idioma ton Farason*. Athens, Collection de l'Institut Français d'Athènes 8.
Anttila, R. 1975. The indexical element in morphology. *Innsbrucker Beiträge zur Sprachwissenschaft*, Reihe Vorträge 12.
Babiniotis, G. D. 1972. To rima tis ellinikis. University of Athens, Philosophical Faculty. Bibliothiki Saripolou 20.
Crothers, J. 1973. *On the abstractness controversy*. Bloomington: Indiana University Linguistics Club.
Dawkins, R. M. 1916. *Modern Greek in Asia Minor*. Cambridge: CUP.
Dawkins, R. M. 1937. The Pontic dialect of Modern Greek in Asia Minor and Russia. *Transactions of the Philological Society* 1937, 15 - 52.
Donegan, P. 1978. On the Natural Phonology of vowels. *Working Papers in Linguistics*, Ohio State University 23.
Donegan, P. and D. Stampe. 1977. On the description of phonological hierarchies.

---

[34] Even at the embryonic stages of Natural Morphology as in Mayerthaler 1977; Dressler 1977a. Cf. later Wurzel 1980b; Dressler 1980, 1981, to appear a, b, c.

CLS book of squibs, ed. by S. E. Fox, 35 - 37. Chicago: University Press.

1979a. The syllable in phonological and prosodic structure. *Syllables and segments*, ed. by A. Bell and J. Hooper, 25 - 34. Amsterdam: North Holland.

1979b. The study of Natural Phonology. *Current approaches to phonological theory*, ed. by D. Dinnsen, 126 - 73. Bloomington: Indiana University Press.

Dressler, W. 1973. Pour une stylistique phonologique du latin. *BSLP* 68. 129 - 145.

1975. Methodisches zu Allegroregeln. *Phonologica 1972*, ed. by W. Dressler and F. Mareš, 219 - 34. Munich: Fink.

1977a. *Grundfragen der Morphonologie*. Vienna: Verlag der Österr. Akademie der Wissenschaften.

1977b. Phonologische Prozeßtypologie. *Studies in linguistic typology*, ed. by M. Romportl et al., 135 - 46. Prague: Acta Universitatis Carolinae, Philologica 5.

1977c. Elements of a polycentristic theory of word-formation. *Wiener linguistische Gazette* 15. 13 - 32.

1980. A semiotic model of diachronic process phonology. *Wiener linguistische Gazette* 22/23: 31 - 94. Reprinted in *Perspectives for historical linguistics*, ed. by W. Lehmann and Y. Malkiel, 93 - 131. Amsterdam: Benjamins, 1983.

1981. Outlines of a model of morphonology, *Phonologica 1980*, ed. by W. Dressler et al., 113 - 22. Innsbruck: Universität.

To appear a. *Morphonology*. Ann Arbor: Karoma Press. (1985).

To appear b. Subtraction in word formation and its place within a theory of Natural Morphology. *Quaderni Semantici* 5(1984) 78 - 85.

To appear c. Subtraction in a polycentristic theory of Natural Morphology. *Rules and the lexicon*, ed. by E. Gussmann. Lublin: Catholic University.

Dressler, W. and J. Hufgard. 1980. *Études phonologiques sur le breton sud-bigouden*. Vienna: Verlag der Österr. Akademie der Wissenschaften.

Dressler, W., W. Mayerthaler, O. Panagl and W. Wurzel. In press. *Leitmotifs in Natural Morphology*. Amsterdam: Benjamins.

Field, T. 1981. Loan-word phonology and phonological rule types, *Phonologica 1980*, ed. by W. Dressler et al., 129 - 36. Innsbruck: Universität.

Fosteris, D. and I. I. Kesisoglou. 1969. *Leksikologion tou Aravani*. Athens: Collection de l'Institut Français 89.

Georgios, C. 1962. *To glossiko idioma Germa Kastorias*. Salonica: Etairia Makedonikon Spoudon 23.

Hyman, L. 1977. Phonologization. *Linguistic studies offered to J. Greenberg*, I., ed. by A. Juilland, 407 - 418. Saratoga: Anma Libri.

Jespersen, O. 1949. Efficiency in linguistic change. *Selected writings by O. Jespersen*, 381 - 466. Tokyo: Senjo.

Kastovsky, D. 1980. Zero in morphology: a means of making up for phonological losses. *Historical morphology*, ed. by J. Fisiak, 213 - 50. The Hague: Mouton.

Kaye, J. 1974. Opacity and recoverability in phonology. *Canadian Journal of Linguistics* 19. 134 - 49.

Kesisoglou, I. I. 1951. *To glossiko idioma tou Oulagats*. Athens: Collection Inst. Franç. 40.

Kretschmer, P. 1805. *Der heutige lesbische Dialekt verglichen mit den übrigen nordgriechischen Mundarten*. Vienna: Hölder.

Labov, W. 1981. Resolving the Neogrammarian controversy. *Language* 57. 267 - - 308.
Linell, P. 1979. *Psychological reality in phonology.* Cambridge: University Press.
Malikouti, A. 1970. *Metaschimatiki morfologia tou neoellinikou onomatos.* Athens: Bibliothiki tis en Athinais philekpaidevtikis etairias 56.
Matthews, P. H. 1972. *Inflectional morphology.* Cambridge: University Press.
Mavroxalividis, G. and L. I. Kesisoglou. 1960. *To glossiko idioma tis Aksou.* Athens: Collection Inst. Franç. 39.
Mayerthaler, W. 1977. *Studien zur theoretischen und zur französischen Morphologie* Tübingen: Niemeyer.

    1980. Morphologischer Ikonismus. *Zeitschrift für Semiotik* 2. 19 - 37.

    1981. *Morphologische Natürlichkeit.* Wiesbaden: Athenaion.

Newton, B. 1972. *The generative interpretation of dialect.* Cambridge: University Press.
Oeconomides, D. 1908. *Lautlehre des Pontischen.* Leipzig: Böhme.
Papadopoulos, A. A. 1955. *Istoriki grammatiki tis pontikis dialektou.* Athens: Epitropi Pontiakon Meleton.
Peirce, C. 1965. *Collected papers.* Cambridge, Mass.: Harvard University Press.
Pernot, H. 1907. *Etudes de linguistique néo-hellénique.* I. *Phonétique des parlers de Chio.* Paris: published by the author.
Schindler, J. 1974. Fragen zum paradigmatischen Ausgleich. *Sprache* 20. 1 - 9.
Seiler, H. 1952. *L'aspect et le temps dans le verbe néo-grec.* Paris: Belles Lettres.

    1958. Zur Systematik und Entwicklungsgeschichte der Griechischen Nominaldeklination. *Glotta* 37. 41 - 67.

    1978 (ed.) *Language universals.* Tübingen: Narr.

Skalička, V. 1979. *Typologische Studien* Braunschweig: Vieweg
Stampe, D. 1969. The acquisition of phonetic representation. *PCLS* 5. 443 - 54.

    1980. *A dissertation on Natural Phonology.* New York: Garland.

Thavoris, A. I. 1980. To proun(e)ikos tou Ironda kai i palaiotita ton gnoston gnorismaton ton voreion Neoellinikon idiomaton. *Dodoni* 9. 401 - 39.
Thumb, A. 1910. *Handbuch der neugriechischen Volkssprache.* 2nd ed. Strassburg: Trübner.
Wang, W. S. Y. 1977 (ed.) *The Lexicon in phonological change.* The Hague: Mouton.
Wurzel, W. U. 1980a. Some remarks on the relations between naturalness and typology. *TCLC* 20. 103 - 13.

    1980b. Ways of morphologizing phonological rules. *Historical morphology,* ed. by J. Fisiak, 443 - 462. The Hague: Mouton.

    1981. Problems in morphonology. *Phonologica 1980,* ed. by W. Dressler et al., 413 - 434. Insbruck: Universität.

    To appear. *Flexionsmorphologir und Natürlichkeit.* Berlin: Akademie der Wissenschaften der DDR. (now: Studia Grammatika 27, 1984).

DID OLD ENGLISH HAVE A MIDDLE VOICE?

THOMAS FRASER

The title of this paper establishes, for those who are familiar with French linguistics, its theoretical framework: the psychomechanics of language, and in particular the theory of verbal diathesis set out by Gustave Guillaume in an article published in 1943, "Existe-t-il un déponent en français?". In this study the author traces the development of the verb system from Latin to French with respect to voice; four types are identified for Modern French — two analytical voices, the active and the passive, the development of the latter being due in part to a change within the system undergone by the Latin -*us* participle, and two synthetic mixed voices; the first of these is derived from the Latin deponents and comprises that small group of verbs which take the auxiliary *être* in the "passé composé" (*entrer*, *sortir*, etc.), the second being the reflexive or pronominal voice with its various sense effects. Since the publication of this article, Guillaume's theory has undergone various modifications, refinements and practical applications, by the author himself in his teaching and by those who have worked within this model.[1]

What characterizes this approach is its dynamic view of the relationship between subject and verb, a view that contrasts with the conception of voice — and particularly the middle voice — inherited from 19th century historical and comparative linguistics. According to this tradition the middle voice is used to indicate that the subject is closely associated with the event expressed by the verb and is deeply interested in its accomplishment. Thus we read, for example, in Marouzeau's *Lexique de la terminologie linguistique* that in the middle voice "... le sujet du verbe est spécialement intéressé à l'action." A similar point of view is expressed — at least in the terms used — by John Lyons (1968, 373): "The implications of the middle (when it is in opposition with the active)

---

[1] Mention should be made of Stéfanini (1962), Moignet (1971, 1980, 1981), Vassant (1980) for French and Hirtle (1965) for English; mention should also be made of Benveniste (1950), who most certainly knew Guillaume's study.

are that the 'action' or 'state' affects the subject of the verb or his interests." Such a psychological approach is, of course, open to different interpretations; can one say, for example, since we have in Sanskrit or in Latin a medio-passive (*marate, morior*) that the personal subject is more interested in his death than in his life, since we have in the two languages an active form for the concept "to live" (*jīvati, vivere*)? It is, of course, difficult, with such interpretations, for the middle voice to be opposed to the active.

This is not the case for Guillaume's definition of the middle voice: he sees it as a mental representation of the subject's position with respect to the verb. Whereas in the active voice the subject is free to initiate and direct the event, or to condition the process, and in the passive, on the other hand, the subject is conditioned by the event, in the middle voice the subject is both conditioner and conditionee.[2] As Moignet (1971: 267) puts it:

> "(...) la voix verbale définit (...) les rapports existant entre un événement et son support personnel — et, plus précisément, dénonce si, dans l'événement considéré, la personne support est pensée comme en ayant l'entière conduction (voix active), ou ne l'ayant que partiellement (voix moyenne), ou ne l'ayant pas du tout (voix passive)..."

Benveniste (1966: 172) points out that in such cases the subject is somehow situated within the event, though he does not elaborate on the question:

> "Dans l'actif, les verbes dénotent un procès qui s'accomplit à partir du sujet et hors de lui. Dans le moyen, qui est la diathèse à définir par opposition, le verbe indique un procès dont le sujet est le siège; le sujet est intérieur au procès."

If we go on now from this grammatical-semantic interpretation of voice to a mechanical interpretation, we can perhaps find a clue to what Benveniste is trying to say. In any voice the subject of a verb stands as a support for the event expressed by the verb, but this event can be viewed either as an operation or as a result. In the first case, where the subject initiates the operation — Moignet would say he is the "cause" of the event — we have the active voice. In the second case, where the result, or effect, of the preceding operation (expressed by the past participle) is

---

[2] Guillaume (1943/1964: 134) writes: "Le moyen est, du point de vue psychique, dans les langues indo-européennes, la conséquence de l'alliance en toute proportion d'une situation qui consiste pour le sujet à *conduire* le procès qu'exprime le verbe et d'une situation inverse plus ou moins oblitérée sous la première, et selon laquelle, dans le procès même qu'exprime le verbe, le sujet apparaît *conduit*."

related to the subject by way of the auxiliary, we have the traditional passive voice. In the middle voice, the subject is the support for an operativity which is then transformed into resultativity by the fact that the limit of the verb's meaning and the limit of the event coincide within the subject. This is perhaps best brought out by an example from French: if we take the French verb "marcher", the subject initiates the operation, and when the event is interrupted a result is obtained notionally even though the process may continue immediately. On the other hand, with a verb like "entrer", a result is only obtained notionally when the event itself is completed.[3] In such cases, where result and operation are related to the same personal support, we may talk in mechanical terms of a middle voice.

Having added this logical dimension to the semantic interpretation given above, I would now like to go on to consider the forms which exteriorize the mental representations, that is, the semiology of voice. It is generally agreed that the Indo-European languages had a specific series of medio-passive morphemes which contrasted with the active paradigm: thus, for example, the well-known Sanskrit opposition between *yajati* ("he sacrifices for someone else") and *yajate* ("he sacrifices for himself"), or again the Latin *-or/-(a)tus sum* inflections expressing both the passive and the active (*loquor/locutus sum*), alongside the active forms. A specifically passive semiology, in the morphology, or the syntax, or both, is a later development in all Indo-European languages.

As regards the Germanic languages, the following facts meet with general agreement: (a) Gothic retains traces of the Indo-European medio-passive, at least in the present tense; (b) Old Norse developed a middle voice by adding a reflexive pronoun to the active form of the verb;[4] (c) Old English had one form inherited from the Indo-European synthetic mixed voice, viz. the verb *hātan*. The dual nature of this verb is illustrated by the following two examples:

(1) het his naman Adam. (*Genesis*, V, 2)
    (And he called his name Adam)

---

[3] To paraphrase Wilmet (1972: 52), with a process like "to walk", the subject can carry out the action, stop, he has walked and he can continue the process immediately. If we take, on the other hand an action like "to enter", the subject can go in, stop, he has gone in — but he cannot continue unless he returns to the point of departure.

[4] This is a case where the semiology reflects the underlying meaning of the form, since it states that the subject is both the initiator or operator of the event and its limit or result.

(2) Wite gere þes ys smyþes sunu hu ne hatte hys moder maria (*Matthew* XIII, 55)
   (Is not this the carpenter's son? Is not his mother called Mary?)

The verb *hātan* translates in turn a Latin active (*vocavit*) and a passive (*dicitur*). With the exception of this isolated instance, the category of voice is restricted in Old English, to the active and the periphrastic passive, formed with one of the two auxiliaries, *beon* or *weorðan*. And yet we find cases where the language seems to be experimenting means of expressing a category it apparently had not entirely lost in the underlying mental system of representation. We therefore find instances of translators rendering Latin deponents by the verb *beon/wesan* + present participle:

(3) syndriglice wæs fram him eallum frignende (Bede, II, 13)
   (He questioned them all separately; Lat. *sciscitabatur*)

There are also a number of cases of verbs, especially those which express a mental process, where a reflexive pronoun appears to express the limit of the verbal event:

(4) þa beþohte he hine (*Luke* XV, 17)
   (Then he thought ...)
(5) ... þa þu þe ondrede (Bede II, 12)
   (... that you were afraid of)

In some instances the verb is to be found in the so-called "impersonal" construction, where the personal support disappears, but to reappear in a form which evokes the result of the notion:

(6) Eac me sceal aþreotan ymbe Philopes (...) to asecgenne (*Orosius* 27, 32)
   (Also it will bore me to talk about Pelops)

One of these forms was to be considerably developed in later English and is now firmly established in the language. This is the progressive form, which corresponds to the interpretation I have given of the middle voice: the subject is in a position where he no longer controls or conditions that portion of the event, no matter how small, which is already accomplished.[5]

The progressive was not, however, part of the verbal system of Old

---

[5] On this point, see Hirtle (1965).

English, and it is only sporadically that it can be said to express the middle voice. In a transitional period such as this, one is led, therefore, to look at the other means the language had at its disposal for the expression of this category. One such means is the system of preverbs that Old English had in common with other Germanic languages, and in particular the preverbs *a-* and *on-*, the latter eventually fusing with the former.[6] Many handbooks and glossaries of Old English consider that *a-* plays no role whatsoever outside that of intensifying particle. A close examination of texts will, however, show quite the contrary. Thus, for example, in the Vespasian Psalter and the hymns in the same manuscript, the verb *cennan* is never confused with *acennan*, and each is used to translate a different Latin verb. The simplex always renders the Latin *parturio* or *pario*, is always transitive, and expresses, literally or figuratively the idea of bearing or producing, as in:

(7) Sehþe cenneþ unrehtwisnesse geecnaþ sar and cenneþ unrehtwisnisse. (V.P. 7, 15)
(Behold, he has brought forth iniquity, conceived mischief and brought forth falsehood.)

The compound, on the other hand, always translates the Latin *nascor* and is always to be found with a passive morphology, *be* + Past participle, as in:

(8) Secgaþ heofenes rehtwisnisse his folce þæt biþ acenned þæt dyde dryhten. (V.P. 21, 32)
(They will declare Heaven's righteousness to his people that shall be born and will say what God has done.)

Examples (9) and (10), taken from St. Matthew's Gospel, confirm the instances from the Vespasian Psalter:

(9) Witodlice heo cenneþ sunu (*Matthew* I, 21)
(Truly she shall bear a son; Lat. *pariet*)
(10) Hwar is se iudea cyning þe acenned is (*Matthew* II, 2)
(Where is he that is born King of the Jews? Lat. *natus est*)

In other words, *cennan* expresses a verbal event in which the subject is the support of an operation, whereas *acennan* expresses a notion in which the subject is seen as being partially conditioned by the event's result.

---

[6] This should not surprise us since it has long been recognized that the preverb *be-* could have a transitivizing function, and that *ge-*, along with other preverbs, played some role — though disputed — in the expression of aspect.

In examples (8) and (10) *acennan* is used in the analytical passive form. In the following two instances the verbs are active in form, and we have clear cases of transitive verbs acquiring, through contact with the preverb *a-*, meanings in which the subject stands as a support for the result of the notion. Thus, whereas the simple verb *cwellan* means "to kill", the compound means "to die", as in:

(11) Sihtric acwæl and Æþelstan feng to Norþhymbra rice (*Chronicle*, 926 D)
(Sihtric died and King Athelstan annexed the kingdom of Northumbria.)

In the following example, the role of the preverb is particularly evident. *Drincan* means "to drink" and is used either transitively or intransitively; *drencan* is the causative of the latter and means "to give to drink", "to inebriate" and by extension "to drown", in which case it is either transitive or else in the analytical passive form, *beon*+past participle; *adrincan*, however, in the active voice, means either "to drink completely, to drink up", where the preverb is an intensifier, or else "to be drowned, to drown oneself". This is the case in the following example:

(12) Her adranc Ædwine æþeling on sæ. (*Chronicle*, 933 E)
(This year prince Edwin was drowned at sea.)

The foregoing examples show that it is necessary to introduce a third factor in the analysis of the middle voice. After the grammatical-semantic and the semiological dimensions, we should also take into account the lexical-semantic interpretation of the verbal notions. It has already been pointed out by Stéfanini (1962: 118—119) in his study on the French reflexive that although the verbs which belong to this category may vary dialectically and historically, there seems to be a natural affinity between the middle voice and certain semantic groups. Two of these — the notions of birth and death — have just been observed, and we can add to these verbs expressing departure from a point, a number of which are constructed with the preverb *a-*:[7]

(13) He þonan afor and his fierd on an oþer fæstre land.
(*Orosius*, 46, 35)
(He left there and led his army to another more secure land.)

---

[7] Notice that in colloquial or slang French we find alongside *s'en aller*, with the same meaning, verbs such as *se barrer*, *se tirer*, *se tailler*, *se casser* in the pronominal form.

(14) ... þæt hie mid sume searawrence from Xerse þæm cyninge sume
   hwile awende. (*Orosius*, 47, 27)
   (... that they would for some time by some stratagem turn away
from Xerxes.)

A corollary notion — that of remaining in a place or continuing in a given state — can also be expressed by means of the compound verb *awunian*, the simplex meaning "to inhabit, to dwell":

(15) And oferwrah mid wetre swencende hie an of him ne awunede.
   (V.P. 105, 11)
   (The waters covered their enemies, and not one remained)

We may also mention here those verbs which express a change of state and whose French and Latin equivalents are respectively reflexive and deponent; in Old English we find the preverb *a-* used to form deadjectival verbs with the meaning "to become *x*", where *x* is the notion expressed by the adjective. Hence we have *adeafian*: "to become deaf"; *adumbian*: "to become dumb"; *aslacian*: "to become slack, to diminish"; *aþeostrian*: "to become dark", therefore "to be eclipsed", as in:

(16) And þy ilcan geare aþiestrode sio sunne ane tid dæges.
   (*Chronicle*, 879 A)
   (And the same year the sun was eclipsed for one hour of the day.)

It is difficult in such cases to use the traditional term "agent" to describe the subject of the verb; the subject is in fact simply the starting point of the verbal notion expressed as a result (see Moignet 1980: 271). Seen in this light, inchoatives are also expressions of the middle voice: since they only evoke the initial instant of the event, the result of this initial instant is obtained immediately the operation begins. Once again the preverb *a-* and the related *on-* can be used for the expression of inchoativeness, hence *slæpan*: "to sleep"; *onslæpan*: "to fall asleep", as in:

(17) Se halga Andreas asette his heafod ofer ænne his discipuli and he
   onslep. (*Blickling Homilies* 235, 13)
   (The holy man Andrew laid his head on one of his disciples and
   fell asleep.)

To this group we can, of course add those basic verbs whose notional content is reduced to an idea of commencement: *aginnan, onginnan*: "to begin".[8]

---

[8] Here again there is an interesting parallel with the main French verb with the same notional content: *commencer* can be used either with the auxiliary *avoir*, or with *être*. Thus: "le film a déjà commencé" *vs.* "le film est déjà commencé".

The quotation by Guillaume (see note 2) suggests that in the middle voice the subject is not completely in control of the operation expressed by the verb, but is partially conditioned by it. Certain notions correspond semantically to this definition, in particular those in which the accomplishment of the operation is dependent on the object. Here again the prefixes *a-* and *on-* seem to play a role. Thus, for example, the verbs *cweðan* and *hwelan* mean respectively "to say" and "to roar"; the compound *oncweðan* could mean either "to reply" or "to resound", while *onhwelan* could mean "to echo"; in both cases the subject of the verb is only partially the "conditioner" of the event. Similarly, in the following example, the preverb transforms the active-transitive verb *bītan* ("to bite") lexically and enables it to express the notion of "tasting" in which the operation depends in part on the genitive object:

(18) He him forbead þæt he þæs næfre ne abite. (*Homilies Wulfstan* 6, 40)

(He commanded that he should never taste that one.)

In example (19):

(19) Onhyrgean we þone blindan. (*Blickling Homilies* 21, 9)
(Let us imitate the blind man.)

the preverb merely reinforces the simplex, both verbs expressing a notion in which the subject depends partly on the object for the conduct of the operation.[9]

As confirmation of the interpretation I have given of such verbs I should mention the behaviour of a certain number of them with respect to the not yet firmly established periphrastic perfect forms. Most of the cases we find of this form in Old English are constructed with *habban* + past participle. In examples (20) to (22), however, taken from the *Chronicle* we find verbs to which *a-* is prefixed used with *beon/wesan*.

(20) Hæfde Hæsten ær geworht þæt geweorc æt Beamfleote and wæs þa ut afaren on hergaþ ... (*Chronicle* 894)
(Haesten had made that fort at Benfleet and had gone off on a plundering raid.)

(21) ... hæfdon miclne dæl þara horsa freten and þa oþre wæron hungre acwolen. (*Chronicle* 894)
(They had devoured most of their horses, and the rest had died of hunger.)

---

[9] It should be noted that Latin has deponent, *imitor*, to express this notion.

(22) ... wæron þa men uppe on londe of agane. (*Chronicle* 897)
(The crews had gone off inland.)

In examples (20) and (21) the contrast with the *habban* forms shows that for the author of this entry the two events in each case are seen from the same viewpoint. In (20) the subject, Haesten, has reached the end of the operation he has initiated — "making a fort" —, but this does not imply any change in the state of the subject; on the other hand, reaching the end of the operation "going off" implies a new state for the subject, and in fact a new linguistic status, hence the choice of the verb *wesan* as auxiliary.[10]

Can we therefore, in the light of the arguments put forward and the examples discussed, give an affirmative answer to the question raised in the title of this paper? It is certainly possible for an underlying mental system of representation to continue to exist despite the disappearance of the semiological system, and the system of voice in Modern French which continues that of Latin shows this to be the case. As Moignet (1980: 271) puts it: "Il serait a priori surprenant qu'une catégorie de langue bien institué en latin eut disparu intégralement sans laisser de trace. La destruction du système sémiologique de la voix latine n'abolit pas le système mental sous-jacent." On the other hand, the varied means of expression of the middle voice that were experimented on by Old English do not seem to point to the existence of a grammatical category. What we can say, however, is that, just as aspect was a grammatical category in Indo-European and became once again part of the English verb system, having gone through a period in Old English where it survived as a lexical category, kept alive by the action of the preverb, so we can point to a similar role for the preverbs *a-* and *on-* in the formation of a lexical middle voice.

BIBLIOGRAPHY

I. *Corpus*

Bede = *The Old English Version of Bede's Ecclesiastical History*, ed. T. Miller, E.E.T.S. 95, 96.
The Blicking Homilies, ed. R. Morris, E.E.T.S. 58, 63, 73.

---

[10] In the same entry in the Parker Chronicle we find two further examples of a periphrastic form of a prefixed verb accompanied by the verb *wesan*: þa Deniscan scipu aseten wæron (the Danish ships had gone aground) and: þæt wæter wæs ahebbad (the tide had ebbed).

Chronicle = *Two of the Saxon Chronicles Parallel*, ed. J. Earle and C. Plummer, Oxford.
Genesis = *The Old English Heptateuch*, ed. S. J. Crawford, E.E.T.S. 160.
Orosius = *The Old English Orosius*, ed. J. Bately, E.E.T.S., S.S.6.
The Vespasian Psalter = *The Oldest English Texts*, ed. H. Sweet, E.E.T.S. 83.
The West Saxon Gospels, ed. M. Grünberg, Amsterdam.
Wulfstan = *The Homilies of Wulfstan*, ed. D. Bethurum, Oxford.

II. Works consulted

Benveniste, Emile
    1950 [1966] "Actif et moyen dans le verbe", *Problèmes de linguistique générale* (Paris, Gallimard), 168 - 175.
Guillaume, Gustave
    1943 [1964] "Existe-t-il un déponent en français?", *Langage et science du langage* (Paris, Nizet/Québec, Presses de l'Université Laval), 127 - 142.
Hirtle, Walter
    (1965) "Auxiliaries and voice in English", *Les Langues Modernes* 59, 4: 25 - 42.
Lyons, John
    (1968) *Introduction to Theoretical Linguistics* (Cambridge, Cambridge University Press).
Marouzeau, Jules
    (^{3}1951) *Lexique de la terminologie linguistique* (Paris, Geuthner)
Moignet, Gérard
    (1971) "Verbe unipersonnel et voix verbale", *Travaux de Linguistique et de Littérature* 9, 1: 267 - 282.
    (1980) "Diathèse verbale. Les verbes fondamentaux en français", *Langage et psychomécanique du langage* ed. A. Joly&W. Hirtle (Lille, Presses Universitaires), 267 - 283.
    (1981) *Systématique de la langue française* (Paris, Klincksieck).
Stéfanini, Jean
    (1962) *La vaoix pronominale en ancien et en moyen français* (Gap, Imp. Louis-Jean).
Vassant, Annette
    (1980) "Lexique, sémantique et grammaire dans la voix verbale en français", *Travaux de Linguistique et de Littérature* 18, 1: 143 - 163.
Wilmet, Marc
    (1972) *Gustave Guillaume et son école linguistique* (Paris, Nathan/Bruxelles, Labor).

THE VOWEL /a:/ IN ENGLISH

HUBERT GBUREK

1. If we compare the classical vowel diagrams of OE, ME, and ModE respectively, we notice that certain vowels are represented in each of them, among them /a:/. But this vowel is represented by different lexical items in every period, e.g. by OE *hām* (which has a different sound in ME and ModE), by ME *name* (which again did not have it in OE and does not have it now), and by ModE RP *harm* (which had different vowels at its earlier stages). It is common in historical English phonology to either consider the development of /a:/ from OE to ModE, or reconstruct the source(s) of ModE /a:/, or deal with the sound change(s) that produced e.g. ME /a:/. Whichever approach we follow, we deal with this particular sound at one period only and lose sight of it once the metamorphosis has taken place.

The subject of this paper will be /a:/ of different periods of the English language and its transitory nature. I will examine its various origins and ultimate destiny when it made room for its successor and, to close the circle, the source(s) of the substitute. Thus phenomena will be linked that have not, to my knowledge, been treated as a unit in handbooks.

At the same time the importance of /a:/ for the English sound system will become evident and an answer will be given to the question whether English (RP) depends on vowel length as a distinctive feature at all.

First, however, I will briefly outline the general framework within which the specific data shall be discussed.

2. Nearly a century ago, philologists like Sweet, Viëtor, and Sievers had the then rather vague notion that every language had its particular 'articulatory basis' (*Artikulationsbasis*), a kind of invariable quality that pervades the phonetic/phonological level over and above the segments that can be isolated.[1] What they had in mind was, I think, what we

---

[1] Cf. Burgschmidt/Götz (1974:203ff).

today call the particular structural type of a language. For the English language this implies as a non-debatable fact that at its birth as a vernacular it had inherited a structure that depended on length-opposition for its vowels. I will further assume, in accordance with the Prague school of structural linguistics, that the system was well balanced or even symmetrical[2] and that there was one pair of open vowels with its place of articulation somewhere in the vicinity of Cardinal Vowels 4 or 5, differentiated by length only. This presupposes a dichotomous (or trichotomous) vowel system at the phonological or lexical level of examination. The question whether the phonetic level has two or three contrastive types, i.e. short monophthongs vs. diphthongs or short monophthongs vs. long monophthongs vs. diphthongs is irrelevant and does not concern us here.[3] This in turn permits the evasion of the terminological battleground and the use of the rather straightforward symbols /a:/ and /a/, which are only 'cover symbols or disguised forms of etymological categories' (Lass).

To introduce my next tenet I begin with a quotation from Penzl (1969:15): 'Significant alternations at a later stage will often provide comparative evidence for an earlier stage of the same language or dialect... The *terminal* value can be used to determine the *initial* values.' (Emphasis mine: HG). But, I would like to add by quoting Lass/Anderson: '...if the living form of a language seems to be a particular structural type, is it not uneconomical (at least) to posit... a major typological break at some point in the history?' (1975:188). Certainly, typological breaks must not, of course, be ruled out as a matter of principle.[4] For lack of evidence to the contrary I will assume that such a break has not occurred so far. If so, I think we are free to modify Penzl and start with an analysis of the *oldest* vowel system. Provided that that analysis is correct, which rests on the assumption that there existed a long vs. short phonemic opposition, it is now permissible to use those findings and apply them to the analysis of more recent periods. (For similar reasoning cf. Lass/Anderson 1975:189.) This yields the preliminary

---

[2] Cf. also Penzl (1969:15): 'Often a symmetrical structure of the phonemic pattern can be assumed.' For the earliest period of English see Trnka (1982:221f).

[3] For this reason a discussion is needless on which of the dichotomous systems that have been proposed is most adequate. Three proposals have become well established: Trager & Smith (1951). Chomsky & Halle (1968), and Lass (1976).

[4] For instance, Czech unlike Polish or Russian eliminated the opposition of hard and soft (palatalized) consonants. Scots (see below) gave up vowel length as a means of lexical opposition.

result that length still carries contrastive significance between (long and short) vowels in ModE.[5]

The link between short and long vowel constituting a contrastive pair did not suffice at times and could not prevent the vowels from changing their place of articulation. Unlike the short vowels, which have not undergone spectacular changes even since IE times, the long vowels have proved to be more fickle. /a:/ in particular time and again became a trouble-maker, when it left its position to merge with its neighbours. But /a:/ being indispensable to the vowel-system, the language never suffered a vacancy in its place. And in order to create the vowel anew, ever fresh sources had to be tapped.

I will now discuss the specific changes which resulted in the loss of /a:/ and its respective restoration from different sources, which in all cases probably set in immediately.

The fate of earlier /a:/ will be dealt with more or less summarily to allow more room for the discussion of the effects the Great Vowel Shift (GVS) had on our vowel. This is justified because on the phonological level historical investigation does not easily succeed in more than offering statements made up of binary oppositions, at least not until the time of the orthoepists. And it so happens that at this point the history of /a:/ is by far the most intricate.

3. Germanic dialects, the so-called Primitive Germanic (PGmc), entered the historical age without /a:/ since IE /a:/ had coalesced in PGmc with /o:/. By a subsequent development the North and West Gmc dialects [6] restored that vowel from the so-called /ē^1/, an open vowel, which was prone to change because the existence of a closer variant /ē^2/ < IE /ei/ sufficed to keep the system in balance. As a probable date for the transition of /ē^1/ > /a:/ the alteration of the name *Suēbi* to *Suābi* in Latin writers ca 500 AD (Krahe/Meid 1969:42) can be cited.

Among the West Gmc languages all the dialects of OE, however, show an interesting deviation. None of them retained West Gmc /a:/. West Saxon had /ǣ^1/ ([æ:] or [ɛ:]) whereas in Anglian and Kentish the vowel merged with close /ē/ ([e:]).[7] (Its retention as /a:/ when followed

---

[5] Only RP and related types of English are meant here. By the same token most dialect types in Britain and the USA are excluded.

[6] Gothic not only can but must be left out of consideration since its history breaks off rather prematurely.

[7] Whether from West Gmc /a:/ or by way of an earlier /æ:/ remains disputed.

by /w/ or a back vowel in the next syllable may be a hint to its phonetic quality but that was no more than a positional variant, an allophone of /$æ^1$/.) It was the existence of a 'hole' in the area of the lowest vowel that led to an interesting sound change that cannot but be explained as a direct and immediate consequence of the preceding loss of /a:/, viz. the monophthongization of the diphthong /ai/, a development not shared by any other Gmc language. In what has become the most probable chronological order of sound changes for OE (cf. Campbell 1974:109) no other sound change can reasonably be thought of as intervening between the two developments. I think the implications therefore are evident:

First, the change of Gmc /ai/ > OE /a:/ was the *premeditated* answer of the language system to the prior failure to retain the West Gmc monophthong /a:/ in OE.

Second, these two developments were no doubt parallel, i.e. they coincided temporarily.

4. The next step takes us right into the ME period. The phenomenon to be here discussed looks, in a way, least exciting of all. I take the lengthening of vowels in open syllables before 1250 to be the central event. It affected all short vowels in open syllables of bisyllabic words and would have occurred no matter whether OE /a:/ had given way by rising to /ɔ:/ south of the Humber or not. Witness for that matter Northern English, where old /a:/ and /a:/ from lengthening merged. Rather than wondering how the language behaved in order to fill a conspicuous 'hole' in its system, this time we have to shift our attention to the question of why Southern English raised OE /a:/ to a position where there was no vacancy thereby possibly creating a 'hole' in the lowest region.

(This is, of course, quite different from the problem with which we were confronted at the previous stage and the one we will meet with when dealing with the GVS.)

How then should the seemingly spontaneous change of Southern EME /a:/ to /ɔ:/ be explained? The explanation is to plead the existence of two allophones, a phonetically back [a:] for the South and a fronted [a:] for the North (cf. Lass 1976:134). This was not reflected in spelling. The spelling system had no means to indicate it nor was there any need to do so. This changed with the advent of the new /a:/. Especially as there were many French loan words among the lexical items with new /a:/, with a traditional spelling to back them, there was no other solution possible but to reserve the use of the graph <a> for old /a/ in open syllables, the newly developed /a:/, and assign the old back vowel [a:] the graph <o>. The abrupt change of spelling traditions thus reflects more properly and more accurately the lengthening of the vowel(s) in open syllables than the change of old /a:/ to /ɔ:/. As for the phonological explanation one can dismiss the theory that 'a "hole in the pattern" existed already in the twelfth century for non-abrupt /a:/' (Plotkin 1972: 61). As long as there were no contrastive pairs made up of /a:/ from lengthening and /a/, which was not the case until final unstressed /ə/ was given up, on the lexical level, the latter could function as the contrastive item to old /a:/, no matter what the respective phonetic values or spellings were like. This implies, furthermore, that there is no need for a chronological order of the two changes since they moved in tandem, and it was rather the new [a:] from lengthening that propelled old [a:] in the direction of [ɔ:] in the South.

5.1. No more than two centuries elapsed before restructuring set in again in the English long vowel system. This time the whole system of English long vowels was set in motion, which justifies the name given to that phenomenon: the Great Vowel Shift. Two questions are of interest at this stage:

1. Since within the first step of the GVS it was phonetically impossible for any vowel affected to enter the position of ME /a:/, how did the system behave?
2. Despite the coherence of the change it was related to a chronological aspect. In other words, where did the movement start and in what order did it proceed? (This has frequently been discussed resulting in the well-known 'pull-chain' and 'push-chain' theories.)

The answer to both questions has a significant bearing on the issue here discussed. I propose to look for an answer within the theoretical framework of sound changes put forward by Martinet (1955). In a paraphrase of Lass (1976:60) this means:

> Every dissolution of the pre-established equilibrium prompts a re-equilibration, and the re-equilibrations do not cycle back to the antecedent condition proper, but to another, similar "point of rest"... The forces prompting re-equilibrations are "imminent", but the defining conditions for particular equilibria are "configurational".

Let us now turn our attention to the conditions prevailing at the time when the GVS began to operate. It has become customary to discuss the GVS together with the surface evidence one can glean from John Hart (1569) since he is the first orthoepist whose description of the long vowels does not present major difficulties. If we compare the late ME system of long vowels to the phonetic values they are given by Hart we get the following correspondences (cf. Wolfe 1972: 33−7 and Lass 1976: 86ff):

Me	Hart	Me	Hart
i:	ei	u:	ou
e:	i:	o:	u:
ɛ:	e:	ɔ:	o:
a:	a:		

The analysis of the comparative data signifies that by 1569: 1. the ME high vowels had been diphthongized 2. the close vowels /e:/ and /o:/ had been shifted to /i:/ and /u:/, and 3. open /ɛ:/ and /ɔ:/ had been raised to /e:/ and /o:/ respectively. But, as for the seventh vowel making up the set of participants in the GVS, Hart does *not* show any raising of ME /a:/. *Its* value remained the same through the late 16th century. This has often been overlooked but it is crucial to any interpretation. It not only shows where the shift did *not* start but also, in my opinion, that /a:/ had been retarded and kept in its position by *the system as such*, because otherwise an intolerable vacancy would have been created for which there was no substitute readily available.

5.2. In the last stage I will have to examine how ME /a:/ eventually was raised and how and when /a:/ was re-introduced especially so as to yield phonemic opposition to /a/.

A few general considerations are appropriate at this point. I have dedicated relatively more space to problems related to the GVS and its aftermath. This is justified not only because this change was more important than the previous ones but also because there is more detailed and datable material available at this stage, which allows us to argue more convincingly for the interrelationship of certain sound changes. In addition, evidence from EModE orthoepists permits us on the one hand to support our reasoning by phonetic data and on the other hand to more strictly separate phonetic from phonological aspects. I will resume my discussion by focusing on such phonetic aspects.

The old /a:/ vs. /a/ opposition operated on a phonetic level that can be described as +long+front+raised vs. +short+front (with raised probably being optional).[8] It was at this stage that a *phonetic* [a:], at first probably front, later on a retracted [ɑ:], developed from different sources, the most important from the point of view of StE RP being the lengthening of the vowel before the voiceless fricatives /f, s, θ/ and in certain nasal environments like /ns/, /nt/, and /mpl/, which can be dated in the mid-to-late 17th century (Lass 1976: 115; Dobson 1957: vol. II, 525).[9] This vowel, however, was an allophonic variant of /a/, its occurrence being regulated distributionally, i.e. restricted to the phonetic neighbourhood mentioned above, so that no minimal pairs resulted from it. In another phonetic environment (on a different level) /a/ developed an allophonic variant before /r/. We depend on this constellation for our new phonemic opposition. We know that the vowel was lengthened in this position, too, most certainly even earlier than before /f, s, θ/ etc.[10] The loss of the liquid /r/, however, is not recorded in the material covered by Dobson.[11] But without it, it would seem, we do not get phonological (only phonetic) opposition of [a] and [a:].

Is it true then that a lexical opposition at the level of the lowest vowel was not re-established until the loss of /r/ led to minimal pairs of the type 'at' vs. 'art' with their phonetic realisations in RP of [æ] and [ɑ:]? If so, English would have remained without that opposition for more than a century or 3 generations (post-Hart until 1700+). I would dismiss this possibility as hardly likely.

The clue to the solution is that there is in discussions of phonological matters a heavy bias in favour of spelling-oriented approaches, which

---

[8] For the long vowel the markers can be deduced from the fact that it joined the front vowels in the GVS. For the short vowel see the discussion in Lass (1976: 105ff).

[9] Occasional earlier [a:] from other sources (Dobson 1957:606 - 10) seems to have been restricted to dialects other than RP since not in a single instance did a merger with old, i.e. ME /a:/ take place in the ancestor of RP.

[10] Dobson (1957:517 - 9) cites Bullokar ca 1580, though in addition to being a vulgarism it seems to have been restricted at first to the position before some consonant groups which had already caused lengthening in OE. Daines (1640) was the first to show it extended to all cases of /r/ plus consonant. Before voiceless spirants, on the other hand, lengthening is not recorded until the end of the 17th century (Cooper, 1685) (Dobson 1957: 525 - 7). Prins (1972: 156f), without evidence from orthoepists, postulates /a : r/ < LME /ar/ < ME /er/ for the 15th century. On the other hand, the end of the 18th century as the date for the general spread of /a:/ in this position would seem to be too late, however. Prins also does not always distinguish clearly enough regular sound changes from isolated or assimilatory instances.

[11] Dobson (1957:992) dates the loss of /r/ not much before ca. 1800.

means that we are liable to arrive at naive notions of what phonetic systems and, for that matter, phonological correspondences at earlier stages of the language really were like (cf. Lass 1975:202).

In our case, assuming the most favourable circumstances, the time-span between the disappearance of ME /a:/ and its re-entering the system from lengthening before certain consonants or groups of consonants can certainly be narrowed to an extremely brief period, maybe even eliminated, since it is probable that the same set of speakers raised the old vowel, simultaneously drawing on a new source for its re-introduction, but only on the phonetic level. The decisive argument for phonological continuity is that EModE [ar] and [a] must be viewed as phonetically independent members of *one contrasting set* regardless of their phonetic realisation or etymology.[12] Thus, and only thus, phonological contrastiveness and at the same time continuity were guaranteed.[13]

This entailed the re-distribution of phonemes. Old oppositions of /a:/ and /a/ in pairs like *bake* ≠ *back* were replaced by *back* ≠ *bark*, whereas *bake* now became opposed to *beck*, as old /a:/, phonetically now [æ:], continued to move on via [ɛ:] to [e:].[14]

6. Reverting now to Martinet, we can put our findings in a more general perspective by stating that: the dissolution of the equilibrium of the pre-GVS-era called for a re-equilibration. The forces of the new balance were imminent as were the configurations. The defining conditions, though, for the eventual re-introduction of the phoneme /a:/ may have evolved somewhat surprisingly.

On the basis of this result it is now safe to add as a conclusion that there has not been so far a typological change in RP of the kind it occurred e. g. in Scots after the operation of 'Aitken's Law', which leaves Scots without phonemic length though with quantity predictable on the surface level (Aitken, 1962). Such a transition can still be ruled out for

---

[12] It would be interesting to speculate whether /e/+/r/ > /ar/ got under way because it was to become a precondition for the evolvement of the new phoneme /a:/.

[13] By the same token /a:/ < /al/ came into opposition with /a/. (I have, however, excluded /a:/ from ME /al/ since no clear cut development seems to be traceable. In ModE RP we have pronunciations presupposing ME /au/ > /ɔ:/ with loss of /l/ as well as those yielding /a:/ without loss of the consonant.) It must be stressed, however, that this does not apply to /a:/ < /a/ plus voiceless fricative. No minimal pairs resulted from this change.

[14] The subsequent loss of /r/ and, less regularly, /l/ can be seen as a stabilizing factor in this chain of developments.

RP. I do not even think that the assumption is justified that there has been so much as a *tendency* in English, to dephonologise the correlation of quantity, (Trnka 1982: 261), or, in the words of Martinet (1955:248) that there was a shift towards 'l'élimination du trait phonologique de quantité vocalique'.

The existence of an opposition /a:/ vs. /a/, which entails the existence of vowel length as a distinctive feature, can be taken to be a characteristic feature of the standard English (RP) sound system, independent of synchronic variants.

REFERENCES

Aitken, A. J. 1962. *Vowel length in modern Scots*. Edinburgh: University of Edinburgh, Department of English Language.

Burgschmidt, E. & D. Götz. 1974. *Kontrastive Linguistik. Deutsch/englisch*. Hueber Hochschulreihe, 23. München: Hueber.

Campbell, A. 1974. *Old English grammar*, repr. from corrected 1st ed. Oxford: Oxford University Press.

Chomsky, N. & M. Halle. 1968. *The sound pattern of English*. New York: Harper & Row.

Dobson, E. J. 1957. *English pronunciation 1500 - 1700*: 2 vols. London: Oxford University Press.

Fisiak, J. 1980. 'The contrastive analysis of phonological systems', *Theoretical issues in contrastive linguistics*. Amsterdam studies in the theory and history of linguistic science, IV. Current issues in linguistic theory, vol. 12, edited by J. Fisiak, 215 - 24. Amsterdam: John Benjamins.

Gimson, A. C. 1970. *An introduction to the pronunciation of English*. 2nd ed. London: Arnold.

Görlach, M. 1978. *Einführung ins Frühneuenglische*. UTB 820. Heidelberg: Quelle & Meyer.

Hart, J. 1569. *An orthographie, conteyning the due order and reason, howe to paint thimage of mannes voice, most like to the life of nature*. Facsimile reprint 1969. Menston: Scholar Press.

Krahe, H. & W. Meid. 1969. *Germanische Sprachwissenschaft*. I *Einleitung und Lautlehre*. Sammlung Göschen, 238, 238a, b. Berlin: de Gruyter & Co.

Lass, R. & J. M. Anderson. 1975. *Old English phonology*. Cambridge: Cambridge University Press.

Lass, R. 1976. *English phonology and phonological theory. Synchronic and diachronic studies*. Cambridge: Cambridge University Press.

1980. *On explaining language change*. Cambridge studies in linguistics, 27. Cambridge: Cambridge University Press.

Martinet, A. 1955. *Economie des changements phonétiques*. Bern: Francke.

Penzl, H. 1969. 'The evidence of phonemic change', *Approaches to English historical linguistics. An anthology*, ed. by R. Lass, 10 - 24. New York: Holt.

Plotkin, V. Y. 1972. *The dynamics of the English phonological system*. The Hague/Paris: Mouton.

Prins, A. A. 1972. *A history of English phonemes*. Leiden: Leiden University Press.
Trager, G. L. & H. L. Smith. 1951. *An outline of English structure*. Studies in linguistics, occasional papers, 3. Norman, Oklahoma: Battenburg Press.
Trnka, B. 1966. *A phonological analysis of present-day Standard English*. Rev. ed. Tokyo: Hokuou Publishing Co.
— 1982. *Selected papers in structural linguistics*, ed. by V. Fried. Janua Linguarum, Series Minor, 88. Berlin/New York/Amsterdam: Mouton.
Weinstock, H. 1976. 'The aims, problems, and value of *A dictionary of early modern English pronunciation 1500 - 1800*', *DEMEP English pronunciation 1500 - 1800. Report based on the DEMEP SYMPOSIUM and EDITORIAL MEETING at EDINBURGH 23 - 26 October 1974*. 8 - 39. Stockholm: Almquist & Wiksell.
Wolfe, P. M. 1972. *Linguistic change and the Great Vowel Shift in English*. Berkeley & Los Angeles: University of California Press.

FRAMING THE LINGUISTIC ACTION SCENE IN OLD AND PRESENT-DAY ENGLISH: OE *CWEÞAN, SECGAN, SP(R)ECAN* AND PRESENT-DAY ENGLISH *SPEAK, TALK, SAY* AND *TELL* COMPARED

LOUIS GOOSSENS

0.1. This paper intends to offer a comparison of the ways in which four present-day English and three Old English verbs frame the linguistic action scene. On the one hand *speak, talk, say* and *tell*; on the other *sp(r)ecan, secgan* and *cweþan*. The original idea was to include OE *tellan* as well, but since its use as a LAV (linguistic action verb) turned out to be marginal in Old English, there appeared to be no point in considering it in a comparative study between high frequency LAVs.[1]

0.2. As the title suggests, the approach is, at least partially, of Fillmorean inspiration. More particularly, it relies on methodological insights gathered in a collective, corpus-based study of the four present-day Eng. verbs which has recently come out in the series Pragmatics and Beyond.[2] In outline, the methodology is as follows. The framing contribution of a given verb is established by studying the syntactic combinations into which the verbs enter and by characterizing the nuclear, semi-nuclear and non-nuclear constituents in terms of the roles which play a part in

---

[1] The frequency in Michael West (1953) for *speak, talk, say* and *tell* is: 1,860, 1,001, 12,278 and 3,550 respectively. The frequency of the OE items in the Toronto Microfiche Concordance to Old English (rough estimate) is: 15,000 for *cweþan*, 5,000 for *secgan* and 2,500 for *sp(r)ecan* (not including any prefixed forms). *Tellan* has less than 250 occurrences, of which only a small minority express linguistic action.

[2] R. Dirven, L. Goossens, Y. Putseys, E. Vorlat (1982). The actual publication date was late October 1983.

the linguistic action scene.[3] The frequency with which a particular role is actualized is equally important (his is why corpus work is an essential ingredient of the methodology). A detailed study of this kind on *speak*, *talk*, *say* and *tell* helped to lay bare the more refined conceptual structurings of the linguistic action scene as framed by these verbs and has given us a deeper insight into the global contribution which our four verbs make to the framing of linguistic action. It is these insights which, I hope, will give us a better undertsanding of *cweþan*, *secgan* and *sp(r)ecan* and of both the similarities and differences between the Present-day and OE counterparts.

0.3. The data for the OE verbs come from three sources. First, I have taken random samplings of 100 instances each from the *Toronto Microfiche Concordance to Old English* for each of the three verbs. Such a 100-instance sample gives a basic insight into the prototypical semantic structure of a verb, but it has to be confronted with other data to check its representativeness. At this point a recent study by Michiko Ogura, *The Syntactic and Semantic Rivalry of QUOTH, SAY and TELL* (Ogura 1981), proved to be a rich supplementary source; it contains a wealth of statistics on the syntactic ('functional' in her terminology) patternings of a considerable number of verbs of saying including the ones that interest us here. And although she does not proceed to a characterization in terms of semantic roles she provides enough data to permit an interpretation of my restricted samplings in the total context of OE *cweþan*, *secgan* and *sp(r)ecan*. My third source then are the entries in BTD/BTS, which, however, thanks to Ogura's study, I had to rely on only marginally.

0.4. The structure of my paper is as follows. In the first section I summarize from *Dirven, Goossens, Putseys, Vorlat* (1983) the framing contributions of Present-day Eng. *speak*, *talk*, *say* and *tell* to the LA-scene. At the same time I outline the conceptual differentiations of the semantic roles that proved to be important in this characterization.

The second section is concerned with the OE data. It includes a justification for selecting (only) *cweþan*, *secgan* and *sp(r)ecan* as counterparts

---

[3] By nuclear constituents we mean *subjects* and *direct objects*; non-nuclear constituents are as a rule prepositional phrases. Semi-nuclear are those prepositional phrases that can be passivized upon. I regard the prepositionless IO in *Tell him that I'm ready* and a simple dative IO in Old English as nuclear.

for the Present-day items (2.1); a presentation and discussion of the three samples from the Toronto Concordance (2.2); an assessment of their representativeness on the basis of BTD/BTS and, especially, Ogura (1981) (2.3); finally an attempt at characterizing the framing contributions of *cweþan*, *secgan* and *sp(r)ecan*. In conclusion, the third section contrasts the verbs under scrutiny and sums up the results of my paper.

1. In order to summarize our findings on the contemporary verbs, I proceed stepwise, characterizing for each verb what roles are frequently actualized by, successively, the active subject (1.1), the direct object (1.2), the nuclear indirect object (1.3), a variety of prepositional phrases (1.4). Adding a number of supplementary observations, I round off with a general characterization of the four verbs in 1.5.

TABLE I: Direct Object Table for *speak, talk, say, tell*

Syntactic/Semantic Characterization	SPEAK	TALK	SAY	TELL
A. The direct object represents the message (utterance) 'described' by the LAV				
1. Direct speech/ DIRECT ENUNCIATION	−	−	+ +	(+)
2. Indirect speech *that*-cl.|INDIRECT	−	−	+ +	+ +
to-inf.|ENUNCIATION	−	−	(+)	+ +
3. *Wh* (*how-*...)-clause/OBLIQUE (CONDENSED) MESSAGE	−	−	+	+ +
4. NP (non-clausal)/CONTENT IDENTIFICATION	+	?	−	+
5. NP/PRONOUNCEABLE ENTITY	+	−	+	−
6. NP/RECITABLE ENTITY	+	−	+	−
7. NP (mainly)/NARRATABLE ENTITY	−	−	−	+
8. NP/QUALITATIVE EVALUATION	+	+	(+)	+
9. NP QUANTIFIED RESPRESENTATION	+	+	+	+
10. NP/TOPIC	−	(+)	(+)	−
B. The direct object represents the code				
1. NP (non-clausal)/CODE	+	(+)	−	−

1.1 For the **active subject** we can generalize over the four verbs. It prototypically harbours the **speaker** (occasionally the **writer**). *Talk* (but not the other verbs) frequently has the role we termed **sender-interactor** (in the more abstract linguistic action schema we adopted), i.e. the speaker is conceived as being essentially involved in linguistic **inter**action, alternating the roles of speaker and **addressee** (as in *we sat down and talked*). The use of a **textual conveyor** (as in *The letter said he had been dismissed*) is markedly more current with *say* and *tell* than with *speak* and *talk*, but even so infrequent.

1.2 The characterization of the **direct object** is the main key to the differentiation between the four verbs. Table I lists the different types of direct objects that can relevantly be distinguished and indicates whether they occur with the verbs under discussion. We adopt the following symbols to indicate frequency:

++ typical and frequent
+ typical but no so frequent in our corpus
(+) possible but rare (or absent) in corpus
? doubtful
− impossible

Examples (for ++ and + only)

A. 1. ++ Just say loudly: "*I'm going to tell the housemaster*".
2. ++ You said just now *that you loved me*.
++ You tell me *this is all lies*.
++ I told him *to do it*.
3. + You did say *when we left Dobson's*.
++ I'll tell you *what you are thinking*.
4. + Speak *your minds* to us.
+ Let Mary tell you *the news*.
5. + Don't speak *Che Guevara's name*.
+ George, who sould be saying *half the speech*.
6. + She spoke *the woman's part*.
+ Would you like me to say *a prayer* now?
7. + I'm going to tell you *a little story*.
8. + He spoke *the truth*.
+ Don't talk *such bloody baloney*.
(+) You didn't say *anything bad* (only in combination with quantification)
+ There was no need to tell Jennie *an outright lie*.

9. + He spoke *a few words*.
    + You mustn't talk *so much*.
    + Can I say *something*?
    + Now you'd better tell us *a bit* about yourself.
10. + If you want to talk *business or something* I can go upstairs.
B. 1. + They're learning to speak *middle class English*.

Without going into details we summarize the most important conclusions that can be derived from this direct object distribution.

— *Speak* and *talk* do not have any direct object which occurs with considerable frequency; on the whole they focus on the linguistic action itself, not on the message. They marginally permit introduction of highly condensed message forms as direct objects (**qualitative evaluation** or some **quantification** of the message). Moreover, *speak*, which can focus on the actual speech production, allows 'recitable' or 'pronounceable' objects or can have the **code** in direct object function. *Talk*, which is the most **topic**-prone of the four verbs, is the only verb that can have the **message topic** in direct object function (though the frequency of such objects is decidedly low).
— *Say* and *tell* do have message focus. However, *say* and not *tell* is to be used for **direct enunciation** (which hangs together with its possible focus on the formal aspects of the utterance/message 'described' by the LAV); *say* can be combined with all speech act types in direct speech, and (witness also its combination with 'recitable' or 'pronounceable' NP objects) can be used to draw attention to the sound properties of the linguistic action described. Alternatively, it can also focus on message content and condense the message into a *that*-clause, in which case it has to be statement-like (it does not, as a rule, permit a *to*-infinitive); further condensation is only marginally possible.

Tell, on the other hand, always focuses on message content, which it can condense as *that*-clause or *to*-infinitive (for 'directives' in *order--tell*), or even further in *wh*-clauses or in **content-identifying** NPs.

1.3 The only verb which permits the addressee in a nuclear indirect object function is, of course, *tell*: *tell* has specialized in addressee focus in present-day English (indeed *tell* showed up with a nuclear IO in nearly 97% of its uses as a LAV, which is even more than the frequency of the message/object). In other words, *tell* as a rule combines message focus with addressee focus (hence its paraphrasability as *inform* (or *order*)); only in its *narrate*-sense can it have mere message focus, the message then being viewed as a **narratable entity**.

1.4 Table II gives a survey of the main prepositional phrases, again with a characterization in terms of the semantic role they incorporate. For reasons of space I only list prepositional phrases which incorporate the topic on which the message bears and those that frame the addressee.

TABLE II: Prepositional phrases with *speak, talk, say, tell*

	SPEAK	TALK	SAY	TELL
A. Prepositional Phrases incorporating ADDRESSEE				
1. *to*-phrases	++	++	+	(+)
2. *with*-phrases	+	(+)	−	−
B. Prepositional Phrases incorporating TOPIC				
1. *about*-phrases	+	++	+	++
2. *of*-phrases	++	+	(+)	(+)
3. *on*-phrases	(+)	(+)	(+)	(+)

Examples (for ++ and + only)

A. 1. ++ Listen to me while I speak *to you*. (RECEPTOR)
  ++ So she always tells me, whenever I talk *to her*. (RECEPTOR-INTERACTOR)
  + I tried to talk *to him*, but he never said a word. (RECEPTOR)
  + I said *to the headmaster* 'Has he got a degree?' (RECEPTOR)
 2. + I must speak *with you* about the events leading to this decision. (RECEPTOR-INTERACTOR)

B. 1. + They spoke *about his funny behaviour at the festival*.
  ++ I thought we were talking *about the children*.
  + You said something *about staying to lunch*.
  ++ Alec wants to tell you *about Myriam*.
 2. ++ Why do you speak *of death*?
  + Let's choose executors and talk *of wills*.

What I want to stress in the first place, is that whatever comes in a prepositional phrase does not incorporate the role(s) on which a given verb primarily focuses. However, high frequency somehow reveals the importance of the role in question for the perspectivization on the LA scene that the given verb produces. In actual fact the + + for *to*-phrases with *speak* and *talk* corresponded to 168 on 580 instances (i.e. 28.97%) and 203 on 901 instances (i.e. 22.53%) respectively. What this amounts to is that *speak* and *talk* often draw the addressee into the perspective, but that this is by no means a prototypical feature. Probably more important is another fact (which is indicated by the specification between brackets after the examples to A1 under Table II), viz. that as a rule those *to*-phrases express an **interactor**-meaning with *talk*, whereas with *speak* they usually harbour a mere **receptor**. This is another confirmation that *talk* primarily focuses on the LA as discourse interaction, whereas with *speak* this does not belong to the prototypical meaning(s).[4]

With respect to the **topic** phrases we restrict ourselves to two observations. First, that they are a frequent, but again not a dominant, feature with *speak* and *talk*, where they can be regarded as minimal, non-focal representations of the message (with *talk* prepositional topic phrases of all kinds occur in 37.84% of the instances in the corpus; with *speak* there are topic-phrases in only 11.55% of the cases). Second, that they are again a frequent, but non-dominant, feature for *tell*, where they are often combined with some direct object expressing the message (note that they become an obligatory feature in the (rare) cases where *inform-tell* has no explicit expression of the message).

1.5 Let me round off with a general characterization of the four verbs, adding a number of additional observations for each of them (there is, of course, no attempt at exhaustiveness).

1.5.1 *Speak* is basically used to focus on the linguistic action itself, which as a rule is viewed as a unidirectional event from speaker to addressee. We can relevantly distinguish three (sub)frames, labelled *speak I*, *speak II* and *speak III* by Vorlat.

In *speak I* the emphasis is on using/uttering (vocalized) language. It can be used i.a. to focus on the speech faculty (*He can't speak any more*) and often combines with manner adverbials to highlight some aspect of the vocalization (*she spoke loudly*). In *speak II* (which is the

---

[4] For the *with*-phrases this was 2.07% for *speak* and 1.55% for *talk*. The fact that *with*-phrases are slightly more current with *speak* than for *talk* (whereas we see the inverse proportion for *to*-phrases) hangs together with the fact that *with* is an explicit marker of a receptor-interactor and hence of less use to *talk*, which, because of its discourse focus, gets receptor-interactor interpretations for the otherwise neutral *to*-phrases already.

most central use of *speak*) the focus is on establishing contact by means of (spoken) language; here we often find addressee-phrases which typically view the addressee as a mere receptor (though occasionally we get *with*-phrases which explicitly mark the addressee as a **receptor-interactor**). The message can be present in a topic-phrase (often in *of*-phrases which appear to represent the topic as merely mentioned). Occasionally the message can be framed as a direct object, but only with considerable condensation and some evaluation (as in *speak the truth*). It also permits the code in a nuclear function (in e.g. *speak French*). *Speak III* is concerned with establishing contact or putting meanings across to a sizable group. It typically combines with adverbials of place indicating the location of the speech event (*He spoke at a meeting in Rotterdam*). Generally *speak* focuses most on the linguistic action itself (it takes even less interest in the message than *talk*). In this respect it is more basic than any other LAV in Present-day English, which explains the unique status of the terms *speaker* and *speech*.

1.5.2 *Talk* is the verb to express linguistic **interaction**, to describe the discourse. Subjects are typically **sender-interactors** (in the same way as *to*-phrases normally harbour receptor-interactors). Correlating with the focus on the interactive process is the fact that *talk* is often accompanied by adverbials highlighting manner dimensions or psychological dimensions of the interaction (e.g. *talk freely, animatedly*). *Talk* does not frame the message as such; but often explicates the topic of the discourse which it describes (in a variety of prepositional phrases, as well as in (nuclear) direct object function, giving rise to a number of paraphrase possibilities such as *discuss, refer to,* or *mention*).

1.5.3 As will have emerged, *say* has greater and more exclusive message focus than any of the other three verbs (though there is, of course, also a clear message focus for *tell*). *Say* can focus on form as well as on content of the message, giving rise to a basic meaning '*utter* (focus on form) or *express* (focus more content-oriented) *something by means of language*'.

When it combines with direct speech all speech act types are possible; when the message is represented by a *that*-clause we only get indirect statements (hence the possible paraphrase with *state*). Correlating with its possible focus on form is the fact that phrases like *say your name* mean 'utter, pronounce your name' (not 'say what your name is') and that we can get a *recite, say aloud*-sense (as in *say prayers, say a speech*). Two more noteworthy facts about *say* are its frequent use as (semi-) performative verb (*It's totally wrong, I say*) and its use with an overtone of an opinion verb (in combination with *so* and *as*; or in the passive, where the **referential topic** is subjectivalized, the rest of the message appearing in the form of a *to*-infinitive).

1.5.4 The main point about *tell* is that in its by far predominant senses (*inform-/order-tell*) it combines focus on message with focus on addressee (only *narrate-tell*, which is highly infrequent, permits omission of the addressee, or its occurrence in a prepositional phrase).

The message appears as a rule with some degree of condensation and focus is on content, never on form. Indirect enunciations show three complementation types (*that*-clauses, *to*-infinitives, rarely indirect questions), *wh-/how*-condensations are considerably more frequent than after *say* and there are extreme condensations where *say* would be impossible (*tell someone the truth; she told me her age*). Topic representation by means of *about*-phrases and (less frequently) *of*-phrases can be regarded as further condensations of the message and (occasionally) as (partial) defocalizations from message focus. Notice that also *tell* occurs frequently in (semi-)performative uses.

2.1 Turning to OE *cweþan, secgan* and *sp(r)ecan*, let me first justify why I have selected only those three verbs as counterparts of the present-day ones.

Establishing rough equivalences, which obviously will have to be refined by what follows, we can equate *cweþan* with *say*, *secgan* with *tell* and *sp(r)ecan* with *speak*. *Tellan* hardly participates in the expression of the LA-scene in Old English, and to the extent that it does it is in its *narrate*-sense, which is more frequently expressed by other verbs in OE (i.a. *reccan*) (this is clearly demonstrated by statistical data in Ogura 1981).[5] With respect to the equivalence *say:cweþan* and *tell: secgan*, the overlap is only partial, but it will do as a first approach. Again I refer to Ogura. Having quoted Marckwardt in connection with the complementary distribution between MoE *say* and *tell*, she continues: "Needless to say, Marckwardt refers to Modern English uses of *say* and *tell*, but if one replaces *say* by *cweþan*, and *tell* by *secgan* in the above statement, it will be a satisfying explanation of the functions of these two OE verbs" (Ogura 1981: i).

As will apear from our investigation, the overlap between *sp(r)ecan*

---

[5] See esp. § 2.9 and tables 11 and 13.

and *speak* is also considerable enough to regard them as each other's (rough) counterparts. The main problem, therefore, seems to be the absence of a counterpart for *talk*. Indeed, *talk* does not come into use before eME (the first quotations for *talk* in the OED are from the thirteenth century), but moreover, there is not a single high frequency verb which perspectivizes the LA scene like *talk*: none of the 74 verbs considered by Ogura can be said to show considerable overlap with *talk*.[6] In actual fact, we shall find that *sp(r)ecan* to some extent shows overlap with it. More importantly, we have to conclude that the OE verbs of *speaking/saying* do not give the same weight to discourse focus in the way they frame the LA scene.[7]

2.2 Let's next turn to our samplings from the Toronto Concordance to Old English, which will give us a fair idea of the way in which *sp(r)ecan*, *cweþan* and *secgan* frame the LA scene.

2.2.1 A look at the first nuclear function, the (active) subject, does not reveal any striking differences with MoE. As a rule it incorporates the speaker (occasionally the writer) of the LA described. The two most important observations to be added concern the expression of the roles sender-interactor by *sp(r)ecan* and of the role textual conveyor.

In some 20 cases[8], the subject of *sp(r)ecan* harbours a sender-interactor (for the other cases with *sp(r)ecan* as well as all instances with *cweþan* and *secgan* it is a mere sender). We exemplify this in (1) and (2).

(1) Leofan men, we rædaþ on bocum þ æt for Adames godnesse... God hine gelogode on fruman in paradyso..., ðær he geseah Godes englas & wið spæc, & wið God sylfne he spæc (W Hom 15 11)

---

[6] For a list of those verbs (among which we find the prefixed derivatives from the high frequency verbs of Old English), see Ogura p. 15. As can be expected, only a few of them have high frequency.

[7] Notice that in our corpus the respective contributions for *speak*, *talk*, *say* and *tell* are 7.21%, 11.21%, 52.72% and 28.86%, whereas in Ogura's (extensive) OE corpus the proportions for *sp(r)ecan*, *cweþan* and *secgan* are 9.67%, 59.53% and 30.80%. Some allowance must be made, however, for the fact that our corpus is based on theatre language and will therefore be somewhat biased towards discourse focus. On the other hand, MoE still has other verbs which focus on the discourse for which there appear to be no counterparts in Old English (e.g. *converse*).

[8] There may be a few more, but in these cases the subject of sentences with *sp(r)ecan* could be interpreted either as a mere sender or as a sender-interactor as e.g. in: ...&þe heofenlice fæder ilome to him (sc. Abraham) spæc for his myclan leafan, ... (...ÆLet 4 (SigeweardB) 247) ('speke to him or spoke with him/talked to him').

(2) ... a eode dauid in to moyse & heo spæcen heom þa betweonon (LS 5 (Invent Cross Nap) 85)

The proportion is higher than for MoE *speak*, because of the absence of a separate counterpart for *talk* pointed out above. The few instances that we get of subjects incorporating the textual conveyor as in (3) all occur with *secgan* (4 times).

(3) Sum fugol is gehaten fenix on leden on arabiscre þeode æfre wuniende. Swiðe ænlic fugol swa swa us secgað bec (ÆCHom 1, 16 (App) 171.22)

Our samplings are too restricted to draw any farreaching conclusions from this, but it may suggest that *secgan*, but not *cweþan* and *sp(r)ecan*, favours this role in subject position (in MoE only *talk* and *speak* do not readily permit it).

2.2.2 Next I want to have a look at the other (i.e. the non-subject) constituents in my samples. I first present the syntactic data for the most important non-subject constituents for the three verbs together. In the following discussion I proceed to a characterization in terms of the semantic categories adopted for MoE in order to arrive at a (provisional) general characterization of my three verbs.

TABLE III: Non-Subject Constituents with *sp(r)ecan*, *cweþan*, *secgan*
Syntactic Characterization

A. Direct Object	SP(R)ECAN	CWEÞAN	SECGAN
1. Direct speech	8	47	18
2. *þæt*-clause	2	35	25
3. *Hu-/hw-/gyf*-clause	2	–	6
4. Accusative NP object	14	5	35
5. Accusative NP + semipredicative complement	–	8	–
6. Genitive NP Object	–	1	–
B. Indirect Obejct			
1. Dative IO	1	2	40
2. *To*-phrase (*to*+dative/dative+*to*)	26	18	–
3. Other prepositional IOs	16	–	1

C. Other Prepositional Phrases			
1. Topic phrases			
1a *be*-phrase	13	1	4
1b *ymbe*-phrase	4	–	1
1c *of*-phrase	1	–	–
1d *on*-phrase	–	–	2
(1e Genitive topic phrase; non-prepositional!)	–	1	2
2. Other prepositional phrases	3	3	3
D. Adverbials			
Manner adverbials (including *swa* (*swa*))	25	4	25

Note: Maximum = 100; in some cases more than one of these possibilities cooccur, though (with a few exceptions) not those under one capital letter.

Before I review these data for each individual verb successively, I want to emphasize that my observations are restricted in various ways. For one thing the samples only represent a tiny fraction of the OE verbs discussed; for another, Old English is not something monolithic, but stretches over several centuries and shows dialectal variation. That is why my generalizations will not make anything of minor details but will look at the broader features of each verb, and will be formulated so that they contradict in no way the more detailed analyses of the syntax of these verbs in Ogura 1981 which I will consider briefly in the next subsection.

2.2.2 (a) *Sp(r)ecan* is basically a one place predicate (i.e. a verb with only one nuclear constituent). The focus is on the verbal action, not on the message. Yet it allows some message focus as is revealed by the 26 instances which have message representation. Some of these can be brought in line with its general focus on the verbal action: the direct speech instances have in 7 cases out of 8 the support of an adverb of manner (*to him þus spræc:*; *freolice he spæc her and ful andrædlice:*; *be heom þus sprǣcon*: etc.), the only other case is (4), where it is already combined with an addressee-phrase.

(4) ... and Judas eft ða spræc to eallum his geferum, Beoð... (ÆLS (Maccabees) 339)

The two *þæt*-clauses are special in their own way: they both report a directive (as appears from the use of the subjunctive, see e.g. (5)). But, of course, this is only a marginal possibility for *sp(r)ecan*.

> (5) He spæcon to Pharaone, Egypta cyninge, þæt he lete faran Israhela folc of Egypta lande (Exod. 6.27).

The two instances under A 3 are different from those with *secgan* in that they border on indirect questions rather than what can be regarded as further message condensations on the scale away from direct speech; (6) is one of these instances.

> (6) Þa wurdon hig mid unwisdome gefyllede and spæcon betux him hwæt hig þam Hælende dydon (Lk (WSCp) 6.11).

It looks therefore as if *sp(r)ecan* marginally permits embedding of both directives and questions.

The accusative NP objects are more numerous and may therefore be more significant to understand the perspectivization contribution of *sp(r)ecan*. Besides pronouns, we mainly get (-)*word*(-) as an object, which appears to serve both as a means to refer to the message in terms of a countable linguistic entity and as a means to produce an evaluative condensation of it (e.g. (7)).

> (7) Ge firenfulle fremde wurdon, syððan hi on worlde wæron acende and heo on life lygeword spæcon (PPs 57.3).

There are, however, no instances which focus on the sound properties of the linguistic action.

Let's concern ourselves next with the indirect object instances. With indirect objects present in 43 instances, *sp(r)ecan* has a fair degree of addressee focus, but it must be emphasized that it does as a rule not permit the addressee to come in a nuclear function (cf. *secgan* in this respect, which does). Another point about addressee phrases is that they frequently refer to a receptor-interactor. Explicit instances in this respect are those with *betweonan*, *betwux* and the like (which occur as many as 7 times and which we have already illustrated in (7) and in (2)). Also those with *mid* appear to be explicit receptor-interactors (there is a single *ongean*-phrase, which is clearly not 'interactive'). As we have already hinted at, this hangs together with an increased contribution of *sp(r)ecan* to the framing of discourse focus. Let me point out, however, that this is only the case in a clear minority of the instances.

The 18 topic phrases are significant; without going into details, I note that together with the direct object instances they provide (some) message representation in 43 cases (there is only one instance in which they occur together). In comparison with the other two verbs *sp(r)ecan* comes out as the most topic-prone item, though topic expression appears to have increased as we proceed to Present-Day English. I add one more observation, which however cannot count as a generalization. The *be*-phrases harbour what we have called a **referential topic**; indeed, the only clear instance of a **propositional topic** (where some sort of message condensation is given) occurs with the only *of*-phrase in our material (quoted here as (8)).

(8) Hio spæcon þam gelomlice betweoxan heom of þises middeneardes forseowennesse and of manegra mihte gewilnunge... (LS 9 (Giles) 354).

This observation is in line with the fact that MoE *speak* has a preference for referential topics (the topic as merely 'mentioned', not 'discussed'). The difference is, however, that it is typically *of*-phrases in Present-day English that introduce referential topics (more elaborate topics usually get *about*).

The comparatively high number of manner adverbials, as I have pointed out already, confirms the focus on the verbal action itself (those occurring with *secgan* do not do so in the same way, the majority of the cases indeed have *swa(swa)*, which can partially be regarded as representing the message). Notice, however, that none of these adverbials unequivocally bears on sound properties of the LA reported. As a final point let me note the absence of instances with the code in a nuclear (direct object) function. But there is one instance where the code comes in a propositional *on*-phrase:

(9) ...þa spræcon hig eac on Ebreisc ... (Nic(A) 56).

Notice also that BTD has a number of instances where a dative/instrumental is used (both *wordum* and *reorde/gereordum*). It would appear from this that also in OE *sp(r)ecan* is the verb to focus on the code, be it that it cannot yet be 'promoted' to direct object function.

2.2.2. (b) Let's turn to *cweþan* next. Clearly *cweþan* has message focus: there are as many as 96 instances where we get a 'direct object' somehow representing the message; the only cases where there is no object are three combinations with *swa* (listed here as manner adverbials, but which can still be said to give a (condensed) representation of the message) and one combination with a genitive which we have listed as a topic phrase.

Among the cases listed as 'direct objects' those with an accusative NP and a semi-predicative complement have to be set apart; (10) is an example. They exemplify a (marginal) development, where *cweþan* reports

(10) Ða cwæð man Swegen eorl utlah ... (ChronE Plummer. 1048.66)

'declarations' (in the Searlian sense). Notice that the semi-predicative element does not agree in case with the direct object (*Swegen eorl* in (10)). It is indeed treated as if it were a direct quotation: in my opinion this enhances the (public) pronouncement character of these instances. As regards the other cases, we find a situation which largely parallels our findings for MoE *say*. Direct speech (47 instances), representing all types of speech acts, is the favoured territory of *cweþan*. As a rule (in 30 out of 45 cases) there is no other constituent going with it, so that it comes fully under focus. *þæt*-clauses come in a high proportion as well; they are typically indirect statements (there are no parallels for the two indirect-questionlike clauses noted for *sp(r)ecan*). A typical feature of Old English is, of course, the opposition indicative: subjunctive, in which the subjunctive is used to underscore the subjective character of the embedded clause (as in (11)) or to report a directive (as in (12))

(11) & se cyng cwæð eac, þæt man nanne ne sloge for læssan yrfe þonne XII pæning weorð ... (LawVIAs 12.3)

(12) ... & cwæð ðæt him wære leofre ðæt he ðæt/land/me/sealde ... (Ch 1445 (HarmD 18) 32)

(though the use of an obligational modal, especially some form of *sculan*, is more current — (13) is an instance of this).

(13) ... swa swa Salomon cwæð ðæt we sceoldon mid urum spedum urum saulum þa ecen gesælinesse begitan (Ch 333 (Rob 11) 7)

The great majority of my instances, however, have plain indicatives. Further, note the significant absence in my sample the *hu-/hw*-clause condensations that occur with *secgan*, and the low number of accusative NP objects. There is only once a pronominal representation of the message; in the other cases we find as direct objects:

— *curs* (where *cweþan* has the sense 'utter as an official pronouncement')

— *gemot* (*cweþan* = 'call (together)')
— *his cwide* ('his say')
— the last case has a compound of *cweðan* (*æfter cwæð* 'renounced')

Addressee phrases are an optional feature with *cweþan* (20/100 in our sample). Clearly *cweþan* has no special addressee focus. Note, moreover, that the addressee as a rule comes in a prepositional phrase (not in a more nuclear simple dative form).

By way of a final observation I want to draw the attention to both the virtual absence of topic phrases (which hangs together with *cweþan*'s message focus) and the absence of manner adverbials (excepting *swa*), which shows that *cweþan* does not focus on the verbal action itself.

2.2.2. (c) Finally, we consider the *secgan* sample. Clearly, this is also a verb which has message focus (all in all 84 instances with a direct object message). In comparison with *cweþan* the higher proportion of more condensed message representations strikes the eye: there are five *hu*-clause and one *swa*-clause condensations (we give one *hu*-clause as an example in (14)), the number of accusative NP objects

(14) We wyllað nu sæcgan be þam ungesæligum Cristes cwellerum, hu forcuðe hi ðohton, þa ða hi feoh sealdon ... (Æ HomM 5 (Ass6) 149)

is strikingly high, and there are as many as 19 instances where the message is represented by *swa* (*swa*), 16 of which have *swa* as the only message condensation (e.g. (15)).

(15) ... and him sylfum gaderiað swa swa us sæde se apostol paulus (ÆHom I, 17 (App) 178.21)

Notice also that, in the majority of cases, the direct speech instances come in combination with other message representations (especially with accusative objects, in relation to which the direct speech can be regarded as an 'expletive addition', as e.g. in (16); or with topic phrases), which correlates with the observation that

(16) þis ic sæde eow ær minre þrowunge: hit is nu gefylled be me (ÆHomI, 15 220.20 [Luke 24]) (in this instance *þis* is cataphoric)

direct speech is primarily (though not uniquely) *cweþan* territory. With respect to *þæt*-clauses the situation appears to be similar to those for *cweþan*. They are embedded statements with predominantly 'plain' indicative, but they also show a fair amount of subjunctives and clauses with *sculan* (seven and three respectively, on a total of 25). Embedded statements are therefore more or less equally divided over *cweþan* and *secgan*.

Of special interest are, of course, the high proportion of accusative objects. The majority (20 out of 35) are narratable or relatable objects (*tacen, swefn, godspel, bigspel* 'parable'- which occurs 5 times-, *geþohtas, wunder, guðgeðingu* 'battle' etc.), which give *secgan* a good deal of *narrate*-character. But there are also as many as eight pronominal objects (*þis, hit,* relatives), two instances with *word,* one with *þing*, one with *þanc* and three with the expression *soð secgan* ('speak, tell the truth'). At least some of these can be paraphrased by 'utter' ('and ne secgað us nenne þanc' and 'ymb hine ... lofsonga word, drihtne sædon').

The next important point about *secgan* is that it often has addressee focus as well (the addressee is conceived as a receptor, not as a receptor interactor. This appears both from the frequency with which the addressee occurs (41 times) and from the fact that the simple dative is the rule (which turns it into a nuclear function). On the whole, however, message focus is more striking than addressee focus, and there is nothing like the near-exclusiveness with which MoE *tell* brings in the addressee.

To round off this discussion let me draw the attention to the nine topic phrases, more current than with *cweþan*, but, as is to be expected, in no way a dominant feature. As a rule those topic phrases cooccur with some other message representation.

2.3 The confrontation of the foregoing analysis with BTD/BTS and with the wealth of material in Ogura will be brief. From BTD I want to signal a few supplementary senses and uses which I have either not pointed out explicitly or which are lacking in my material. I simply list them with minimal comment.

Sp(r)ecan
— BTD gives clear instances of *sp(r)ecan* 'exercise the faculty of speech', e.g.

(16) Dumbe *spræcon* (Mk. Skt. 7, 37)

— It lists a number of accusative objects which we do not get in our material and which characterize the nature of the message (*ræd* 'counsel', *bysmer* 'blasphemous language' etc.). For some of these a paraphrase with 'utter, pronounce' is possible.

— *Sp(r)ecan* is paraphrasable by 'mention' in:

(17) Of ðæm beorgan ðe we ær spræcon
(Ors. 1, 1; Bos. 17, 44)

— It has two embedded statement examples; (18) is one of them.

(18) Hie spræcon, ðæt hit betere wære (Ors. 2, 3; Sw. 68, 8)

— It lists technical senses for *sprecan æfter, on, ymb* ('sue for, make a claim against, lay a claim to')

Cweþan

— There are a few additional possibilities for accusative objects (*lofsang, word* and the pronominal items *hwæt, wiht*)

— We get a passive instance which can be rendered by 'be called':

(19) On ðære stowe ðe is cweden Ægeles þrep (Chr. 455; Erl. 13, 23; etc.)

— A phrase which is used with special discourse function is the combination cweðs ðu la = cwyst ðu la = '0?', 'sayest thou?' (Latin 'numquid?')

Secgan

— There is a context in which *secgan* is predicated over words and is paraphrasable as 'mean':

(20) Cantica cantorum, ðæt segþ on Englisc ealra sanga fyrmest (Ælfr. T. Grn. 7, 42)

— *Secgan* shares the pattern accusative object + semi-predicative adjunct with *cweþan*; note, however, that the syntactic integration is greater with *secgan* in that there is accusative agreement:

(21) Hie hine scyldigne sægdon (Blickl. Homl., 173, 33) ('declared him guilty')

— In the entry for *secgan* we also get the combination *secgan on* (w.acc. or dat.) meaning 'to ascribe to a person, lay to the charge of, accuse of, attribute to'.

Ogura (1981), as I said earlier, has ample statistical data which refine the restricted observations in my own sample. A full integration of these statistics is beyond the scope of this paper. Moreover, she does not give exhaustive exemplification, so that it is not possible to proceed directly to interpretations in terms of semantic roles. Let me restrict myself to the statement that her statistic material for *secgan* and *cweþan* covers i.a. the 'direct object' (differentiated into 'direct speech', 'indirect speech', 'indirect question', 'accusative', 'accusative + predic.'), 'dative' and 'to + dative-phrases' for important samples of OE poetry (with the surprising proportion 357 *cweþan* vs. 404 *secgan*)[9] and for OE prose (4777 *cweþan* vs. 2252 *secgan*)[10], and that nothing in her results affects fundamentally the observations that we have derived from our samples.

2.4 As the last step in this section I now proceed to a characterization of *sp(r)ecan*, *cweþan* and *secgan* successively.

2.4.1. The primary focus with *sp(r)ecan* is on the linguistic action itself: it reports the very fact that some speaker/speakers uses/use language (which in some contexts amounts to saying that they dispose of the capacity for speech). In a considerable number of cases (though not as a rule) it focuses on linguistic interaction, on the discourse; the speaker is then a sender-interactor, and the addressee (which is as a rule present then) a receptor-interactor. Another point is that manner adverbials can come in to characterize the LA described. *Sp(r)ecan* has a limited capacity for bringing in the message as well (as direct speech, *þæt*-clauses reporting a statement or a directive and even indirect questions, though for all of these *sp(r)ecan* is on the whole exceptional). Somewhat more current are condensations of the message in direct object function (and therefore in semantic focus), especially those that give some idea of the nature of the message. Sometimes those condensations are 'pronounceable entities'; as a result the focus of *sp(r)ecan* shifts to sound aspects of the LA described.

As was already suggested, the addressee is often drawn into the picture as well, with a variety of prepositional phrases (hence not in a nuclear syntactic function). Some of these prepositional phrases are uniquely or predominantly associated with the receptor-interactor role (*betweonan*;

---

[9] See Ogura, table 21, p. 57. Ogura suggests as a (plausible) explanation the greater usefulness of *secgan* in alliteration. It may also hang together with a movement away from the commoner word in poetic diction (which at the time was certainly *cweþan*).

[10] See Ogura 1981, tables 24 (p60) and 26 (p61).

mid), others are neutral in this respect (*to*; *wið*). Of the three OE verbs considered, *sp(r)ecan* is the one that most often draws in a topic phrase (but never in a nuclear function, and with a frequency that is still on the low side). Those topics are as a rule of the referential kind.

Sp(r)ecan is also the verb which can be used to focus on the code, though that role cannot come in a direct object function.

2.4.2. *Cweþan* has very outspokenly message focus. It is the favoured item to introduce direct enunciations (of all speech act types), even if those are not its exclusive territory. It is also very currently used to frame indirect enunciations, which have to take the form of indirect statements (when the subjunctive is used it emphasizes the subjective character of the reported statement or corresponds to an original directive; in the latter case we can also have a *þæt*-clause containing an obligational modal, especially *sculan*). Indirect questions are probably impossible with *cweþan*.

Further condensations of the message are not current. Some of the accusative NPs which it permits are correlatable with a sense 'utter', 'pronounce', pointing to a possible focus on publicly announced message types. There is also a marginal condensation pattern correlating with a sense 'declare', which is also connected with this public announcement dimension. Addressees with *cweþan* are an optional but not infrequent feature. Note that they are as a rule framed by prepositional phrases. Note also the rarity of topic phrases.

2.4.3. *Secgan* also has message focus, but preferably has the message in some form of condensation. This does not mean that direct speech is totally uncommon, but that mostly we get *þæt*-clauses which run parallel with those for *cweþan*, that *hu-/hw*-clauses (a further form of condensation) are possible, and that there is a high proportion of accusative NP objects.

Among those NP objects the ones representing the message as a narratable entity are strikingly frequent, hence a possible *narrate*-sense for *secgan* (also with less condensed message representations). A few accusative objects invite an *utter*-sense (hence *secgan* can marginally focus on sound aspects of the message). The other striking point about *secgan* is a marked but incomplete degree of addressee focus (their frequency is considerable, though not very high; and they are realized by a dative, not by a prepositional phrase). Topic phrases occur considerably more often than with *cweþan*, but not so often as with *sp(r)ecan*.

We also noted a possible preference for *secgan* when it comes to subjectivalizing textual conveyors.

3. In conclusion let me sum up contrastively how *sp(r)ecan*, *cweþan* and *secgan* compare with *speak*, *talk*, *say* and *tell*.
— The most striking difference is the absence in Old English of a high frequency verb that focuses on linguistic action as discourse. The contribution to discourse focus, it is true, appears to be greater for *sp(r)ecan* than for *speak*, yet *sp(r)ecan* is more like MoE *speak* than like *talk*.
— *Sp(r)ecan* is most like *speak*, because it also focuses primarily on the LA (and possibly the speech faculty as such). It often draws in the addressee, and, less frequently, the message, especially in the form of an object NP characterizing the nature of the message, or in a topic phrase. Sometimes *sp(r)ecan* and *speak* take pronounceable entities as their objects. They can both be used to draw the code into the perspective.

There are, however, differences. *Sp(r)ecan* (still) marginally allows less condensed message representations, including direct enunciations. It is also more discourse oriented, as was pointed out above, which affects the interpretation of both subjects and addressee phrases. *Speak*, but not *sp(r)ecan* allows the code in a (nuclear) direct object function. Finally, there appears to be no real parallel in Old English for *speak* III (which emphasizes public use of language in front of a sizable group), though, of course, the sense is not incompatible with *sp(r)ecan*; on the other hand, there are one or two marginal meanings for *sp(r)ecan* which are not parallelled by *speak*.
— In the pairs with message focus *cweþan* is more like *say* and *secgan* like *tell*. *Cweþan*, like *say*, is most outspoken in its message focus, and has direct enunciation objects as its favoured territory; it easily takes embedded statement clauses, but not more condensed message forms. It can optionally be combined with addressee phrases, and rarely with topic phrases. *Secgan*, like *tell*, also has message focus but takes more condensed message forms than *cweþan*; it easily takes narratable entities as its object, which correlates with a *narrate*-sense. Moreover, it is the item in Old English that comes closest to having addressee focus (it is the only verb of the three that has it in a simple dative). As far as topic phrases are concerned, they are an optional feature for both *secgan* and *tell*. On the other hand, there are noteworthy differences. Direct speech is not in the same way the near-exclusive territory of *cweþan* as it is for *say*. As regards *secgan*, it does not nearly combine message and addressee in over 90% of its uses like *tell*; hence there is no room for

an *'inform'-secgan* parallelling *inform-tell*. Moreover, *secgan* embeds directives only as statements, there is therefore nothing like *'order'-secgan*. Finally there are, of course, a number of minor uses not shared by the so-called pairs.

Summing up, whereas MoE has among its high frequency verbs an item which has 'linguistic action as discourse' as its specific focus (*talk*), a second one which is virtually uniquely associated with direct speech message focus (*say*), and a third one which centrally combines addressee and (condensed) message focus (*tell*), there are no items in Old English with the same specificity.

This absence may at least partially explain why such important changes have occurred in the field of English LAVs (the introduction of *talk*, the wide ranging expansion of *tell*, and the important shift in the framing contribution for *say*). Why *cweþan* was lost is another story which I don't want to go into here, but as Ogura suggests it certainly hangs together with a considerable degree of 'functional overlap' in Old English.

In this context the relative stability of *sp(r)ecan-speak* may after all be the most striking fact.

REFERENCES

Bosworth, J. and T. N. Toller. 1898. *An Anglo-Saxon dictionary*. Oxford: University Press (=BTD).

Dirven, R., L. Goossens, Y. Putseys and E. Vorlat. 1982. *The scene of linguistic action and its perspectivization by speak, talk, say and tell*. (Pragmatics and beyond III: 6) Amsterdam: Benjamins.

Fillmore, C. J. 1977. "The case for case reopened". *Grammatical relations*. Edited by P. Cole and J. Sadock (Syntax and semantics, vol. 8.), 59 - 81. New York: Academic Press.

1977b. "Topics in lexical semantics". *Current issues in linguistic theory*. Edited by R. W. Cole. 76 - 138. Bloomington and London: Indiana University Press.

A microfiche concordance to Old English. Compiled by Antonette Di Paolo Healey and Richard L. Venezky. Toronto: The Dictionary of Old English Project, Centre for Medieval Studies, University of Toronto, 1980.

Ogura, M. 1981. *The syntactic and semantic rivalry of quoth, say and tell in Medieval English*. Hir akata City: Kufs Publication, Kansai University of Foreign Studies.

Toller, T. N. 1921. *An Anglo-Saxon dictionary. Supplement*. Oxford: University Press (=BT S).

West, M. 195 3. *A general service list of English words with semantic frequencies and a supple mentary word-list for the writing of popular science and technology*. London: Longman.

LEXICAL RESTRUCTURING: RULE LOSS VERSUS RULE INTERSECTION; EVIDENCE FROM ITALIAN

RITA DE GRANDIS

I INTRODUCTION

In Italian, the majority of verbs take an -o ending in the 1 st. person singular of the Present Indicative

E.g.; (1) *léggo+o* [léggo] "I read"
        dic+o   [díko] "I say"

However, there is a small group of verbs -the so-called irregular verbs- that present the following characteristics:
1. verbs with 1 st. person singular (Present Indicative) -yo ending at t_1, that is, in Old Italian, and the same -yo ending at t_2, that is, in Modern Italian.
    E.g.; (2) t_1 and t_2 (Old and Modern Italian)

    piak+yo [pyáčco] "I like"
    cuok+yo [kuóčco] "I cook"
    cuk+yo [kúčo]   "I sew"
    tak+yo   [táčco]   "I am silent"
    giak+yo [ğáčco]   "I lie"

2. verbs with 1 st. person singular (Present Indicative) -yo ending at t_1, but an -o ending at t_2.
    E.g.; (3) a-t_1-(Old Italian)
    tem+yo [témyo]   "I fear"
    dorm+yo [dórmyo] "I sleep"
    fug+yo   [fúğo]   "I run away"
    (3)b-t_2-(Modern Italian)
    tem+o   [témo]
    dorm+o [dórmo]
    fug+o   [fúggo]

3. verbs that constitute a very small group, and that present the same alternation as group (3). The particularity of this rather small group is that the -*yo* ending in Old Italian appears in a *non-contracted*, and the -*o* ending, in Modern Italian, appears in a *contracted* form E.g.; (4)a-t_1-(Old Italian) non-contracted forms

sap+yo [sáččo] "I know" (Old Tuscan)
(cf. Jensen, 1971: 47)
ab+yo [áǧǧo] "I have" (Old Tuscan)
(cf. Jensen, 1971: 42)
fak+yo [fáččo] "I make"
(4)b-t_2-(Modern Italian) contracted forms
s+o [so]
h+o [o]
f+o [fo] (Literary form)

In this paper I will study the alternation between the -*yo* ending and the -*o* ending in the 1 st. person singular (Present Indicative) in the groups mentioned above.

In order to account for the alternation between the -*yo* and the -*o* endings two approaches could be taken into consideration. Firstly, such an alternation is explained in classical historical linguistics as a change from one class of verbs, that is, the -*yo* class, into another class, the -*o* class (Meyer-Lübke 1955, Tekavčič 1972). Secondly, in generative phonology, it has been generally assumed that diachronic phonological changes could be described synchronically, within an ordered hypothesis. In this paper, I will show the inadequacies of a synchronic analysis such as the one supported by these hypotheses. I will argue for a third approach, which I call following Wang 1969, the rule intersection and lexical diffusion hypotheses. I will show the superiority of these notions over the rule addition and rule loss notions.

Section 2 of this paper consists of an analysis and critique of the rule addition and rule loss hypotheses. In section 3, I present an analysis that provides evidence in favour of the rule intersection and lexical diffusion hypotheses.

II. RULE ADDITION AND LOSS HYPOTHESES

According to the rule addition and loss hypotheses, changes in grammar can be regarded as changes *in rules*. A change in rules could manifest itself as the placement of a new rule in the grammar, that is, as *rule addition* (King, 1973) or, as the disappearence of a rule from the grammar, that is, as *rule loss* (King, 1969. page 46—49). Rule addition occurs when the phonological component contains a rule that it did not contain before and, rule loss when a phonological rule disappears from the grammar.

The alternation between the *-yo* and *-o* endings in the 1 st. person singular (Present Indicative) could be handled by means of these notions. Under the rule addition hypothesis, the grammar, as a synchronic model, adds a new rule, which must be ordered at the end of the phonological rules, but prior to the low level phonetic rules (King, 1973). Thus the phonological rule (1) is added, which applies in a lexically specified class of verbs:

(1) $\begin{Bmatrix} \check{e} \\ i \end{Bmatrix} \rightarrow y/\_\_\_+V$

E.g.; /piakĕ+o/ "I like" /piakyo/ [pyáčco]

    [+rule(l)]
    /dormi+o/ "I sleep" /dormyo/ [dórmyo]
    [+rule(l)]

Notice that rule (1) will account for the *-yo* ending in:

    piakyo[piáčco] (group 2))
    *temyo [témyo] (group 3.a)
    *sapyo [sáčco] (group 4.a)

but it will not account for the failure of the *-yo* ending in:

    temo [témo] (group 3b.)
    so   [só]   (group 4b.)

Diachronically, verbs that took the *-yo* ending at t_1 (Old Italian), lost the *-yo* ending at t_2 (Modern Italian). This is the case for the forms studied here. So, a question arises: How would the hypotheses at work explain this fact? In order to account for the failure of the *-yo* ending in groups 3b. and 4b. at t_2, that is, in Modern Italian, the rule loss hypothesis claims that therefore, the alternation between the *-yo* and *-o* is lost.

Note that sound changes such as rule loss type of change seem to obey general principles on paradigm conditions. Kiparsky in 'Historical Linguistics' (1968), studies different types of sound change and, considers that rule loss represents an extreme case of simplification of the grammar. Moreover, he proposes a principle governing paradigm conditions that reads as follows: (b) Allomorphy tends to be minimized in a paradigm. So, on the assumption that this principle is valid, one could say that in the verb morphology of Italian, there is a strong tendency to regularize two morphological classes into one class, that is, the *-yo* and the *-o* forms are regularized into the *-o* form for the 1 st. person singular (Present Indicative). Thus, *temyo and *sappyo (groups 3a. and 4a.) are *-yo* verbs, which are reanalized as *-o* verbs. In addition, King, in 'Rule Insertion' (1973), in studying Kiparsky's paradigm conditions related to the order of phonological rules in a synchronic grammar, states that the order of rule application tends to go from a marked order to an unmarked one and, that such a tendency increases regularity at the surface level. Hence, the loss of rule (1) will support the unmarked order, whereas the *-yo* forms derived phonologically by means of rule (1) represent the marked order. Therefore, King's notion of rule application towards unmarkedness gives support to Kiparsky's principle on paradigm regularization.

Furthermore, to claim that rule (1) is rule loss requires evidence that rule (1) has lost its phonological environment and has become morphologized. In regard to this problem, Vennemann, in 'Phonetic Analogy and Conceptual Analogy' (1972), posits conditions under which a rule is considered rule loss. He states that a rule must be considered rule loss when the phonetic or phonological environment is no longer present and has been replaced by a morpho-syntactically conditioned environment. Moreover, morphologized rules arise from situationes where new rules have been added to the grammar. In accordance with this argument, rules that lose their phonological environment are morphologized rules and they are subject to loss. The loss of a morphonologized rule, therefore, increases paradigmatic regularization. Notice that this concept is closely related to Kiparsky's condition. Therefore, under Vennemann's notion of rule loss, the phonological rule (1) that explains the alternation between the *-yo* and the *-o* endings contains morphological information, that is, it applies in the 1 st. person singular and 3rd. person plural of the Present Indicative of a lexically specified class of verbs:

E.g.: *piaccio*   [pyáčo]   (1st. singular)
                                                          (group 2)
     piacciono [pyáččono] (3rd. plural)
       *temio   [témyo]   (1st. singular)
                                                          (group 3a.)

*temiono [témyono] (3rd. plural)
*sapio   [sáččo]   (1st. singular)
                            (group 4a.)
*sapiono [sáččono] (3rd. plural)

With this in mind, I reformulate rule (1) as follows:

(1) $\begin{Bmatrix} ĕ \\ i \end{Bmatrix} \rightarrow y / \underline{\quad} +V$
$\qquad\qquad\qquad +\text{verb}$
$\qquad\qquad\qquad +\text{present}$
$\qquad\qquad\qquad +\text{Indicative}$

Notice, however, that this morphologization condition imposed upon rule (1) needs further research in Italian. Observe, for example that rule (1) will be considered rule loss in groups (3b.) and (4b.):

E.g.; temo   [témo]   (1st. singular)
      temono [témono] (3rd. plural)   (group 3b.)
      so   [só]   (1st. singular)
      sonno   [sónno]   (3rd. plural)   (group 4b.)

but it will not be considered rule loss in groups 3b. and 4b. as shown above. This situation will give rise to the problem that the same rule will be marked as [+loss] and [−loss] in the same synchronic grammar as groups 2, 3b. and 4b. indicate. Furthermore, rule (1) seems to apply to other lexical categories such as nouns, where the rule has not become morphologized and, consequently, is not subject to loss.

E.g. braccio [bráččo] "arm"
     giovane [ǧóvane] "boy"
     viaggio [vyáǧǧo] "trip"

As we can see, the loss of a morphologized rule in a synchronic description seems to be a very special rule whose behaviour is highly idiosyncratic. In sum, I state that the phonological rule (1) has become morphologized. Therefore, the -yo forms that the present grammar of Italian contains show the presence of an ancestral rule, (rule (1)), which in turn has become morphologized when another rule, a rule of vowel contraction, has been added to the grammar as I will demonstrate later.

At this point, it is worthwhile considering that the rule addition and rule loss result in a restructuring process. According to these notions, with the addition and the loss of a rule a lexical item is restructured, that is, the underlying representations are restructured. "Restructuring takes place when previous changes have removed or attenuated the evidence for positing some rule or rules, so that the original underlying representations have become too abstract for the child to recover" (Sommerstein, 1977: 238).

The language acquisition hypothesis supports this lexical or phonological restructuring. Within this framework, the restructured underlying representations are organized in different autonomous synchronic grammars. To illustrate this argument, it is claimed that a child learning language will only have access to one underlying representation. For example, a child is capable of knowing either /temĕo/ or /temo/, but he is unaware that the form /temo/ comes from /temĕo/ at the underlying level of representation. Furthermore, although the rule addition and rule loss hypotheses incorporate diachronic change into a synchronic description, they organize the restructured levels into autonomous grammars that are not necessarily related to diachronic facts. According to this synchronic autonomy, the underlying form /temĕo/ which will yield /temyo/ by means of rule (1), will belong to grammar$_1$. Likewise, the loss of rule (1) will produce a restructure dunderlying form such as /tem+o/ which will, similarly, belong to grammar$_2$.

In spite of the fact that these two underlying representations are organized independently, into two different grammars, they are indeed related to two stages of the evolution of the language. Grammar$_1$ accounts for the -*yo* forms in Old Italian and, Grammar$_2$ accounts for the -*o* forms in Modern Italian. Notice, however, that a form such as *piakyo* [pyáččo] (group 2) contains the -*yo* ending in Old Italian, and in Modern Italian. This will show that rule (1) is still active in the domains of Grammar$_2$. On the contrary, forms such as *temo* and *so* (groups 3b. and 4b.) will show that rule (1) is lost. Then, how will a synchronic description handle these forms? Will it posit a feature [+rule(1)] for the forms that present the -*yo* ending at t_2, that is to say in Grammar$_2$?.

As we can see, despite the fact that the loss of rule (1) has erased the -*yo* ending at t_2 from groups 3b. and 4b., the -*yo* suffix has not been erased completely from all of the morphemes. Therefore, the rule loss hypothesis as applied to a synchronic description fails since the presence of the -*yo* forms in subsequent autonomous grammars leads to a very complex description, which is far from reaching generality and simplicity. The concept of morphologized rules is taken as valid and so the rule loss, however, their application to a synchronic framework results in a taxonomic device lacking in theoretical validity. The synchronic account of restructuring does not capture the nature of the development of the alternation between the *-yo* and *-o* endings in the lexicon. The use of rule addition and rule loss result in a contradiction. For example, a verb such as *piakyo* [pyáčč̌o] must be marked as still undergoing [+rule(l)] in Grammar₂ when all the other forms of Grammar₂ are marked as not undergoing [+rule(l)]. Therefore, we need an adequate hypothesis that will reflect the restructuring process arising from the alternation between the *-yo* and *-o* endings. I will now claim for a diachronic analysis in terms of rule intersection and lexical diffusion. This approach is not only more consistent with the known facts but also, and more importantly, it does not require the levels of restructuring organized in subsequent synchronic grammars.

III. RULE INTERSECTION AND LEXICAL DIFFUSION HYPOTHESES

It will be remembered that the rule addition and rule loss hypotheses as applied to a synchronic description do not explain in an adequate manner the restructuring process carried out in the lexicon. From the language acquisition point of view all that the morphologized rule (1) does is introduce a redundant alternation into the root, since a child learning language by not learning rule (1) restors the uniformity of the paradigm. *Temyo* symbolizes the *-yo* class and *temo* the *-o* class. What the child knows is a morphological class rather than a phonological rule being morphologized, and restructuring the underlying representations. Furthermore, despite the fact that a synchronic description such as this advocates for its independence from historical facts, Grammar₁ and Grammar₂ are directly related to Old and Modern Italian. Those items such as *piakyo* [pyáčč̌o] (group 2) that historically have not undergone the alternation described above, are marked diacritically as irregular with respect to **restructuring**.

The superiority of a third approach, in terms of the rule intersection and lexical diffusion hypotheses lie in the fact that items such as *piakyo* [pyáčč̌o] are not considered irregular. On the contrary, they have not been restructured because the loss of rule (1) does not affect all the items simultaneously but in a gradual manner. By using this approach, the forms that did not seem to have undergone restructuring are now regarded as *residues* of a restructuring process prevented from running its complete course. Therefore, what is described **synchronically** as irregular can now be explained diachronically more appropriately.

Within this framework, the alternation between the *-yo* and *-o* endings is explained in terms of a *rival rule*, that is, a rule that competes with another rule, which applies to the same set of morphemes. As mentioned, the rule addition hypothesis, considers that when a rule has been added to the grammar it will apply to all the items simultaneously. However, as the data illustrates in groups 2, 3b., and 4b., rule (1) has not affected all of the morphemes as expected.

According to the rule intersection and lexical diffusion notions, a phonological rule takes place in time and, rules could be added or lost from the grammar, as the rule addition and rule loss claim. However, when a rule is added to the grammar it does not apply simultaneously to all items but in a gradual manner, from item to item, until all the forms have been reached. In the period of operation of a rule, such a rule could be intersected by another rule that operates on the same morphemes. This *newer rule* will take the place of the previous rule, therefore, the prior rule was prevented from completing its action. When a situation as the one just described arises, *residues* might be left in the lexicon of a grammar, which in turn, eventually will disappear, when the newer rule will have completely applied. Under this diachronic approach, rule (1) is present in the grammar, and another rule, a rule of *vowel contraction*, takes its place:

(2) e+o
    i+o

According to Foley in, *Foundations of Theoretical Phonology* (1977) vowels tend to contract. The contraction of two elements depends on the similarity of the elements. Contraction is based on strength assuming that phonological segments are related by their inherent strength. The contraction of vowels is formalized in a *vowel parameter*, which is based on observation of phonological processes such as *elision*, *apocope*, *contraction* etc. Elision, for example, indicates relative phonological strength among vowels since weak elements drop before strong elements. Foley notes that in Spanish /e/ drops while /o/ remains in the plural formation of nouns.

E.g., *papel* "paper" from *papele
    papeles "papers"
    amigo "friend"
    amigos "friends"

Considering now the nasalization rule, the nasalized reflex represents a stronger vowel than the unnasalized etymon:
E.g., in French i+ẽ (cinq)

e+ã (cent)
u+õ (un)

Regarding the vowel system in Romance, Foley establishes the following relative phonological strength scale: *Romance parameter* i e u o a
$$\overset{\leftarrow}{1\ 2\ 3\ 4\ 5}$$
In the *Romance parameter*, *a* represents the strongest vowel with a numerical value assigned as 5 and, *i* represents the weakest vowel with 1 as numerical value. Furthermore, the Romance parameter is governed by parochial conditions, which are language specific and these parochail conditions establish that each language has a different strength hierarchy on which contraction is based. For example the parochial condition for the Latin Vowel Contraction Rule is $\gamma=1$, that is, identical vowels ($\gamma=0$) contract and vowels differing by only one unit, but not vowels differing by two or more units.

E.g., nihil   niil   nil ($\gamma=0$)
      amao   amo   ($\gamma=1$)
      moneo idem   ($\gamma=2$)
      audio   idem   ($\gamma=3$) (Foley: 79)

With regard to Italian, Foley states a parochial condition as $\gamma=3$, that is, not only a+o contract but e+o and i+o. E.g., *amicoi-i "friend" (singular) amici "friends" (pl.) The parochial condition established by Foley as $\gamma=3$ holds for Modern Italian. This degree of contraction represents a stage ahead in the parochial condition of the *Italian Vowel Contraction Rule*, since earlier stages of Italian had a parochial condition as $\gamma=2$. Forms such as *temyo and *sappyo (groups 3a. and 4a.) illustrate that in Old Italian the parochial condition was $\gamma=2$. By the same token, in Modern Italian, forms such as temo and so (groups 3b. and 4b.) demonstrate that the parochial condition is $\gamma=3$. Hence, the Italian Vowel Contraction Rule comes from the Latin Vowel Contraction Rule and, the parochial condition of the former has been relaxed from $\gamma=1$ (Latin) to $\gamma=2$ (Old Italian) and $\gamma=3$ (Modern Italian).

With this in mind, rules (1) and (2) are viewed as being both present in the grammar; the newer rule (2) is diffusing through the lexicon and replacing the older rule (1). When rule (2) applies to underlying representation like /sapĕ+o/, it blocks rule (1) and *so* is obtained. Compare the derivations (i) and (ii) below: (i) /sapĕ+o/ U.R. (ii) /sapĕ+o/ U.R. /saypo/ Rule (1) /sapo/ Rule (2) ... Other rules ... Other rules [sáččo] Phonetic form [so] Phonetic form

The historical priority of rule (1) over rule (2) is independently justified. Meyer-Lübke in, *Grammatica della Lingua Italiana*, reports that verbs in *-yo* are being lost nowadays and they tend to be regularized along with the verbs in *-o*. "Ma nella lingua antica le trace dell' *i* sono ancora numerose, mentre nella moderna diminuiscono sempre piu" (p 176).

Consequently, rules (1) and (2) are responsible for the alternation between the *-yo* ending and the *-o* ending in the same lexical item. The notion *lexical diffusion* explains why at a given point in time we should expect to find morphemes with dual pronunciations. The presence of doublets in groups 3 and 4 represent *residues* of rule (1). Eventually, rule (2) will eliminate the residues left by rule (1) as for example group 2, and the *-o* ending will take over the *-yo* ending.

IV. CONCLUSION

As was stated at the beginning of section 3, I believe that the alternation between the *-yo* ending and the *-o* ending in 1st. person singlar (Present Indicative) is best handled by a diachronic approach that considers rules in their time of operation, that is to say the derivational time. This approach accounts for the lexical restructuring more efficiently than a synchronic approach. The priority of rule (1) over rule (2) is attested historically and predicts that there is a tendency to increase the *-o* ending. The rule intersection and lexical diffusion hypotheses were shown not to suffer from the inadequacies that a synchronic framework has.

REFERENCES

Bybee, J. 1980. Morphophonemic change from inside and outside the paradigm. *Lingua* 50. 45 - 49.

Foley, J. 1977. *Foundations of theoretical phonology*. Cambridge: University Press.

Harris, James W. 1973. Morphologization of phonological rules; an example from Chicano Spanish. *Linguistic studies in Romance languages*, ed. by R. J. Campbell et al., 117 - 20. Washington, D. C.: Georgetown University Press.

Hooper, J. B. 1974. Rule morphologization in natural Generative Phonology. *Natural Phonology*, ed. by A. Bruck et al., 160 - 70. Chicago: CLS.

Jensen, F. 1970. *The Italian verb*. Chapel Hill: University of North Carolina.

King, R. 1968. *Historical linguistics and Generative Grammar*. Englewood Cliffs: Prentice-Hall.

1973. Rule insertion. *Language* 49. 551 - 78.

Kiparsky, P. 1971. Historical linguistics. *A survey of linguistic science*, ed. by W. O. Dingwall, 577 - 659. College Park: Linguistic Program, University of Maryland.

―――― 1974. Linguistic universals and linguistic change, *A reader in historical and comparative linguistics*, ed. by A. R. Keiler, 338 - 67. New York: Holt.

Meyer-Lüebke, W. 1955. *Grammatica Storica della Lingua Italiana*. Loescher Editore.

Newton, B. 1971. Ordering paradoxes in phonology. *Journal of Linguistics* 7. 31-53.

Sommerstein, A. H. 1977. *Modern phonology*. London: Arnold.

Tekavčić, P. 1972. *Grammatica Storica dell'italiano*, vol. 2 Morfosintassi. Bologna: Societa editrice il Mulino.

Vennemann, T. 1972. Phonetic and conceptual analogy. *Schuchardt, the neogrammarians and the transformational theory of phonological chagne*, ed. by T. Vennemann and T. H. Wilbur, 181-204. Frankfurt: Athenäum.

Wang, W. S-Y. 1969. Competing changes as a case of residues. *Language* 45. 9-25.

THEORIES OF SOUND CHANGE FAIL IF THEY TRY TO PREDICT TOO MUCH

JADRANKA GVOZDANOVIĆ

*To Roddy
for teaching me to see
the underlying lines.*

0. Introduction

If we are to have a theory of sound change that can satisfy the requirement of falsifiability so that it be considered scientific, what sort of predictions can we expect such a theory to make?

Substantive predictions, stating which sounds are most likely to occur in the languages of the world, are not falsifiable as long as they are based on the attested segment inventories. Also substantive predictions about sound change based on phonetic considerations, such as asymmetry of the speech organs, can at best be probabilistic. A probabilistic theory of sound change cannot be refuted by unpredicted sound change, even though it cannot account for it either.

What is needed is a theory of sound change that can state more that only probabilities. In order to be falsifiable, it must also state possible restrictions.

Phonetic restrictions on sound change, which are based on universal impossibilities of articulation or coarticulation, are predictable from the linguistic point of view, and cannot account for all of the observed restrictions on sound change. Apparently, additional systematic restrictions are operative, too.

What are systematic restrictions on sound change based on? On the distinctive feature patterning, I am going to claim here. All of the systematic restrictions which have been reported in the phonological literature can be analysed as derived from the distinctive feature patterning of the languages under consideration. Given the distinctive feature patterning of a language, then restrictions on possible sound change can be formulated, but it cannot be predicted whether or which sound change will take place. This is due to a variation and partial unpredictability of the conditioning factors, and to the abductive mechanism of language learning (cf. Andersen 1973), which mediates between speech perception and its analysis, and yields unpredictable outputs in potentially ambiguous cases.

A restrictive theory of sound change must survey conditioning factors and mechanisms of change, and state possible systematic restrictions on them.

1. Conditioning factors and mechanisms of change

1.1. Phonetic conditioning

Phonetic conditioning factors of sound change originate from speech production and are made possible and restricted by speech perception.

Speech production may influence sound change in universally predictable ways (hence its 'naturalness', cf. Hooper 1976), due to asymmetry of the speech organs (cf. Martinet 1955) or ease of articulation (cf. Jespersen 1922). The articulatory phenomena characteristic of speech production are translated into shifts within the acoustic space (cf. Labov, Yaeger and Steiner 1972), which occur in universally predictable ways, unless they are prevented by speech perception, reflecting the underlying language system.

There are two main phonological reasons why sound shifts may be prevented:
a) because the slots that would become filled by a sound change are filled already,
b) because the distinctive feature patterning of a given system restricts the possibilities of feature changes.

Given the fact that distinctive speech sounds are analysed in terms of distinctive features, the first reason is included in the second one. The second reason, that of feature patterning, may have consequences not only for the effectuation of a given change, but also for its direction. For example, it is one of the phonetically motivated principles of vowel shifts that back vowels shift to the front (cf. Labov, Yaeger and Steiner 1972: 106). Greenberg (1966: 514) established that this is one of diachronic universals indeed, and in particular that in unconditional sound change, "of the two vowels /i/ and /ü/, /i/ may originate from /ü/ but not /ü/ from /i/". However, in Hungarian from the tenth to the fifteenth centuries we do encounter rounding of front vowels (cf. Kálmán 1972), as a consequence of which /ü/ did originate from /i/. Why not vice versa? The fact that there was an open slot in the /ü/ position (because the original /ü/ was lowered to /ö/) obviously cannot give an answer as to why this open slot was not filled from the /u/ side, in a 'natural' phonetic way.

The only answer can be found in the fact that Hungarian already had rounded vowels at the point at which the change took place. This means that preceding the change, the Hungarian system had the following feature patterning:

(1a) the articulatory feature patterning of Hungarian preceding the /i/→/ü/ change

```
        _back_+
       /
_rounded_+
    i           u
    e       ö   o
    ε           α
```

(1b) the acoustic feature patterning of Hungarian preceding the /i/→/ü/ change

```
        _grave_+
       /
  _flat_+
    i           u
    e       ö   o
    ε           α
```

We can observe a feature hierarchy in Hungarian, which occurs in an isomorphous way both in the articulatory and the acoustic features. By this hierarchy, [±back] is dominating and [±rounded] subordinate in the articulatory vowel features, and [±grave] is dominating and [±flat] subordinate in the acoustic ones.

What would a change of /u/ into /ü/ have entailed? A change of a relevant dominating feature specification.

And what did the change of /i/ into /ü/ entail? A change of a relevant subordinate feature opposition. (By 'relevant' I mean throughout 'distinctive for the given major set of segments', in casu: vowels.)

We can see that sound change is restricted by the existing feature hierarchy. The fact that it is feature hierarchy indeed which exerts influence on sound change can be shown only if the given effect is not found in systems which are not characterized by the same hierarchy. I have shown elsewhere (cf. Gvozdanović 1983a) that this is indeed the case, as can be illustrated on the basis of the Dutch 'predicted' development of /u/ into /ü/ in approximately the same period as the Hungarian /i/→/ü/ change, but due to the fact that Dutch had no such hierarchy preceding the change, and consequently no restrictive influence of the distinctive feature patterning on general phonetic tendencies.

1.2. Sound change based on the sound system vs. sound change based on meaningful units

There is a basic difference between sound change which is based on the sound system, and sound change which is based on meaningful units. Whereas sound change which is based on the sound system reflects its organization in the sense of restrictions imposed by the existing hierarchies (such that a change of a dominating distinctive feature is possible only if its subordinate distinctive features change also), sound change which is based on meaningful units reflects the organization of the lexicon, the syntax, or the morphology of the changing system, its productivities, or similarities in general. Sound change based on the meaningful units of a language may disregard the existing phonological hierarchies.

The difference between change based on the sound system and change based on meaningful units can be illustrated by two different possibilities of elimination of rounded front vowels in a language: either by making them unrounded front, or by making them rounded back. In both cases, one of the two distinctive features involved in rounded front vowels, nl. [±rounded] and [±back], is eliminated, but in the first case it is [±rounded] which is eliminated, and in the second case, [±back]. What is the difference?

We have seen in the preceding section that rounded front vowels are characterized by distinctive feature specifications of [±back] and [±rounded] in such a way that [±back] is the dominating feature and [±rounded] the subordinate one. Unrounding of rounded front vowels equals elimination the subordinate feature specification. Defronting of rounded front vowels, on the other hand, equals elimination of the dominating feature specification, but preservation of the subordinate one. The former type of change reflects the organization of the phonological system, whereas the latter type of change does not reflect it. The latter type of change can only be based on meaninfgul units.

I have come to understand these regularities by studying the Kajkavian dialect of the Yugoslav city of Zagreb, which is my own native dialect. The Zagreb Kajkavian dialect is based on the Kajkavian dialect of the surroundings and influenced by the standard Serbo-Croatian language, which is based on the Neoštokavian dialect. As a result of this influence, Zagreb Kajkavian has eliminated the rounded front vowels which are still found in at least some of the surrounding Kajkavian local dialects in two ways: either by changing them into unrounded front vowels (i.e. /ü/→/i/ and /ö/→/e/) or by changing them into rounded back ones (i.e. /ü/→/u/ and /ö/→/o/). The regularity underlying these two types of elimination of rounded front vowels can be illustrated by the following examples.

(2) Elimination of rounded front vowels in Zagreb Kajkavian:

original Kajkavian	Zagreb Kajkavian	Standard Serbo-Croatian	
[künštler]	[kinštler]	[umjetnik]	'artist'
[kük]	[kuk]	[kuk]	'hip'

These two Kajkavian words have a different origin: whereas [künštler] is a borrowing from German, [kük] is a word of Slavic origin. Standard Serbo-Croatian has an own derivative pendant of the first word, and an equivalent of the second one. This means that on the basis of its lexicon, Standard Serbo-Croatian could not have influenced the Zagreb Kajkavian pronunciation of the first word, whereas it could have influenced the pronunciation of the second word. In the absence of a lexical conditioning of sound change in the course of adaptation (by which the Kajkavian words were adapted to the similar Standard Serbo-Croatian ones by changing /ü/ and /ö/ into /u/ and /o/), phonological conditioning took place determining that the dominating feature specification cannot be changed without consequences for the subordinate one, and that — consequently — if only one feature specification is to be changed, it can only be the subordinate one. Hence the change of /ü/ into /i/, and of /ö/ into /e/.

The fact that sound change which is based on meaningful units need not follow the restrictions imposed by the organization of the sound system holds for the lexicon as much as it does for morphology and syntax. The regularity which is operative here aims at relating one meaning to one form. This is a restrictive tendency, too.

Next to conditioning sound change, the tendency of having one form attached to one meaning may have a preservative effect as well. This is attested not only in spoken language, but also in writing within a given scribal tradition. What we often encounter in manuscripts is preservation of the unchanged lexical form of the word, whereas sound change may be found in desinences. A concrete example of it is found in the Slavic manuscript *Code slave 11* of the National Library of Paris, dating from the end of the fourteenth century. Its scribe presumably did not distinguish between /e/ and /i/, but he continued to distinguish them in the writing of lexical stems (apparently knowing how they used to be spelled), whereas he sometimes interchanged them in desinences and particles.

The mechanism of sound change is always restricted by the existing system in one way or another. Whatever the source of sound change may be — the trial-and-error process of language acquisition (termed 'abduction' by Andersen 1973), adaptation, or expressive formation, the initial stage of sound change reflects the organization of the changing system. This may be overlayered by later stages, but it may also remain overtly visible, as in the prosodic system of the Serbo-Croatian local dialect of Dubrovnik.

In the sixteenth century, the Serbo-Croatian dialect of Dubrovnik was basically Štokavian (with Čakavian influences due to a population mixture), but of an older type than the Neoštokavian dialect, which had undergone a series of phonological and morphological innovations preceding that period. One of those innovations was a regressive accent shift which yielded the rising tonal accent, as opposed to the unshifted falling tonal accent, occurring only in the initial position of a prosodic word (for a definition of the prosodic word, cf. Gvozdanović 1980: 12). The final syllable never kept the accent, and there was a prosodic word boundary there. The Neoštokavian system could (as it still can) be analysed as having tone, with the accent predictable from tone and prosodic word boundaries. The rising vs. falling tone of Neoštokavian occurred on long and short vowels, the long ones being single phonological segments due to their opposition to the corresponding sequences (cf. also Gvozdanović 1983b: 68). Each vowel formed a syllable nucleus.

Dubrovnik was different from that. Its poetry from that time shows that a syllable nucleus could contain two vowels as well (cf. e.g. [meu] 'between', which counted as one syllable). The long vowels of the local dialect of Dubrovnik were not opposed to the corresponding sequences, which means that they could themselves be analysed as sequences. At that time, the local dialect of Dubrovnik did not distinguish tone in short syllable nuclei (consisting of a single vowel), but only in long ones (constiting of a vowel sequence as its nucleus), which could have the accent either on the first or on the second vowel of the syllable nucleus.

In the sixteenth and seventeenth centuries, Dubrovnik underwent sociolinguistically conditioned extensive Neoštokavian influences. One of them triggered the accent retraction, which started in word-final syllables. The retracted accent was rendered as rising on the prefinal syllable if that syllable was long. If it was short, there was no tonal distinction. Originally short prefinal syllables were lengthened under the retracted accent if the final syllable was short. Only in that case did they become rising. The output of the first stage of the accent retraction correspondingly agreed with the existing system.

(3a) Neoštokavian in the sixteenth century:

[vòda] /vòda/ 'water, nominative singular' (ˋ) denotes the rising tone on a short vowel, (ˇ) denotes the falling tone on a short vowel, (ˊ) denotes the rising tone on a long vowel, (ˆ) denotes the falling tone on a long vowel, and (‾) denotes vowel length.
[vòdē] /vòdē/ 'water, genitive singular'
[vŏdu] /vŏdu/ 'water, accusative singular'
[lòpata] /lòpata/ 'spade, nominative singular'
[gláva] /gláva/ 'head, nominative singular'
[glávē] /glávē/ 'head, genitive singular'
[glâvu] /glâvu/ 'head, accusative singular'
[pítala] /pítala/ 'ask, feminine active past participle'.

(3b) Dubrovnik in the sixteenth century:

[vóda] /voòda/ The same translations as above. In the phonological notation, (ˊ) denotes the accent.
[vŏdē] /vòdee/
[vŏdu] /vòdu/
[lopăta] /lopàta/
[gláva] /glaàva/
[glávē] /glaàvee/
[glâvu] /glàavu/
[pītăla] /piitàla/.

In the further course of the developments, the accent retraction proceeded into all positions, and the pronunciation rules of Neoštokavian were taken over by which a long vowel was systematically differentiated from the corresponding sequence. In the final result, tone emerged as a vowel feature in the same way as in Neoštokavian. The result of the first stage of the development was preserved and rendered as the rising tone on a long vowel and the falling tone on a short one, respectively.

(3c) Dubrovnik after the change:

[vóda] /vóda/   The same translations and notation as in (3a).
[vǒdē] /vǒdē/
[vǒdu] /vǒdu/
[lòpata] /lòpata/
[gláva] /gláva/
[glávē] /glávē/
[glâvu] /glâvu/
[pítala] /pítala/

2. Phonological restrictions on sound cnange

2.1. Syntagmatic restrictions

Sound change is not only restricted by the feature patterning of a given system. It is also restricted by the segmentation characteristic of that system, as was shown already by the Dubrovnik case demonstrated in (3b) above.

Phonological segments are sets of distinctive features — and this is why they are directly related to the feature patterning. Following Ebeling (1960: 67), I define the phonological segment as a set of distinctive features for which the fact that they are grouped together is relevant in this sense that the same features constitute different linguistic forms according as they are grouped together differentially.

We have seen on the basis of the Dubrovnik case discussed above that the initial stage of sound change obeys the segmentation principle characteristic of the system undergoing the change. In the next stage, the same principle may either be preserved or changed. Its preservation may be taken as a proof of the relevance of the existing segmentation principle.

Preservation of the original segmentation principle but change of the prosodic one is found in the southeastern part of Slavonian Serbo--Croatian, which also underwent Neoštokavian influences. In Slavonian Serbo-Croatian, there is no systematic distinction between long vowels and the corresponding sequences. Each sequence of two identical vowels is pronounced as a single long vowel, even if there is an intervening morpheme boundary between them, as in the following example.

(4a) Slavonian Serbo-Croatian:

[gra] /gra/ 'beans, nominative' (⌢) denotes vowel length.
[grā] /gra-a/ 'beans, genitive'

In the period directly preceding the Neoštakavian influence, Slavonian had phonetic rising and falling tones only on long syllable nuclei, where they were due to a differential accent placement either on the first or on the second vowel of a sequence. These phonetic tones differed from the Neoštokavian ones by a breaking of fundamental frequency which occurred between the high-pitched and the low-pitched part of a long syllable nucleus having a tonal accent (cf. Ivšić 1911: 151 etc.). This breaking reflected the segmentation principle.

As a result of the Neoštokavian influence, the southeastern part of Slavonian retracted the accent by one phonological vowel (which could be a half of a phonetic one). The retracted accent was reinterpreted as a low tone, and the unretracted accent as a high tone. The low vs. high tone is a vowel feature there, as is also shown by its phonetic realization (cf. also Ivić's somewhat different notation, 1958: 291).

(4b) Southeastern Slavonian equivalents of the Neoštokavian ones:

[vòda]   /vòda/   The same translations as in (3a). Phonetically, (ˋ) denotes the short rising tonal accent, (ˮ) denotes the short falling one, (´) denotes the long rising one, (ˆ) denotes the long falling one, and (˜) denotes the broken rising one (of somewhat unclear phonetic quality). Phonologically, (ˋ) denotes the low tone, and (´) the high one.
[vodẽ]   /vodèe/   /vs. vodeé/
[vŏdu]   /vódu/
[lòpata] /lòpata/
[gláva] /glaàva/
[glāvẽ] /glaavèe/ /vs. glaaveé/
[glâvu] /gláavu/
[pítali] /piìtali/

The segmentation principle of a given language is its principle of linear feature ordering. At least in its initial stage, sound change is restricted by the existing linear ordering of the distinctive features of the anguage undergoing the change.

2.2. Paradigmatic restrictions

Paradigmatic restrictions in phonology distinguish the set of possible changes from the set of impossible ones in a given language. What are the impossible sound changes? My hypothesis about them is the following one: if sound change is based phonologically, it cannot involve a dominating distinctive feature without involving its subordinate ones. This restriction can be violated only if sound change is based on the meaningful units. As far as I can see, this is the only possible falsifiable hypothesis about sound change, and it should be put to a test as such.

Also seemingly strange sound changes are within the set of the possible ones because they do not violate this restriction. For example, nasal changes in Polynesian languages, as discussed by Harlow (1983). They go in different directions, viz. /n/ merges with /ŋ/ in Colloquial Samoan yielding the velar nasal /ŋ/, /ŋ/ merges with /n/ in the Bay of Plenty Maori yielding the dental nasal /n/, and /ŋ/ merges with /k/ in the South Island Maori yielding the velar consonant /k/. Harlow discussed these changes in terms of Foley's (1977) weakening and strengthening hierarchies, and stated that the /n/→/ŋ/ change can be analysed as weakening, and /ŋ/→/n/ as strengthening, but that there are problems analysing the /ŋ/→/k/ change as strengthening in Foley's terms. This is why I am going to elaborate the Maori changes here, leaving the Samoan one for another occasion (cf. Gvozdanović, to appear).

First of all, Foley's strength hierarchies (of the type: stops (1), spirants (2), nasals (3), liquids (4), glides (5), and vowels (6)) are not universal. There are language-specific deviations from them which can only be formulated in terms of the phonological feature specifications (e.g. in languages in which glides are opposed to the corresponding vowels, they are weaker that liquids and nasals; an example of it is found in Serbo-Croatian). Second, Foley's strength hierarchies are entirely derivable from the distinctive features. Again, with language-specific deviations in terms of feature patterning.

We can now proceed to discuss the Maori changes of /ŋ/ in terms of the distinctive features involved. This discussion makes sense only if Harlow's analysis of /ŋ/ as a single segment (and not a sequence of a nasal and a velar) is correct indeed. I assume that this is the case in view of the distributional properties of the language (cf. Harlow 1983: 100).

THEORIES OF SOUND CHANGE   193

In order to be able to discuss the elimination of /ŋ/ in the Bay of Plenty Maori (henceforth: MAB) and the South Island Maori (henceforth MAS), I shall first present a distinctive feature analysis of the Maori which still has /ŋ/. The acoustic analysis of the Maori phonological system was forwarded to me by Harlow in a letter dated July 20, 1981. I shall present it here with minor modifications due to predictability, and add the corresponding articulatory analysis (based on the Chomsky and Halle features, 1968).

(5a) The articulatory features of Maori.

	i	e	a	o	u	p	t	k	m	n	ŋ	h	r	f	w
consonantal						+	+	+	+	+	+	+	−	+	−
vocalic	+	+	+	+	+								−		−
high	+	−			+										
back	−	−		+	+										
low			+												
anterior						+	+	−	+	+	−	−		+	+
coronal						−	+	−	−	+	−	−	+	−	−
nasal						−	−	−	+	+	+				
continuant						−	−	−	−	−	−	+		+	

(5b) The acoustic features of Maori:

	i	e	a	o	u	p	t	k	m	n	ŋ	h	r	f	w
consonantal						+	+	+	+	+	+	+	−	+	−
vocalic	+	+	+	+	+								−		−
diffuse	+	−		−	+										
compact	−	+	−			−	−	+	−	−	+	+	−	−	−
acute	+	+	−	−	−	−	+		−	+			+	−	−
nasal						−	−	−	+	+	+				
continuant						−	−	−	−	−	−	+		+	

The acoustic pendant of [±back] would be [±grave], and the articulatory pendant of [±acute] would be [±anterior] as a vowel feature as well. There is a discrepancy between the two matrices there, and it is possible that the articulatory one should be revised. I shall leave the matrices as they are, however, because these features are not at issue in the discussion of the nasals.

We can see that there is a regularity in the matrices by which a feature may be predictable in combination with a '+' specification of another feature, and distinctive in combination with its '−' specification or predictable specification. Such an asymmetry equals hierarchy. Apparently, the hierarchy treats a '−' specification in the same way as predictable specification, and distinguishes it systematically from the corresponding '+' specification. This is a case of markedness in the structuralists' sense (cf. also Andersen 1975:70 for the same notion of markedness, but a less restricted notion of hierarchy). The notion of hierarchy presented in the first section of this paper can now be further developed as follows:

(6) Phonological hierarchy equals asymmetrical patterning by which a feature is predictable in combination with the marked term of another distinctive feature, and distinctive in combination with its unmarked term. 'Marked' equals the '+' specification, and 'unmarked', the corresponding '−' and predictable specifications. In a hierarchical relation as defined above, the former feature is subordinate, and the latter, dominating.

Hierarchy is a case of paradigmatic feature ordering, which may occur throughout the matrix. Which hierarchies can in this way be established for Maori?

(7a) The articulatory feature hierarchies of Maori:

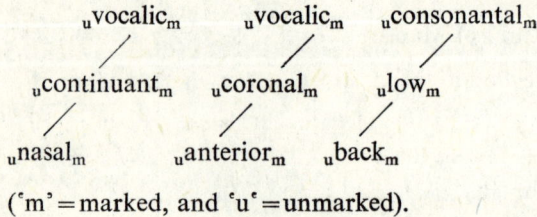

('m' = marked, and 'u' = unmarked).

(7b) The acoustic feature hierarchies of Maori:

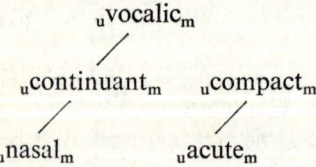

([±compact] and [±acute] are unordered with respect to [±vocalic] and [±consonantal], cf. also comments on 5b above.)

The Bay of Plenty Maori (MAB) eliminated /ŋ/ by letting it merge with /n/. In terms of markedness only, this seems hard to understand on the basis of the articulatory features involved, because a change of

THEORIES OF SOUND CHANGE   195

[−coronal] into [+coronal] is a change of an unmarked segment into the corresponding marked one. We can understand such a change only if we take the entire system into account and evaluate the change in terms of the hierarchies involved, both in the articulatory and in the acoustic features.

(8a) The articulatory feature hierarchies of the Bay of Plenty Maori following the /ŋ/→/n/ change:

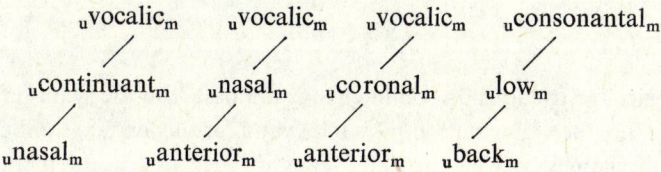

(8b) The acoustic feature hierarchies of the Bay of Plenty Maori following the /ŋ/→/n/ change:

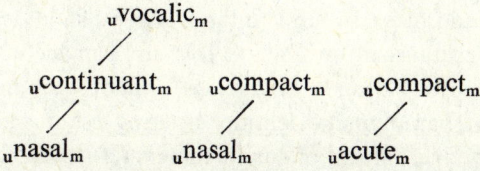

In the articulatory features, MAB had a change of the dominating feature [±coronal] in the context of [+nasal], and the subordinate feature [±anterior] changed, too, and became subordinate with respect to [±nasal] as well. In the acoustic features, MAB had a change of the dominating feature [±compact] in the context of [+nasal], and the subordinate feature [±acute] changed, too. In that case, however, the dominating feature [±compact] became dominating with respect to [±nasal] as well. What is the difference between the articulatory and the acoustic features due to? Possibly to an analytic difference, but also possibly to the fact that in the acoustic features, a dominating feature changed in the direction 'marked'→'unmarked', by which a conditioning feature (i.e. [±nasal]) could become subordinate to it. This must further be investigated.

The MAB change of /ŋ/ into /n/ has increased the amount of predictability in both the articulatory and the acoustic features, without violating the level restrictions imposed by the existing hierarchies.

The South Island Maori (MAS) eliminated /ŋ/ by letting it merge with /k/. It was a change of [+nasal] into [−nasal] in the context of [+consonantal, −coronal, −anterior, −continuant] in the articulatory features, and a change of [+nasal] into [−nasal] in the context of [+consonantal, +compact, −continuant] in the acoustic features. The resulting segment inventory of MAS is the same as that of MAB, and the resulting feature hierarchies are consequently the same, too. This shows that the same structural change can be reached by different processes, which are predictable only to the extent that they do not involve a dominating distinctive feature without involving its subordinate ones.

2.3. Conclusion

Phonological restrictions on sound change are based on the syntagmatic ordering (i.e. the segmentation principle) valid for the language undergoing sound change, and on the paradigmatic ordering (i.e. the hierarchies) valid for the distinctive feature system of that language.

These orderings underlie the phonological constraints on sound change discussed in the literature, e.g. rule transparency as formulated by Kiparsky (1982, 2nd:75), and add restrictiveness to them. They also underlie the strength hierarchies established by Foley (1977) and can account for phenomena for which the strength hierarchies cannot account.

Finally, the principles of paradigmatic feature ordering established above underlie the abductive mechanism of sound change (cf. Andersen 1973) and show why sound change cannot be merely inductive (i.e. based on the language data) and deductive (i.e. based on the general principles of ordering). The phonological system — and language system in general — is as a rule only partially ordered. Only the ordered parts of the system are by nature restrictive, and the restrictions imposed by them can be satisfied in various ways, as we have seen above.

REFERENCES

Andersen, H. 1973. Abductive and deductive change. *Language* 49. 765-93.
———. 1975. Variance and invariance in phonological typology. *Phonologica 1972*, ed. by. W. U. Dressler and F. V. Mareš, 67-78. München/Salzburg: Fink.
Chomsky, N. and M. Halle. 1968. *The sound pattern of English*. New York: Harper and Row.
Ebeling, C. L. 1960. *Linguistic units*. The Hague: Mouton.
Foley, J. 1977. *Foundations of theoretical phonology*. Cambridge: University Press.
Greenberg, J. H. 1966. Synchronic and diachronic universals in phonology. *Language* 42. 508-17.

Gvozdanović, J. 1980. Tone and accent in Standard Serbo-Croatian, with a synopsis of Serbo-Croatian phonology. Vienna: Österreichische Akademie der Wissenschaften, Schriften der Balkankommission XXVIII, Wien.

— 1982. On establishing restrictions imposed on sound change. *Papers from the 5th International Conference on Historical Linguistics*, ed. by A. Ahlqvist, 85-97. Amsterdam: Benjamins.

— 1983a. Patterning of distinctive features in relation to variability. *Proceedings of the 13th International Congress of Linguists*, ed. by Sh. Hattori and K. Inove, 611-617. Tokyo: Gakushin University.

— 1983b. Typological characteristics of Slavic and non-Slavic languages with distinctive tonal accents. *Dutch contributions to the 9th International Congress of Slavists*, ed. by A. G. van Holk, 53-108. Amsterdam: Rodopi.

— 1983c. Variability in relation to the language system with special emphasis on the Zagreb Kajkavian dialect. *General Linguistics*.

— to appear. Markedness and ordering at various levels. *Synchronic and diachronic linguistics*, ed. by U. Pieper and G. Stickel. The Hague: Mouton.

Harlow, R. B. 1982. Some phonological changes in Polynesian languages. *Papers from the 5th International Conference on Historical Linguistics*, ed. by A. Ahlqvist, 98-109. Amsterdam: Benjamins.

Hooper, J. B. 1976. *An introduction to Natural Generative Phonology*. New York/San Francisco/London: Academic Press.

Ivić, P. 1958. *Die serbokroatischen Dialekte, ihre Struktur und Entwicklung*. The Hague: Mouton.

Ivšić, S. 1911. Prilog za slavenski akcenat. *Rad Jugoslavenske Akademije Znanosti i Umjetnosti* 187. 133-208.

Jespersen, O. 1922. *Language: its nature, development and origin*. London: Allen and Unwin.

Kálmán, B. 1972. Hungarian historical phonology. *The Hungarian language*, ed. by Benkő, L. and S. Imre, 49-83. The Hague: Mouton.

Kiparsky, P. 1982. Explanation in phonology. *Explanation in phonology*, ed. by P. Kiparsky. Dordrecht: D. Reidel. [Reprinted from Peters, S. 1972. Goals in linguistic theory. Englewood Cliffs, N. J.: Prentice Hall, Inc. 189-227].

Labov, W., Yaeger, M. and R. Steiner. 1972. *A quantitative study of sound change in progress*. Philadelphia: U.S. Regional Survey.

Martinet, A. 1955. *Economie des changements phonétiques*. Bern: Francke.

Weinreich, U. 1953. *Languages in contact*. New York: Linguistic Circle of New York.

CHANCE AND NECESSITY IN DIACHRONIC SYNTAX – WORD ORDER TYPOLOGIES AND THE POSITION OF MODERN PERSIAN RELATIVE CLAUSES

HUBERT HAIDER

0. *Introduction*

The development of Modern Persian relative clauses is instructive for the study of syntactic change. A relative clause construction gets changed into a general particle construction for nominal attributes. Clauses which are embedded in this attributive construction function as relative clauses again. Even more instructive it is for typological reasons. Modern Persian relative clauses seem to be exceptional with respect to typological generalizations established for the word order types It is an SOV language and should have prenominal instead of postnominal relative clauses.

It is the aim of this paper to show that this 'exceptionality' is only apparent and an artefact of the method of description. It can be shown that every step in the development is in full agreement with general principles of the theory of grammar, and so is the result in Modern Persian. In the first part of the paper I argue for a replacement of autonomous word order typology by a more general account for 'types': 'Types' are viewed as the result of fixing some crucial parameters of grammar in a default manner. As an exemplar case I use Vennemann's Principle of Natural Serialization and show how it can be derived from a general theory as the combined result of two simple and independently necessary principles.

In the following section (2) I extend this method to the serialization properties of relative clauses.

In section (3) I lay out an analysis, according to which the Modern Persian relative clause is an instance of a postnominal particle construction, and hence is postnominal by grammatical necessity.

Section (4) is devoted to a brief outline of the history of this construction, within a main perspective: I want to isolate the general grammatical factors that lead to the final result, the general postnominal attribute construction in an SOV language.

Chance and Necessity factors in diachronic change are contemplated in (5) and related with the foregoing discussion.

1. Autonomous theories of word order, i.e. theories that analyze serialization as a primitive phenomenon, independent of the whole set up of a grammatical system, suffer from two basic shortcomings, *insufficient coverage* of data and *explanatory inadequacy*. Prototypical examples of theories of that type were put forth by Vennemann (1974, 1975) and Lehmann (1973). They try to analyze serialization-patterns in terms of instantiations of one primitive principle, e.g. the Principle of Natural Serialization of Vennemann's:

(1)

$$\{\text{Operator }(\{\text{operand}\})\} \Rightarrow \begin{cases} [\text{operator }[\text{operand}]] \text{ in XV languages} \\ [\text{operand }[\text{operator}]] \text{ in VX languages} \end{cases}$$

(Vennemann 1974:10)

As pointed out by Mallinson/Blake (1981:406), Vennemann's or Lehmann's principles are consistently fulfilled by not more than 40% of the languages under investigation. In a diachronic perspective languages are consistent only about one fifth of the time. This calls for a principled way of dealing with exceptions. It is necessary to demonstrate on *independent* grounds why a given language is exceptional. Otherwise such a language simply invalidates the principles. It is justly criticized by Watkins (1977:439) as a misuse of typology to assume that the reason for inconsistency of the serialization patterns of a language is due to its being 'in transition'. Circularity can be avoided only if the transitory characteristics can be derived from a general theory of grammar.

If a general theory is needed anyway, the question arises, why the correlation among word order patterns could not be derived also from it.

This is the point of view I want to argue for in this paper. The success of such a move would overcome the second shortcoming as well, the insufficient explanatory adequacy: As is well known, serialization patterns are correlated with other areas of grammar, as e.g. the presence or absence of a morphological case system. Secondly languages differ with respect to the rigidity of serialization, which again correlates with other properties of the grammatical system of the respective language. Finally it should be remembered that "so many phenomena of word order are not in any sense syntactical" but "may serve a purely iconic function". (Watkins 1977:440)

If the degree of grammatically determined serialization properties varies, depending on the general grammatical set up of a language, there is no hope to find a consistent theory of word order. Since word order will reflect only partly strictly grammatically determined patterns, just as well as patterns of preference for those areas that are left open for extra-grammatical influences, as e.g. the cognitively motivated order of animate nouns preceding inanimate in languages with free word order (for German cf. Haider 1982).

I take it as justified by the low explanatory success of the autonomous-system view to switch the perspective and view word order as an *epiphenomenon* of independent principles of grammar.

Within an elaborated theory of grammar, as e.g. the theory of Government and Binding (Chomsky 1981), it is very easy to derive the effects of the Principle of Natural Serialization (1) from principles relating to case assignment.

Case is assigned under government and government is directional. Fixing this parameter — i.e. directionality — yields the basic types of XV vs. VX languages:

In order to be syntactically wellformed a NP must be assigned (abstract) case. But case can be only assigned to an NP that is *ortholateral* to its case-assigning element (e.g. verb, preposition, etc.), i.e. on the proper side of its governor:

If the verb governs to the right, the NP must be preceded by the verb and vice versa.

How do crosscategorial patterns arise?

The answer is that the *default* option — unique directionality for all governing elements, immediately leads to most of the patterns accounted for by (1)

(2) i) O V   a) [NP   A]   ii) V O   a) [A   NP]
                     AP   AP

         b) [NP   P]   b) [P   NP]
                     PP   PP

         c) [NP   N]   c) [N   NP]
                Gen NP   Gen NP

In (2) A, P, N are case-assigning elements. In German for instance adjectives govern Dative and Genitive, prepositions all cases except Nominative, and nouns are the government-context for adnominal Genitive. The immediate consequences of the default option for directionality are the following:

(3) a) VSO: Prepositions — N+Gen. directionality: rightwards
 b) SVO: Prepositions — N+Gen. rightwards
 c) SOV: Postpositions — Gen.+N leftwards

It is the serialization within APs (2i, a); 2ii, a)) — a phenomenon which is neglected in the various treatments of word-order — that gives us the *indirect* reason for the correlation between the basic position of the verb and the position of the *attributive* adjective.

It is a frequently observable property of elements which agree with other elements that they have to be *adjacent* to each other. Take for instance German adjective phrases:

(4) a) Der Mann ist { stolz auf seine Kinder
 auf seine Kinder stolz
 'The man is { proud of his children
 of his children proud'
 b) der auf seine Kinder *stolze Mann*
 'the of his children proud man'
 c) * der *stolze* auf seine Kinder Mann
 'the proud of his children man'

It is the violation of adjacency which rules out (4c), because a PP-complement may otherwise, e.g. in predicative constructions like (4a) precede or follow the adjective. Due to the rigid complement-structure of English, — complements follow their heads — English does not allow complex attributive APs. The English equivalent of (4b) is just as ungrammatical as (4c). If an adjacency requirement holds in a given language this entails a particular serialization. As indicated in (2), adjectives, being governing elements, require an ortholateral NP-complement, i.e. an NP to the left in OV languages and vice versa.

Taken together with the adjacency requirement, this entails prenominal position of the attributive AP in XV and postnominal in VX languages, because this is the only order where adjacency is possible. That adjacency is a crucial concept universally will become still more transparent with relative clauses. Even this sketchy exposition is enough to give an idea how word order phenomena can be dealt with as *epiphenomena* of independently motivated principles:

Directionality of government and the adjacency requirement are sufficient to cover the most frequent word order syndromes:

(5) a) VSO: Prepositions   —   N+Gen.   —   N+Adj.
    b) SVO: Prepositions   —   N+Gen.   —   N+Adj.
    c) SOV: Prepositions   —   Gen.+N   —   Adj.+N

(cf. Hawkins 1979:625)

In (5a, b) directionality of government is rightwards, in (3b) leftwards. The types in (5) are the result of setting the parameter of directionality in a *default* manner, i.e. uniformely. It is just as well possible, however, that the value of the parameter is fixed differently for one or the other category, e.g. for P, i.e. prepositions instead of postpositions in (5c), as in Amharic.

That deviances of this kind are marked options not just in theory becomes clear in view of the fact, that constructions resulting from marked options are more constrained: In English and in Scandinavian languages (e.g. Swedish, Icelandic) preposition stranding is possible, but not in Dutch or German. This is a consequence of the divergence between the basic OV pattern of Dutch and German (cf. Koster 1975) and pre- instead of postpositions.

6) a)   who did you wait for — ?
   b)   He was waited for —.
   c) * Wen hast du auf — gewartet
   d) * Er wurde auf — gewartet

Since a gap, i.e. "—" in (6), is licit only if it is properly governed (cf. Chomsky 1981, "Empty Category Principle"), i.e. governed by a verb or an element that governs like a verb, the ungrammaticality of (6c, d) follows then from the marked government property of P in German or Dutch.

Deviation from the 'types' in (5) may have other reasons than marked fixing of parameters as well. It can be the result of an impoverished system.

Let us take e.g. the frequent case of SVO & Prepositions & N+Gen, but Adj+N, as in English, Swedish, Danish, etc. If adejctives do not assign case any more in a particular language simply for the fact that there is no case left that would be assignable by an adjective, i.e. oblique cases like Dative or Genitive, the adjacency requirement becomes less important as a trigger for serialization.

In English for instance the serialization of A+N can be viewed as the last remnant of its SOV-predecessor Old English. Since oblique cases got lost in the course of the development, adjectives dropped out of the set of case-assigning elements, hence there do not occur any longer adjective phrases with bare NP complements, hence adjacency is endagered only with PP complements. Obviously these were too small a class of adjectives to trigger the change in serialization. So due to the lack of the grammatical trigger, u.e. restoring adjacency, the old pattern is conserved although this leads, ironically enough, to a loss in expressibility: Complex APs are impossible as attributes. This shows very clearly that internal grammatical principles override functional principles like 'ease of communication'

The preceding paragraphs are intended not so much as factual claims but rather as a brief illustration that the application of finer grained concepts will not only produce the same results but make available methods that are superior in handling exceptions: Exceptions can be tackled in various ways, relating them to marked options of parameter values or by showing that the 'ideal types' are not more than clusterings, resulting from favourable combinations of principles. But it needs closer scrutiny and detailed analysis to find out that what looks like an exception is just a system with the same degree of overall optimality, i.e. a combination of favourable principles but with slightly different inventory, as e.g. the position of adjectives and the inventory of Case. In the main part of this paper I want to demonstrate that what looks like an exceptional feature of Modern Persian is an artefact of the crude methods applied in word order typology. It will turn out that what appears to be an exeptional feature, i.e. the order of relative clauses, is a straighforward consequence of the very same principles that lead to the clusterings of the 'ideal types' in (5). What makes Modern Persian appear exceptional in word-order surveys is the neglection of a crucial fact, a particle construction. The properties of this construction interfere with the above-mentioned principles and make it impossible to view a Modern Persian relative clause on a par with, let us say, an English counterpart.

This is a third case of 'exceptionality'. Exceptionality as an artefact of the method of description. The occurrence of this third type shows very clearly that word-order-typology cannot be viewed as a self-supported discipline.

2. Word order typology and the position of the relative clause.

According to the following typological statements (6), an SOV-language with postnominal relative clauses is exceptional.

(6) a) There seems to be a very strong correlation between basic word order and Head/RC order, which can be stated as follows:
VO languages have Head-RC, order
OV languages have RC-Head order (Mallinson/Blake p. 273)
b) With few exceptions, a language has postnominal restrictive RCs if and only if in the basic word order of the language verbs precede their objects (Downing 1978:383)
c) Greenberg (indirectly)
U 24: If the relative expression precedes the noun (...) either the language ist *postpositional* (emphasis H. H.) or the adjective precedes the noun or both
U 4: With overwhelming greater than chance frequency, languages with normal SOV order are *postpositional* (emphasis H. H.)
Consequently:
(If the adjective does not precede the noun) with overwhelming greater than chance frequency languages with normal SOV order have *prenominal* relative clauses.

That prenominal RCs match the structural requirement of SOV languages can be infered from the theory of phrase-structures. Such a theory was worked out by Jackendoff (1977). The basic concept is the notion 'projection'. Every phrase is a projection of its head.

(7)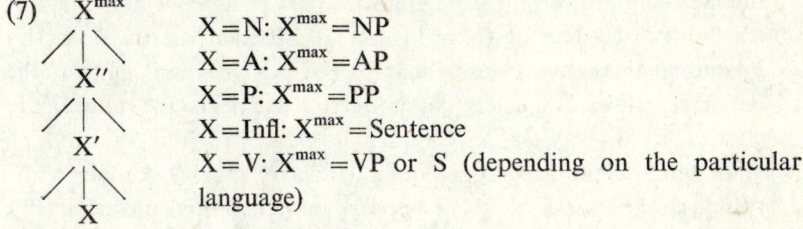

$X = N: X^{max} = NP$
$X = A: X^{max} = AP$
$X = P: X^{max} = PP$
$X = Infl: X^{max} = Sentence$
$X = V: X^{max} = VP$ or S (depending on the particular language)

A phrase is built up from its head by adding specifiers and complements. The structure is determined by the position of these elements.

(8) a) $\bar{\bar{X}} \rightarrow \{[\text{Spec } \bar{X}] [\bar{X}]\}$
b) $\bar{X} \rightarrow \{X \text{ Complement}\}$

The curly brackets in (8) indicate that the categories are unordered. A particular order is assigned by the particular grammar. On the assumption that [Spec $\bar{X}$] and 'Complement' must be each adjacent to the head, the serialization of (8a) and (8b) are interdependent.

What is essential, however, is the uniformity of structure imposed by (8) in the default case: For a specific category, *all* specifiers will precede or follow the head, and the same hold for *all* complements, the other way round. With respect to its complement-status, adnominal Genitive is on a par with a RC. Hence it is again the directionality of government which determines indirectly — due to uniformity of categorial structure — the prenominal occurrence of RCs in SOV languages.

But the default case — categorial uniformity — can be overridden by other principles one of which is the adjacency requirement: The following quotations can be subsumed under the general statement:

(9) Relative pronouns that agree with the head must be adjacent in the base position

A. Only postnominal RCs may contain an obligatory initial relative particle or nominal that is not generally present in that position in the corresponding unmarked simple sentence (relative particle=particle or pronoun or NP that contains the relative pronoun or complementizer)
D. In prenominal RCs there is never an obligatory clause initial marker. (There may be a clause final marker)

Downing (1977: 166 - 67)

F. A relative pronoun in a postnominal relative clause is always placed in clause-initial position (sometimes as part of a NP which contains it), either preceding or following the relative particle, if any. (IU)
I. Postnominal relative clauses contain relative pronouns only if the language allows (other) initial nonverbal elements in subordinate clauses. (IU)
K. With few exceptions, if postnominal relative clauses contain a distinctive verbal affix, the verb appears in clauseinitial position. (IT)

Downing (1978: 390 - 91)

It is this adjacency requirement which is the crucial cue for the explanation of the development and history of the Modern Persian RCs.

3. *Modern Persian Relative Clauses*
The basic characteristics are:

(10) a. postnominal
   b. the clause is introduced by the standard complementizer for embedded clauses 'ke' (comparable to English 'that')
   c. restrictive RCs are preceded by a particle,
   d. occurrence of resumptive pronouns, except for subjects and objects

Since there is no agreement involved between head-noun and RC — there are no relative pronouns — the question arises why RCs are postnominal in Modern Persian.

The answer which I propose is very simple. RCs are postnominal in Modern Persian because a Modern Persian RC is an instance of an attributive construction, which is postnominal. For this attributive construction — in traditional terminology; 'ezafe' — construction — I want to show that it is postnominal by grammatical necessity.

3.1. Ezafe

Any attributive constituent follows the nominal head with a particle — transliterated by 'e' — intervening:

(11) $[N - Part - attribute]_{NP}$
   a) N — p. — AP: ab-e   garm   — hot water
                 'water'   'hot'
   b) N — p. — PP: ruz-e   ba?d az an etefag   — the day after
                 'day'   after that incident'   that incident
   c) N — p. — NP: ketab-e   hasan   — Hassan's book
                 'book'   'Hassan'

The most general syntactic analysis for the examples presented in (11) is (12):

(12) $[N - p. - X^{max}]$

If (12) is the correct structural analysis for 'ezafe' we expect that sentential constituents appear at the position of X^{max} in (12), which is the case indeed.

(13) a) in matlab (in)ke *dar inhare* bāū sobbat karde ast
      'the claim that thisabout with her (he) talked'
      'the claim that he talked about it with her'
   b) in matlab ke *dar bareas* bāū sobbat karde ast
      'the claim that about it with her (he) talked'
      'the claim that he talked about with her'
   c) in matlab i-ke dar bareas ba ū sobbat karde ast (restrictive version of 13b)

The attributive clause (13a) is kept distinct from the relative clause just by means of different pronouns. In (13a) it is the enclific demonstrative 'in', whereas in (13b) the resumptive pronoun 'as' = 'it' occurs.

The presence or absence of 'i' in (13b) and c) respectively depends on the restrictive or appositive quality of the RC. The particle *ke* in (13) is the standard complementizer particle for embedded clauses, comparable to English *that*. Embedding a clause under (12) leads immediately to a typologically well-attested RC-pattern (cf. Schwartz 1971:142).

(14) N [$_\bar{s}$ Par [......ø/Pronoun ....]]

In Modern Persian the pattern (14) is an instance of 'ezafe', hence the 'ezafe'-particle intervening between N and $\bar{S}$. In traditional grammars (cf. Windfuhr (1979)), however, the ezafe-particle and the particle that occurs with RCs is transliterated differently, the former with 'e' the latter with 'i'. This is misleading.

First of all, these particles are not spelled at all in Modern Persian, due to the use of the Arabic alphabet, which does not spell vowels.

Secondly, 'e' is no basic phoneme. Modern Persian has a 3-element vowel system a-u-i with phonemic length distinction. Unstressed 'i' is reduced to 'e'. (cf. Lentz 1958:183). Therefore the 'e' of ezafe is analyzed here as unstressed 'i'. The analysis proposed here accounts also for the lack of 'i' in appositive or non-restrictive relative clauses. Restrictive RCs are constituents of an NP, hence instance of ezafe of Modern Persian. Non-restrictive RCs are rather of a parenthetical nature (cf. Emonds (1979)) and no constituents of the NP they refer to, hence not instance of ezafe, hence without 'i'. Last but not least, it is only the ezafe-analysis of RC's which explains why they are postnominal. If RC's were independent of ezafe (cf. Lehmann 1977/78) their postnominal position would be mysterious.

4. The development of the ezafe-construction

Since I have presented elsewhere (Haider/Zwanziger 1984) a detailed diachronic analysis, I will concentrate here on the essential traits. The development of 'ezafe' can be traced back until Old Iranian. In Avestan and Old Persian we find a particular type of RCs, RCs without a verb, termed nominal RCs in traditional grammars.

(15) Yt. 10.17

  miðrem ... yō nōit kahmāi aiβi.draoxðō
  Mithra (acc) ... who (nom) (is) not deceived by anyone

Sentences like (15) have been suspected to have arisen by copula-ellipsis. But there are cases which are problematic for the ellipsis hypothesis, like e.g. (16).

(16) Yt. 5.38
   gandareβem   yim   zairi.pāšnəm
   Gaṇdarva$_{Acc.}$ who$_{Acc.}$ golden heeled

The relative pronoun in (16) is marked Accusative, not Nominative, as would be required if there were a copula. But there are also cases where, according to handbooks (cf. Bartholomae 1979) the 3rd person neuter singular pronoun 'yat' occurs:

(17) Yr. 9.4
   aēbiiō yazataēibiiō yat aməšaēibiiō spəntaēibiiō
   these deities$_{dat.pl.m.}$ which Aməša spntas are

It is handbook knowledge that in nominal RCs in Younger Avestan the relative pronoun agrees in Case with the head noun if it is Accusative or Nominative (and sometimes in Instrumental) but is replaced by 'yat' in all the other cases. The crucial point is the analysis of 'yat'. It always occurs as 'yat', i.e. although there is also the plural from 'yā', which we would expect if the head noun is plural and 'yat' is the neuter pronoun.

In these analyses (cf. Seiler 1960) it is overlooked that the complementizer particle in Avestan is 'yat' too. Given that the 'yat' we find in nominal RCs is the complementizer 'yat' there is no reason to assume that it should agree in number, of course.

It is this very reanalysis — Relative Pronoun to Complementizer — which is crucial for the later development.

Let us take a sentence like (18):

(18) Yt. 17.18
   staota ašəm yat xahištəm
   praised righteousness$_{Acc.}$ that the highest value (is)

There are three analyses, synchronically speaking, compatible with (18).

(19) yat: a) pronoun, 3rd p. sg. Nominative (copula deleted)
   b) pronoun, 3rd p. sg. Accusative (no copula) (no copula/copula deleted)
   c) complementizer

It is easy to see how these three analyses can arise. (19a) is the basic construction. The RC is a standard relative clause and the verb, being a copula, is elided. Nevertheless it is still responsible for the Nominative: Nominative is dependent on the presence of a finite verb (cf. Chomsky 1981: 264).

The analysis (19b) is a result of interpreting the sentence as non-elliptic. Since there is no verb then, there is no element to assign nominative. Since the head noun is Accusative and 'yat' can be interpreted as Accusative, this Accusative can be interpreted as assigned by case-agreement, similar to the agreement found with attributive adjectives.

This analysis entails, however, that there is no sentence-boundary between the elements that agree with each other, because case-assignment is blocked by sentence boundaries. It is this very analysis that yields (17).

The third analysis (19c) is also a consequence of the opacity of case-assignment to 'yat', due to the lack of an overt verbal case assigner. Since the Case of the relative pronoun plays no role for the interpretation of nominal RCs — they are predicative — 'yat' can be reanalyzed as the complementizer particle. This results e.g. in (20).

(20) V.5.39
   ahmi aŋhuuō   yat astuuainti
   (in) this life (loc., sg., m) that (a) material (one is)

The analysis (19b) and c) are inconsistent, however; If 'yat' is a complementizer it entails the *presence* of a sentential constituent, if a relative pronoun gets case by agreement it entails *the absence* of a sentential boundary. Since examples like (17) are clear instances of agreement, a consistent structure-assignment of nominal RCs in Younger Avestan requires a reanalysis of 'yat' as a specific particle, distinct from its complementizer function.

This is the crucial point in the development, and this is also the point where the chance factor enters for a second time, the first being the particular reanalyses (19b) and c). In this situation there are several options available.

1. Generalizing 'yat' for all nominal RCs, leading to a homonymy: 'ya*t*' = attributive particle or complementizer
2. Avoidance of nominal RCs, making them obsolete
3. Generalizing 'ya*t*' as attributive particle and promoting another complementizer to the standard complementizer.

The choice among these options is a forced choice, forced by the reanalysis that had happened already due to the opacity of case assignment.

What has happened is the choice at option 3. The reasons for this choice seem to be the following: Generalizing 'ya*t*' to the attributive particle results in a structurally articulated attributive construction which allows to circumvent the problems resulting from the decay of the inflection-system in a free word order language (cf. Haider/Zwanziger (1983) on Middle Persian).

It is easy to see why this resulted in a *postnominal* construction: The 'ezafe' — and option 3 is the origin of 'ezafe' — is the result of a re-analysed relative clause. This reanalysis involved case-agreement. Case-agreement entails that the reanalyzed RC is constituent of the NP that gets case assigned to. Case is morphologically realized on the head noun and spreads to other constituents.

Avestan RCs have sentence-initial relative pronouns that agree with the head noun. Hence they have to be adjacent to the head, which is possible only in *postnomial* position. Hence reanalysis was possible only in *postnominal* position and consequently 'ezafe' originated in *postnominal* position. Right from the beginning, the 'ezafe' comprised NP, PP and AP attributes, since these occurred also in the nominal RCs. It is a matter of grammatical necessity that this developing new construction became fully general, comprising all maximal projections, i.e. clauses too. Again this was a development fully in line with the decay of the case system: It offered a possibility to make up for the loss of case distinctions in the pronominal system.

Speaking of 'matter of grammatical necessity' means that in the particular situation there was no way to avoid the most general interpretation since a restriction that, let us say, would allow attributive clauses as 'ezafe' and keep RCs distinct from it, could not be expressed with the means available in the system of the particular grammar.

4.1 *The complementizer origin of the ezafe-particle*

Empirical evidence as well as theoretical considerations corroborate the analysis that the element 'yat' which occurs in Young Avestan RCs is not the pronoun but the complementizer:

1. There is no number agreement, although there exists a plural form of 'ya*t*', namely 'yā' (cf. 17)
2. In Middle Persian we find a new complementizer 'ka' (the source of Modern Persian 'ke'), 'ya*t*' becoming obsolete as a complementizer.

These two facts receive an immediate explanation, if it is the complementizer 'yat' that gets confined to the 'ezafe' — constructions.

3. It is a typologically common characteristic of RC-patterns, that the

complementizer may replace the pronoun, as e.g. in English.

(21) a) the book which/that I bought
b) the man $\begin{cases} \text{*that's father I know, ...} \\ \text{whose ...} \end{cases}$
c) a book $\begin{cases} \text{*about that I would not write a review} \\ \text{about which ...} \end{cases}$

The examples (21 b, c) show that 'that' is the complementizer not the demonstrative pronoun. A demonstrative pronoun can occur within PPs, but the complementizer only sentence initially.

4. A sentence initial relative pronoun serves two functions:

It marks the sentence boundary and its case signals the syntactic relation to the verb. In copulative RCs the latter function is redudant. So without loss it can be reinterpreted as the element that marks the boundary of an embedded clause, the complementizer.

5. *Chance & Necessity*

Every generation of speakes of a languages L has to acquire the grammar of L. The grammar of L is a particular instantiation of universally available principles, which we may take to be one element of human biological endowment, the language faculty. (Chomsky 1982:

The universal principles that form the language faculty are called Universal Grammar (UG).

"The grammar of a language can be regarded as a particular set of values for the parameters (associated with the principles H.H.), while the overall system of rules, principles, and parameter is UG." (Chomsky 1982: 7).

The acquisition of a grammar L requires — among other tasks as e.g. learning the vocabulary etc. — the fixing of the value for the parameters.

Language change is the result of fixing parameter(s) in a way that differs from the previous generation, i.e. the very same phenomenon is analyzed differently.

An instructive example is the choice of the basic pattern in a system with various patterns:

German exhibits a characteristic variation, the verb-second phenomenon. In main clauses the finite verb occurs in second position in embedded clauses it is clause-final. This means there are two different positions for the finite verb, depending on main or subordinate clause. Consequently there are two options for the choice of the basic position, subordinate is basic or main clause position is basic.

In any case the particular choice is bound to a particular value of the directionality parameter, since in main clauses the verb tends to *precede* the objects but in subordinate clauses it *follows* them. So if the parameter is fixed 'rightwards', the main clause pattern is taken as basic and with 'leftwards' it is the pattern of the subordinate clause. If Proto-Germanic was an SOV language with a verb-position-variation similar to existing Germanic languages (as e.g. Dutch, German), then the rise of SVO patterns as e.g. in Scandinavian languages, reflects a switch in the value for the directionality parameter.

It must be borne in mind that radically different grammars may yield widely overlapping outputs. Hence the 'language' of two generations is the same, but the grammars differ. But since the newly fixed parameter is related with other parameters or with the fixing of the very same parameter in different instances, this may trigger ongoing change or what has been dubbed drift by Sapir.

Due to reasons external to a subsystem of grammar it may turn out that the value for a particular parameter that was chosen by the previous generations is not so readily available any longer since the data from which the value was inferred changed. Given that there are several options available, neither of which is optimal, the choice will be random. This is the *chance factor* in the acquisition. Of course there are external chance factors as well: If sound shift or loss affects particular sounds, it is a factor of chance if these are involved in the inflectional system, so that the system gets affected.

The *necessity* I refer to is the implementation of the newly structured subsystem in the whole system of grammar.

5.1 *Chance & Necessity in the development of 'ezafe'*

There are at least two crucial chance factors involved: The possibility to delete the copula (as an independent rule of the grammar) and the homonymy of the complementizer with some forms of the relative pronouns.

This made it possible to reanalyze a sequence of Noun — Relative Pronoun — Predicate either as sentential, i.e. as N+RC, or N+non-sentential attribute.

For the RC there was again the option for analyzing the initial element as pronoun or complementizer.

It was the structure of the Case-system — only structural cases could be spread (i.e. Nominative and Accusative, cf. Haider 1985) that lead to a split: There was no consistent analysis any longer for nominal RCs in Young Avestan, so they had to be interpreted as a *non-sentential* attributive construction. When the reanalysis from 'yat' had been extended to 'yo' resulting in 'yim' (Acc. Sg. masc.) a sentential analysis was clearly precluded by the way case-assignment works. As an immediate consequence of this subcase, the whole construction is characterized as non-sentential, by necessity since case-assignment does not "cross" sentence boundaries. But this has repercussions for the cases where 'yat' appears. A coherent structural assignment to nominal RCs entails that 'yat' gets shifted into a non-sentential environment. Since it is a particle but not in a complementizer position any longer, a new function must be assigned to it: This new function is the 'ezafe'.

If we view this from a broader perspective we can again distinguish between chance and necessity.

It is a matter of chance that the 'ezafe'-construction developed, but it is a matter of necessity that it developed *postnominally*, because it is the result of the reanalysis of a relative clause and the particular reanalysis of a relative clause and the particular reanalysis could happen only postnominally: The reanalysis — i.e. replacing case assignment for the pronoun by case spread-required the RC to be a constituent of the NP. Since RCs that agree with the head have to be adjacent, and since the relative pronouns occur sentence initially in Avestan, the RC had to be postnominal.

Hence a RC that is a constituent of the NP to the head of which the RC belongs is postnominal.

The fact that 'yat' is confined exclusively to 'ezafe', by replacing the homonymous complementizer may be a consequence of the avoidance of having sequences of homonymous elements with different functions, which would have occurred in embeddings of clauses under NP:

(22) [N – ya*t*   [$_S$yat [...]]]

The replacement of 'yat' in (22) is then generalized. This kind of avoidance is observable also in English (double-ing filter) or in Italian (double infinitive filter), (cf. Ross, 1972; Riemsdijk/Williams 1981: 177 and references cited there).

6. Concluding Remarks

If this analysis is correct it turns out that Modern Persian relative clauses are not so exceptional at all. They are an instance of a very general construction. It is a particle construction and therefore *adjacency* is not at stake here. Thus there is no link to the directionality factor of government. The serialization of attributes is independent. It is the oversimplified data-classification in word-order typologies, which does not care for the grammatical details of a construction, and therefore runs into problems with cases of that type.

It is not sufficient to compare functions — i.e. relative clause equals relative clause, etc., to get insight into the "great underlying groundplans". These may turn out as the result of setting the values of the main parameters in the grammatical systems in one or the other default manner.

REFERENCES

Bartholomae, Ch. 1979. *Altiranisches Wörterbuch*. Berlin: de Gruyter.
Chomsky, N. 1981. *Lectures on government and binding*. Dordrecht: Foris.
—— 1982. *Concepts and consequences of the theory of government and binding*. Cambridge, Mass.: MIT Press.
Downing, B. 1977. Typological regularities in postnominal relative clauses, *Current themes in linguistics*, ed. by F. Eckman, 163-194. New York: Wiley and Sons.
—— 1978. Some universals of relative structure, *Universals of human language*, IV, ed. by J. H. Greenberg, 375-418. Stanford: Stanford University Press.
Emonds, J. 1979. Appositive relatives have no properties. *Linguistic Inquiry* 10. 211-43.
Greenberg, J. H. 1963. Some universals of grammar with particular reference to the order of meaningful elements, *Universals of language* ed. by J. H. Greenberg, 73-113. Cambridge, Mass.: MIT Press.
Haider, H. 1982. Dependenzen und Konfigurationen — Zur deutschen V-Projektion. *Groninger Arbeiten zur Germanischen Linguistik* 21. 1-60.
—— 1985. The case of German, *Studies in German Grammar*, ed. by J. Toman. Dordrecht: Foris.
Haider, H. and R. Zwanziger. 1984. Relatively attributive: the development of the 'ezafe' — construction from Old Iranian to Modern Persian, *Historical syntax*, ed. by J. Fisiak. Berlin: Mouton.
Hawkins, J. 1979. Implicational universals as predictors of word order change. *Language* 55. 618-48.
Jackendoff, R. 1977. *$\bar{X}$-syntax: a study of phrase structure*. Cambridge, Mass.: MIT Press.
Koster, J. 1975. Dutch as an SOV-Language. *Linguistic analysis* 1. 111-36.

Lehmann, Ch. 1977/78. Ya-ye esarat — Zur Grammatik des persischen Relativsatzes. *Indogermanische Forschungen* 82. 97-106.
Lehmann, W. P. 1973. A structural principle of language and its implications. *Language* 49. 47-66.
Lentz, W. 1978. Das Neupersische. *Handbuch der Orientalistik, I/IV/1: Linguistik*, ed. by B. Spuler, 179-221. Leiden: Brill.
Mallinson, G., B. Blake. 1981. *Language typology*. Amsterdam: North Holland.
Riemsdijk, H. van, E. Williams. 1981. NP-structure. *The Linguistic Review* 1. 171-217.
Ross, J. R. 1972. Double-ing. *Linguistic Inquiry* 3. 61-86.
Schwartz, A. 1971. General aspects of relative clause structure, Stanford: *Working Papers on Language Universals* 6. 139-71.
Seiler, H. -J. 1960. *Relativsatz, Attribut und Apposition*. Wiesbaden: Harrassowitz.
Vennemann, T. 1974. Theoretical word order studies: results and problems. *Papiere zur Linguistik* 7. 5-25.
—— 1975. An explanation of drift. *Word order and word order change*, ed. by Ch. Li, 269-306. Austin: Texas University Press.
Watkins, C. 1977. Towards Proto-Indo-European syntax: problems and psuedo-problems. *Indo-European Studies* III, ed. by C. Watkins, 437-67. Cambridge, Mass.: Harvard University.
Windfuhr, G. 1979. *Persian grammar*. The Hague: Mouton.

UMLAUT AS A HARMONY PROCESS

CAMIËL HAMANS

1. Introduction

In a recent article Halle and Vergnaud (1981) discuss harmony processes. They distinguish two types: dominant and directional harmony. Dominant harmony spreads a feature in both directions whereas directional harmony propagates a feature in one direction only, from left to right or from right to left. For the description of dominant harmony they make use of an autosegmental framework, in which an autosegment can be associated with segmental slots in a more or less classical way. For directional processes they propose a metrical theory, in which the feature specification of the designated terminal node is copied by a rule on to the root of the tree and percolates downwards from there to all terminal nodes of the tree.

Halle and Vergnaud do admit that harmony processes agree in many respects, but because of descriptional simplicity they propose two different systems. Intuitively this idea is not very attractive. In spite of the different kinds of harmony and assimilation, that occur in various languages, they are of the same nature. In fact all harmony processes can be characterized in the same way: the occurrence of a special feature determines the value of the same or corresponding features in a restricted domain for instance a word or a foot. Because of this idea I would suggest that all kinds of harmony processes have to be described within one and the same framework.

1.1. Non linear phonology

In the last ten years research done on stress and tone showed that the classical model of linear generative phonology, the SPE model, was inadequate. In the SPE model stress has been described by a cyclically operating stress rule, which gives an absolute stress value to all the qualified vowels of a word. This approach produced values from 1 stress up to 4. The predicted differences, in for instance, 3 stress and 4 stress appeared not to be observable. Moreover, stress is not an absolute feature, but a relative property. Therefore a metrical theory has been developed.

Within this theory the stress pattern of a word is represented in binary branching trees, where the nodes are labelled *s* (strong) or *w* (weak). These labels do not have a fixed phonetic or absolute interpretation. *S* means that the node labelled *s* is dominant in stress with respect to a node labelled *w*. The element, which is dominant within a certain domain, is called the designated terminal node. Words, such as *canoe*, *police* and *pontoon* get the following metrical structure.

(1a)
```
         /\
        w   s
        ca  noe
        po  lice
        pon toon
```

It will be evident that this tree represents the stress pattern of these words. Words, such as *canyon*, *caper* and *system* have stress on the first syllable. An appropriate tree for these examples would be

(1b)
```
         /\
        s   w
        can yon
        ca  per
        sys tem
```

In words with more syllables, such as *phonology*, *elephant* and *monopoly*, there are more stressed syllables. The primary stress in *phonology* is on the second syllable, the secondary stress lies on the last. Therefore, this syllable must be *s*, but must have a lower degree of strength than the second. An appropriate tree for *monopoly* and *phonology* could be

(1c)
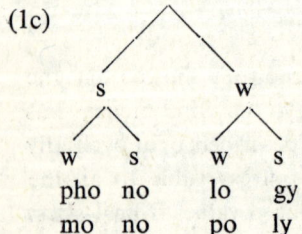

The *s* node under *s*, which is the designated terminal element, is stronger than the *s* under *w*. So we get the right stress pattern. For *elephant* we need another structure. For instance

(1d)

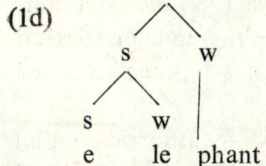

In this example the secondary stress is on the last syllable as well. The tree shows this: *w* under another node is weaker than an 'independent' *w*. Theoretically, *elephant* or *mountebank* could be described by other trees.

*(1e)

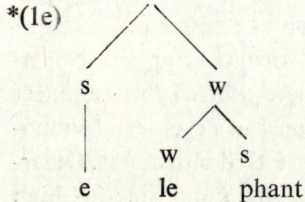

Such a tree is not allowed: of two sister nodes [N1, N2], N2 is strong if and only if it branches.

As will be clear the terminal nodes of these trees stand for syllables. This is not the only element used in metrical phonology; the other element is the *foot*. A foot structure is needed to describe the difference between *w*-labelled syllables. In English, for instance, there are two different types of weak syllables: the first one cannot be reduced, whereas the second can. Therefore there must be a distinction between the structure of *gymnast* and *modest*. According to their stress pattern there is no difference between these two examples, but the last syllable in *modest* is reduced, whereas the last syllable of *gymnast* cannot be reduced. That is why we award the foot status to both of the syllables of *gymnast* and only to the first syllable of *modest*:

(1f)

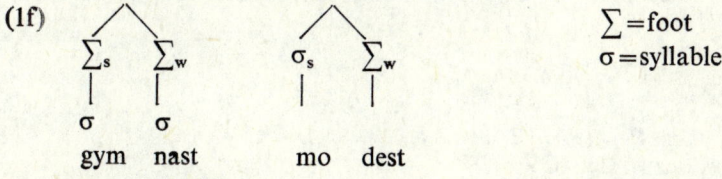

Only syllables that are not a foot and are unstressed, can be reduced. By accepting a foot level we can group the syllables together, as I did in fact in the tree of *phonology* and *monopoly*. There are at least four theoretical possibilities for feet structure, but that is not important here. By means of these feet we can represent the rhythmic or metrical stress pattern of polysyllabic words. That is why this approach is called metrical phonology.

Autosegmental phonology has been invented for the description of tones, especially of contour tones. Contour tones, which are opposed to level tones — tones that show a constant pitch — involve a change in pitch. Contour tones, which are often put on only one vocalic segment, can be rising, falling, rising-falling, falling-rising etc. In the standard generative phonology it is very difficult to describe these changes adequately. In SPE the words are divided in segments. Each segment is an unordered set of specified features, which can be seen as a representation from points in time to states of the articulatory organs. Normally these states are constant. Only features like delayed release reflect a change. If we want to account for changing tones in a classically phonological framework, we have to make use of these kind of features. Otherwise a segment could be [+high tone] and at the same time [− high tone].

Tones can spread over more segments. This means that e.g. vowels without a specified pitch can get one, if they are for instance preceded by a tone-bearing segment. This tone can spread over the whole word. From this phenomenon it has been concluded that the feature tone could be removed from the segments and placed upon an autonomous level, from which they can be associated with the possible tone-bearing segments. Such a proposal can also solve the problems with features describing changes, for instance contour tones.

In an autosegmental theory there are at least two different levels, called tiers. On this tiers different classes of features can appear. The features of each level are unspecified with respect to these on other levels. Since all tiers together give the possibility for a phonetic interpretation, there must be a mechanism of association between the different tiers. In a schematic representation this can be described as follows:

(2a)

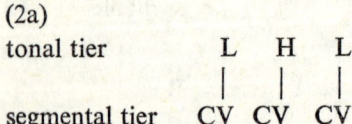

If there are less tones than tone-bearing slots, a tonal element will be associated with more vowels on the segmental tier:

(2b)
```
    L   H   L
    |   \   /\‾‾\‾‾\
    CV  CV CV CV CV
```

If there are more slots on the tonal tier than tone-bearing elements on the segmental tier, several tonal elements will be linked to one segmental slot, yielding contour tones:

(2c)
```
    L H L
    |  V
    CV CV
```

(2d)
```
    H L H
    V   |
    CV  CV
```

Since association can be applied according to language specific criteria, from right to left, left to right or both, the autosegmental framework is suited for describing dominant harmony. Halle and Vergnaud (1981: 1 - 5) show how dominant harmony in Kalenjin can be represented in an autosegmental way.

Kalenjin has two sets of vowels, one with the feature [+ ATR] (=advanced tongue root) and one without. If there is a [+ ATR] vowel in the word, whether in the root or in the affix, all [− ATR] vowels become [+ ATR]. If there are only [− ATR] vowels in the word, they remain so. For example, in kI-a-gɛr (I shut it) all vowels are [− ATR]; in kI-a-bar-In (I killed you) also. In ki-a-ge:r-in (I see you) and in ki-a-ger-e (I was shutting it) all vowels are [+ ATR], because of the dominant vowels of the morphemes ge:r and e. Underlying representations of these words can be sketched in a simplified way as follows:

(3a)   [+ ATR]   (3b)   [+ ATR]
             | |
          kI-a-gɛr-e   kI-a-gɛ : r In

The dominant feature spreads over the whole word and changes the vowels to the appropriate value

(3′)
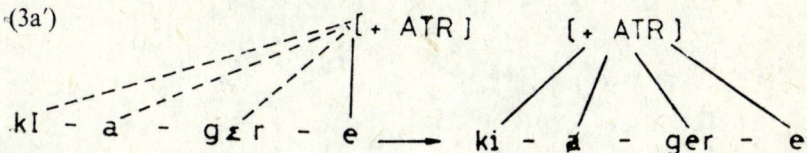

(3b')

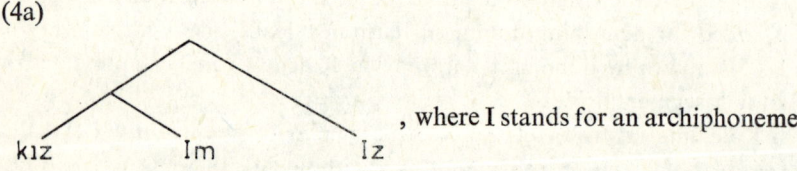

Direction harmony propagates in one direction only. Therefore Halle and Vergnaud propose a metrical system for the description of this kind of harmony. In Turkish, for instance, the value of vowels in suffixes agrees with that of the immediately preceding vowel. This rule is not completely correct, but for the example it will do. So in Turkish the vowels of the suffixes in gurur-un-uz (your pride) and in kız-ım-ız (our girl) have been determined in the last resort by those of the stem. The underlying form of kızımız is:

(4a)

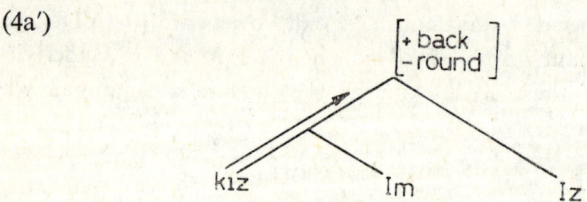

, where I stands for an archiphoneme

The feature $\begin{bmatrix} + \text{back} \\ - \text{round} \end{bmatrix}$, which comes from ı, goes to the top of this tree, according to Halle's and Vergnaud's idea:

(4a')

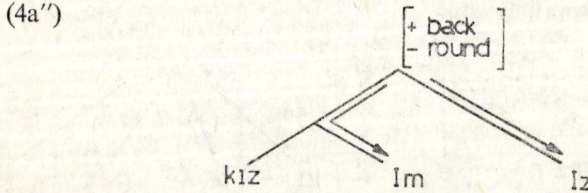

Thereupon it percolates downwards to all terminal nodes and gives them the appropriate feature value:

(4a'')

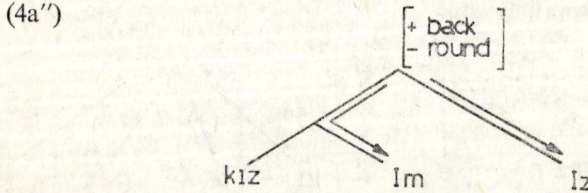

2. Counterarguments

2.1. Turkish

There are not only intuitive counterarguments against Halle's and Vergnaud's proposal. There are factual counterarguments as well. For instance their description of Turkish vowel harmony is rather incomplete. They do not only account for the exceptions to the normal rule of progressive assimilation (cf. Clements and Sezer (1982)), but also overlook the fact that there are instances of regressive vowel assimilation. This type of harmony is very interesting, because it mainly works in recent loanwords. This rule, which is not a very productive one, applies to loanwords, that become current. Lewis (1978^3: 16 - 17) gives the following examples:

(5a) imparator (emperor)   < Serbo-Croat imperator
      menecer (manager of a football < English manager
      team)
      madalya (medal)   < Italian medaglia
      ütüv (sterilizer)   < etüv < French étuve
      apolet (epoulet)   < French épaulette

Regressive vowel harmony also applies to compounds:

(5b) bu gün (this day)   > bugün > bügün (büğün)
      o bir (the other)   > öbir (> öbür)

These examples show that vowel harmony in Turkish can work from right to left too, although Halle and Vergnaud consider Turkish vowel harmony as a prototype of directional harmony. From the given loanwords we may conclude that not only progressive vowel harmony in Turkish is productive, but also regressive.

2.2. Umlaut

Another famous example of directional and local vowel harmony is umlaut. Umlaut could be considered therefore as another prototype of Halle's and Vergnaud's directional harmony. Traditionally umlaut has been described as a kind of regressive vowel assimilation operating on adjacent syllables. Both elements of this description appear to be incorrect. Boer (1924^2: 58&169) already mentioned umlaut in trisyllabic forms (*zahari-zeheren*). In my description of umlaut in Roermond (see below) we will find many, also recent, examples of umlaut operating in non-adjacent syllables, for instance: *computer-compüterke, hamburger-hämburgerke* (*-ke* is the diminutive suffix).

Umlaut is not typical for Germanic languages and not necessarily regressive. McCormick (1981: 127)[1] shows that in Sinhalese there was a rule of progressive umlaut at one time:

(6) Sinh. sevel (moss) cf. Pali sēvāla
     poho (quarter of cf. Pali upōsatha
     a lunar month)
     dolos (twelve) < *dolasa

3. Umlaut in Dutch and German

In Dutch, e.g. Standard Dutch, there have been three types of umlaut (cf. Van Bree 1977: 234). At the moment umlaut is not productive anymore, neither in phonology nor in morphology. Except for several dialects umlaut operated in short vowels only. Between Old Germanic and Proto Germanic there existed a-umlaut, a lowering rule; in the same period there was a raising umlaut, conditioned by ĭ, ī, j, ŭ or NC. Between Proto Germanic and Old Western Germanic there existed a rule of i-umlaut, a fronting rule. These rules did not occur, as foresaid, at one and the same moment. Each of these rules covered centuries. Since there are not that many written testimonies from the Pre-Old Dutch period, it is impossible to prove that the development of umlaut was gradual and diffuse; but because we do not accept, other kinds of processes than we encounter now, according to Labov's uniformitarian principle, these Dutch umlaut processes must be considered as lexical diffuse. So we have to specify in the various stages of the lexicon the words, to which the different umlaut rules can apply.

Later in the history umlaut, especially i-umlaut, has been expanded to words without an umlaut condition. In German the plural of the following words received for instance an umlaut, although there was no umlaut factor, i.e. no i/j in these plurals at any stage of the historical derivation:

(7a) German Wolf (wulf) — Wölfe
      Nagel (nail) — Nägel

---

[1] McCormick states that there are no examples of umlaut occuring between non-adjacent syllables. I don't agree with her. My examples of umlaut in Roermond will show that umlaut can also occur between non-adjacent syllables. There are examples kown from German too, e.g. Bruder-Brüderlich.

In the dialects of Dutch Limburg, a province in the south-eastern part of the country, the same phenomenon turns up (cf. Royen 1953: 16).

(7b) Limburg sjaop (sheep) — sjäöp
boum (tree) — buim

At this moment these rules seem no longer productive[2], but there was a time that they were. So we have to specify not only the words to which the umlaut applies under certain phonological conditions, but also the words, on which the same rule operates without that condition.

Since the plural morpheme in these dialects, at least in some cases, only consists of the feature [-back], which causes a change from [a:] into [ɛ:], and from [ɔ] into [ʌ] etc., an autosegmental framework offers a possible description for this phenomenon. On the autosegmental tier we could introduce a floating segment [-back], which spreads over the segmental slots. I would suggest to incorporate this spreading rule in the lexicon as well. So we do not only have words in the lexicon marked for umlaut, but also a lexical rule. In this way we can account for the originally dynamic and now, in some cases, fossilized character of umlaut. It will be clear that Halle and Vergnaud, who describe directional vowel harmony within a metrical theory, get into difficulty when they want to describe this kind of umlaut in a metrical way. In the examples given under (7) there is no designated terminal node with the feature [-back]. Therefore this feature cannot be copied and percolated.

4. Umlaut in Roermond

In the dialect of Roermond, a small town in the Dutch province Limburg, we meet the same phenomenon. However, in Roermond there exists only umlaut without a plural suffix.[3] Because I go on with diminutives in this dialects, I shall also give these forms here.

---

[2] In Hamans (in prep.) I will show that in the dialect of Roermond, a town in the centre of the province Limburg, there are indications that analogically extension of umlaut has not disappeared completely.

[3] There are a few examples of umlaut and a plural suffix:

peštoor	(parish-priest)	pešteurs	
keplaon	(chaplain)	kepleuns	(Schmitz 1978: 8)
broor	(brother)	breurs	(Kats 1939: 155)

One of my informants gave the plural forms *pesteur* and *kepleun*. I suppose that these are the regular forms and that the suffix -*s* is a borrowing from the standard Dutch.

(8a) long vowels   singular   plural   diminutive

   1. oe→uu (u:→y:)   voes (fist)   vuus   vuuske
   2. oo→eu (o→ø)   voot (foot)   veut   veutje
   3. ou→ui (ɔu→∧y)   boum (tree)   buim   buimke
   4. ao→äö (ɔ:→∧:)   haof (garden)   häöf   häöfke
   5. aa→ae (a→ɛ)   naagel (nail)   naegel   naegelke

(8b) short vowels

   1. ŏe→ŭu (u→y)   kŏef (forelock)   kŭuf   kŭufke
   2. o→u (v→œ)   štómp (stump)   štuup   štuupke
   3. o→ö (ɔ→∧)   štop (stopper)   štöp   štöpke
   4. a→e (a→æ)   tak (branch)   tek   tekske

As these examples show umlaut in Roermond is a kind of fronting, as it is in German.[4] Umlaut in the plural is no longer productive (but cf note 2), whereas umlaut in the forming of diminutives is the normal process. Therefore, the words have to be marked in the lexicon for a plural without a suffix and a floating feature [-back]. Since there are words in this dialect that can get a plural without a suffix but with a change in tone, the specification [-suffix] and [-back] must be added both to the lexical entries. It is impossible to describe this phenomenon in the Halle and Vergnaud framework, because there is no designated terminal node which has the specification [-back]. So we cannot copy this feature from this non-existing node. Feature percolation is therefore excluded as well.

Jo Kats, who wrote a dissertation on the dialect of Roermond (1939), already showed that plural formation with umlaut is no longer productive,[5] whereas diminutive formation with umlaut is. I shall give here some of the words, he mentioned in his glossary. I shall add some examples from my own research (these examples are marked +).

---

[4] There are a few exceptions to the normal rules:

hóntj	(dog)	huunj	huuntje	
móntj	(mouth)	muunj	muuntje	(Kats 1939: 154/5)
štat	(town)	štaej	stetje	

In fact *stat* isn't a counterexample: in the plural lengthening takes place, as in Dutch (*stad-steden*). I can't explain the examples *hontj* and *montj*.

[5] Some of my informants (cf Hamans in prep.) showed to have intuitions from which one can conclude that the umlaut rule in the plural has not disappeared completely. They said, for instance, that the plural of *astronaut* should have been *astronuit*, but unfortunately it has become *astronaute*, like in Dutch.

(8c) oe→uu   hoes (house)   hoezer   huuske
              +ragout   ragouts   raguuke
     oo→eu   boot (boat)   boote   beutje
                                     +beut⁶
              +gool (goal)   goole   geulke
     ou→ui   kous (stocking)   kouse   kuiske
              +astronaut   astronaute   astronuitje
     ao→äö   baog (arch)   bäög   bäögske
                                     +boage
     aa→ae   kraan (tap)   kraane   kraenke
              naas (nose)   naaze   naeske
              +garnaal (shrimp)   garnaale   garnaelke
     ŏe→ŭu   stŏep (steps)   stŭup   stŭupke
                                     +stŏepe
              broek (mother-hen)   broeke   brŭukske
     ó→u   vós (fox)   vus   vuske
                                     +vósse
              mót (moth)   mótte   mutje
     o→ö   dolk (dagger)   dolke   dölkske
              +tolk (interpreter)   tolke   tölkske
     a→e   +wak (hole in ice)   wakke   wekske
              +alm (Alpine pasture) alme   elmke
              muuzzekant (musician) muuzzekante   muuzzekentje

These examples are convincing. It seems, from this list, that umlaut only occurs between adjacent syllables. This is not the case.

(9) vader (father) — vaederke
    nóttaares (notary) — nóttaereske
    appel (apple) — eppelke
    partner — pertnerke
    corner — cörnerke
    dokter (doctor) — dökterke
    komkommer (cucumber) — komkömmerke
    computer — compuuterke
    scooter — scuuterke

---

[6] This is the only example in which all my informants gave a more 'conservative' answer than those of Kats. I suppose that Kats made a mistake, because all my older informants gave *beut*. On the other hand, the fact that Roermond is now a well known centre for aquatics possibly influenced the return of this form.

auto (car) — uiteke
Opel (a trade-mark) — eupelke

As can be seen from the examples *nóttaares*, *komkommer* and *computer*, umlaut does not take the whole word:

(10) maššenis → *mešseniske (engineer)
šoeffäör → *šuuffäörke (driver)
arties → *ertieske (artist)
kappietaalis → *keppietaeliske (capitalist)
haoveneer → *häöveneerke (gardener)
astronaut → *estreunuitje (astronaut).

In a classical autosegmental framework one tries to solve this problem by stipulating opaque segments. In fact Halle and Vergnaud could do the same in their metrical approach, if not, the feature would percolate downwards to all terminal nodes. Unfortunately there is no natural class of opaque segments or blockers. Another possible solution would be to allow umlaut between nonadjacent syllables, only if the intermediate syllable contains e schwa. This proposal does not hold water.

(11) operátie (operation) → operaetieke
nátie (nation) → naetieke
bálie (court) → baelieke

These diminutives are not commonly used. Not all my informants gave these forms; some people gave the Dutch forms, whereas others answered that diminutives of these words do not exist.

However, these forms suggest that umlaut occurs in the foot adjacent to the suffix (cf. Liberman and Prince (1977) and Selkirk (1980)). This suffix does not contain a normal umlautfactor, e.g. a *i* or a *j*. Maybe the *k*, which is slightly palatalized, can be considered as the conditioning factor (cf. Peé 1936–38: 1, 53–60). Otherwise we have to introduce a floating feature [-back].

It is not that surprising that the foot can be the domain of vowel harmony. Hayes (1981) showed that stress feet form the domain for directional vowel harmony in Eastern Cheremis. Zubizaretta (1979) has argued that the dependence of Andalusian vowel harmony on stress requires that the harmony domain be identified with the metrical stress foot.

5. Description

For Dutch there is independent evidence for a foot level (cf. Van der Hulst (1981), Van der Hulst and Moortgat (1981), Neyt and Zonneveld (1981a & b) and (1982)). This evidence has been found in the very complicated stress system of Dutch. The stress system of the Roermond dialect is not different. So we may assume that this evidence is valid for this dialect too. There is some discussion about the exact nature of the Dutch feet. Van der Hulst and Moortgat (1981) argue for unbounded feet, whereas Neyt and Zonneveld (1981) do for binary-branching ones. I could give a description in terms of the Van der Hulst and Moortgat system, but I shall borrow the foot and superfoot system, defended for Dutch by Van Nes (1982), since this system is very similar to that of Selkirk (1980). My trees can be transformed into unbounded ones rather easily. We get the following trees

(F means foot, F' superfoot and W word):

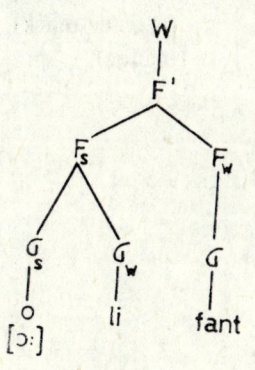

ólifant   (elephant)
cárnaval   (carnival)
hámburger   (hamburger)
rádio   (radio)

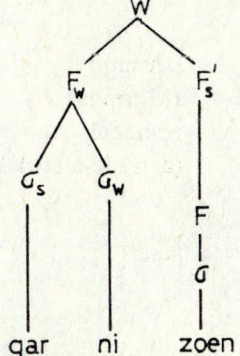

garnizóen   (garrison)
abrikóos   (apricot)
astrokáut   (astronaut)
ledikánt   (bed)

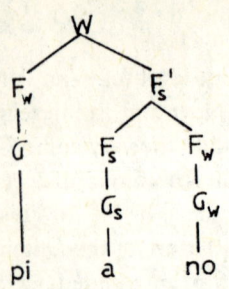

piáno (piano)
mecáno (meccano)
nirwána (nirvana)
pyjáma (pyjamas)

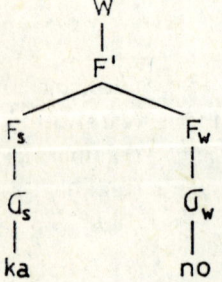

kátie (nation)
bálie (court)
Vólvo (a trade-mark)
káno (canoe)

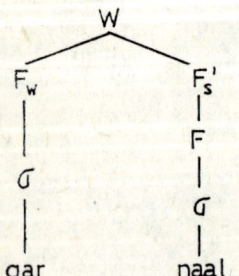

garnáal (shrimp)
mormóon (Mormon)
mongóol (mongol)
Talbót (a trade-mark)
[bö]

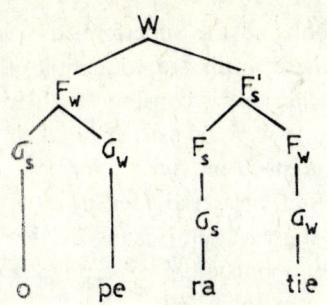

operátie (operation)
consultátie (maternity centre)
dromedáris (dromedary)
proclamátie (proclamation)

This description seems to explain almost all data. The diminutives are:

(12i) olifentje
carnavelke
hemburgerke
radieuke/raedieuke
(12iii) piaeneuke/pianeuke/piaeneke
mecaneuke
nirwanaeke
pyjaemaeke/pyjamaeke
(12v) garnaelke
mormeunke
mongeulke
Tolbeuke

(12ii) garnizuunke
abrikeuske
astronuitje
ledikentje
(12iv) naetieke
baelieke
Völveuke/Volveuke/Völveke
kaeneuke
(12vi) operaetieke
consultaetieke
dromedaeriske
proclamaetieke

The conclusion must be that umlaut takes the adjacent foot or superfoot (*hemburgerke, raedieuke, piaeneuke, pyjaemaeke, naetieke, baelieke, Völveuke, kaeneuke, operaetieke, consultaetieke, dromedaeriske* and *proclamaetieke*). The superfoot has been chosen in case the last foot was weak, but not consequently: **ölifentje*, **cernevelke* etc.). The exceptions to this general rule are: *piaeneke* and *Völveke*. These forms are not difficult to explain. The vowel of the penultimate syllable has been reduced. A reduced vowel cannot take umlaut.

It is clear that umlaut cannot operate on the whole word in this dialect. Forms such as

(13) ebrikeuske
estreunuitje
gernizuunke
euperaetieke

are impossible.

In my opinion, the choice between the foot and the superfoot, as in (12i & iii) is an individual one. Almost all these words are not common in this dialect, so the informants applied the rule according to their preference. It can be said that the informants were consistent in their choice, only the word *hamburger* caused a problem. One informant, who always applied umlaut to the adjacent foot, answered *hamburgertje*, the Dutch form, and *hemburgerke* as well. I suppose that it is the Anglo--American influence, which gave him the opportunity to change a *hamburger*, with an [a], into a real *hamburger*, with an [æ].

As my last examples showed, umlaut works within a domain. Therefore a metrical approach would do. However I showed before that a metrical approach cannot describe the plural formation. Since at least some of my informants have intuitions about the relation between plural and diminutive formation, I have to combine these two theories. Following ideas of Clements and Huang, Van der Hulst and Smith (1982: 40−41) suggest that an integration of metrical and autosegmental structure could be possible. They propose a structure like

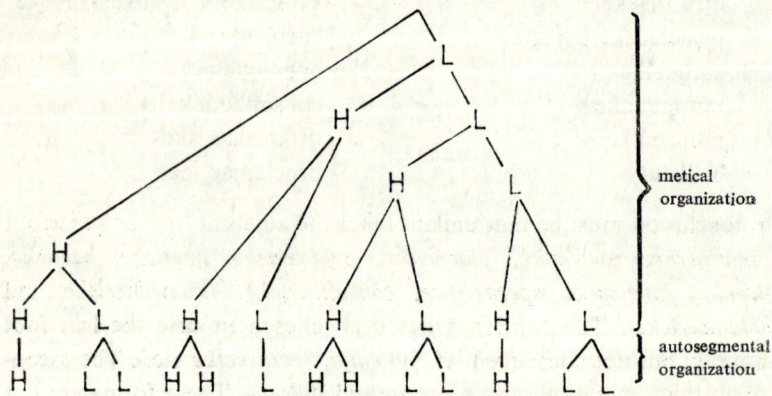

This structure has been made for tonal phenomena, not for umlaut. I would suggest that a slight modification of this type of structure, which has not been worked out yet, can handle all I discussed here.

BIBLIOGRAPHY

Boer, R. C. 1924². *Oergermaansch handboek*. Haarlem: Tjeenk Willink.
Bree, C. van 1977. *Leerboek voor de historische grammatica van het Nederlands*. Groningen: Wolters-Noordhoff.
Clements, G. N. and E. Sezer. 1982. "Vowel and Consonant Disharmony in Turkish", in: H. van der Hulst and N. Smith, eds. *The structure of phonological representations* Part II. Dordrecht: Foris. 213-255.

Halle, M. and J. R. Vergnaud. 1981. "Harmony processes", In: W. Klein and W. Levelt, eds. *Crossing the boundaries in linguistics.* Dordrecht, Boston and London: Reidel. 1-22.
Hamans, C. In preparation. "Achteruitgang van het dialect".
Hayes, B. 1981. *A metrical theory of stress rule.* Doctoral dissertation, MIT Cambridge, Mass. Rev. version distributed by IULC Bloomington, Indiana.
Hulst, H. van der 1981. "Die structuur van fonologische representaties" *Glot* 4. 1-33.
Hulst, H. van der and M. Moortgat. 1981. "Prosodische fonologie en de accentuatie van Nederlandse woorden, of: Leeft het Nederlands op grote voet?". In *Verslag van de 156e vergadering van de Nederlandse Vereniging voor Fonetische Wetenschappen.* Amsterdam. 1-25.
Hulst, H. van der and N. Smith. 1982. "An overview of autosegmental and metrical phonology". In: H. van der Hulst and N. Smith, eds. *The structure of phonological representation* Part. I. Dordrecht — Cinnaminson: Foris. 1-45.
Kats, J. 1939. *Het phonologisch en morphonologisch systeem van het Roermondsch dialect.* Roermond — Maaseik: Romen and Zonen.
Liberman, M. and A. Prince. 1977. "On stress and linguistic rhythm". *Linguistic Inquiry 8*. 249-336.
Lewis, G. L. 1978[3]. *Turkish grammar.* Oxford: Clarendon Press.
McCormick, S. 1981. "A metrical analysis of umlaut". In: *Cornell Working Papers in Linguistics 2.* 127-137.
Nes, J. J. van 1982. "Een parametrisch verschil tussen de klemtoonsystemen van het Nederlands en het Engels". *Glot* 5. 285-310.
Neyt, A. and W. Zonneveld. 1981a. "Metrische fonologie: klemtoon en clitics in het Nederlands". In: *Verslag van de 156e vergadering van de Nederlandse Vereniging voor Fonetische Wetenschappen.* Amsterdam. 26-37.
Neyt, A. and W. Zonneveld. 1981b. "Die aantrekkingskracht van -baar". *Glot* 4. 215-228.
Neyt, A. and W. Zonneveld. 1982. "Metrische fonologie — de representatie van klemtoon in Nederlandse monomorfematische woorden". *Die Nieuwe Taalgids* 75. 527-547.
Peé, W. 1936-38. *Dialectgeographie der Nederlandsche Diminutiva.* Tongeren: Michiel-Broeders.
Royen, G. 1953. *Taalrapsodie.* Bussum: Paul Brand.
Schmitz, J. 1978. *Kleine spraakkunst van het Roermonds dialect.* Roermond: St Christoffel.
Selkirk, E. O. 1980. "The role of prosodic categories in English word stress". *Linguistic Inquiry* 11. 563-605.
Zubizarretta, M. L. 1979. "Vowel harmony in Andalusian Spanish". In: K. Safir, ed. *Papers on syllable structure, metrical structure and harmony processes.* Cambridge, Mass.: MIT Working Papers in Linguistics 1.

DIVERGENT PATTERNS OF WORD ORDER CHANGE IN CONTEMPORARY FRENCH

MARTIN B. HARRIS

Scholars of French have long noted alternatives to the 'canonical' SVO word order traditionally attributed to that language, in particular structures in which the subject and/or the object and/or indeed certain other types of complement also can be extracted from their 'normal' position and located either to the left or to the right of the 'core' sentence, this consisting now of the verb and any non-dislocated NPs, with an appropriate co-referential clitic being, in general, affixed to the verb in respect of each dislocated NP. Thus, to make use once again of a much-cited example, a sentence such as

(1) je le lui ai donné moi le livre à Pierre

may be analysed as a 'core' sentence comprising a verb and three co-referential clitics (now by common consent seen as bound prefixes) followed by the subject, object and prepositional complement (indirect object) in right-dislocated position.

As has already been observed, the frequent occurrence of such sentence types, and of comparable left-dislocated structures, has been widely described (see in particular Müller-Hauser 1943). In the last decade or so, however, they have attracted particular attention, both within the context of general syntactic theory (Rodman 1974, Hirschbühler 1975, Cinque 1977, Larsson 1979) and in the context of greatly increased interest in problems of word order and word order change. The purpose of the present paper is to look again at the developments which appear to be in progress in French, and to try to present the data which has been amassed by a number of scholars within a wider theory of word order change; in particular, it seems appropriate to reconsider an analysis I presented earlier (Harris 1976, 1978) in the light of two alternative hypotheses presented subsequently, those of Joelle Bailard (1982) and Knud Lambrecht (1981), with a view to formulating an integrated description of the position in contemporary French. It will be suggested that there are (at least) two competing strategies of change in operation in the language at the present time, both with clear parallels attested and described in many other languages, and that it is by no means obvious which strategy will prevail — or, indeed, whether any alternative to the canonical order will wholly prevail in the foreseeable future, given the particular cultural position in which French currently finds itself.

Let us consider first the position of right-dislocated structures, which are those which form the primary focus of attention in my own earlier work and that of Bailard. At the purely descriptive level, it no longer seems contentious to assert that one alternative intrasentential order in modern French, minor but by no means insignificant (17% of the tokens within a substantial sample recently presented by Bill Ashby (Ashby 1982: 34)), is verb initial (given the analysis of clitic pronouns as bound prefixes noted earlier). The emergence of a verb-initial pattern in a language whose canonical order has been SVO is by no means unexpected cross-linguistically, a fact observed by Theo Vennemann in 1974. Two important questions remain, however: is the newly emergent order VSO or VOS — a question primarily addressed by Bailard (1982) — and, more generally, why should a right-dislocated order be in the process of being grammaticalised in French at the present time,[1] rather than simply remaining as a heavily marked option for use in the case of afterthoughts and the like?

The most honest answer to the first question seems to be that the matter is unresolved, or rather that there is no general *syntactically governed* preference for VSO or VOS when the two relevant NPs are indeed the subject and the direct object and when there is no special factor binding one or other of these constituents particularly closely to the verb. (These caveats are important.) One of Bailard's examples (1982: 22) indicates clearly this point:

(2) (her 25) elle l'aimait bien Marie sa mère

This sentence is indeed ambiguous, as Bailard notes; so too is

(3) elle l'aimait bien sa mère Marie

In other words, with a verb like *aimer* where there is overlap between the class of possible subjects and the class of possible objects, and where the surface syntactic structure takes the form of an 'orthodox' subject

---

[1] Noting that such a development is relatively frequent cross-linguistically, as we have just done, is not of course at all the same as attempting to explain why such a development takes place in a particular language at a particular time.

and direct object, there are apparently no *syntactic* grounds for choosing between VSO and VOS.

In making this claim, I am in effect reverting to the more open position I first proposed in 1976, and retreating from the more definite prediction of an eventual preference for VSO order found in Harris 1978. The reason for this is that, in the latter case, I attached undue importance to sentence tokens in which one of the right-dislocated NPs was in fact a disjunctive personal pronoun. As Bailard (1982: 22) implicitly reminds us, it is unwise to make general statements about word order in the light of specific examples in which the constituents under discussion are, conceivably at least, distinguished in respect of some other variable. Specifically, personal pronouns may well be less 'heavy' than lexical NPs, as Bailard suggests, and thus — in the absence of some other factor such as stress, discussed below — may well tend to precede other nominal elements. Accordingly, in

(4) je la déteste moi Marie (=Bailard's (23))

'moi' would, by this analysis, precede 'Marie' because of this general tendency for 'heavier' nominals to follow less heavy elements such as personal pronouns, thus yielding in this case a VSO order,[2] the unmarked order in such instances. This would not, however, constitute proof of the emergence of VSO as the preferred order in verb-initial sentences in French.

On the evidence currently available, however, the 'stronger' version of the VOS claim advanced by Bailard does not seem to be tenable either. Close examination of her principal examples (1982: 21) reveals that none of them is of the type represented by (2) and (3) above.

In some cases, the valency of the main verb requires a prepositional phrase within the core sentence in order to complete its sense (a point aken up again below)[3] and it therefore may not be dislocated; thus, for tnstance, while

(5) il est allé au cinéma Jean (=Bailard's (9))

---

[2] The personal pronoun may of course also appear in final position. For a discussion of the prosodic factors which might cause this to be so, see below.

[3] Bailard's examples (12) and (20)
   (12) il est parti sans sa serviette Jean
   (20) ? il est parti Jean sans sa serviette
lie outside the scope of the present discussion, since 'sans sa serviette' is not only a wholly optional complement but also one which cannot be cliticized. For the record, (20) seems quite acceptable to me. A similar point concerning 'circumstantial' adverbials of time, place etc. is made by Larsson 1979: 86.

is acceptable (5a) is not:

(5a) *il est allé Jean au cinéma (=Bailard's (17));

in some cases, one nominal is the complement of one verb whereas the subject is the subject of the entire complex, thus

(6) il a fait tomber un oeuf Jean (=Bailard's (10))

but not (6a):

(6a) *il a fait tomber Jean un oeuf (=Bailard's (18));

and in some cases the main verb is lexically empty and it is only the 'direct object' which gives it any meaning, thus

(7) il a eu un accident Jean (=Bailard's (7))

but not (7a):

(7a) *il a eu Jean un accident (=Bailard's (15)).

Similar points can be made about all the examples which purport to show that the emerging verb-initial order is VOS rather than VSO. In fact, I submit, they do not demonstrate this, but rather show that there are specifiable syntactic grounds, some of which I have tried to indicate above, which may cause the subject to follow rather than precede other nominal elements within the sentence. To reiterate: when the two NPs in a sentence are, in surface structure, a subject and a direct object respectively, and where the class membership of these two categories may overlap, there seem to be no syntactic grounds for postulating a preference for VSO or VOS in French at present.

There is one other point which should be made before leaving Bailard's data on this topic. It is essential to distinguish right-dislocated sentences in which every cliticizable nominal does in fact have a co-referential clitic affixed to the verb — and it is to these sentences that my own work has been directed — from those where one or more potential clitics do not in fact appear. Thus example (5a) is rendered acceptable by the addition of a clitic *y* within the core sentence, both 'Jean' and 'au cinéma' now being available for dislocation (and either order being possible):

(8) il y est allé Jean au cinéma

Conversely, because cliticisation of *un accident* is ruled out,[4] (9) is as

---

[4] Both because 'avoir in accident' is, as we have already seen, one semantic unit and, more generally, because of the restrictions on the use of anaphoric and cataphoric pronouns (and determiners) in the case of non-specific NPs. (For discussion, see for example Gundel, 1975: 79ff. and Lambrecht, 1981: 61 and 84.)

unacceptable as (7a) above:

(9) *il l'a eu Jean un accident.

We shall return to this point below, in our discussion of Lambrecht's work, where we shall note that only nominals which *can be and are* cliticized may be right-dislocated in French. It is perhaps just worth recalling at this point that it is precisely these clitics which ensure that in the overwhelming majority of cases (and quite unlike our atypical example (2)!), a sentence which may in principle be interpretable as either VSO or VOS is in fact capable of only one interpretation. (And there are even strategies for interpreting examples like (2): cf. Larsson 1979: 95.) The clitics, which are marked for case, disambiguate the nouns and/or disjunctive pronouns, which are not (Harris 1978: 119–20).

Finally in this part of the paper, let us pose again the question as to what factor or factors have led to the progressive grammaticalisation of verb-initial structures in French. Here, the characteristic phrasefinal stress pattern of French does indeed seem, as Bailard suggests, to be crucially relevant. Essentially, the principal stress within a French sentence occurs at the end of the 'core' sentence, with one or more 'parenthetical' elements tolerated thereafter. Such 'parenthetical' elements may include, as we have seen, nominals with various functions,[5] in a structure which was surely in origin an 'afterthought mechanism', where this term is to be interpreted broadly to include any word order used to make more explicit, or to elaborate on, the value of an element expressed earlier in some more restricted way (e.g. by a pronoun) (and hence not *always* 'de faible valeur informative', *pace* Larsson 1979: 18). Such nominals were of course frequently co-referential with the subject, direct object, etc. of the 'core' sentence, and (secondarily) were also often co-referential with the topic (theme) of the sentence.[6] (The reasons why right-dislocated sentences in French do not seem to be best analysed as instances of topicalisation are discussed below.) From the starting point of a phrase-stress-final language readily tolerating right-dislocated

---

[5] Subject always (*pace* Larsson 1979: 150) to the constraint that there is a co-referential clitic pronoun available and utilized. The solution to the problems of examples like Larsson's (135) (p. 149) is to incorporate *ce/ça* within the inventory of 'clitics', a decision which can in any event be independently justified.

[6] It will be noted that we depart at this point from the analysis presented by Bailard (1982: 27), in that we do not see this structure primarily as a means of topicalization. It remains the case, however, that the subject in particular very often *is* the topic.

nominals (among other elements), it is but a short step to a newly integrated pattern where one or more 'dislocated' nominals is reincorporated within the intonation contour, the nominal in question being then in the most prominent position. A nominal functioning as subject (and hence very frequently marking the topic also) is particularly likely to be assimilated in this way — the structure being 'used' to the point of being 'abused' — and it is no accident that it is sentences of the type

(10) je (ne) sais pas moi and
(11) on y va nous

which are the most thoroughly grammaticalised of the right-dislocated structures. For all these reasons, the emergence of VSO/VOS as a widely used word order in modern French need not surprise us.

Leaving now right-dislocated sentences on one side for the time being, we shall look at a recent analysis of left-dislocation,[7] that of Knud Lambrecht. Lambrecht argues convincingly that left-dislocated sentences in French represent a major, and widely attested, method of indicating the topic of the sentence, where 'topic' is understood in the very broad sense of 'given' or 'situationally evoked' or simply 'inferrable' (Lambrecht 1981: 60—5; cf. also Larsson 1979: 12). Thus, as Lambrecht observes (62) 'if neither A nor B have been thinking or talking about B's father, sentence, (12) would be an unacceptable sentence in Non--Standard French'

(12) Ton père il attend devant la porte (=Lambrecht's (76a)).

Sentences of this type — that is, with one or more topicalised NPs left-dislocated — are widely found in contemporary spoken French. It is not wholly clear from Ashby's data just *how* common they are, because Ashby, in claiming (1982: 41) that 'the Tours data ... support Lambrecht's hypothesis that French is becoming a topic-prominent language', has grouped left-dislocated ('topic') and right-dislocated ('antitopic') structures together, an analysis we shall reject shortly. However, if we recall that only 17% of tokens containing both a clitic and a co-referential NP are verb-initial (*op. cit.*: 34), whereas in another sample of sentences in which the subject always referred to 'given' material, 47% of the tokens contained both a clitic and a co-referential NP, we might perhaps infer that around a third of the relevant sentences in this large corpus of contemporary spoken French are left-dislocated topic senten-

---

[7] Lambrecht also deals with right-dislocation. We shall return below to his views on this matter.

ces. It is therefore beyond dispute that left-dislocated structures, topic sentences, are a major rival to SVO sentences in contemporary French.[8]

One other important fact must be noted, in view of the claims we shall make shortly. Lambrecht reports the view of Li and Thompson (1975: 463) that in topic-prominent languages 'the topic ... is not determined by the verb; topic selection is independent of the verb' and demonstrates clearly that this is the case for left-dislocated sentences in contemporary French. 'Topics', he states (1981: 53) 'are syntactically independent of the verb and its semantic-syntactic structure' ... 'unlike subjects and objects, topics cannot be assigned a place in the relational structure of the proposition.' (It should be noted that Lambrecht is here using topic in its narrow sense, *i.e.* to exclude antitopics, in contradistinction to the analysis of Ashby just described.) What this means is firstly that left--dislocated NPs (which in English in particular may be preceded by a 'topic-establishing' expression, cf. Rodman 1974: 443 and Lambrecht 1981: 56) are not marked for case (though there is normally a subsequent co-referential clitic[9] where one is syntactically possible) and, secondly, more importantly, such NPs (whether or not there is in due course a co-referential clitic) are wholly independent of the syntactic framework imposed on the core sentence by the verb, or rather by the entire predicate. In such cases, of course, co-referential clitics are by definition precluded. As a straightforward illustration of the first point, consider:

(13) La plage i-faut y-aller quand i-fait chaud (=Lambrecht's (63))

and as instance of the second, we may take Lambrecht's three examples (his 67 (a) — (c)):

(14) (a) Leurs cousins, les Becker, c'est la même chose
(b) La prison y-a pas à se plaindre
(c) Tandis que le suisse-allemand faut s-lever tôt alôrs

---

[8] The very large corpus studied by Müller-Hauser (1943), at an earlier date and drawn from written material, suggests that, except where the dislocated nominal is a disjunctive pronoun (cf. p. 195), the two structures (ie. right and left-dislocation) occur approximately equally (cf. p. 242). In the case of personal pronouns, left-dislocation is considerably more frequent. If it is nevertheless the case that in Ashby's data, thirty years later and spoken, left-dislocated structures are noticeably more widely found than right-dislocated (verb-initial) structures, this is most suggestive as to the direction of change in the contemporary language.

[9] Or an 'anaphoric' noun, cf. Hirschbühler 1975: 159—60 and Larsson, 1979: 130. Consider for instance his example 16 (b): La *grande blonde* qui est là-bas, je pense qui j'ai déjà vu *cette-tête-là* quelque part. The 'anaphora' in question is very often an instance of hyponymy: cf. Larsson 1979: 44.

and from Hirschbühler (1974: 17):

(d) Oh, tu sais, moi, la bicyclette, je n'aime pas me fatiguer.

So long as the hearer can establish a link between the topic and the rest of the sentence, processing presents few if any difficulties. We shall return below to parallels between this situation as described in contemporary French and other recent analyses of left-dislocation/topicalisation in other languages.

Lambrecht's discussion of left-dislocated structures, then, seems wholly convincing, and complements in an illuminating way the "verb initial" analyses of Bailard and myself. As has emerged from what precedes, however, Lambrecht is also concerned with right-dislocated structures, which he calls 'antitopics', a term chosen because 'it captures nicely the parallelism that obtains between the topic construction and the construction under analysis in this section' (*op. cit.*: 76). In a review of Lambrecht's work (Harris, 1983), I have cast considerable doubt on this parallelism (and see also Larsson 1979:82), largely on syntactict grounds. Firstly, there is the major difference already alluded to: 'antitopics' *must* have a preverbal co-referential clitic, and therefore must be cliticizable (*i.e.* only certain prepositional phrases [10] may participate in this structure in addition to subjects and direct objects). Secondly, all appropriate case markers (*i.e.* prepositions) must appear overtly, so we may contrast:

(15) I-faut y-aller quand i-fait chaud, à la plage (=Lambrecht's (96) with (13) above.

In respect of the pragmatics of antitopic sentences too, it seems to me, the 'parallelism' alluded to by Lambrecht is not always easy to pin down. All are agreed that (left) topicalisation is appropriate only when the referent is 'given' (in the very broad sense defined above). Antitopics, on the other hand, 'appear to be an entirely regularised and conventionalised way of appealing to the addressee's ability to "take referents for granted" even when these are *not* immediately accessible in memory' (*op. cit.*: 93), and the last few pages of Lambrecht's monograph contain an interesting discussion of 'right-dislocated' sentences which appear to be wholly natural (in some cases, the most natural) ways of formulating a

---

[10] As Lambrecht points out with a wealth of examples, an expansion of the use of certain clitics, especially *y*, has greatly increased the range of prepositional phrases which may be cliticized in non-standard French.

particular utterance but where the normal criteria for topicalisation are not met. Interestingly enough, it does seem possible to me to 'save' all Lambrecht's own examples, by means of a (wholly plausible) extension of the principle of 'inference' mentioned earlier; I am reminded once again of the discussion of 'associative anaphora' and related concepts in Hawkins (1978: 123ff.). More problematic for an 'antitopic' analysis, it seems to me, are the very simple cases of right dislocation such as those in (10) and (11) above, repeated here for convenience:

(10) je (ne) sais pas moi
(11) on y va nous

Of course, here too it might be argued that the referent of all personal pronouns (discussed as a special case by Larsson 1979: 19—20), proper names, etc. is necessarily inferrable from the context; as indeed is, or should be, the referent of any 'definite' NP (even if only by being unique in the speaker/hearer's world) — and of course nonspecific NPs are not in general right-dislocated.[11] All in all, however, I think it is the 'conventionalised' nature of so many utterances of this type, coupled with the major syntactic constraints on what may be right-dislocated, which call the parallelism between 'topics' and 'antitopics' into question and lead me to conclude that my original analysis of verb-initial structures in syntactic terms may well be correct, at least in terms of the putative ultimate outcome of the particular change in progress. In other words, what was originally a pragmatically controlled structure is in the process of being grammaticalised, an initial verb being followed by those elements which are cliticizable within the structure of contemporary French. And this is of course the VSO/VOS order discussed in the first part of this paper.

We are now in a position to summarise the situation in contemporary French, as follows. The original canonical word order, SV(O), is still widely attested in French, particularly in more formal registers and/or when the subject of the sentence refers to 'new' rather than 'given' information. Alongside this order, there exists a frequently used topic-initial order, often now fully integrated prosodically with the rest of the sentence (Müller-Hauser 1943: 193—5), such a structure being of a

---

[11] Recall note 4 and also Bailard's examples (30) and (31) (1982:24)

(30) *Elle était venue une fille
(31) *Elle était à deux pas une ferme

type widely attested in the world's languages. Thirdly, there exists also a verb-initial order, occurring less often but still in significant quantities, which no doubt began life as a pragmatically controlled 'afterthought' mechanism (broadly defined), and which is progressively grammaticalising in French, for reasons and in ways which seem to be partly general and partly specific to the relevant *état de langue*.

The final part of this paper will look briefly at certain more general considerations relating to the sentence types we have been discussing here, and to the various changes which appear to be in progress. Firstly, as far as the left-dislocated structures are concerned, the passage from subject-prominence to topic-prominence,[12] with the topic tending very strongly to occur in leftmost position (Li and Thompson 1975: 465) is in no way an unexpected development. Topics are of course discourse notions, which are in principle independent of the syntactic framework imposed by the predicate and, as Vincent (1979:5) rightly notes, there is a clear reason why they should occur initially: 'there is an iconic relation between the primary role of the topic as establishing the focus of the discourse and its sentence-initial position.' (See Harris 1984 for further discussion of this point within the context of a general review of the causes of word order change.)

Equally, the fact that left-dislocated elements such as we have been discussing are not in general marked for case is again a widely attested phenomenon. In a brief but illuminating survey of the position in a number of other languages, Larsson (1979: 110ff.) demonstrates that the use of the 'unmarked' form, (for example, the 'nominative' case[13] or its equivalent) of the left-dislocated nominal is quite general. She is primarily concerned, however, as were earlier Rodman (1974), Hirschbühler (1975) and Cinque (1977), to determine whether left-dislocated elements of the type under discussion here are base-generated or transformationally derived, Ross (1973) having argued on the basis of German examples where case marking *is* retained on the relevant nominal that their origin is transformational. In fact, it seems clear that Larsson is absolutely correct to assert that, in syntactic terms at least, the term "left-dislocation" as we have been using it in fact covers two

---

[12] The converse tendency, for topics to become identified with the grammatical subject, lies outside the scope of the present paper.

[13] The 'unmarked' form may not of course necessarily be that which is traditionally labelled 'nominative'. For a discussion of the distribution of 'I' and 'me' (etc.) in this light, see Harris (1981); cf. also Cinque 1977: 400 fn. 5. 'Me' etc. are certainly *not* best analysed as 'accusative', *pace* Rodman 1974: 458, fn. 8.

distinct processes (cf. also Cinque 1977: 411), which she refers to as 'Topicalisation' and 'Left Dislocation' (see in particular pp. 115−22). In the former case, the element moved to the left remains an integral part of the basic sentence and retains its case marking (and hence in her terms is transformationally derived); in the latter case, the element is not marked for case and may indeed, as we have seen, have no grammatically definable links at all with the predicate. Such nominals are of course base generated. We thus find in German [14] both

(a) Der Professor (nom) dem (dat) habe ich gedankt and
(b) Dem Professor (dat) dem (dat) habe ich gedankt

the former being (in Larsson's terminology) Left Dislocation and the latter Topicalisation. (A comparable distinction is found in the case of left-moved objects in Spanish preceded or not by personal *a*.) Although the latter does not appear to be particularly frequent in French where the dislocated element is a disjunctive pronoun − the large corpus studied by Müller-Hauser 1943 reveals (p. 187) only one dubious example − Larsson does note instances such as:

(16) Au foutebole, on y joue dans des endroits spéciaux (=Larsson's (20)) and:
(17) De la résistance, il n'y avait rien à en dire (=Larsson's (21))

where the left-moved element is a full NP [15] and comparable examples are discussed by Lambrecht (1981: 68ff.) under the rubric 'contrastive'.

---

[14] I am grateful to Andreas Jucker for an illuminating discussion of the German data. For a recent detailed survey of both right- and left-dislocation in German, see Altmann 1981, especially pp. 119−25.

[15] Larsson continues with convincing evidence that these two structures are wholly independent of one another and that a core sentence which has undergone "Topicalization" can still be subject to "Left Dislocation", but only in that order. Compare Larsson's (53) with (55) (pp. 120−1)

(53) *De cette affaire (Top), Jean (LD), elle ne lui en a pas encore parlé
and
(55) Jean (LD), de cette affaire (Top), elle ne lui en a pas encore parlé
Cf. once again Cinque 1977: 407 fn. 13, and also Lambrecht 1981: 72. A variety of important syntactic consequences noted by both Larsson and Cinque hinge on the distinct status of the two types of left-moved nominals. Interestingly, Cinque suggest (*op. cit*: 411) that one of the structures (his 'Hanging Topic', cf. note 16) is not found in English. Certainly, whereas
Peter, we can depend on him
seems quite acceptable, the same is surely not true of
*On Peter we can depend on him
This tends strongly to support Cinque's view.

We thus have in French not two constructions but three: two sub-types of left-dislocation and also right-dislocation. The formal parallelism which Lambrecht noted between his 'topics' and his 'antitopics', and which we cast doubt upon earlier, seems in fact to be between the (relatively minor) subgroup of his 'topics' (those which he labels 'contrastive') which have undergone 'Topicalisation' (in Larsson's terminology) and his 'antitopics', that is, between left- and right-moved elements *which remain explicitly grammatically linked to the core sentence*, and, very often at least, within a single intonational contour. Larsson's 'Left-Dislocated' structures — which include virtually all the examples involving disjunctive pronouns, and the majority of all other left-moved nominals — are formally quite distinct, in that the links between such elements and the core sentence are semantic — or, to be more exact, pragmatic — and may not, as we have seen, be syntactically definable at all.[16]

There seem to be far less problems with right-dislocation. We have already seen that only elements which can be, and are, copied by means of a clitic within the core sentence may occur in this position.[17] Given their presumed origin as afterthoughts or elucidators, it is self-evident that the core sentence must have been grammatically complete in itself, with an overt filler for each slot required by the predicate in question. As the right-dislocated structure has progressively grammaticalised, this situation has persisted and seems likely to do so in future, given the perceptual advantages of having a filler (the clitic) at the first appropriate point in surface structure even when additional lexical material is to be added later within the newly integrated VSO/VOS sentence order. (For a discussion of the parsing of sentences from left to right, see Fodor 1979). It is in this light that the unacceptability of example (5a), discussed at length above, should be interpreted.

This paper deliberately leaves on one side the semantic and pragmatic differences between left- and right-dislocated structures. An informative but inconclusive discussion can be found in Müller-Hauser 1943: 196ff., her main proposal being that left-dislocated structures have a 'valeur

---

[16] Just to increase the terminological confusion further, we should note that what Cinque 1977 refers to as 'L(eft) D(islocation)' is that construction which does require clitic copies, ie. Larsson's 'Topicalization'. Larsson's 'Left Dislocation' he refers to as 'Hanging Topic'.

[17] Cf Rodman 1974: 460: 'A right-dislocated element must have an anaphor in the main clause'.

d'opposition' while right-dislocated structures have a 'valeur de qualification' (197). Even this distinction is not however always made (200): in fact we are simply dealing with 'des tendances de la langue' (202). Furthermore, she makes the clear point (195) in respect of left-dislocation — and we would add once again the same point in respect of right-dislocation — that very often (particularly with disjunctive pronouns) grammaticalisation is complete and there is no special value to be found. Equally, we make no suggestions as to the different values of the two sub-types of left-dislocation identified by Larsson, except the obvious one that her "Left-Dislocation" is enormously wider in scope than the alternative (her "Topicalisation") simply because the dislocated element, the topic, need only have pragmatic links with the core sentence.

The position in contemporary French, then, is extremely complex. The statistically most frequent alternative to the canonical word order is a Topic-initial structure, the development of which is, both in general and in detail, very much in line with widely attested changes in other languages. At the same time, an alternative verb-initial word order (VSO/VOS) has made some progress, and we have suggested that while the use of afterthoughts and elucidators is itself clearly a general phenomenon, the reasons why right-dislocated structures have been so readily grammaticalised in French have to be sought in the particular structure, especially the prosodic structure, of the language in recent years. (In this sense, we have moved forward from the point reached in Harris 1983.) A great deal of work is now needed, following on from that of Lambrecht, to establish precisely the pragmatic conditions under which these distinct structures are used by native speakers, and also the styles and registers to which each is appropriate, since by no means all grammatical variants are acceptable in all contexts. Detailed examination is called for also of the genesis of the topic-initial and verb-initial structures in modern French, the former certainly reflecting the re-emergence of a pattern favoured centuries earlier within the history of the language (Harris, 1976: 37–9). Surveys such as those of Ashby give us sociolinguistic data on the progress (or otherwise) of the available alternatives. It may be that variation of the type discussed here is in fact a relatively stable situation in the contemporary language. Certainly, it remains an open question as to whether, and if so when, either of these structures will come to be perceived as the 'normal' word order in French and a particular change seen as 'completed'. Given the inevitable linguistic conservatism of a literate society with a long cultural tradition, such an outcome may well be long delayed.

REFERENCES

Altman, H. 1981. *Formen der 'Herausstellung' im Deutschen; Rechtsversetzung, Linksversetzung, Freies Thema und verwandte Konstruktion.* Tübingen: Max Niemeyer Verlag.

Ashby, W. J. 1982. The drift of French syntax. *Lingua* 57. 29—46.

Bailard, J. 1982. Le français de demain: VSO ou VOS? *Papers from the 5th International Conference on Historical Linguistics,* ed. by A. Ahlqvist, 20—28. Amsterdam: Benjamins.

Cinque, G. 1979. The movement nature of left dislocation. *Linguistic Inquiry* 8.2. 397—412.

Fodor, J. 1979. Superstrategy. *Sentence processing: psycholinguistic studies presented to Merrill Garrett,* ed. by W. E. Cooper and E. C. T. Walker, 249—79. Hillsdale, N.J.: Lawrence Erlbaum.

François, D. 1974. *Français parlé: analyse des unités phoniques et significatives d'un corpus recueilli dans la région parisienne.* Paris: SELAF.

Gundel, J. K. 1975. Left dislocation and the role of topic-comment structure in linguistic theory. *Working Papers in Linguistics* 18. 72—131. Ohio State University.

Harris, M. B. 1976. A typological approach to word order change in French. *Romance syntax: synchronic and diachronic perspectives,* ed. by M. Harris, 33—53. Salford: University of Salford.

— 1978. *The evolution of French syntax: a comparative approach.* London: Longman.

— 1981. It's I, it's me: further reflections. *Studia Anglica Posnaniensia* 13. 17—20.

— 1983. Review of Lambrecht (1981). *Romance Philology.* XXXVII, I, 86-92.

— 1984. On the causes of word order change. *Lingua,* 63, 175-204.

Hawkins, J. A. 1978. *Definiteness and indefiniteness: a study in reference and grammaticality prediction.* London: Croom Helm and Atlantic Highlands: Humanities Press.

Hirschbühler, P. 1974. La dislocation à gauche comme construction basique en français. Actes du Colloque Franco-Allemand de Grammaire Transformationnelle 1. *Etudes de Syntaxe,* ed. by C. Rohrer and N. Ruwet, 9—17. Tübingen: Max Niemeyer.

— 1975. On the source of lefthand NPs in French. *Linguistic Inquiry* 6.1. 155—65.

Lambrecht, K. 1981. *Topic, antitopic and verb agreement in non-standard French.* Amsterdam: Benjamins.

Larsson, E. 1979. *La dislocation en français: étude de syntaxe générative.* Lund: CWK Gleerup.

Li, C. N. and S. A. Thompson. 1975. Subject and topic: a new typology of language. *Subject and topic,* ed. by C. N. Li, 457—89. New York: Academic Press.

Müller-Hauser, M. -L. 1943. *La mise en relief d'une idée en français moderne.* Geneva: Droz and Zurich: Eugen Rentsch.

Rodman, R. 1974. On left dislocation. *Papers in Linguistics VII.* 437—66.

Ross, J. R. 1973. A fake NP squish. *New ways of analyzing variation in English,* ed. by C. -J. Bailey and R. W. Shuy, 96—140. Washington, D. C.: Georgetown University Press.

Vennemann, T. 1974. Topics, subjects and word order: from SXV to SVX via TVX. *Historical linguistics*, 2 vols. ed. by A. Anderson and C. Jones, 339—76. Amsterdam: North Holland.

Vincent, N. B. 1979. Word order and grammatical theory. *Linear order and generative theory*, ed. by J. Meisel and M. D. Pam, 1—22. Amsterdam: Benjamins.

ARTICULATORY MODES AND TYPOLOGICAL UNIVERSALS: THE PUZZLE OF BANTU EJECTIVES AND ASPIRATES*

ROBERT K. HERBERT

1.0 Introduction

Systematic research in the field of language universals has stimulated wide interest in recent years, due partly to the convergence of data and goals from a number of diverse fields of inquiry, including experimental phonetics, child language, comparative linguistics, synchronic variation, language pathology, pidginization, etc. A great deal of this interest can be traced to Jakobson's (1941) postulation of the "panchronic laws of solidarity". In the United States, this approach has been championed in numerous works by Joseph Greenberg (e.g. 1966, 1970a, b, c) and by various members of the Stanford Phonology Archive and the Stanford Universals Project. (Cf. Greenberg, Ferguson, and Moravcsik 1978.)

The goal of phonologists studying universals is to provide a complete framework within which to view and to classify phonetic and phonological segments and processes in all human languages. This taxonomic feature is a necessary prerequisite to arriving at *explanations* for the behaviour of speech sounds (Ohala 1980). Further, as Jakobson (1958) pointed out, such studies of phonological universals form the touchstone of validity for all reconstructed systems. The interaction of processes of change as well as the directionality of change should provide insight into the problems of reconstruction:

> When for any class of sounds we can develop an overall theory concerning their patterning, phonetic characteristics, and dynamic tendencies, we will have

---

* This research was supported in part by an American Council of Learned Societies postdoctoral fellowship and a Faculty Research Grant from the State University of New York. Research facilities provided by the Department of Linguistics at the University of the Witwatersrand, Johannesburg are gratefully acknowledged. Participation in ICHL VI was made possible by a grant from the Foundation of SUNY-Binghamton.

made a contribution toward more accurate, realistic, and phonetically detailed reconstruction. (Greenberg 1970c:138)

In this sense, increased knowledge and sophistication, especially within the phonetic sciences, should enable researchers to select among alternative reconstructions and to replace simple correspondences and assertions such as "X became Y" or "X developed into Y" with principled statements of explanation.[1] Distinguishing between conditioned and unconditioned sound change, it is apparent that explanation has more commonly been achieved in instances of the former, wherein the influence of contiguous or neighboring sounds has been invoked to explain *why* X became Y. In cases of unconditioned change, the most frequently provided explanations include considerations of phonemic pressure and pattern symmetry, markedness, "drift", language contact phenomena, etc. Such explanations are seemingly less valued than explanations of conditioned changes. In practice, however, the two approaches to explanation often overlap, a natural consequence of our poor understanding of perceptual, processing, and related factors.

In this brief paper, a puzzle involving the conditioned appearance and relationship between two phonetic types, *viz*. ejectives and aspirates, will be considered. The approach employed here has come to be known as "processual", attending to both synchronic and diachronic factors. The primary interest is not theoretical, but it involves the application of this method, and the data are drawn from Southern Bantu languages. The discussion illustrates once again the complex interaction between synchronic universals and diachronic process and between typology and universals. Operating with the assumptions that it makes sense to proceed from the simple to the complex and that conditioned changes are, in some sense, "easier" to explain, the presentation begins with examples of conditioned developments in a single phonetic environment, following a nasal consonant, and then proceeds to a discusson of broader phonetic concerns.

1.1 *Definition of terms*

Part of the following discussion relates to similarities between ejectives and aspirates and it is therefore essential to provide working definitions

---

[1] There remains the larger question of whether true explanation is possible within linguistics, a question which hinges on the definition of *explanation*. In the realm of historical studies, actuation remains the most vexing problem. Cf. Jeffers (1974) for a discussion of explanation in historical linguistics.

of these terms. Ejective consonants are voiceless obstruents with abrupt onset produced with an upward movement of the closed glottis. Air in the oral cavity is compressed by this action and there is thus a heightening of supraglottal pressure during articulation. Oral closure is released prior to glottal closure, and there is frequently a significant interval between the release of oral closure and the onset of vocal fold vibration, on the order of 35—80 msec. However, there is wide variation in the actual interval and in the degree of oral pressure. A description of this variation would need to refer to facts of inherent specifications (e.g. it is easier to compress a small body of air and there is therefore a preference for back ejectives), language-specific articulatory facts (e.g. the ejectives of Southern Bantu are much weaker than those of Caucasian languages), style (ejectives seem to function as a marker of formal style in some languages), social marking (e.g. in some Southern Bantu languages ejection seems stronger for females than males), etc.

While ejectives are relatively uncommon, aspirated consonants are indeed common, and it has been asserted that the unmarked state for voiceless stops is aspirated (Givon 1974), although this is surely too strong a statement. Aspirated consonants are frequently described by reference to an "extra puff of air" following release; Ladefoged (1971) noted that such descriptions are inherently unsatisfying since the "extra puff" could be achieved by more than one mechanism. The essential aspect of articulation seems to be a relatively unconstricted glottis, with the vocal folds in voiceless position both prior to and during release of closure. In some languages, the fundamental aspect is this position *during release*, which accounts for the delay in voice onset time (Lisker and Abramson 1964). Catford (1968, 1977) noted that there is frequently an increase in oral pressure during the articulation of an aspirated consonant as opposed to level or falling pressure in the production of unaspirated stops. Aspirated stops also differ from plain stops in that the vocal folds are in the position for voicing or at least significantly narrowed during the articulation of the latter; state of the glottis thus seems to be the primary aspect of the *aspirated*: *unaspirated* opposition.

There are certain important similarities in ejectives and aspirates. Both involve specified glottal sets during oral occlusion, both involve increased supraglottal pressure during articulation, and both are typically characterized by delays in voicing following release of *supraglottal* occlusion. In these features, both sound types are set apart from plain voiceless consonants. Indeed, ejection is occasionally termed "supraglottal aspiration" (Russian *s nadgortannym pridyxatel'nom*)

(Catford 1977). There is no articulatory continuum of the sort *unaspirated-aspirated-ejective* since the state of the glottis varies most widely for aspirates (relatively open) and ejectives (closed). Greenberg (1970c) described similarities in the origin and patterning of ejectives and implosives, which are not germane to present purposes.

2.0 Post-Nasal Consonants

There is a strongly marked preference among nasal-oral sequences that points to the unmarked status of sequences of homorganic nasal plus (simple) voiced stop (ND). This preference is attested in diachronic evolution, synchronic variation, inventory constraints, cross-language frequencies, etc. Other sequence types (NT, NTS, NZ) occur, but these are less common and many processes, both synchronic and diachronic, conspire to produce phonetic and phonological inventories comploded only of (ND). Such processes include positional assimilation of the nasal (or rarely the oral) consonant, voicing, hardening of fricatives to affricates and/or affricates to stops, deimplosion etc. Surveys of such processes are important in that they point to a single direction of development toward the unmarked (ND). The reverse processes occasionally occur, but they are rare and other facts exist which explain these apparent anomalies. Thus, such counterexamples do not invalidate the notion of universal, but demonstrate rather that single universals do not exist *in vacuo*. Ultimately, it will be necessary to study the interaction of universals to account for processes of development.

There are, however two reported processes that counter the general tendency toward (ND) sequences: ejectivization[2] and aspiration. The situation with regards ejectives is that some languages are reported to develop ejectives from post-nasal voiceless obstruents, (e.g. Zulu (Doke 1926). Ejectives and implosives thus differ in that implosives tend to become plain voiced stops in this environment although there are examples where they are maintained, but implosives never develop in this position. The situation concerning aspiration is doubly problematic since some languages show the expected pattern of deaspiration ($NT^h \rightarrow NT$) where

---

[2] The term *ejectivization* is recognizably deficient since it suggests that the ejective quality is a secondary articulation and that this process operates upon plain conconants whereas in fact the term refers to the replacement of a plain consonant with its ejective counterpart.

as others exhibit development of aspiration (NT→NT^h). Such conflicting tendencies require investigation since the goal of processual research is to discern, where possible, universal directions of development.

2.1 Aspiration

Loss of Aspiration

In a typological survey of spiration, Devine (1974) noted that the normal state for voiceless consonants in contact with preceding sonorants is unaspirated. On the basis of examples such as Tarascan /N+ ptcčk/→ →[mb nd nj nǰ ŋg] and /N+p^h t^h c^h č^h k^h/→[mp nt nc nč ŋk], he suggested that it might be best to regard *voiced-voiceless-aspirated* as a sliding scale of consonantal complexity.

Within Bantu, the phenomenon of post-nasal deaspiration is not frequently reported, due in part to the general uncommonness of underlying aspirates within the family. This pattern is presented in the treatment of clicks within Southern Bantu, e.g. in Zulu aspirated clicks are replaced by simple nasal clicks after a nasal whereas in Xhosa they simply lose their aspiration: /N+ ŋ^{h}C^{h}ŋ^h/→[ŋ̩ŋ^{c}ŋ^h]

Development of Aspiration

The aspiration of post-nasal voiceless stops is common, both synchronically and diachronically, within Bantu, e.g. Sotho:

phaha 'wild cat' (cf. Xhosa mpaka)
thapo 'rope, string' Xh. intambo)
motho 'person' Xh. muntu)
likhong 'firewood' Xh. izinkuni)

Hinnebusch (1975) reconstructed the phonetic processes by which Swahili *mp nt nk > p^h t^h k^h. He posited a two-stage model involving nasal devoicing and deletion. In this model, a period of nasal devoicing (NC̃→ →NN̥C) occurred and speakers reinterpreted the period of noisiness as postaspiration rather than the typologically uncommon preaspiration:

```
              *NC
               |
              NNC  (unattested)
               |
              NNCʰ (unattested)
             /      \
           NCʰ       NCʰ
          /   \       |
         Cʰ    Nʰ     Nʰ
```

Hinnebusch's model,[3] involving an original articulatory motivation followed by reinterpretation, has been generally accepted as plausible (Herbert 1979) although the precise status of his unattested stages remains unclear; they may represent periods of variation prior to the phonologization of one particular variant. The process of post-nasal aspiration occurs in several Bantu zones: among the Southern languages it occurs in all groups except Nguni[4] so that *mp nt nk > Shona $mɦ$ $nɦ$ $ɦ$, Venda p^h t^h k^h, Sotho p^h t^h k^h, Tswa $mɦ$ $mɦ$ $ɦ$, Copi p^h t^h k^h (Guthrie 1967 - 70).

2.2. Ejectivization

The second counterexample to the general evolutionary preference for (ND) sequences is ejectivization, e.g. in Zulu /N+p^h t^h k^h f s [→]mp' nt' $ŋk'$ f' nts' ntt'] and Bantu *mp nt nk > mp' nt' nk'. On a cross-language basis, the process of ejectivization is rare, occuring only within the Nguni group (Zulu, Ndebele, Xhosa, Swazi, etc.). No simple articulatorily based model such as that proposed for aspiration presents itself here.

Several preliminary points require mention. First, it will not suffice to refer to similarities between ejectives and aspirates since the Nguni case involves not only post-nasal ejectivization but also loss of aspira-

---

[3] I am grateful to Erhard Voeltz for the information that Panconcelli-Calzia (1915/16) provided a model which approximates that of Hinnebusch in broad detail.

[4] There are six groups of languages recognized within Southern Bantu (Guthrie's Zone S). They are represented here by Shona (Manyika) (S13), Venda (S21), Sotho (S33), Tswa (S51), and Copi (S61); the Nguni group (S40) is represented below by data from Zulu (S42), Xhosa (S41), and Swazi (S43). In former classifications, Shona was assigned to a separate Zone T, and the remaining five groups to the Southeastern Zone. There are good reasons motivating such a distinction, some of which are mentioned below.

tion. That is, Bantu *$p\ t\ k > p^h\ t^h\ k^h$ except* under nasal influence when they become $p'\ t'\ k'$. There is good reason to suspect that the development of aspiration on simple voiceless stops is older than post-nasal ejectivization since the former involved all Southeast Bantu languages whereas the latter is restricted to the Nguni group.

Both aspiration and ejectivization affect voiceless consonants exclusively. Further, both developments serve to "heighten" the voicelessness of these consonants in the sense that they "check" other processes such as voicing, which is the most common process affecting post-nasal stops. Thus, it might be suggested that both ejectivization and aspiration are perceptually motivated processes. While there is no evidence to counter this proposal, there is no direct evidence to support it and the fact that one "heightened" type (aspirates) is replaced by another (ejectives) is vexing although it might be possible to argue that *voiceless-aspirated-ejective* be regarded as a sliding scale of complexity.

Phonetically, the ejectives in Zulu are only weakly ejected. Doke (1926) reported weak or absent ejection for many informants except in careful, emphatic speech. The same facts are described by Selmer (1933). In modern Zulu, especially urban varieties, it is possible to find speakers who seem to lack ejectives entirely. These sounds thus differ from the typical Amerindian or Caucasian ejectives where the glottal release is rather prominent.

Also of probable importance in explaining the ejective pattern is the role of aspiration, ejectives, and so-called implosives as areal features in Southern Bantu. While the unrestricted aspiration of Bantu stops can be reconstructed for the Southeastern languages, aspiration is typologically uncommon in Bantu, rarely arising in similar fashion.[5] Similarly, implosives are largely confined to this area, and the click consonants occur in no other Bantu languages. It is well-established that clicks entered Bantu languages through contact with Khoisan, probably Hottentot, languages. An essential difference between clicks on the one hand and ejectives, aspirates, and implosives on the other is that clicks occur mainly in borrowed words whereas the latter are regular developments from Proto-Bantu consonants. Lanham (1964) and Westphal (1963) have described the linguistic and cultural prehistory of southern Africa. It is possible that, in addition to the enormous influence on

---

[5] It occasionally occurs that a specific environment will induce aspiration on voiceless stops; the most common such environment in Bantu seems to be that preceding one of the Proto-Bantu "super-close" vowels, e.g. Makua (P31) *$p > > p^h/-i$, but elsewhere *$p > v$.

Bantu phonemic systems and lexicon, the contact situation might have resulted in the development of a Southern Bantu "articulatory mode". The nature of such a mode would involve a predilection for glottalic consonants, clicks, aspirates, etc.[6]

Some support for the notion of ejection as an articulatory mode or "family universal" (cf. Lass 1975) derives from the fact that in several languages ejection is characteristic of all voiceless obstruents. For example, Bailey (1976) reports that in Copi, which has a rich consonant inventory, ejection is optional with plain voiceless consonants, which are opposed to voiceless aspirates, implosives, and "voiced aspirates". In Phuti, postnasal voiceless consonants are rare since $N \rightarrow \emptyset /\_C$, but they are ejective when they do occur in Sotho borrowings; the plain voiceless stops are "slightly ejective" and are opposed to aspirates, voiced stops, and implosives (Mzamane 1949). Bantu *$mp\ nt\ nk > b\ d\ g >$ $> p\ t\ k > p'\ t'\ k'$ in Sotho although, as Tucker (1929) noted, the ejection is an optional feature of these consonants.[7]

Returning to the puzzle of post-nasal ejective consonants in Zulu and other Nguni languages, it is suggested that this process can be understood by reference to two basic typological facts. The first is the universal tendency for voiceless obstruents in contact with preceding nasals to be unaspirated (although this preference is counteracted in the Southern Bantu language groups). The second typological fact refers to the articulatory mode of Southeastern Bantu in which weak ejection is characteristic of plain voiceless stops and affricates. Thus, in place of the simple formula *$mp\ nt\ nk > mp'\ nt'\ nk'$ or the phonological rule $[+\text{aspirate}] \rightarrow$ $\rightarrow [+\text{ejective}]/N\_$, one needs to understand a two-stage process:

(1) deaspiration
(2) ejectivization of plain voiceless obstruents.

Such an analysis has the advantage of bringing Nguni within a single typological class insofar as aspiration is concerned:[8] as mentioned earlier,

---

[6] This proposal has much in common with Westphal's (1963) notion of "phonation areas".

[7] The same variation is characteristic of Southern Bantu implosives: the bilabial varies from a voiced bilabial fricative to a lenis stop to a true (weakly) imploded stop.

[8] It is noted that deaspiration of post-nasal consonants is a Nguni innovation; other Southern languages show the opposite pattern. However, it is perhaps significant that Nguni is the only group in which *$p\ t\ k > p^h\ t^h\ k^h$ without further development whereas in the other groups they are weakened, e.g. Venda $\Phi\ r\ h$.

aspirated clicks unambiguously lose their aspiration in this group. Swazi, another Nguni language, deaspirates post-nasal stops, but only *nt* is subject to ejectivization: **p t k > p^h t^h k^h*; **mp nt ŋk > mp nt'/nt ŋk* (Ziervogel 1952). It may be significant that in Swazi, with its non-ejective mode, there is a tendency to voice post-nasal stops, e.g. /mp/ tends to be [mb]. For some speakers, Bantu **mp nt nk* and **mb nd ng* are thus not distinguished in some styles of speech.

By way of provisional summary, the data concerning the process of post-nasal ejectivization reported for Nguni languages have been briefly considered. It has been proposed that in lieu of such a process, which counters the evolutionary preference for (ND) sequences, the data exhibit a process of despiration and an "articulatory mode" wherein all nonaspirated voiceless obstruents are subject to ejectivization. This ejection is most clearly marked on post-nasal consonants, but optional throughout the system in most languages. The stronger ejection following nasal consonats may be related to timing considerations, or the ejective quality of these consonants may function in preserving their voicelessness as suggested by the Swazi data.

3.0 Articulatory Modes

The question which arises at this point relates to the exact nature of an articulatory mode. The concept is cited with some frequency in the literature, especially by authors who have at some time been associated with the University of Edinburgh. There is some variation in the use of this concept, but the basis notion seems to be that material for language acquisition involves the articulatory mode/set for a particular language/dialect. One may say that articulatory mode refers to *general phonetic principles governing the articulation of a particular language variety*. These modes are frequently associated with voice qualities, and anyone who has heard much spoken Zulu cannot fail to have been impressed by the "breathy voice" of many speakers. There is no reason why the concept of articulatory mode might not be extended to include, for example, the ejective tendency of many Southern Bantu languages. Such an approach has much in common with the formalization as a "low level phonetic realization rule" although it is difficult to specify what these two different conceptualizations of ejection entail.

Assuming the validity of a notion such as an articulatory mode of ejection in Southern Bantu, its origins are necessarily buried in prehistory. It is tempting to speculate, however, that its origin might lie in language contact. There is excellent evidence for wide Bantu-Hottentot contact, which included widescale replacement of Hottentot languages by Bantu languages (Westphal 1963). It is not unreasonable to hypothesize, on the basis of extant Hottentot languages, that the contact languages was characterized by considerable complexity in phonation types; e.g., the presence of clicks seems to imply the presence of glottalic consonants. Further evidence suggestive of a contact basis for the ejective mode is the fact that Hottentot words for 'cow', 'sheep', and 'milk' are borrowed in all Southern Bantu languages except Shona, which has reflexes of Bantu terms for these items. This opposition between Shona and the other Southern languages is the same found for the ejective mode, i.e. the opposition between voiceless consonant types in Southern Bantu tends to be between aspirates and ejectives, except in Shona where neither type occurs. There are other features distinguishing the two sets of language groups, and some of these may derive from contact. Evidence for a relatively late origin for the ejective mode comes from the fact that the Proto-Bantu voiceless stops are not ejectives in any of these languages: they were aspirated in early times (pre-contact) and not subject to this phenomenon.[9] The aspirated stops were liable to further development, but the aspiration typically reappears under nasal influence, e.g. Venda $*p\ t\ k > \Phi\ r\ h$ and synchronically $/N+\Phi\ r\ h/ \rightarrow [p^h\ t^h\ k^h]$.[10] Had the ejective mode been present in earlier forms of Southern Bantu, ejection would have inhibited aspiration since the two phenomena are mutually exclusive.

In a stimulating article, Lass (1975) proposed the notion of "family universal", which has obvious affinities with the concept of articulatory mode. Briefly, Lass took issue with the generative phonology conception of universal marking constraints, which had asserted that certain features and sounds will be less common among the world's languages, lost over time, later acquired by children, etc. He considered the cases of front rounded vowels in Germanic and retroflex stops in Dravidian, both marked sound types, and he proposed that these sounds are neither marked nor unmarked in their respective language families: they are simply part of the inventory. Germanic languages such as Swedish work

---

[9] The dating of this contact is uncertain since there is some disagreement among the archaeological, linguistic, and folklore evidence, but a time depth of about 500 years can be assumed.

[10] This process is now morphophonological; the nasal appears only in restricted environments, e.g. before monosyllabic stems and when it represents the first person singular object marker.

as well as Germanic languages without front rounded vowels, and Lass suggested that markedness theory could then be reduced to a weak statement of statistical probability with no inherent content. Herbert (1978) examined the Lassian notion of "family universal" and, citing data involving clicks and geminate consonants, argued that these segments exist only in opposition to less marked types. That is, clicks and geminates occur and are stable in certain languages, but if the simple stops undergo spirantization, we expect that the geminate counterparts will be "reinterpreted" as simple stops. The set of predictions provided by markedness theory is borne out in such cases. Marked segment types may develop within a language (e.g. as the result of introducing an umlaut process) or increase in number (e.g. if new forms are subject to an existing umlaut process), but the development of marked types cannot be context-free. In such a situation, markedness predictions would be falsified. For example, the shift $*i \rightarrow y$ cannot occur as an unconditioned sound change unless $*X \rightarrow i$.[11] The reverse process, $*y \rightarrow i$, should by contrast be common both in historical development and acquisition.

Applying these principles to ejective consonants, the prediction is that ejective consonants should preserve this feature only in the presence of non-ejective counterparts. The unconditioned process $C' \rightarrow C$ should be common whereas $C \rightarrow C'$ should be uncommon unless other shifts occur within the consonantal system replacing the plain consonants. In the absence of plain voiceless consonants, it is expected that ejectives will be reinterpreted as such. Unfortunately, it does not seem possible to reconcile the Southern Bantu data with this approach. Consider, for example, the stop inventory of Venda (Doke 1954):

p'	t	t'	k'
p^h	t^h	t^h	k^h
b	d̂	d	g
mb	n̂d	nd	ng

The same four distinctions are present in the affricate series. Such an inventory seems "ripe" for reinterpretation, yet there is every indication that it is stable and has been so for generations. Such a situation is typical of Southern Bantu languages.

Several points require mention before abadoning markedness theory at this point. First, although ejection is a stable feature over time, it is

---

[11] This view obviously has much in common with Martinet's concept of push and drag-chains.

phonetically optional. This is usually stated explicitly in grammatical descriptions, or it is reported that ejection is "not very prominent". My impression is that ejection varies with speech style, being most noticeable in careful speech. Second, there are very few studies of acquisition of a Southern Bantu language, and these deal only with morphology (Kunene 1979, Suzman 1980). However, informal observation suggests that children do not noticeably mark ejection either. Third, it has been noted that within Southern Bantu ejection exists in opposition to aspiration. Both are generally unknown in Shona, although there are Shona dialects where both occur or where aspiration alone occurs; no dialect, it seems, presents ejectives in the absence of aspirates. This intriguing fact may point to a special status of ejection in Southern Bantu. A fourth fact to consider is that ejection in Southern Bantu seems to differ phonetically from ejection elsewhere to that extent that glottalization, when present, is not very marked: the degree of supraglottal pressure created is not very great and a separate glottal release is seldom heard. Fifth, the "least marked" stop type, plain voiceless consonants, does not occur in the same languages generally.[12]

It is tempting, on the basis of the above, to propose that Southern Bantu ejectives are not "typical ejectives". What ejection means for Southern Bantu is that in the articulation of unaspirated voiceless obstruents the vocal folds are brought rather closer together than is typical for plain voiceless consonants. The opposition *aspirated: unaspirated* is interpreted as *relatively large glottal opening: relatively restricted/closed glottis*. Ejection, in this sense, differs from its usual meaning. If so, such a difference may reflect the difference between articulatory mode and phonetic realization rule. This attempt at a solution to the problem of ejection in Southern Bantu, viewing it as a phonetic mode, is not any more satisfying than describing a language with the vowel inventory /y ø u o a/ as having an articulatory mode for roundness in vowels. No such vowel inventory exists, and markedness theory, incorporating bases in articulatory and preceptual phonetics, claims it cannot exist. However, as Roger Lass once informally observed: one doesn't disprove the egg-laying nature of the duck-billed platypus by producing a picture of one or even a dozen not laying eggs.

The lack of content in its predictive value is what led Lass to reject markedness theory of generative phonology. The theory is, he claimed,

---

[12] There are a few Southern Bantu languages which appear to present simple voiceless stops, e.g. /K/ in Zulu; these are in fact "semi-voiced".

devoid of intrinsic content to the extent that it cannot reconcile metatheoretical considerations of simplicity with language-internal economy of phonological systems.

There is no apparent way to reconcile the phonetic mode of Southern Bantu with universal considerations of markedness in consonant types. One approach might be to analyze the ejective consonants as underlying plain consonants that are realized with optional surface ejection. Thus, there would be no contradiction of markedness predictions at the underlying level. However, this is a disguise rather than a solution to the problem. There seems to be good reason to believe that the underlying contrast is between ejective and aspirated types and that the realization rule effects weakening of the ejective consonants.

Obviously, a single example such as the above does not invalidate markedness theory. Rather, this example points to the need for more precise definition of the terms *articulatory/phonetic mode* and the status of such concepts, if any, within phonological theory. In the absence of any explanation for the ejective mode of Southern Bantu, all we can do at present is to note, using Lass' metaphor, that Southern Bantu is "that kind of beast" and that ejectives are "like gizzards in chickens", i.e. simply part of the inventory.

REFERENCES

Bailey, R. A. 1976. *Copi phonology and morphotonology*. Unpublished B. A. Hons. thesis, University of the Witwatersrand.

Catford, J. C. 1968. The articulatory possibilities of man. *Manual of phonetics*, ed. by B. Malmberg, 303 - 33. Amsterdam: North-Holland Publishing Co.

— 1977. *Fundamental problems in phonetics*. Edinburgh: Edinburgh University Press.

Devine, A. M. 1974. Aspiration, universals, and the study of dead languages. *Working papers in language universals*. 15. 1 - 24.

Doke, C. M. 1926. The phonetics of the Zulu language. *Bantu Studies*, Special Number.

— 1954. *The Southern Bantu languages*. London: Oxford University Press.

Givón, T. 1974. Rule un-ordering: generalization and degeneralization in phonology. *Papers from the parasession on natural phonology*, 103 - 15. Chicago: Chicago Linguistic Society.

Greenberg, J. H. 1966. Synchronic and diachronic universals in phonology. *Language* 42. 508 - 17.

— 1970a. Language universals *Current trends in linguistics*, ed. by T. Sebeok, 3. 61 - 112. The Hague: Mouton.

— 1970b. The role of typology in the development of a scientific linguistics.

Theoretical problems of typology and the Northern Eurasian languages, ed. by L. Dezsö and P. Hajdu, 11 - 24. Budapest: Akademiai Kiadó.

1970c. Some generalizations concerning glottalic consonants, especially implosives. *IJAL* 36. 123 - 45.

1978. Diachrony, synchrony, and language universals. *Universals of Human Language*, ed. by J. H. Greenberg et al., 1. 61 - 91.

Greenberg, J. H., C. A. Ferguson, and E. A. Moravcsik (eds). 1978. *Universals of human language*, 4 vols. Stanford: Stanford University Press.

Guthrie, M. 1967 - 70. *Comparative Bantu*. 4 vols. Farnborough: Gregg International Publishers.

Herbert, R. K. 1978. Another look at meta-rules and "family universals". *Studies in African linguistics* 9. 143 - 65.

1979. Typological universals, aspiration, and post-nasal stops. *Proceedings of the ninth international congrees of phonetic sciences*, II, 19 - 26. Copenhagen: University of Copenhagen.

Hinnebusch, T. 1975. A reconstructed chronology of loss: Swahili class 9/10. *Proceedings of the sixth conference on African linguistics*, ed. by R. Herbert, 32 - 41. Columbus: Ohio State University Working Papers in Linguistics.

Jakobson, R. 1941. *Kindersprache, Aphasie und allgemeine Lautgesetze*. Uppsala: Språkvetenskapliga Sällskapets i Uppsala Förhandligar.

1958. What can typological studies contribute to historical comparative linguistics? *Proceedings of the eighth international congress of linguists*, 17 - 35. Oslo: Oslo University Press.

Jeffers, R. J. 1974. On the notion "explanation" in historical linguistics. *Historical Linguistics II*, ed. by J. M. Anderson and C. Jones, 231 - 55. Amsterdam: North-Holland Publishing Co.

Kunene, E. C. L. 1979. *The acquisition of siSwati as a first language*. Unpublished Ph. D. dissertation, U.C.L.A.

Ladefoged, P. 1971. *Preliminaries to linguistic phonetics*. Chicago: University of Chicago Press.

Lanham, L. W. 1964. The proliferation and extension of Bantu phonemic systems influenced by Bushman and Hottentot. *Proceedings of the ninth international congress of linguists*, 383 - 91. The Hague: Mouton.

Lass. R. 1975. How intrinsic is content? Markedness, sound change, and "family universals". *Essays on The Sound Pattern of English*, ed. by D. Goyvaerts and G. Pullum, 475 - 504. Ghent: Story-Scientia.

Lisker, L. and A. Abramson. 1964. A cross-language study of voicing in initial stops. *Word* 20. 384 - 422.

Mzamane, G.I.M. 1949. *A concise treatise on Phuti with special reference to its relationship with Nguni and Sotho*. Fort Hare Papers 1(4). Special volume.

Ohala, J. 1980. Introduction, symposium on phonetic universals in phonological systems and their explanations. *Proceedings of the ninth international congress of phonetic sciences*, III, 181 - 5. Copenhagen: University of Copenhagen.

Panconcelli-Calzia, G. 1915/16. Objektive Untersuchungen über die stimmlosen Nasale im Ndonga. *Zeitschrift für Kolonialsprachen* 6. 257 - 63.

Selmer, E. 1933. *Experimentelle Beiträge zur Zulu Phonetik. Avhandlinger utgitt av det Norske Videnskaps-Akademi i Oslo* II, No. 1.

Suzman, S. M. 1980. Acquisition of the noun class system of Zulu *Papers and reports on child language development* 19. 45 - 52.

Tucker, A. N. 1929. *The comparative phonetics of the Suto-Chuana group of Bantu languages.* London: Longmans, Green and Co.

Westphal, E. O. J. 1963. The linguistic prehistory of southern Africa: Bush, Kwadi, Hottentot, and Bantu linguistic relationships. *Africa* 33. 237 - 65.

Ziervogel, D. 1952. *A grammar of Swazi.* Johannesburg: Witwatersrand University Press.

VELAR SEGMENTS IN OLD ENGLISH AND OLD IRISH

RAYMOND HICKEY

The purpose of this paper is to look at a section of the phoneme inventories of the oldest attested stage of English and Irish, velar segments, to see how they are manifested phonetically and to consider how they relate to each other on the phonological level. The reason I have chosen to look at two languages is that it is precisely when one compares two language systems that one notices that structural differences between languages on one level will be correlated by differences on other levels demonstrating their interrelatedness. Furthermore it is necessary to view segments on a given level in relation to other segments. The group under consideration here is just one of several groups. Velar segments viewed within the phonological system of both Old English and Old Irish correlate with three other major groups, defined by place of articulation: palatals, dentals, and labials. The relationship between these groups is not the same in each language for reasons which are morphological: in Old Irish changes in grammatical category are frequently indicated by palatalizing a final non-palatal segment (labial, dental, or velar). The same function in Old English is fulfilled by suffixes and /or prefixes. This has meant that for Old English the phonetically natural and lower-level alternation of velar elements with palatal elements in a palatal environment was to be found whereas in Old Irish this alternation had been denaturalized and had lost its automatic character. Here one has the reverse influence of a higher sound structure level on a lower one: palatalization was originally a phonetically conditioned phenomenon in pre-Old Irish and became morphologized when it took over the function of distinguishing grammatical categories such as case, number, etc. After this point the natural assimilations of place of articulation were blocked as palatalization and non-palatalization were used for morphological contrast.

Now to consider actual velar segments let me begin with Old English. The inventory of obstruents was as follows.

(1) /k/, /g/, /x/

The phonetic segment /γ/ also existed but only as a phonotactically predictable variant of the voiced velar stop. This in itself is remarkable as Old English has voicing of voiceless fricatives in intervocalic position generally (note /f/→/v/, /s/→/z/, /θ/→/ð/). The expected voicing of /x/ is not found which may be due to the progressive loss of /x/ in intervocalic position (compare pre-Old English *seχan with West Saxon seon 'to see') which then allowed the /γ/ as a contextually predictable variant of /g/. Note that the voicing which can be seen here is an example of intervocalic lenition which is also found in Irish throughout its entire history. The scope open to lenition is determined by the configuration of the remaining segments. Thus /k/ does not have a voiced allophone in Old English as there is already a /g/ segment on a phonological level, nor does it alternate with /x/ for similar reasons.

I wish to maintain this position although it may smack somewhat of teleology and to substantiate it later on. But first to an apparent objection to it. There seem to be cases of phonemic overlapping in Old English if one considers forms such as

(2) *fāg*; *fāh* 'blood-stained', 'variegated'

Both of these are orthographic forms occurring in Beowulf.[1] Now assuming that the grapheme *g* represents /g/ and *h* /x/ then it might seem that one has both an independent phoneme /x/ and a phone [x] which is an allophone of /g/. But this unlikely situation turns out to be quite simple to resolve if one considers two processes operating at different levels from each other. First one has lenition which operates obligatorily on intervocalic segments and optionally on final ones. This would give

(2)a *fāg* → /faːγ/

Now on a phonetic level one has final devoicing in Old English. If final lenition does not operate then the phonetic form of (2) a is

(2)b *fāg* → /faːg/ → [faːk]

If both lenition and final devoicing operate then it is

(2)c *fāg* → /faːγ/ → [faːx]

---

[1] See Wrenn (ed.) (³1973: 133 for *fāh*; 147 for *fāg* and 125 for the inflected form (*on*) *fāgne* (*flōr*)).

The second of the orthographic forms in (2) would then be a representation of the final form in (2)c.

Supportive evidence for the interpretation just given can be found in Modern German. In colloquial Northern German, words such as *Tag* 'day' *Zug* 'train' have alternative pronunciations, the second being less standard but nonetheless common for that.

(3) Tag→/ta:k/∼/tax/
    Zug→/tsu:k/∼/tsux/

Here one has a parallel to the /fa:k/∼/fa:x/ situation, final devoicing alone in the first instance, lenition and devoicing together in the second.[2]

Apart from the processes of lenition and final devoicing a third is also operative in Old English and determines the phonetic form which velar segments take. This is assimilation to the place of articulation. Both velar stops have fronted allophones before front vowels. But again the particular allophone is conditioned by the remainder of the phoneme inventory. While /k/ has the allophone [tç] (>Modern English /tʃ/)[3] before front vowels (not all instances of course, notably not with those where the front vowel resulted from mutation (Campbell, 1959:174) cf. *cyning* /kynink/)

(4) *ćoesan* 'to choose'; *curon* 'chose (pl.)'

---

[2] In a comment on the oral version of this paper Wolfgang Wurzel suggested that the German forms in (3) arose through analogy with other forms showing [γ] intervocalically. Thus [ta:γəs] 'day-GEN' would have yielded [tax] in the nominative by analogy. He rightly pointed to the existence of sets of forms like [ta: γəs] and [ta : k] which he would see as a paradigm without analogical spread of the intervocalic [γ] to final position (and devoicing) in the nominative. To suggest that analogy is at work here is the same as maintaining that there are no instances of final fricative and intermediate plosive (as plosives are original). Final fricativization is then optional lenition (or analogical spread if one likes) and the lack of it is lenition failing to operate (or no analogical spread). The non-existence of final fricatives and intermediate plosives is due to a prohibition on lenition which blocks it in final position if the language does not have it in intermediate position. As this is a more general statement on the notion of positional weakening of segments it is to be preferred to the analogy analysis for while it accounts for the situation in (3) it does not explain the non-occurrence of final fricative and intervocalic stop. It should be added that in the variety of German mentioned one may well have final fricative and intervocalic stop. This is however due to two varieties of German mixing with the final fricative of Low German being taken over into High German but the intervocalic stop of the latter being retained.

[3] For a treatment of this split (in phonemic terms) and its subsequent development through Middle English to Modern English see Penzl (1947, esp. 34f.).

/g/ has a fricative allophone [j]

(5) ġeotan 'to pour'; guton 'poured (pl.)'

This corresponds to the situation which is still found in present-day Swedish (Malmberg (1971:98)) and in central dialects of German (Meinhold and Stock (^{2}1982:165)) where however the fricative realization can also occur before back vowels.

In Old English the allophony of the voiced velar stop was complicated by the existence of the voiced palatal affricate [dʒ] (Modern English /dʒ/). This appear as the reflex of a geminate /gg/ before high vowels. Its occurrence is restricted to medial position (and final position where this is the result of apocope)..

(6) secʒan 'say'; hecʒ 'hedge'
compare Old High German hegga 'enclosure'
Old Saxon seggian[4] 'say'
   (Kluge-Mitzka (^{21}1975:619+296))

It is unclear to what extent one should posit two voiced velar stop phonemes, one short and one long. Against this one could point to short and long /k/ and /k:/ which show the same allophony (including affricativization). In addition there are some cases where both /g/ and /g:/ have an affricate allophone after front vowels. These instances have been the subject of considerable comment. Consider the forms which Lass and Anderson (1975:145ff.) examine.

(7) secʒan < *sæggjan 'say'
    menġan < *mæng jan 'mix'

The position which they maintain is that in both forms of (7) the occurrences of /g/ were 'protected'.[5] In the first there was a double /gg/ where the first /g/ then represented a strong segment protecting the second one from lenition to /j/. In this view /j/ is a lenited element whereas /dʒ/ is not. In the second instance the nasal has a similar 'protecting' influence,

---

[4] I give the Old Saxon forms for this as it shows the West Germanic consonant doubling already.
[5] Lass and Anderson (1975: 163) define their notion of protection as follows 'given a weakening environment, or a process of lenition independent of some specific environment, the most likely condition under which lenition will fail is if the segment (otherwise) affected is contiguous to another strong segment'. For the purpose at hand suffice it to say that stops and nasals are strong segments in the view of Lass and Anderson.

inhibiting the lenition of /g/ to /j/, thus leaving it as /dʒ/ as in the first form. I basically agree with this position but would prefer a more phonetic account rather than appeal to a putative protective effect. With both geminates and post-nasal single consonants one has a period of closure longer than with post-vocalic single consonants. The long closure enables the tongue to advance to the point of articulation for the following /j/ with ease. In both cases velar closure formed the onset of the occlusion and with closing jaw movement the point of closure was brought forward so that on release it was palatal giving assimilation to place of articulation. The fact that with forms such as *menĝan* the initial stage of occlusion was nasal is irrelevant as this would not effect the assimilation in place of articulation. From the point of view of tongue configuration geminates and nasal-plus-single-consonant clusters are the same. The sound produced on release of the tongue from a palatal position was an affricate due to the absorption of /j/ (a palatal fricative) into it. This could only have not been the case if /j/ had syllabic prominence and resisted absorption but this is known not to have been so.

To conclude then I will maintain for my purposes here that /dʒ/ was a fronted allophone of a former /g:/ and that the latter had overlapped with /g/ when this was in a post-nasal environment. Note that the velar intervocalic allophone of /g/, viz. [ɣ] did not exist for /g:/ which retained its stop character despite the weakening environment as in

(8) *frogga* 'frog'; *dogga* 'dog'

At this stage let me switch to Old Irish to show how the processes just considered affected velar segments there. The inventory of velar obstruents for Old Irish is as follows.[6]

(9) /k/, /g/, /x/, /ɣ/
Exx. *caillech* /kal,əx/ 'witch'
    grád   /grɑ:ð/ 'love'
    ech   /ɛx/   'horse'
    togu   /tɔɣu/   'choice'

Phonemic overlapping in Old Irish occurred abundantly. This is because voicing and fricativization are found regularly both as the result of (i) intervocalic position of segments and (ii) the morphological processes which require consonants to be voiced or fricativized to indicate gram-

---

[6] See Thurneysen (1946: 74) for detailed remarks on both the consonant inventory and lenition.

matical categories. The latter is of course a development of the former but for purposes of classification one must distinguish whether voicing and fricativization occur for phonetic or morphological reasons.

The forms of overlap are as follows: /g/ represents /k/ intervocalically and sometimes word finally (phonetic lenition)

(10) *bucae* /buge/ 'softness'
    póc /po:g/ 'kiss'

/x/ represents /k/ after morphological lenition

(11) *a chrann* /ə xran:/ 'his tree'

Though here one can regard the change as phoneme substitution as with /k/ to /g/ in

(12) *a crann* /ə gran:/ 'their tree' (modern spelling: *a gcrann*)

where the substitution of one segment for another indicates the desired grammatical category. The appearance of [ɣ] for /g/ is phonetic, it being the intervocalic realization of the stop as in Old English. But with the development of morphological lenition this phone was raised to the level of a phoneme as it now contrasted with /g/ initially.

(13) *a ghrád* /ə ɣra:ð/ 'his love'
cf. *a grád* /ə gra:ð/ 'her love'

The two velar fricatives were then possible in word initial position but only as a result of morphological lenition. Here one can see how an important role in the morphology of a language can secure the position of phonological segments throughout a language's history. The function of distinguishing the third person, masculine and feminine, singular and plural is obviously very basic and despite the significant changes in the phonology of Irish since the time of Old Irish, the method of distinguishing the various forms of the third person possessive pronoun has remained the same: fricativization for the masculine singular, no change for the feminine singular and voicing or nasalization for the plural. This has maintained /x/ and /ɣ/ in initial position with respect to /k/ and /g/. Throughout the course of the history of Irish the word-internal, or more precisely the morpheme internal development has been as follows: the voiced velar fricative was vocalised in this position just as in English. Morpheme finally it was also lost. The voiceless velar fricative survived but only in morpheme final position where it commonly occurs in Modern Irish.

This corresponds to an earlier stage of English as the standard modern language has vocalised /x/ as well, but to a later one than that where the voiced velar fricative disappeared. It is to be expected that this would be the case because the final stage of lenition, that is vocalization, is reached more quickly by voiced segments such as [γ] than voiceless ones such as [x].[7]

At this point a few general remarks about the phonotactics of velar segments in Old English and Old Irish seem appropriate. In both Old English and Old Irish the weakest position for fricatives and simultaneously the strongest one for stops is the morpheme initial position. Old English as well as the other Germanic languages has lost /x/ in this position (Campbell (1959:180f.)). It has either fused with /h/ or disappeared entirely. For example

(14) hlāf /xla:f/→/l̥a:f/→/louf/ 'loaf'
meaht /meəxt/→/mɪxt/→/mi:t/→/mait/ 'might'
hēah /hæ:əx/→/hi:x→/hi:/→/hait/ 'high'

There is a third possibility, that of labial shift, which I will deal with presently.

In Irish the voiceless velar fricative has been retained for the morphological reasons given above. It has also been kept distinct from /h/. Again there may be a motivation for this. In Old Irish, as in the present-day language, there is a morphological process of prefixing /h/ before a vowel in certain cases (Thurneysen and Hickey (forthcoming : V.1.5.)), for example after the feminine singular third person possessive pronoun and the plural article. This does not occur after the corresponding masculine pronoun so that where there is no initial consonant in a word (i.e. where lenition cannot fulfil its distinctive function the two forms are nonetheless distinct.[8]

(15) a arcat /ə harəgəð/ 'her silver'
/ə arəgəð/ 'his silver'

/h/ has yet a further source in Old Irish as the lenited form of /s/ and later on as that of /t/ after the loss in Irish of interdental fricatives due to

---

[7] See Hickey (forthcoming: I.5.) for an extensive treatment of lenition.
[8] This is a morphological intepretation which is suggested by the function of lenition and prefixed (h) in Modern Irish but which appears to be justified for Old Irish as well, where however (h) did not alternate with zero (i.e. non-lenition) but with gemination (Thurneysen (1946: 150 - 153)), something which has been lost in Irish with the decline of phonologically long segments.

vocalization, or shift to /γ/, of voiced interdental fricatives, and reduction to /h/ of voiceless ones. The consideration here of phonotactics concerns not only the position of a segment within a morpheme but also the segments which adjoin immediately on it. Why this is impotrant can be seen from Old Irish. To go by the orthographic evidence there appears to have been in Old Irish, and there certainly is in the modern language, a restriction on two plosives occurring together, the same holds for sequences of two fricatives as well; this applies within morpheme boundaries.[9] But in Irish, either Old or Modern, there are no single consonant suffixal morphemes such as the tense or plural markers /t/∼/d/ and /s/∼/z/ of English so that double plosive or fricative sequences do not occur at morpheme boundaries either. In pre-Old Irish the sequences of two plosives developed into sequences of a fricative and plosive.

(16) *ocht* 'eight'   cf. Latin *octo*
     in-nocht 'tonight'   *noctis* gen. of *nox*

The development of /kt/→/xt/ is by far and away the most common. In fact the sequence /ɔxt/ represents one of the most frequent and productive suffixes in Modern Irish denoting abstract nouns and nouns of action. Note also that in the prehistory of the two languages Old Irish shared this particular source of the voiceless velar fricatives with Old English as the Germanic languages altered earlier sequences of /kt/, attested abundantly in Latin, into /xt/, compare the Old English forms for the words in (16).

(16) *niht*   'night'
     eahta 'eight'

Lastly on phonotactics mention should be made of nasals. In both Old English and Old Irish there were three nasals at the labial, dental, and velar positions. An additional palatal nasal was found in Old Irish as part of the palatal series of consonants. The velar nasal was only found in both languages in a final position just as in the present-day forms of both languages. But in Old Irish there was, and in Modern Irish there is, an additional circumstance which violated the normal condition that velar nasals were morpheme-final. One of the consonant mutations of Old Irish required that a homorganic nasal be substituted for an initial voiced

---

[9] Note that a source of double plosive clusters, i.e. Latin, did not donate forms with these to Irish as opposed to English which in Middle English received them with words like *direct*, *apt*, etc.

consonant under given grammatical conditions. This did not conflict with the phonotactic distribution of non-mutated consonants with labials and dentals, as /m/ and /n/ occurred initially anyway, but it did with velars leading to morpheme initial occurrences of the velar nasal /ŋ/ when this was the result of mutating /g/.

(17) *a nga* /ə ŋa/ 'their spear'

Turning now to assimilation in Old Irish one can contrast it with Old English. It will be remembered that assimilation to the place of articulation of a front vowel in Old English led to different allophones being used than before back vowels and that the allophones were also conditioned by the existence or non-existence of other palatal segments in the language. In Old Irish the situation is quite different. The state of affairs obtaining there is that there are not only a couple of palatal segments but a whole series. The situation in pre-Old Irish may have been somewhat similar to that of Old English but by the time of the first records of Old Irish palatalization has advanced from a phonetically motivated low-level assimilatory phenomenon to a central morphological process in the language. All consonants with the exception of /h/ come in pairs of palatal and non-palatal segments. For those consonants where the tongue is not the active articulator, i.e. for labials, palatalization is correlated by lip tension and a tongue position for a high front vowel giving a brief /j/-glide or release and non-palatalization is correlated by an unrounded high back vowel giving a /ɯ/-glide on release.

The significance of this for the realization of consonants is that before a front vowel one has a palatal phone but one which resembles the velar segment in all other respects, that is the palatal counter part of a velar stop is not a fricative or an affricate. /g/ has the palatal counterpart /gʲ/ not /j/, /k/ has /kʲ/ and not /tɕ/. In fact the latter segment does not exist in Old Irish nor does its voiced counterpart /dʑ/. But there are two segments which are articulatorily very similar to them. These are /tʲ/ and /dʲ/ which are however the result of palatalizing the dentals /t/ and /d/ respectively and are unrelated to the velars /k/ and /g/. The existence of morphological palatalization in Old Irish has meant that assimilation of consonants to high front vowels only took place if the morphological category demanded it. There was no automatic realization of say /x/ as [ç] after high front vowels as in present-day High German. /x/ only had one allophone [x], but there also existed a separate phoneme /xʲ/. This situation had an effect on vowel realization. Assuming that the orthography represents monophthongs reasonably accurately[10] then a form such as

(18) *tech* /t̪, ɛ x/ [11] 'house'

had a mid front vowel flanked by a palatal and velar consonant respectively. But the modern pronunciation shows that lowering has taken place due to the velar /x/ which follows the vowel leading to the pronunciation /t̪, ax/. This may in fact have been the case in Old Irish already; it is uncertain as the orthography does not allow one to conclude this. The point I wish to establish is that velar segments cause vowel lowering. But not only velars could cause this. As all consonants had palatal equivalents the distinction of palatal and non-palatal segments assumed systematic importance and a process of secondary velarization of non-velars set in. The sounds where the velarization was most obvious (and is in the present-day language) were sonorants, above all dental sonorants as the formants caused by voicing (in an oral configuration for velar resonance) are auditively quite perceptible. These were articulated with lowering of the tongue body and raising of the back towards the velum with closure formed by the apex behind the teeth, assuming that the velarization which characterizes the realization of non-palatal sonorants in the present-day language was already established in Old Irish.

(19) *rún* /ru : n̪/ 'secret'
    lón /ɫo : n̪/ 'provision'

Now there are cases where the vowel before the velarized sonoran is at least orthographically the same as that in (18), that is mid-front

(20) *cenn* 'head'
    penn 'pen'

If the forms in (20) are parallel to that in (18) then the pronunciation which one would expect to result would be

(20)a *cenn* /k, an̪/
    penn /p an̪/

---

[10] See Greene (1976) for a consideration of Old Irish diphthongs.
[11] As Prof. E. Hamp rightly remarked in the discussion the expected form of this noun should be [tɛɣ] (see Hamp (1973) where he deals with this). But in Old Irish there is devoicing of final velars after unstressed syllables. This is true up to the present-day language but here only [x] and [g̊] occur finally after unstressed syllables so the realization of [g̊] as [k̊] is in fact the only synchronic evidence of the situation in Old Irish. The form [tɛx] incidentally also shows how final devoicing spread in some cases to monosyllables.

but the modern language shows

(20)b *ceann* /k, a : n/
 peann /p, a : n/

with the vowel both lowered and retracted. It would seem correct to assume that the vowel was first shifted to /a/ and then to /a:/ the latter being the retraction found before sonorants where velarization was and is most acoustically prominent. A similar retraction is evident in English, albeit at a much later stage (17th. century) after the labio-velar fricative /w/ as in *was* /wɔz/ (Wełna (1978:235f.) Ekwall ([4]1965: 23)). The position with Modern English forms such as /bɔ : l/, /tɔ : k/, etc. is somewhat more complicated inasmuch as there was not a simple shift of /a/ to /ɔ:/ but first a diphthongization of the low central vowel to /au/ as a result of the velar /ł/ in Late Middle English (Wełna (1978: 192)) and then a monophthongization of this to /ɔ:/ as part of the wider change of the Great Vowel Shift. The velar /ł/ which resulted in the development of the /u/ on-glide in the first place in Middle English was vocalized unless in final position (contrast the two forms given above); due to hypercorrection and the influence of spelling /l/ was introduced or reintroduced into words such as *fault* (< French *faute*), *almost* (for earlier *a'most*).

If one looks at the environment in which syllable final /l/ disappeared in Late Middle and Early Modern English then one sees that this contains consonants of two sorts: labials and velars. The explanation is simple. /l/ disappears when contact between the tip of the tongue and alveolar ridge is no longer made and the vowel which corresponds to the articulation of the /l/ remains, in this case /u/. When followed by an alveolar the /l/ is likely to be maintained as contact between apex and alveolar ridge is necessary for the following consonant. Nonetheless one could take the standpoint that the consonants before which /l/ does not survive fall into some sort of grouping opposing the set of consonants (alveolars) before which /l/ is maintained.

There would appear to be supportive evidence that this is the case. Of all the major articulation groups mentioned at the outset two of them, labials and velars, appear to either act together or to interact. Interaction is to be seen in the alternation of velars and labials diachronically. Consider first the English examples

(21) *hlahhan* /l̥axən/→/la : f/ 'laugh'
 rūh /ru : x/→/r∧f/ 'rough'

They represent the third possibility for the development of /x/ in English mentioned earlier. Note that in English a velar fricative changes to a labial fricative and that is there is no change in manner of articulation. In Old Irish a shift from /p/ to /x/ is found as in

(22) *secht* /ṣ, ɛ xt/ 'seven'
cf. Latin *septem*

It is not certain whether the change was /p/ to /k/ and then /k/ to /x/ or /p/ to /f/ and then /f/ to /x/. If the double plosive restriction was already operative at the time then the view that /p/ shifted to /f/ first is to be favoured. Furthermore evidence of labial to velar shift in Germanic shows that it occurs with fricatives and not so often with plosives. In Old High German it is clear that the shift involved /p/ to /f/ first. Consider

(23) OHG *nift* 'niece' → ModHG *Nichte*

cf. Latin *neptis* 'grand-daughter'

The interaction of labial and velar segments was captured in the early Jakobson and Halle feature system (Jakobson and Halle (1956: 31)) by the use of the term [grave] which was dropped in the later Chomsky and Halle set of distinctive features (Chomsky and Halle (1968: 304ff.)) which were ostensibly based on articulatory parameters and was later on again suggested (for example in Ladefoged (1972: 44)) as it accounted for the interrelationship observed to exist between labials and velars. This does not however explain why labials have shifted in some cases and not in others. Consider the form in (23) again. It shows the shift whereas the word for 'nephew', *neve* does not. A suggested explanation might be that /f/ shifted to /x/ to yield the segment sequence /xt/ word-finally which both in German and in Irish was a favoured sequence of segments in final position, thus the occurrence of /xt/ in Old Irish as well:

necht 'grand-daughter' (+niece?)
Contributions to a dictionary of the Irish language. Letters N-O-P (1940:19))

Lastly I should point to the possibility of co-articulation which existed for velars and labials which is deserving of mention here. In Old English the operation of Verner's Law left certain intervocalic instances of a voiced velar fricative with simultaneous lip rounding i.e. /ɣw/. The verb sēon 'to see', mentioned at the beginning, while losing the intervocalic /x/ early on, retained a segment here when this had been voiced due to Verner's Law, as in the preterite of the verb. The attested forms show a splitting up of this voiced intervocalic segment so that one has one of two possibilities

(25) sǣgon /-ɣ-/ 'saw (pl.)'
sāwon /-w-/ 'saw (pl.)'
(Quirk and Wrenn (1957: 128))

which evidence the relatedness of labial and velar articulations.

REFERENCES

Campbell, A. 1959. *Old English grammar.* Oxford: Oxford University Press.
Chomsky, N. and M. Halle. 1968. *The sound pattern of English.* New York: Harper and Row.
Contributions to a dictionary of the Irish language. Letters N-O-P. 1940. Dublin: Royal Irish Academy.
Ekwall, E. 1965. *Historische Neuenglische Laut- und Formenlehre.* Berlin: de Gruyter.
Greene, D. 1976. The diphthongs of Old Irish. *Ériu* 27. 26 - 45.
Hamp, E. 1973. On voicing in Old Irish final spirants. *Ériu* 24. 171 - 172.
Hickey, R. forthcoming. *The phonology of Modern Irish.*
Jakobson, R. and M. Halle. 1956. *Fundamentals of language.* The Hague: Mouton.
Kluge, F. and W. Mitzka. 1975[21]. *Etymologisches Wörterbuch der deutschen Sprache.* Berlin: de Gruyter.
Lass, R. and J. Anderson. 1975. *Old English phonology.* Cambridge: Cambridge University Press.
Malmberg, B. 1971. *Svensk fonetik.* Lund: Gleerups.
Meinhold, G. and E. Stock. 1982[2]. *Phonologie der deutschen Gegenwartssprache.* Leipzig: Bibliographisches Institut.
Penzl, H. 1947. The phonemic split of Germanic *k* in Old English. *Language* 23. 34 - 42.
Quirk, R. and C. L. Wrenn. 1957[2]. *An Old English grammar.* London: Methuen.
Thurneysen, R. 1946. *A grammar of Old Irish.* Dublin: Dublin Institute of Advanced Studies.
Wełna, J. 1978. *A diachronic grammar of English.* Part one: Phonology. Warsaw: PWN.
Wrenn, C. L. (ed.) 1973. *Beowulf.* London: Harrap.

ON THE SEMASIOLOGIZATION OF PHONOLOGICAL RULES: THE SEMIOTIC EVOLUTION OF FINNISH CONSONANT GRADATION

EUGENE HOLMAN

Introduction

In this presentation I would like to discuss the process of evolution by which Baltic-Finnic (BF) consonant gradation has developed from a phonologically to a morphologically and pragmatically conditioned rule in the Finnish grammatical system. My discussion consists of two parts. First I would like to present my views on the ontology of morphologization as a phase in the evolutive dynamics of a rule which is part of a semiotic system. Second, I would like to give an examplification of these views by tracing the genesis and evolution of the alternation of intersyllabic consonantism, traditionally referred to as consonant gradation, from early Proto-Finnic to contemporary Finnish.

In a recent publication devoted to the ontology of morphologization, Wolfgang Wurzel emphasizes that the process is no mere consequence of the interaction of phonological and morphological levels of language (Wurzel 1980). Rather, he asserts, the morphological facts and principles concerned "hold for a field of facts which show especially clearly how the individual components of a language system with their different and partially contradictory principles not only interact, but also counter-act..." (Wurzel 1980: 443).

If I understand Wurzel correctly, he is implying that the patterns which obtain when phonological rules become morphologized are but specific instances of more general principles governing the emergence of higher level elements in hierarchically organized systems. Specifically, the morphologization of phonological rules signifies the consolidation within the language system of a higher level source of variability characterized by two essential properties. Firstly, being the product of interaction as well as counteraction, its specificity is only indirectly connected with the properties of the lower units from which it has emerged. It is thus heterogeneous with respect to them. Secondly, a morphologized phonological rule is a higher level source of variability, for which reason the necessarily further reaching ramifications it has on the structure of the system after it has become consolidated as a part of it must have the capability of being exploited to further the system's overall functional aims, the most important of which is to serve more efficiently as a vehicle of communication.

With respect to the first characteristic, the morphologization of a phonological rule provides a linguistic system with a semiotically more powerful entity. Whereas the primary function of phonological rules is to differentiate, that of the morphological rules which emerge from them is to codify and transmit information immediately pertinent to the morphological and syntactic levels. In this sense any instance of morphologization is a case of semasiologization: a source of variability has been provided with the capability to transmit information directly pertaining to the more complex levels of linguistic organization.

As to the second characteristic, the exploitation of a morphophonemic rule has two dialectically opposed facets. In the short term, the increase in variability a morphophonemic rule brings with it enhances the functional potential of the system by providing it with new sources of redundancy. The fact that a specific morphosyntactic class was signalled by a single linguistic element at an earlier phase of the system, but by an interplay of elements in the phase immediately following the morphologization of a phonological rule, may be seen as having two consequences. First, it provides the system with new opportunities to rid itself of dysfunctional elements. Second, it offers the system favorable conditions for implementing any sound changes which have been "lurking in the background" but impeded from actualization because of their potentially dysfunctional consequences. In the long term, however, the variability which is a consequence of the operation of a morphophonemic rule after it has become productive in its own right and is thus no longer dependent on a specific phonological environment is itself dysfunctional. Its potential for enhancing the ability of the system to function becomes a matter either of its restriction and ultimate elimination by analogical levelling or, alternatively, of its further semasiologization to serve as a source of variability on still more complex organizational levels of the linguistic system. Thus, it could be argued, morphologization is but one phase in the life cycle of a linguistic rule.

The linguistic literature abounds with examples of morphologized phonological rules which have subsequently been shunted out of the system by analogical levelling. There are far fewer examples of the alternative strategy, the further semasiologization of a morphophonemic rule to the status of what might be considered as a morphosyntactic, a morphosemantic, or even a morphopragmatic rule.

In the following I shall present data documenting one example of further semasiologization: the evolution of the lenition of intersyllabic consonantism, collectively known as consonant gradation, from Pre-Finnic to contemporary Finnish.

The genesis of Baltic-Finnic consonant gradation

The obstruent system which has been reconstructed for Pre-Finnic was relatively simple. It appears to have consisted of the three occlusives */p/, */t/, */k/, the three sibilants */s/, */š/, and */ś/, and possibly the two fricatives */δ/ and */δ'/ (Posti 1953).

From the standpoint of its inventory of phonological units this system appears to be characterized by the uneconomical use of its resources since it is not based on the exploitation of any clearly correlative oppositions. Indeed, its communicative potential can only be appreciated by an appeal to the morpheme structure conditions which prevailed during its period of validity. Specifically, virtually all of the root morphemes of the language system which it served were bisyllabic and this structural restriction allowed the intersyllabically occurring obstruents to participate in a correlation of length, as well as to cluster with both one another and the other consonants of the sytem. Of crucial importance from the standpoint of the subsequent development of BF intersyllabic consonantism, however, is the fact that addition of a syllable closing consonant to a polysyllabic sequence, the final syllable of which was bimoric, had no effect on the phonological properties of the consonantism initiating the syllable. A reconstruction of the situation is given in (1):

(1) Reconstruction of selected aspects of early Proto-Finnic intersyllabic on the phonetic and phonematic levels:

*/akka/ ['ak : a] 'old woman' */akkan/ ['ak : an] 'idem gen. sg.'
*/loka/ ['loka] 'mud' */lokan/ ['lokan]   ' „   „   „ '

The phonologization of Baltic-Finnic consonant gradation

The far-reaching sound changes which are so important a part of the development from Pre-Finnic to late Proto-Finnic resulted in a drastic simplification and reorganization of the obstruent system. The result was the reduction of the obstruent system to four members; the voiceless occlusives */p/, */t/, and */k/, and the single sibilant */s/. Parallel to this simplification of the obstruent system a regular, phonetically conditioned alternation of quantity began to establish itself with respect to intersyllabic consonantism. In conjunction with the natural phonetic process of lenition which affects intersyllabic consonantism when a non-initial, unstressed monomoric open syllable is transformed into a closed bimoric one in conjuction with suffixation, intersyllabic consonantism was gradually lenited. By the end of the late Proto-Finnic period a situation seems to have emerged in which the original short intersyllabic occlusives */pp/, */tt/, */kk/ had acquired shortened or weakened allophonic variants. Most significantly, however, the variation was conditioned by purely phonetic factors, and its only semiotic significance appears to have been that of an index of mastery of a specific set of pronunciation norms. An approximation of this later situation is given in (2):

(2) Partial reconstruction of the phonology of consonant gradation in late Proto-Finnic

*/akka/ [ˈak : a] */akan/ [ˈakˑan]
*/loka/ [ˈloka] */lokan/ [ˈlokan̪]

Examination of (2) reveals that late Proto-Finnic was characterized by a two way opposition with respect to the length of intersyllabic consonantism on the phonematic level, but by a much more complex state of affairs on the phonetic level. The reconstructed phonetics given in (2) are but an attempt to capture what must have been a highly volatile and dynamic state of affairs, the resolution of which must have involved a delicate interplay between intrasystemic and extrasystemic pressures.

With respect to intrasystemic pressures it should be noted that despite the fact that the system in question was characterized by two phonematic degrees of length at three points of articulation, the acoustic and articulatory characteristics of the sounds in question played a completely different role in the case of those intersyllabic occlusives which were originally long than they did in the case of those which were originally short. A long occlusive was weakened within the framework of a phonological system which opposed intersyllabic long and short occlusives on the phonematic level, but did not oppose short intersyllabic occlusives to any articularly cognate in an analogous manner. Despite differences in the phonological substance of the sounds concerned, the phonological system itself can be seen as having imposed a natural limit on the degree to which a long intersyllabic stop could be shortened, while imposing no corresponding limit on the weakening of short intersyllabic consonantism. Consequently, the phonetic properties of short intersyllabic occlusives, both individually and in their interaction with contiguous sounds, played a crucial role in determining the different courses of phonetic development embarked upon by the weakened versions of each instance of intersyllabic consonantism involving a short occlusive. The lenited versions of long occlusives, in constrast, evolved systematically towards their natural limit, this being phonetic and phonematic merger with the short stops.

With respect to extrasystemic pressure it is worth noting that various strategies for interpreting the alternations concerned semiotically seem to have provided some of the oldest and most salient isoglosses in the disintegrating late Proto-Finnic speech community. It is of some interest to observe that the two peripheral BF languages, Vepsian and Livonian, evolved from dialects of late Proto-Finnic in which the alternations in question never succeeded in establishing themselves as anything more than low-level phonetic rules, cf. the Vepsian equivalents of the Finnish forms under discussion: /ak/: /akan/ and /loga/ : /logan/. Thus, the different semiotic interpretations of the rule as indices of specific pronunciation norms appear to have been reflected in the early fragmentation of the Proto-Finnic speech community into dialects.

In the dialects of Proto-Finnic from which Finnish proper has emerged, the process of language standardization resulted in the establishment and reinforcement by the mass media and public institutions of a phoneme /d/ as the weakened grade of intersyllabic /t/, even though there was virtually no justification in the dialects the standard serves for the selection of this particular sound. There is no reason to doubt similar extrasystemic impositions from above to have participated in the establishment of the astounding array of alternatives characterizing the contemporary BF languages and dialects with respect to the sounds which have become established in them as the weakened alternates of short intersyllabic consonantism.

In the dialects of late Proto-Finnic from which Finnish has evolved the interplay between intrasystemic and extrasystemic pressures resulted in the emergence of two typologically different types of consonant gradation: alongside of the older quantitative gradation, according to which intersyllabic consonantism alternated with a shortened variant, a newer qualitative gradation evolved, according to which one sound alternates with another one. These two types of alternation may be symbolized algebraically as $XX : X$ (cf. *akka : akan*) and $X : Y$ (cf. *loka : loan*).

The entire inventory of gradational alternates found in contemporary standard Finnish is given in (3):

(3) OVERVIEW OF FINNISH CONSONANT GRADATION [1]

Table of strong and weak gradational alternates

Strong grade	Weak grade	Stem in strong grade	Stem in weak grade
pp	p	oppia 'to learn'	opin 'I learn'
tt	t	ottaa 'to take'	otan 'I take'
kk	k	nukkua 'to sleep'	nukun 'I steep'
p	v	saapua 'to arrive'	saavun 'I arrive'
lp	lv	kelpaan 'I quality'	kelvata 'to quality'
rp	rv	arpoa 'to draw lots'	arvon 'I draw lots'
mp	mm	lempia 'to love'	lemmin 'I love'
t	d	kutoa 'to weave'	kudon 'I weave'
ht	hd	tahtoa 'to want'	tandon 'I want'
lt	ll	yltää 'to reach'	yllän 'I reach'
rt	rr	kertoa 'to tell'	kerron 'I tell'
nt	nn	kantaa 'to carry'	kannan 'I carry'
k	ϕ	lukea 'to read'	luen 'I read'
uku	uvu	puku 'suit'	puvun 'suit gsg'
uku	u'u [uwu]	liukua 'to glide'	liu'un['liuwun] 'I glide'
yky	yvy	kyky 'ability'	kyvyn 'ability gsg'
lk	l	alkaa 'to begin'	alan 'I begin'
rk	r	purkaa 'to undo'	puran 'I undo'
lke	lje	kulkea 'to go'	kuljen 'I go'
rke	rje	särkea 'to break'	sarjen 'I break'
hke	hje	rohkenen 'I dare'	rohjeta 'to dare'
nk [ŋk]	ng [ŋ:]	hankaan 'I rub' [ˈhaŋka:n]	hangata 'to rub' [ˈhaŋ:ata]

Of interest is the fact that quantitative gradation remains restricted to the same three sounds it involved in late Proto-Finnic, while qualitative alternation has, in accordance with the factors already discussed, evolved into a veritable maze of loose psychologically rather than phonetically motivated links connecting specific sounds and clusters.

---

[1] The following sequences of consonants fo not participate in consonant gradation: *tk*, *sp*, *st* and *sk*, e.g. *itkeä* 'to cry' vs. *itken* 'I cry', *vispaan* 'I whip' vs. *vispate*, *kestää* 'to endure' vs. *kestän* 'I endure', *laskea* 'to count' vs. *lasken* 'I count'. The sequence *hk* shows some vacilation with respect to gradation: between the first and second syllables of some stems it is not usually subject to gradation, e.g *uhkua* 'to overflow' vs. *uhkun* 'I overflow', *ähkyä* ~ *ähkiä* 'to groan' vs. *ähkyn* ~ *ähkin* 'I groan'. For other stems having the identical structure there is a gradation pattern *hk* vs. *h:vihkiä* 'to dedicate' vs. *vihin* 'I dedicate', *pyyhkiä* 'to wipe' vs. *pyyhin* 'I wipe'. For many noun stems with the cluster *hk* there is free variation between a gradated and a non-gradated variant: *vihko* 'notebook' vs. *vihkon* or *vihon* 'of the notebook', *nahka* 'leather' vs. *nahkan* or *nahan* 'of the leather'.

The significance of the development from the standpoint of the semasiologization of the rule of consonant lenition, the source of the variation in question, is that whereas in late Proto-Finnic the semiotic significance of the rule was to indicate the norm with which a specific speech act was associated, in those dialects of the language from which Finnish has evolved it assumed the status of an essentially phonologically conditioned rule. Mastery of the grammar of these dialects thus meant learning that some instances of short intersyllabic consonantism signaled the fact that the word concerned was extended by one of the suffixes which closed a syllable. Other instances of the same consonant meant that the form concerned was not extended by one of the same suffixes. This alternation affected a considerable number of lexical items, thus enriching the system with a quantum increase in allomorphy which, in turn, signaled a qualitative enhancement in the communicative potential of the system. Specifically, many crucial morphosyntactic oppositions in Finnish frequently involve a form having an open final syllable being opposed to one having a closed one, e.g. the differences between singular and plural, resultative and irresultative aspect (indicated by the case of the object), and the difference between participant and non-participant in the speech act. For all root morphemes having intersyllabic consonantism subject to gradation, the morphosyntactic oppositions in question are, so to speak, presignalled by whether the intersyllabic consonantism occurs in the weak or the strong grade. Consonant gradation thus assumes a semiotic role as an index of specific morphological oppositions.

Alternations of this scope, however, are not without their dysfunctional aspects. In (3) we see clearly that the intersyllabic -p-, -t-, and -k- are simultaneously the weak alternates in quantitative oppositions as well as the strong alternates in qualitative oppositions. Since all root morphemes did not have intersyllabic consonantism participating in gradation we see that in spite of the semiotic function consonant gradation assumed, it simultaneously littered the morphology with an abundance of disturbing alternations. These divided the inventory of root morphemes into three distinct classes from the standpoint of their morphophonemic behaviour.

The first class was characterized by alternations of the type encountered in *akka* : *akan*. Here a phonologically conditioned alternation of intersyllabic consonantism was analogous to an already existing phonematic opposition. Thus, a speaker was confronted with the fact that some instances of short intersyllabic consonantism were variants of long consonantism, while others were not.

The second class was characterized by alternations of the type encountered in *loka* : *loan*, presumable [loka] : [loγan] at an earlier stage of the language. Here the intersyllabic consonantism of the strong grade coincided with the intersyllabic consonantism of the weak grade of the first class, but the intersyllabic consonantism it exhibited in the weak grade was uniquely associated with it.

The third class was characterized by a lack of any alternation. This is seen in the notes accompanying (3) where various instances of intersyllabic consonantism such as -tk-, and -ps-, not to mention both long and short fricatives and sonorants, are completely outside of these alternations.

The morphologization of consonant gradation

As might be expected, this situation was considerably simplified by Systemzwang and analogical levelling in many BF dialects, specifically those which gave rise to Vodian, Izurian, Estonian, and the more easterly dialects of Karelian. The evolution of these descendants of late Proto-Finnic is characterized by the analogical extension of gradation to all instances of intersyllabic consonantism, as in Vodian /matka/ 'trip' /madgā/ 'idem gen. sg.'[2] The evolution of Finnish, in contrast, has been characterized by a stubborn effort to make order out of the madness by using a variety of strategies. Let us consider a few of them.

Finnish paradigms contain forms with possessive suffixes. These constitute a functionally equivalent class, the phonological exponents of which exhibit one of two fundamentally different basic shapes. One involves the addition of a purely autonomous syllable, cf. the preceding example, while the other involves the addition of a syllable-closing consonant followed by an autonomous syllable, e.g. *akkamme* 'our old woman'. In virtually all Finnish dialects as well as in the standard language the phonologically conditioned allomorphy which the different shapes of the possessive suffixes would demand by virtue of their different phonological shapes has been eliminated. In (4) we see part of the paradigm for the possessed forms of *akka*:

(4) akkani 'my old woman'   *akkamme* 'our old woman'
    akkasi 'your old woman'   *akkanne* 'your (pl.) old woman'
    akkansa 'his/her old woman' *akkansa* 'their old woman'

---

[2] In Vodian the development of consonant gradation in conjunction with other sound changes has resulted in it having the status of a remarkably consistent marker of morphological relationships, cf. (matkā) 'trip part. sg.', '(madgā' idem gen. sg.

Notice that 4 out of the 6 forms (underlined) are characterized by strong rather than the expected weak consonantism. Of equal interest is the fact that all of these forms are morphologically polysemic, serving additionally as the genetive/accusative singular as well as the nominative plural, that is to say, as forms which have the weak grade in the non-possessed forms.

The statistically more frequent verbal endings, some of which have phonological shapes coinciding with those of the possessive suffixes (cf. 1st and 2nd pers. plural in (4)) have not undergone this type of leveling. Thus, consonant gradation serves marginally as a means for distinguishing the members of nominal paradigms from those of verbal paradigms. The root *sylke-* 'spit', for example, exhibits different gradational behaviour in conjunction with the suffix *-mme* depending upon whether it is the base of a nominal paradigm (cf. *sylkemme* 'our saliva') or a verbal paradigm (cf. *syljemme* 'we spit').

Additional instances of morphologization are the consequences of what might be characterized as iconic constraints as well as of the inevitable loss of conditioning factors.

An example of iconic constraints is provided by the behaviour of verbal stems derived from roots by a process which already subjects their stem final intersyllabic consonantism to gradation. In example (5) the verbal stem *patukoi-* 'to whip' is a relatively recent derivative from the noun *patukka* 'rawhide' by a process which automatically shortens intersyllabic consonantism. Even though the personal ending *-mme* is normally associated with the weak grade, here the intervention of a second instance of gradation would destroy the iconic link between *patukka* and its derivative. Compare *patukoin* 'I whip' and *patukoi* 'he whips' with *jaoin* 'I divided' (from *jakaa* 'to divide') and *jakoi* 'he divided'.

An interesting example of the loss of a conditioning factor is provided by the loss of word final and specific intersyllabic */k/'s. The sound change in question took place only after consonant gradation had become firmly established as a source of phonological variation, for which reason its demise complicated the grammar with numerous instances of gradation which lacked a synchronic motivation. Thus, the intersyllabic consonantism of the pre-Finnish forms */tarvek/ 'need' and */tarpeken/ 'idem, gen. sg.', is motivated by phonological factors, whereas that of their reflexes in the modern standard language, *tarve* : *tarpeen* is not.

Summarizing, we see that reduction of paradigmatic allomorphy, iconic constraints, and loss of conditioning factors have resulted in a compromise of the semiotic task consonant gradation was once charged with on the phonological level while, at the same time, these factors have allowed it to assume new and more complex tasks as indicators of the morphological and semantic affiliations of the forms affected by it.

The further semasiologization of consonant gradation

In contemporary standard Finnish consonant gradation exhibits a tendency to assume an increasing number of highly specialized although indisputably marginal morphosemantic and morphopragmatic functions. One of the most important of these is service as a means available for dividing the lexicon into strata characterized by specific functional-stylistic valencies. The different gradational behaviour of potentially gradatable intersyllabic consonantism serves as a concrete index of whether a specific lexical item is affective or neutral, e.g. *pupu* 'bunny' (: *pupun*), cf. *papu* 'bean' (: *pavun*); cognate proper or common, e.g. *Into* ' <male given name>' (: *Inton*), cf. *into* 'enthusiasm' (: *innon*); endosystemic or exosystemic, e.g. *sampo* 'mythical magic mill', (: *sammon*) cf. *tempo* 'tempo' (: *tempon*). It is interesting to note that the above remarks hold for nominal stems only, the verbal system is characterized by different sources of fully productive non-motivated gradation, some of which have also assumed morphopragmatic functions, but limitations of space prevent further discussion of this question.

Conclusion

The foregoing discussion documents dramatically the manner in which consonant gradation has, from the standpoint of Finnish as a functioning hierarchically structured semiotic system, assumed a succession of increasingly complex semiotic functions. More importantly, however, it demonstrates how morphologization is but one stage in the semiotic evolution of a source of linguistic variability.

REFERENCES

Posti, Lauri. 1953. From Pre-Finnic to late Proto-Finnic. *Finnisch-Ugrische Forschungen* 31. 1 - 91.
Wurzel, W. U. 1980. Ways of morphologizing phonological rules. *Historical morphology*, ed. by J. Fisiak, 443 - 62. The Hague: Mouton.

ANOTHER EXPLANATION FOR THE DEVELOPMENT OF s BEFORE l IN NORWEGIAN*

ERNST HÅKON JAHR

1.0. The problem to be discussed in this paper is the development of *s* to *š* before *l* in Norwegian.[1] This particular phenomenon has been the object of some interest in recent years, and various explanations have been offered to account for the change of *s* before *l*.

1.1. The problem under consideration can be stated like this: Why does *s* in Norwegian change to *š* before *l* in words like *slem* 'naughty', *slå* '(to) strike, beat', *Oslo* 'Oslo', but not before *n*, like in *snakke* 'talk', *snø* 'snow' and *snar* 'quick'?

1.2. James Foley claims that the explanation for this cannot be of a phonetic nature, but has to be phonological. He writes (1973: 51):

"The conversion of s to *š* cannot be attributed to phonetic influences since *l* and *n* are both dentals, and in any case conversion of dental *s* to palatal *š* looks more like dissimilation than assimilation. In short, there is no phonetic explanation for the palatalization of *s* before *l* but not before *n*. But there is a phonological explanation: *l* is phonologically stronger than *n*, and *s* is strengthened by proximity to *l* but not by proximity to the relatively weaker *n*; the strengthened *s* then manifests itself as *š*."

Foley repeats this explanation in his 1977 monograph.[2]

1.3. John J. Ohala (1974: 254 - 56) objects to this explanation. First he points out that the notion of 'strength' is undefined, and second,

---

* I would like to thank Thomas Hoel, Ove Lorentz, Theo Vennemann, Kjel Venås and Geirr Wiggen for useful comments. Thanks are also due to Merle Horne and Kay Wikberg for correcting my English. None of them should, however, be held responsible for remaining mistakes and shortcomings.

[1] 'Norwegian' in this context means Standardized East Norwegian, the variety found in text books on Norwegian (e.g. Marm/Sommerfelt 1967).

[2] Cf. also Smith 1981: 587. Both Foley 1973 and 1977 contain certain mistakes in the given Norwegian data and I will use this opportunity to correct them:

1973, P. 51: *Oslo* is given the pronunciation [ošlo], it should be [ušlu], or — as shown later in this paper — [ušļu].

1977, p. 37: *snø* [snø:] 'snow' turns up incorrectly as *snå* [sno]. This mistake is re-that there *is* a phonetic explanation to the change of *s* to *š* before *l*. This explanation is, however, not articulatory, says Ohala, and criticizes the "tendency many phonologists have of thinking of phonetically-plausible processes as being primarily those involving articulatory assimilation."

Ohala refers to Einar Haugen (1942) where Haugen suggested, in Ohala's words, "some of the elements which make this a phonetically plausible change". Ohala's explanation goes like this:

> "In all likelihood the [l] in the [sl] cluster became partially devoiced yielding [sl̥l]. [l̥] is acoustically a fricative — in fact, it is very much like the fricative [ʃ], as can be seen from the spectra of the fricatives [s], [ʃ], [l̥] [which Ohala presents in an illustration on p. 255]. This is true even though [ʃ] and [l̥] are very different in articulation. Thus, auditorily [sl̥l] could also appear to be [sʃl]. Probably there was then an acoustic assimilation of the [s] to the following fricative, yielding either [l̥l] or [ʃl]... The reason [s] didn't become [ʃ] before [n] is because if the same partial devoicing of the [n] had occurred in the [sn] cluster, it would not yield a fricative sounding anything like [ʃ], and the fricative it would yield, [n̥] has extremely low intensity and wouldn't cause [s] to assimilate to it."

Ohala's explanation seems very convincing, especially since he can support it with spectrograms showing that [l̥] is more similar to *š* than to *s*.

1.4. Roger Lass, however, has launched two objections to Ohala's explanation, in his 1980 monograph *On Explaining Language Change*. Lass first makes a point of the fact that "spectrographic similarity (to a phonetician) does not necessarily equal perceptual similarity" (p. 40), and argues against Ohala that English speakers perceive the Welsh voiceless lateral fricative either as [l] or as [fl], but not as [šl]. Lass' second objection is that in many English dialects we find devoiced /l/ after initial /s/, but still no dialect of English has turned [sl] into [šl], as should have been expected if Ohala's explanation to

---

peated on p. 111 and again on p. 114, where we also find two cases of *strom* [strom] 'stream' instead of the correct *strøm* [strøm]. On p. 37 we find the word *slags* [šlaks], with the translation 'blow'. It should have been *slag* [šlaːg] = 'blow'. *Slags* with the pronunciation [šlaks] is genitive case of another noun *slag*, which is used with the meaning 'kind(s) of': *hva slags* 'what kind of', *alle slags* 'all kinds of' etc. The most important mistake is, however, the given pronunciation of the adjective *norsk* 'Norwegian'. Foley (p. 37 and again on p. 113) gives the pronunciation [noršk], and uses this example to show "The Norwegian palatalization of *s* to *š* after *r*" (p. 37). The actual pronunciation is [nɔšk]. *r* is never found before *š*, and the *rs* combination (in the written language) is always pronounced [š].

the Norwegian phenomenon is correct. Lass concludes that

> "even if Ohala's case is plausible on the face of it (as one possibility), he has given us no particular reason to believe it. That is, he has adduced neither a necessary nor a sufficient condition for the transition from [ɬl] to [šl]; he has provided no reason why anything at all should happen, or if something did, why it should be just that. (...) All he has shown is that given a particular theory, it could have happened, maybe" (p. 41).

1.5. In a review article of Lass' book, Esa Itkonen (1981: 691) makes a brief remark on Lass' objections to Ohala, and rather resignedly comments on Lass' scepticism in this way: "It is clear that nothing within the limits of the possible could satisfy L [ass]."

2.0. So, where do we stand? Is Foley's more abstract explanation the right one, or does Ohala's more concrete approach account better for what happens to *s* before *l* in Norwegian? Or — is Lass' deep scepticism to Ohala appropriate?

2.1. Lass' objection to Ohala is valid enough, I think, even if it perhaps seems strange to use English speakers' interpretation of a Welsh sound as an argument. But we can support Lass' argument here with a good example from Norwegian itself, to show that acoustic similarity between two sounds does not necessarily mean that the language users interpret them as the same sound or phoneme. In East Norwegian dialects we find a retroflex flap. Although it acoustically is very similar to the flapped *r*, everyone interprets it as an *l*. It is also popularly referred to as "tjukk l" ('thick l'). This happens in spite of the fact that the retroflex flap also has the status of a phoneme, as can be shown with the minimal pair test (cf. Jahr 1978).

2.2. The main mistake Ohala makes, however, is to confuse an old diachronic development with a synchronic rule given in modern text books on Norwegian. Perhaps it is more accurate to say that we face two diachronic developments here, one old and completed several hundred years ago (covering the change from Old Norse to the modern Norwegian dialects), and another ,still on-going, change in standardized East Norwegian. The new change is of course the one that has to be specially mentioned in modern text books on Norwegian. The rule that Foley tries to explain is the modern one, and Ohala then confuses this modern rule with the old change of Old Norse /sl/ (and /tl/) to the various manifestations of these consonant clusters in the modern dialects. This old change was described by Einar Haugen 1942, where he suggested this development of Old Norse /sl/ and /tl/ to the modern dialect forms:

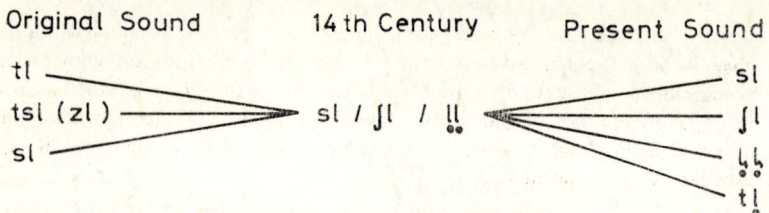

(In an "Author's Comment" on a reprint (1972) of his 1942 article, Haugen has modified this scheme slightly.)

Ohala (1974) presents an explanation to the present day rule along the same line as Haugen explained the old development from Old Norse /sl/ (and /tl/). Ohala's intermediate stage [sll] may be necessary and even correct when it comes to this old change. But it is obviously wrong as an explanation for the modern treatment of *s* before *l* in the standardized variety of Norwegian described in those text books where Foley found his examples (Popperwell 1963, Marm/Sommerfelt 1958).

2.3. So, to sum up, two separate phenomena are confused in the Foley-Ohala discussion. The first phenomenon is the development and change of Old Norse /sl/ and /tl/ to the various realizations observable in the modern Norwegian dialects. The second is an on-going change, usually referred to as a synchronic phonological rule, which accounts for the change of *s* to *š* before *l* in standardized East Norwegian. These two phenomena should not be mixed up, and can of course not be given the same explanation. While the first one dates back to the 14th century, the second one started only a century ago. I will not discuss the first one further here, but refer to Haugen's treatment 1942, since it is the second one that was the starting point of the Foley-Ohala discussion.

3.1. Oslo speech is divided into two major varieties, often referred to as the East (popular, working class) variety and the West (educated, upper class) variety. While the popular Oslo dialect is in close linguistic relation with the rural dialects surrounding the capital, the upper class variety historically is a mixture of Norwegian and Danish linguistic features. It developed towards the end of the 18th and the beginning of the 19th century, and was based on written Danish with respect to word forms and morphology, but with a predominant Norwegian sound system and Norwegian prosody. 'Spelling pronunciation' was widespread in this variety until about 1900. Although the upper class variety has had some influence on popular Oslo speech, the main direction of influence in phonetics and phonology has been the opposite: features from popular, working class speech have made their way into the educated and upper class variety.

3.2. The sound š is a good example of this tendency. In the second half of the 19th century, upper class speech did not exhibit š before *l*, but — as a result of spelling pronunciation — this cluster was pronounced [sl]. In the working class dialect, however, š was used before *l*. To use š before *l* was then a conspicuous feature of popular speech, and therefore considered vulgar among speakers of the upper class variety.[3]

3.3. During the last century, upper class Oslo speech has changed in the direction of popular speech. Speakers of the upper class variety have gradually picked up features from the working class dialect. As a consequence the phonetic and phonological difference between the two varieties of Oslo speech is smaller today than it was one hundred years ago. This development is presumably caused by the general development of Norwegian society, and perhaps also in part by official Norwegian language planning (cf. Jahr 1983).

The use of š in upper class speech has increased as a result of this development, despite the vulgarity that has stuck to the š pronunciation of the *sl* cluster.

3.4. We could perhaps stop here, and say that when the cluster *sl* is now pronounced with š even in upper class or educated speech, it is a result of the heavy influence from popular speech over the last hundred years.

This 'explanation' is, however, not particularly satisfactory. On the contrary, we are left with the question 'why just š in the *sl* cluster'? Another, earlier exclusive feature of popular speech is the use of retroflex flap. This feature has also been on the increase in upper class speech, while another 'vulgar' feature — initial stress in many polysyllabic loan words (cf. end of note 8) — still is kept effectively out of standardized speech. So why š in the *sl* cluster? The answer lies in another important sound change that has spread from popular speech to upper class speech during the present century and especially in the after war period (Jahr

---

[3] A special feature of š in Oslo speech is the interesting 'expressive' use of this sound, i.e. the use of š instead of *s* initially before another consonant. By substituting š for *s* one can give a word an additional expressive meaning which the word does not have with just a 'clean' *s* (cf. Broch 1927). Although this stylistic use of š originated in popular speech, it was earlier especially expressive in the upper class variety because š was generally not as frequently used there as in popular speech.

1981). This change concerns the system of lateral sounds, and has occurred, it seems, without any social notice. This change in the lateral system is of great importance to the question under discussion here, and a study of this sound change finally gives us the key to a plausible explanation of why s today changes to š before l in standardized East Norwegian.

4.1. James Foley (1973) claimed that what causes the actual change in the sl cluster is the phonological 'strength' of l, since we have slem [šlem] 'naughty', but snø [snø:] 'snow', and both l and n are dentals — according to Foley. But Foley is clearly mistaken here. If he had read the text books more carefully, he would have noticed that the l after š is not dental. Popperwell (1963: 57) does in fact say — and this is quoted also by Foley (1977: 114) — that "[s] does not occur before [l] in the same syllable but is replaced by [ʃ]", and Popperwell fails to mention that the l here is retroflex, but his information is actually given in the transcription of his examples: slapp [ʃlap:] 'slack', slå [ʃlɔ:] '(to) strike' etc. Then the question is whether it is the changed s that causes the l to change to [ḷ], or whether perhaps the l was retroflex in the first place and by a regressive assimilation changed s to š. In order to decide which of these two possibilities is the right one,

either: sl > šl > šḷ
or: sl > sḷ > šḷ [4]

we have to take a closer look at the lateral system of the Oslo dialect (both varieties).

4.2. Around 1880 the phonological system had two distinct laterals, dental l and retroflex ḷ, the latter being a possible pronunciation in words with the cluster rl, as in perle [pæ:ḷə] 'pearl'. But also [pærlə] was a common pronunciation in upper class speech at that time. In popular speech, however, [ḷ] was also found after š in the sl cluster (Larsen 1907: 74). Today we can observe that a sound change is taking place and that the retroflex ḷ is used among young people in almost every position earlier held by dental l. The only important exception [5] is l following the back vowels [a] and [ɔ], where we find a 'dark', velarized dental l, [ł],

---

[4] Or, more accurately, sl > sḷ > ṣḷ. However, speakers of Oslo dialect today, myself included, do not distinguish between [š] and [ṣ]. I have therefore used š throughout this paper.

[5] Another obvious exception is when l follows the dentals n, d or t, e.g. in anlegge 'establish, start', handle '(to) act', Atle 'Atle' (proper name), etc.

very similar to the English *l* in words like *full*, *bell*.[6] The development from dental *l* to retroflex *l* went through an intermediate stage, where [!] had replaced dental *l* especially after [u] and [u̯].[7]

The development of the lateral system can be illustrated in this way:

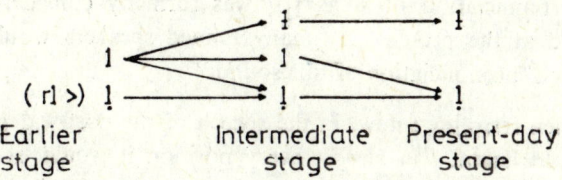

Earlier stage / Intermediate stage / Present-day stage

(The earlier stage is described by Western 1889, the intermediate stage by Vogt 1939 and the present-day stage by Jahr 1981).

4.3. As mentioned above, this still on-going change in the lateral system seems to happen without social notice, i.e. it is not socially stigmatizing to replace dental *l* with retroflex *l*.[8] However, to pronounce the

---

[6] It is therefore incorrect when modern text books on Norwegian claim that there is no 'dark' *l* in Norwegian, see Marm/Sommerfelt 1967: 9, Popperwell 1963: 52 - 53 (cf. Jahr 1981: 330).

[7] This intermediate stage confused the linguists that made the first structural phonological descriptions of Norwegian in the 1930s. Then they found unexpected use of retroflex *l* in words where they expected dental *l* (see Vogt 1939).

[8] The relation between the l-allophones [l] and [ḷ] is, however, an interesting example of how a sound change may have sociolinguistic impact and also of how a sociolinguistic feature may stop an on-going change.

Around 1880, when dental *l* was the most frequently used *l*-allophone, the difference between [l] and [ḷ] was minimal. They were both dentals, i.e. they had the same primary articulation. But after back vowels the *l* was coloured by these vowels and became velarized. The secondary articulation was thereby different, but that was not enough to differentiate these *l*'s as two sounds. *Today*, when the most frequently used *l*-allophone is retroflex, and not dental, the dental, velarized *l* we find after back vowels differs from the usual *l* not only in secondary articulation, but also in primary. This means that the two ballophones have becme so different that they can easily be distinguished, and their distribution has become socially significant. Old speakers of e.g. popular Oslo dialect tend to use the velarized *l* not only after [a] and [ɔ], but also after [u], while the young generation use retroflex *l* after [u].

However, the rapid progress of retroflex *l* seems to be effectively stopped by an important sociolinguistic factor. The use of retroflex *l* after (stressed) [a] and [ɔ] will to most Oslo speakers be unacceptable because it will give the impression of a dialect of rather low social status south east of Oslo (the Southern østfold dialect). The retroflex *l* after [a] and [ɔ] is one of the most salient features of this dialect,

s before *l* as *š* has up till now been considered popular and vulgar. The *š* in the *sl* cluster has been looked upon as 'an ugly sound' by speakers of upper class Oslo speech. This judgement is reflected in most text books on Norwegian, and f.ex. Popperwell (1963: 57) states:

> "The pronunciation of *sl* as [ʃl] was formerly considered vulgar, (...) and at the present day many refined speakers would avoid a too 'thick' pronunciation of this sound."

4.4. When retroflex *l* now, in the speech of the post-war generation, has replaced dental *l* in almost every position it would of course be phonemically uneconomical to maintain dental *l* in the *sl* cluster as an exception. And when dental *l* had changed to retroflex *l* here, not even the negative sociolinguistic evaluation of the *š* sound could prevent the *s* in the *sl* cluster from assimilating to the retroflex *l* yielding *š* as the result.

4.5. The change in the lateral system originated in popular speech and spread from there to upper class speech, but the interesting fact is that this spreading could happen so totally without social notice. Only when this unnoticed change resulted in a more frequent use in upper class speech of the socially stigmatized *š* in the *sl* cluster, and consequently — to most young speakers of the upper class variety — made the [sl] pronunciation almost impossible, could it be noticed that a change had taken place. The *š* sound in the *sl* cluster now had to be socially recognized as 'natural'.

The new social status of the [šl] pronunciation is evidenced in an interesting discussion about the *sl* cluster in a daily Oslo newspaper in 1978 (Jahr 1981: 333). The participants in the discussion, which went on for more than a month, were speakers of the educated or upper class variety. They all agreed that the only possible pronunciation of words like *slå* and *slem* was with *š* today, but they disagreed about *Oslo*, the name of the capital. This disagreement is not at all surprising. When the capital regained its old name in 1924 (before 1924 it was called *Kristiania*)

---

and it is often referred to as 'østfold *l*'. That there really *is* some kind of barrier against retroflex *l* after [a] and [ɔ], is evidenced from the fact that if the [a] and [ɔ] are unstressed, then a following *l* can be retroflex. In unstressed position a retroflex *l* after [a] and [ɔ] does not give the same low dialect impression as it does in stressed syllables. Therefore, we can find *ballétt* 'ballett', *salóng* 'drawing room', *alàrm* 'alarm' with retroflex *l*, because here the stress is on the final syllable (i.e in upper class speech; in popular speech the stress is on the initial syllable in these words, and consequently, they are pronounced with [l], not [ḷ]).

the stigma on š in the *sl* cluster was still very strong. Consequently the name was pronounced [uslu] by speakers of the upper class variety, but [uṣ̌lu] by speakers of the popular Oslo dialect. Today [uslu] is not very frequently used, but some people still consider it the only correct pronunciation.

5. *Conclusion.*

Then James Foley was right when he said that the *l* in the *sl* cluster was the main cause of the change of *s* to *š*. But it was not any abstract phonological 'strength' of the *l* that was essential. When the change of dental *l* to retroflex *l* in the lateral system also yielded retroflex *l* in the *sl* cluster, then *s* assimilated to the retroflex *l*, with *š* as the result also in educated upper class speech.[9]

REFERENCES

Broch, O. 1927. Lyden [š] som ekspressivt middel i Oslo-målet. *Festskrift til Hjamar Falk*, 30. desember 1927 fra elever, venner ag kolleger. 1 - 12. Oslo: Aschehoug [Reprinted in Jahr/Lorentz (eds.) 1981, 146 - 57].
Foley, J. 1973. Assimilation of phonological strength in Germanic. *A Festschrift for Morris Halle*, ed. by S. R. Anderson and P. Kiparsky, 51 - 8. New York: Holt.
Foley, J. 1977. *Foundations of theoretical phonology*. Cambridge: University Press.
Haugen, E. 1942. Analysis of a sound group: *sl* and *tl* in Norwegian. PMLA 57. 879 - 907. [Reprinted in Studies by Einar Haugen, The Hague:/Paris. Mouton, 1972, 115 - 41].
Itkonen, E. 1981. Review of Lass 1980. *Language* 57. 688 - 97.
Jahr, E. H. 1978. The sound 'retroflex flap' in Oslo. *Proceedings of the Twelfth*

---

[9] Vennemann (1972: 186) sets up the following rules for Norwegian (Oslo), Northern German and Standard German ($ stands for syllable boundary):

a) s→š/$−l
b) s→š/$−{l r m n w}
c) s→š/$−{l r m n w p t}

and claims that they reflect "three degrees of generality of the same phonological process" based on phonetic analogy:

a) s→š/$− $\begin{bmatrix} +^c\text{sonorant} \\ + \text{liquid} \end{bmatrix}$
b) s→š/$− [+^{c}sonorant]
c) →š/$− C

If my explanation of the change of *s* to *š* before *l* is correct, Norwegian does not fit into this picture.

International Congress of Linguists, Vienna 1977, ed. by W. U. Dressler and W. Meid, 785 - 8. Innsbruck: University.

Jahr, E. H. 1981. L-fonema i Oslo bymål. In Jahr/Lorentz 1981. 328 - 44.

Jahr, E. H. 1983. How to succeed in language planning: the influence of a century's language planning on upper class speech in Oslo. *Nordlyd. Tromsø University Working Papers on Language and Linguistics* 7. 46 - 64.

Jahr, E. H. and O. Lorentz (eds.) 1981. *Fonologi/Phonology*. (Studies in Norwegian Linguistics 1) Oslo: Novus.

Larsen, A. B. 1907. *Kristiana bymål*. Kristiania: Utgit av Bymålslaget.

Lass, R. 1980. *On explaining language change*. Cambridge: University Press.

Marm, J. and A. Sommerfelt. 1958 (1967). *Teach yourself Norwegian*. New York: Hodder and Stoughton. (New edition 1967).

Ohala, J. J. 1974. Phonetic explanation in phonology.. *Papers from the Parasession on Natural Phonology*, April 18, 1974, ed. by A. Bruck et al., 251 - 74. Chicago: CLS.

Popperwell, R. G. 1963. *The pronunciation of Norwegian*. Cambridge: Cambridge University Press/Oslo: University Press.

Smith, N. S. H. 1981: Foley's scales of relative phonological strength. Goyvaerts, D. L. (ed.): *Phonology in the 1980's*. Story-Scientia Linguistics Series 4. E. Story-Scientia, Scientific Publishers, 587 - 95.

Vennemann, T. 1972. Phonetic analogy and conceptual analogy. *Schuchardt, the Neogrammarians, and the transformational theory of phonological change*, ed. by T. Vennemann and T. H. Wilbur, 181 - 204. Frankfurt/Main: Athenäum Verlag.

Vogt, H. 1939. Some remarks on Norwegian phonemics. *Norsk Tidsskrift for Sprogvidenskap* XI. 135 - 44. [Reprinted in Jahr/Lorentz (eds.) 1981, 187 - 95].

Western, A. 1889. Kurze Darstellung des norwegischen Lautsystems. *Phonetische Studien II*. 259 - 82. [Translated into Norwegian in Jahr/Lorentz (eds.) 1981, 79 - 96].

WILHELM SCHERER'S
ZUR GESCHICHTE DER DEUTSCHEN SPRACHE
A MILESTONE IN 19TH-CENTURY LINGUISTICS

KURT R. JANKOWSKY

At the time after Jacob Grimm's enormous and almost unanimously applauded achievements, there seems to have been left very precious little room, if any room at all, for his linguistic successors of the immediately ensuing several decades to bring about truly significant contributions of their own. By and large the impression seems to have prevailed that the grand old master had laid the solid foundations for Germanic linguistics so securely that no part of the general framework was in need of major supplementation, let alone of substantial, or even radical, revision. The course for further research appeared to have been firmly set. There was, in the perception of the majority of contemporaries and successors alike, by no means a scarcity of worthwhile tasks and objectives to be persued, it is true, but these tasks and objectives were concerned, at best, with filling in the details into an otherwise definitively established framework.

And then along came Wilhelm Scherer. Not that he tried to dismantle, or to belittle, the achievements of Grimm and of all those who had labored within his fold. On the contrary, he had studied Grimm's voluminous work in great detail and had developed for it not only a thoroughly adequate understanding, but also a genuinely admiring appreciation. His elaborate study of 1865 (Scherer 1865) on Jacob Grimm's life and work is a very convincing, and lasting, testimony to it, probably not matched, and certainly not surpassed, by any other study on Grimm to this very day.

And yet, it was precisely Scherer's comprehensive knowledge of, his unsurpassable familiarity with, every facet in Grimm's linguistic thought and the moving forces behind it that he came to recognize the shortcomings and weaknesses of the linguistic procedures as introduced, extensively demonstrated, and adhered to unalteringly by Jacob Grimm.

Scherer knew Grimm personally from his student days in Berlin. The impressions registered by Scherer on their fairly numerous encounters were "sweepingly overpowering" (Schröder 1890: 105). And there are indications that Grimm likewise had more than an inkling of the great promise exhibited by both conduct and quality of performance of the very young student (ibid. — Cf. also Hoffory 1887: 646). At the time of their personal meetings, however, no critical discussion of any section of Grimm's work occurred, neither publicly nor in their private conversations.

On the other hand, Scherer did not shy away from uncompromising controversy even at a very early age. I would like to refer, e.g., to the clash with his first teacher of major influence, Franz Pfeiffer, under whom he had studied Germanic philology in Vienna from 1858—60. Pfeiffer's methodology concept had a disillusioning effect on him. In disgust, Scherer went to Müllenhoff in Berlin, "um Methode zu lernen" (Schröder 1890: 105), to acquire the appropriate linguistic method. His break with Pfeiffer became irreparable when he publicly took sides with Karl Müllenhoff against Pfeiffer in the notorious feud of the *Lachmann Schule* and Pfeiffer, principally over the question as to the origin of the Nibelungenlied: Were there many authors — so Müllenhoff — or was there only one — so Pfeiffer — ? Müllenhoff did teach Scherer THE method, but he also accomplished something else for Scherer which proved to be of at least equal importance. He launched Scherer's career into an orbit of instantaneous fame. Müllenhoff, commanding a widely acknowledged reputation of the highest order, selected Scherer, the unknown student, still far away from acquiring his Dr. phil. degree, to be his collaborator in the prestigeous as well as ambitious plan for a critical edition of the *Denkmäler deutscher Poesie und Prosa aus dem VIII. — XII. Jahrhundert*. The good results of Scherer's endeavors in the common project were generously acknowledged by Müllenhoff who called Scherer, in the "Vorrede" to the edition of 1864, "his friend, a collaborator as he only could wish to have."

Scherer's contribution was hailed as a "philologische Musterarbeit", an exemplary piece of philological research, "with truly astonishing scholarship, with unprecedented power of combination and generalization" (Körner 1916: 477). Later in his life Müllenhoff expressed serious doubt as to whether he would have been able to carry out his editorial projects without the limitless enthusiasm and inexhaustible, powerful drive of his student-friend to perform.

To the work undertaken in connection with the *Denkmäler* Scherer owed both his doctoral degree (1862) and his habilitation (1864) as well as the topic for his academic inaugural address at the University of Wien (1864), entitled "Der Ursprung der deutschen Literatur" (Heinzel 1907: 146—47).

Some of the factors mentioned above carry a decisive weight concerning the main characteristics and the appropriate understanding of Scherer's earliest, and only, major linguistic investigation, *Zur Geschichte der deutschen Sprache*, which first appeared in 1868 and in a second edition ten years later in 1878.

I will refer back to three items which I consider of utmost importance for the topic at hand. First, Scherer studied method under Karl Müllenhoff whom a friend and contemporary characterized as a scholar who combined "creative phantasy and the most exacting critical rigor" (Hoffory 1887: 646). Next, Scherer's first major approach to the German language was launched within a framework of objectives where linguistic and literary viewpoints quite naturally coexisted. And third, prior to the publication of the *Geschichte*, Scherer's reputation as a first-rate scholar had been firmly established.

The first two items largely contributed to the peculiar qualities of the book, the third item was the vital precondition for its widest possible circulation immediately upon its appearance.

Grimm and Scherer had in common that they both considered it as the chief objective of language studies to explain the development of the nation through the explanation of the development of its language. Philology is, in the words of Scherer, "the great work of national self-recognition which cannot be achieved in any way other than by historical means" (Scherer 1865: 221). Hence, in the German grammar, as a part of this philology, there must be encoded "a history of the intellectual life to the extent as it is reflected in the language" (ibid.).

Both Grimm and Scherer, as true "Kinder der Romantik", were guided to a significant degree by a national, sometimes nationalistic framework of thought. But while Grimm contented himself with the ceaseless search for facts and their often less than deep-rooted interrelation, Scherer aims much further than that. He strives to seek out the hidden intellectual causes of related items in successive language stages, and he is satisfied only if and when he has reached as far back as is feasible and possible. Thus, while Grimm stopped at Gothic as the Germanic ancestor language — or at least equated it in his practical work with Proto-Germanic — Scherer insists on a more thorough investigation of Old High German and ascribes to it a far greater importance for the reconstruction of Proto-Germanic than Grimm had done (Scherer 1865: 215. — Cf. also Werner 1886: 864).

Scherer enlarges his theoretical framework as against Grimm and many of his contemporaries, notably Schleicher, in that he does away with the notion that language formation and language decay are successive stages in language history. "Ich meinerseits habe überall nur Entwicklung, nur Geschichte wahrgenommen" (Scherer 1868: X).

Grimm showed lesser interest in more recent language stages. He considered them less productive for his main objective to unravel the intellectual history of his nation. This disinterest is due to his belief that the forces of decay are at work and do not make it worthwhile for the scholar to advance from the early Middle Ages too close to modern times. Scherer, on the other hand, interprets what Grimm called decay as a decrease of form tied to an increase of meaning (Scherer 1875: 108) and hence does not see any need for a restriction to an older time period only. On the contrary, the investigation of both language and literature of the most recent times is of crucial importance to him. Since language and literature are to be approached by an identical methodology and since conditions prevailing at modern times are not basically different from those prevailing at older times, the research effort has to encompass a space of time as far back as possible and as close to the present time as possible.

In Scherer's view, Grimm's time frame has to be extended even into the direction of the past. Jacob Grimm was reluctant to leave the field of Germanic languages in search for substantiation via linguistic information from other Indo-European languages. Scherer strongly insists on always obtaining corroborating evidence from the entire IE language family.

It should be obvious from the foregoing that Scherer's objectives were more ambitious than those of Jacob Grimm and that he wanted the investigation to proceed in a markedly different way. The mere fact-finding period of such giants like Grimm had to come to an end, and it had to be replaced by an all-out effort to ascertain the causes behind the facts and the causes that interrelate these facts.

Scherer is all for the accumulation of facts, but he is dead set against letting it become the pivotal point of language investigation: "Wir sind es endlich müde, in der blossen gedankenlosen Anhäufung wohlgesichteten Materials den höchsten Triumph der Forschung zu erblicken" (Scherer 1868: VIII).

Although the deviation from Grimm in matters of general concepts is far from being peripheral, it is the difference in methods that has to be termed truly revolutionary. And it is here that Scherer has exercised an unprecedented influence on all activities in Germanic and Indo-Germanic linguistics at his time.

Scherer looked in vain for a model of a linguistic analysis using a methodology which relied on that employed by the natural sciences. Zimmer (1879: 324) stresses this point: "Ein zukünftiger Geschichtsschreiber der germanischen Sprachwissenschaft wird ... anerkennen müssen, dass die durch Schleicher eingeführte aber vielfach nur äusserlich angewendete Methode der naturwissenschaftlichen Forschung erst durch Scherers Hand in der Sprachwissenschaft ihre volle Verwertung gefunden hat." And Scherer himself (1875: 108) is even more specific:

> ... in dieser gegenseitigen Befruchtung von Natur- und Geisteswissenschaft schärfen sich die Begriffe und verfeinern sich die Methoden. Und es ist kein Zweifel, dass die Sprachforschung wesentlichen Nutzen ziehen kann aus dem Vorbilde von Darwins Theorie. Das ist, so viel ich sehe, bis jetzt wenig geschehen. Der einfache methodische Grundsatz, das Nahe, Erreichbare möglichst genau zu beobachten und daran den ursächlichen Zusammenhang zu studieren, um ihn in die Vergangenheit zu projizieren und so deren Ereignisse zu begreifen, ist noch lange nicht in seiner Wichtigkeit erkannt.

Such a sporadic utilization of a potentially powerful principle was entirely unsatisfactory for him. He was content with nothing less than an all-out effort. All through the 19th century, natural science had gained, in an almost uninterrupted chain of success, one triumph after another, and these achievements were obtained on the basis of consistent observations of facts and a consistent application of a rigorous methodology. Never for a moment did Scherer believe, as some of his contemporaries and successors have done, that linguistics is a natural science. He refers, e.g., to Schleicher as professing "the strange inconceivable opinion that linguistics is no *Geisteswissenschaft*, but a natural science" (Scherer 1875: 107). But he did believe that linguistics as a historical science is in some major respects closely related to the natural sciences in that they both pursue similar objectives and may employ similar methods. By discarding the notion that language formation and language decay are succeeding developmental stages and by replacing it with the notion of constant uniform language development, he created the theoretical precondition for the search of regularity features in the development of language. These regularity features are accessible via a natural scientific method. By his refusal to approach linguistics in separation from its neighboring disciplines, he opened up new avenues for gaining insights into hitherto unfathomable linguistic conditions via factors adduced from other sciences. A case in point is his full-fledged exploration of sound physiology, of sound production, and of acoustics in order to be able to throw new light on historical sound transitions. Bechtel (1888: 167) and also Körner (1916: 479) comment on it. In both instances reference is made to Scherer's heavy reliance on Ernst Brücke's sound physiology, a fact which Scherer himself indirectly comments on in his *Geschichte* (1868: IV): "Was ich anstrebte, hat vielfaches Wohlwollen schon während der Arbeit erfahren. Namentlich haben Prof. Brücke und Prof. v. Miklosich mich teils in Erlangtem bestärkt, teils durch Rat und Belehrung gefördert." He rejected Grimm's preoccupation with the letter and turned his attention, instead, to the exhaustive study of all sound properties from all possible vantage points. He drew the logical conclusion from these deliberations and called for the minute observation of speech factors in the living languages spoken at his time, especially in the dialects. Findings from these observations, so he argued and convincingly demonstrated, are transferable to older language stages and constitute the only reliable procedure to reach beyond the mere enumeration of language facts and come to grips with the ultimate problem of identifying the underlying causal factors.

While assigning to language physiology its appropriate place of importance for shedding light on language history, Scherer did not lose sight of the supplementary force at work in bringing about language changes. Sound transitions caused by physiological factors account for only part of the form discrepancies among succeeding language stages. A sizeable number of forms undergo transformations caused by interference from psychological forces which create new utterances via analogy, irrespective of the physiological properties involved.

Scherer has by no means been the first to recognize how powerful the influence of analogy is on language change. He has paid ample tribute to Rudolf von Raumer (cf., e.g., Scherer 1868: 38—39) and others as his predecessors in this regard. But no one before him can claim to have employed the notion of analogy as consistently and as extensively as he has done. Besides, it was Scherer who first erected the proper framework for a meaningful and objective application of analogy to language change, since it was he who directed the linguists' attention to the fact that the conditions under which languages change have remained essentially the same throughout historical times. Same causes lead to same effects:

This axiom, basic to all natural scientific investigation, has been proven by Scherer to be of equal importance also for the science of linguistics. Retracing each securely established linguistic fact to its causing forces must become, so he demands, the core effort of the linguistic investigator: "'Gleiche Ursachen, gleiche Wirkungen' ist, wie wir schon mehrfach bestätigt gefunden haben, ein Axiom der Sprachwissenschaft so gut wie der Naturwissenschaften" (Scherer 1875:109). In his *Geschichte* (1868: VII–VIII) there is a similar reference to the need for the linguist to observe and determine the "Wirkungsweise historischer Kräfte überhaupt.... Allgemeine vergleichende Geschichtswissenschaft ... würde ... besagen: ... dass ein systematischer Kopf ... seine Kenntnisse unter dem Gesichtspunkt der Kausalität zu ordnen unternähme."

The search for causes will not, and cannot, come to a halt whenever the borderline of an adjacent discipline is reached. Scherer utilizes the insights of geology, borrows applicable procedures from many related fields if and when he recognizes in the course of his analysis that such actions are mandatory for obtaining farthest-reaching results. He cautions against overspecialization. The researcher cannot afford to be too narrowly specialized. There is need for division of labor since precision requires expertise. But there is also the necessity to avail oneself of the combined expertise acquired in several disciplines, either by one individual scholar or by several of them. "Neben Arbeitsteilung auch eine neue Arbeitsvereinigung" (Dilthey 1886:139). There is no doubt that Scherer's wide-ranged approach to the investigation of language phenomena and his matching achievements would be unthinkable without a comparable broadness of his basic qualifications in many related disciplines. Numerous contemporaries of his elaborate applaudingly, with unrestricted, unenvious admiration, that he easily outdistances any of his peers by his power of combination, by his mostly unerring intuition, and the capability of detecting the common link in seemingly disparate factors from different fields and disciplines.

Scherer's *Geschichte der deutschen Sprache* in many respects is the illustration of most of the tenets briefly discussed in the above. With his monumental work he does not — did not even intend to — and cannot, replace Grimm's 4 volumes of *Deutsche Grammatik* (1819–37). Grimm's findings are, as far as they go, supplied with the stamp of approval even by Scherer himself, as he, e.g., undertook to prepare in 1869 a new edition of Grimm's *Deutsche Grammatik* (Scherer 1869). But on the other hand, Scherer's *Geschichte* went far beyond Grimm's in that its appearance propelled, as it were, language studies out of its stagnation. With it he inaugurated a new era by creating new perspectives for the formulation of objectives and by placing into the hands of his successors a set of powerful methodological tools which have revolutionized the practices of linguistic research in the Germanic languages and also contributed greatly to far-reaching improvements in IE studies in general.

The foregoing statement is true even though it is an indisputable fact, asserted by Johannes Schmidt, one of the contemporary reviewers of Scherer's work, that almost half of the results presented in the book, were doomed to be outdated by the time it had appeared: "Etwa die Hälfte des mit ungewöhnlich umfassender Sprachkenntnis geschriebenen Buches war von Anfang an unhaltbar" (Schmidt 1887: 12). But the same reviewer also reaches the conclusion: "Die Abschnitte des Buches, welche sich in erreichbaren Regionen bewegen, haben in die ganze Entwicklung der germanischen und indogermanischen Sprachforschung tief eingegriffen, sie haben vielleicht von allem, was Scherer geschrieben hat, die nachhaltigste Wirkung geübt" (Schmidt 1887: 12).

Schmidt's appraisal, on the one hand exceedingly positive, on the other hand somewhat condoningly negative, is typical for almost all of the many evaluations that have appeared between the time of the first edition of the book in 1868 and the year 1936, 50 years after Scherer's death (Seckel 1936: 111—15).

The negative component in these appraisals requires a word of explanation. This may best be initiated by another comment from Johannes Schmidt found in the same context as the comments already quoted. Scherer's book contains, according to Schmidt, "ein Programm von schwindelerregender Universalität" (Schmidt 1887: 8). Its overall objective aims at nothing less than to present, now in the words of Scherer himself, "the origin of our nation from a particular perspective ... By physiological analysis and uniform characterization I have come up with an explanation of the sound form of our language, which constituted an introduction to the entirety of the human personality, which showed moral motives as effective forces and identified the unconditional passionate devotion to ideal objectives as the monumental foundation that gave our nation and our language its first individual existence" (Scherer 1868: IX).

To judge the book on these premises can of course not lead to a favorable result, the less so as Scherer himself fully realized that the objectives of such a program were plainly unobtainable. In the second edition of 1878, which appeared without many revisions, with only few deletions, and precisely 176 pages of more or less casual additions, the foregoing quotation is footnoted with essentially this remark: "Diese Auffassung hat sich leider nicht bewährt" (Scherer 1878: XIII).

Not that I would want to say that the entire proposition should be termed outrageous or at least utopean. There was much thought behind every word that Scherer wrote. And the reasoning behind that proposition is spread throughout his work; it is by no means restricted only to the initial phase of his scholarly career. It surfaces, e.g., in sentences like these: "Die deutsche Philologie solle der Nation einen Spiegel vorhalten." "Die deutsche Philologie ist eine Tochter des nationalen Enthusiasmus" (E. Schmidt 1894: 1).

Towards the end of his life Scherer was preoccupied with completing work on his *Poetik*, a truly grandiose project of long standing, undoubtedly his most ambitious design, which by 1886 had already progressed further than its planning stages: "Im Sommer 1885 begann mit der ersten Ausarbeitung einer Vorlesung über 'Poetik' ... ein früh gefasster und weitaussehender Plan zu reifen, der nichts geringeres als eine Ausdehnung des Machtgebietes der Philologie und die Neubegründung einer empirischen Ästhetik anstrebte" (Schröder 1890: 109—10). It was to be built uniformly on the two main components of German philology, namely German literature and German language.

A scholar of as many extraordinary achievements as Wilhelm Scherer should not be, and need not be, judged by those of his projects that did not fully mature or did not materialize at all, even if they should strike us as futile from the very start. If we stick to the large number of projects which he has completed in his short life span of 47 years, we have more than enough to praise. The same should hold true for our attitude towards the *Geschichte der deutschen Sprache*. In the light of the wealth of useful, innovative, and inspiring information which a patient and attentive reader even of the enlightened 1980s will find in the 507 pages of the book, we should be willing today to accept the conclusion at which Julius Hoffory arrived in his obituary tribute to Scherer on the basis of his personal acquaintance with him: "His weaknesses and his deficiencies are of an entirely insignificant nature if viewed in relation to his strengths" (Hoffory 1887: 653).

Many contemporary scholars did not fully agree with Hoffory's summary statement. I would like to mention here only one, highly representative, group of those contemporaries, the Neogrammarians or *Junggrammatiker*, who are especially indebted to Scherer's work, mainly to the *Geschichte*, as the indispensable stepping stone for their own important, and highly influential, achievements.

None of the Neogrammarians, neither the four Indo-Europeanists Karl Brugmann, Berthold Delbrück, August Leskien, and Hermann Osthoff, nor any of the four Germanists Wilhelm Braune, Friedrich Kluge, Hermann Paul, and Eduard Sievers, fail to give credit to Scherer for his many achievements. In the "Vorwort" to the *Morphologische Untersuchungen*, Volume 1, written in 1878 by Osthoff and Brugmann, which constitutes the linguistic credo of the group, Scherer is accorded a place of honor by several highly favorable references being made concerning the impact of his studies on Neogrammarian theory and practice. For instance: "Seit dem Erscheinen von Scherer's Buch 'Zur Geschichte der deutschen Sprache' (Berlin 1868) und wesentlich durch die von diesem Buch ausgehenden Impulse hat sich die Physiognomie der vergleichenden Sprachwissenschaft nicht unbeträchtlich verändert" (Osthoff-Brugmann 1878: III).

Another sample passage praises as Scherer's "Verdienst, die Frage, wie die sprachlichen Umgestaltungen und Neugestaltungen sich vollziehen, nachhaltig angeregt zu haben" (Osthoff-Brugmann 1878: XI). Osthoff-Brugmann add on, specifying: "... das eine, alle Irrtümer in Schatten stellende und kaum hoch genug anzurechnende Verdienst kann ihm niemand streitig machen" (ibid.).

Even Hermann Paul, in spite of his devastating review of Scherer's second edition of 1878, has many favorable things to say of Scherer's importance as an initiator and mover of crucial ideas (Paul 1879: 308).

One must read, and re-read, Scherer's book to understand what Paul, and others, meant by ascribing to Scherer the power of initiating crucially important ideas. After all, it is not by furnishing a corpus of data that he has earned a place among the greatest of the 19th-century linguists, but by providing a mental framework within which his successors could procure many of their achievements. And in this sense Wilhelm Scherer's overwhelmingly stimulating, even provocative work *Zur Geschichte der deutschen Sprache* is indeed a very important milestone in 19th-century linguistics.

REFERENCES

Bechtel, Fritz. 1888. Wilhelm Scherer. *Beiträge zur Kunde der indogermanischen Sprachen* 13. 163 - 72.

Dilthey, Wilhelm. 1886. Wilhelm Scherer zum persönlichen Gedächtnis. *Deutsche Rundschau* 49. 132 - 46.

Grimm, Jacob. 1819 - 37. *Deutsche Grammatik*, vol. 1 - 4. Göttingen: Diederichsche Buchhandlung.

Hoffory, Julius. 1887. Wilhelm Scherer. *Westermanns Monatshefte* 62. 646 - 53.
Heinzel, Richard. 1907. Rede auf Wilhelm Scherer. *Kleine Schriften von Richard Heinzel*, ed. M. H. Jellinek and C. von Kraus, 145 - 63. Heidelberg: C. Winter.
Jankowsky, Kurt R. 1972. *The Neogrammarians. A re-evaluation of their place in the development of linguistic science*. The Hague: Mouton.
Körner, Josef. 1916. Wilhelm Scherer (1841 - 1886). Zur 30. Wiederkehr seines Todestages. *Neue Jahrbücher für das Klassische Altertum, Geschichte und deutsche Literatur* 37. 475 - 85.
Meyer, Richard Moritz, ed. 1888. Wilhelm Scherer, *Poetik*. Berlin: Weidmannsche Buchhandlung. New ed. by Gunter Reiss. Tübingen, 1977.
Müllenhoff, Karl. 1864. Vorrede. *Denkmäler deutscher Poesie und Prosa aus dem VIII. - XII. Jahrhundert*. Berlin: Weidmann.
Osthoff, Hermann and Karl Brugmann. 1878. Vorwort. *Morphologische Untersuchungen auf dem Gebiete der indogermanischen Sprachen* 1. III - XX.
Paul, Hermann. 1879. Review of Wilhelm Scherer, *Zur Geschichte der deutschen Sprache* (Berlin: Weidmannsche Buchhandlung 1878). *Jenaer Literaturzeitung*. 307 - 11.
Scherer, Wilhelm. 1865. *Jacob Grimm*. Berlin: Georg Reimer.
    1868. *Zur Geschichte der deutschen Sprache*. Berlin: Franz Duncker.
    ed. 1869. Jacob Grimm, *Deutsche Grammatik*. Berlin: F. Dümmler (2 vols. only).
    1875. Review of W. D. Whitney. *Die Sprachwissenschaft*, transl. by Julius Jolly (München: Th. Ackermann, 1874). *Preussische Jahrbücher* 35. 106 - 11.
    1878. *Zur Geschichte der deutschen Sprache*. Berlin: Weidmannsche Buchhandlung.
Schmidt, Erich, ed. 1894. "Wissenschaftliche Pflichten. Aus einer Vorlesung Wilhelm Scherers". *Euphorion* 1.1 - 4.
Schmidt, Johannes. 1887. Gedächtnisrede auf Wilhelm Scherer. Abhandlungen der Königlichen Akademie der Wissenschaften zu Berlin, 3 - 19. Berlin: Georg Reimer.
Schröder, Edward. 1890. Wilhelm Scherer. *Allgemeine Deutsche Biographie* 31. 104 - 14.
Seckel, Dietrich. 1936. Wilhelm Scherer. Zu seinem 50. Todestag am 6. August. *Deutsche Rundschau* 248. 111 - 15.
Werner, J. M. 1886. Wilhelm Scherer. *Zeitschrift für Allg. Geschichte* (Stuttgart) 3. 862 - 67.
Zimmer, Heinrich. 1879. Review of Scherer, *Zur Geschichte der deutschen Sprache* (Berlin: Weidmannsche Buchhandlung, 1878). *Beiträge zur Kunde der indogermanischen Sprachen* 3. 324 - 31.

PROTO-INDO-EUROPEAN CONSONANTISM: METHODOLOGICAL AND FURTHER TYPOLOGICAL CONCERNS

BRIAN D. JOSEPH

The traditional view of the consonantal inventory of Proto-Indo-European, as put forth, for example, by Brugmann 1904, posited four series of stops, a voiceless unaspirated series, a voiced unaspirated series, a voiceless aspirated series, and a voiced aspirated series. For instance, at the dental point of articulation, the sounds *t, *d, *th, and *dh were reconstructed, with similar sets posited for the other points of articulation as well. As is now well-known, the evidence for the voiceless aspirated series (*ph, *th, etc.) was not overwhelming — the number of "good" cognates with these elements was markedly small, with the best examples coming from Indo-Iranian, and in many cases the Indo-Iranian voiceless aspirates could be shown to be secondary developments of a sequence of voiceless unaspirated stop plus laryngeal. Similar problems were noted with regard to one member of the voiced unaspirated series, the labial stop *b. Because of such considerations, many scholars have now reacted these elements as part of the Proto-Indo-European segmental inventory and have worked instead with three series of stops with a gap (or near-gap) in the labials — this is the "3-way" system of, for example, Lehmann 1952: (ignoring the question of the gutturals)

p	t	k	k^w
(b)	d	g	g^w
b^h	d^h	g^h	g^{wh}.

Such a step, though, has presented other problems, especially the oft-made observation that the resulting system is unbalanced and worse yet, is typologically unparalleled (Jakobson 1958 and others following him). The major problem is the putative existence of a voiced aspirated series without a corresponding voiceless aspirated one. This particular problem has led to (at least) four types of responses:

a. attempts to restore the Brugmannian system (e.g. Szemerényi 1967)
b. redefinition, within a "3-way" system, of the voiced aspirated (*dh) series as voiced spirants (e.g. Prokosch 1938, Peeters 1971, and others)
c. denial of the relevance of typological information and thus the acceptance of either a 3-way or a 4-way system (e.g. Dunkel 1981)
d. revision of the phonetic reality of the 3-way system to yield a typologically suitable reconstruction (e.g. Hopper 1973, 1977a, 1977b, Gamkrelidze and Ivanov 1973, Gamkrelidze 1981).

The problem of the Proto-Indo-European consonantal inventory thus is a most complex one, and anyone wishing to take one of the above four positions — or any other conceivable one — has really to argue against all the other possible positions. In as short a paper as the present one, such detailed argumentation simply is not feasible. However, a few important methodological questions bearing on this general issue can be examined. The importance of these questions lies in the fact that under one possible — and, I would argue, reasonable — resolution of them, the traditional reconstruction, i.e. that of Brugmann, can be maintained without (too much) further ado, thus rendering revisions and redefinitions unnecessary at least for Proto-Indo-European, the stage of the language reachable through the comparative method; speculations regarding the pre-Proto-Indo-European state-of-affairs would be largely unaffected.

The methodological side of the Proto-Indo-European consonant system issue has already received some attention in the literature. For example, Dunkel 1981, in a cogent dicussion of possible methodological pitfalls in the typologist approach to the Proto-Indo-European consonantism question, criticizes those who take the rarity of *b in Proto-Indo-European to be equivalent to its complete absence and accordingly revise the phonetic reality of the reconstructed system so as to make such a gap occur at a typologically natural spot (e.g. in a voiceless glottalic series at the labial point, in the schema of Hopper 1973). Similarly, he also takes to task those who rely too heavily on typological observations to provide checks on reconstructions, on the grounds that "typology will in fact never be in a position to make such statements [of absolute nonexistence for some feature], because it will never have studied all human languages" (p. 564). Szemerényi 1967, on the other hand (and others, e.g. Hopper 1981, partly in his own defense), gives his general approval to the uses to which typology has been put in discussions of the Proto-Indo-European consonant system (up to 1967 at least) and even uses Jakobson's observation that languages with distinctive aspiration also have a phoneme /h/ to justify his reconstruction of a single "laryngeal" consonant with the phonetic value [h].

Despite remarks such as these, there are still further methodological questions to be addressed. In particular, two additional important issues can be identified:

1. the type of evidence which counts as relevant "input" for the comparative method
2. the type of units which the comparative method yields for the proto-language.

As the discussion to follow indicates, these two issues are interrelated, especially when their relevance to the question of the Proto-Indo-European consonant system is explored.

To start with the first issue, it must be noted that typically, onomatopoetic words, loan words, and expressive vocabulary are in general excluded from consideration in the comparative method. As is well-known, a good many of the reconstructed roots for Proto-Indo-European with a *b or a voiceless aspirate involve just these types of words, for example: *kha- 'interjection of laughter' and basis for verbs, as in Sanskrit *kakhati* 'he laughs heartily' or Greek *kakházō* 'laugh' (Pokorny IEW 634); *phu-k- 'blow' (IEW 847), *pha^{x}mph- 'swell' (IEW 94, there labelled a "Lautnachahmung"); *baba-/*balbal-/*barbar- 'word for unarticulated, meaningless speech' (IEW 91); *ăbe/ŏl- 'apple' (IEW 1) where the vowel variations suggest the possibility of a loan. Accordingly, the usual practice has been to ignore forms such as these in compiling the phonological inventory of Proto-Indo-European, leaving the situation noted at the outset that there is just a small number of what most scholars would consider to be "good" cognates with these sounds.

It is fair, though, to question this practice. Laon words can certainly become so solidly entrenched in a langage that native speakers are not aware of their origin, even if they contain "nonnative" sounds. The case of English words with /ž/ borrowed from French provides a clear instance of this type. Also, it is often hard to judge the age of loan words accurately, especially very old ones, so that it is not always clear if a given loan word should be excluded.

Similarly, Proto-Indo-European, like all known languages, must have had expressive forms, affective usages, and onomatopoetic words — the need for such elements in a language seems simply to be a fact about the context in which human communication takes place and the nature of the humans engaging in that communication. Since it seems rather unlikely that human nature has changed considerably since Proto-Into-European times, roughly 6500 years before present, it can safely be assumed that Proto-Indo-European had expressive vocabulary and onomatopoetic words.

Such elements are certainly notoriously irregular with regard to sound change and are susceptible to iconic recreation and reformation at any time as well as shaping by culture-specific "definitions" of iconicity. Nonetheless, certain aspects of these words can often enter into the normal transmission of language from generation to generation; to that extent, these words can show the same stability diachronically that the nonexpressive sectors of the lexicon do. This last fact was noted by Meillet, for example, who wrote (1967:106) regarding the form *kha for the noise of laughter "this is an onomatopoeia ... but this does not interfere with the application of phonological laws". Given all the foregoing, the comparative method provides the only possible way of gaining any insights into what those Proto-Indo-European expressive and onomatopoetic forms must have looked like. For that reason, they should not be discounted as potential input to the comparative method.

It is therefore quite likely that Proto-Indo-European had voiceless aspirates, and probably a *b* as well, at least in expressive and affective words and in onomatopoetic forms. Interestingly, this conclusion is accepted by Bomhard (1981) one of the leading proponents of the "glottalic hypothesis" under which the phonetic reality of a three series consonant system for Proto-Indo-European is revised to include a glottalic series (à la Hopper et al.). Bomhard (p. 354) states: "the voiceless aspirates found in the onomatopoeic words are probably the only ones that should be assigned to Indo-European and are to be regarded here simply as non-phonemic variants of the plain voiceless stops".

Bomhard's statement, however, merits a closer look. For one thing, it is important to note that it is not uncommon for certain sounds in a language to have a restricted, specifically expressive function. Such is the case with the labial stops in Iroquoian, as pointed out by Mithun 1982, with the voiced palatal aspirate *jh* in Sanskrit, as noted by Dressler 1969, and to a certain extent with the sounds *ts* and *dz* in Modern Greek as well, as argued by Joseph 1982a, b, 1984. The parallels between these restricted function sounds and the case of the Proto-Indo-European voiceless aspirates and *b* is instructive. Like Proto-Indo-European *b, Sanskrit *jh* fills what would be a gap in an otherwise symmetrical system; like the Proto-Indo-European voiceless aspirate series, the Iroquoian expressive sounds range over a whole class of sounds, the labial stops, and are not just a single isolated sound. Even more striking parallels with Modern Greek are taken up in more detail below.

Moreover, what does it mean to say, as Bomhard does, that the voiceless aspirates in Proto-Indo-European were "nonphonemic variants"? This leads directly into the second issue mentioned above concerning the synchronic status of phonological elements reconstructed for the proto-language. Unless this is taken to mean that the voiceless aspirates were in free variation with unaspirated stops, a claim which is tantamount to begging the question of synchronic status since "free variation" is an inherently unexplanatory move, there seem to be (at least) two possible interpretations of Bombard's statement.

Translating Bombard's statement into classical phonemic terms, one would have to say that there was, for example, an allophone [ph] of the phoneme /p/, and that the occurrence of this allophone was conditioned not by some aspect of its surrounding phonetic environment, as is usually the case, but instead by a lexical fact, namely the fact that the word containing the /p/ was an expressive or onomatopoetic word. Similarly, translating Bomhard's statement into generative phonology and systematic phonemic units, one would have to posit a rule converting an underlying /p/ into a surface [ph] in words marked with an appropriate feature such as [+EXPRESSIVE]. Furthermore, this rule would have to be optional for at least some words, since unaspirated [p] seems to have occurred in such words in Proto-Indo-European as well, to judge from reconstructions such as *pū-, variant of *phu- 'blow' (Pokorny IEW 847), or *paaˣmpɲ-, variant of *phaamph- 'swell' (Pokorny IEW 94). Thus in either framework, the appearance of voiceless aspirates in expressive words in Proto-Indo-European is really a lexical fact, not conditioned by anything other than the nature of the lexical item containing the appropriate sounds. Essentially, then, one is dealing with lexical instances of voiceless aspirates, whether they are "disguised" as "nonphonemic variants" or not. Accordingly, at the very least, some of these lexical voiceless aspirates should properly be considered to be systematic phonemes synchronically in Proto-Indo-European.

At this point, the interrlatedness of the two methodological issues discussed so far becomes important. Any loan words that may have been present in Proto-Indo-European with *b* or with a voiceless aspirate would have lent systemic support to the phonemic interpretation of *b* and voiceless aspirates in expressive words, since they would have constituted independent evidence for the status of these sounds as distinctive phonological elements. Some possible candidates here include *ăbe/ŏl- 'apple' (IEW 1), whose extreme vocalic variations suggest a nonnative word, and *math-/moth- in words for gnawing, biting worms and vermin (IEW 700), where the "non-core"-vocabulary nature of the word suggests the possibility of a loan (and note that Finnish *matikka* 'little worm' seems to be borrowed from an Indo-European language) and the distribution of the cognates (Armenian *mat'il* 'louse' and Germanic, e.g. Gothic *maþa* 'worm, mite') would point to a very early entry into Indo-European.

In addition, some instances of *b's that are allophonic (in the classical phonemic sense) might well be reassignable as underlying, i.e. phonemic, units, given the general approach being outlined here. One likely instance is the *b in *[-bd-], the surface form of the zero-grade of the root *ped- 'foot; go, step' (IEW 790), i.e. underlying /pd-/, where the *b* has arisen via a regressive voice assimilation rule. This form is a good candidate for being considered to have been relexicalized with an underlying /b/, because, to judge from its occurrence in compounds in Indo-Iranian (Sanskrit *upa-bd-a-* 'trampling', Avestan *fra-bd-a-* 'forefoot') and Greek (*epí-bd-ai* 'day after a festival'), the relationship in meaning between the full-grade forms of the root *ped- and the zero-grade *bd- may have been somewhat tenuous (cf. especially the Greek form).

Similarly, some allophonic voiceless aspirates, in particular those that appear to be conditioned by contact with a preceding *s, as in *skhel- 'stumble' (Sanskrit *skhal-ate* 'stumbles', Armenian *sxal-em* 'I stumble', Pokorny IEW 929), may also be analyzable as containing underlying voiceless aspirates. While the aspiration in these roots could be the result of independent developments in the individual languages — Burrow (1973:72, 393) refers to several such roots in Indic as showing "spontaneous aspiration" — there are many cases where the forms in two or more languages agree in showing reflexes of aspiration, as with *skhel- noted above or with Sanskrit *sphūrj-ati* 'bursts forth' and Greek *spharagéomai* 'burst with a noise' both from a root *(s)p(h)erəg- 'spring' (IEW 996). Thus the possibility cannot be ruled out that such allophonic aspiration was already present in Proto-Indo-European, conditioned by the preceding *s* in such roots.

Moreover, with many of these roots with an initial *s̑* plus voiceless aspirate cluster (12 of the 23 Pokorny lists) the *s* is the so-called "*s*-mobile"; since the conditions which favored the presence or absence of the *s* in these roots are not retrievable given our current state of knowledge (though many interesting possibilities have been put forward), it seems that we must accept it as likely that some surface aspirated forms of these roots would have lost the underlying *s* which conditioned the aspiration. Such a situation seems to occur with *(s)p(h)el- 'split' (IEW 985) attested in forms such as Sanskrit *sphaṭ-ati* 'tears' and Greek *sphalássein* 'to cut, to prick' but also, with aspiration but with no *s*, Sanskrit *phal-ati* 'bursts, springs apart' and the extended form Greek *phel-g-únei* 'be without understanding'. Such forms show that the originally allophonic aspiration, in some occurrences, was opaque and thus susceptible to reanalysis as being underlyingly present; such a reanalysis would have been facilitated by any independent instances of voiceless aspirates in expressive words, in loan words, and the like.

Similar considerations hold for voiceless aspirates which seem to be the result of a voiceless stop plus laryngeal, as in the second person singular perfect ending *-tha from the earlier and possibly synchronically underlying sequence */-tH$_2$e/; the equation of Sanskrit *vet-tha* with Greek *ois-tha* 'you know', where both languages show aspiration in the ending, suggests that the ending may have been aspirated on the surface already in Proto-Indo-European, and without strong synchronic support at that stage for the internally reconstructed underlying morphological form */-tH$_2$e/ noted above, that surface voiceless aspirate would have been another candidate for emergence as an underlying segment through relexicalization.

Thus with just slight modifications to some of the standard assumptions that are made about the nature of the input to the comparative method and the synchronic status of the units arrived at by applying the comparative method, one reaches a very different picture of the consonant system of Proto-Indo-European, where this designation represents, by definition, that stage of the protolanguage just prior ot the break-up into the individual branches. The view that emerges is of lanaguage that indeed did have a *b and in addition had a voiceless aspirate series, just as the traditional reconstruction would have it. All that is different in this view is the recognition of special functional status for many occurrences of these sounds, just as is the case with certain (classes of) sounds in Iroquoian, Sanskrit, or Modern Greek. While it is fair to ask why just these sounds and not others should have had such a special status, it does not seem that we can ignore their existence anymore than we could say, for example, that there was no *ts* or *dz* in Modern Greek.

In fact, to close on a different sort of typological note, the parallel between the situation with Modern Greek *ts* and *dz* and the Proto-Indo-European situation with *b and the voiceless aspirates is striking indeed. Modern Greek has *ts* and *dz* in numerous expressive and onomatopoetic forms such as the diminutive suffixes *-útsikos*, *-ítsa* and *-ítsi*, the adjectives *kutsós* 'lame, and *tsevdós* 'lisping', the verb *tsak-ízo* 'crack' derived from the noise word *tsak*, the sound symbolic verb *tsimbó* 'pinch', and others; in addition, these sounds are to be found in Greek in numerous relatively recent loans, such as *dzudzés* 'dwarf' and *dzámba* 'for free' from Turkish, *klotsó* 'kick' from Italian, and many more; finally, there is even one instance of a *ts* in Modern Greek which is derived historically from a reduction of *-θis-*, just as Proto-Indo-European had forms like the perfect ending *-tha derived from earlier *-tH$_2$e. The relevant form is *kats-* 'sit' which arose via syncope and spirantal dissimilation from the fuller form, the aoristic stem *kaθis-* (cf. Ancient Greek *kathízō*), and is now perhaps best treated as a new lexical stem with *ts* as an underlying element (cf. the imperative singular *kátse* 'sit!' or the first person plural subjunctive *na kátsume* 'let's sit'). The comparison of the Modern Greek phonological system with that of Proto-Indo-European, then, provides another case in which the present can guide us in understanding the past.

REFERENCES

Arbeitman, Y. and A. Bomhard (eds.) 1981. *Bono Homini Donum*: *Essays in historical linguistics in memory of J. Alexander Kerns*. Amsterdam: John Benjamins B. V.

Bomhard, A. 1981. Indo-European and Afroasiatic: new evidence for the connection. In Arbeitman and Bomhard 1981, Part I. 351 - 474.

Brugmann, K. 1904. *Kurze vergleichende Grammatik der indogermanischen Sprachen*. Strassburg: Trübner. (Reprinted 1970).

Burrow, T. 1973. *The Sanskrit language*. London

Dressler, W. 1969. Altindisch (jh). *Die Sprache* 15. 168 - 70.

Dunkel, G. 1981. Typology versus reconstruction. In Arbeitman and Bomhard 1981, Part II. 559 - 69.

Gamkrelidze, T. 1981. Language typology and language universals and their implications for the reconstruction of the Indo-European stop system. In Arbeitman and Bomhard 1981, Part II. 571 - 609.

Gamrelidze, T. and V. Ivanov. 1973. Sprachtypologie und die Rekonstruktion der gemeinindogermanischen Verschlüsse. *Phonetica* 27. 150 - 56.

Hopper, P. 1973. Glottalized and murmured occlusives in Indo-European. *Glossa* 7. 141 - 66.

1977a. The typology of the Proto-Indo-European segmental inventory. *Journal of Indo-European Studies* 5.1. 41 - 54.

1977b. Indo-European consonatism and the 'new look'. *Orbis* XXVI. 1. 57 - 72.

1981. 'Decem' and 'Taihun' languages. An Indo-European isogloss. In Arbeitman and Bomhard 1981, Part, I. 133 - 41.

Jakobson, R. 1958. Typological studies and their contribution to historical comparative linguistics. *Proceedings of the Eight International Congress of Linguistists*, ed. by E. Sievertsen, Oslo

Joseph, B. 1982a. Phonesthemes in Greek and the Balkans. Paper read at Third Annual Conference on Balkan and South Slavie Linguistics, Indiana University, April 1982.

1982b. Ya tin idieteri Θesi tu [ts]/[dz] stin eliniki fonologia (On the special position of [ts]/[dz] in Greek phonology). To appear in *Proceedings of Third Meeting of the Department of Linguistics, University of Thessaloniki*.

1984. Balkan expressive and affective phonology - the case of Greek *ts/dz*. *Papers for the V. Congress of Southeast European Studies*. Columbus: Slavica Publishers, 227 - 237.

Lehmann, W. 1952. *Proto-Indo-European phonology*. Austin: University of Texas.

Meillet, A. 1967. *The Indo-European dialects*. University, Alabama: University of Alabama Press Translated from 1922 French edition by S. Rosenberg; Alabama Linguistic and Philological Series No. 15.

Mithun, M. 1982. The synchronic and diachronic behavior of plops, squeaks, croaks, sighs, and moans. *International Journal of American Linguistics* 48. 49 - 58.

Peeters, C. 1971. A phonemic redefinition of Indo-European voiced aspirates. *Indogermanische Forschungen* 76.

Prokosch, E. 1938. *A comparative Germanic grammar*. Baltimore: Linguistic Society of America.

Pokorny, J. 1959. *Indogermanisches etymologisches Wörterbuch*. Bern: Francke (=IEW).

Szemerényi, O. 1967. The new look of Indo-European: reconstruction and typology. *Phonetica* 17. 65 - 99.

THE PLACE OF SAUSSURE'S 'MÉMOIRE' IN THE DEVELOPMENT OF HISTORICAL LINGUISTICS

E. F. KONRAD KOERNER

0.0 *Introductory observations*
Recent translations into Russian (1977) and Italian (1978) of Ferdinand de Saussure's *Mémoire sur le système primitif des voyelles dans les langues indoeuropéennes*, which had first appeared in Leipzig in December 1878 (Saussure 1879), may be taken as an indication of the continuing interest in an appreciation of Saussure's contribution to comparative-historical Indo-European linguistics. I do not know of any other book in linguistics of the last quarter of the 19th century that has been translated in recent years, with the exception of Hermann Paul's *Prinzipien der Sprachgeschichte* of 1880 (5th revised edition, 1920), which had translations into Russian and Japanese in 1960 and 1965, respectively. But Paul's book was a contribution to general linguistics rather than historical linguistics as the title of his book may suggest, and as such it was much less quickly outdated as is common in a field in which new discoveries and advances make yesterday's findings obsolete tomorrow. The fact that Saussure's *Mémoire* did not share the fate of most other studies of the period calls for special reasons, and I am hoping that the present paper will offer at least a few of these.

0.1 *Eary reactios to Saussure's 'Mémoire'*. There are indications that Saussure's 300-page study on the sound system of Proto-Indo-European made a notable impact on linguistic circles of the time, though perhaps not the impact that the young author might have hoped for. We may recall that when the book was published, Saussure was just 21 years old, and a student of linguistics at the University of Leipzig for barely four semesters; indeed, when he defended his thesis on the absolute genitive in Sanskrit in February 1880, it is said that one of his examiners assumed that he was a young relative of the well-known author of the *Mémoire*! But apart from Saussure's precocity, there were other factors that hampered the immediate success and the acceptance of the ideas he proposed in the *Mémoire*. Despite the fact that he was a student of the *Junggram-*

matiker, notably Karl Brugmann (1849 - 1919), the prime mover of this group of young 'revolutionaries' in historical-comparative linguistics at the time, Brugmann did not concur with the main tenets of Saussure's argument, although he was impressed by his breadth of coverage, circumspection, and "nicht gewöhnliche Combinationsgabe". Indeed, Brugmann (1879a:774) felt that Saussure had proposed a purely aprioristic scheme (rein aprioristische Construction), which did not hold water, and he was not convinced that Saussure's proposals would have to lead him to a substantial revision of his own views (cf. also Brugmann 1879b:261 - 262, and the relevant quotations in Redard 1978:33).

Hermann Osthoff (1847 - 1909), Brugmann's close collaborator during the 1870s and 1880s, expressed himself in a much more hostile manner to Saussure's theories in several articles published in volumes 2 and 4 of *Morphologische Untersuchungen* in 1879 and 1881, qualifying them as a 'total failure', 'radical error', and the like (cf. Redard 1978:35 for details). Gustav Meyer (1850 - 1900), another member of the group, incorporated part of Saussure's findings in his *Griechische Grammatik* of 1880 (3rd enl. ed., Leipzig: Breitkopf & Härtel, 1896), without ever mentioning the source of the series of the Indo-European ablaut he was basing his work on. In short, it can be said that, at least in its initial phase, Saussure's *Mémoire* did not find the reception within the immediate circle of the Leipzig linguists one might perhaps have expected. However, other reviewers of the book who were either opposed to the Young Turks at Leipzig or abroad and thus far removed from the scientific quarrels among German scholars, seem to have agreed on at least one trait of Saussure's *Mémoire*, namely, that it was theoretically very demanding, that the author had a penchant for algebraic formulae, and that the argument was difficult to follow because of a predilection for abstraction. Thus August Fick (1833 - 1916), the head of the Göttingen linguistic circle which included, inter alios, Hermann Collitz (1855 - - 1935), reviewing Saussure's book at considerable length, noted Saussure's fondness of 'mathematische Formulierungen' (1880:420), but concluded, after having criticized a number of points of detail in Saussure's argument:

> Die etwas künstliche Anordnung des Stoffs und eine eigentümliche Vorliebe des Verf[assers] für mathematische Formulierungen erschweren das Studium des sonst klar geschriebenen Werkes, wer aber die Mühe nicht scheut, wird sich durch mannigfache Belehrung und Anregung reichlich entschädigt finden. (Fick 1880: 239)

The Celtologist, (Sir) John Rhys (1840 - 1915), writing for a more general audience in a British monthly, likewise noted, in his very positive review:

> The work is so technical and the reasoning so complicated that it is very difficult to give any idea of it excepting to those who have had a thorough training in Aryan glottology [i.e., Indo-European linguistics]; but it may at once be said that it is the most important and epoch-making work that has appeared since [Johannes] Schmidt's [(1843 - 1901)] [*Zur Geschichte des indogermanischen*] *Vocalismus* [2 vols., Weimar: H. Böhlau, 1871 - 75] was published. (Rhys 1879: 234)

We may also cite a similar opinion by the French Latinist and comparative linguist Louis Havet (1849 - 1925), who in fact wrote the most extensive review of Saussure's *Mémoire*, but had similar misgivings, arguing that it had "un defaut grave: il est extraordinairement dur à lire". Havet found that Saussure was abusing abstract designations and was engaging in an excessive use of (at times newly coined) technical terms, concluding his complaints by stating that "Ainsi, M. de Saussure fait suer sang et eau à ceux qui le lisent" (Havet 1978 [1879]: 107). However, apart from these criticisms, Havet's review of Saussure's book was very favourable indeed, leading to a life-long friendship and correspondence between the two scholars (cf. Redard 1976).

There is still at least another review of the *Mémoire* that deserves being mentioned, namely, the one by the young Polish linguist Mikołaj Kruszewski (1851 - 87), which appeared in Russian in 1880. It also included an account of Brugmann's "Nasalis sonans" article of 1876, but it is obvious that Saussure's *Mémoire* was far more attractive to the theoretically inclined Kruszewski, who regarded Saussure's book as an important contribution to the method of phonology, and in fact as marking a new phase in the study of Indo-European phonology (Kruszewski 1978 [1880]:444 and 450, respectively). (I may also mention in parenthesis that the *Mémoire* inspired Kruszewski's work in various ways; apart from leading him to study questions of ablaut in Indo-European, especially in Slavic, Kruszewski — and his mentor and collaborator Baudouin de Courtenay — took from the *Mémoire* a number of concepts and terms, such as 'phoneme', 'alternation', and 'zero'. Indeed, Kruszewski translated 'phoneme' into Russian as 'fonema' and proposed to use it as a phonological term in contradistinction to 'zvuk' "sound", a distinction which made history in linguistics.)

In sum, we may say that outside the narrow circle of the Leipzigers Saussure's work was well received when it was first published. It is true that in France Saussure's proposal found a untiring critic in Paul Regnaud (1838 - 1910), a professor of Classics and comparative grammar at the University of Lyon (e.g., Regnaud 1889, 1890, 1891), but it seems that Regnaud's attacks on Saussure's system of the proto-Indo-European vowels were ignored by most of his contemporaries, probably for the simple reason that the younger generation of Indo-Europeanists had long since rejected the basic assumptions of August Schleicher (1821 - 1868) in matters of PIE phonology, to which Regnaud still subscribed.

0.*2 The reception of Saussure's 'Mémoire' during the late 19th and early 20th century*. Ignoring for the moment the peculiar reception Saussure's theories received from scholars such as Hermann Möller (1850 - 1923) and Albert Cuny (1869 - 1947) — it will concern us later in this paper — we may note that members of the next generation of Indo-Europeanists, notably Saussure's former student at the Ecole Pratique des Hautes Etudes in Paris, Antoine Meillet (1866 - 1936), and two German scholars, Wilhelm Streitberg (1864 - 1925) and Herman Hirt (1865 - 1936), had a particularly high opinion of the *Mémoire*. Hirt can be said to have been the first scholar to fully incorporate Saussure's findings in his monograph of 1900, *Der indogermanische Ablaut*; already in 1885, the brilliant comparative linguist Heinrich Hübschmann (1848 - 1908), one of Saussure's former teachers at Leipzig, was close to accepting Saussure's theory part and parcel had it not been for an error on Saussure's part in taking Lat. *agō* and the like as an aorist present of **Aǵ-* (Hübschmann 1885:2 - 3; cf. Mayrhofer 1981:26 - 27, n. 75). Hirt, for his part, regarded Saussure's *Mémoire* as "ein bahnbrechendes Werk, noch heute von grösster Bedeutung", some two generations after its publication (Hirt 1927:XXV), thus echoing Streitberg's opinion expressed in his obituary of Saussure of 1914:

> Das Buch ist de Saussures Meisterwerk: noch heute, nach einem Menschenalter, wirken Inhalt und Form mit derselben bezwingenden Macht wie am Tage des Erscheinens — von wieviel sprachwissenschaftlichen Werken, auch solchen höchsten Ranges, kann man das Gleiche sagen? (Streitberg 1966 [1914]: 103)

Last but not least, reference should be made to Meillet, in particular to his influential *Introduction à l'étude comparative des langues indo-européennes*, which first appeared in 1903, and which bears the inscription "A mon maître Ferdinand de Saussure à l'occasion des vingt-cinq ans écoulés depuis la publication du *Mémoire* ... (1878 - 1903)", an inscription that was retained in the many subsequent editions of the text. As a matter of fact, this book remained for Meillet Saussure's major achievement, and not the posthumus *Cours de linguistique générale*, with the result that even after the latter's appearance, Meillet associated the well-known phrase (wrongly ascribed to Saussure, though undoubtedly in his spirit) that language is a system 'où tout se tient' with the *Mémoire*. (Cf. the 8th ed. of his *Introduction* (pp. IX [=1903:X], 475, and elsewhere; and Brogyanyi 1983, for details.)

In 1887, Saussure's *Mémoire* was republished in Paris; at this time, Saussure contemplated accompanying the new edition with an attack on his detractors (cf. Redard 1978:36). One may speculate who or what circumstances persuaded Saussure to suppress his ill feelings toward those who did neither understand nor appreciate his accomplishments. It could have been the recognition he received from scholars outside the narrow circle of the *Junggrammatiker*, notably Havet, Fick, and Hübschmann, all between 9 and 24 years his seniors, and perhaps by the opinion expressed by the doyen of Indo-European linguistics at Leipzig, Georg Curtius (1820 - 85), in a personal letter of 1884: "Lange habe ich nichts der Art gelesen, was mich so entschieden überzeugt hat."[1]

0.3 *The third phase in the reception of the 'Mémoire'*. The phase following Saussure's death in 1913 may well be regarded as the most important period in the development of the discussion of the PIE phonological system, a phase which has not yet come to a close. Saussure's *Mémoire* may be said to have played an important role in this discussion, which in fact began as early as in 1879, though more as a fairly weak undercurrent as we may see later on. There were a number of reasons for the slow posthumous recognition of Saussure's work in Indo-European linguistics. For example the *Cours* of 1916, owing to its seeming anti-historical bias, tended to detract from the fact that Saussure's life-time contribution lay almost exclusively within diachronic linguistics. Also the hostile feelings toward anything German of the period during and following the First World War made the work of a French Swiss scholar rather attractive as it appeared to oppose the traditional kind of linguistics widely associated with Germany. As a result, among many of the new generation of linguists Historical Linguistics became a side-issue and the preoccupation of a comparatively small number of experts. This development is clearly reflected in most histories of linguistics. If they mention Saussure's *Mémoire* at all, they present it as something

---

[1] Curtius was not referring to the *Mémoire*, whose rigor might well have exceeded his tastes and comprehension, but to an article of 1884, "Une loi rythmique de la langue grecque", of which Curtius had taken notice, one year before his death, which had probably been precipitated by the 'war of monographs' between him and his former students concerning the sound laws and the analogy principle during 1885. — The quotation is taken from Redard (1978: 36).

of marginal interest, focussing instead almost their entire attention on the work that in fact did not have his imprimatur and, as we have come to understand in recent years, does not reflect his true intentions. In short, it has become customary to refer to a Saussure who wrote the *Mémoire* in his youth, and another who is the author of the *Cours*, which brought about a revolution in modern linguistics, with the result that even the large portions devoted to diachronic linguistics it contains are patently passed over in silence.

It would exceed the frame of the present paper to show, as Cristina Vallini (1969) has already done to some extent (pp. 49ff.), that in fact there is no justification for the traditional conception of the existence of 'deux Saussure' (cf. Redard 1978), but that the early work is consistent with his later, largely unpublished theories. Perhaps it should be stated in the present context that the critical edition of the *Cours*, carefully compiled by Rudolf Engler, contradicts affirmations in the text as edited by Bally and Sechehaye, including those frequently attacked ones according to which synchrony and diachrony are supposed to be regarded as two subjects apart: Nothing could have been more contrary to Saussure's view on the proper relationship between these two 'points de vue'.

We know from the *Cours* the central role that the concept of 'system' has played in Saussure's linguistic theory. But if we analyse his *Mémoire* carefully, we will notice that the same notion is basic to Saussure's argument therein as well. Indeed, we may say that in the *Mémoire* 'system' is the 'clé de voûte', the key stone holding the entire edifice together. Interestingly enough, while others referred to Saussure's book as the *Mémoire* for short, he himself preferred to refer to it as his *Système des voyelles*, with a capital 'S' (cf. Watkins 1978:61). Moreover, Saussure justified the title of his book in the following terms, at the same time indicating his approach to the subject matter:

> Etudier les formes multiples sous lesquelles se manifeste ce qu'on appelle l'*a* indo-européen, tel est l'objet immédiat de cet opuscule: le reste des voyelles ne sera pris en considération qu'autant que les phénomènes relatifs à l'*a* en fourniront l'occasion. Mais si, arrivé au bout du champ ainsi circonscrit, le tableau du vocalisme indo-européen s'est modifié peu à peu sous nos yeux et que nous le voyions se grouper tout entier autour de l'*a*, prendre vis-à-vis de lui une attitude nouvelle, il est clair qu'en fait c'est le *système des voyelles dans son ensemble* qui sera entré dans le rayon de notre observation et dont le nom doit être inscrit à la première page. (Saussure 1879 [1878]= *Mémoire* p. 1; emphasis added: KK)

Similarly, and quite revealingly I believe, Saussure ends his book with the following paragraph, in which he discusses special instances of the possible presence of this elusive PIE *a* or, rather, in Saussure's analysis, *e*:

> Cette inconstance de la voyelle [in western Indo-European languages] révélerait, dans d'autres circonstances, la présence du phonème *A*; mais si telle est la valeur de l'ε dans ἀFέξω, la relation de cette forme avec *vákšati*, *ukšáti*, ἀύξω, aussi bien que sa *structure considérée en elle-même* cessent d'être compréhensible pour nous. (*Mémoire* p. 283; emphasis added: KK)[2]

This concept of system is not simply what is implied by expressions such as 'le système de Curtius' (*Mémoire* p. 2), 'système de Schleicher' (pp. 3 - 4), and the like, which refers merely to the hypothesized inventory of the sounds of a language, but, as will become evident in the subsequent discussion, a system of relationships of phonemes. Indeed, we may discover in Saussure's *Mémoire* the source of his later definition of phonemes as "des entités oppositives, relatives et négatives" (Saussure 1931 = *Cours* p. 164; cf. Saussure 1968:268). Already the first paragraph of his *Mémoire* cited above suggests this.

1.0 *Saussure's Argument in the 'Mémoire sur le système primitif des voyelles dans les langues indo-européennes'*

Before delineating the manner in which the *Mémoire* made an important contribution to linguistics, both historical and theoretical, let us first present the main tenets of Saussure's argument, his approach having been signalled in the introductory paragraph of his work, namely, to investigate the various reflexes in the attested languages of what has been generally regarded as the common Indo-European *a*, with all other vowels of the system being considered only in relation to this phoneme, but with the result that eventually the entire system of Indo-European vowels is established.

Saussure proceeds in a most rigorous fashion. He discusses — and discards — one proposal after another made by Curtius, Schleicher, Fick, and others, in part also those by his teachers, including Brugmann and

---

[2] Watkins (1978: 67), who quotes the second half of the sentence, argues that the phrase 'structure considérée en elle-même' italiziced in the citation constitutes "la véritable source" of a part of the famous statement at the end of the *Cours*, for which Engler was at a loss to find a textual basis in the critical edition (p. 515): *la linguistique a pour unique et véritable objet la langue envisagée en elle-même et pour elle-même.* (*Cours*, p. 317). This is undoubtedly an overinterpretation, but it merits further investigation in the light of the entire context of Saussure's argument, both in the *Mémoire* and elsewhere in his writings, published as well as unpublished.

Osthoff. Subsequently, he adduces evidence for his own views, and this with a precision that must have astounded his contemporaries, and which impresses us still today. I am quoting just one example from the English translation, provided by Winfred P. Lehmann in 1967, to illustrate Saussure's style of scientific discourse. In this passage from chapter II of his *Mémoire* in which he proposes to separate the 'old' from the 'true', by lifting "tout l'humus moderne que différents accidents avaient amassé sur lui", Saussure, after having established the various correspondences between root vowels found in what he terms the northern languages, e.g., Germanic and Slavic, and the southern languages, such as Latin and Greek, proceeds as follows:

> How then could the *a* and *o* of the languages of the South have arisen from one and the same original *a*? By what miracle could this old *a* be coloured to *o*, *and never to a*, precisely in all the times that it is found in the company of an *e*? — Conclusion: the dualism of *a* and *o* is original, and it must be that in the single *a* of the North two phonemes were confused.
>
> Confirmation: when a root contains *a* in Greek or Latin, and when this root is found in the languages of the North, one observes in the first place *that this a never alternates with e*, as is the case when the Greek replies by an *o*. Thus Goth. *vagja* = Gk *okhéō*, *hlaf* = Gk (*ké*)*klopha* are accompanied by *viga* and *hlifa*. But *agis*(*a*-) = Gk *ákhos*, or *ala* = Lat. *alo* do not have a parent form with *e*. On the other hand, the roots of the latter type have one characteristic, unknown to the first type: the ability to lengthen their *a* (*agis*: *ōg*, *ala*: *ōl*), of which we will have to take account below.
>
> Brugmann has designated with a_1 the prototype of the European *e*; his a_2 is the phoneme which we have called *o* up to now. As to this third phoneme which is the Greco-Italic *a* and which constitutes one half of the *a*'s of the languages of the North, we will designate it by the letter *A*, after noting well that it is neither the *e*(a_1) nor the *o*(a_2). — Excluding for the time being the other possible kinds of *a*, one obtains the following table:[3]

Langs. of the North	Primordial state	Greco-Italic
e	a_1	e
⎰	a_2	o
⎱a	A	a

At first sight, it may appear to be an over-interpretation to claim that

---

[3] Source: Lehmann (1967: 233). I have ventured to introduce a couple of *Verschlimmbesserungen* into the translation on the basis of my understanding of the French original (*Mémoire* pp. 51 - 52), where, among other things, certain phrases are in italics, but which Lehmann presented in regular type. (The emphasis in the original appears to me to underscore the forcefulness of Saussure's manner of argumentation.)

Saussure's use of 'state' (état) in this table has any significance. But if one follows his argument more closely, it becomes evident that he is primarily concerned with establishing an 'état de langue' in his *Mémoire*, namely, that of the Proto-Indo-European vocalic system, and not with delineating its evolution. Indeed, one indication of this intention is Saussure's regular use of the term 'phoneme' in his work instead of 'son', a usage which is the first of its kind in the history of linguistics, even though the term itself had not been invented by Saussure, as Hjelmslev (1970:125) holds. Saussure wanted to signal by this that he is not concerned with matters of phonetic realization; as a matter of fact, he rarely makes a reference to phonetic detail in his book (cf. Polomé 1965:10, and n. 7), preferring instead an algebraic notation devoid of phonic substance. From what will become clear below, we may say that Saussure's *Mémoire* is structuralist in approach, and that it constitutes in essence a contribution to structural linguistics 'avant la lettre' and not merely to historical-comparative linguistics as it is commonly understood.

However, this understanding of the *Mémoire* is of a much later date, and it required the work of kindred spirits such as Louis Hjelmslev (1899 - 1965) to fully appreciate this endeavour on Saussure's part (cf. Hjelmslev 1970:123 - 28, for details). In the context of the present paper this essential trait of Saussure's argument must remain a matter of lesser consideration, although it should be clear that his theory of PIE ablaut cannot be understood without the concept of language as a rigorously organized system underlying it (cf. also Schmidt-Brandt 1967:2; Vincenzi 1976). For the field of Historical Linguistics, which at the time was almost identical with linguistics *tout court*, Saussure's *Mémoire* must now be regarded as introducing a revolution, even though it is safe to speak of 'une victoire retardée' or 'tardive', since, as we have seen in the introduction (0.1 - 0.2 above), most of Saussure's contemporaries did not grasp the full implications of his theories, and a number of distinguished scholars, including Brugmann, did not see the necessity of revising their inventory of the PIE sounds in accordance with Saussure's findings. As will become clear from what follows, however, there were, apart from Saussure's quasi algebraic approach to the subject, other reasons which explain the difficulty Saussure's contemporaries, not least the *Junggrammatiker* with whom he had been associated for some time, experienced in accepting his proposals.

1.1 *Saussure's revisions of the PIE vocalic system*. We have already hinted (1.0 above) at Saussure's general procedure in dealing with the problem of the PIE vocalic system. However, we cannot fully appreciate his in fact audacious innovations unless we present ourselves what had been, until the mid-1870s, received opinion.

Until about that period, Indo-Eruopean linguistics, despite a number of statements by their proponents to the contrary, was essentially 'Sanskrito-centric' (cf. Mayrhofer 1983: 130—36 passim). This meant that, in matters of phonology especially, linguists clung to the belief that Sanskrit, which, until the decipherment of Hittite during the early decades of the 20th century, supplied the comparative linguist with the oldest data, was in effect reflecting the earliest state of Indo-European. As a result, the inventory of PIE vowels was regarded as consisting of three vowels only, which could either be long or short:

$$i \quad u$$
$$a$$

Since Greek and Latin for instance displayed a five-vowel system, this was accordingly interpreted as representing an innovation of the part of these (classical) European languages, usually regarded as a degeneration of the primordial state; cf. the following correspondences taken from Arlotto (1972: 118):

Sanskrit	Greek	Latin	Indo-European
(a) ad-mi "I eat"	(e) ed-omai "I will eat"	(e) ed-ō "I eat"	(*e) *ed- "to eat"
(ā) prā-ta "full"	(ē) plē-res "full"	(ē) plē-nus "full"	(*ē) *plē- "to fill"
(a) aṣṭa "eight"	(o) oktō "eight"	(o) octō "eight'	*(o) *oktō "eight"

and so on, where there are still two other correspondences in Greek and Latin to Sanskrit a and $\bar{a}$, which are also a and $\bar{a}$, respectively. The i/u/a vowel triad, however, had been codified in Schleicher's *Compendium* of 1861 (pp. 134—35), and was widely accepted for several years after Schleicher's death in 1868. Indeed, his *Compendium* was reedited twice (1871 and 1876) by two of his former students, Johannes Schmidt (1843—1901) and August Leskien (1840—1916), and thus continued its influence in the teaching of Indo-European phonology. The rejection of the PIE vowel triad and the acceptance of a much more variegated system of both short and long vowels in Indo-European was one of the main accomplishments of the younger genertaion of comparative-historical linguists during the later 1870s. But Saussure was not satisfied with a simple enlargement of the vowel triad to a five-vowel system as the classical languages may have suggested, namely:

$$\begin{matrix} i & & u \\ e & & o \\ & a & \end{matrix}$$

However, this view of the PIE vowel inventory had become widely accepted about the same time that the *Mémoire* appeared. Saussure did not appear to subscribe to this configuration of the vocalic system of Indo-European and, as a result, made it difficult for his contemporaries to appreciate and, furthermore, to accept his own proposals. As a matter of fact, these came, as Szereményi (1980: 115), notes, at the worst possible time.

Without adducing much evidence for his hypothesis, Saussure claimed (*Mémoire* p. 135) the following: First of all, the basic root vowel in PIE is /e/ rather than /a/ or a variety of vowels; this was the a_1 that we noted earlier, and which both in the northern dialects and Greco-Italic are represented by *e* (cf. *Mémoire* p. 52). He had earlier noted that the high vowels *i* and *u*, like the nasals and liquids, could take on (semi-)vocalic function, and therefore (p. 8) he put them together in one group as 'coefficients sontantiques': Depending on the presence or absence of the *e* within the root, *r l m n* become sonants, and *i* and *u* take on consonantal function.[4] (We are long since used to calling these sounds 'resonants'.) In other words, Saussure argued that all root vowels consist of combinations between the basic PIE *e* and a resonant or 'sonant coefficient'. Under certain conditions, this *e* was ejected (quantitative ablaut), leading the resonants to take on syllabic function, and under others, it alternated with *o* (qualitative ablaut), represented by a_2 in earlier theories (such as those by Brugmann).

In addition to alternation with *o*, *e* could simply disappear altogether, thus producing the following results at the 'degré zéro' (zero grade); example:

*peik->*pik- *penk->*pn̥k and *pet->*pt- (without a vowel)

In addition to the six sonorants or resonants mentioned above, however,

---

[4] When Saussure speaks of "*i* et *e* passent de l'état *symphthongue* à l'état *autophthonge*" (*Mémoire* p. 8) — note also the use of 'état' in the present context!, it seems to me that he is using a terminology (meaning "functioning as a consonant" and "functioning as a vowel", correspondingly) created by the French phonetician A. Dufriche-Desgenettes (cf. *Phonetica* 33. 222 - 31 [1976], pp. 227 - 28).

Saussure hypothesized the presence of two more 'coefficients sonantiques', which he symbolized as A and $\underset{\smile}{O}$ respectively, both sounds which could appear on their own only at the so called zero grade of a root form, and would produce a and $\underset{\smile}{o}$ respectively — the latter being of course different from the o_1 in the ablaut relation (and should therefore be identified as o_2) or — and this should be highlighted here: shwa. Saussure (*Mémoire* p. 178) described the latter as a 'voyelle indéterminée' and as "une *espèce d'e muet, provenant de l'altération des phonèmes A et $\underset{\smile}{O}$*" (italics in the original).

These two added sonant coefficients play a central role in Saussure's argument, as he sets up the following combinations to obtain the series of long vowels:

$e + A = \bar{e}$ and $\bar{a}$, and $e + \underset{\smile}{O} = \bar{o}$

As Saussure does not specify the phonetic quality of his A, this 'sonant coefficient' can produce both $\bar{e}$ and $\bar{a}$; $\bar{o}$ can also be the result of the apophonic $o + A$ or $o + \underset{\smile}{O}$. At any rate, all long vowels are products of the original e plus a coefficient, and hence not original as having independent existence. Examples:

*bheA- = *bhā- cf. Gk fā-mi (Attic Gk: fēmi) "I say"
*bhA- (zero grade) cf. Gk fă-mén "we say"
*deO- cf. dō- "(root of) to give"
*dO- (zero grade) cf. Gk do-tós "given"

No doubt, Saussure operates with what we nowadays refer to as 'underlying forms', deriving the actual attested forms through specific rules. By the same method, Saussure (*Mémoire* p. 248) sets up the rule "*Le groupe* sonante $+^A$, *précédé ou placé au commencement du mot, se change en* sonante longue, *quel que soit le phonème qui suit*" (italics in the original), so that $\bar{\imath}$ and $\bar{u}$ as well as the long sonorants $\bar{\underset{.}{n}}\ \bar{\underset{.}{m}}\ \bar{\underset{.}{l}}\ \bar{\underset{.}{r}}$ are derived from $i^A, u^A, \underset{.}{n}^A, \underset{.}{r}^A$, and so on, or, in notation suggested by Saussure only in 1891 (cf. Saussure 1922: 603), sonant plus shwa. In effect, it would seem that Saussure was the first abstract phonologist in that he was operating with hypothetical constructs and indirect (distributional) evidence.

From his *Mémoire* at least, it is quite clear that the shwa was supposed to have vocalic rather than consonantal quality,[5] and Mayrhofer (1983:

---

[5] Interestingly enough, the great English phonetician Henry Sweet (1845 - 1912), in his review of the *Mémoire*, calls the sonant coefficients A and $\underset{\smile}{O}$ 'consonants' or 'consonantal elements' (Sweet 1880: 160). One may wonder whether it would be correct to say with Jonsson (1978: 2n. 1) that "we have to do [here] with an

144n. 91) may be justified in his hesitation to accept the view expressed by others that in his 1891 observations Saussure was in fact modifying his earlier interpretation. This question is relevant in the subsequent discussion of PIE phonology (cf. 1.2 below); but what is important to emphasize in the present context is that Saussure had developed a fairly abstract and rigid system of phoneme combinations which allowed him to produce the various attested forms in individual Indo-European languages. As Szemerényi (1980: 115) has pointed out, Saussure did not present much in terms of evidence for his theory except for hinting at such incidents in Greek and Sanskrit which may be explained by his assumptions. The beauty of the matter is that much of what Saussure advanced on theoretical and structural grounds was subsequently shown to be correct, to the extent that we may be right in saying that with Saussure's *Mémoire* a new phase in the history of Indo-European phonology had been set in motion.

1.2 *Saussure's contribution to the laryngeal theory*. It is not surprising that Saussure's discussion of PIE vowels contained one or the other error, though none substantial enough to lead to a rejection of his theory as a whole. We have already hinted at the fact that Saussure was not much concerned with phonetic detail in his argumnet; this may have indeed been a point of strength rather than weakness, as some modern phonologists may well be ready to admit. But in Saussure's time, when linguists were beginning to take note of articulatory phonetics, this attitude might easily have been subject to criticism. August Fick, in his review of the *Mémoire*, was one of the first to point to the difficulty of deriving both a and e from $e+A$; I guess we would today call Saussure's hypothesis 'counter-intuitive' on this issue and lacking in symmetry. Saussure had considered such a combination of $a_1 a_1 (ee)$ "parallèle aux combinaions $a_1 A$, $a_1 i$, $a_1 n$ [i.e., *eA, ei, en] etc.", but he argued in fact that this would lead to 'contre-sens' (*Mémoire* p. 141). Fick (1880: 437), however, felt, although he conceded that his "Begeisterung für das Analogieprincip nur schwach ist" (p. 436), that a 'coefficient sonantique' E parallel to Saussure's A and O was indeed desirable, at least as long as one admitted the original existence of an unaccentuated e in addition to Saussure's 'fundamental e'.

---

anachronism or a misinterpretation under the influence of the later consonantal theory", without indicating what he meant by 'later'. However, Sweet (p. 158) refers to Möller's (1879) review of Kluge (1879), where in fact the consonantal hypothesis was first enunciated (see 1.2 below for details).

But as we noted in the introductory part of this paper (0.1–0.**3**), most Indo-Europeanists of the last quarter of the 19th and the first quarter of the 20th century ignored Saussure's theory of sonant coefficients, and it was only some fifty years after the publication of the *Mémoire* (and 14 years after his death) that the significance of Saussure's proposals was fully recognized. The path of recognition was long and slow, and the fact the first scholars to see the light were outside the mainstream of Indo-European linguistics did not help to further it.

Shortly after the appearance of Saussure's book, the Danish Nordist Hermann Möller (1850–1923), who also worked in Semitic and in fact adhered to the Indo-European-Semitic hypothesis so ardently combatted by Schleicher and dismissed by the generation of Indo-Europeanists following him, proposed, in a review of a book by Friedrich Kluge (1856–1926)

> ein consonantisches element ..., welches die eigenschaft hatte, ein vorangehendes oder (im anlaut) folgendes a_1 (das in der letzten zeit der grundsprache ein $ä$ gewesen sein wird) in reines $ā$ zu verwandeln, und das mit vorhergehendem vocal a zu reinem langem $ā$ zusammenschmolz. (Möller 1879: 150).

In the same review, Möller suggested that in order to justify the alternation in Gk $θη$-/$θε$-, it would be required that a third sound, E, should be added to Saussure's sonant coefficients A and $Q̣$ (Möller 1879: 151, n. 1), quite in line with Fick's suggestions mentioned earlier. However, in contrast to Fick (1880: 438), for whom these coefficients were "von Haus aus Vocale", Möller had hypothesized them to be consonantal in nature. Henry Sweet (1845–1912), also reviewing Kluge's (1879) book, though together with Saussure's *Mémoire*, proposed by following Möller's lead to regard A as a voiced glottal trill, with E being characterized by a palatalized, and O by a velarized articulation (Sweet 1880: 161). In the meantime, Möller was shifting his position: While he had hypothesized "A [as] die tönende, E die tonlose kehlkopfspirans?, O das kehlkopf-*r*?" in 1879 (p. 151n. 1), he connected the Indo-European sounds in question with Semitic in the following year by suggesting that we have to do with "wahrscheinlich gutturale von der art des semitischen, A=ālef, der tonlose verschlusslaut, und E wahrscheinlich der entsprechende tönende verschlusslaut" (Möller 1880: 492n. 2).

However, Möller did not draw the conclusions from his own observations for almost forty years (cf. Möller 1917: 4–5 and 53), and since his 94-page monograph on the laryngeal consonants of Indo-European and Semitic was not regarded as sound in scholarship with regard to much of the data presented therein to bolster the claim for an early Indo-European-Hamito-Semitic genetic relationship, Möller's proposals remained largely ignored. (For a detailed analysis of Möller's suggestions, see Szeremény 1973: 5—8.) Eventually, his laryngeal hypothesis of 1879 found adherents, though not before the early years of the 20th century. Thus in 1907 his former student Holger Pedersen (1867—1953), at that time sympathetic to the Semitic-Indo-European hypothesis, tried to adduce evidence that PIE shwa[6] derived from a consonant.[7] By that time, Möller (1906/7) had proposed, on the basis of Semitic, a theory of altogether five similar sounds, which, in the preface to his Comparative Semitic-Indo-European Dictionary (Möller 1911: VI), he called 'laryngeals', in fact stating that "die von F. de Saussure für das Vorindogermanische erschlossenen 'phonèmes' entsprechen den semitischen Laryngalen". One may wonder whether this remark and related observations by Möller led the French scholar Albert Cuny (1869—1947), another strong believer in the original genetic relationship between Afro-Asiatic and Indo-European (called 'Nostratic' by Pedersen), to assert that Saussure had, at least since 1891, thought of the shwa as having consonantal function (Cuny 1912: 119; cf. Szemerényi 1973: 8—10, for a thorough refutation of this common assertion).

But Cuny made a number of much more striking observations in his 1912 article, which followed an earlier dissatisfaction with Möller's views on the relationship between Indo-European and Semitic. Indeed, this article contains a series of important observations, of which only few will be mentioned here (cf. Szemerényi 1973: 13—15 and Jonsson 1978: 3—4 for details):

(1) The Indo-European proto-language must have contained altogether three *consonantal* laryngeals (E, A, O; $ə_1, ə_2, ə_3$ or H_1, H_2, H_3, depending on notational preference) instead of Saussure's two *vocalic* Q

---

[6] Mayrhofer (1981: 29 - 29, note 81) supplies evidence for his suggestion that the term 'schwa' was first introduced by August Fick; since he refers only indirectly to the possibly first appearance of the term in print, reference is made here to Fick's paper, "Schwa indogermanicum", (Adalbert Bezzenberger's [1851 - 1922]) *Beiträge zur Kunde der indogermanischen Sprachen* 3. 157 - 65 (1879).

[7] Pedersen had been under the influence of Möller's views from very early on in his scholarly activity (from 1893 onwards, if not earlier); cf. the bibliography of his major writings in H. Pedersen, *A Glance at the History of Linguistics, with particular regard to the historical study of phonology* ed. with an introduction by Konrad Koerner (Amsterdam & Philadelphia: John Benjamins, 1983), xxiii-xxx. — For details on Pedersen's contribution to the laryngeal theory, cf. Szemerényi 1973: 11 - 12 and 15).

and $\underset{\sim}{A}$. (The series of three such 'coefficients' had been suggested as early as 1879 by Möller and 1880 by Fick.)

(2) Cuny allowed for a certain flexibility in the matter concerning the consonantal quality of these laryngeals, however, Thus he had noted that in sequences of sonorant+laryngeal+obstruent, it is always the sonorant that becomes vocalic, e.g., *sterə-* : *str̥ətos*, which of course means that the laryngeal is less inherently vocalic than the sonorant. However, in the absence of a sonorant, the laryngeal, following the loss of a vowel, is vocalized, e.g., *sāg-* standing for (in Saussure's notation) *seAg-* has its counterpart in *səg-* (for *săg-*), having the formula *sAg-* underlying (Cuny 1912: 102—103). This flexibility allows Cuny (p. 120) to show that Greek for instance had a series of three vocalic schwas.

(3) In addition to Saussure's suggestions, in particular the one made in 1891, according to which an unvoiced spirant derives frequently from *t*+laryngeal, Cuny added further evidence for the original presence of laryngeals in Indo-European, in Indic as well as in Balto-Slavic (Cuny 1912: 117—20; cf. Szemerényi 1973: 13—14).

Cuny's argument, if followed closely, reveals at least two major traits: first, he is very much indebted to Saussure's (and also to Möller's) findings; second, we may note a considerable increase in phonetic-phonological sophistication. What in addition deserves to be pointed out is that mainly *internal* evidence, i.e., evidence deriving from attested language material of Indo-European, was supplied for the laryngeal hypothesis. The fact that the laryngeal theory, as it is more generally called today, had originally been inspired by findings made in Semitic does not contradict this statement, though the fact that its main proponents subscribed to the pre-Indo-European genetic relationship with Hamito-Semitic, appears to have made it difficult for mainstream Indo-Europeanists to accept the theory. Therefore, further evidence was required to lead the laryngeal theory to victory, and it came from a former student of Antoine Meillet, Jerzy Kuryłowicz (1895—1978) in 1927, two generations after the publication of Saussure's *Mémoire*.

It is no exaggeration to state that Kuryłowicz's connection between Indo-European shwa and a sound actually found in Hittite, an Indo-European language older than Greek or Sanskrit as far as the available data is concerned, which could be compared with the hypothesized Proto-Indo-European phoneme (Kuryłowicz 1927), could not have been undertaken without the work of another researcher. The evidence adduced by Kuryłowicz had not been available to either Saussure or his early followers like Möller, Cuny, or Pedersen. Indeed, it was only several years after Saussure's death in 1913 that the tablets of cuneiform inscriptions, discovered during excavations near the Turkish village of Boğaz Köy during 1905—1907, had been deciphered and identified as Indo-European, namely, by the Czech scholar Bedřich Hrozný (1879—1952) in 1915 and the following years.

Kuryłowicz (1927) had examined Hittite words whose etymological connection with other Indo-European languages such as Greek or Latin was beyond doubt. He chose examples where Saussure had predicted the original presence of a sonant coefficient, in particular the A, and could establish the following correspondences among others, where Hittite has the laryngeal $ḫ$:

Greek a*nti* = Hittite $ḫ$anti   "in front"   < *Aa*nti*
Greek a*rges* = Hittite $ḫ$arkis   "white"   < *Aa*rges*
Latin $pāsco$ = Hittite pa$ḫ$sanzi   "protect"   < *pa$A$sk-

The above examples prove another hypothesis made by Saussure, namely, that if (originally) the laryngeal preceded the vowel, the result is a short a, and a long one, if it follows. As a result, it could no longer be doubted that early Indo-European contained laryngeals at one time of its development, traces of which can be found in the various attested languages. In this way, we may say that Kuryłowicz's work vindicated Saussure's theory, which from then onwards has become more and more generally accepted by historical-comparative Indo-Europeanists.

Of course, Kuryłowicz's paper of 1927 was not a one-shot enterprise; on the contrary, as Szemerényi (1973: 15—19 and especially note 40) has shown, he published a flurry of studies to establish his proof on a very broad basis of philological evidence himself, and a number of other scholars followed his lead in quick succession. Among them, mention should at least be made here of Emile Benveniste (1902—1976) and his important work of 1935, in particular his theory of the basic structure of the Indo-European root, and Walter Couvreur's massive monograph of 1937 *De hettitische $ḫ$*, which for the first time accounted for the fact that the Hittite laryngeal occured sometimes in a simple, sometimes in a double consonant. Both Benveniste and Couvreur (cf. also the latter's 1939 paper) based their argument largely on Saussure's *Mémoire*, seeking, as Möller, Pedersen, Cuny, and Kuryłowicz had done before them, to adduce further proof to the basic correctness of Saussure's theories. As Polomé in his formidable survey of the history of the laryngeal theory has shown (Polomé 1965: 14ff.), the work of Kuryłowicz, Benveniste, Couvreur and others was first met with a lack of sympathy and comprehension similar to the fate of the *Mémoire* during Saussure's life-time, namely, that the hypotheses were characterized as 'constructed', 'aprioristic', 'too audacious to be true', and the like. History appears to be repeating itself.

2.0 Concluding remarks

In this paper, it has not been my intention to trace the history of the laryngeal theory; this has been done already very competently by others (e.g., Polomé 1965; Szemerényi 1973; Jonsson 1978). Nor did I mean to indicate the role that Saussure's proposals concerning the structure of the Indo-European vowel system have played in the development of this theory, by simply suggesting that he had given the initial impetus to research undertaken by others. The reason for this is simple: I believe that Saussure had much more to offer to Historical Linguistics than an initial suggestion which was subsequently proved to be right, although this may be no small contribution by itself. Indeed, we all have witnessed that with the advent of the so-called Chomskyan 'paradigm' hundreds of linguists and would-be-linguists have been engaged in tossing out 'theories' almost daily, frequently withdrawing them a few weeks later themselves before others had time to refute them.

In Saussure's case we have to do with something much more profound and valuable. Apart from the fact never to be overlooked that his argument was based on a considerable amount of verifiable data, Saussure presented his theory of the PIE vowel system in a highly organized fashion, proceding with a step-by-step interpretation of the material together with his reasoning about the data. Most importantly, he put forward a theory arrived at not merely in a wholly deductive fashion deriving from the premise that the vowel system of any language must be a complete system of relationships, but at the same time by adducing inductively, as much as was possible at the time, anything that could lead to substantiating the veracity of his general assumption. That he produced a hypothesis of consequence was therefore not simply the strike of genius — which is nevertheless true of course, but the result of a considerable familiarity with the available data, the tools of the craft, and a particularly lucid mind. This last-mentioned criterion may be the key to Saussure's success, distinguishing himself from the great majority of his contemporaries and, we may add, followers. Saussure was very conscious about this, and critical especially of the linguists of his day who evidently lacked the capacity which he regarded as vital to the advancement of the field. In an unpublished draft of a letter probably dating from the 1890s, when he was planning on writing a book on the principles of linguistic science, Saussure stated:

> Je veux malgré cela résumer quel est pour moi l'exact état des preuves, car ce que je déteste chez tous les Germains comme [aussi Holger] Pedersen [cf. his book mentioned in note 7 for instance], c'est la manière subreptice d'amener la preuve, et de ne jamais la formuler, comme si la preuve de leurs réflexions les dispensait de mettre à nu leur opération logique. (Quoted from Watkins [1978: 65])

What me may learn from Saussure's example for Historical Linguistics as well as for the study of language in general is the following:

(a) The analyst must lay bare, to himself and others, the entire *procedere* of his argument; his approach must be clearly presented and well reasoned.

(b) Historical-comparative linguistics is not a field of mere data gathering and ordering, a barren positivistic enterprise as has been common at least since the 1870s, but a subject which can only advance significantly if it admits the setting-up of hypotheses which must be substantiated by subsequent research.

(c) Language in general is an ordered whole; as a result, the tools of analysis must be used on the assumption of the basic systematicity of the data. These and other ideas have become familiar to us through the *Cours de linguistique générale*, although the manner in which it was compiled has left the impression on three generations of linguists that Saussure was holding Historical Linguistics in low esteem.[8] However, a close reading of Saussure's *Mémoire sur le système primitif des voyelles* makes these points very clear, indeed offering us in hindsight a proof for the desirability of a sound combination of theory and empirical evidence, of deduction and induction, in historical linguistic research. That his *Mémoire* has still today not yet lost its original lustre may be taken from recent evaluations of this work (e.g., Vincenzi 1978; Watkins 1978), and a recent announcement (Gmür 1980: 4) of a comprehensive dissertation devoted to this pioneering work.

---

[8] Thus, ever since the availability of Rudolf Engler's critical edition of the *Cours* (Wiesbaden: O. Harrassowitz, 1967 - 74), it should have become clear to everybody that the various statements in the text as compiled by Charles Bally and Albert Sechehaye concerning the clash between synchrony and diachrony for instance have no foundation in Saussure's lectures as recorded by his students.

REFERENCES

Arlotto, Anthony. 1972. *Introduction to historical linguistics.* Boston: Houghton Mifflin (2nd printing, University Press of America, 1981.)
Benveniste, Emile. 1935. *Origines de la formation des noms en indo-européen.* Vol. I. Paris: A. Maisonneuve. [Actually published in 1936.]
Brugmann, Karl. 1876. Nasalis sonans in der indogermanischen Grundsprache. (Curtius') *Studien der griechischen und lateinischen Grammatik* 9. 285 - 338. [Abridged English transl. in Lehmann (1967:191 - 96).]
— 1879a. Review of Saussure 1879. *Literarisches Zentralblatt für Deutschland* 29, coll. 773 - 74.
— 1879b. Nachschrift [of June 1879]. *Morphologische Untersuchungen auf dem Gebiete der indogermanischen Sprachen* 2. 161 - 62.
Brogyanyi, Bela. 1983. A few remarks on the origin of the phrase 'ou tout se tient'. *Historiographia Linguistica* 10. 143 - 47.
Couvreur, Walter. 1937. *De hettitische ḫ: Een bijdrage tot de studie van het indo-europeesche vocalisme.* Louvain: Muséon. [French summary, 381 - 91.]
— 1939. Le hittite et la doctrine de F. de Saussure. *Revue hittite et asianique* 5. 132 - 41.
Cuny, Albert. 1912. Notes de phonetique historique: Indo-européen et sémitique. *Revue de Phonétique* 2. 101 - 132.
Fick, August. 1880. Review of Saussure 1879. *Göttingische gelehrte Anzeigen,* Stück 14 (7. April 1880). 417 - 39.
Gmür, Remo. 1980. *Das Mémoire von F. de Saussure.* Bern: Institut für Sprachwissenschaft, Universität Bern.
Havet, Louis. 1879. Review article on Saussure 1879. *Journal de Genève* 47 (50e année), Supplement, 1 - 2 (25 Feb. 1879). [Cited after reprint in *Cahiers Ferdinand de Saussure* 32. 103 - 122 (1978).]
Hirt, Herman. 1900. *Der indogermanische Ablaut, vornehmlich in seinem Verhältnis zur Betonung.* Straßburg: Karl J. Trübner.
— 1927. *Indogermanische Grammatik.* Vol. I. Heidelberg: C. Winter.
Hjelmslev, Louis. 1970. *Language: An introduction.* Transl. from the Danish by Francis J. Whitfield. Madison-Milwaukee-London: Univ. of Wisconsin Press.
Hrozný, Bedřich. 1915. Die Lösung des hethitischen Problems: Ein vorläufiger Bericht. *Mitteilungen der Deutschen Orient-Gesellschaft zu Berlin* 56. 17 - 50.
— 1916 - 17. *Die Sprache der Hethiter: Ihr Bau und ihre Zugehörigkeit zum indogermanischen Sprachstamm: Ein Entzifferungsversuch.* Leipzig: J. C. Hinrichs.
Hübschmann, Heinrich. 1885. *Das indogermanische Vocalsystem.* Straßburg: Karl J. Trübner.
Jonsson, Hans. 1978. *The Laryngeal Theory: A critical survey.* Lund: C.W. K. Gleerup.
Kluge, Friedrich. 1879. *Beiträge zur Geschichte der germanischen Conjugation.* Straßburg: Karl J. Trübner.
Kruszewski, Mikołaj. 1880. Novejšija otkrytija v oblasti ario-evropejskogo vokalizma [Recent discoveries in the field of Indo-European vocalism]. *Russkij Filologičeskij Vestnik* (Warsaw) 4. 33 - 45. [A review article on Brugmann (1876) and, in particular, Saussure (1879). Italian transl. in Vincenzi 1978. 441 - 50.]

Kuryłowicz, Jerzy. 1927. ə indo-européen et ḫ hittite. *Symbolae Grammaticae in honorem Ioannis Rozwadowski*, vol. I. 95 - 104. Kraków: Drukarnia Uniwersytetu Jagiellońskiego.

Lehmann, Winfred Philipp (ed. & transl.) 1967. *A reader in nineteenth-century historical Indo-European linguistics*. Bloomington & London: Indiana Univ. Press.

Mayrhofer, Wolfgang. 1981. *Nach hundert Jahren: Ferdinand de Saussures Frühwerk und seine Rezeption durch die heutige Indogermanistik*. Heidelberg: C. Winter.

―― 1983. Sanskrit und die Sprachen Alteuropas: Zwei Jahrhunderte des Widerspiels von Entdeckungen und Irrtümern. *Nachrichten der Akademie der Wissenschaften in Göttingen, I: Philologisch-historische Klasse*, Jahrgang 1983, Nr. 5. 121 - 54. Göttingen: Vandenhoeck & Ruprecht.

Meyer, Gustav. 1880. *Griechische Grammatik*. Leipzig: Breitkopf & Härtel. (3rd rev. & enl. ed., 1896.)

Möller, Hermann, 1879. Review of Kluge 1879. *Englische Studien* 3. 148 - 64.

―― 1880. Zur Conjugation: *kunþa* und das *t*-praeteritum. Excurs: Die Entstehung des *o*. (Paul&Braune's) *Beiträge zur Geschichte der deutschen Sprache und Literatur* 7. 482 - 534. ["Excurs" on pp. 492 - 534.]

―― 1906/7. *Semitisch und Indogermanisch*. 1. Teil: *Konsonanten*. Copenhagen: H. Hagerup. Repr., Hildesheim: G. Olms, 1978).

―― 1908. Die gemein-indogermanisch-semitischen Worttypen der zwei- und dreikonsonantigen Wurzeln und die indogermanisch-semitischen vokalischen Entsprechungen. (Kuhn's) *Zeitschrift für vergleichende Sprachforschung* 42. 174 - 91.

―― 1911. *Vergleichendes indogermanisch-semitisches Wörterbuch*. Göttingen: Vandenhoeck & Ruprecht. [See esp. Preface on pp. xviii-xxi.]

―― 1917. *Die semitisch-vorindogermanischen larygalen Konsonanten*. (= *Mémoires de l'Académie Royale des Sciences et des Lettres de Danemarl*, 7e série, 4: 1.) Copenhagen: A. F. Høst & Søn. (With a French summary).

Osthoff, Hermann. 1879. Kleine beiträge zur deklinationslehre der indogermanischen sprachen II. *Morphologische Untersuchungen auf dem Gebiete der indogermanischen Sprachen* 2. 1 - 147.

―― 1881. Die tiefstufe im indogermanischen vocalismus. *Ibid.* 4. 1 - 406.

Paul, Hermann. 1880. *Principien der Sprachgeschichte*. Halle/S.: M. Niemeyer. (5th rev. ed., 1920.)

Pedersen, Holger. 1907. Die indogermanisch-semitische Hypothese und die indogermanische Lautlehre. *Indogermanische Forschungen* 22. 341 - 65.

Petersen, Walter. 1939. Hittite ḫ and Saussure's doctrine of the long vowels. *Journal of the American Oriental Society* 59. 175 - 99.

Polomé, Edgar (Charles). 1965. The laryngeal theory so far: A critical bibliographical survey. *Evidence for laryngeals*, ed. by Werner Winter, 9 - 78. (Bib., 44 - 78.]

Redard, Georges. 1976. Ferdinand de Saussure et Louis Havet. *Bulletin de la Société de Linguistique de Paris* 71: 1. 313 - 49. [Publication of correspondence between Saussure and Havet.]

―― 1978. Deux Saussure? *Cahiers Ferdinand de Saussure* 32. 27 - 41.

Regnaud, Paul. 1889. *Esquisses du véritable système primitif des voyelles dans les langues d'origine indo-européenne*. Paris: E. Leroux.

—— 1890. Le véritable système vocalique indo-européen: Preuves et déductions nouvelles. *Revue de Linguistique et de Philologie comparée* 23. 63 - 89, 183 - 87.

—— 1891. *Observations critiques sur le système de M. de Saussure*. Gray/Haute Savoie: Bouffaut Frères.

Rhys, (Sir) John. 1879. Review of Saussure 1879. *The Academy* (London, 27 Sept. 1879), 234 - 35.

Saussure, Ferdinand de. 1879. *Mémoire sur le système primitif des voyelles dans les langues indo-européennes*. Leipzig: B. G. Teubner. [Actually published in December 1878.] (Repr., Hildesheim: G. Olms, 1968.)

—— 1891. Contribution à l'histoire des aspirées sourdes. *Bulletin de la Société de Linguistique de Paris* 7. CXVIII (1892). [Summary of a paper presented at the 'Séance du 6 juin 1891'. Repr. in Saussure 1922. 603.]

—— 1916. *Cours de linguistique générale*. Ed. by Charles Bally & Albert Sechehaye, with the collaboration of Albert Riedlinger. Lausanne & Paris: Payot.

—— 1931. *Cours...*. 3rd corrected ed. Paris: Payot. [All other editions follow this one.]

—— 1922. *Recueil des publications scientifiques*. Ed. by Charles Bally & Léopold Gautier. Geneva: Editions Sonor; Lausanne: Payot; Heidelberg: C. Winter. (Repr. Geneva: Slatkine, 1970.)

—— 1967 - 68, 1974. *Cours de linguistique générale*. Edition critique par Rudolf Engler. Wiesbaden: O. Harrassowitz.

—— 1977. Memuar o pervonačal'noj sisteme glasnyx v indoevropejskix jazykax. *Trudy po jazykoznaniju* by F. de Saussure, ed. by A. A. Xolodovič, 302 - 562. Moscow: Progress. [= Russian transl. of Saussure 1879.]

—— 1978. *Saggio sul vocalismo indoeuropeo*. Edizione italiana a cura di Giuseppe Carlo Vincenzi. Bologna: Cooperative Libraria Universitaria Editrice. [= Italian transl. of Saussure 1879.]

Schleicher, August. 1861 - 62. *Compendium der vergleichenden Grammatik der indogermanischen Sprachen: Kurzer Abriss einer Laut- und Formenlehre der indogermanischen Ursprache*. Weimar: H. Böhlau. (4th ed., prepared by August Leskien & Johannes Schmidt, 1876.)

Schmitt-Brandt, Robert. 1967. *Die Entwicklung des indogermanischen Vokalsystems: Versuch einer inneren Rekonstruktion*. Heidelberg: Julius Groos.

Streitberg, Wilhelm. 1914. Ferdinand de Saussure. *Indogermanisches Jahrbuch* 2. 203 - 213. (Repr. in *Portraits of Linguists* ed. by Thomas A. Sebeok, vol. II, 100 - 110. Bloomington & London: Indiana Univ. Press, 1966.)

Sweet, Henry. 1880. Recent investigations of the Indogermanic vowel-system. *Transactions of the Philological Society 1880 - 81*, 155 - 62. (Repr. in H. Sweet, *Collected papers* ed. by Henry C. Wyld, 141 - 47. Oxford: Clarendon, 1913.)

Szemerényi, Oswald. 1973. La théorie des laryngales de Saussure à Kuryłowicz et à Benveniste: Essai de réévaluation. *Bulletin de la Société de Linguistique de Paris* 68. 1 - 25. [Transl. from the English by Michel Lejeune.]

—— 1980. *Einführung in die vergleichende Sprachwissenschaft*. 2nd rev. ed. Darmstadt: Wissenschaftliche Buchgesellschaft. [First ed., 1971.]

Vallini, Cristina. 1969. *Problemi di metodo in Ferdinand de Saussure indoeuropeista.* Pisa: P. Mariotti.
Vincenzi, Giuseppe Carlo. 1976. 'Sistema' e 'fonema' nel primo Saussure. *Studi italiani di Linguistica teorica ed applicata* 5. 229 - 51.
— 1978. Introduzione del Curatore. Saussure 1978. xix-xciv.
Watkins, Calvert. 1978. Remarques sur la méthode de Ferdinand de Saussure comparatiste. *Cahiers Ferdinand de Saussure* 32. 59 - 68. [Appendice, 68 - 69]

INDO-EUROPEAN NUMERALS
AND THE SEXAGESIMAL SYSTEM

WITOLD MAŃCZAK

Nearly a century ago, Johannes Schmidt (1890), famous for his "Wellentheorie", was concerned with the difference which seemed to him to exist in various Indo-European languages between the numerals 20—60 and the numerals 70—90, cf. Lat. *sexaginta* but *septuaginta*, Greek ἑξήκοντα but ἑβδομήκοντα, Old Irish *sesca* but *sechtmoga* or Gothic *saihs tigjus* but *sibuntehund*. According to Schmidt this difference was due to the influence of the Babylonian sexagesimal system, which, he thought, was also responsible for the difference between Goth. *twalif* and the numerals of the type *fidwortaihun* (the word meaning '13' not being attested in Gothic) as well as for the fact that the Germ. equivalent of I.-E. *$\hat{k}mtom$ meant not only '100' but also '120', because 12 is a fifth of 60 and $120 = 2 \times 60$. From all these facts, Schmidt drew the conclusion that the primitive homeland of the Indo-Europeans had been somewhere in Asia, not too far away from Babylon.

Johannes Schmidt's theory was criticized, among others, by Sommer (1951: 23 and 57ff.), Rosenfeld (1956—1957: 201 and 206ff.) and Szemerényi (1960: 2 and 151), but many linguists sympathized with it, e.g. Jacobsohn (1927: 86), Hirt (1932: 114), Eis (1950: 118), Brunner (1951: 88), Schönfeld (1954) or Devoto (1958: 73). It is also significant that Pisani, who criticized Schmidt's theory before the war (1932), in 1964 called his pre-war paper a "peccatum iuventutis" and approved the theory in question: "È notevole che, dove le lingue germaniche, tutte o in parte, si discostano dal baltico, ciò avvenga per 12 o per 60: negare qui l'influsso di un sistema duodecimale-sessagesimale di numerazione, che si è incrociato con quello decimale, mi pare assurdo: tanto più che di questo sistema abbiamo tracce anche nel valore '120' che in ant. nordico compete a *hundrađ*, la parola per '100' nel senso di una serie compiuta."

The purpose of this paper is to present a new argument against Schmidt's theory. First of all, I would like to draw attention to the fact that from the point of view of frequency of occurrence there are important differences among numerals. According to the frequency dictionary of Italian words by Juilland and Traversa (1973), the frequency of the Italian numerals is as follows:

uno	9334	undici	—	venti	43	cento	37
due	814	dodici	10	trenta	19	duecento	—
tre	234	tredici	5	quaranta	6	trecento	—
quattro	116	quattordici	5	cinquanta	19	quattrocento	—
cinque	58	quindici	17	sessanta	—	cinquecento	6
sei	30	sedici	—	settanta	—	seicento	—
sette	29	diciassette	5	ottanta	—	settecento	—
otto	28	diciotto	—	nonanta	—	ottocento	—
nove	9	diciannove	—			novecento	—
dieci	60						

In Italian, as in other Indo-European languages, there are four series of numerals: 1—10, 11—19, 20—90 and 100—900. If we divide each of these series into a lower half and an upper half, it will be evident that the frequency of occurrence of lower numerals in each of these series is larger than that of higher numerals:

Numerals	Mean frequency	Numerals	Mean frequency	Numerals	Mean frequency	Numerals	Mean frequency
2—5	311	11—15	7	20—50	87	100—500	9
6—10	31	16—19	1	60—90	0	600—900	0

In order to calculate the mean frequency of the lower half of the series 1—10, I took into account only the numerals 2—5, since the dictionary by Juilland and Traversa does not make a distinction between the numeral `one` and the indefinite article.

It is useful then to compare the Latin numerals with their equivalents in some Romance languages because, in the Indo-European language family, the Romance languages occupy a unique and privileged position since Latin, which is the Romance proto-language, is attested, while Proto-Germanic, Proto-Slavic and so on are not.

Latin	Portuguese	Spanish	French	Italian	Rumanian
unus	um	uno	un	uno	unu
duo	dois	dos	deux	due	doi
tres→	tres	tres	trois	tre	trei
quattuor	quatro	cuatro	quatre	quattro	patru
quinque	cinco	cinco	cinq	cinque	cinci
sex	seis	seis	six	sei+	șase+
septem	sete	siete	sept	sette	șapte
octo	oito	ocho	huit	otto	opt

novem	nove	noueve	neuf	nove	nouă
decem	dez	diez	dix	dieci	zece
undecim	onze	once	onze	undici	unsprezece +
duodecim	doze	doce	douze	dodici	doisprezece +
tredecim	treze	trece	treize	tredici	treisprezece +
quattuordecim	catorze	catorce	quatorze	quatotrdici	paisprezece +
quindecim	quinze	quince	quinze	quindici	cincisprezece +
sedecim	dezasseis +	dieciseis +	seize	sedici	şaisprezece +
septendecim	dezassete +	diecisiete +	dix-sept +	diciassette +	şaptesprezece +
duodeviginti	dezoito +	dieciocho +	dix-huit +	diciotto +	optsprezece +
undeviginti	dezanove +	diecinueve +	dix-neuf +	diciannove +	nouăsprezece +
viginti	vinte	veinte	vingt	venti	douăzeci +
triginta	trinta	treinta	trente	trenta	treizeci +
quadraginta	quarenta	cuarenta	quarante	quaranta	patruzeci +
quinquaginta	cinquenta	cincuenta	cinquante	cinquanta	cincizeci +
sexaginta	sessenta	sesenta	soixante	sessanta	şaizeci +
septuaginta	setenta	setenta	soixantedix +	settanta	şaptezeci +
octoginta	oitenta	ochenta	quatrevingts +	ottanta	optzeci +
nonaginta	noventa	noventa	quatrevingt- -dix +	novanta	nouăzeci +
centum	cento	ciento	cent	cento	o sută +
ducenti	duzentos	doscientos +	deux cents +	duecento +	două sute +
trecenti	trezentos	trescientos +	trois cents +	trecento +	trei sute +
quadringenti	quatrocentos +	cuatrocientos +	quatre cents +	quattrocento +	patru sute +
quingenti	quinhentos	quinientos	cinq cents +	cinquecento +	cinci sute +
sescenti	seiscentos +	seiscientos +	six cents +	seicento +	sase sute +
septingenti	setecentos +	setecientos +	sept cents +	settecento +	şapte sute +
octingenti	oitocentos +	ochocientos +	huit cents +	ottocento +	opt sute +
nongenti	novecentos +	novecientos +	neuf cents +	novecento +	nouă sute +

Analogical forms are marked by crosses. It is easy to see that there is a connection between resistance to analogical change and frequency: the groups of numerals 1−5, 11−15, 20−50 and 100−500 show fewer analogical forms than the groups 6−10, 16−19, 60−90 and 600−900 respectively, which are less frequently used:

Numerals	Percentage of analogical forms
1−5	−
6−10	8%
11−15	20%
16−19	90%
20−50	20%
60−90	35%
100−500	68%
600−900	100%

Returning to Schmidt's theory, it is first of all necessary to point out that Schmidt was wrong in believing that there was a difference between the numerals 20−60 and 70−90 in Latin, Greek and Old Irish, that e.g. Lat. *sexaginta*, Greek ἑξήκοντα and Old Irish *sesca* were derived from cardinals, whereas Lat. *septuaginta*, Greek ἑβδομήκοντα and Old

Irish *sechtmoga* contained an ordinal as the first term. In reality, the Latin, Greek and Old Irish numerals 20—90 are all derived from cardinals, as Brugmann realized in 1890, as did several other scholars (Pieri, Jacobsohn, Pisani, Kent, Sommer) after him, cf. Szemerényi (1960: 3). On the other hand, it is a fact that there is a difference in some older Germanic languages between the numerals 20—60 and 70—90, cf. Goth. *twai tigjus*, etc. and *sibuntehund*, etc., but *sibuntehund, ahthautehund, niuntehund* have nothing to do with the Babylonian sexagesimal system. In reality the Gothic numerals 20—60 are as archaic as the Old Church Slavic numerals 20—90 (*dъva desęti*, etc. until *devętь desętъ*), while the Gothic numerals 70—90 are neologisms due to the analogy of *taihuntehund* '100', and *taihunte-hund* '(τὸ τῶν) δεκάδων ἑκατόν' had to be formed after Goth. *hund* < *$\hat{k}mtom$ began to mean not only '100' but also '120'. There is nothing strange in the fact that *sibuntheund* '70', *ahtautehund* '80' and *niuntehund* '90' were formed on the model of *taihuntehund* '100' if one takes into account that 1° in the Italian texts which Juilland and Traversa used in compiling their frequency dictionary *cento* '100' was attested 37 times, whereas *settanta* '70', *ottanta* '80' and *nonanta* '90' were not attested at all, 2° the Romance (Portuguese, Spanish, etc.) numerals 20—50 show 20% of analogical forms, whereas the percentage of analogical forms among the numerals 60—90 is 35%. In addition, the "Kluft" that Johannes Schmidt saw between Goth. *saihs tigjus* '60' and *sibuntehund* '70' has nothing to do with the Babylonian sexagesimal system because similar differences can be found between the lower and the higher numerals of the series 1—10, 11—19 and 100—900, since in each of these series the higher numerals are less frequently used and thus are less resistant to analogical change.

Until now this connection between the analogical development of numerals and their frequency has been illustrated by examples from Romance languages, but it is not difficult to find similar examples in other languages. As far as the series 1—10 is concerned, it may be mentioned that in Old Church Slavic the numerals 1—4 retain a conservative character, whereas the numerals 5—10 show innovations: *pętь, šestь, sedmь, osmь, devętь, desętь*. The same applies to Lithuanian, where the inflection of *keturi* '4' was extended to the numerals 5—9: *penki, penkios, šeši, šešios, septyni, septynios, aštuoni, aštuonios, devyni, devynios*. In Albanian the inherited forms of the numerals 6—10 were replaced by nouns with a suffix -*t*-: *gjashtë* '6', *shtatë* '7', *tetë* '8', *nëntë* '9', *dhjetë* '10'. Among the Ossetic numerals 1—10 there is only one innovation, namely *farast* '9' (<*far-ast* 'after eight'). In Sanskrit, '6' is expressed not only by *ṣáṭ* but also by *páñca caikaṃ ca* '5+1'; similar additive phrases occur in Romany (Gipsy), too. Returning to Romance languages, it is worth while to mention the fact that in Modern Spanish the ordinals 1—5 (except *segundo* 'second') are inherited, whereas all higher ordinals (*sexto, séptimo, octavo*, etc.) are borrowed from Latin. In Finno-Ugric only the numerals 2—6 are common for all of these languages, whereas some higher numerals are of foreign origin.

As to the series 11—19, it may be mentioned that according to Lejeune (1981) Latin *duodeviginti* and *undeviginti* are due to an Etruscan influence.

As far as the series 20—90 goes, it deserves to be mentioned that after the eleventh century the inherited English numerals 60 and 80 were replaced by *threescore* and *fourscore*, containing *score* of Scandinavian origin. According to Rosenfeld (1956—1957: 211) in some modern Low German dialects the highest dialectal numeral is 30 or 50, while the higher numerals are replaced by High German forms. In Russian the numeral corresponding to Old Church Slavic *devętь desętь* '90' was replaced by the neologism *devjanosto* < *devętьno sьto* (see my article on *Russe devjanosto* to appear in the Festschrift for Petar Skok). Already Brugmann knew that in Indo-Iranian the numerals 20—50 were old forms in *-śat(i), -sat(i)*, while the numerals 60—90 were innovations in *-ti*. Jacobsohn (1927: 91—2) mentions two Finno-Ugric dialects one which shows the numerals 70—90 in *-das* and the other, the numerals 80—90 in *-sāt*; both *-das* and *-sāt* are of Old Iranian origin.

The only conclusion that could be drawn from all these facts is that analogical development is conditioned by frequency: in every series of numerals the lower numerals, which are more frequently used, preserve a more conservative character than the higher numerals, which are of less frequent usage. Therefore, it occurs in some Indo-European as well as non-Indo-European languages that in the series 20—90 there is a difference between the structure of the lower and that of the higher numerals, but there is no reason for ascribing it to an influence of the Babylonian sexagesimal system. One thing more deserves to be stressed. Meillet and some other scholars (among them Rosenfeld, 1956—1957: 211) believed that the numerals 60—90 were lacking in Proto-Indo-European because in the historical period these numerals are more differentiated than the numerals 20—50. This opinion is false. There is no reason for thinking that the Proto-Indo-Europeans knew the numerals 20—50 and 100 but did not know the numerals 60—90. The difference between the numerals 20—50 and the numerals 60—90 is comparable to that between the singular and the other numbers, the present and the other tenses, the indicative and the other moods, the positive and the other degrees, and so on. It is easier to reconstruct the singular, the present, the indicative or the positive than respectively the other numbers, tenses, moods or degrees, because the singular, the present, the indicative and so on are more frequently used and therefore more resistant to analogical development than the other numbers, tenses, moods and so on. But there is no reason for thinking that Proto-Indo-European knew no other forms than those of the singular, no other forms than those of the present, no other forms than those of the indicative and so on. *Mutatis mutandis*, the same applies to the numerals. There was no gap between the numerals 20 — 50 on the one hand and 100 and higher numerals on the other. The fact that in the historical period the numerals 60 — 90 are less homogeneous than the numerals 20 — 50 is quite natural and has a very simple explanation: the numerals 60 — 90 just were less frequently used than the numerals 20 — 50.

REFERENCES

Brunner, K. 1951. *Die englische Sprache. Ihre geschichtliche Entwicklung*, II. Halle/Salle: Niemeyer.
Devoto, G. 1958. *Scritti minori*. Florence: Le Monnier.
Eis, G. 1950. *Laut- und Formenlehre des Mittelhochdeutschen*. Heidelberg: Winter.
Hirt, H. 1932. *Handbuch des Urgermanischen*, II. Heidelberg: Winter.
Jacobsohn, H. 1927. Zahlensystem und Gliederung der indogermanischen Sprachen. *KZ* 54. 76 - 99.
Juilland, A. and V. Traversa. 1973. *Frequency dictionary of Italian words*. The Hague: Mouton.
Lejeune, M. 1981. Procédures soustractives dans les numérations étrusque et latine. *BSL* LXXVI. 241 - 48.
Pisani, V. 1932. Il sistema sessagesimale e i numerali indeuropei. Reale Accademia Nazionale dei Lincei. Rendiconti della Classe di Scienze morali, storiche e filologiche, ser. VI, vol. VIII, fasc. 3 - 4. 148 - 66.
       1964. Review of O. Szemerényi, *Studies in the Indo-European system of numerals*. *Archivio glottologico italiano* XLIX. 150 - 6.
Rosenfeld, H.-Fr. 1956 - 1957. Die germanischen Zahlen von 70 - 90 und die Entwicklung des Aufbaus der germanischen Zahlwörter. *Wissenschaftl. Zeitschr. der E. M. Arndt-Univers. Greifswald* VI. 157 - 215.
Schmidt, J. 1890. *Die Urheimat der Indogermanen und das europäische Zahlsystem*. Berlin.
Schönfeld, M. 1954. *Schönfeld's historische grammatica van het Nederlands*. 5th ed., verzoorgd door... A. van Loey. Zutphen: Thieme.
Sommer, F. 1951. *Zum Zahlwort*. Munich: Beck.
Szemerényi, O. 1960. *Studies in the Indo-European system of numerals*. Heidelberg: Winter.

ABSOLUTE VS. RELATIVE COMPARISON: TYPOLOGY AND DEVELOPMENT

T. L. MARKEY

Categorically, there are two fundamental types of comparison: absolute and relative. Typically, absolute comparison is comprised of the set: positive, comparative, and superlative, e.g., Engl. *big — bigger — biggest*. Relative comparison, on the other hand, is a qualification of absolute comparison and denotes intermediary degrees between the positive, comparative, and superlative, e.g., Engl. *rather big — rather bigger — rather the biggest*.[1]

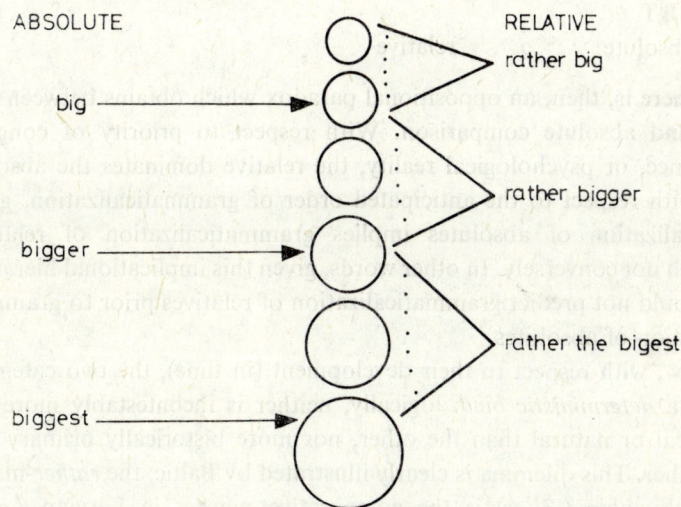

The initial link in the chain is the relative (*rather big*) in reference to the positive (*big*), and the ultimate link is, of course, the superlative. Something is either *big* or *not big* (...*rather big*) or intermediary between

---

[1] The absolute relative (*rather the biggest*) may well be starred for American speakers, but, I am told, would seem to represent a Received Standard expression of understatement for British speakers. Here, I would like to thank my colleagues for discussion and some data, particularly Benjamin Stolz for leading me through the Slavic material; Derek Bickerton for creole data, Sasha Lehrman for pointing out the importance of the Baltic dilemma, and the staff of the Middle English dictionary at The University of Michigan for once again putting their rich resources at my disposal. The classic work to date on degree is, of course, Dwight L. Bolinger's *Degree Words* (1972).

the two (=*rather big*). Relative, *rather*-degrees either approach absolute degrees or are ranged as intermediary degrees between absolute degrees.

Relative comparison is primary and takes cognitive precedence and prominence over absolute comparison. The perception of relative distinctions provides to inferential basis required to formulate absolute distinctions.

In terms of implicational hierarchies, however, absolute comparison implies relative comparison. Absolute degrees (as shown on the above diagramme) form the points of reference required for the formulation of relative (intermediary) degrees. Absolutes are the boundary signals of relatives.

Thus, relative comparison dominates absolute comparison, while absolute comparison implies relative comparison:

relative (d̃)   absolute (d̃)
BUT
absolute ⊃ relative

and there is, then, an oppositional paradox which obtains between relative and absolute comparison. With respect to priority of congitive inference, or psychological reality, the relative dominates the absolute, but with respect to the anticipated order of grammaticalization, grammaticalization of absolutes implies grammaticalization of relatives, though not conversely. In other words, given this implicational hierarchy, we would not predict grammaticalization of relatives prior to grammaticalization of absolutes.

Now, with respect to their development (in time), the two categories form a *deterministic bind*: logically, neither is incontestably more economical or natural than the other, nor more historically primary than the other. This dilemma is clearly illustrated by Baltic: the *rather*-marker in Lithuanian (*-ókas*) is the comparative marker in Latvian (*-aka-*), or vice versa (in time), see Stang (1966: 267–8) and infra.

Absolute and relative comparison would appear to be derivationally interdependent, yet transformationally unrelated. Absolute degrees form points of essential reference for designation of relative degrees, while, in turn, relative degrees entail the prior existence of absolute degrees if relative degrees are to have referential meaning. Nevertheless, the one category is not a formal derivation of the other. The absolute is prototypical; the relative the distortion. Having been first given the absolute, it is easier to recognize the relative than, conversely, having been first given the relative to recognize the absolute. From this, one infers that the relative is more susceptible to variation (both formal and semantic) than the absolute. These observations would seem to deny the efficacy of a dependency or generative approach to an analysis of their historical development and deployment.

It is highly significant to note that marginal and emerging languages (argots, pidgins, creoles) have absolute, but not relative, comparison. Relative comparison marking thus appears to represent a later stage in linguistic development. The absence of relative comparison in creoles and its presence in languages with well established histories and expanded grammatical complexity (e.g. English, Romance, Slavic) lends further support to the bioprogram notion of language origin and development as articulated by Bickerton (1981). While broaching a not altogether invidious circularity in this regard, the lack of relative comparison in creoles points to the prototypical character of absolute comparison.[2]

Absolute comparison articulates a quantificationally limited propositional calculus and is cognitively serial and conceptually enumerative. Note that the superlative may be perceived as marking the *n*th-term of a series, cf. Germ. *-st* in *best* and *zwanzigst*. If this serialization is viewed as distributional and case is employed to mark the non-standard, then the case marker is generally a partitive, e.g. Finno-Ugric *-m-/-n-* formants. In such instances, the predication that X is bigger than Y is based on the presupposition that Y is distributed in X. Absolute comparison is thus a serial concept wherein the standard is both more accessible and has greater prominence (higher standing) in an implicational hierarchy than the non-standard: the compared implies the non-compared. The standard is therefore *naturally* less marked than the non-standard. Moreover, a marked standard is constructionally iconic, while an unmarked standard is not: failure to mark the standard leaves it structurally symmetrical with the positive, cf. *X is big, Y is not* (*big*) and *X is bigger, Y is not* (*big*). The range of marking conventions for absolute comparison includes at least (possibly also only) the following conventions: *case* (e.g. Finno-Ugric, Uto-Aztecan), *reduplication* (e.g. Polynesian, Melanesian), *qualifiers* (e.g. Romance, Polynesian), *deictic focus* (e.g. Polynesian, Melanesian, Ngadha, Japanese), *negation* (e.g.

---

[2] The crux of the circularity should be obvious: prototypes define creoles and creoles define prototypes. That is, the linguistic structures of creoles are regarded as prototypical, and prototypes form the essence of the bioprogram, so that structures not found in creoles are not prototypical and not part of the bioprogram.

Welsh, English, Sranan, Malay), *verbs* (e.g. some Kwa languages, some Melanesian languages), *contextual inference* (e.g. Swahili, also with deictic focus via *kuliko* 'where there is'), and *superlatives in contextual coreference* (e.g. Engl. *both are just great, but which is greatest?*). For further details and discussions, see Markey (1981: 18–20), Puhvel (1973).

We infer that absolute comparison is conducted by a restricted set of paradigmatic procedures. In the following survey of data from specific languages, it will be demonstrated that, in contrast to absolute comparison, relative comparison is conveyed by an unlimited set of syntagmatic freezes. Moreover, it will be shown that, while absolute strategies tend to be etymologically transparent, relative markers tend to be etymolovically opaque. Moreover, it appears that these discrepancies are univtersal:

ABSOLUTE COMPARISON	RELATIVE COMPARISON
limited paradigmatic strategy	unlimited syntagmatic freeze
etymologically transparent	etymologically opaque

With respect to *rather*, relative comparison, there is a clear-cut dialectal distinction between French and Italian on the one hand and the other Romance languages on the other hand. French and Italian reflect the syntagm *plus+tostus* lit. 'more burned' (Fr. *plutôt*, It. *piuttosto*), while the other langages have 'more better' (Sp. *más bien*, Rum. *mai bine*, Port. *mais bom*), or other qualifier options, e.g. Sp. *un poco, un tanto, algo*, Catal. *bastant* 'suffice'. The *plutôt*-syntagm is not descended from Classical Latin, which marks *rather* with *paulo*+Adj-comparative, e.g. *paulo celer-ius* 'rather quickly'. Recall that Lat. *paul(l)us* 'few', properly a diminutive, is virtually always singular, while *paucus* idem is virtually always plural, the source of Sp. (etc.) *poco*. Both are from IE *pow-l/k-o-*, cf. Goth. *fawai* 'few'. *Plutôt* is an Italian innovation, as is *tôt* 'soon', from Vulgar Latin *tostus* 'quickly', attested in French since the 10th century (*Eulalie*). Note OFr. *tostein, tosteinement* 'quick, quickly' in early Italianized texts.

For *rather*, Slavic predominantly reflects the OCS phrase *do syti* 'to satiety', cf. Lat. *satis* 'enough', e.g. Pol. *dość, dosyć*; Cz. *dosti*; Serbo-Croatian *dosta*; Bul. *dòsta*; while Russ. *dovol'no* (*On govorit dovol'no xorošo po-russki.* 'He speaks Russian rather well.'), OCS *dovolĭnŭ*, derive from the syntagm *do-+volja* 'to+will', cf. *voliti* 'wish, prefer'. Macedonian employs the "more" prefix *po-* (*po-dobre* 'rather well'). Gk. *mãllon* (with infinitives and with expressive gemination of *-l-*) is

properly the absolute comparative of *mála* 'very, quite', cf. Lat. *multus* <
IE *ml̥-tos*, Lith. *milns*, as a general strenghening term. Greek seems to
have remained at a somewhat primitive stage of relative comparison
development.

In Welsh, *rather* receives a multiplicity of translations: *braidd* (MW
breid, breyd, cf. MBr., MdBr. *bre* 'difficulty') 'rather, somewhat',
hytrach 'rather', *go* 'rather, somewhat', *lled* 'partly, rather'. MW *breid*
originally signified 'hardly, scarcely, with difficulty', and implementation
as *rather* is a 19th century innovation. *lled* also covers 'half, partly', cf.
MdIr. *leath-chrua* (∼ *scoth-chrua*) 'rather hard'. *go-* 'partly, somewhat' is
prefixed to nouns, generally diminutives, cf. *go-bant* ∼ *lled-band* = *go* +
pant 'small hollow, low place'. Of particular interest is *hytrach*, a fusion
of *hyt-rac* 'until on account of', where *rac* is used with the equative
with causal meaning. When applied to nouns (station), *hyt* signifies
'length', and when applied to verbs (motion) it denotes possibility of
approach, i.e. 'until'. Note *V+hyt y nos* 'until the night'. Extent of
station (length) is paralleled by extent of motion in time (until), cf. use
of the same markers for the distributive and iterative in Uto-Aztecan.
Thus, W *hytrach*, properly deictic in scope, reveals the nature of a prominent subsidiary value of relative qualifiers, namely, signification of
approximation of an absolute value and, hence, their role in expressing
boundary conditions.

Rather-marking and its history and development is somewhat more
complicated in Germanic than in the other European languages reviewed so far. This complexity is quite possibly a reflection of belated
attempts to convey relative comparison in Germanic. Indeed, the more
archaic forms and conventions are found in the core of the Germanic
speech community, while the periphery attests numerous innovations
and loans, as well as, possibly, instances of relexification.

English *rather* as an adjective qualifier is a late 16th/early 17th century
innovation, for *rather* is historically the comparative of OE *hraþ(e)*
'quick(ly)', now abandoned. Engl. *rather* may, in fact, be a relexification
of Fr. *plutôt* 'quick(ly)' → 'rather', but a survey of the evidence in favor
of this supposition need not detain us here. Sw. *tämlig(en)*, Dan., Nw.
temmelig are loans from MLG *tem(m)elik* (*tāmelĭk, tĕmelĭk*) or Du.
tamelijk, cf. MdG *ziemlich* 'rather' < Gmc. **tāmi-*, a derivative of
verbal **tem-*, ultimately from IE **d-/om-*, the timber word, cf. Lat.
domus. The original significance was apparently 'zusammenfügen',
so Falk-Torp (1960: 125*d*), also Pokorny (1959: 198). Note that *ziemlich*
applies only to the positive: *ziemlich besser, ziemlich das Beste* are un-

grammatical. In the higher degrees, *ziemlich* is replaceable by *wohl*, which implies doubt on the part of the speaker, while *wohl ziemlich* (*gut*) in the positive anticipates agreement on the part of the speaker. In Bavarian and Alemannian, *ziemlich* is (dialectally) replaceable by *halt*, a fossilized form of OHG *halto* 'very'. In contrast to *ziemlich*, *halt* enters the higher degrees of absolute comparison: *halt besser*, *halt am Besten*. Late OHG *halt halto* adv. 'very' is presumably related to OIc. *heldr* (MdIc. *heldur*, Far. *heldur*, Dan., Sw., Nw. *heller*, NNw. *helder*), and *heldr* is then properly the comparative of a Gmc. **hald-* **haldiza-*), cf. Goth. *haldis* 'rather, sooner'. Note that ME *helder/hildire* and the like, cf. MdEngl. (northern) dial. *helder*, were borrowed from Scandinavian. This is further evidence for the later evolution of *rather*-markers in English, see De Vries (1962: 221a). Gmc. *haaldiza, lit. 'more very', itself a qualified intensive, became a relative qualifier. Scand. *heller* expresses preference, as does MdG *halt*, but *heller* does not qualify adjectives. When negated, *heller* translates as 'either': Sw. *inte han och inte han heller* 'not him and not him either'. The ultimate origin of Gmc. **hald-* is unclear, though possibly from IE **k^e/ol-* 'sloping, inclined, slanting', cf. Lith. *šalìs*, Toch. A *kälts-*, B *klants-/klänts-* 'sleep', actually 'lean (against)', but this would seem to be a more likely source for OIc. *hallr*<*halþaz 'sloping, slanting'. The suggestion by Falk-Torp (1960: 346) of a relationship with OIr. *calath* 'hard', while ingenious, is improbable due to semantic difficulties despite reference to OE *tylg* 'rather' and Goth. *tulgus* 'firm, solid'. MdG *ganz* (and *ganz*+Adj 'rather+Adj') was originally uniquely High German, but was dispersed to all the other dialects, except English, in the course of the Middle Ages. MDu. *gansch* is the basis for Dan., Sw. *ganska(e)*, while MDan. *gantze* derives from Middle Low German. There is the well-known semantic disparity between Norwegian and Swedish: *ganska(e)* signifies 'quite' in Norwegian and 'rather' in Swedish. In all dialects, *ganz* (and the like) is restricted to the positive: *ganz besser* and *ganz am Besten* are ungrammatical. Falk-Trop (1960: 300) contend that the further etymology is "durchaus dunkel", while Kluge-Mitzka (1967: 231 – 232a) bravely derive it from an IE **ghwon-*, cf. Lith. *ganà* 'enough', OCS *goněti* 'to suffice', Arm. *yogn* 'multum', etc. Early dialectal contamination with the 'suffice, sufficient, enough' group or within that group (Goth. *ga-nauhan*, *ga-nohs*, OIc. *gnógr*<IE **(e)nek-/enk-*) seems highly likely.

A summary of the Germanic data, with particular attention to English, is now appropriate. At its earliest stages, English apparently lacked or failed to develop proper *rather* -markers. Note that, as a fusion language, English is the most creole-like of any of the Germanic dialects. It either borrowed *rather*-markers (i.e. Scand *heldr*) or, apparently, relexified them (i.e. *rather* 'more quickly, quicker' < OFr *plustots* 'more quickly, quicker' < VLat. *plus tostus* 'more quickly/burned'). For Continental Germanic, High German was the dynamic progenitor of acceptable *rather*-markers: *halt, ziemlich, ganz*. High German supplied the other Continental dialects with *rather*-markers. In Scandinavian, however, *held*, formally the comparative of HG *halt*, was presumably original, but as such was never a *rather*-qualifier of adjectives. The etymologies of *halt* and *ganz* are opaque, and while the etymology of *ziemlich* is clear enough, the semantic twists required to adapt it and shift it from the semantic field of 'fit together, build' to yield a moderating qualifier of adjectives ('rather') would seem considerable. Germanic *rather*-marking is analytic and syntagmatic, as in the bulk of the other languages surveyed here. The Germanic evidence points to a probable anteriority of absolute comparison over relative comparison. Note, too, that in Germanic dialects *rather*-marking is generally restricted to the positive: *ziemlich* and *ganz* are not coupled with the comparative or the superlative. Indeed, even in English, *rather*-marking in the superlative would seem to be a late, socially motivated analogical extension based on *rather*-marking in the comparative. Then, too, in the other languages reviewed here, *rather*-marking in the comparative is exceptional: it is generally restricted to the positive.

From the above survey, we conclude that the underlying semantic focus of *rather*-markers — and this may well be universal — is: 1) *sufficiency* (*satis*), 2) *approachability* (e.g. W *hytrach*), or 3) *partiality* (somewhat), all of which are subsumed by the notion of approximation. *Rather*-markers would seem to be universally signs of approximate valuation, and thus absolute comparison markers would seem to be etymologically and transformationally independent from relative markers and relative comparison marking strategies. Nevertheless, for the reasons indicated above, relative and absolute comparison are cognitively interdependent.

This cognitive interdependence would seem to have surface manifestations in Baltic. That is, in Baltic, perturbations in the relative comparison system would seem to have entailed perturbations in the absolute comparison system, or, conceivably, the converse may have been true: perturbations in the absolute system entailed perturbations in the relative system.

The precise historical character of the relationship between the Latvian absolute comparative -aka- and the Lithuanian *rather*-marker -oka- has never been entirely clear. Cf. Lith. *ger-ókas* 'rather good' and Latv. *lab-âks* 'better'. The Lithuanian absolute comparative is formed by suffixing -esni- to the positive (-esnis m., -esnė f., -iau n.). A relative comparative is derived from the absolute comparative by inserting an *l*-diminutive: *ger-ėl- ėsnis* 'somewhat, rather better'. For relative comparison, Latvian employs *diezgan* 'rather, enough' +Adj. The following pattern emerges:

	Abs. Comp.	Rel. Comp.
Lith.	-esni-	-óka-
Latv.	-àka-	diezgan+Adj

The originality of -āka- as an absolute comparative formant is belied by relics such as Latv. *vaĩrs=vaĩrâk* 'more', which reflects *-is-, the Indo-European comparative *-y-/os-) in the zero grade, originally a sign of the intensive. Cf. OPr. *tāl-is* (1x), *tāls* (2x) 'farther' and Lat. *magis*. Lithuanian has retained the old comparative in the relic *pãstaras* 'last'. Cf., similarly, preservation of an archaic competetive alternant in the Gothic directional *fruma* 'former'. Lith. -esnis can be analyzed as containing -es-+-ni-<IE *-yes-+-ᵉ/on-, cf Gth. -izin- and Gk. -i(s)on-. To this one would anticipate a Latv. *-ešņs, but this is phonotactically impluasible for Latvian. Stang (1966:268) contends that, despite the impressive comparative evidence that can be marshalled in its favor, lack of any trace of suppletive comparison in Lithaunian obviates a clear-cut Indo-European heritage for Lith. -esnis.[3] Recall, too, that the original superlatives are no longer viable in Baltic, see Stang (1966 268 - 70) for details.

In view of the comparative evidence, employment of -āka- as an absolute comparative marker is clearly secondary. The Lithuanian diminu-

---

[3] I tend to agree with Stang. If, indeed, -esne (<*-is-+-ne-) were an inherited form and had the status quo been maintained, then absence of suppletion is rather extraordinary. It seems more reasonable to consider this an innovation, a compound of the original comparative -is- + the negative particle -ne-. The negative particle frequently figures in the formation of the comparative, e.g. Engl. *than*< OE *pŏ*, inst. of the def. art., +*ne*; MW *no(c)*<IE *no-k. The original would have been something like "X-very not (Y)"→"more X than Y". The negative value (i.e. the diminutive) associated with relative -oka- (-aka-) comparisons and the reciprocity between the absolute and relative as outlined below may also have played a role in reshaping the inherited absolute comparative.

tive comparative (e.g. *ger-ėl-ėsnis*, cf. *dařžas* 'garden': *daržēlis* 'little garden') and evidence from the dialects provide clues as to a formal and semantic source. Selonian Latvian attests pejorative diminutives in -*āka*-, e.g. *teļāks* 'bad calf' and note the same value of -*ēko*- as a variant of -*āka*-/-*oka*-: Lith. *pélekas*, Latv. *pęlȩ̃ks* 'grey'. Cf., similarly, use of diminutive *paulo* in Latin relative comparison (*paulo celerius*).

However, mere identification of a formal and semantic source, so often passed off as probative in historical studies, is never really a linguistically sufficient explanation of development. Invocation of phonological causality and/or plausibily to explain morphosyntactic change (the phonatactic implausibility of a Latv. **-ešņs*) is equally unsatisfactory. Adequate explanation of change and change types, of typology and development, should be firmly grounded in the observation of cognitive patterns and implicational networks, typically ranged as hierarchies.

As a preface to a further, deeper analysis of the Baltic situation, we may reiterate our findings so far as follows. At the outset, we noted the oppositional paradox that obtains between relative and absolute comparison with respect, on the one hand, to cognitive prominence and, on the other hand, to implicational priority. We have also noted that the absolute is the prototype, the relative the distortion; that absolute and relative are derivationally interdependent, yet transformationally unrelated; that absolute comparison is typically derived from a limited set of paradigmatic strategies, while relative comparison arises from an unlimited set of syntagmatic freezes (e.g. Fr. *plutôt*); that absolute strategies tend to be etymologically transparent and synthetic, while relative strategies tend to be etymologically opaque and analytic; and that marginal and emerging languages — and here fusion languages such as English might well be added — have absolute, but not relative, comparison. *Rather*-comparison is developmentally and historically secondary to absolute comparison and tends to be defective: it is generally restricted to the positive (*rather good*). In its typically syntagmatic formulation, relative, *rather*-comparison tends to be indiscriminate and, correspondingly, diverse in selecting etyma to express an underlying notion of approximation as relativity. This indiscretion in etyma selection for marking conventions is reflected by the general etymological opacity of *rather*-markers.

Here, we should interject a word or two about the relationship that is generally presumed to obtain between relative comparison (*rather good*) and preference (*I would rather have X than Y*). There has, I believe, been a great deal of confusion on this issue, and mainstream grammarians have somehow failed to penetrate the heart of the matter. Relative comparison expresses a conditional modality: a relative degree term *de natura* signifies approximation of some absolute values as a goal (whether present on the surface or not) but is itself conditioned by the very approximation it conveys. In qualifying adjectives, *rather*-markers ultimately reference station words (N's). By the same token, terms of intention, such as preferential *rather*, signal approximation of the absolute of some decision as a goal: *I would rather have X than Y > I have chosen X*. Without going into further detail, we assert that preferential, intentional *rather* is the volitional, verbal mode or verbal reification of the *rather* of relative comparison, the *rather* of qualitative approximation. The one is the flip of the other, and this contention is borne out by the derivational history of the Slavic forms, such as Russ. *dovol'no < do- + volja* 'to will', reviewed above.

From these typological generalizations — and they should be regarded more as rules of thumb than as obiter dicta, we infer that, generally speaking, the relative vs. the absolute stand in a constructionally inverse relationship to one another: the analytic relative is less marked and more highly grammaticalized than the more marked and less highly grammaticalized synthetic absolute. Cf., similarly, the polar opposition that obtains between signification of possession by juxtapositioning (*John house* = NN) and possession marking on the verb (*John has a house* = = NVN), see Seiler (1981) for details and a full discussion:

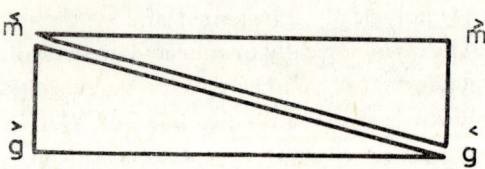

((NN) (*John house*) (NVN) (*John has a house*))
Relative Comp. Absolute Comp.
approximation goal
analytic synthetic
syntagmatic paradigmatic
etymological opacity etymological transparency
COGNITIVE PROMINENCE COGNITIVE NON-PROMI-
Implied by Abs. Comp. Implies Rel. Comp.

where *m* denotes degrees of marking and *g* degrees of grammaticalization.

In these terms, relative comparison is the flip of absolute comparison and vice versa. Recall, once again, the flip-flop opposition between the two categories in terms of cognitive prominence vs. implicational priority. The possible transition from one to the other, a flip, would thus be a discontinuous reversal without trace and without discernible intermediary residue. Just so, the transition between absolute comparison with *-is- (*-yes-) and relative comparison with *--/oka- in Baltic, that is, the replacement of an original absolute comparative in *-is- in Latvian by a relative comparative in /--/oka-, in reality a diminutive employed to denote (originally) the partialness of, the approximation to, some absolute quality.

Finally, then, the point is that, it is only by viewing the cognitive and implicational relationships, as well as the relative degrees of markedness and grammaticalization, that obtain between interconnected, if not developmentally parallel, grammatical categories that we can adequately interpret change and the developmental and, I presume, programmatic and highly principled patterns that change erects. We cannot persist in merely mapping a surficial linearity, but must probe the depths of certain semantic foci, the modalities of constructional iconicity, the significance of observable implicational hierarchies and degrees of cognitive prominence, and seek to define the precise character of the relationship between naturalness and simplification. It is only then that we can hope to come to grips with the dynamics of change, be it continuous or discontinuous, natural or abnatural. We must, in fine, attempt to discover and determine the character of processual universals in language origins and development and move away from the old (primarily Greenbergian) opposition between categorical universals and preconceived typological contingencies.

REFERENCES

Bickerton, Derek. 1981. *Roots of language.* Ann Arbor: Karoma.
Bolinger, Dwight L. 1972. *Degree words.* The Hague: Mouton.
Falk, Hjalmar and Alf Torp. 1960. *Norwegisch-Dänisches etymologisches Wörterbuch.* 1 - 2. Heidelberg: Winter. 2nd ed.
Kluge, Friedrich and Walther Mitzka. 1967. *Etymologisches Wörterbuch der deutschen Sprache.* Berlin: de Gruyter. 20th ed.
Markey, T. L. 1981. Diffusion, fasion and crealization: a field guide to developmental linguistics. *Papiere zur Linguistik* 24. 1. 3 - 37.
Pokorny, Julius, 1959. *Indogermanisches etymologisches Wörterbuch.* Berne-Munich: Franke Verlag.

Puhvel, Jaan. 1973. Nature and means of comparison in Proto-Indo-European grammar. *Journal of Indo-European Studies* 1. 2. 145 - 54.
Seiler, Hansjakob. 1981. *POSSESSION as an operational dimension of language*. (Arbeiten des Kölner Universalien-Projekts, Nr. 42.). Cologne: Institut für Sprachwissenschaft.
Stang, Christian. 1966. *Vergleichende Grammatik der Baltischen Sprachen*. Oslo: Universitetsforlaget.
Vries, Jan De. 1962. *Altnordisches etymologisches Wörterbuch*. Leiden: E. J. Brill. 2nd ed.

DIACHRONIC MORPHOLOGIZATION:
THE CIRCUMSTANCES
SURROUNDING THE BIRTH, GROWTH, AND
DECLINE OF NOUN INCORPORATION

MARIANNE MITHUN

A large number of geographically and genetically diverse languages share a powerful morphological process kwnown as noun incorporation. The process compounds a verb stem with a noun stem to yield a complex verb stem, like So:ra: *tem-* 'sell' *+-jo:-* 'fish' > *tem-jo:* 'fish-sell'. It has often been assumed that lexical constructions were merely arbitrary formal alternatives to the syntactic rules of more analytic languages. All languages with noun incorporation, however, invariably contain syntactic analogues to such constructions as well. If we know, for example, that one can say in So:ra:, *tem-jó-te-n* 'she fish-sells', then we can correctly predict the existence of a grammatical sentence something like *ɔjó:n tém-te* 'she sells fish'.

It is well known that languages do not tolerate perfectly equivalent alternatives for long. The morphologization involved in noun incorporation must be functional, or else it could not coexist so systematically beside its syntactic counterparts. In fact, an examination of the process across languages indicates that speakers always incorporate for a reason. The reason is not always the same, however. Incorporation is used for four different, but related functions. The functions fall into an implicational hierarchy, which in turn indicates the path along which the process evolves in language.

1. Type I: Backgrounding within the Predicate

If a language shows any incorporation at all, it will contain basic lexical compounds. Lexical compounding is always done for a reason. It is a means of creating a unitary lexical item to represent a nameworthy, unitary concept. In English, for example, *grocery-shopping* and *ditch-*

digging have an institutionalized, nameworthy status that compounds like *penshopping* and *basement-digging* lack.

The kind of compounding termed incorporation, in which a noun stem and verb combine to form a complex verb stem, has a significant effect on the noun involved. Incorporated nouns do not refer. Rather, they qualify the host verb. If I tell you that I am going grocery-shopping, I am not referring to particular groceries, but rather qualifying the type of shopping I plan to do. Because they do not refer, nouns in such compounds are not normally associated with markers of definiteness or number. I would not say, for example,

(1). *I am going $\begin{bmatrix} \{ \begin{smallmatrix} \text{some} \\ \text{the} \end{smallmatrix} \} \end{bmatrix}$ groceries shopping.

Incorporated nouns also have no syntactic status as clausal arguments, although they may qualify the semantic patient, instrument, or location of their host verb. For this reason, they bear no case markers.

The degree of cohesion between the constituents of the compounds is primarily a function of the overall morphological character of the language. In more analytic languages, the noun and verb may retain their formal identity as separate words, although they function syntactically and semantically as a single unit. In more synthetic languages, they fuse immediately into a single word so that in many cases, even speakers are unaware of the precise boundaries between the constituents.

1.1. Composition by Juxtaposition

Kusaiean, a Micronesian language, contains a large number of verb-object or 'incorporated object' constructions. The verb and noun remain separate words, but behave as a single constituent syntactically and semantically. Compare the two sentences below.

Kusaiean	(2)a.	Nga	twem	mitmit	sac.
Micronesian		I	sharpen (tr)	knife	the
Lee 1975		'I am sharpening the knife'.			
	(2)b.	Nga	twetwe	mitmit.	
		I	sharpen (intr)	knife	
		'I am knife-sharpening'.			

The phrase *mitmit sac* 'the knife' in 2a functions as a direct object, so it appears with the transitive form of the verb *twem* 'sharpen'. In 2b, however, the noun *mitmit* is not an argument of the sentence at all, but rather qualifies the verb. The verb thus appears in its intransitive form *twetwe*. Lee notes, "The derived intransitive verb *twetwe* can be used to refer to all sorts of sharpening. It can be used with regard to sharpening a knife, a pencil, an ax, or anthing that can be sharpened ... The included object restricts the range of potential reference of a verb". (1975:277)

Since the incorporated object is not referential, it cannot be accompanied by markers of definiteness or number.

(2)c. Nga   twetwe   mitmit   sac.
     I   sharpen tr   knife   the

The intransitive status of the verb-noun compounds is confirmed by the form of instrumental and nominalizing constructions. An insrumental suffix *-kihn* can occur with intransitive verbs but not transitives.

(3).   taptat 'to take out' (intr)
        taptapkihn 'to take out with'
        tahpuhk 'to take out' (tr)
        *tahpuhkkihn

The *-kihn* can be suffixed to incorporated object constructions, just like intransitives.

(4).   taptap kaki kihn 'to take out coconut meat with'

Transitive verbs require a nominalizing suffix when functioning as nominals.

(5)a. Sah el twem   mitmit   sac   ke   yot   se.
     Sah he sharpen (tr) knife   the with stone a
     'Sah is sharpening the knife with a stone.'

(5)b. Twem*iy*en   mitmit sac ke   yot   se
     se sharpen-*nom*-cnt knife   the with stone   a

        sel Sah ah arlac pathlac.
        by Sah the very longtime
     'Sah's sharpening of the knife took a long time'.

Intransitive verbs can serve as nominals with no change in form.

(5)c. Twetwe   lal Sah ah arulac wo.
     sharpen (intr) clsf Sah the very   good.
     'Sah's sharpening is very good'.

Incorporated object constructions, like intransitive verbs, can serve as nominals just as they are.

(5)d. Sah   el   twetwe   tuhla.
      Sah   he   sharpen (intr)   ax
      'Sah sharpens axes.'

(5)e. Twetwe   tuhla lal   Sah ah arulac wo.
      sharpen (intr)   ax   cllsf Sah the very good.
      'Sah's ax-sharpening is very good'.

Although the verb and noun remain separate words, a number of facts reflect their formal bond. Directional suffixes like *-lah* 'away', often used as aspectual markers, immediately follow transitive verbs.

(6)a. El   twem*lah*   mitmit   sac.
      he   sharpen-*away*   knife   the
      'He has sharpened the knife'.

In incorporated object constructions, however, such markers follow the entire verb-noun complex.

(6)b. El   twetwe   mitmit*lac*.
      he   sharpen   knife-*away*
      'He has knife-sharpened.'

(The alternation in form between *-lah* and *-lac* represents the effect of vowel harmony. The sequence ah is used orthographically to represent [æ], while the sequence ac is used for [ɛ].)

Manner adverbs, including the interrogative *fuhkah* 'how', can appear before the object of a transitive verb.

(7)a. El   twem   *upac*   mitmit   sac.
      he   sharpen (tr)   *diligently*   knife   the
      'He is diligently sharpening the knife'.

(8)a. Kom ac   twem   *fuhkah*   mitmit   sac?
      you will   sharpen (tr)   *how*   knife   the
      'How will you sharpen the knife'?

In incorporated object constructions, however, the adverbs cannot separate the verb-noun unit; they must follow it.

(7)b. El   twetwe   mitmit   *upac*.
      he   sharpen (intr)   knife   *diligently*.
      He is diligently knife-sharpening'.

(8)b. Kom ac   twetwe   mitmit   *fukhah*?
      you will sharpen (intr)   knife   *how*
      'How will you knife-sharpen?'

A large number of languages follow this pattern. A verb stem and noun stem are juxtaposed to form an especially tightly bound constituent. Although the constituents retain their separate identity as phonological words, the construction functions as a unit syntactically and semantically.

1.2. Morphological Compounding

In Lakhota, a Siouan language of South Dakota, nouns may be compounded with verbs to denote institutionalized, nameworthy activities.

Lakhota   (9).   chą-lé
Siouan   wood-gather
Redbird p.c.   'to gather firewood'

                (10). chą-pá-ile
                       chą-pá-ile
                       'to make fire with a fire drill'

As in Kusaiean, the nouns do not refer to specific entities, such as particular logs. They lose their individuals salience with their syntactic role, and simply qualify the type of action denoted by the compound.

Compounds are very likely to change in meaning over time because they do constitute complete lexical items. The compounds below were provided by Boas and Deloria in 1939 with the first glosses listed. Ella Deloria, a Lakhota speaker herself, was born late in the nineteenth century. The second glosses were provided by an excellent but much younger speaker, born in 1957.

Boas and   (11). pte-'átųwą
  Deloria   buffalo-look for
  1939/   'to scout for buffalo' > 'to round up cows'
Redbird
  p.c.   (12). pte-kté
  (1983)   buffalo-kill
                       'to kill buffalo' > 'to slaughter cattle'

In Lakhota, incorporated nouns behave as part of the verb with respect to phonological processes. Stress regularly falls on the second syllable of Lakhota words (with certain well defined exceptions). As can be seen above, the incorporated nouns enter into the determination of stress.

Word-internal phonological processes also operate across the noun-verb boundaries. Note the loss of final -*e* and subsequent shift of *t* to *l* in the incorporated noun below, for example.

Redbird   (13).   chąl-níyą   chąté 'heart'
p.c.   heart-beat
                      'he beats his wife'

                (14).   chąl-wášte
                      heart-good
                      'he is happy'

The examples above indicate the tendency toward semantic specialization of lexicalized compounds. Their meanings are not simply the sum of the meanings of their components. They are created as the names of specific concepts, so they are lexicalized with only a portion of their possible meaning.

Although such compounding may be a productive process, speakers are aware of which combinations exist, that is, have been lexicalized, and which are merely potentially grammatical.

2. Type II: Backgrounding within the Clause

A large number of languages with Type I incorporation, in which a verb and noun stem combine to form an intransitive verb, have a second type of incorporation as well. In this type, a verb and noun combine, as in Type I, to yield a unitary lexical item. The incorporated noun does not refer, but rather qualifies the verb. It has no syntactic status as an argument of the clause, and is unmarked for definiteness, number, or case. Unlike Type I compounds, however, constructions of this second type are not necessarily intransitive. Instead of reducing the valence of the verb, this type of incorporation permits another argument of the clause to occupy the case role vacated by the incorporated noun. The result is a lexical device for manipulating case relations within clauses.

In the late nineteenth century, Edward Horace Man found a large number of Type I compounds in Nicobarese, a Khmer-Nicobar Austro-asiatic language of India. They refer to institutionalized activities, and are often somewhat idiomatic.

Nicobarese (15). pem-omhòin
Khmer-Nicobar   drink-tobacco
Man 1888 - 9   'to smoke'

    (16). wi-lâyan-düe
        make-decorate-canoe
        'to have a canoe decorated with flags'.

A number of compounds, however, function to background one argument of a clause by incorporating it, while foregrounding another by advancing it to the case role vacated by the incorporated noun. Most of these compounds are transitive verbs whose surface direct objects would be oblique were it not for incorporation.

    (17). taiha-onglônga
        cut-neck
        'to behead'

    (18). kalōapa-mat
        tickle-skin/surface
        'to smear with turmeric'

    (19). wi-kentâng
        make-fence
        'to enclose'

Some of the Type II compounds are intransitive. Without incorporation their subjects would be oblique.

    (20). chē-kaletâk
        shiver-tongue
        'to stammer'

    (21). orēh-chakâ
        shead-face (N)
        'to proceed in advance'

Type II compounding thus provides lexical alternatives which allow the speaker to assign primary case roles to the most significant arguments under discussion.

3. Type III: Backgrounding within Discourse

A number of languages which show incorporation of Types I and II show a third type of incorporation as well. Languages with this third type share a set of interrelated characteristics, however, They are typically polysynthetic, with obligatory pronominal affixes within the verb. Since the pronominal affixes are usually sufficient for keeping case relations clear within the clause, external nominals are necessary only for initially identifying arguments, not for grammaticality. Such languages typically show a very high proportion of verbs to nominals in discourse. Perhaps for this reason, verbs in these languages typically carry much of the semantic load, that is, they usually bear markers for such tense, aspect, directional, voice, transitivity, etc. distinctions as the language systematically encodes.

Since case relations in such languages are established by pronominal affixes, word order is available for a different function. In these languages, it is generally exploited to manipulate the presentation of information. Constituents are ordered according to their importance to the discourse. New, significant information tends to appear near the beginning of the sentence, whether it be represented by nouns, verbs, adverbials, or some other type of constituent. Elements which are clear from context and not in special focus are simply not mentioned.

Often in these languages, verbs appear which would normally be qualified by the presence of a nominal argument, yet the particular nominal might represent known information or entities which are only incidental to the discourse as a whole. A separate nominal constituent referring to this information would inappropriately sidetrack the attention of he listener. The solution is incorporation. Incorporated nouns are not salient constituents in themselves, that would distract the audience and obstruct the flow of information. Their presence is sufficient, however, to narrow the scope of a verb. This third type of incorporation permits, then, the backgrounding of known or incidental information within discourse.

Tewa, a Tanoan language of New Mexico, shows all three types of incorporation. Numerous compounds denote institutionalized activities.

Tewa	(22).	ʿi-ʿa̢:gen-suwɛh
Tanoan		he-gruel-drank
Dozier 1953		'he drank gruel'

Harrington	(23).	ʿà-koŋ-hen^y impı̀ʾyè
1947		we-buffalo-hunting went
		'we went buffalo hunting'

It also contains compounds of Type II, in which the incorporation of one noun permits another to advance to a primary case role.

Dozier   (24). na-p̓oh-kê:mù:
                   he-skull-thick
                   'he does not learn rapidly'

Harrington (25). nà̧-tsí:-hè:
                   she-eye-sore
                   'her eyes were sore'

Tewa also makes use of incorporation to background known information in discourse. In the text below, the first time the hair is mentioned, it appears as a separate noun at the beginning of the sentence. The second time, it is still a separate noun, but no longer sentence-initial. The third time it appears, it is incorporated.

Harrington (26). ʼWę́m fóʼè: rı̧́ntcą́ę nų̀ʼ. nà̧:
                   hair me-throw   I

ʼòpíʼírí   ʼò:ʼų̧́ ą́ęndì   ʼòpíʼíríʼ.
there-to-   that-I-may-
where-you-are   climb

hèrì ʼì-ʼą̧nᵘų́kè: wę́m *fóʼè*:   ʼóntc ą̀ęnų̧ ...
and the-girl   ʼa *hair*   she/her-threw

Hèrìhòʼ   ʼìtcùðèʼìrì   ʼì-ʼą̧nᵘų́ké:
and-so   the-witch   the-girl

ʼó:-*fóh*wìðíˆ dèʼè   ʼìhè:rì ...
she/her-*hair*-throwing when ...

(And then the witch said to the girl...)
"Throw me a hair, so that I might climb up to where you are." So the girl threw her hair... And so as the girl was throwing it (the hair) to the witch', (she stuck a little stick into the middle of her head.)

Since so many different nouns could represent known information. Type III incorporation is usually distinguished by its high productivity. The resulting compounds are still lexicalized, however, and speakers recognize whether a particular combination actually exists in the language or is merely a potential word.

4. Type IV: Classificatory Backgrounding

A number of languages with Types I, II, and III incorporation, have a fourth type as well. This fourth type is in some ways a combination of the other three. Like all of them, it combines a noun stem and verb stem to derive a complex verb stem. The incorporated noun is not an argument of the sentence, but rather qualifies the verb. Like Type II, it does not necessarily lower the valence of the verb, because it can be used to derive transitive verb stems. Like Type III, it plays a significant role in the presentation of information in discourse, by permitting the backgrounding of established information. In this fourth type of incorporation, a salient entity can be first introduced with an independent noun phrase while a more general noun stem is simultaneously incorporated to narrow the scope of the verb. Once the argument has been thus identified, the generic, incorporated noun stem is sufficient to quality verbs in subsequent discourse.

Since relatively general nouns are incorporated for this purpose, a classificatory system often results. A well defined set of incorporable nouns becomes established, which imply sets of entities with certain properties, such as liquids versus flexible objects versus granular substances, of animals versus inanimate objects versus abstract entities.

Ngandi, an Australian aboriginal language of Eastern Arnhem Land, ahows all four types of incorporation. Numerous Type I compounds denote unitary events, activities, or states. In these constructions, verbs usually incorporate their semantic patients, although on occasion they incorporate instruments or locations.

Ngandi (27). ṇi-yul-mak-burkayi-yuŋ
Austrialian   Msg-person-good-really-abs
Heath 1978   'he is a well behaved person'

(28). gu-ja-daŋic-maṇiñ'-d-i-ni
BU-now-fire-make good-aug-refl-PCon
'it was burning well'

(29). ñaru-miṛ'-ñil'-bo-m
we/him-jail-confine-aux-past punc
'we locked him up'

The language makes considerable use of Type II incorporation. Ngandi is basically ergative, so subjects of transitive sentences appear in one case, the ergative, while objects of transitives and subjects of intransitives appear in another, called the nominative. Type II incorporation permits otherwise oblique arguments to assume nominative status.

The verb may be intransitive, as below.

(30). ñar-ga-loŋ-ŋutŋut
1pl.ex.-subord-head-thick
'we have headaches'

(31). ŋa-ganam-dam
1sg-ear-be closed up
'I am deaf'

The verb may be transitive, as below.

(32). Baru-ga-maŋa-gulk-d̠-i
3pl/3msg-subord-neck-cut-aug-past punc

ni-wolo ni-yul-ø-yun.
Msg-that Msg-aboriginal-nom-abs

'They hanged that aboriginal.'
('They nec-cut that aboriginal.')'

(33). Bu-wolo-yuŋ, na-ṛaŋ-guruŋ-gič-uŋ
BU-that-abs Fsg-his-mother in law-all-abs

ø-giban-yowk-da-ni ...   o-moyŋo'-du ...
3Msg/3Fsg-nose-apply-aug-pres A-red ochre-inst

'(The boy) rubs red ochre onto the nose of
his (prospective) mother-in law.' (Then, if
she bears a child, she will give it to her
(prospective) son-in-law.)

The primary case roles of the aboriginal and the mother-in-law can be seen from the pronominal prefixes on the main verbs, which show agreement with them.

The use of Type II incorporation in discourse can be seen below. The narrator is describing an emu hunt. The first mention of the emus is made with an independent noun. Thereafter, they retain nominative status because of appropriate choice of appropriate lexical compounds. The compounds introduce new entities without demoting the emus to a lesser case role.

(34).   ñar-ič-ŋa-čini   "A-wurpaṇ-gič
        1pl.ex.-mind-hear-pres A-emu-allative
        'We think, "I am going hunting for emus."

        ŋa-ṛuḍu-ŋ'. ñara-ja-waṇḍa-ṛič ...
        1sg-go-fut   1pl.ex./A-now-track-look for
        We go looking for tracks ...

        Ñar-ič-ŋa-čini   a-ja-ñawk,
        1pl.ex.-mind-hear-pres A-now-speak,
        We think we hear them talking.

        ñara-ja-yaŋ-gaṛu-ni.
        1pl.ex./A-now-voice-chase-pres
        We follow the sound of their voices.'

The nominative status of the emus can be seen in the pronominal prefixes at the beginnings of the verbs. The noun *wurpaṇ* 'emu' is of the A class. The final -*a*- of the pronominal prefix *ñara*- shows agreement with a noun of this class. *Waṇḍa* 'track' and *yan* 'voice' are of the GU class. Agreement with these would be shown by the pronominal prefix *nargu*- (>*ñaru-/ gu*).

The lexical choice is indeed functional. An alternative exists.

(35).   Gu-yaŋ-ø-yuŋ   ñaru-ga-gaṛu-ni.
        GU-voice-nom-abs 1pl.ex./GU-sub-chase-pres
        'We follow the sound of their voices.'

(Heath notes that the absolutive marker 'indicates that the constituent to which it is attached occurs in a sentential context as an argument (not as a predicate) but retains its formal autonomy-in particular, it is not incorporated into the verb as a compounding initial.' (1978: 49)

Ngandi also shows Type III incorporation, in which old information is backgrounded in discourse, in contrast to new information, which first appears in independent nominals. The passage below is taken from the account of the emu hunt cited earlier. When mention is first made of the legs of the emu, an independent (GU) noun appears clause initially. At the second mention, the legs appear later in the clause, because they are no longer in focus. At the third mention, they are incorporated.

(36).   Gu-ḍarpič-gi-burkayi   ñara-ga-yaw,
        GU-upper leg-loc-really 1pl.ex/A-sub-spear
        'We spear them right in the upper leg.

ñar-ga-wut,
1pl-.ex.-subord-throw spear
We throw spears

ñar-ja-ram-da-ni   gu-darpič-gi.
1pl.ex.-now-spear-aug-pr GU-upper leg-loc
and spear them in the upper leg.

bugan'! a-darpič-doŋk.
there!   A-upper leg-break
There! Their upper legs break.

Ngandi also shows the fourth type of incorporation. An independent noun may be used initially to introduce an entity, while a generic noun stem is simultaneously incorporated to qualify the verb. Thereafter, the generic stem alone is sufficient to qualify subsequent verbs in the discourse.

(37). Gu-na-ji-ri   gu-bata-jambaka'-wič-uŋ
       GU-that-kind-imm GU-com-can-having-abs
       'He drinks (liquid-eats) that kind of liquid

gu-jark-ø-yuŋ,   gu-na-ji-ñ-uŋ
GU-water-nom-abs GU-that-kind-ø-abs
in the can (i.e. beer) and that kind (in) the

gu-bottle-garngarŋ'-yuŋ   ni-bun-ŋu-čini.
GU-bottle-big-abs   3msg-water-eat-pres
big bottle (i.e. hard liquor).

The generic stems are classificatory, in that each can be incorporated in place of a semantic class of nominals. Heath notes that one pair of such classificatory nouns is found in a number of languages in the area. In Ngandi, the pair is -*bulku*- 'ripe or cooked object' and *diku* 'raw, potentially edible but not yet ready to eat objects'. After catching and cleaning the emu, the hunters in the narrative cited above put the body into an oven to bake. When it is done, they remove it.

(38). O-wolo   a-walŋa-yuŋ
       A-that   A-body-abs
       'Then we remove the (cooked) body

       ñara-ja-*bulku*-wiri'.
       1pl.ex./A-now-*cooked*-dig out
       from the oven.'

When incorporated in this way, the stem *ḍiku* 'raw etc.' is frequently extended to imply fallen, fainted, collapsed, unconscious, or dead persons. In the text cited below, a group has gone out looking for a certain man, who is first mentioned by name then referred to by pronominal prefixes during the search. When they find him, he is dead.

(39). baru-ja-ṇa-y   ṇi-ja-*ḍiku*-yo-y
3pl/3Msg-now-see-punc 3msg-now-*raw*-lie-Pcn
'They saw him lying (dead).'

(They made a coffin for him.)

baru-*ḍiku*-goṛt-i,
3pl/3Msg-*raw*-put in-past punc
They put it (the dead body) in,

baru-ja-*ḍiku*-ga-n-di,
3pl/3Msg-now-*raw*-carry-aug-pcon
then they carried it (the dead body),

baru-*ḍiku*-goṛt-i.
3pl/3msg-*raw*-put in-past punc
they put it (the dead body) in.

(They went along with horses. Then they thought, "Well, we will not do it this way, we will get a boat.")

mala'-ič-wolo ṇi-ni-ñ-uŋ   ṇi-yul-yuŋ
at that time Msg-that-ø-abs Msg-man-abs
Then we will get that (dead)

ŋaru-ga-mi-yaŋ ṇi-ni-'-yuŋ
1pl.in/3msg-sub-get-fut Msg-this-ø-abs
"man and take him (back)."

ŋaru-ja-*ḍiku*-ga-n,
1pl.in/3Msg-now-*raw*-carry-fut

baru-ja-ga-ŋ, police station   ṇa-ki-ñ
3pl-3Msg-now-carry-past punc p.s. there
They took him then, they took him (the dead

baru-ga-*ḍiku*-wal-kubu-ŋ.
3pl/3Msg-sub-*raw*-enter-caus-past punc
man) into the police station.'

5. The Evolution of Incorporation

A comparison of noun incorporation across related languages indicates that incorporation is not simply present or absent from a language for all time. Many families contain some languages with incorporation and others without it, such as the South Munda family (Pinnow 1966), the Mayan family (Robertson 1980, Dayley 1981), and the Australian Aboriginal languages (Dixon 1980). The way in which such a process could arise is indicated by certain tendencies present in both incorporating and nonincorporating languages.

5.1. The Origin of Incorporation

Hopper and Thompson (1980) pointed out that there is a perceptible tendency in a number of languages for verbs and indefinite direct objects to coalesce. They cite examples from Hungarian, in which verbs with definite objects bear special transitive markers, while those with indefinite objects have none. A similar situation exists in Turkish. Definite direct objects precede their verbs and bear an accusative case marker.

Turkish   (40)a. Ahmet öküz-ü aldı.
Lewis 1967   Ahmet ox-acc buy-past
                     'Ahmet bought the ox.'

Indefinite direct objects normally bear no case marker at all. The *in*definite article *bir* 'one/a' is optional.

         (40)b. Ahmet (bir) öküz aldı.
                 Ahmet an   ox   buy-past
                 'Ahmet bought an ox.'

When the indefinite object marker is omitted, a generic reading is possible.

         (40)c. Ahmet öküz aldi.
                 Ahmet ox   buy-past
                 'Ahmet bought oxen.'
     or: 'Ahmet engaged in ox-buying.'

Such constructions are used exactly like the Type I compounds exemplified by Kusaiean. The noun, unmarked for definiteness or case, is not refential, but, instead, qualifies the verb, narrowing its scope to an activity directed at a certain type of object.

The nouns and verbs in these constructions retain their identity as phonological words, but syntactically, they behave as a unit. This fact is demonstrated by the position of focussed elements. The normal focus position in Turkish is immediately before the verb, as below.

Zimmer p.c.
(41)a. Bir çocuk kurd-u *sopa-ile* öl-dür-dü.
a child wolf-acc stick-inst die-caus-past
'A child killed the wolf with a stick'

In these special constructions, however, focussed elements cannot separate the noun-verb unit. They precede the entire compound.

(41)b. *Sopa-ile* kurd öl-dür-üyor-dü.
stick-inst wolf die-caus-hab-past
'He used to kill wolves with a stick.'

Turkish thus shows both the general tendency for verbs and indefinite directs to coalesce, and the exploitation of this coalescence for a backgrounding of the object to qualifier status.

5.2. The Development of the Process

Once basic noun-verb compounding becomes established in a language, the path along which incorporation can develop is indicated by the implicational hierarchy shown in sections 1—4. The fact that all languages with Type IV compounding also have Types III, II, and I, all those with III also have II and I, and all those with II also have I, suggests that the process evolves in ordered stages. It probably begins as in Turkish, with the coalescence of frequently occurring noun-verb combinations. The combination of a noun and verb stem becomes a productive mechanism for creating new intransitive verbs to denote nameable activities or events. The incorporated noun loses its individual salience within the predicate and simply narrows the scope of the verb (Stage I). Once this process has become established, it may be extended to background nouns within a clause, while advancing an otherwise oblique argument into the primary case role vacated by the incorporated noun (Stage II). In polysynthetic languages of a specific type, the process may be exploited still further to background nouns representing old information in discourse (Stage III). Finally, the development of the process may advance one more step. As a larger set of nouns come to be backgrounded for the various purposes outlined above, a special set of generic nouns becomes established, which are incorporated in place of more specific nouns (Stage IV).

The fact that the hierarchy has diachronic reality is confirmed by a comparison of genetically related incorporating languages. Most families contain an assortment of languages with varying repertoires of incorporation types. Mayan, for example, contains languages with no incorporation, such as Ixil and Aguatec (Robertson 1980), languages with only Type I, such as Kanjobal, Mam, and Chuj (Dayley 1981), and at least one language with both Types I and II, Yucatec (Bricker 1978). The Australian languages include some with no incorporation, such as Dyirbal (Dixon 1972), some with productive Type I, such as Walmatjari and Yir-Yoront (Dixon 1980), some with Types I and II, such as Pitta-Pitta (Blake 1979) and Guugu-Yimidhirr (Dixon 1980), and still others with productive Types I, II, III, and IV, such as Ngandi and Gunwinguu (Oates 1964). The Siouan family, which contains numerous languages with Type I compounding, such as Lakhota, is distantly related to the Caddoan family and to the Northern Iroquoian languages, all of which show Types I, II, III, and IV incorporation.

6. Decay

Once incorporation begins to develop in a language, is it destined to evolve along this path without interruption? If such were the case, all languages should have reached Stage IV by now, and exhibit all types of incorporation. A comparison of the productivity of the process across languages indicates that its development can be arrested at any point.

6.1. Decay at Stage I

When the development of incorporation ceases at Stage I, a language is simply left with an ever shrinking pool of lexical compounds. Speakers stop creating new ones, and, as time passes, the repertoire of existing compounds grows steadily smaller due to natural processes of lexical replacement. The compounds that remain become increasingly opaque. Phonological change obscures the forms of their constituent stems, semantic change, which operates on compounds as unitary lexical items, obscures the semantic relationship between free and constituent stems, and lexical change obscures the identity of the constituents, as their free cognates are replaced by new words.

Kharia, a Munda language of India, provides an example of such a state. Although verb-noun compounding is no longer productive in this language, a few relics remain of an earlier productive period in which verb stems were compounded with noun stems implying certain patients or instruments.

Kharia Munda Pinnow 1966	(42).	gu'j-te wash-hand 'to wash hands'
	(43).	gu'j-ḍa' wash-water 'to wash (using water)'

In all lexical items, a certain amount of phonological assimilation is likely to take place over time. The compound below shows this trend.

(44). gujuŋ (<gu'j-juŋ)
wash-feet
'to wash feet'

6.2. Decay at Stage II

When the development of incorporation in a language is arrested at Stage II, the results are similar to those left by decay at Stage I. Speakers no longer create new combinations, so the pool of compound lexical items slowly shrinks over time, and the remaining compounds become increasingly opaque due to normal processes of phonological, lexical, and semantic change. The compounds are of two types, however: those which simply combine a verb and patient, instrument, or location to form a unitary intransitive verb denoting a unitary concept, and those which affect case relations within the clause.

Kunjen, an Australian language, shows only very slight traces of incorporation. None at all was apparent in the texts collected by Sommer (1972), but he cites a few compounds in his grammar. Note how idiomatic the Type I compounds are below.

Kunjen Australian Sommer 1972	(45).	or arṭe- cold/dew — cook/burn 'to singe the hair or fur off a dead animal, or heat a spear rod to straighten it'
	(46).	adnd-ambi- interception-steal 'to hide'

The Type II compounds he cites are somewhat more transparent, although still specialized semantically. Many involve body parts.

(47). eg-erŋa-
head-scrape
'to sharpen the end'

(48). eg-urñḍa
head-bump
'to batter to death'

(49). aŋaŋal-afa-
image-fetch
'to photograph'

6.3. Decay at Stage III

Decay at Stage III is much like that at Stages I and II. A large store of compound lexical items exists for backgrounding entities within a predicate, a sentence, or discourse. At a certain point, speakers cease creating new combinations, however, although they continue to use the existing ones. Normal processes of phonological, lexical, and semantic change reduce the transparency of the existing compounds, and over time, lexical replacement diminishes the stock of compounds of all types.

Kamchadal, a Chukotko-Kamchatkan language of Siberia, showed signs of such a state when W. Jochelson recorded texts in 1900. A few compounds of Types I and II remain to show that such compounding was once a productive process.

Kamchadal (50). tkaɬxaɬqazáɬkecan
Chu-Kam   I-arrow-make-shall
Worth 1961   'I shall arrow-make'

(50). qazwoŋtnoke
nettle-gather
'to gather nettles'

Type III incorporation is extremely rare in texts. Most texts show none at all. One rare example from Jochelson's texts involves the noun *caxl*- 'feast'. Ememqut manages to get married. When he brings his wife home, he fixes up the house, then decides to arrange a feast.

Kamchadal (52). Hácyeq Emémqut *cález* ksqázoan.
Worth 1961 began Ememqut *feast* to arrange
'Ememqut began to arrange a feast.'

During the feast, however, he becomes angry with his wife.

Cáxłez ktkílın.
feast was abandoned
'The feast was abandoned.'

The wife returns to her parents. After a long time, Ememqut begins to think of his wife again, and goes to see her. At first he is not let in, but after he works for his father-in-law for six years, his wife is returned to him. The pair return to their house and Ememqut again arranges a feast.

Ténaq k*cáx*qazoknan.
again he-*feast*-arranged
'Again he arranged a feast.'

This time the feast is old information, so it is backgrounded by incorporation. The extreme rarity of such discourse manipulation indicates that Type III incorporation is no longer a productive process either.

A number of facts indicate that both the creation of such complex lexical items and their manipulation are relatively difficult operations. The use of common Type I and II compounds does not appear to be especially difficult. They are simply learned as lexical units and are used as such. The use of incorporation to background information in discourse appears to be somewhat more difficult, however. Usually a much larger repertoire of combinations is involved, and perhaps some sense of their internal structure.

Type III incorporation appears to be one of the last linguistic skills to be acquired by children. Children learning Mohawk as a first language still do not use incorporation for discourse purposes as late as age six, although by this age they have mastered most of the complex morphology and order constituents appropriately according to their importance to the discourse. (Mithun ms.) Young adult native speakers of Mohawk who prefer English, and use it more often, tend to use compounds of Types I and II almost as often as other speakers, but use Type III incorporation considerably less than older, admired speakers. In fact, perhaps the most salient feature of the speech of highly respected speakers is the high frequency and wide variety of such incorporation. Parks has reported that in Pawnee, 'Younger speakers incorporate nouns much less than older speakers; in fact, whenever it is optional, younger speakers usually do not incorporate.' (1976: 250)

Conversely, the creation and use of Type III compounds appears to be on of the most fragile aspects of polysynthetic languages. It appears to be one of the earliest processes to disappear in the course of language loss. Comparison of a dying dialect of Cayuga, in Oklahoma, with a thriving dialect in Ontario, showed that one of the most salient differences was the degree of synthesis used, and especially the amount of incorporation. The speaker of the moribund dialect used a few very common compounds of Types I and II, but did not tend to use incorporation to background established information in discourse. (Mithun and Henry ms.) Weltfish noted such a tendency in Pawnee as well. 'The rapid disintegration of the langage presents a dismaying spectacle ... In the simplified dialect now so commonly spoken many of the modal distinctions are neglected and the process of noun incorporation almost wholly disregarded ... The dominant tendency of classic Pawnee to compound and integrate ideas into one complex is also falling into disuse. Conversations with older people indicate that this type of integration has a very real aesthetic value for speakers of the older language.' (1937: vi) Comrie noted a similar trend in modern Chukchi, another Chukotko-Kamchatka noted a similar trend in modern Chukchi, another Chukotko-Kamchatkan language. 'With respect to incorporation in Chukchi, it should be noted that while this syntactic device is very common in traditional tales, it is much less frequent in current writing, and virtually absent in translations from Russian, i.e. incorporation seems to be on the wane in the modern language.' (1981: 250) Incorporation is a fragile process.

6.4. Decay at Stage IV

When incorporation ceases its development at Stage IV, results are much like those left by earlier decay. Compounds remain which permit speakers to background entities within the predicate, the clause, and the discourse. A fourth type of compound remains as well, however. These are sets of classificatory verbs, whose form is determined by certain properties of their accompanying arguments. Over time, the pool of all of the compounds grows smaller, and their internal constituent structure more opaque, due to normal processes of phonological, lexical, and semantic change. Although no new classificatory segments are added to roots, new nominals which come into the language are still assigned to the appropriate class.

Haida, a Na-Dene language of British Columbia and Alaska, shows a limited set of basic noun-verb compounds.

Haida　　　　　(53).　L tc ǫ́anu-ga-da-gAn
Na-Dene　　　　　　　they *fire*-be-cause-temp
Swanton 1911　　　　　'they had fire'

More frequent than such incorporation, however, is the appearance of one of a set of classificatory elements in the position otherwise occupied by an incorporated noun, directly preceding the verb stem. Swanton notes, 'On account of the extended use of these classifiers, incorporation of the noun itself is comparatively speaking rare. It is here represented by the use of the clasifiers which express the subject of the intransitive verb, or the object of the transitive verb as a member of a certain class of things, the principle of classification being form.' (1911: 216) He lists 36 of these.

(54).　táia tc!îs-　L!　　　　　xid-ás
cranberries they *box*-pick up-participle
'They picked up a whole box of cranberries.'

(55).　tcǫ́tga　　　　lA la
ground squirrel　he it
　　　　t!a-lgŭ́l-s
flexible coiled object-go. around–participle
'He put a ground squirrel about her as a blanket.'

The classificatory segments are sufficient in themselves to qualify the verb if their implication is clear from context.

(56).　lA dAñ-k!ú-stA-sgoañ-añagani
he by pulling-*short obj*-stem-for good-tmp
'He pulled it (the spear) out for good.'

(57).　lA dañ-*gi*-dji-L xa-gAnAsi
he by pulling-*thin material*-stem-toward-past
'He pulled out the canoe.'

Sapir remarks (1915: 541) that several and perhaps all of the classifiers are old noun stems. Krauss adds that 'this is not obvious from the available data, though not improbable' (1968: 203) since they begin with consonant clusters similar to those beginning noun (and verb) stems.

7. Revitalization of a System

Once productive incorporation processes begin to decay, the system is not necessarily destined to disappear entirely. Remnants of incorporation processes frequently resurge as productive systems of affixes.

Koryak, a Chukotko-Kamchatkan language of Siberia, still had numerous examples of Types I, II, and III incorporation at the turn of the century, when Bogoras recorded a large corpus of texts. Type I compounds denote institutionalized, unitary concepts.

Koryak
Chu-Kam
Bogoras 1917

(58). *atta'm*-t vá-yk n
bone-spit out-3abs pres
'to spit out bones'

(59). *čil*- nm lulätik n
tongue-lick-past
'he licked with the tongue'

Type II compounds permit the promotion of otherwise oblique arguments to a primary case role, absolutive.

(60). *lawt* nt ykin
head-do something
'to wring the neck of'

(61). t -ma!ñ -*láwt* -p ktik n
I-much-*head*-suffer
'I have a headache'

Incorporation is also used in Koryak texts to background established information. The first time fire is mentioned in the sequence below, it is new and in focus, so it appears as a separate noun at the beginning of the clause. The second time it is established, so it is backgrounded by incorporation.

(62). 'Milhón qanalagátča.' Ga*milh*nálinat.
fire   bring out   they-*fire*-carry-dupst
'Bring out the fire.'   They carried it (the fire) out.

In the exchange below, the housetop and the cache are backgrounded at second mention.

(63). Éwañ, ʻYas: qaḷkaitɪñ gawyis: qíwa.ʼ
said, *housetop-to* (go and) eat something
ʻShe said, "Go to the upper storeroom and eat something."

Éwañ, ʻYáqk nau, nɪ*yas: qalqa*čáčaqenau.ʼ
said, what for? they-*housetop*-taste of
He said, "What for? Those provisions taste of the upper storeroom."

Éwañ, ʻOlh wét n gawyis: qíwa.ʼ
said, *cache-to* (go and) eat something
She said, "Go to the cache and eat something."

Éwañ, ʻYáqkinau, *nolho*čáčaqenau.ʼ
said, what for? they-cache-taste of
He said, "What for? Those provisions taste of the cache."ʼ

In his grammar of Chukchee (and Koryak), Bogoras (1922) also notes the existence of a set of derivational suffixes which, when added to nouns, form verbs. The suffixes add meanings such as ʻto eatʼ, ʻto fetchʼ, ʻto take off (clothing)ʼ, ʻto put on (clothing)ʼ, ʻto search for (as in hunting)ʼ.

(64). ith lhuykɪn ʻto eat whaleskinʼ
ithɪlh-ɪn ʻwhaleskinʼ

a'sóykɪn ʻto eat cooked fishʼ
á's- ʻcooked fishʼ

(65). qatap-ñɪt ykɪn ʻto catch winter fishʼ
qatáp ʻwinter fishʼ

ilvá-ñit ykin ʻto hunt wild reindeerʼ
ilva ʻwild reindeerʼ

The suffixes are used in discourse much as incorporation, to background established information. When a new topic is introduced, a separate noun used. Thereafter, it is bound. In the passage below, two magpies are criticizing Amamqut, who feeds on inappropriate food.

(66). A'ttay pná, qoyay pná, qoyáatvag lñón!
with dog's with reindeer reindeer hoof
inner skin inner skin

Got, títaq múyu mɪta'*ttayípn*ula?
off, when we we on *dog's inner skin* have fed?

Qunam nutak uíña anélh *y pn*uka.
even in the no not eating inner
country inner skin

Lígiqai mɪna'*ttayípn*ula.
much less we have fed on *dog's inner skin*.

'He is feeding on dog's inner skin, on reindeer inner skin. (He is consuming) a reindeer-hoof! Off! When have we fed on dog's inner skin? Even when wandering in the open we do not eat (reindeer) inner skin. Much less do we eat dog's inner skin.'

The suffix u/o (subject to vowel harmony), functions exactly like an incorporating verb. In fact, Bogoras provides no explanation of why he has chosen to term the set mentioned above suffixes rather than verb stems. Presumably, it is because they never appear without a preceding noun stem.

In general, languages with well developed, productive incorporation have some verbs which do not incorporate, usually for semantic and pragmatic reasons, some which may or may not, depending on context, and some which never appear without an incoporated noun. Verbs in this last category are usually rather wide in scope, and take much of their meaning from their associated arguments, such as 'to be nice', 'to consume', etc. Because they require qualification to narrow their scope, they become constituents of a large set of lexicalized compounds. At some point, either phonological changes obscure the relation between their incorporating and their independent forms, or their independent form disappears from the lexicon, through normal processes of lexical replacement. The result is a set of verbs like those mentioned above, which appear only in compounds. (Bogoras 1922 points out the similarity between the suffix -*u* 'eat' and the verb *yu/nu*.) Speakers continue to form new compounds by analogy to the existing ones, and a system of affixation develops.

A number of languages have developed extensive systems of affixation which function much like the incorporation of other languages. Some especially good examples of such languages are several families in the

Pacific Northwest (Washington State and British Columbia), such as Wakashan (Nootka, Nitinat, Makah, Kwakiutl, Bella Bella), Chemakuan (Quileute, Chemakum), the numerous Salish languages, Kootenai, and Kathlamet.

Swedesh (1948) noted over 400 suffixes in Nootka alone. In modern Nootka stems are clearly differentiated from suffixes both positionally and phonologically, although semantically, the difference is much more subtle. Pairs exist like the stem *hawa* and the suffix -'*is*, both meaning 'eat', or *mak* -/-*Ha* 'buy'.

Of course numerous stem-suffix combinations denote conceptually unitary activities or events.

Nootka (67). tas-i : l
Wakashan   trail-make
Sapir and   'making a trail'
  Swadesh 1939

Numerous combinations similar to Type II incorporation also exist.

(68). čaḥ-o : λ
      cut with an adze-(on) face
      'they become wrinkled faced'

(69). 'oyi wikqo: to : to : h-čap-i : k
      so that they might not head-sore-given to
      'so that they might not always be headsore'

The suffixes are used much like Type III incorporation to background established information in discourse. New topics are introduced by separate nouns. Thereafter, they appear bound.

(70). čiči'aλatwe'in čiyop 'o'i-h'aλatok.
      his now, it is *intestines* now they were
      said, began to cut after his

      'owi : we' in čisna : kšiλ p̓a : im.
      he was first get to have chiton
      it is said   *intestines*

      'ah' a : 'aλ hiyiqtop hinin'aλ či-ỳi : ḥ'aλ.
      thereupon all kinds now came were after
      now   of animals   *intestines*

'Then they began to cut his intestines, which they were intent on getting; the Chiton (a mullusk) was the first to get intestines. All kinds of animals came to get intestines.'

Nootka also makes use of affixation reminiscent of Type IV incorporation. In the sentence below, the noun base classifies the predicate while an external noun identifies the actual patient.

(71). *naẏaqnakši'aλ   me'iλqac'isok.*
child-have-now   *little boy of* (her)
'She gave birth to a little boy.'

Affixation in Nootka thus serves essentially the same types of functions as incorporation in other languages. It provides a means of backgrounding entities within a predicate, within a clause, or within discourse. Is there any evidence of a diachronic connection between the suffix system and incorporation? In fact, there is. Although in most cases, stems and semantically related suffixes are not cognate, Sapir and Swadesh uncovered a set of stem-suffix pairs which are related, some within Nootka itself, others across neighboring languages Nootka and Kwakiutl, and others across neighboring but genetically unrelated languages Nootka and Quileute or Chemakum. Some have verblike meanings, while others are more like substantives.

Wakashan/   (72).   N. -p'ał 'smell'
Chemakuan   K. -p'ala 'smell',
Swadesh 1948   -pa 'taste'
                          peq 'to taste' (stem)

                          N. -mùt 'left over part'
                          mut- 'to bite off'
                          mutk 'to cut off'
                          K. -mut 'refuse'

Swadesh found the system quite productive. 'Although one finds a few obsolescent suffixes, most are in free and flexible use.' (1948: 118). He also suggested that the source of the suffixes were probably roots, as his data, cited above, indicate. 'It is not impossible that we have here in part the residue of an older structural stage when stems and suffixes were not so rigorously differentiated.' (1948: 118).

An older, decaying incorporation system can thus give way to a productive system of affixation. After a certain period of time, the relation between stems and affixes is no longer discernible, as in the Salish languages and Eskimo.

8. Conclusion

The foregoing sections have demonstrated that noun incorporation is not merely an arbitrary formal alternative to syntax. Rather, it is a type of functional morphologization. In all cases, speakers use incorporation for a reason. It permits the backgrounding of entities with respect to a predicate, a clause, or a portion of discourse.

The process originates, develops, and fades, according to a predictable pattern. It first arises from a general tendency in language for verbs and their indefinite direct objects to coalesce. At this first stage, incorporation consists essentially of the combination of a verb stem and noun stem to derive an intransitive verb stem denoting a conceptually unitary activity or event. The incorporated noun loses both its semantic salience and its status as an argument of the sentence. It is backgrounded to qualifying status within the verb. Once such a process has become established within a language, it may develop into a second stage. As one noun is incorporated into a verb, another may be promoted into the case position it has vacated. Such a process provides a mechanism for advancing an otherwise oblique argument into a primary case role. While it backgrounds one argument within the clause, it foregrounds another, more significant one by allowing it to assume subject or direct object status. Once this second stage has become established, the process may evolve still further. Incorporation may be used to background known or incidental information within discourse. Incorporation at this state is generally characterized by its especially high productivity, since a large repertoire of nouns can represent established information. Finally, once the process has become a productive mechanism for the arrangement of information in discourse, a fourth type of incorporation may evolve. Relatively generic noun stems may be incorporated in place of sets of more specific nominals. When an entity is first introduced, a generic noun may be incorporated to qualify the verb, while a separate more specific external noun phrase identifies the argument. Thereafter, the incorporated generic noun is sufficient to qualify subsequent nouns and retain the entity within the sphere of discourse.

Differences in the productivity of incorporation in various languages indicate that the development of the process may be arrested at any point. Languages in which this occurs are simply left with an ever diminishing pool of compounds of the types that were once productive. These relic forms become increasingly opaque over time due to natural processes of phonological, lexical, and semantic change.

Once incorporation is no longer productive, the system is not necessarily destined to disappear entirely. Frequently noun or verb roots which were once especially productive in incorporation, and therefore appear as constituents of a large number of relic compounds, develop into productive affixes with functions much like those they assumed during incorporation. They serve to background established or incidental information within predicates, clauses, or portions of discourse.

I am especially grateful to Stanley Redbird, of Rosebud, South Dakota, for sharing his expertise on his language, Lakhota, to Mary Haas, for her comments on Nootka, to Karl Zimmer, for his comments on Turkish, and to Wallace Chafe for very useful discussion of an earlier draft of the paper.

REFERENCES

Blake, Barry. 1979. Pitta-Pitta. *Handbook of Australian languages*, ed. by R. M. W. Dixon and Barry Blake, 182 - 242. Canberra: The Australian National University.
Boas, Franz and Ella Deloria. 1939. *Dakota Grammar*. Memoirs of the National Academy of Sciences XXIII. 2.
Bogoras, Waldemar. 1917. *Koryak Texts*. American Ethnological Society V. 1922. *Chukchee*. Handbook of American Indian languages Part 2, ed. by Franz Boas, 631 - 897. *Bureau of American Ethnology Bulletin* 40.
Bricker, Victoria. 1978. Antipassive constructions in Yucatec Maya. *Papers in Mayan Linguististics*, ed. by Nora C. England, 3 - 24. Columbia: University of Missouri.
Comrie, Bernard. 1981. *The languages of the Soviet Union*. Cambridge: Cambridge University Press.
Dayley, Jon. 1981. Voice and ergativity in Mayan languages. *Journal of Mayan Linguistics* 2. 2. 3 - 82.
Dixon, R. M. W. 1972. *The Dyirbal language of North Queensland*. Cambridge: University Press.
　　 1980. *The languages of Australia*. Cambridge: University Press.
Dozier, Edward. 1953. Tewa II: Verb structure. *International Journal of American Linguistics* 19. 118 - 27.
Harrington, John P. 1947. Three Tewa texts. *International Journal of American Linguistics* 13. 112 - 6.
Heath, Jeffrey. 1978. *Ngandi grammar, texts, and dictionary*. Canberra: Australian Institute of Aboriginal Studies.
Hopper, Paul J. and Sandra A. Thompson. 1980. Transitivity in grammar and discourse. *Language* 56. 251 - 99.

Krauss, Michael E. 1968. Noun-classification systems in Athapaskan, Eyak, Tlingit and Haida verbs. *International Journal of American Linguistics* 34. 3. 194 - 203.

Lee, Kee-dong. 1975. *Kusaiean reference grammar*. Honolulu: The University Press of Hawaii.

Lewis, G. L. 1967. Turkish grammar. Oxford: The Clarendon Press.

Man, Edward Horace. 1888 - 9. A Dictionary of the Central Nicobarese Language. Delhi: Sanskaran Prakashak. [Reprinted 1975: K. M. Mittal.]

Mithun, Marianne. ms. The acquisition of polysynthesis. Presented to the annual meeting of the American Anthropological Association, Washington, D. C. 1982.

Mithun, M. and Reginald Henry. ms. Language moribundity: the incipient obsolescence of Oklahoma Iroquois. Presented to the 43rd International Congress of Americanists, Vancouver 1979.

Parks, Douglas. 1976. *A grammar of Pawnee*. New York: Garland Press.

Pinnow, Heinz-Jurgen. 1966. A comparative study of the verb in the Munda languages. *Studies in comparative Austroasiatic linguistics*, ed. by Norman H. Zide, 96 - 193. The Hague: Mouton and Co.

Ramamurti, G. V. 1931. *A manual of the So:ra: (or Savara) language*. Madras: Superintendent, Government Press.

Robertson, John S. 1980. *The structure of pronoun incorporation in the Mayan Verbal complex*. New York: Garland Press.

Sapir, Edward. 1915. The Na-Dene languages, a preliminary report. American Anthropologist, n. s., 17. 534 - 58.

Sapir E. and Morris Swadesh. 1939. *Nootka texts*. Special Publication of the Linguistic Society of America. Philadelphia: University of Pennsylvania.

Sommer, Bruce A. 1972. *Kunjen syntax: a generative view*. Canberra: Australian Institute of Aboriginal Studies.

Swadesh, Morris. 1948. A structural trend in Nootka. *Word* 4. 106 - 119.

Swanton, John R. 1911. Haida. *Handbook of American Indian Languages*, Part 1. ed. by Franz Boas. Bureau of American Ethnology Bulletin 40. Washington D. C.: Smithsonian Institution.

Weltfish, Gene. 1937. *Caddoan texts*. New York: G. E. Stechert.

Worth, Dean Stoddard. 1961. *Kamchadal texts collected by W. Jochelson*. The Hague: Mouton and Co.

FOR A DIACHRONY-IN-SYNCHRONY ANALYSIS

RUTA NAGUCKA

What is by Lyons (1977: 621) referred to as diachrony-in-synchrony is somehow narrower a concept than I am going to use in this paper. For him the languages of two or three generations spoken within the same speech community during the same span of time can be noticeably different (and usually are): 'at any one time, certain forms, lexemes or expressions will strike the average member of the language-community as old-fashioned and ... other forms, lexemes or expressions may strike him as new and not fully established'. It is in this sense that diachrony enters into synchrony. But this is just a starting point of what I understand by this term; I shall argue that it is not only 'old-fashioned' structures used by the older generation that are synchronically relevant but also many other ones whose synchronic meaning and function can be better accounted for on the basis of their origins and history, although superficially they are not felt as clearly obsolete.

It is generally assumed that diachronic information should be irrelevant in the synchronic study of the language; the native speaker, taken to be a sufficient and often the only source of information, is usually unaware of historical aspects of a given structure or simply ignorant of them. What is of relevance to synchronic analysis is the native speaker's intuition, feeling, and introspection. According to current attempts to formalize all necessary information of this nature in order to explain a usual synchronic meaning of some structure, linguists often postulate, propose, suggest, etc. most sophisticated speculative hypotheses. As long as such hypotheses are formally successful and psychologically convincing little criticism should be expected of them. In practice, very few solutions have fulfilled these requirements, and few have satisfied all linguists even of the same theoretical orientation. Some kind of compromise offered by Hankamer (1977) seems to be a way out here. He claims that 'we must give up the assumption that two or more conflicting analyses cannot be simultaneously correct for a given phenomenon' (583—4). His main arguments are based on the assumption that the child while acquiring his language does not have any ability to choose between two conflicting analyses but that he 'constructs conflicting analyses'. His theory of multiple analysis has far-reaching consequences with respect to linguistic change in general and mechanisms of syntactic change in particular.

The concept of diachrony-in-synchrony in its modified wider sense and Hankamer's hypothesis of multiple analyses serve as an introductory background against which I shall try to show that diachronic interpretation of synchronic data can contribute to a better understanding of language and that a diachronic analysis supplementary to a synchronic one (conflicting though they may be) is a legitimate procedure.[1] I shall pursue these two points in the following sections by examining their implications in the syntactic analyses of such structures as:

(1) It is bad for him to smoke
It is wicked for him to smoke
It is usual for hats to be worn
... Saudi Arabian pressure was making it difficult for them to join the Sinai peacekeeping force (*Newsweek* March 1, 1982)
... it is all too easy for doctors to fall into cold and dehumanized approach to their practice (*Newsweek* March 1, 1982)
(2) I want very much for John to come[2]
I would like very much for John to come

The ModE structure *for-NP-to-V* as exemplified in sentences (1) and (2) has often been syntactically and semantically scrutinized to prove or disprove theoretical concepts of transformational grammar on the one hand, and on the other hand, to search for the best, intuitively acceptable, interpretations of the structure itself considered within the system of the language (obviously, the English language). These hypotheses differ

---

[1] I have adopted this approach in my previous research on obsolete syntactic constructions in English (forthcoming) and have found it rewarding.

[2] These sentences are quoted after Lightfoot (1977: 212); there are, however, occurrences of *want-for-NP-to-V* which do not seem to be fully acceptable in all variants of the language. 'Thus for many people (myself included), such examples as (7) and (8) are fully acceptable:

(7) we want very much [$_{\bar{S}}$ *for* [$_{-NP}$ pictures of each other] *t o be on sale*]
(8) the men expected [$_{\bar{S}}$ *that* [$_{-NP}$ pictures of each other] *would be on sale*]'

(Chomsky 1977: 73), while a sentence

He wants for me to leave

would not be used in British English (cf. Quirk et al. 1973:739).

sometimes in minor formal points, sometimes in basic assumptions. In the subsequent presentation I shall attempt to draw clear distinctions between the analyses of the *for-NP-to-V* pattern offered so far, and further, to consider any possibility for them to be integrated into a 'multiple analysis'.

Since Rosenbaum's doctoral dissertation on the grammar of English predicate complement constructions (1967) it has been customary to consider the *for-NP-to-V* as a complement sentence in the underlying structure. Starting with this concept Lakoff (1970: 128 ff.) was interested in showing that some verb and adjective complements are derived from the same deep structure and through the same rule; for example, out of the following

(3) I need to know that
(4) It is necessary for me to know that

o know that and *for me to know that* are both traceable to *it-for-I-to-know-that*. For Postal (1971) the underlying structure of the complement sentence is somehow taken for granted and what he elaborates is the rule called tough-movement which is responsible for the derivation of sentences such as:

(5) It was difficult for Tony to hit Jack
(6) Jack was difficult for Tony to hit

Postal also noticed the structural ambiguity of the *for-NP-to-V* structure so that a sentence like (5) could be understood either as

(5) a. It was difficult for Tony (to hit Jack)

or as

(5) b. It was difficult (for Tony to hit Jack)

The semantic difference between these two is 'real though subtle' and the ambiguity of 'a not understood type' (29). It seems that it was this point that made Chomsky analyse this construction within the specified subject condition (1973). However, Chomsky himself found this proposal unsatisfactory and in his article on wh-movement (1977: 102−3) suggests the following underlying structure

X is easy (*for us*) [$_{\bar{S}}$ *for PRO to please Y*]

for

(7) *John is easy* (*for us*) [*to please*]

It is essential for our further discussion to stress Chomsky's opinion of this solution when he says, 'Our assumptions lead us to suppose that each of the competing familiar analyses is in part correct: that is, X =John — the subject is generated in place — but there is a movemen' rule applying to Y, namely, *wh*-movement.' Thus for (7) we get

John is easy (for us) [s̄ [*who for*] *PRO to please t*]

In the same collection of articles, i.e. *Formal syntax*, still a different approach has been claimed: the tough-movement rule seems possible for Culicover and Wexler (1977: 43) only if the Binary Principle is adopted. I shall not go further into various other solutions; those mentioned so far have su+ced for our purpose, I hope.

As pointed out at the beginning, there are several ways to solve the problem of the derivation of the *for-NP-to-V* pattern, and there are several reasons of theoretical significance for which this construction has been investigated (e.g. wh-movement, traces and conditions on rules, variables in transformations, etc.). In all the proposals, however, *for* is treated as a complementizer and the structure itself as the complement, taken by a group of adjectives (*hard, tough, easy, difficult*, etc.) and verbs (*want, would like, hate, desire, prefer*). It has been observed that the structure is ambiguous. It should be borne in mind that all the views of the derivations of the *for-NP-to-V* type and all the assumptions which support these various hypotheses have been conceived to explain what seems to be an intuitively obvious meaning in contemporary situations. That none of the proposals is unquestionably satisfactory is not being denied. For the moment, we shall leave these synchronic considerations and turn to some proposals made from the diachronic point of view that are relevant to this question.

In his investigations of the origin of raising rules in English, Ard takes the example of the *for-NP-to-V* structure (*for-to* complements, according to him) to prove his point that the transformation used to derive these complements in Old English was different from the one used to generate the same type of complement in Modern English. In order to avoid this rather unwelcome solution that makes a linguist postulate two radically different transformations, one for Modern English and the other for some period in the past, that would account for 'similar surface structures with similar meanings' (1976: 3), he uses a modified form of Montague grammar and finds it rewarding. In conclusion he emphasized that one of the consequences of this reanalysis is a possibility of treating the whole *for-NP-to-V* complement as a single cinstituent unit. It seems that Ard's diachronic explorations have been undertaken to explain both old and modern aspects of the problem. Although not clearly stated, diachronic considerations enter unnoticeably into analyses of modern contemporary data.

Three months before Ard read his paper during the parasession on diachronic syntax, Lightfoot had presented his concepts at the Second International Conference on Historical Linguistics. These concepts focussed primarily on the base component and were illustrated by the use of the word *for* in the structure *for-NP-to-V*. Through an elaborate investigation taking into account a number of apparently disconnected changes, Lightfoot says that 'if we argue on historical grounds that the simultaneity of a set of changes occurring in the 16th century is accounted for by postulating a grammar treating *for* as a deep structure preposition, then it follows that the grammar of modern English must treat it the same way unless there is evidence of a later change whereby *for* was re-analysed as a COMP' (1976: 29). The discussion of *for* has been resumed by Lightfoot in his monograph *Principles of diachronic syntax* (1979: 186 ff.), the conclusion of his new arguments, however, being the same, i.e. that *for* 'has been a preposition throughout its history as a clause-introducer' (195). Also in this case diachronic information conditions, in a sense, an interpretation of the *for-NP-to-V* construction in Modern English, as far as the status of *for* is concerned. For simplicity of the exposition, I shall not mention other aspects no matter how important they are and only add that Lightfoot's views differ from those of Stockwell (1976: 32), who claims that *for* did become a complementizer. A kind of compromise solution is given by Visser when he says that *for* is a natural

> 'introduction to a complement to the verb, noun or adjective in the preceding *it*-phrase ... so that the syntactical unit in which it occurs can be apprehended as 'it is good for him, to go', and not as 'it is good, for him to go.' Among the later instances, however, there are a few in which it is possible that 'for him to go' is a close unit in which *him* is pre-eminently realized as the subject of the infinitive, and *for* is 'inorganic'' (Visser 1966: 968).

Withoug going into details of Visser's presentation of the problem under scrutiny it will suffice to point out that his interpretation and the historical data he has collected are widely employed in work of any historical linguist of English.

Throughout this section I have tried to show the variety of hypothetical solutions and the difficulty, if not the impossibility, of choosing between the competing analyses (Lightfoot 1979: 210) on the diachronic plane, which has also some interpretative significance for contemporary data.

How do we know, then, which hypothesis to follow? Or perhaps, what would make us decide that one is 'better' than the other? Such and similar questions seem unanswerable unless new, more adequate, textual data are provided as evidence for or against one of the hypotheses. Therefore, I shall try to test the plausibility of Hankamer's multiple analyses, making use of the results of diachronic and synchronic investigation supplementing them with my own observations and commentaries.

Putting together the main approaches presented in the previous sections we can distinguish two main trends: one is to analyse *for-NP-to-V* as a complement of sentential origin; the other is to treat *for-NP-to-V* as a prepositional phrase. The former dominates in synchronic studies of contemporary English; the latter seems to prevail in diachronic studies. In both tendencies, however, whether looked at from a synchronic point of view or from a diachronic point of view, the *for-NP-to-V* structure is assumed to be somehow ambiguous. Those who are for the complement view admit that a sentence like (1)

It is bad for him to smoke

can be also understood as

(1) a. To smoke is bad for him
b. It is bad for him — to smoke

with *for him*, a prepositional phrase, being a complement to the adjective *bad*. On the other hand, those who in principle advocate the preposition view do not exclude a possible restructuring of *for* as a complementizer. We can now extend either of the views through the integration of all the information provided by both analyses. It is conceivable that the sort of multiple analyses and interpretation will account for the intuition about this structure more adequately.

As a complement the *for-NP-to-V* construction is taken for a sentence which superficially may belong to usually encountered clause types (cf. Quirk et al. 1973:723); *for-NP* has a function of the subject, *to-V* is a nonfinite verbal predicate which may be followed by an object, adverbial, subject or object complement, depending on the verb class. The deep structure of such a clause-complement has been differently formulated, which is of lesser importance for the immediate purpose. If the structure under analysis is a transform of a deep sentence it should be semantically interpreted as such: in this way *for him to smoke* in sentence (1) would be meant to express the meaning *he smokes*. This is perhaps a fairly satisfactory explanation of *for-NP-to-V* when the structure is embedded into a sentence referring to present/past temporal relations, or rather referring to real situations something like

It's bad — he smokes = it is a bad thing that the smokes
It was bad — he smoked = it was a bad thing that he smoked

If a hypothetical condition is meant, then this interpretation is difficult to assume, e.g.

(1)c. It would be bad for him to smoke
It would be bad — he smokes (?) = *It would be a bad thing that he smokes

and we would rather understand (1)c. as

It would be a bad thing if he smoked

This brings us to assume that the interdependencies between the two clauses are very tight. This English structure, a superficially timeless proposition, is rendered into Polish as

Źle (jest), że pali[3] — It is bad for him to smoke
Źle (było), że palił — It was bad for him to smoke
Byłoby źle gdyby palił — It would be bad for him to smoke

where the translational equivalents do make temporal distinctions. This point is of considerable importance for the complement view interpretation: the complement clause derived from an underlying sentence would be temporally interpreted in accord with general laws operating on non basic sentences. It follows that the main clause, *it's bad*, *it's difficult*, *it's easy*, etc., expresses a kind of general evaluation of somebody's action, state, behaviour, etc., to the effect that the speaker evaluates the thing somebody does: I believe that what you do is {bad, difficult, easy ...}, in my opinion the fact that you do × is a {bad, difficult, easy ...} thing, I approve of ..., I disapprove of ..., etc.

What I am aiming at is to show that if we assume the complement view, the *for-NP-to-V* structure, derived from a deep sentence, should be liable to be paraphrasable into *that-S*, e.g. for (1) we would expect

It's bad that he smokes
It's wicked that he smokes
It's usual that hats are worn, etc.

---

[3] There are, of course, other semantic equivalents such as *palenie mu szkodzi*, *palenie jest dla niego szkodliwe*, etc. which are also formally distinct from their English counterparts.

Although some of the *that-S* sentences sound foreign to English ears and are hardly acceptable there are some adjectives which easily permit *that-S* complement as well as *for-NP-to-V* structure, for example

It is necessary that you should obey him
It is necessary for you to start at once

In the past the *that-S* construction is quite common and frequently encountered in such contexts as

(8) nys hit na god þæt man nime bearna hlaf and hundum worpe (Mt. 15.26 after Visser 1966:822) 'it is not meet to take the children's bread, and to cast it to dogs'
(9) Nu is þearf mycel,
þæt we fæstlice ferhð staðelien (Elene (426)
'Now there is much need (great need) to set our hearts firmly'
(10) hit gede(fe) bið, þæt mon his winedryhten wordum herge (Beowulf 3174) 'it is fitting that a man should extol his friendly lord in words'

to mention only OE instances. It is not only the structural shape of this clause, i.e. *that-S*, that is of interest but above all the use of the subjunctive. The introductory, main clause being evaluative in meaning 'expresses the speaker's attitude of mind concerning the activity in the subject clause by declaring it good, correct, advisable, desirable, probable, necessary, preferable, proper, just, fair, etc., or the reverse' (Visser 1966: 821). Because of well known processes the modally marked form in the *that-S* clause was fading into desuetude in the Early New English period. Later, the occasional uses of the subjunctive in such structures are considered stylistically marked and restricted to literary or dialectal variants of the language. It seems plausible that at the time the subjunctive was losing its ground because of the transparency principle being at work here, there was a tendency to substitute (not to restructure) *that-S* by *for-NP-to-V*, which construction in its structurally different shape functioned side by side with the *that-S* clause. Take for example the following OE sentences

(11) god ys us her to beonne (Mt. 17.4 after Visser 1966:955) 'it is good for us to be here'. Nis na god ðisum men ana to wunienne (Aelfric tr. Genesis 2.18 after Visser 1966:955) 'it is not good that the man should be alone' (cf. (8))
(12) us is mycel þearf to witenne (after Visser 1966:955) 'there is much need for us to know' (cf. (9))

(13) Ne is gilefed ðe to habanne lafe broðor ðines (Mk. 6.18 after Visser 1966:955) 'it is not lawful for thee to have thy brother's wife' (cf. (10))

In (11) through (13) the adjective is followed by a NP in the dative (functionally similar to later *for-NP*) and *to*+N (gerund) (much later restructured into the *to* infinitive). For a hypothesis that attempts to account for this complex change see Lightfoot (1977, 1979). It is easy to see that the two patterns have semantically much in common as in both the introductory adjective is of the evaluating type. There are, however, noticeable differences: in *that-S* the speaker concentrates more on somebody's activity which he qualifies as good or bad, correct or incorrect, etc.; in the dative construction the speaker is more concerned with the effect or the impact of the activity upon the experiencer. That this difference was not always taken as semantically significant is best illustrated by rendering a sentence in Mt. 17.4 which runs

it is good for us to be there

either by

(14) god ys us her to beonne (after Visser 1966:955)

or by

(15) god his þæt we her sie (after van der Gaaf 1904:5)

In Old English there is one more variant which in a sense combines that *that-S* clause with the dative, for instance

(16) God bið men ðæt he sie butan wife (Pastoral Care 397/17) 'It is good for a man to be without a wife'
(17) him is micel nie(d)ðearf þæt hie mid oftrædlicum gebedum ða scylde adiligien (Pastoral Care 397/14) 'it is very necessary that they efface the sin with frequent prayer'

In sentence (16) the meaning is very clearly expressed: the speaker says not only what according to him is good but also for whom this something is good. It is more specific than either of the preceding variants. It may also happen that an utterance is of a general maxim-like type in which neither the 'experiencer' of something nor the 'agent' of something is given. Structurally, in the introductory clause there is no NP in dative, and the evaluating adjective is followed by *to*+gerund, e.g.

(18) hit is god godne to herianne 7 yfelne to leanne (Bede 2/10) 'it is good to praise the good and blame the bad'

From the above examples it may be inferred that in Old English there are four formally different patterns used to express basically the same meaning with different degrees of the speaker's involvement in the act of evaluating. They are

a. Evaluating adjective *that-S* (subjunctive)
   god his þæt we her sie (15)
   (the fact that we are here is evaluated as good in general)

b. Evaluating adjective *to-N* (gerund)
   god ys us   her to beonne (14)
   (the fact of being here is evaluated as good for us)

c. Evaluating adjective *that-S* (subjunctive)
   god bið men   ðæt he sie butan wife (16)
   (the fact that a man is without a wife is evaluated as good for him)

d. Evaluating adjective *to-N* (gerund)
   hit is god   godne to herianne (18)
   (the fact of praising the good is evaluated as good)

It is within this general pattern, typical of Old English, that one may look for the explanation why there are two competing views: complement interpretation vs preposition intepretation. Now I should like to go into this problem in some detail and to show that the competition is only apparent, not real at all, and that the two hypotheses can be reconciled. Of particular importance is the fact that a structure like

(1) It is bad for him to smoke

might be understood either as *it is bad* ... or *it is bad for him* ... This observation made on different occasions (Visser, Lakoff, Stockwell, etc.) tacitly admits the complement view on the one hand and the preposition view on the other hand. Each interpretation can be traced back to its OE structural and semantic sources: in this way sentence (1) is interpretable as 'the fact that he smokes is bad', 'I, the speaker, believe that his smoking is a bad thing', and the like stating explicitly the speaker's evaluation of some event (his smoking), similarly to the intepretation of the OE *that-S* pattern (a) (and partly pattern (d)). What can be said about this thesis is that semantically the ModE and OE sentences seem to be very similar. If we accept that this is so the complement view would be then additionally grounded with the historical material. It might be argued, however, that semantic similarity is not a sufficiently convincing criterion in view of the formal differences: OE *that-S* — ModE *for-NP-to-V*. But in spite of these surface differences there is no conflict, it seems, between their corresponding deep structures.

The other interpretation of sentence (1), i.e. the preposition view, takes into account not so much the evaluation of something as such (this something is bad) but the evaluation of something with reference to somebody: 'smoking is bad for him', 'I assume (believe) that smoking is harmful to him (not necessarily to other people)', etc. It is this meaning that underlies the *for-NP* understood to be the preposition phrase, which hypothesis has been proposed and strongly defended by Lightfoot on the basis of a thorough analysis of the historical material.[4] Here again, OE examples can be adduced in favour of this interpretation, chiefly pattern (b) (and partly pattern(c)) in which dative referring to the person who 'is a goal' of the speaker's evaluation is explicitly expressed.

It would be interesting and worthwhile pursuing this problem further to show what were the principles and the mechanisms operating throughout the centuries which resulted in the changes responsible for the ModE shapes of the structure, if this were the main goal of the discussion. All that needs to be said in this connection is the fact that the process was active during the period of the vast majority of structural changes such as: the rise of modals as a distinct cateogry, the rise of the verbal infinitive, the disappearance of the subjunctive, etc. which incited in one way or another syntactic modifications. It is probably the case that all four patterns that were used in Old English are a source of the ModE *for-NP-to-V* structure. What is less obvious is the nature of the process which grammaticalized the old meaning in a new and different way.

Describing how the English language was in the past is but one of several aspects that have to be considered when analysing contemporary material. Diachronic facts (and hypotheses about them as well) have their own life and internal logic, as has been illustrated by the OE examples. Furthermore, the results of diachronic studies need not be in agreement with the results of synchronic studies on the same problem; both can be correct since both are derivable by differently motivated rules. Nevertheless, it may well be that the (conflicting) results are not

---

[4] The view taken here is not following Lightfoot's claims and his argumentation pertaining to the origin and the development of ModE *for-NP-to-V*; the principle idea, however, about the *for-NP* as the preposition phrase is his and in my opinion is of relevance to the problem at hand.

For a recent attempt to explain the rise of the *for-NP-to-V* construction see Fischer (forthcoming).

mutually exclusive but rather mutually complementary in the sense of multiple analysis proposed by Hankamer. If we are to capture all the aspects of subtle semantic regularities as well as idiosyncracies of contemporary structures a synchronic and diachronic treatment seems to be required. However conflicting the hypotheses may look, these are conflicts in which, it seems, you can split the difference: one side and the other, diachrony and synchrony, are going to win.

REFERENCES

Ard, Josh. 1976. Rebracketing in diachronic syntax and Montague grammar. *Papers from the Parasession on Diachronic Syntax*, April 22, 1976, ed. by Sanford B. Steever, Carol A. Walker, Salikoko S. Mufwene, 1—8. Chicago: Chicago Linguistic Society.

Chomsky, Noam. 1977. On wh-movement. *Formal syntax*, ed. by Peter W. Culicover, Thomas Wasaw, Adrian Akmajian, 71—132. New York: Academic Press.

Culicover, Peter W. and Kenneth Wexler. 1977. Some syntactic implications of a theory of language learnability. *Formal syntax*, ed. by Peter W. Culicover, Thomas Wasaw, Adrian Akmajian, 7—60. New York: Academic Press.

Fischer, Olga. Forthcoming. The rise of the *for NP to V* construction: an explanation. To appear in 1984 in a memorial volume for Professor Barbara Strang, ed. by G. Nixon.

Hankamer, Jorge. 1977. Multiple analyses. *Mechanisms of syntactic change*, ed. by Charles N. Li, 583—607. Austin: University of Texas Press.

Lakoff, George. 1970. *Irregularity in syntax*. New York: Holt, Rinehart and Winston.

Lightfoot, David. 1976. The base component as a locus of syntactic change. *Current progress in historical linguistics*, ed. by William M. Christie, Jr., 17—32. Amsterdam: North-Holland.

Lightfoot, David. 1977. On traces and conditions on rules. *Formal syntax*, ed. by Peter W. Culicover, Thomas Wasaw, Adrian Akmajian, 207—237. New York: Academic Press.

Lightfoot, David. 1979. *Principles of diachronic syntax*. Cambridge: Cambridge University Press.

Lyons, John. 1977. *Semantics*. 2 vols. Cambridge: Cambridge University Press.

Nagucka, Ruta. Forthcoming. *An integrated analysis of syntax and semantics of obsolete English constructions.*

Postal, Paul M. 1971. *Cross-over phenomena*. New York: Holt, Rinehart and Winston.

Quirk, Randolph, Sidney Greenbaum, Geoffrey Leech, Jan Svartvik. 1973. *A grammar of contemporary English*. London: Longman.

Stockwell, Robert P. 1976. Discussion on Lightfoot's paper (1976). *Current progress in historical linguistics*, ed. by William M. Christie, Jr., 32—34. Amsterdam: North-Holland.

Visser, F. Th. 1966. *An historical syntax of the English language*. Part 2. Syntactical units with one verb. Leiden: E. J. Brill.

SOURCES

Bede — *The Old English version of Bede's Ecclesiastical history of the English people*, ed. by Thomas Miller. Part I. 1. E.E.T.S. O.S. 95. 1959.
Beowulf — *Beowulf and the Fight at Finnsburg*, ed. by Fr. Klaeber. 3rd ed. Boston: D. C. Heath. 1950.
Elene — *Elene. An Old English poem*, ed. by Charles W. Kent. Boston: Ginn. 1889.
Pastoral Care — *King Alfred's West-Saxon version of Gregory's Pastoral care.* Part II. ed. by Henry Sweet. E.E.T.S. O.S. 50. 1958.
van der Gaaf — W. van der Gaaf. *The transition from the impersonal to the personal construction in Middle English.* Heidelberg: Carl Winter's Universitätsbuchhandlung. 1904.
Visser — F. Th. Visser. *An historical syntax of the English language.* Part 2. Syntactical units with one verb. Leiden: E. J. Brill. 1966.

ON THE POSSIBLE CLUSTERS OF mb, nd, AND g IN PROTO-JAPANESE

FRED C. C. PENG

Purpose

In 1975, when Nomoto reported that words like *obi* 'belt' in Tsuruoka all have a nasal quality vocoid preceding the obstruent, resulting in [ɔ~bi] and the like, I began to suspect, then, that there might have been at one time in the past a full-fledged nasal consonant that existed as a segment in the said environment in such cases, and that the pre-obstruent nasality as a homorganic nasal segment was probably much more prevalent in all dialects of Japanese than was hitherto reported, the Tsuruoka instances being merely the accidental 'discovery' of the remnants of such proto-nasals.

If I am to pursue this line of thinking, it means that some kind of reconstruction will have to be employed — a reconstruction that will establish the consonantism which will show that many single obstruents as in *obi* were indeed nasal-obstruent clusters in the past. The first method that could be utilized is of course the Comparative Method which would compare cognates from various dialects which have the pre-obstruent nasality in the forms compared. However, most scholars in Japan differ in their opinions regarding the phonetic nature of the nasality, although all of them agree that the pre-obstruent nasality exists in Tohoku (northeastern) dialects. As a matter of fact, evidence of the nasality can be traced back to as eaerly as 1932 when Ogura reported that in Sendai (a Tohoku dialect) people often nasalized the vowel preceding a voiced consonant, as in [kãdo] 'angle' and [ãbɯ] 'horsefly' (Ogura (1932:27), the equivalents (i.e., cognates) of which in the Tokyo (or other southern) dialects are devoid of the nasality. In view of this observation, it is rather difficult to reconstruct nasal-obstruent clusters on the basis of the comparison of nasalized and oral vowels alone. For instance, if I were to compare the following cognates, I do not think I could come up with any clusters other than saying that perhaps the nasalized and oral vowels were at best, at one time, members of the same nasalized phonemes, a conclusion that would certainly be hard to defend when other factors are taken into consideration.

Tohoku	Tokyo	English Gloss
ãbɯ	abu	horsefly
kãdo	kado	angle
ãgɯrɯ	agaru	to rise

It is for this reason that I have decided not to employ the Comparative Method for the time being — at least, until such time as the evidence of nasal-obstruent clusters is properly established.

This decision leaves me with two other choices; namely, documentary investigation and the Internal Reconstruction. I prefer to take the latter on the ground that the Japanese writing system is not apt to indicate nasality. The purpose of this paper, therefore, is to apply the method of Internal Reconstruction to a single dialect, viz., the Tokyo (standard) variety, where some cognates can still be found, in order to reconstruct the proposed nasal-obstruent clusters.

Internal Reconstruction

There are forms in standard Japanese that diplay the alternation of a consonant (usually a stop) and a cluster of the same consonant plus a homorganic nasal preceding it. In such instances, a morpheme boundary more often than not exists at the point where the alternation can occur. Examples follow:

First Morpheme	Second Morpheme	Resultant
me- 'female'	tori 'bird'	me-ndori 'hen'
o- 'male'	tori	o-ndori 'cock'
me 'eye'	tama 'ball'	me-ntama 'eyeball'

The hyphen in the resultant forms indicates the morpheme boundary in each case. In case there is doubt as to the accuracy of the morpheme cuts, let me point out that the morphs *me-* and *o-* (which function as prefixes) occur elsewhere without any change in shape, as in *me-su* 'female species' and *o-su* 'male species', which is to say that it is inconceivable to consider *men-* and *on-* as being the morphemic alternants of *me-* and *o-*, respectively. Thus, the morpheme boundary firmly identifies *-ndori* as the morphemic alternant of *tori*. By the same token, it might be plausible to establish *tama* and *ntama* as variants of the same morpheme, except that in the case of *me-ntama* 'eyeball' not only is the morpheme *me* 'eye' a free form (hence, a word by itself), as against the prefix *me-*

'female' which is a bound form (hence, not a word by itself), but also the /t/ phoneme in *tama* 'ball' does not undergo morphophonemic alternation (i.e., is not voiced as in the case of *tori* 'bird') in the environment given; however, elsewhere the /t/ phoneme of the same morph *tama* does undergo the same kind of morphohpnemic change, provided the environment is intervocalic, as may be evidenced by the following example: *ame* 'candy', *tama* 'ball', and *ame-dama* 'candy ball'. It follows that there is an alternative form for 'eyeball' which is *me*-dama wherein the same morphophonemic change (i.e., voicing of the /t/ phoneme) occurs. What this means is that there are now three allomorphs of the morpheme *tama* 'ball', viz., *tama, dama*, and *ntama*.[1]

So far, only cases with morphophonemic alternation at the morpheme boundary have been considered; in such cases, the alternation results in (1) the appearance of an extra nasal phoneme and/or (2) the voicing of an otherwise voiceless stop. But the alternation may be reversed in that a nasal segment disappears as a result of the addition of a morpheme at a distance. Examples of this nature are few but the following is an intriguing one:

ko-mbu 'seaweed' *tya* 'tea' *ko-bu-tya* 'seaweed tea'

All this suggests that the alternants in each instance are, historically speaking, allomorphs that descended from one and the same proto-form which is to be reconstructed. For the time being, the analysis below of the above mentioned morphemes will suffice:

Proto-form	Proto-form	Proto-form
╱ ╲	╱ ╲	╱ ╲
-bu -mbu	tama dama	tori ndori

If this analysis is essentially correct, it is of interest to observe that a similar kind of alternation occurs in forms that involve no morpheme boundary at the point of alternation. But more interesting is the fact that, these forms are doublets, which is to say that they are in 'free variation'[2] as it were. Examples are:

Single	*Cluster*	*English Gloss*
tabi	tambi	every time
tobi	tombi	jumping; flying
togaru	toŋgaru	to taper

---

[1] However, an alternative solution is to regard the /n/ segment as a c̲o̲n̲tracted form of *no* 'of'. Thus, *me-ntama* results from *me-no-tama* 'the ball of eye'.

[2] Sociolinguistically, there should not be any free variation. However, in the present context, free variation is taken to mean that native speakers are not conscious of any difference in meaning, although they may use the words on different occasions.

Such being the case, I am inclined to believe that the clustering of a nasal and an obstruent (wherein the nasal is assimilated to the obstruent) was a widespread phenomenon at one time in the past, so much so that in the light of the above analysis the sequence of *mb, nd,* and *ŋg* in modern Japanese must be regarded as the remnants of prevalent phoneme clusters that have undergone changes over the past centuries. To support this inference, let me offer two more examples as evidence: (a) *ta* 'rice paddy' vs. *ta-mbo* 'rice field' and (b) *tombo* 'dragonfly'. Note that in (a) there is a morpheme boundary, though no morphophonemic alternation is possible, that is, there is no such form as *ta-bo*, and that in (b) not only is there no morpheme boundary but also there is no 'free variant' such as *tobo*. The reason for this seemingly irregular pattern in sound change is, for the time being, not so important. The main point here is that the cluster is retained in those instances and that it has not changed (i.e., not denasalized) into an oral single obstruent as in the other cases.

So far, I have only touched upon certain evidence for a possible internal reconstruction of the three clusters. Let me now move on to the actual reconstruction itself. To do so, I shall rely on modern Japanese verb paradigms. Synchronically, Japanese verbs can be divided into two groups: (i) vowel verbs (cf. *tabe-ru* 'to eat') and (ii) consonant verbs (cf. *suber-u* 'to slide'). If the latter is further divided in accordance with the kind of consonant ending that goes with the verb stem, the following paradigms of eleven classes obtain:

	Non-past	Past	Negative Derivation
1.	kaø-u 'to buy'	kat-ta	kaw-a-nai
2.	kat-u 'to win'	kat-ta	kat-a-nai
3.	kak-u 'to write'	kai-ta	kak-a-nai
4.	tob-u 'to fly'	ton-da	tob-a-nai
5.	—	—	—
6.	tog-u 'to sharpen'	toi-da	tog-a-nai
7.	yom-u 'to read'	yon-da	yom-a-nai
8.	sin-u 'to die'	sin-da	sin-a-nai
9.	—	—	—
10.	kar-u 'to cut'	kat-ta	kar-a-nai
11.	sas-u 'to stab'	sasi-ta	sas-a-nai

Note that in (1) although the final consonant does not manifest in the non-past form, it appears in the negative derivation as /w/ which is a bilabial. Judging from the consonantism in the paradigms, especially with respect to stem-finals in (2) and (3), /w/ may be restored to $\hat{g}p$. Thus, the verb stem in (1) may be reconstructed as *kap- where ø in all modern forms of Non-past Indicative is the reflex of *p which has survived as /w/ in their derived negatives, such as *au* 'to meet' and *aw-a-nsi* or *iu* 'to talk' and *iw-a-nai*, but is assimilated to /t/ in the past form.

This much reconstruction, of course, is not enough to enable one to see the remnants of the three clusters in the paradigms. It is, therefore, of great importance to look into the next classes of verbs, as they will shed a different light. That is, although (5) is missing, (4) and (6) have preserved the original consonatisms to a considerable extent to which, if the above evidence of clustering is added, (4) and (6) can be reconstructed to show the clusters involved; the reconstructions are greatly facilitated when (7) and (8) are also taken into account. Let me, therefore, first point out what the preserved, orginal consonantisms are and, then, move on to the reconstructions of the verb paradigms.

Note first that in both Non-past and Negative Derivation, except for (1) the stem-final consonant is preserved throughout. So, there is no problem to assume that all verbs, originally in the proto-forms, had a stem-final consonant. This observation has been recognized by all scholars, be they Japanese or not. The problem lies in determining the consonantism involving this stem-final element which, traditionally, has been thought of only as a singleton. Thus, (4) and (6) according to the extant view in the literature are said to have *tob- and *tog- as their reconstructed protostems. But I wish to take exception to this view, arguing that the stem-final element in those verbs was not a single obstruent; rather, it was a cluster consisting of a voiced stop and a hormorganic nasal that precedes the stop. I have already presented certain evidence. So, let me proceed to the next observation.

Observe now that the past tense is indicated by a morpheme that synchronically comprises two allomorphs, viz., /-ta ~ -da/. The conditioning factors are fairly obvious, that is to say, phonological:-*ta* is preceded by a voiceless consonant and -*da*, by /n/, except for (3) and (6) where the environments can be said to be identical (e.g., *tuk-u* 'to arrive' and *tui-ta* vs. *tug-u* 'to pour' and *tui-da*). The usual explanation in synchronic morphology for (3) and (6) is to say that the past tense morpheme first undergoes an assimilation process (i.e., voicing) when it is suffixed to the stem of (6) where the stem-final consonant is a voiced stop, a process that is salient to (3) because the stem-final consonant in this case is a voiceless stop. The explanation, then, asserts that after the assimilation is completed, the stops in (3) and (6) undergo a morphophonemic change, becaming /i/ in both cases.

This kind of synchronic explanation, of course, can be reformulated in the style of generative phonology by setting up a Voicing Rule which affects only verbs in (6) but not verbs in (3), a rule that is to be *followed by* another rule which may be called, for the sake of convenience, something like Syllabic Rule (or Vocalic Rule) which affects both (3) and (6) by changing a nonsyllabic (or nonvocalic) segment into a syllabic (or vocalic) segment (i.e., /i/). These rules, again, can be stated "elegantly" in the form of distinctive features, but the important point, if one adheres to the older version of generative phonology, is the *ordering* of the rules; otherwise, the voicing of the past tense in (6) would not result from the application of the rules. That is, if the second rule is applied first, whereby both /k/ and /g/ in (3) and (6), respectively, would change to /i/ creating an identical environmet, such as *kai-* or *toi-*, that would certainly render the first rule inapplicable.

Given these illustrations of first the Structuralist explanation and then of the Generativist explanation, there is no doubt that the latter simply *imitates* the former by changing the format of presentation (e.g., from conditioning factors to enviromnents, from allomorphs to features, and from morphophonemic alternations to rules). If there is any difference at all, it may be found in the repeated but groundless claims that the generativist view not only reflects historical developments of the language concerned but also characterizes the phonological competence of its native speakers. For instance, in Harms (1968:1), he says: "Ultimately, ..., generative phonology seeks to provide a general theory explaining the competence of the native speaker in the sounds of his language." Hence, it is also claimed that there exists some sort of psychological reality in the rules and "systematic phonemes," whereas structuralists using exactly the same materials have made none of these claims (cf. Peng 1972 and 1975 for a detailed discussion of this controversy). But, as I shall demonstrate below, generativists have gone widely off the mark on all claims, although this is not the place to discuss the ideal speaker-hearer's phonological competence and the psychological reality of whatever kind. For instance, generativists equipped with their rules and "fancy" but complicated notations would never be able to discover (or even observe) that (4) and(6), unlike (1) through (3), are historically different in that they contained a cluster, rather than a single obstruent, in the stem, a discovery (or observation) that is of utmost importance in historical linguistics, because it is precisely this kind of discovery that led de Saussure to his reconstructions of the now well-known Proto-Indo-European laryngeals (although the phonetic nature of these laryngeals have been modified since de Saussure's discovery). If this analogy is valid, is there any further evidence for my reconstructions of the clusters? The answer is "Yes". Here are the traces.

Notice that (4) resembles (7) and (8) in two very important respects; namely, the preservation of the nasal and voicing of the consonant in the past tense. The connection between the nasal segment and the voicing phenomenon is the key which, coupled with the stem-final element in Non-past and Negative Derivation, has enabled me to conclude that verbs in (4) and (6) originylly comprised a cluster in the stem and that the nasal is kept in Past for verbs like (4) but has been lost for verbs like (6), whereas the voiced stop remains intact in both Non-past and Negative Derivation for (4) and (6). This conclusion is supported by forms like *tombi* 'jumping, and *tombo* 'dragonfly where the cluster *-mb-* is well preserved.

While there is no denying that *tombi* is related to *tob-u* as cognates, since its alternant *tobi* also exists in free variation as was pointed out earlier, *tombo* may not be so related synchronically, on the ground that *tombo* is probably made up of **to-mbo*, historically speaking, which resembles *ta-mbo* 'rice field' rather than *tombi* or *tob-u*, although synchronically no linguist would dare analyze it as morphemically *to-mbo*. In this connection, I have yet to see in the literature, other than my own analysis presented above, that *tambo* is morphemically analyzed as *ta-mbo*- most materials, e.g., Ono (1980:56 and 77), have analyzed it as *tamb-o* with *ta* as a separate morpheme. That my analysis is more plausible may be seen in the fact that in Niigata it is pronounced as *ta-na-mbo*, where *-mbo* is clearly cut from *ta*, and that in yet another dialect there is a form *ari-mbo* 'ant' which corresponds to *ari* in many other dialects, including the standard dialect of Tokyo; the existence of *ari-mbo* supports the idea that *tombo* was historically made up of *to-mbo*.

Given these observed pieces of evidence, it is clear beyond a doubt that the nasal preserved in Past must be restored to the verb stem in Non-past and Negative Derivation, which is to asy that the proto-stem of (4) must be reconstructed as **tomb-*. Likwise, the proto-stem of (6) may also be reconstructed as **toŋg-* exept that there is no nasal preserved in the past form, viz., *toida*. However, the voicing of consonant in the past tense morpheme, which is caused none other than by the "missing" nasal, as may be evidenced by (4) and supported by (7) and (8) ,is intact in all verbs of (6) e.g., *kag-u* 'to sniff' which becomes *kai-da* where the verb stem is identical with that of (3). But there is one problem in the reconstruction of *tog-* to **toŋg-*, not only because there is no nasal preserved in the past form but also because there is an additional segment, viz., /i/, which must be accounted for historically. How to account for the introduction of /i/ in the past form is, of course, the objective of the next paragraphs.

First, observe that the additional segment, /i/, is synchronically regarded as alternating with the velar stop in (3) or (6), an alternation that must be disregarded if the said reconstruction is to be carried out smoothly, because historically such should not be the case; that is, the velar stop never alternated with /i/ in the past but only looks as if it alternated with /i/. Why? The answer is crucial here, as it must establish the fact that the velar stop was somehow lost due to sound change (and possibly grammatical change as well), but more importantly that when and during the period the velar stop existed it did not alternate with /i/. What is needed, therefore, is some sort of indication that the added /i/ does not (synchronically) alternate with the stem-final element elsewhere. Alas, verbs in (11) are indeed instances of such an indication, which means that /i/ was an added rather than alternating segment. This distinction is important, because if /i/ had been an alternating segment (with the velar stop) at some point in the past, as it does today, having nothing to do with sound change, some sort of phonetic consideration between /i/ and the velar stop would be in order, such as the consideration of an original sound that split into /i/ and /k/, on the one hand, and /i/ and /g/, on the other, for verbs like (3) and (6), respectively, Such a consideration, however, is implausible, because it could not explain the existence of /i/ in (11), which clearly does not alternate with /s/ (and never has). But if /i/ is regarded as an added segment in the inflection of the past tense, for reasons that will be presented later, all that needs to be done is to posit that a consonant was lost some time in the past for verbs in (3) and (6) but not for verbs like (11), because the stem-final segment, /s/, is well preserved, and therefore the reconstruction is to restore that lost consonant in each case, which is [k] for verbs in (3) and [g] for verbs in (6), except that [g] must be preceded by an homorganic nasal, [ŋ], as was stated above.

Likewise, /i/ must be restored in the inflection to the past forms of the remaining verbs of (1), (2), (4), (7), (8), and (10), a restoration that can be well attested by historical documents going back ot the Heian period (794 - 1184 A.D.). As a consequence, the reconstructed paradigms look more or less like the following:

	Non-past	Past	Negative Derivation
1.	*kap-u 'to buy'	*kap-i-ta	*kap-a-nai
2.	*kat-u 'to win'	*kat-i-ta	*kat-a-nai
3.	*kak-u 'to write'	*kak-i-ta	*kak-a-nai
4.	*tomb-u 'to fly'	*tomb-i-ta	*tomb-a-nai
5.	—		
6.	*toŋg-u 'to sharpen'	*toŋg-i-da	*toŋg-a-nai
7.	*yom-u 'to read'	*yom-i-da	*yom-a-nai
8.	*sin-u 'to die'	*sin-i-da	*sin-a-nai
9.	—	—	—
10.	*kar-u 'to cut'	*kar-i-ta	*kar-a-nai
11.	*sas-u 'to stab'	*sasi-ta	*sas-a-nai

Second, a question may now arise as to why the added /i/ was needed in the first place. The answer is very simple: It was needed as a derivational suffix. However, due to morphological change, it has become an inflectional suffix, because in modern Japanese the /i/ phoneme is a morpheme in the verb paradigms well preserved in all of Infinitive and several forms of Gerund which correspond to those in Past. These two paradigms are listed below:

	Infinitive	Gerund
1.	kaø-i	kat-te
2.	kat-i	kat-te
3.	kak-i	kai-te
4.	tob-i	ton-de
5.	—	—
6.	tog-i	toi-de
7.	yom-i	yon-de
8.	sin-i	sin-de
9.	—	—
10.	kar-i	kat-te
11.	sas-i	sasi-te

All this suggests that what is morphologically analyzed as Infinitive, that is, the suffix /i/, in modern Japanese, was originally part of the derivation to connect the stem with the past tense and the gerundic morpheme in Proto-Japanese verb paradigms, but due to sound change /i/ is now lost in many forms of Past and Gerund, except in (3) and (6).[3] As a matter of fact, there is evidence in many historical documents to attest this claim. It follows that like all forms in Past, those in Gerund may also be reconstructed to the extent that *mb*, *ŋg*, and *i* are restored, as in the following reconstructed paradigms of Infinitive and Gerund.

	Infinitive	*Gerund
1.	*kap-i	*kap-i-te
2.	*kat-i	*kat-i-te
3.	kak*-i	*kak-i-te
4.	*tomb-i	*tomb-i-de
5.	—	—
6.	*toŋg-i	*toŋg-i-de
7.	*yom-i	*yom-i-de
8.	*sin-i	*sin-i-ide
9.	—	—
10.	*kar-i	*kat-i-te
11.	*sas-i	*sas-i-te

The reconstructions of Infinitive and Gerund further support the assumption stated earlier that the stem-final velar stop in (3) and (6) never alternated with the /i/ phoneme as they seemingly do today in modern Japanase, because /i/ was a derivation suffix and, therefore, is not at all the result of a sound change that split a common (proto-) phoneme into /k/ and /i/, on the one hand, and /g/ and /i/, on the other, a split that has been erroneously believed, until now, to have occurred in the past by many historical linguists, Western scholars in particular (cf. de Chene 1979:509). That the /i/ phoneme served as a derivational suffix in Proto-Japanese (because it appeared in both paradigms of

---

[3] The loss of /i/ in Past and Gerund has resulted in what Japanese philologists call *Onbin* which is a historcial process of sound change seen in forms like (2), e.g., *kat-i-ta kat-ta* (for Past) and *kat-i-te kat-te* (for Gerund) or in forms like (7), e.g., *yom-i-da yon-da* (for Past) and *yom-i-de yon-de* (for Gerund). Synchronically, however, *Onbin* may also be used to mean morphophonemic change, as in *iti* 'one' and *hatu* 'shot' resulting in *ippatu* 'one shot' where the ultimate vowel of 'one' is lost and /t/ and /h/ are mutually assimilated to the geminated (i.e., lengthened) /pp/. For the difference between inflection and derivation, see Nida (1949: 99).

Infinitive and Gerund) *but* is regarded instead as an inflectional suffix in Infinitive is based on the analysis prevalent in (synchronic) Japanese linguistics that the /i/ in Infinitive and the /i/ in Gerund have nothing to do with each other morphologically; once they are linked to the same historical source, however, it is easy to see, as I have shown above, the morphological change from Proto-Japanese (derivational suffix) to modern Japanese (inflectional suffix).

The reconstructions based on modern Japanese verb paradigms, however, have yet to touch on the cluster *-nd-*, because there is simply no trace of a verb in modern Japanese that ends in /d/. Consequently, it is impossible to determine from contemporary data whether or not there were verbs at one itme in Proto-Japanese that comprised the cluster in the stem. Moreover, there also remains a problem concerning (9) which is "missing" in all paradigms. The reason is that for many modern Japanese speakers the phoneme /g/ in (6) is replaced by the phoneme /η/, and therefore, as far as they are concerned (cf. Susuki-Jinushi 1967: 69), verbs in (6) do not exist; instead, such verbs are included in (9). This being the case, to those speakers, *tog-u* naturally becomes *toη-u*, *tog-a-nai* is *ton-a-nai*, and *tog-i* is replaced by *toη-i*, although the rest of the paradigms, e.g., Past and Gerund, remain the same, that is, /i/ appears to alternate with /η/ which, again. as a nasal conditons the voicing of the consonant in the suffix for each paradigm.

Be that as it may, the substitution of /η/ for /g/ in (6) will not alter the reconstructed results; rather, it renders firm credence to the existence of the cluster in that for the /g/ speakers, it was the nasal element of *-*ng-* tha' disappeared, but the converse was the case for the /η/ speakers, although both groups have maintained the /i/ phoneme in Past and Gerund on account of the fact that the cluster *-*ng-* was velar, having undergone the same fate of sound change as the /k/ phoneme in (3).

What should be done about the cluster *-nd-*, then, since no trace is left in modern Japanese verbs? I suggest that the data presented at the beginning of this section be now taken into consideration, namely, the morphemic alternants of *tori* and *ndori* 'bird' and of *tama*, *ntama*, and *dama* 'ball', albeit they are all nouns. This resort to nouns, rather than to verbs, is inevitable, because in conducting internal reconstructions, one has to work with whatever evidence that is left; no restoration is feasible when there is no material to work on. In view of the above observation and analysis, I belive I have now sufficient ground on which on reconstruct three clusters from the data made available above, which are:

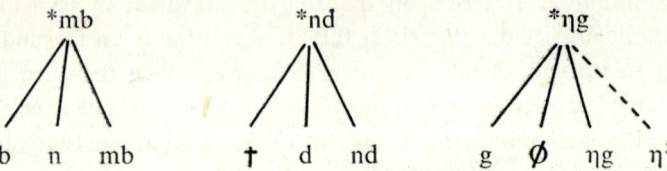

Hence, *tama* < *ntama* "ball"; *tori* < **ndori* 'bird'; *-bu* < **-mbu* 'sheet'; *tabi* < **tambi* 'every time'; *tobi* < **tombi* 'jumping; flying'; and of course *togaru* < **toŋgaru*.

What this means is that the cluster in each case lost its nasal element, on the hand, and the voicing of th obstruent element, on the other, in word-initial position (cf. *tama* and *tori*) but has, in intervocalic position, either remained intact in some instances (cf. *tambo* and *tombo*) or lost only the nasal element in most of the other instances (cf. *tabi*, *to-bu*, and *tog-u*);[4] for the remainder, however, either the nasal element is preserved but the voiced obstruent is lost (cf. *ton-da*), in which case, something else, viz., /i/, is lost with it, thereby constituting the loss of an entire syllable, or both are loIt (cf. *toi-da*). The conditioning of the latter changes may, therefore, be considered morphological.

IMPLICATIONS

What are, then, the implications of reconstructing the clusters? Put differently, what bearing does the above sound change have on the diachronic phonology of Japanese? I think two important implications may be mentioned here. Important, because they are indicative of profound consequences that will no doubt follow after the reconstructions are made known which, as a result, will not only improve the historical perspective of Japanese linguistics (in parcular, Japanese philology) but also greatly enhance the probability of classifying Japanese with Tamil, as proposed by Ono (1980) and others, on the one hand, as well as with Austronesian, proposed by many though without any conclusive evidence. The dual classification suggests that Japanese may be the "missing link" between Dravidian and Austronesian.

---

[4] This phoneme as a reflex of *ŋg in modern Japanese is dialectal and, therefore, is not meant to be on a par with the other reflexes.

The first implication has two aspects: one, the traditional approach to Japanese syllable structure (hence, phonotatics) as being based solely on the (C)V pattern must now be modified, when dealing with Proto-Japanese. The (C)V pattern is the foundation for the Japanese writing system the study and explication of which have been the "soul and body" of Japanese philology for many centuries. This is because most Japanese linguists think that Japanese syllable structure has remained unchanged for more than a millennium, except for syllables like /wi/, /yi/, /we/, /ye/, /wu/, and /wo/ [5] which have been lost for quite some time. But the reconstructed clusters will most certainly alter this picture, because it purports that there were syllables in Proto-Japanese which comprised the clusters, viz., of the CCV type where the first C was a nasal and the second C, a voiced stop, before or during the time when or even after the *kana* syllabary was invented.[6]

The existence of the nasal, in word-initial position or elsewhere, was of course not noticed at first when the *kana* syllabary was invented (during the Peian period), although there is evidence that prior to that, when Chinese characters were still being used to transliterate Japanese, the nasal in some cases was transcribed with a separate but comparable Chinese character that has an initial nasal. For instance, *dak-u* 'to embrace' in modern Japanese was transliterated with three Chinese characters, 武太伎 for the Infinitive *dak-i*, the first character being for the indication of a nasal (cf. Murayama 1973: 71). This example (taken from *Man'yoshu* believed to have been written during the Nara period [694–792 A.D.] using only Chinese characters) would, thus, appear to support the reconstructions above, suggesting that *dak-i* or its non-past Indicative form, *dak-u*, had indeed at one time *ndak- as its stem, although Murayama following the traditional view has regarded the transliteration as reflecting three CV syllables, viz., *mudak-i*, thereby reconstructing 'embrace' to something like *mendak- where he considers the firs

---

[5] Theoretically, there are supposed to be 50 *kana* syllables in the Syllabary chart. However, a syllabic nasal was added in the Middle Age during the Muromachi Period (1392–1466 A.D.), making the syllabary to consist of 51 syllables. In contemporary usage of the Syllabary chart, only 45 (51 less 6) are actually employed.

[6] In addition, one may wish to add CVC as a pattern to account for words like *tombo* and *toŋgaru*, in which case, the second C is either a nasal or a voiceless stop (e.g., *kat-ta* which is the past tense of several non-past forms). The issue, however, falls outside the purview of this paper.

Chinese as indicating a prefix (which he reconstructed as *mə-), *not* for the phonetic value of the pre-consonantal nasality, and that the pre-consonantal nasality was just a transitional phenomenon which occurred when the prefix was attached to the stem *dak-*. In other words, Murayama ignored the possibility that the stem might have had the shape of *ndak- and that the first Chinese character, like the third one, might have been meant to indicate just a single segment (i.e., the pre-consonantal nasal, in the case of the first character, but the suffix, in the case of the third character) rather than a whole syllable (to stand for an assumed prefix, in the case of the first character, but subsume both the stem-final /k/ and the suffix /i/, in the case of the third character), although the Chinese rendition of the said characters during that period (700 – 800 A.D.) did begin with a bilabial instead of dental or alveolar sound (for the first character) but with a velar stop (for the third character). Put differently, I wish to point out that the Chinese characters employed to transliterate Japanese in the example cited were intended to approximate only the pronounciation and, therefore, that the first character did not mean to indicate a whole syllable but rather a single segment that was a nasal; the fact that the author of the passage was forced to employ a character that seemed to stand for a whole syllable is because there is no Chinese character that could be pronounced with a nasal alone. The following diagrams will ullustrate the difference between Murayama's view and mine:

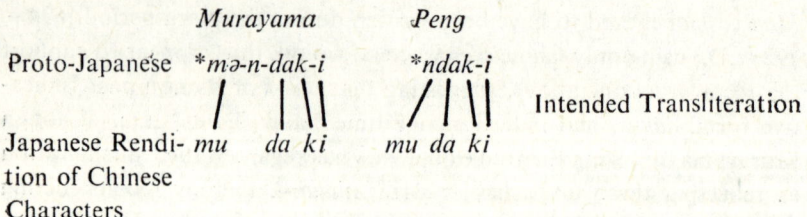

In view of this discussion, I think it would be difficult for Murayama to justify the existence of a prefix like *me- in Proto-Japanese, when a grammatical system of that sort was not prevalent other than a few sporadic instances (Murayama 1973: 72 – 5), because all the cited instances can be readily reinterpreted as containing one of the reconstructed clusters, instead of the prefix. Besides, what is the meaning of such a prefix, if there was indeed one in the historical documents? As long as no provisions of meaning and other prefixes are available, it is probably best that clusters like *mb-, *nd-, and *ŋg- are recognized in the syllable structure of Proto-Japanese and that the prefix be done with altogether.

Given this aspect of the first implication, I am now in the position to point out its second aspect which is that the voiced/voiceless contrast in modern Japanese probably resulted from the loss of the nasal in the clusters or the disappearance of such a cluster as the conditioning factor of voicing due to the sound changes stated above. For instance, if *ndak-u is taken to be the proto-form of 'to embrace', the loss of the nasal would force the obstruent in the form to be in contrast with the (voiceless) obstruent of another form, say, *tak-u 'to cook', thereby constituting a secondary split between [d] and [t] which were originally members of the same phoneme. Likewise, the losses of -k- in (3) and -ŋg- in (6) of the verb paradigms as conditioning factors of -ta and -da, respectively, yielded another instance of secondary split of the same phoneme, thereby resulting in minimal pairs like *toi-ta* (past tense of *tok-u* 'to solve') and *toi-da* (past tense of *tog-u* 'to sharpen') not to mention that the loss of the nasal in the Non-past form of *toŋg-u 'to sharpen' is still another instance of secondary split resulting in the voiced/voiceless contrast of /k/ and /g/ in modern Japanese.[7]

The second implication, however, is much more abstract and involved and, therefore, needs more evidence. That is, it pertains to the reclassification of Dravidian and Austronesian (or Malayo-Polynesian) languages and thus requires data from them to substantiate the reclassification. Nevertheless, the consonantisms shown in Dravidian (especially Tamil) and most of the Austronesian languages resemble the consonantism reconstructed above for Proto-Japanese. If this implication proves to be far-reaching, I will not be surprised that Proto-Japanese as reconstructed here holds the key for reconsidering the current groupings of Asian languages. More importantly, it will help solve the pending issue of genetic relationship of Japanese with Altaic languages.

---

[7] The history of the development of the voiced/voiceless contrast in Japanese is, actually, much more involved than what I have described. For instance, if *ndori 'bird' has changed to *tori*, the loss of the nasal should be followed subsequently by the devoicing process in initial position, although the change of *ndama 'ball' to (me-)ntamd 'eyeball' seems to suggest that the devocing process took place prior to the loss of the nasal. However, if we follow the alternative solution suggested in footnote 1, then *ndama will not be the reconstructed photo-form of *tama* 'ball'. I plan to take this matter up on a separate occasion.

Conclusion

I have in the preceding sections reconstructed three clusters on the strength of internal evidence alone. The technique of Internaal Reconstruction was regarded as more applicable in this case, on the ground that the comparative data within Japan in all dialects gave no hint of the existence of a nasal segment in each of the clusters, although the results yielded did clarify and help settle the long-disputed report in the literature as to the phonological nature of the nasalized vowels in Tohoku dialects. In fact, there is also evidence of similar nasalized vowels in Okinawan dialects. The results internally reconstructed can be extended to support the genetic relationship between Tamil and Japanese, on the one hand, which is being sought by Ono and his Japanese colleagues, and possibly between Austronesian languages and Japanese, on the other, which is to say that Proto-Japanese may have been the "missing link" between Dravidian and Austronesian.

While the purpose of my paper set forth at the beginning was not the determination of either the genetic relationship of Tamil and Japanese or of the classification of Japanese dialects on the basis of their genetic relationships, but rather the reconstruction of three possible clusters by testing once again the power of Internal Reconstruction, I believe the effect of the reconstruction can be felt throughout the history of Japanese. What this means is that if the internally reconstructed clusters are indeed so valid, they may prove to be as important a discovery in the history of Japanese linguistics as the Proto-Indo-European laryngeals were in the history of Indo-European linguistics originally suggested by de Saussure.

I may add then that given the validity of the reconstructed clusters, the three techniques often used in historical linguistics are not as equipollent as have been hitherto assumed to be; that is, for certain data, Internal Reconstruction may be better suited and more accurate for producing and interpreting the anticipated results than the Comparative Method or even the examination of historical documents, although needless to less they more often than not complement one another.

REFERENCES

Harms, R. T. 1968. *Introduction to phonological theory*. Englewood Cliffs: Prentice Hall.

Murayama, H. 1973. *Nihongo no kigen* (The origin of Japanese). Tokyo: Kobun Do.

Nida, E. A. 1949. *Morphology: the descriptive analysis of words.* Ann Arbor: University of Michigan Press.

Nomoto, Kikuo. 1975. "How Much Has Been Standardized over the Past Twenty Years?" in *Lanbuabe in Japanese Society: Current Issues in Sociolinguistics*, pp. 33 - 70, Fred C. C. Peng (ed.), Tokyo: University of Tokyo Press.

Ogura, S. 1932. *Sendai hogen onin ko* (Phonological study of the Sendai dialect). Tokyo: Toko Shoin.

Ono, Susumu. 1980. *Sound Correspondences between Tamil and Japanese*, Tokyo: Gakushuin.

Peng, F. C. C. 1972. Review of *Introduction to phonological theory* by R. Harms. *Lingua* 30. 262 – 74.

―――. 1975. The place of generative phonology in the history of linguistics. *The First LACUS Forum 1975*, ed. by A. and V. Maddai. Columbia, South Carolina: Hornbeam Press.

Susuki-Jinushi, Toshiko. 1967. *The Structure of Japanese, Studies in Linguistics*, Occasional Papers 11, Dallas, Texas.

ARE THERE DYSFUNCTIONAL CHANGES?

ANNA GIACALONE RAMAT

1. Functional explanations have been much favoured among the various explanations put forward for language change and, as R. Lass (1980: 66) has pointed out, seem to have some special attraction for linguists, although he personally does not support them. Take, for example, O. Jespersen (1949: 15) and his definition of language as "a purposeful activity tending toward ease and distinctness". More recently, M. Harris in his contribution to the Vth International Congress on Historical Linguistics (1982: 5) held that change can be explained "in terms of an inherent tendency of human beings to impose an order on the data which they encounter and experience and to organize and reorganize the material at their disposal coherently and economically".

H. Lüdtke (1980: 5) has also viewed language change as a consequence of human beings' desire to minimize the effort needed in communication (both productively and receptively) and to facilitate the process of language acquisition. As Harris rightly points out, recourse to principles of this kind — which are not specific to language but rather human tendencies governing perception of and, generally, learning about reality as an ordered and systematized whole — may be said to constitute an explanation of *why* certain changes take place and not merely a description of *how* they come about (even though, admittedly, this is not a "fully predictive deductive-nomological explanation", an issue I do not wish to explore here).

While agreeing with the general framework outlined above, my intention in this paper is rather to examine some aspects of language change which would seem *not* to comply entirely with the overall pattern of economy and functionality. Two basic positions may be adopted in any research strategy designed to test for functional language changes:

1) examples can be sought of "functional" changes which introduce regularity and confirm the trend, something which has been done by scholars in various schools, including, for example, the description of

such features of language change labelled "allomorphy reduction",
1) examples can be sought of "functional" changes which introduce regularity and confirm the trend, something which has been done by scholars in various schools, including, for example, the description of such features of language change labelled "allomorphy reduction", "maintenance of meaningful oppositions", etc. [1]

2) consideration may be given to what, at least hypothetically, may be considered non-functional: in other words, examples may be sought of changes which functional forecasts rule out completely or which should in theory not be productive. If such examples *do* occur, then the internal or external circumstances that bring them about need to be examined.

2. A satisfactory definition of the term "function" would be opportune before embarking on research of this nature. The truth is that, although function as a factor in language change has had a very respectable position in the history of linguistics from the Prague School to Martinet and so on, little attention has been paid to defining what function is. Moreover, there has been constant confusion inasmuch as the functionality of a particular language change has been construed of *either* in terms of the system, with its balanced internal relationships, *or* in terms of the speaker's strategy whereby he reorganises data and searches for an optimal grammar.

In a brief discussion about "dysfunction" R. Lass (1980: 86—88) states that we do not know what is pathological, inadequate or unsuccessful for a language because we do not know of any language "abortions" so that we cannot even say what is good and successful. In other words, neither dysfunction nor function can be defined. I believe, however, that even in the absence of a formally defined and explanatory theory of functional change or of a general taxonomy of functions, we may still

---

[1] R. Lass (1980: 69 et seq.) discusses various types of "functional explanation": preservation of contrast, minimization of allomorphy, avoidance of homophony and criticises them inasmuch as they are "totally non predictive" and concludes (p. 71): "the theory of functional change (if there is any such thing) is apparently so constructed that almost anything can be a supporting example and nothing can be a counter-example". But also for those who do not share this pessimistic view of the explanatory power of functionalism, the problem arises that all languages ought to adopt functional solutions and develop in a uniform and direct way, direct as regards their application. In reply to this objection it may be said that two different dialects may give priority to different functions, or that two languages may implement a function using a set of existing options (multiple-strategy principle).

examine "functionally non-efficient changes" and try to find reasons why languages should follow "bad choices".

One way of approaching the notion of dysfunction might be to examine all those theories put forward to define the concept of "possible human language", such as Chomsky's Universal Grammar or Keenan's Language Universals. These theories make it possible, at least in principle, to forecast the acceptable features of human languages, and at the same time to make a number of predictions about the potential results of language change. We might then define a dysfunction with reference to the violation of some principle of Universal Grammar. But a "dysfunctional" change, in this sense, ought not to occur because its result would not be among the various phenomena that make up a possible human language.

In actual fact, this would seem to be too strong and too easily falsifiable a position. Neither Chomsky nor Keenan manage in fact to rule out the occurence of certain "violations" of universals.[2]

A weaker formulation would be to consider those changes which deviate from general language change patterns as dysfunctional. The problem is then to define "general language change patterns", which should take form of generalizations about the probability of certain phenomena occurring.

3. The introduction of the concept of naturalness may, I feel, be helpful when dealing with these problems, since some linguists posit a criterion of naturalness underlying phonological and morphological changes. According to Mayerthaler (1981: 173—74) this concept may be projected on all components of a grammar and may constitute the basis of a linguistic theory.

The concepts of "natural" and "functional" need to be distinguished, although, of course, they do overlap very obviously and frequently. Generally speaking, we expect natural morphology to be functional as well, as stated by Dressler (1981). One difference between the two concepts lies in my opinion in the extra-linguistic factors constituting the reference framework of both. Functionality refers directly to com-

---

[2] According to L. Campbell, "Explaining Universals and their Exceptions", in E. Traugott et al. Papers from the IVth ICHL, Benjamins, Amsterdam, 1980, 17—26, exceptions to language universals, in their turn deriving from restrictions on the production and perception of human languages, are to be sought in social factors. Universal and natural features — Campbell observes — are generally determined by internal factors, but are often complicated by external factors of a socio-cultural nature.

munication, stressing that language is a communicative and semiotic system. And I would add that it may also be directed towards social aspects of language: in this sense it is language specific.

Naturalness refers to bio-psychological characteristics of human beings and is therefore universal. For example, natural phonology refers to processes of articulation and/or perception, natural morphology and syntax to cognitive processes. The naturalness of a phenomenon may be identified on the basis of such parameters as widespread diffusion, ease of acquisition and frequency of occurrence of change (Mayerthaler, 1981: 1). Indeed a rule of such widespread diffusion as the assimilation of nasals to the following obstruents is both a natural (synchronic) rule and a natural language change (see Lass 1980: 31 for the problem of exceptions).

A natural change is not necessarily functional within a given system, however. Unlike the concept of naturalness, functionalness cannot be defined absolutely, removed from consideration of relevant systems.[3]
For example Sanskrit vocalism is characterized by a change of IE *e* and *o* to *a*, a rather frequent change if we consider other Indo-European languages like Germanic, Baltic and Slavic languages. But the effects of such changes were *both* a non-functional impoverishment of the apophonic system which was at the time still totally viable (with loss for example of the distinction between *e*-grade and *o*-grade in cases like *rocate* < **leuketai* and *ru-roca* < **louk-*) *and* a loss of opposition between 1st and 3rd person sing. Perfect endings. Thus lengthening occurring in 3rd person sing. Perfects like *cakāra* and *jajāna* (= gr. γέγονε) in Vedic texts (which was only later extended to the 1st person sing: Thumb-Hauschild II, p. 279) can be interpreted as an attempt to introduce a functional distinction between 3rd and 1st persons, as a case in other words of "preservation of contrast" (Lass: 1980: 69) rather than as a case of 'Brugmann's law', which is highly questionable.

On the other hand, the preservation of functional morphological distinctions (plural marking, for example) may give rise to unnatural phonological rules. Of course, this unnaturalness arises when we consider synchronically cases where the original naturalness has been lost (for example in the English plural using an Umlaut, *feet* or *geese*, the phono-

---

[3] Naturalness can in fact depend on contextual values: cfr. the concept of markedness reversal (Markiertheitsumkehrung) in Mayerthaler 1981. For a slightly different concept of naturalness which includes considerations of language specific properties see Wurzel 1983.

logical context has been completely lost: Dressler 1977a: 26). In such cases, functionality would seem to outdo naturalness, i.e. there is a morphological priority over phonological transparency.

4. Zero-processes and subtractive morphological processes. With reference to possible conflicts between naturalness and functionalness I would like now to deal with what are known as zero-processes and subtractive morphological processes which take precisely the opposite direction of the more common "additive" morphological operations, which add one or more segments to the base or modify the base by means of lengthening or "ablaut".[4]

An example from the field of inflexions is the genitive plural of some classes of nouns in Slavic languages: Czech Nom. Sing. *žena* "lady wife" Gen. Plur. *žen*; Nom. Sing. *mešto* "town" Gen. Plur. *mešt*. Here the effect of phonological change is to produce a result running counter to the dominant morphological patterns.

Diachronically speaking I feel that this is a subtractive process because a phonological segment has been deleted without leaving any trace whereas synchronically there is a contrast between a zero marker in the gen. plural and a non-zero marker elsewhere (Mayerthaler 1981: 25 speaks of counter-iconic symbolization of the morphological category).

As analogous developments, I take plurals of *a*-feminines in Northern Italian dialects (cfr. Jaberg, 1936, map 19), where diachronically Latin inflectional endings have been lost, resulting in a subtractive pattern: Milanese *la candela, i candel*; *la scala, i scal*. In both cases diachrony can be said to explain unnaturalness inasmuch as the origin is traced.

In the field of derivational morphology we may quote agentive nouns with no suffix in German such as *Senn, Linguist*. Natural change ought to favour the addition of suffix *-er* of agentive nouns, as has occurred for *Dolmetscher* from *Dolmetsch* and indeed besides *Senn* we can find *Senner* already, whereas *Linguistiker* does not yet seem to have had any success.

Generally speaking, derivations with no observable suffix are liable to be discarded owing to their lack of perceptive clarity (Mayerthaler 1981: 123), whereas in actual fact there are cases where they impose themselves as a successful and productive process.[5]

---

[4] Under the label "non-additive operations" Mayerthaler (1981: 110) brings together subtractive processes such as abbreviations: *auto* for *automobile*, acronyms: USA, and "modulatory" processes — Ablaut, Umlaut and zero-processes).

[5] It might be objected that what is significant in the derivational process is in fact the transformational process which consists in changing the grammatical category.

In modern Italian there is a development of postverbal nouns with no specific suffix. Probably this is the commonest formation used when introducing new words into the language. And it has a base in very old formations common to the entire Romance area (Malkiel 1977: 73 et seq.).[6]

The list of nouns formed in this way is very long (Tollemache, 1954, Dardano 1978). The following are a few examples:

candeggio from *candeggiare* "to bleach" not **candeggiamento*
degrado from *degradare* "to degrade" not **degradamento*: *degradazione* with a different meaning.
revoca from *revocare* "to revoke" not *revocazione*.[7]

To what can we attribute the success of a formation which, given the general characteristics of morphology, was on paper not likely to be successful? We may think perhaps of the fact that it satisfies the trend to limit the number of syllables in a word, a trend which in recent decades has developed remarkably (and which also brings about such abbreviated forms as *auto, metro, cine* and so on). For this reason, new no-suffix type formations are preferred to the two more common verb-to-noun markers *-zione* and *-mento*, which add two syllables to the verb stem. But we ought to take another factor into consideration namely that the exact nature of the derivation is clear to the linguist but not to the speaker: the relationship verb→noun is in fact synchronically reversible inasmuch as "the naive speakers" may interpret it as a noun→verb relationship.[8] Indeed non-systematic experiments carried out with Italian students

---

The presence of an explicit marker (a suffix) denoting the process is not really very relevant (according to Guilbert, 1975: 164 et seq.) For example, the process in English called "conversion" (e.g. *to look, to have a look*) is not marked by any suffix. This does not, however, invalidate the fact that a derivational rule not involving any suffix (or other derivation marker) is less natural, or "unsuited" and consequently we should expect it to be unproductive. Some examples of the productivity of these rules may be explained bearing in mind a number of historical and social factors which bring about a conflict between naturalness and functionality.

[6] In Italian there is also another class of postverbal no-suffix forms acting as agentive nouns: *mangia, arruffa, brighella*: a list of these often regional and jocular words may be found in Tollemache 1954: 146 et seq., see also Migliorini 1957, 82 et seq. Some linguistis have considered these as forms of the present indicative or the imperative, but it is more plausible that it is a zero-suffix of agentive nouns, a much less widespread and unproductive formation than agentive nouns formed with the suffix *-tore*.

have shown that a form which has a recognizable suffix — whether nominal or verbal — is considered to be derived: thus *accordare* is considered as being derived from *accordo* (historically the verb precedes the noun) and a series tends to be developed of the type *carica caricare caricamento*.

These developments tend to support the assumption that additive morphology is more natural and conforms more satisfactorily to speakers' analytical strategies. It is, however, necessary to distinguish between the interpretation supplied by speakers in any concrete circumstances (synchrony) from the initial developments of derivatives (diachrony). From the diachronic point of view we may speak of non-additive morphology and look for the reasons behind the incidence of this type in functional principles related to the size of the words.

From what has been said so far however it would clearly be arbitrary to equate unnatural linguistic changes with dysfunctional changes.

5. Other (possibly) dysfunctional changes. Studies of language change usually analyse adult native speakers' utterances alone, inasmuch as they have a complete command of language. But when attempting to identify possible dysfunctional changes it is legitimate to expect interesting data from child language, from natural second language learning and from the study of pidgins and creoles as well as from the process of language death. The advantage of these areas is that in them language change may be studied in circumstances which are, as it were, favourable as regards quantity, speed of development, and presence of spontaneous innovations for which there is very little data available with normal languages.

From what has been mentioned above, a general tendency emerges whereby the morphological component is reformulated in more simple ways for those languages which have complex morphological inflexions and indeed reference is often made to *simplification* as a general feature of the areas in question (9).

But a number of big problems remain to be resolved:
1) to what extent may we consider simplification functional inasmuch as it brings about an improvement in communication and decreases the speaker's effort? Too drastic a simplification would seem liable to damage

---

[7] In the last century, postverbal forms with zero-suffix were criticised by purists in such registers as the language of legislation and they proposed *rimborsazione* and *revocazione* instead of *rimboros* and *revoca*: cfr. De Mauro, 1976: vol. II, p. 421 and Tollemache, 1954, 9 et seq.

communication or even prevent it taking place. Many examples of unsuccessful communication come from the efforts of second language learners and are due, at least in part, to the drastic reduction of the grammatical system.

2) is it legitimate to speak of simplification if we look merely at surface structure, classifying the various developments such as omission of the article, plural markers, case endings and so on?

When studying individual cases of language learning we should not forget that simplification is a speaker's strategy resulting in less complex output and we should take into account the social and psychological factors which induce a person to simplify his speech.

The interaction between the various components of a grammar may represent a remedy and a solution for the reductive effects of simplification, as Trudgill (1976—77) has shown with the notion of "simplification with cost": the loss of morphological elements may be compensated for in another component such as the syntactic component. This is what has happened in the Romance languages, where the loss of morphological information as a result of phonetic changes in the final part of the word is "compensated" for by the development of a much more fixed word order (10). By resorting to similar syntactic devices the English language has largely adjusted to the inconveniences deriving from loss of declensions.

Cases of simplification with cost do not seem to compromise then in any definitive way the system's functionality: the compensation that we find in them seems to represent a therapy for restoration and maintenance of functionality. We might then posit that changes where there is no compensation in other components of a grammar may be labelled as "dysfunctional".

But we have still to clarify two points: 1) it is not true that every simplification requires compensation elsewhere, 2) we cannot expect that all changes move towards simplification.

Synchronically speaking, for instance, the allomorphic variations in the morphological component may seem pointless, inasmuch as there is no difference in meaning or function despite the difference in form. For example, when N. Dorian notes the trend in the Celtic area of Sutherland to reduce the large variety of means to indicate number in

---

[8] M. Leumann, too, (1944: 132) observes that in the case of *pugna* and *pugnare* linguistic awareness of Latin speakers took the verb to be derived from the noun, whereas in actual fact the reverse is true.

the noun system, resorting to the generalisation of one suffix in most cases (Dorian 1981: 136—137), the simplification with no compensation that seems to arise from such changes does not seem to be dysfunctional: quite the contrary it would seem designed to create an isomorphic relationship between meaning (function) and form. Clearly this is no more than an application of the principle of "one meaning one form" a typically functional principle. In psycholinguistic terminology we can speak of an application of speakers' tendencies to impose a rational order on data which has been proposed as an explanation of language change by Harris (1982, see also Itkonen 1982).

Language change does not, however, only proceed in the direction of simplification: cases can also be found of changes which produce an increased discrete surface marking of meanings which previously were less distinct. For example, in both the Germanic and Romance languages, and perhaps not entirely independently, an article has developed from demonstrative forms, systematically realizing definiteness marking at a surface level which had not been explicitly expressed prior to this (Ramat: 1984). The development of new connectives to indicate various types of subordination (see for example Wiegand 1982) may illustrate the same tendency, which works in the opposite direction to simplification construed as a reduction of surface elements, but equally reflects a trend towards isomorphism between form and function. This principle thus comes to be reconfirmed as an essential feature of the morphological component's make-up. It may be added that isomorphic relationships are natural within a theory of naturalness (Mayerthaler 1981: 22 et seq) and organisational principles of communication can be based on them, as Slobin has proposed (11).

6. To sum up, in the examples discussed so far we have found no cases of dysfunctionality but rather instances of inconvenient changes to which a particular language has found a remedy. Consequently, we have not progressed very much towards a definition of dysfunctional change.

Nevertheless, precisely in the field of connectives we may quote examples of the loss of formal distinctions related to semantic and functional distinctions. In this light, in a previous paper. I examined the use of an invariable element *che* in colloquial Italian registers where I argued that

---

[9] Meisel 1980: 37 considers various simplified code data and introduces a distinction between *restrictive simplification* which is the type which might possibly relate to dysfunctional changes and *elaborative simplification* which is more concerned with the maximum generalisation of rules.

it was a complementizer used to suggest a connection between utterances without specifying the relative, causal and temporal nature of the link, so much so that it deserved the name "polyvalent *che*" (Giacalone Ramat 1982). It is an uncompensated simplification as compared with standard Italian which differentiates using differently functioning connectives. This change, which certainly does not encourage isomorphism between form and meaning, might be considered a dysfunctional change.

Another example might be loss of productivity in derivational suffixes, which according to Dressler (1977 b) is a characteristic feature of language death situations. It might be objected that this fossilization is compensated for lexically by the introduction of loan words from another (dominant) language which carry out the communicative requirements in question. But we do have an instance of dysfunction if we accept that a major function in morphology and particularly in word formation is lexical enrichment and if in a given language it actually stops. In language decay we may find changes which heavily reduce the language system: in Walser dialects spoken south of the Alps verb paradigms tend to be reduced to infinitive and past participle forms, all other forms being constructed by means of the auxiliaries *be*, *have* and *do*. This is an extreme development of a tendency also observable in Swiss dialects and in further German areas, where the preterite is lost and in present tense periphrastic constructions of the type *do*-auxiliary+infinitive are currently used alongside "normal" present forms. But in language decay such optional periphrastic forms with *do* tend to become the norm, since the speakers regard them as a convenient means of avoiding difficult inflections (Giacalone Ramat 1979 b). The results of such changes are an impoverished language structure, not impoverished in absolute, but certainly in relation to standard German verbal conjugation.

The net result of our research on dysfunctional changes is at the end of the day rather scant (even though, plainly, I do not pretend to have exhausted all the examples, having merely tried to indicate a few possible

---

[10] The development of so-called analytical forms in the Romance languages has been interpreted in two ways: 1) a surface interpretation which takes phonetic change to be the "trigger" which brought about a fixed word order, 2) a "deep" interpretation which sees these changes as a coherent alignment with the developing SVO sentence type, which established a fixed word order and made endings less necessary and which also encouraged the development of prepositions consistent with the new SVO type (Antinucci 1977). In actual fact, there is no contradiction between the two interpretations: the second achieves a higher degree of generalisaton and for this reason may be considered more interesting.

types). What we have found is that a variety of solutions have been adopted to cater for potentially dysfunctional changes: in particular, the decreased complexity of the morphological component is matched by increased complexity in the syntactic component.

7. Nevertheless, for a proper assessment of the concepts of function and dysfunction it seems we must consider *sociolinguistic* dysfunctionality. The fact that a language is used by a linguistic community is *per se* proof that it is functionally appropriate to be used as such. This would seem to be blatantly obvious but there are a number of limitations:
1) progressive restriction may occur in functions tied to a particular language variety in a particular community, a phenomenon which often precedes the death of a language. In such a case we may speak of a functionality decrease in a language, a kind of "maladaptation to the speakers' needs" (precisely what Lass, 1980: 84 wishes to exclude);
2) the community's restricted use of a language may be accompanied by phenomena of language disgregation: massive interference by a dominant language, increases in the number of semi-speakers whose grammar contains many examples of changes deviating from the norm. The result of these changes will be a "bastardisation" of the language which in some cases may contribute to hastening the demise of the language in question (Hill and Hill 1977; Giacalone Ramat, 1979 a).

Put more concisely, a combination of socio-political factors may make a language effectively less functional and less adequate. It does not seem that we can accept the opinion of those who see no relationship between the restriction in use of a language as a means of communication and the decline and decay of its linguistic devices. I do not wish to deny by this that the *causes* of language death as a social phenomenon are external to language: I believe they are to be sought not so much in rapid social change, in the process of industrialization or in changed economic circumstances, but rather in poor social control, in the high number of semi-speakers, particularly among young people, to whom the dying language is not transmitted within the family.

---

[11] Slobin 1977, 186 et seq. presents "four basic ground rules to which a communicative system must adhere if it is to function as a full-fledged human language". These goals are: 1) be clear (in the sense of striving to maintain a one-to-one mapping between underlying semantic relations and surface forms); 2) be humanly processible in ongoing time; 3) be quick and easy; 4) be expressive. The tension between these four factors is present — according to Slobin — in all situations affecting language change: child development, historical change, language contact, depidginization or creolization.

This conclusion confirms the need to take "social" factors into account, ("social" in the broad sense of the term) when speaking about language functions. A language may become dysfunctional *both* sociolinguistically when it is no longer used by its speakers in the functions for which it was used by previous generations *and* linguistically more or less in the same circumstances.

In child language and second language learning examples of dysfunctionality are gradually ousted as the learning process proceeds. In language death, on the other hand, these phenomena are not reabsorbed but tend on the contrary to accumulate.

REFERENCES

Antinucci, F. 1977. *Fondamenti di una teoria tipologica del linguaggio.* Bologna: Il Mulino.
Campbell, L. 1980. Explaining universals and their exceptions. *Papers from the IVth ICHL*, ed. by E. Traugott et al., 17–26. Amsterdam: Benjamins.
Dardano, M. 1978. *La formazione delle parole nell'italiano d'oggi.* Roma: Bulzoni.
De Mauro, T. 1976. *Storia linguistica dell 'Italia unita.* Bari: Laterza.
Dorian, N. 1981. *Language death. The life cycle of a Scottish Gaelic dialect.* Philadelphia: University of Pennsylvania Press.
Dressler, W. 1977a. *Grundfragen der Morphonologie.* Wien: Verlag der österreichischen Akademie der Wissenschaften.
— 1977b. Wortbildung bei Sprachverfall. *Perspektiven der Wortbildungsforschung*, ed. by H. E. Brekle and D. Kastovsky, Bonn: Bouvier Verlag.
— 1981. On word formation in Natural Morphology. *Wiener Linguistische Gazette* 26. 3–13.
Giacalone Ramat, A. 1979a. *Lingua, dialetto e comportamento linguistico. La situazione di Gressoney.* Aosta: Musumeci.
— 1979b. Language function and language change in minority languages. *Journal of Italian Linguistics* 4. 141–62.
— 1982. Explorations on syntactic change. Relative clause formation strategies. *Papers from the Vth ICHL*, ed. by A. Ahlqvist, 283–92. Amsterdam: Benjamins.
Guilbert, L. 1975. *La créativité lexicale.* Paris: Larousse.
Harris, M. B. 1982. On explaining language change. *Papers from the Vth ICHL*, ed. by A. Ahlqvist, 1–14. Amsterdam: Benjamins.
Hill, J. and K. Hill. 1977. Language death and relexification in Tlaxcalan Nahuatl. *International Journal of the Sociology of Language* 12. 55–69.
Itkonen, E. 1982. Change of language as a prototype for change of linguistics. *Papers from the Vth ICHL*, ed. by A. Ahlqvist, 142–8. Amsterdam: Benjamins.
Jaberg, K. 1936. *Aspects géographiques du langage.* Paris: Droz.
Jespersen, O. 1949. *Efficiency in linguistic change.* Copenhagen: Munksgaard.
Lass, R. 1980. *On explaining language change.* Cambridge: Cambridge University Press.

Leumann, M. 1944. Gruppierung und Funktionen der Wortbildungssuffixe des Lateins. *Museum Helveticum* 1. 129–51.
Lüdtke, H. 1980. Sprachwandel als universales Phänomen. *Kommunikationstheoretische Grundlagen des Sprachwandels*, ed. by H. Lüdtke, 1–19. Berlin: de Gruyter.
Malkiel, Y. 1977. The social matrix of Paleo-Romance postverbal nouns. *Romance Philology* 31. 55–90.
Mayerthaler, W. 1981. *Morphologische Natürlichkeit.* Wiesbaden: Akademische Verlagsgesellschaft Athenaion.
Meisel, J. 1980. Linguistic simplification. A study of immigrant workers' speech and foreigner talk. *Second language development*, ed. by S. W. Felix, Tübingen: Narr.
Migliorini, B. 1957. I nomi maschili in *-a*, in *Saggi linguistici*, 53–108. Firenze: Le Monnier (First published in 1934).
Ramat, P. 1984. Es war ein König in Thule ... Dem sterbend seine Buhle...: on the rise and transformations of morphosyntactic categories, *Historical Syntax*, ed. by J. Fisiak, 351–79. The Hague: Mouton.
Thumb, A. and R. Hauschild. 1959. *Handbuch des sanskrit.* Dritte Aufl. Heidelberg: Carl Winter.
Tollemache, F. 1954. *I deverbali italiani.* Firenze: Sansoni.
Trudgill, P. 1976–77. Creolization in reverse: reduction and simplification in the Albanian dialects of Greece. *Transactions of the Philological Society* 1977, 32–50.
Wiegand, N. 1982. From discourse to syntax. *Papers from the Vth ICHL*, ed. by A. Ahlqvist, 385–93. Amsterdam: Benjamins.
Slobin, D. 1977. Language change in childhood and history. *Language learning and thought*, ed. by J. Macnamara, 185–214. New York: Academic Press.
Wurzel, W. 1983. Thesen zur morphologischen Natürlichkeit. *Zeitschrift für Germanistik* 2. 196–208.

THE INDO-EUROPEAN ORIGIN
OF THE BALTO-SLAVIC -ē- AND -ā- PRETERITE

JENS ELMEGÅRD RASMUSSEN

As is well known, the two preterite formations of East Baltic, the ē-preterite and the ā-preterite, are in complementary distribution in Modern Standard Lithuanian,[1] while the Latvian standard language has only -ā- and Latvian dialects are found to agree with the general picture of Lithuanian.[2] The forms of Old Prussian are not all entirely clear, but quite possibly only the ē-preterite is attested, a situation that may reflect loss of the ā-type.[3]

While some Lith. ē-preterites may well reflect a sequence *-i̯-ā- (e.g. sakýti, prt. sãkė, and ē-preterite with j-presents),[4] there is no global phonological possibility of reducing the two types to one common source. Despite the modern complementary distribution, there must be a morphological justification for the choice of either -ē- or -ā- in a given form, and certainly the specific appearance of the resulting forms in which -ē- and -ā- are tied to different root structures, demands an explanation.

One very significant fact was brought forward many years ago by Endzelin[5] and later elaborated upon by Stang[6] and Kølln,[7] viz. the

---

[1] On the details of the rules regarding the Lithuanian preterite as contrasted with the present see the beautiful survey in W. P. Schmid 1966.
[2] On Latvian see W. P. Schmid 1967. Divergences between Lith. and Latv. can be accounted for by recognizing 'das Vordringen der ē-Präterita im Litauischen, der ā-Präterita im Lettischen' (ibid. 122).
[3] The examples of ā-preterite given by Stang 1966: 375 are all somewhat insecure: kūra 'bawet' may be a present form, cf. Endzelin 1944:178; lymu-/lima-/līma 'broke' may be from a stem with derivative -ā-, as may imma 'took', cf. Trautmann 1910: 290, pro-wela 'betrayed' may have *-ē- like Lith. výlė (if this is not from *-i-ā-, cf. prs. vı̃lia), cf. billa, bela, byla beside billē 'said'. However, the comparisons /līmā-/: Latv. l̦imu 'ich knickte' and -wela: Latv. vilu, -vylu (Endzelin 1944: 177f) are quite impressive.
[4] Cf. -ėjo, -ójo from verbs (ė̃ti, -óti etc.
[5] Endzelin 1910:18f sub degt; 1922:567 with n. 3, 667f; 1938:190.
[6] Stang 1942:189, 1966:376f.
[7] Kølln 1969, esp. the conclusion p. 63.

existence of both formations with the same verb, and with a functional opposition: In Lith. and Latv. dialects, *deg-* 'burn' has a transitive *ē*-prt. and an intransitive *ā*-prt.,[8] and in fact *ē*-preterites are practically always transitive, while *ā*-preterites may be both transitive and intransitive, but, as pointed out by Kølln,[9] they are almost always *ineffective*, i.e. indicating an action that leaves the object unaltered.[10] This situation is very strongly reminiscent of the IE opposition of active and middle, if for no other reason, because it is an opposition of verbal voice, and this was the voice opposition the IE verb had. One may indeed cite quite good parallels from more well-preserved IE languages, cf., from Greek, transitive and effective *kaíō* 'I burn', intransitive *kaíomai*, and transitive but ineffective *dérkomai* 'I see'. In a first draft of the present paper it was, therefore, my intention to prove this point; in the meantime, however, the view that the *ē*-preterite represents the IE active, the *ā*-preterite the middle, voice has appeared in print in Gert Klingenschmitt's penetrating study of the Armenian verb.[11] While I agree with the outstanding representative of the school of Indo-European studies emanating from the city of Erlangen on the central point regarding the original nature of the opposition, I hold a somewhat different view on most of the details. As a consequence, the present paper will not so much try to demonstrate that the opposition active : middle *is* at play, but will rather discuss exactly *how*.

According to Klingenschmitt, the transitive preterite stem **degē̂-* is formed from the corresponding present stem **deg-e-* on the analogy of the verb 'to be', in which a present **esti* stands beside an inherited imperfect **ēst* (i.e. IE **e-h₁es-t* with the augment otherwise only known from

---

[8] The specific forms are given by Endzelin, cf. the references in note 5. On the whole question cf. also the detailed survey by Kazlauskas 1968.362—65.

[9] See the examples collected and discussed by Kølln 1969:33ff and Stang 1966: 385. W. P. Schmid's rejection (1967:122) of the view that the choice of *ē* and *ā* depends on the verbal voice is invalid, if the stem-formation of the present with which the preterite is correlated in Schmid's analysis, is itself largely dependent on the verbal voice.

[10] In Kølln's terminology, *effective* is employed in a sense that includes both what is normally called effective (effective verbs being such that bring about or cancel the very existence of an object, like *dig a hole, put out a fire*) and what is generally referred to as *affective* (affective verbs denoting a change in the state of an independently existing object, as *shoe a horse*), cf., e.g., Marouzeau 1951:12 and 83. I am indebted to my colleague Svend Erik Rosenberg for enlightenment on this point.

[11] Klingenschmitt 1982:3—5 with notes 5—8.

Indo-Iranian, Greek, Armenian, and Phrygian). The imperfect is continued by OChS *bě* and, in part restructured, OPr. *be, bei, bēi* (cf. *dai* from *dā-* 'give'), both with a secondary *b-* taken over from associated forms like the infinitives *byti, būton* etc., cf. OHG *bim* vs. Goth. *im*. I am in no doubt that this analysis represents a major breakthrough in Balto-Slavic diachrony as far as the verb 'be' is concerned. For the ē-preterite it is highly suggestive too, and it may look particularly persuasive if the 2sg forms are picked out for demonstration: Before the special Baltic *and* Slavic restructuring of the thematic 2sg prs. form to *-ei̯* (athematic *-sei̯*, on the analogy of which Slavic reshaped the thematic ending to *-esei̯*),[12] pre-Balto-Slavic had the IE form in *-esi* which coincided exactly with the whole of the 2sg prs. *ési* 'you are'; then, after the elimination of the augment, except for the verb 'be' where it had been fused with the root to give *ẽs*, the thematic ipf. *degẽs* was changed to *degẽs* so that the forms rhymed in both tenses. This would indeed explain why the analogical -ē- did not hit the root segment instead. In point of fact a system

esi	ẽs		esi	ẽs
degesi	degẽs		degesi	dẽges

is rather more likely than

esti	ẽst		esti	ẽst
degeti	dẽget		degeti	dẽget

to result from a copying of the inflexion of 'be'.

In this explanation, the key role played by the 2sg in its Indo-European, not its reshaped Balto-Slavic, form indicates that the creation of the ē-preterite was anterior to the disintegration of the Balto-Slavic unity also. And in fact both -ē- and -ā- are found in Slavic too, namely as the basis of the Slav. imperfect, cf. OChS *vezě-aše* 'was driving' : *zъva-aše* 'was calling' agreeing with the Lithuanian types *vėžė* 'drove' : *lĩko* 'was left over'. The special Slavic form of the imperfect is no doubt due to restructuring after the aorist inflexion of durative verbs in derivative -ā- as convincingly argued by Bech.[14] The main point of interest here, however, is merely that both -ē- and -ā- belonged to Common Balto-Slavic.

In Klingenschmitt's analysis,[14] the -ā- proceeds from enlarged forms

---

[12] Rasmussen 1981:18–21.
[13] Bech 1971:8–29, esp. 13–17.
[14] Loc. cit. (n. 11).

of the middle. According to Klingenschmitt, this 'Medialparadigma des urindogermanischen athematischen Wurzelaorists' had a 1sg in *-$h_2$ãm with a circumflex vowel produced by the encounter of the ending *-h_2a with an element *-om, this giving, in Greek, the further reshaped 1sg middle ending -omān and, in Balto-Slavic, a form *-ãn, on whose reanalysis as *-ã-n the whole paradigm of the ā-preterite is supposed to be based. As for Gk. -omān, I would rather take this to be restructured from the thematic middle (whence also athematic -mān), IE *-a-h_2, with an ending /-h_2/, the zero-grade of //-H_2e//, selecting the thematic vowel /-e-/, here coloured to -a- because next to h_2.[15] This would of course not give a circumflex, but there is no way of telling which intonation -mān would have, had it been accented. With regard to the Balto-Slavic ā-preterite I consider a totally different explanation more likely.

It is doubtlessly significant that the ā-preterite selects the zero-grade of the root while the ē-preterite is linked to root shapes that do not easily go into the zero-grade. The ā-prt. is certainly sometimes the continuation of the aorist middle, cf. Lith. lĩko, kir̃to 'cut' from verbs which in IE formed nasal presents (Ved. riṇákti, kṛntáti). This again indicates that the opposition -ē- : -ā- reflects, in some fashion, the IE opposition of active vs. middle. I think the ultimate solution has been given by Jasanoff, though not for these specific languages. In his book 'Stative and Middle in Indo-European' Jasanoff calls attention to the interesting fact that the paradigms continuing the IE middle reflect the thematic vowel as a constant *-o- in Gothic, Hittite, and Tocharian.[16] In this

---

[15] The rest of Proto-Greek /-omān/ is pure analogy: /-m-/ is from the present ending /-mai/ (where it is already analogical on the active /-mi/), the final /-n/ is from the active /-o-n/, the whole segment /-mān/ being added to the thematic stem anew. — The nature of Klingenschmitt's element *-om is not entirely clear; on p. 4 it is expressly identified as a deictic particle with Ich-Deixis seen also in the personal pronoun *eĝ-óm 'I', but the parallel treatment of 2sg *-th_2e-es (p. 6) seems to indicate that the thematic secondary active ending *-o-m may also be involved. Incidentally, if all the Vedic pronouns ah-ám, tu-ám, ay-ám etc. contain this element, there is nothing particularly ich-deiktisch about it (unless, of course, ahám is taken as the analogical basis of all the rest). I agree with Klingenschmitt, of course, in rejecting the comparison of the ē-preterite with the Greek /-ēn/-aorist which is constantly intransitive (Kl. p. 3[5]).

[16] Jasanoff 1978:47f. Jasanoff no doubt rightly dismisses the Baltic evidence for persistent *-o- (vẽda, -ame, -ate), cf. the near-persistent -e- in Slavic. I doubt, however, that this is to be explained by the open pronunciation of /e/ after /i̯/ in Lithuanian, and by the development i̯o > i̯e in Slavic; both may be very simple cases of paradigmatic levelling, and the different direction of the levelling may be purely accidental.

one may see a true reflexion of the PIE situation, taking the e/o interchange of Greek, Italic, Celtic, and Phrygian to be analogical on the active.[17] Since IE o gives BSl. a, we may perhaps add Balto-Slavic to the list, provided the length of ē : ā can be explained as secondary.

For the long -ē-, Klingenschmitt's analogy with 'be' may, but only just may, be the correct solution, for -ā- we must think of something else. The BSl. aorist — and the Slavic imperfect is certainly modelled on the sorist — had apparently received the inflectional segments of the thematic imperfect, cf. OChS *nese* vs. Vedic *ā́naṭ* 'brought, reached' from *$e\ h_2nek̂-t$, and consider the endings of the Lithuanian preterite -*iaũ*, -*iaĩ*, -*ė* etc. and -*aũ*, -*aĩ*, -*o* etc., in which -*ė*- and -*ā*- are plainly enlarged by the segments -*ù*, -*ĭ*, -*a* (-*úo*-, -*ĭe*-, -*a*-) of the thematic present.

I therefore suggest as a solution for both the ē and the ā preterite that a BSl. 3sg ipf. act. *$vež-e$[18] (from IE prs.inj.act. *$u̯ég^h$-e-t after the loss of final stops), middle *$vež-a$ (from *$u̯ég^h$-o-to through levelling to *-o-t after the active) were simply expanded by the endings -e-, -a again, this giving first the hiatic sequences *-ee-, *-aa-, later the long circumflex vowels -$\tilde{e}$-, -$\tilde{a}$-. This is no doubt a repercussion of the steady generalization of thematic forms: when athematics like the aorist *neć- received an extra -e, so did thematics like the imperfect *vež-e. In the synchronic analysis the whole segment comprising the thematic vowel + the personal ending proper was no doubt felt as the regular ending to be added to the synchronic stems. This gives the forms later emerging as OChS *nese* and Lith. *vėžė*, OChS ipf. *vezė-aše*. Of these, the former is an aorist, the

---

[17] Jasanoff posits *-e- for the middle of the 2. person, however, cf. his reconstructions 2sg *bhéretar, 2pl *bhéredhu̯e (p. 52). The reason for this is not stated very clearly in Jasanoff's book, but the references to (1) Toch. A *aräṣt*, B *erṣt(o)* 'you call forth' (47), (2) a Baltic thematic ending *-ei of the 2sg, and (3) Latv. dial. 2pl ipv. in -et (both 48) suggests that this is the material on which the claim is based. Now, all of this may simply reflect the state of affairs of the active: the Toch. forms are 2sg act., so that the old middle ending *-th₂e may simply have been added to the stem of an old forms in *-e-si; Baltic '-ei' should no doubt be -ai, cf. OPr. -sai (and see the reference in n. 12); and why cannot Latv. -et be active *-e-te?

[18] I write the Balto-Slavic reflexes of the IE palatals as *ć and *ź because (1) the degree of palatality was probably intermediary between Lith. š, ž and OPr., Latv., Slav. s, z, and certainly less than the 'cerebralization' product of *s (Lith. and Latv. š, Slav. x), and (2) Trubačev 1973:310—13 draws attention to (pre-) Slavic loanwords in Lith. with /st/ for (later) Slav. /s/ from IE *k̂, in which Trubačev convincingly sees an attempt to render a Slav. pronunciation [ts]. This means, then, that the IE palatals had preserved their original occlusion in Balto-Slavic, having been merely opened to the state of affricates.

latter an imperfect, simply because the IE stem *$h_2ne\hat{k}$- is the stem of an aorist, while *$u\acute{e}\hat{g}^h$-e- is a present stem. The restriction of the long ē-vowel to the imperfect in Slavic is obviously due to the fact that IE had almost no thematic aorists (only two cases are secured),[19] while the thematic formation was *the* present stem formation from the earliest times.

In the ā-preterites that exhibit ablaut of the root vowel a thematic basis is excluded. The forms *kirta, *lika, *ǵuva are therefore obviously 3sg middle forms of the aorists, cf. Vedic (secondarily normalized with active endings) ákṛta-h, áh(u)va-t, Skt. arica-t. Here the ablaut grade, the intransitive emaning of most of the examples (the stem *kṛt-o- forming an exception as a deponent with active meaning also in the RV: 1.63.4 ví dásyūm̐r yónāv ákṛto vṛthāṣáṭ 'winning at will, you smote the Dasyus in their camp'), and the o-form of the 'ending' all work together in pointing to middle forms of root aorists whose existence in PIE can be independently secured.

There is one big problem in this: If the preterite lĭko is from the aorist *middle*, why then is the present liēka,[20] apparently a continuation of the full-grade alternant of the aprist *active*, IE *e-leik^w-t? I think the answer to this has been indicated by the Erlangen school again. Vedic forms like gámati, kárati, vánate are not, as supposed by Renou,[21] representatives of a special category intermediary between indicative and subjunctive with a 'valeur mi-réelle mi-modale' (1932: 15), but are simply, as demonstrated by K. Hoffmann,[22] regular subjunctives of root aorists; due to the largely subjective choice between subjunctive and indicative, there were many contexts in which the difference did not really matter (thus they could both be used of the future), or where we have no clues for knowing which is meant. Therefore, Gk. leípō, Lith. liekù,[23] or Goth. qimiþ, Lith. gḗma, and OChS nesetъ, Lith. nèša, Ved. náśat are in origin no doubt aorist subjunctives. In this light, the question about the apparent difference of verbal voice between liēka and lĭko can be answered: I have the audacity to declare that they both reflect middle forms of the root aorist, only lĭko is from the indicative, while liēka is from the subjunctive.

---

[19] IE *e u̯id-é-t 'saw' and *e h₁ludʰ-é-t 'went'; see Cardona 1960, esp. 123.
[20] On the relation of liēka to OLith. liēkti see the remarks in the chart given below (no. 3).
[21] Renou 1932 passim.
[22] K. Hoffmann 1955 (=1976:384–86). See also Narten 1968:114.
[23] But only indirectly in this form, see the chart below.

Already in PIE, the subjunctive displayed a semi-independent status with regard to ablaut of the root segment: it simply has full grade all through, irrespective of the ablaut properties of the corresponding indicative. This situation is most probably due to levelling: both the normal type act.sg. *$k^w ér$- : mid. *$k^w r̥$- (Ved. á-kar : á-kr̥ta) and the ´acrostatic` type *$stéu̯$- : *$stéu̯$- (Ved. stáuti : stave) chose the short-vowel full-grade alternant for the sbj. of both voices: *$k^w ér$-e-t(i) : *$k^w ér$-e-to(r) and *$stéu̯$-e-t(i) : *$stéu̯$-e-to(r), cf. Vedic kárat(i) : kárte like stávat : stávate; cp. also the fact that the Gk. future which in the main continues IE subjunctive forms, has e-grade as its characteristic vocalism: édomai, eleúsomai etc. I suspect that the subjunctive middle had the same e/o interplay of the thematic vowel as the active and that this was further instrumental in the decline of the constant -o- of tFe middle in a fair number of languages.

This explanation of a number of verbal forms on the basis of the IE middle only concerns the stem formation. As to the endings, IE middle endings are nowhere reflected in the whole of Balto-Slavic.[24] The most reasonable explanation of this is probably that the active endings were generalized at some point in time anterior to the disintegration of the Balto-Slavic unity.

There remains the question of the relation between the two ā-stems seen in the OChS ipf. zъva-aše and the aor. zъva, corresponding to which Lithuanian has only the type kir̃to. Due to the fact that Balto-Slavic consists of two branches only, it is of course very difficult to reconstruct the final phase of the BSl. unity from which they both proceed. However, the following is, I suspect, a fair guess:

From the aorist active *neć-, the subjunctive -neć-e- assumed the function of the present (and future, and old function of the sbj.); when the aor. *neć- took on the thematic ending giving 3sg *neć-e, so did the preterite of the present stem, this giving the imperfect *neć-e-e as described above. With verbs of this inflexion, the ipf. could now just as well be seen as derived from the aor. by the doubling of its 3sg desinential segment. This seems to have had repercussions for the middle: the 3sg mid. aor. ind. *ẑuv-a ´called` had a different ablaut makeup from its subjunctive which was *ẑav-e- (IE *$ĝ^h áu̯h$-e-to[r]). On the analogy of aor. *neć-e : *neć-e-e, the aor. *ẑuv-a generated an ipf. *ẑuv-a-a. It is possible that the later generalization of long -ā- for both the aorist and

---

[24] OPr. 1sg -mai, 1pl -mai, 2pl -tai are obviously modelled on the 2sg -sai on which see the reference in n. 12. On Gk. /-mai/ cf. n. 15.

the imperfect reflects a straightforward development of *-a-e to *-a-a in the aorist with *-e added from the type *neć-e, but it may also be a matter of analogy from the aorist of 'be', Lith. bùvo, from IE *$bʰuáh_2$-t,[25] cf. OLat. sbj. (from aor. inj.) *fuat*. It is impossible to know whether the difference aor. *-a: ipf. *-a-a still existed in the final period of Balto-Slavic. My suggestion is merely that at some prestage of Proto-Slavic, be it before or after the point indicated by the term Balto-Slavic, it did exist.

The remains only to sum up the hypothesis of the present paper by indicating the specific forms of a number of selected verbal inflexions which, either directly or in some reshaped guise, are continued by the forms of Baltic and Slavic:

1. *$u̯éĝʰ$- 'convey'.
    Prs. stem *$u̯éĝʰ$-e/o-
    Act.: prs. ind. *$u̯éĝʰ$-e-ti > prs. *véžet(i): OChS vezetъ, Lith. vẽža.
        ipf. *e $u̯éĝʰ$-e-t > ipf. *veže→*veže-e: OChS ipf. vezě-aše,
                                                                    Lith. pr t.vẽžė.
        sbj. *$u̯éĝʰ$-ē-t(i)→ +
    Mid.: prs. ind. *$u̯éĝʰ$-o-tor→ +
        ipf. *$u̯éĝʰ$-o-to→ + (or Baltic type *deg-ā-?)
        sbj. *$u̯éĝʰ$-e-to(r)→ +
    Aor. stem *$u̯éĝʰ$-s-/*$u̯éĝʰ$-s-
    Act.: aor. ind. *e $u̯éĝʰ$-s-t > aor.: Serb. ChS 1sg věsъ.
        sbj. *$u̯éĝʰ$-se-t(i)→ +
    Mid.: aor. ind. *e $u̯éĝʰ$-s-to→ +
        sbj. *$u̯éĝʰ$-se-to(r)→ +

2. *$h_2nek̂$-/*$h_2enk̂$- 'reach'.
    Prs. stem *$h_2énk̂$-/*$h_2ánk̂$- not continued in BSl.
    Aor. stem *$h_2nék̂$-/*$h_2n̥k̂$-
    Act.: aor. ind *e $h_2nék̂$-t > aor. *neć-→*neć-e-: OChS nese.
        sbj. *$h_2nék̂$-e-t(i)→prs. (-fut.) *neć-e/o-: OChS nesetъ,
        Lith. nẽša; with ipf. *neć-e→*neć-e-e: OChS nesě-aše.
    Mid. aor. stem not continued in BSl.

3. *$lei̯kʷ$- 'leavel'.
    Prs. stem *$linékʷ$-/*$linkʷ$- in Lith. dial. (Pagramantis) link (Fraenkel LEW 37tf), now liñka (Zinkevičius 1966:349), obviously from *link-ti; cf. OPr. polīnka 'Bleibt'.
    Aor. stem *$léi̯kʷ$-/*$likʷ$-

---

[25] Unshortened Lith. -o reveals circumflex *-ã̄ from *-ā + thematic -a, cf. above.

Act.: aor. ind *e léik̑ʷ-t→ +
sbj. *léik̑ʷ-e-t(i)→ +
Mid.: aor. ind. *e likʷ-ó (*-tó)→aor. *lik-a, to which ipf. *lik-a-a: Lith. lìko.
sbj. *léik̑ʷ-e-to(r)→prs. *léik̑-e-, in Lith. early reshaped after the athematic *linkti: OLith. liẽkti, Mod.dial liẽkta, Mod. Standard liẽka. See Specht 1935:87 - 89; liẽka is thus not a direct continuation of the thematic form of the sbj.

4. *ĝʰaṷh- 'call'.
Prs. stem uncertain, if *ĝʰuh-éi̯-e/o-(Ved. hváyati) not continued in BSl.
Aor. stem *ĝʰáṷh--/*ĝʰuh-'
Act. not continued in BSl.
Mid.: aor. ind. *e ĝʰuh-ó (*-tó)>aor. *ẑuv-a, to which ipf. *ẑuv-a-a: OChS aor. zъva, ipf. zъva-aše.
sbj. *ĝʰáṷh-e-to(r)→prs. (-fut.) *ẑav-e-: OChS zovetъ.[26]

I have here only been concerned with the very basic parts of the verbal inflexion. As is well known, a great multitude of individual verbs present special problems that must be tackled on a more local basis. What I do claim to have shown by my suggestions are two things: (1) That the classical picture of the IE verb as still quite well preserved in Indo-Iranian and Greek is a useful point of departure also for the explanation of the Baltic and Slavic verb; and (2) that the developments here presented go very smoothly through a common intermediary stage. The preterite formations of Baltic and Slavic, for all their differences in the details, presuppose quite an impressive array of common innovations as compared to the reconstructed IE proto-language. Inflexional endings and inflexional analogical processes are not normally borrowed. A possible alternative explanation would be creolization: Baltic grammar with Slavic lexicon or vice versa. However, both branches display a considerable degree of expansive force over quite some territory so that it is not very likely that one of them should have been thus totally dominated by the other. And indeed, if the concept of a Balto-Slavic unity does correspond to the reality, things ought to look the way they do.

---

[26] I have not entered a Balto-Slavic middle-voice dimension in the chart, because it is highly probable that it had been obliterated by this time (cf. above). It cannot be completely excluded, however, that the Baltic preterites in -ē- and -ā- with the same verb are remains of a Balto-Slavic *living* category. One may think of the situation of Verner's Law with the English verb: who would dream of reconstructing a relatively recent prestage with an all-pervading alternation now seen only in *was* : *were* if he had no independent knowledge of the truth?

REFERENCES

Bech, Gunnar. 1971. Beiträge zur genetischen idg. Verbalmorphologie. *HFM*. 44,5. København.
Cardona, George. 1960. *The Indo-European thematic aorists*. Yale Ph.D. Diss.
Endzelin, J. 1910. Zum lettischen präteritum. *KZ* 43. 1–41.
    1922. *Lettischen Grammatik*. Riga: Gulbis.
    1938. *Latviešu valodas skaņas un formas*. Riga: Universitāte.
    1944. *Altpreussischen Grammatik*. Riga: Latvju Grāmata.
Fraenkel, Ernst F. 1955–65, (=LEW). *Litauisches etymologisches Wörterbuch*, Bd. I-II. Heidelberg: Winter.
Hoffmann, Karl. 1955. Vedisch *gámati*. *MSS* 7. 89–92. [Reprinted in Hoffmann 1976: 384–86].
Hoffman, Karl. 1976. *Aufsätze zur Indoiranistik* (Hrsg. Johanna Narten). Wiesbaden: Reichert.
Jasanoff, Jay. 1978. *Stative and middle in Indo-European*. IBS 23. Innsbruck: University.
Kazlauskas, J. 1968. *Lietuvių kalbos istorinė gramatika (kirčiavimas, daiktavardis, veiksmazodis)*. Vilnius: Mintis.
Klingenschmitt, Gert. 1982. *Das altarmenische Verbum*. Wiesbaden: Reichert.
Kolln, Herman. 1969. Oppositions of Voice in Greek, Slavic, and Baltic. *HFM* 43, 4. København.
Marouzeau, J. 1951³. *Lexique de la terminologie linguistique*. Paris.
Narten, Johanna. 1968. Das altindicshe Verb in der Sprachwissenschaft. *Die Sprache* 14. 113–34.
Rasmussen, Jens Elmegård. 1981. Blandede morfologiske problemer i indoeuropæiske enkeltsprog (I). Præliminær version. *Arbejdspapirer udsendt af Institut for Lingvistik*, Kobenhavns Universitet II. København. (Separate pagination.)
Renou, Louis. 1932. A propos du subjonctif védique. *BSL* 33. 5–30.
Schmid, W. P. 1966. Baltische Beiträge IV. Zur Bildung des litauischen Praeteritums. *IF* 71. 286–96.
Schmid, W. P. 1967. Baltische Beiträge V. Zur Praeteritalbildung im Lettischen. *IF* 72. 116–22.
Specht, Franz. 1935. Zur Geschichte der Verbalklasse auf -ē. *KZ* 62. 29–115.
Stang, Chr. S.1942. *Das slavische und baltische Verbum*. Oslo: Skrifter ... Akademi, Hist.-filos. Klasse 1942, No. 1.
    1966. *Vergleichende Grammatik der baltischen Sprachen*. Oslo-Bergen-Tromsö: Universitetsforlaget.
Trautmann, Reinhold. 1910. *Die altpreussischen Sprachdenkmäler*. Göttingen: Vandenhoek & Ruprecht.
Trubačev, O. N. 1973. Leksikografija i etimologija. *Slavjanskoe jazykoznanie. VII Meždunarodnyj s'ezd slavistov*. Varsava, avgust 1973. g. *Doklady sovetskoj delegacii*, 294–313. Moskva: Nauka.
Zinkevičius, Z. 1966. *Lietuviu dialektologija*. Vilnius: Mintis.

VARIABILITY IN WORD FORMATION PATTERNS AND PRODUCTIVITY IN THE HISTORY OF ENGLISH

SUZANNE ROMAINE

It is well known that the number of suffixes in English has increased through borrowing, while others have lost their productivity. I propose to examine one case which has involved an extension in the productivity of a suffix; namely, *-ness*. This suffix is used to form abstract nouns from adjectives (e.g. *good→goodness*, OE *gōd→gōdness*).

The successful spread and productivity of *-ness* is partially accounted for by the fact that it managed to attach itself to native as well as non-native roots and was able to compete with certain French suffixes, especially *-(i)ty* (e.g. *delicacy-delicateness, frailty-frailness* etc.). Other linguistic factors correlated with its productivity have to do with the phonological requirements of the non-native suffixes, e.g. stress placement (*visible→visibility*) and alteration in the stem vowel or consonant (*extreme→extremity, eccentric→eccentricity*. Perhaps the most important extralinguistic factor, however, is genre. I will argue that the great increase in *-ness* formations in the Middle English period is connected with particular genres of discourse where nouns denoting abstract qualities are found in abundance; it is also the case that these genres contain a high rate of foreign to native words. Thus the rise of new genres provided a locus from which an increasing number of *-ness* formations could spread.

I will also address myself to some of the methodological and theoretical issues which arise in trying to relate variability in patterns of word formation to productivity and morphological change.

1. *A brief historical sketch of the development of -ness and -ity*

By way of a brief historical introduction to the problem I would like to comment only very sketchily on the development of the suffixes *-ness* and *-ity* (for fuller discussion, see Romaine, forthcoming).

Looking first at Germanic developments, we can see that the reflexes of this nominalizing suffix found their greatest foothold in Old High German and Old English. The suffixes *-ness* in modern English and *-nis* in modern German are related to Gothic *-assus/-inassus*, as in the example, *þiudinassus*. The suffix acquired its present /n/ through a shift in word boundary in the *n*-stem verbs to which it was attached. In Old English it was used to form abstract feminine nouns, along with other suffixes like, *-hood, -dom, -scipe*. Competition among these was resolved largely in favor of *-ship* and *-ness*, the latter being the most productive. The suffix *-ity*, which is morpho-semantically cognate with *-ness* makes its appearance in 14-15th century loanwords from French, and later, in loanwords from Latin.

Some examples of the development of *-ness* in English and other Germanic languages are given below:

Gothic: weak verbs in -*a/ōn* + *assus*
                                    -*inōn*
e.g. *þiudanon* 'to rule' → *þiudinassus* — 'kingdom'
OHG: *galihnissi* → NHG *Gleichnis*
       finistarnissi → NHG *Finsternis*
OE: *forgifeness* V → N
      yfelnes Adj → N

OE abstract noun formation suffixes: *-ness, -hood, -dom, -scipe* e.g. *drunkenscipe, drunkennesse, drunkenhede*.

2. On productivity and productiveness

A number of scholars have suggested that *-ness* is fully productive Jespersen (1924), for example, says it is possible to add the suffix to any adjective or adjectival word. Indeed, its productivity extends beyond the scope of adjectives, as can be seen in the examples below:

Modern English

formations from major categories: *goodness, jackassness, wellness*
- minor categories: *muchness, threeness, whyness, betweeness*
- phrasal/semi-phrasal: *broken-heartedness, fedupness, up-to-dateness, know-nothingness*
- fully lexicalized: *witness, business, wilderness*.

Some of these examples are nice exceptions to a principle which Aronoff puts forward in arguing for a word-based morphology within generative grammar. As far as -*ness* is concerned, Aronoff (1976:21) is wrong when he says that only major classes can be the product of word formation rules and that only these form classes can be used as bases in the formation of derivatives. At the other end of the productivity cline are fully lexicalized forms, such as *wilderness*, etc., which are long established in English. This is a good demonstration of the inverse relationship between productivity and lexicalization (cf. Bauer 1983:88).

The opposite state of affairs prevails in modern German, where many of the OHG formations have disappeared, and most of the modern formations were established by 1800. As in English, there is a competing French suffix, -*ität*, which applies mainly to foreign bases. Unlike English, however, -*nis* never really extended itself to foreign bases and most of the formations are deverbal. There are a total of 428 derivations in Mater's reverse dictionary (1971), more than 3/4 of which are compounds or derivatives of only 29 bases. Word forms in -*ität* account for nearly as many of the total abstract noun formations (48% as compared to 52% in -*nis*). From a comparative historical perspective it is clear that not only has -*ness* met its most productive locus in English, but the same is true of -*ity* compared with its productivity in French. In French there are a total of 797 words ending in the suffix -*ity* (of these 94 end in -*té*). In English there are a total of 1926 (of these 134 formations end in -(*e*)*ty*, e.g. *safety*). Nouns ending in -*ity* in English account for 33% of the total number of -*ness* and -*ity* formations in English (N=5902), while those ending in -*ness* account for 67%. The difference between English and French on the one hand, and English and German on the other is quite striking.[1]

So far I have spoken of productivity (or productiveness) as if it were a coherent and well-understood phenomenon; this is, however, far from the truth. Common to most of the implicit definitions, however, is some notion of frequency. Looking at dictionaries, as I have just done, gives us a retrospective idea of productivity; that is, a dictionary lists the existing products or established lexemes which have arisen via the application of various word formation rules. Or, in other words, it tells us which words are actual, but not which words are possible. It is impossible to talk about productivity in any meaningful sense without taking into account phonological, syntactic, semantic and pragmatic factors.

---

[1] The English data come from Lehnert's reverse dictionary (1971), and the French from Juilland (1965).

Aronoff's approach to the problem of productivity relies on the assumption that the morphological form of the base is the most important factor. He compared the difference in the number of *-ness* and *-ity* formations which obtain when the suffixes are attached to two distinct classes of adjective. Using a rhyming dictionary he calculated that there are approximately five times as many words of the type, *perceptiveness* as those of the form *perceptivity*. Other bases, however, show the opposite.

Aronoff's approach still does not deal with the question of occurrent vs. possible lexemes and whether the productivity of *existent types* bears a regular relationship to productivity of *possible types*. Aronoff (1976:37) argues that speakers of a language have intuitions about productivity, which entail the notion "likelihood of being a word of the speaker's active vocabulary". I have explored this dimension of productivity in order to see what the limits of inter-subjective agreement are in this area of the lexicon. On this occasion, however, I must confine myself to reporting that the factor of morphological type of base is itself a *dependent*, not an independent variable in productivity. Speakers' intuitions about the possibility of forms in *-ness* and *-ity* are variable, not only according to individual words, but also from speaker to speaker (cf. Romaine, 1983) for a fuller discussion of the data from intuitions). I concluded from my experiments that speakers do not equally share a common lexicon (whatever that may be) any more than they share a common grammar. Nor do speakers have equal access to its rules of word formation. It is arguable how much, if indeed any, of this individual variability can or need be incorporated into a model of grammar.

There are, of course, other factors besides morphological type of the base which have to be considered in the question of productivity. These are listed below.

Factors associated with productivity in *-ness* and *-ity*
i. Morphological type of the base: *-ous, -ive, -able, -al, -ible, -ile, -ic*.
ii. Phonological: consonant alterations: *opaque/opacity*
    stress shift: *authentic/authenticity*
    vowel shift: *sane/sanity*
    divine/divinity
    verbose/verbosity
    profound/profundity
    brief/brevity
iii. Meaning: syntactic/grammatical:
    the meaning of a deadjectival nominalization is simply that the suffix marks a change in form class from one category to another.

pragmatic/stylistic:
non-referential associations of a suffix;
learned vs. unlearned
semantic: *-ness*.

His kindness amazed me (=the fact that he was/the extent to which he was kind) Kindness is a virtue (quality or state of being kind).

Under the heading of phonological factors come stress shift, vowel shift and consonant alternations. In order to use *-ity* forms a speaker must control this part of the morphophonemics of English. Speakers will tend to avoid using words whose pronunciation the yare not sure of. Another important factor is meaning. I use the term in its broadest possible sense to refer not just to referential meaning or semantics, but also to pragmatics and syntax. To take the last of these first, we can distinguish (following Bauer 1983: 185 - 9) between the grammatical vs. lexical meaning of a word formation process. The syntactic meaning of a deadjectival nominalization is simply that the suffix marks a change in form class from one category to another. Even though *-ness* applies to a wider range of base types and form classes than *-ity*, the end result of derivation is a noun. This is not true for *-ity*, however. And again, some of the formations which it creates are exceptions to Aronoff's major form class principle. The su+x *-ity* can combine with a preposition as in *uppity* (cf. *snippety, lickety-split, flippity-flop, blankety-blank*, etc.). In the case of *uppity* and *snippety*, the pragmatic meaning seems to be 'snobbishness' or 'pretentiousness'.

Aronoff (1976:39) suggests that there is a simple relationship between meaning and productivity: a morpheme whose meaning is more semantically coherent will be more productive. The meaning of *-ness* nominalizations can be stated, as indicated above, in terms of a choice between two operations on the base. The semantics of *-ity* derivatives is not nearly so coherent, and more widely divergent. A great many of the established lexemes ending in *-ity* have strayed from their original abstract sense to denote concrete count nouns, and now have a collective or technical sense. The semantic wanderings of deadjectival formations in *-ity* appear to have followed a course from abstract to concrete as sketched out in Figure 1 (p. 456).

The root sense of many *-ity* formations is abstract, i.e. a noun denoting a state, quality or condition, e.g. *nobility* in the sense of 'nobleness', the quality or state of being noble. Some of these formations then became used as nouns denoting occupations, offices, titles or positions signifying the abstract qualities of the titles or positions signifying the abstract

Figure 1: Semantic route for -*ity* formations

Abstract			Concrete	
states/conditions/qualities		things	offices, titles, persons, occupations	collectivities
humanness	nobleness			
	oddness	oddity	nobility	humanity
Germanness	royalness			Germanity
	curiousness	curiosity	royalty	
	antiqueness	antiquity	admiralty	Christianity
			squiralty	society
		wilderness	shrievalty	polity
			celebrity	authority
				sorority
	holiness		holiness	nationality
	highness		highness	
busyness				business

qualities of the occupations, e.g. *admiralty*. Some formations acquired a sense of collectivity or totality of people belonging to an occupation or who have the quality of being associated with it, e.g. *humanity, Christianity* etc.

This semantic itinerary is established for -*ness* too, although the number of -*ness* formations which have strayed from their original abstract sense is far fewer. There are cases where -*ness* formations became used as titles connected with occupations, e.g. *highness*. We can see that where competing -*ness* and -*ity* nominalizations exist, they often occupy different semantic spaces, e.g. *humanness* refers to the quality of being *human*, while *humanity* refers to the collectivity of humans; *antiquity* refers to an old object or time period, while *antiqueness* refers to the state of being antique. Many words of course spread themselves out over more than one slot in this semantic space; for example, *curiosity* can denote the state of being curious, but it can also denote an object having the quality associated with the adjective. *Curiousness*, however, can only denote the quality or state. The fact that the semantics of -*ity* formations is less predictable and less regular than that associated with -*ness* formations is implicated in productivity since people will tend not to use words whose meaning is unclear to them. Throughout Indo-European there seems to be an association between the concepts of abstractness and collectivity on the one hand, and between the semantics of abstractness/collectivity and feminine gender on the other (cf. Baldinger 1950).

Aronoff (1976:56) predicts that it will be impossible for there to be two words with the same meaning and the same root in one person's lexicon at the same time. Others, like Givón (1979) have also suggested that some possible formations will be blocked if there is already an existing lexeme with that meaning (the so-called 'Regel der besetzten Stelle' or pre-emption by synonymy). Blocking doesn't prevent coining; it acts only as a brake on institutionalization Formations in *-ness* often appear in the semantic slots of nouns formed with other abstract deadjectival noun forming suffixes. The individual limits and differences in semantic distinguishability between pairs such as *sincereness/sincerity* and *chasteness/chastity*, *stableness/stability* remain to be investigated.

3. *Productivity from a diachronic perspective*

So far my considerations of the problem of productivity have been largely synchronic. The use of dictionaries and informants' judgements in the study of word formation are in my view essential, but we need texts too to explore other aspects of productivity, where informants have no intuitions. Dictionaries record all actual lexemes and informants give possible lexemes, but both without regard to genre. And productivity is not simply a matter of synchrony or frequency. Even though the average speaker of a language is neither an etymologist nor a student of historical morphology, one cannot understand the present day distribution of *-ness* and *-ity* without a consideration of diachrony. How is it that competing patterns of word formation establish themselves? It is well known that vocabulary statistics can serve as stylistic profiles, but are types of word formation patterns social and stylistic markers?

If trying to define the limits of the lexicon and variability in word formation patterns is problematic synchronically, these tasks are even more so diachronically. Presumably individual variability was as great as it is now, although we do not have the intuitions of informants. Nor are there dictionaries in the early stages. We do know, however, from examining texts that a great deal of variability in spelling and other matters was tolerated before standardization and the appearance of codified norms in dictionaries and grammars. Even though the OED records the dates of entry, these are unreliable, and these dates give us only a rough idea of what the possibilities for an individual in speech and writing were in a particular time period. Again, there is no reason to believe that the actual lexemes in existence at a given time reflect the range of possible lexemes. And we have no idea how familiar an unrecorded but possible item would be to the average person.

A good starting point for comparing the lexical resources available at different stages in the history of English is to look at renderings of the same text over a span of several centuries. This at least enables us to keep topic and genre constant and focus attention on the various devices available for lexicalization of the subject matter. This sort of analysis is possible to do with *De Consolatione Philosophiae* by Boethius. There have been a great many translations of Boethius over the last 500 years not only into English but most of the European languages. The translation by King Alfred in roughly 880 A. D. was the first of the vernacular translations. About another 100 years later Notker produced a translation into OHG. In the 13 - 14th centuries four French versions were produced, one of which, that by Jean de Meun, probably served as the model for Chaucer's translation into Middle English in roughly 1300. Several centuries later in 1593 Queen Elizabeth's Englysshing of Boethius appeared. There has been a more or less continuous tradition of translation from OE to modern English, and in comparing the versions produced by Alfred, Chaucer and Elizabeth we cover a time span of 700 years.

The process of comparing translations requires a number of assumptions, some of which are arguable. One has to consider the semantic and pragmatic resources of the system into which new meanings, new functions and devices for encoding them make their entrance. Word formation rules are optional devices, which can be exploited or avoided as a stylistic resource. Potential semantic slots for lexicalization can always be circumvented by paraphrase or borrowing.

However, I take it as a working principle that such a comparison is a reasonable approach in studying patterns of word formation diachronically. As a beginning I looked at the number of *-ness* formations used in each of the three versions. These are given in Table 1. Alfred used 87 forms; of these 20, or 23% are still in use today. Chaucer only uses 59, 41 (or 69%) of which are still in use; but at this stage there are also a great many *-ity* forms. In Chaucer there are 52. The ratio of *-ness* to *-ity* nominalizations is 53% to 47%. Of the *-ness* forms used in Alfred, 11 of these are matched by Chaucer. In her translation Queen Elizabeth uses *-ness* and *-ity* formation in equal proportions (38 of each). Only four of the *-ness* formations she uses have continuity with Chaucer's and Alfred's forms. She uses fewer *-it* forms (types) than Chaucer; 18 of these match his.

Table 1: *-Ness* formations in Alfred's, Chaucer's and Queen Elizabeth's translations of Boethius

De Consolatione Philosophiae

ALFRED	CHAUCER	ELIZABETH
87 -*ness*	59 -*ness* 53%	38 -*ness* 50%
	52 -*ity* 47%	38 -*ity* 50%

I will discuss in detail here only a few examples of the kind of results this type of comparison yields. First, let's take a case where there is continuity in a form from Alfred to Elizabeth: *sweetness* and *bitterness*. Compare the equivalent texts below:

Alfred: wið swiðe monige *biternesse* is gemenged sio *swetness* þisse worulde.
Chaucer: þe *swetnesse* of mannes *welefulnesse* is yspranid wið many *bitternesses*.
Elizabeth: the *swetness* of mans lyfe with how many *bitternesses* is it mixt.

The comparison here seems at first glance relatively straightforward since the texts are reasonably close matches, but even this simple case is quite complicated and illustrates the difficulties involved in this type of analysis. If we look at the occurrences of *swetness* elsewhere in Alfred, Chaucer and Elizabeth, we find that another possibility is open to Elizabeth, who sometimes uses *doulcenes* where Chaucer and Alfred use *sweetness*. This is made possible by borrowing and native suffixation. Another case in which we can see an increase in the possibilities open to both Chaucer and Elizabeth is in the translation equivalent of Alfred's *godnes*, where Chaucer and Elizabeth also have the option *goodness*, but sometimes use *bounty*. And in some cases where Chaucer uses *goodness*, Elizabeth uses *bounty*.

In the above passage Chaucer uses a form, *welefulnesse*, which does not appear in the equivalent portion of either Alfred's or Elizabeth's text. For *welefulnesse*, Elizabeth has *felicitie*, a form which is not used by Chaucer in this prose text, but which he does use in end-rhymed position in the *Pardoner's Tale*. In other places where Elizabeth has written *felicite*, Chaucer has *blisfulnes*, sometimes *blyþenes*, and Alfred *bliþnesse*. Furthermore, where Chaucer has *blisfulnes* or *welfulnes*, Elizabeth sometimes has *blessdnes* or *happynes*.

Another case concerns the equivalents used by Chaucer and Elizabeth for Alfred's *fæstnes/fæstrædnes/unfæstrædnes*. Chaucer has three choices, *stedfastnesse*, *stablenesss* and *stablete*. When Chaucer writes *unstableness*, Elizabeth has *unstabilitie*. In addition to the French form *stability*, which Chaucer and Elizabeth share, Elizabeth also has *con-*

*stancy*m which is sometimes the equivalent of Chaucer's *stablete* or *stableness*. Elizabeth also uses the term *mutabilitie* where Chaucer writes *unstableness*, although in some cases where Chaucer uses *mutabilitie*, these are matched by the use of *mutabilitie* in Elizabeth; but Chaucer also uses *chaunge* or *chaungying*.

Figure 2: Lexical resources in Alfred, Chaucer and Elizabeth

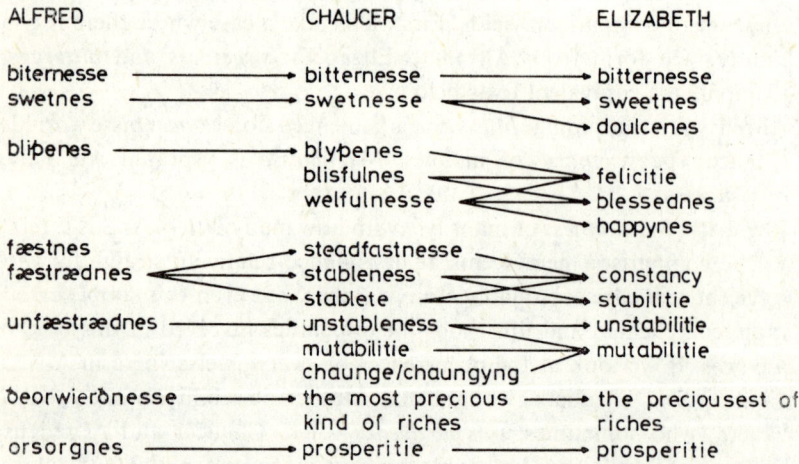

In just these few cases we can see quite a dramatic (and in some instances, wholesale) reshuffling of lexical resources. Firstly, we find borrowings such as *stability* and *stable* which compete with native established forms like *steadfastness*. Sometimes these borrowings integrate themselves into native patterns of word formation as in *stableness* and *unstableness*. Others of this type are Chaucer's *frailness* (*frailty*) and *purenes* (*purete*) and Elizabeth's *doulcenes*. In other cases borrowing leads to suppletion, e.g. *felicitie*, which has no corresponding adjective — not yet, at least, *dignitie*, and *prosperitie*, which replaces native *orsognes*. In some cases resources for lexicalization are enriched as in the case of the forms *stableness/stability*, in other cases reduced or made less transparent. Some of the *-ness* lexicalizations in Alfred have to be paraphrased by Elizabeth and Chaucer due to loss of words from Old English, e.g. ðeorwierðnesse. This continual waxing and waning of lexical resources leads to the renewal of some lexical fields by total or partial relexification with foreign material.

Another factor to be considered in comparing lexical resources from one time period to another is that of individual choice in relation to both the linguistic resources of the system and the semantic and pragmatic constraints imposed on referentiality and expressivity by the genre; or in other words, the constraints on what can be said and how it can be said. Presumably most of the -*ity* formations available to Chaucer were available to others writing at the same time, while those writing earlier or later had somewhat different resources, even though individuals may not choose equally from these. This can be seen clearly in Romaine, forthcoming, where I have compared the data from the Boethius translations with two translations of the *Polychronicon* produced within a short time span of another and which fall between the dates of Chaucer's and Elizabeth's texts of Boethius. I will report here only that it is fairly easy to establish that the two translations follow very different strategies in rendering the Latin into Middle English. On the whole, the unknown translator adheres to Latin-based word choices, introducing may new words, opting wherever possible for a literal translation of the Latin into Latinate-English equivalents. Trevisa, on the other hand, exploits the possibilities of native English word choice to a much greater extent. Trevisa uses a total of 50 nouns ending in -*ness*, compared to the unknown translator's 13; and Trevisa uses only 7 forms in -*ity* compared to the other 44 forms. Using a measure of vocabulary distinctiveness based on the percentage of -*ness* or -*ity* forms out of the total of both, Trevisa's translation scores 79% -*ness* (compared to the unknown translator's 14%) and 21% -*ity* (compared to the unknown translator's 86%).[2]

Comparisons of this type show the enormous range of possibilities open to an educated author/translator writing in the 15th century. The fact that English has borrowed not only a great many words from Latin and French, but also absorbed their derivational system meant that the English writer could draw on four distinct sub-systems of derivational morphology, as indicated in the matrix below (p. 462).

Massive borrowing in the Middle English period disrupted the prevealing native patterns of word formation illustrated in Figure 3 in a number of ways. Firstly, it led to a decline in native affixation processes; this affected the inherited OE system of prefixation more so that suffixation. Secondly, it led to greater lexicalization, competing variants and a fragmenting of the semantic and morphological transparency of a great many lexical fields. Not only did competing formations with the same base such as *fragileness/fragility* appear, but pairs such as *clearness/clarity*, and semantically related sets such as *madness/insaneness/insanity*

---

[2] These figures are based on the First Book.

Figure 3: Subsystems of derivational morphology in English

	SUFFIX	
BASE	foreign	native
foreign	1 fragility	2 fragileness
native	3 oddity	4 oddness

began to appear in great numbers. Almost as soon as French words (and later Latin) were introduced into English, native prefixes and suffixes were added to them, making formations of the second type possible. As soon as sufficient lexical was borrowed for foreign word formation patterns to be transparent and isolable, they could be used productively with both native and newly borrowed foreign words. For the educated, the second and third types of patterns were never a problem; knowing the derivational systems of both foreign and native words made mixing the two possible, especially in translating works from Latin and French into English. Authors such as Chaucer and Wyclif experimented with these types of formations very early. Wyclif, for example, uses *feersness* and *feerste* and *bareyness* and *bareynte* side by side within the same text (both from 1382; *bareynte* is used to translate Latin *sterilitas*). *Feersness* is an example of Type 2 and *bareynte* an example of Type 3. This is quite common in texts of this period; for example, in the *Cloud of Unknowing* we find "in sobirness and in puretie and in depnes of spirite" (Ch. 47). Very often when new formations are introduced, they are glossed, such as in *Ancrene Riwle*, "cherite pet is luve", and Trevisa "sikernesse and surete". The repetition of two synonymous forms, one native and one foreign, is still used in legal registers, where there is a high proportion of French and Latin vocabulary. A number of *-ity* formations owe their appearance to the exigencies of meter and appear first in poetry. They contrast with synonyms of native formation used elsewhere where rhyme isn't an important factor.

4. *The creolization hypothesis*: *support from the lexicon and derivational morphology*

So just how much influence did foreign patterns of word formation have on English? To answer this question one must presuppose some coherent criteria for distinguishing between what is foreign and what is native. Few are aware of the classification problem posed by Type 2 and 3 patterns of word formation, which create words which are neither fish nor fowl etymologically speaking. Others such as Koziol (1937:17) recognize a class of so-called *Zwitterbildungen* ,which includes both these types.

From vocabulary statistics scholars have drawn very different conclusions about the extent and nature of French influence on patterns of word formation. At one extreme, we find those such as Einekel, who was one of the earliest to argue for the influence of French on English syntax, claiming that English retains its basically Germanic character in the area of word formation since the native element constitutes the core of the lexicon and is more basic and frequent. He says (cited in Koziol 1937:9) that the

Fügungsart des heutigen Englischen ist entstanden durch Weiterentwicklung altheimischer Fügungsweise und fremder Sprachgeist ist nur in wenigen Fällen wahrscheinlich, in noch weniger Fällen, sicher beweisbar. Die Bausteine stammen also zwar in ziemlicher Menge aus dem Auslande aber das Gebäude selbst wiest heimischen Stil auf und gerade in den wichtigsten Teile des Baues finden wir auch die geringste Zahl frem der Bausteine.

At the other extreme, linguists such as Bailey and Maroldt (1977) have argued that the influence of French on the development of English was pervasive enough to cast its continuity into doubt. Certainly if one attaches any significance (I myself don't) to the claim of glottochronologists than an accelerated rate of lexical turnover and change is indicative of some abnormality or discontinuity of transmission (cf. for example, Hall's 1959 statistics on rate of lexical retention and change in Neo-Melanesian), then Baugh's observation on the loss of 85% of vocabulary from OE should at least have sparked off some serious attempts to validate relexification. But no one has yet collected the detailed evidence in the area of word formation to support reasonable arguments for or against the creolization hypothesis. And little attention has been paid to the systematic effects of borrowing upon the lexicon cross-linguistically in an effort to compare what happened in English with what happened in German as a result of borrowing from French and Latin, or indeed with what happens in lexical restructuring annd expansion in creoles.

Thanks, however, to Mühlhäusler's work (1979) on the structure of the lexicon in Tok Pisin, we are in a position to offer a preliminary comparison. If we take a grand overview of the historical growth of the English lexicon from OE to present, it is clear that lexical affiliation changes in accordance with both historical depth and differentiation into social and stylistic varieties. The differential use of patterns of word formation can be use to characterize styles in so far as the parameter of individual choice can be subsumed under this heading. In this respect the structure and growth of the English lexicon shares some similarities with Tok Pisin as described by Mühlhäusler (1979:317), where renewed heavy influence from English is leading to instability in urban varieties. This is manifested in the loss of stable conventions about lexical information and the disintegration of structured lexical fields, an increase in the number of suppletive lexical items, and replacement of existing items with loans. It is not sufficient to say that English underwent heavy borrowing without recognizing the fact that borrowing in the lexicon may take place in different ways, diffuse through a language at different rates in accordance with social and stylistic factors, and affect different languages in qualitatively different ways. The extent to which English allows type 2 and 3 formations is notable in the Germanic (and no doubt other) branch(es) of Indo-European. I have already noted the remarkable success both *-ness* and *-ity* have had in English as compared to German.

Much more work remains to be done on the extent to which patterns of neology vary in accordance with style and time-depth. Of inestimable importance in the history of English, however, is the fact that certain literate genres rely heavily on the use of abstract nominalizations particularly religious and philosophical discourse. And it is in Middle English translations of works such as these where *-ity* and new hybrid *-ness* formations are introduced.

Conclusion

My concluding remarks will be mainly methodological. There has been an unfortunate tendency to polarize research into word formation into two camps, one which is generative and synchronic, and the other, diachronic and philological. Now that there is increasing interest in morphology and lexical matters, and the role they play in grammar and linguistic theory, it seems appropriate to reconsider questions of morphology in innovative ways with a pluralistic methodology which is not wedded to a dichotomy between synchrony and diachrony. I hope I have at least pointed the way to a new dimension in the study of morphology and the problem of productivity by taking into account the questions of productivity, individual choice and variability in patterns of word formation.

REFERENCES

Aronoff, M. 1976. *Word formation in generative grammar.* Cambridge, MA: MIT.
Bailey, C. -J. and K. Maroldt. 1977. The French lineage of English. *Langues en contact: pidgins, creoles,* ed. by J. Meisel, 21—53. Tübingen: Gunter Narr Verlag.
Baldinger, K. 1950. *Kollektivesuffixe und Kollektivebegriff.* Berlin: Akademie Verlag.
Bauer, L. 1983. *English word formation.* Cambridge: CUP.
Baugh, A. 1957. *A history of the English language.* New York: Appleton-Century-Crofts.
Givón, T. 1979. Prolegomena to any sane creology. *Readings in Creole Studies,* ed. by I. Hancock, 3 - 37. Ghent, Belgium: E. Story-Scientia P. V. B. A.
Hall, R. A. 1959. Neo-Melanesian and glottochronology. *International Journal of American Linguistics* 25. 265 - 7.
Jespersen, O. 1924. *The philosophy of grammar.* London: Allen and Unwin.
Juilland, A. 1965. *Dictionaire inverse de la langue française.* The Hague: Mouton.
Koziol, H. 1937. *Handbuch der englischen Wortbildungslehre.* Heidelberg: Winter.
Lehnert, M. 1971. *Rückläufiges Wörterbuch der englischen Gegenwartsprache* Leipzig: VEB.
Mater, E. 1971. *Rückläufiges Wörterbuch der deutschen Gegenwartsprache.* Leipzig: VEB.
Mühlhäusler, P. 1979. *The growth and structure of the lexicon in New Guinea pidgin.* Pacific Linguistics. Series C. No. 52.
    1982. Etymology and pidgin and creole languages. *Transactions of the Philological Society* 1981. 99 - 118.
Romaine, S. 1983. Style, productivity and morphological change in the history of English: or, why d elicateness hath very properly given way to delicacy and why perfectness hath not prevailed. *Transactions of the Philological Society.*
    1983. On the productivity of word formation rules and the limits of variability in the lexicon. *Australian Journal of Linguistics.* 3: 176 - 200.

TEXTS

Babington, C. 1869. (ed.). *Polychronicon Ranulphi Hidgen Monachi Cestrensis; together with the English translation of John Trevisa and of an unknown writer of the fifteenth century.* London: EETS.
Morris, R. 18 68 (ed.) *Chaucer's translation of Boethius's "De Consolatione Philosophiae".* London: Early English Text Society.
Pemberton, C. 1899. (ed.) *Boethius De Consolatione Philosophiae Englisht by Queen Elizabeth 1 593.* London: Early English Text Society 113.
Sedgefield, W. J. 1899 (ed.) *King Alfred's Old English version of Boethius De Consolatione Philosophiae.* Oxford: Clarendon Press.

REGIONAL VARIATION IN 19th CENTURY BLACK ENGLISH IN THE AMERICAN SOUTH

EDGAR W. SCHNEIDER

1. *Introduction*

One of the many issues discussed in recent years in connection with the dialect spoken by lower-class black Americans, though a relatively marginal one, is the extent and nature of regional speech variation in "Black English". With respect to the South, especially the rural areas, it is natural to assume that such variation exists. C. M. Wise observed already in 1933:

> The speech of the Virginia negroes is considerably different, and that of the Carolina Negroes somewhat different, from that of Negroes in the rest of the South. Not that the rest of the South has homogeneous Negro speech; but in the rest of the South Negro speech is sufficiently homogeneous for general treatment. (218)

We can expect that future analyses of the *Linguistic Atlas of the Gulf States* will help to clarify this point, yet it is clear that lexical and phonological differences will be found. The situation seems to be different with respect to the speech of blacks living in urban ghetto areas of the North, which seems to be "not greatly affected by geography" (Wolfram 1969:219). This assessment is based upon the fact that a number of sociolinguistic studies of urban black communities in the North have yielded a high degree of uniformity in grammatical patterns at distant places all over the country. Labov speculates that "It is quite possible that many of the features which differentiate Southern dialects disappear in the contact situations of the Northern cities, and the resulting form, stripped of the differentiating rules, is therefore uniform by default.", (Labov et al, 1968, I:6).

The data which I am going to present cannot contribute to a solution of these synchronic questions, but they will be of specific interest in the light of the above observations. I want to demonstrate that systematic regional differences on the levels of grammar and inflectional morphology existed in the speech of southern blacks in the 19th century. The data presented are based upon an analysis of the "slave narratives" compiled by the Federal Writers' Project in the mid-1930's, a collection of more than 2 000 interviews with very old ex-slaves (Rawick 1972). The collection is described and evaluated linguistically by Yetman (1967), Schneider (1981: 46 - 57) and Brewer (1982), who rates it finally "an irreplacable source of morphosyntactic data" (52). Its linguistic reliability, at least for these linguistic levels, has been conceded by scholars of various linguistic camps (Brewer 1973, 1974, 1982; Fasold 1976; Dillard 1972: 41, 64; Viereck 1979: 21). The question for which period they are valid needs a word of comment, however. In the strict sense, these texts represent of course nothing else than the speech of old, mostly uneducated blacks in the 1930s. When we consider, however, that the informants were at that time in their 80s or 90s, or even older, that they acquired their speech patterns in the decades and years preceding the Civil War, and that recent sociolinguistic research has shown that especially with uneducated lower-class informants the speech patterns learned in their youth tend to be persistent throughout their lives (Labov 1970: 35; Wolfram/Fasold 1974: 89), we can assume quite safely that the speech of these ex-slaves preserves mid-19th c. black dialect, or, as Brewer puts it, "elements of the pre-Civil War linguistic system" (1974: 31).

My corpus consists of interviews with 104 ex-slaves from 9 southern states, viz. 12 each from North Carolina, South Carolina, Georgia, Alabama, Mississippi, Tennessee, Missouri, and Texas, and eight from Arkansas. The methodology of selection is described in detail in Schneider 1981: 57 - 65). In short, the interviews were selected randomly from those in the collection meeting three conditions established beforehand: linguistic quality, determined by a pre-test which rates the interviewers, lifelong residence of the informant in the same state, and minimum length of the interview of two pages of direct speech.

The regional factor as analysed in this study demands further explanation. For two reasons lying in the nature of the materials, it is not possible to establish a grid of localities in the manner of a dialectological atlas. First, there are very few informants who spent their whole lives at the same place. Most of them moved once or twice, though only within the area, often from a rural place to the nearby urban center. Second, in almost all states the places of interviews are not distributed

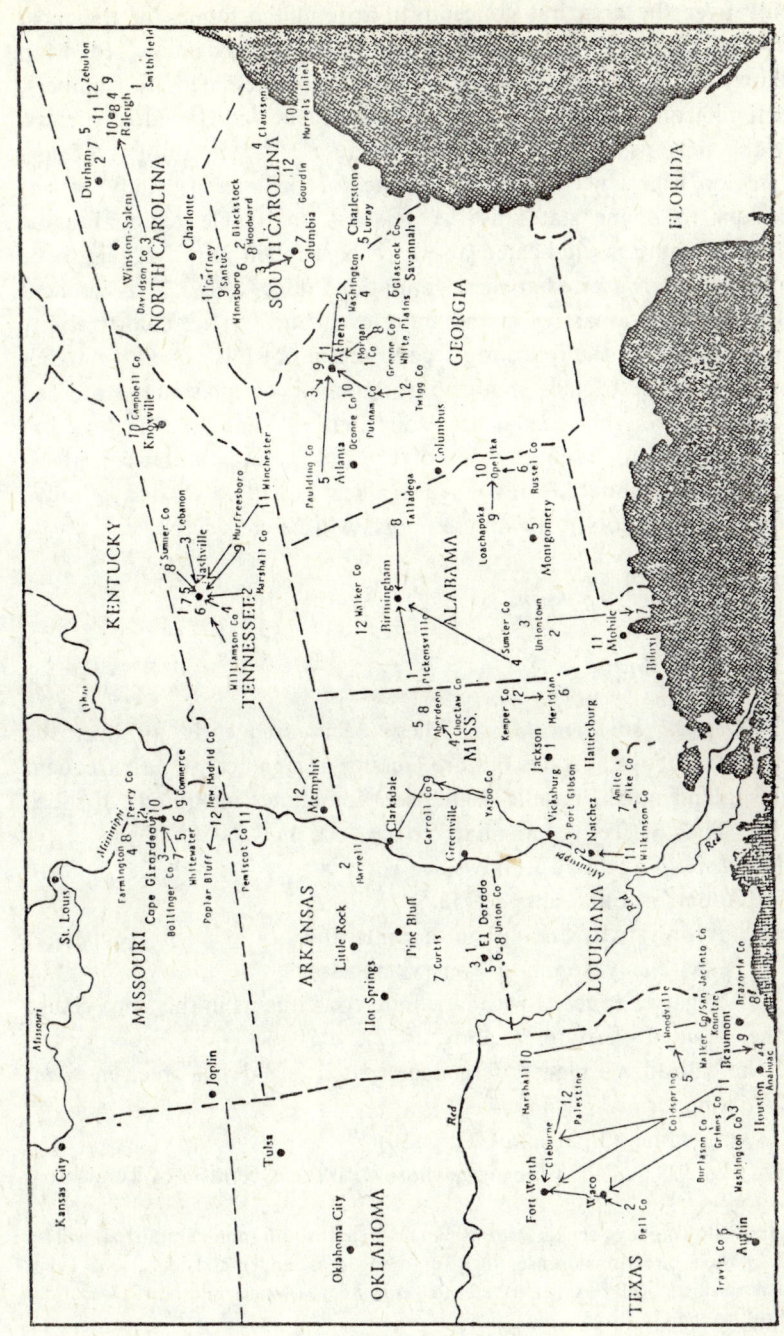

Map 1: Informants' places of residence

evenly over the area but concentrate around the homes of the most active interviewers, leaving some counties completely uncovered. Map 1 shows the home places of the informants represented by numbers, and significant changes of their place of residence, indicated by arrows. For the reasons noted above, and because a larger amount of text per region was a necessary prerequisite for the present study, it was necessary to define states as the smallest analysable regional units, with the limitations indicated above to be kept in mind. It has to be emphasized, however, that these limitations affect only the assignment of forms to sub-areas below the state level, but not the comparability between states. In the following second section of this paper, a number of regionally restricted linguistic forms will be presented, ordered according to roughly similar areal distributions, and the third section will be devoted to a summarizing division of the area under consideration. Only nonstandard forms with a significant quantitative or qualitative regional distribution in the anlysed areas will be considered.[1]

2. Regionally varying forms

2.1. Southern forms

2.1.1. General southern forms. These occur frequently all over the southern and coastal states but are lacking or significantly less frequent in the inland north, usually Tennessee, sometimes including Missouri.
2.1.1.1. The perfective auxiliary *done*, as in

(1) *I done told* you all I knows.
    (Anderson Furr, Ga., p. 352)[2]

is used by only two Missouri informants and not at all in Tennessee, but it is extremely common everywhere else.
2.1.1.2. Negative concord with indefinite constituents in the same clause as the negated verb (cf. Labov 1972), e.g.

(2) he call all his niggers tergedder en tell 'em dey is free, en *doan'* b'long ter *nobody no mo'*.
    (Emmaline Kilpatrick, Ga., p. 10)

occurs over 91 % of the time everywhere with the exception of Tennessee,

---

[1] In the following text, regional terms like north and south (non-capitalized) will be used in their directional sense, relative to the area under consideration. Thus, "northern states" will be taken to refer to Tennessee, Missouri, and North Carolina, "south" to the Gulf states, etc.

[2] All examples are taken from Rawick 1972.

where the rule is applied in only 61.7% of all possible cases (cf. Appendix, table 1).

2.1.1.3. In Tennessee, Missouri and Arkansas, 65.6% of the informants use *ain't* to replace *be* or *have* + a negative, each of them on the average 2.9 times. This is considerably less than in the other states taken together (excluding North Carolina, which will be treated separately with respect to this form), where *ain't* is used by 78.3% of the informants, averaging 4.8 times each (cf. Schneider 1981: 265 for detailed figures).

2.1.1.4. Nonstandard relative pronouns (*what*, the zero-subject and simple personal or possessive pronouns in this function) tend to concentrate in the southern, standard pronouns in the northern states (cf. table 1). For example, *what* is more frequent than its standard counterparts *who/which* everywhere except in Tennessee and Missouri; in North Carolina the ratio of both is about the same.

2.1.1.5. The following example illustrates the so-called "pronominal apposition", or the use of a "pleonastic pronoun":

(3) *Marse Peter he* makes a speech
    (Lucy Ann Dunn, N.C., p. 208f.)

This nonstandard construction is used most frequently in the southern states situated by the Gulf of Mexico, less regularly in the relatively more northern states, and by only one informant in Tennessee (cf. table 1).

2.1.2. *South-southeastern forms.* This group comprises forms with a main extension ranging from Mississippi eastward, usually to Georgia or South Carolina. Outside this area, they are found much less regularly.

2.1.2.1. The form *us* as the subject pronoun of the first person plural dominates in the range of southern states from South Carolina via Georgia and Alabama to Mississippi and holds a strong position in Texas, too. On the other hand, it occurs only sporadically (with one informant each) in Arkansas and Missouri and is lacking completely in Tennessee and North Carolina. Map 2 illustrates this distribution.

2.1.2.2. Among the reflexive pronouns of the third person plural, *theyselves* is the typical southern form, being the only one in Mississippi (with seven informants) and Alabama (with one informant), dominating in Georgia and occurring occasionally in Missouri (2 informants), South Carolina, Tennessee and Arkansas (one informant each). Standard English *themselves* was recorded with two Arkansawyers and one ex-slave each from North Carolina, South Carolina, Georgia, Tennessee and Texas. *Theirselves* will be mentioned later.

2.1.2.3. Two interesting negative structures were found only in the central south. The more strongly deviating variant of negative concord affecting indeterminate constituents not in the same clause but in a following subordinate clause was noticed only in Georgia and Alabama. If a negative subject precedes the verb, the latter is negated only in North Carolina (3 instances), Georgia (1), Alabama (2) and Mississippi (1).

2.1.2.4. The vowel prefix *a-* precedes a verbal ing-form most frequently in the range of southern states (Mississippi: 9 informants; Alabama: 6; Georgia: 8; South Carolina: 5) and in Missouri (9), less often in North Carolina, Arkansas and Texas (3 each), and not at all in the Tennessee corpus.

2.1.2.5. My corpus contains 35 instances of nonstandard comparisons of adjectives and participles (such as *worser, bestes', terriblest, beatenest*), which are heavily concentrated in the south, primarily in South Carolina, Georgia, and Alabama, and slightly less in Mississippi and Texas (cf. table 1).

2.1.3. South Atlantic forms. Here we find a few presumably old linguistic forms which are strongly rooted in and almost restricted to the Carolinas and Georgia, an early settled area with an old plantation culture which corresponds to the „Coastal Southern" area of Gordon Wood's (1971) well-known division of southern dialects. I want to remark only in passing that this coincidence gives important evidence on the history of these forms (cf. Schneider 1983a, 1983b), which, however, is not the topic of the present paper.

2.1.3.1. A perfective three-verb-cluster of the form *had done* + past participle or *is/was/be done* + past participle occurs 43 times in my corpus with four informants from North Carolina, two from South Carolina, eight from Georgia, and one each from Mississippi and Arkansas.

2.1.3.2. Map 3 illustrates the relative share of *-s* and zero as present tense verb endings in the first and second person singular and the third plural (the grammatical persons which have no *-s* in Standard English and yielded enough instances for a breakdown) in each of the states. Two different inflectional systems can be observed. In the Carolinas and Georgia, a dialectal system with the *-s*-morph strongly dominating in all grammatical persons almost everywhere prevails. On the other hand, the standard zero ending in these persons is dominant in all the states situated by and west of the Mississippi river, with Tennessee being closest to the standard inflectional pattern. The state of Alabama, lying between these two clear-cut areas, displays pressure from both,

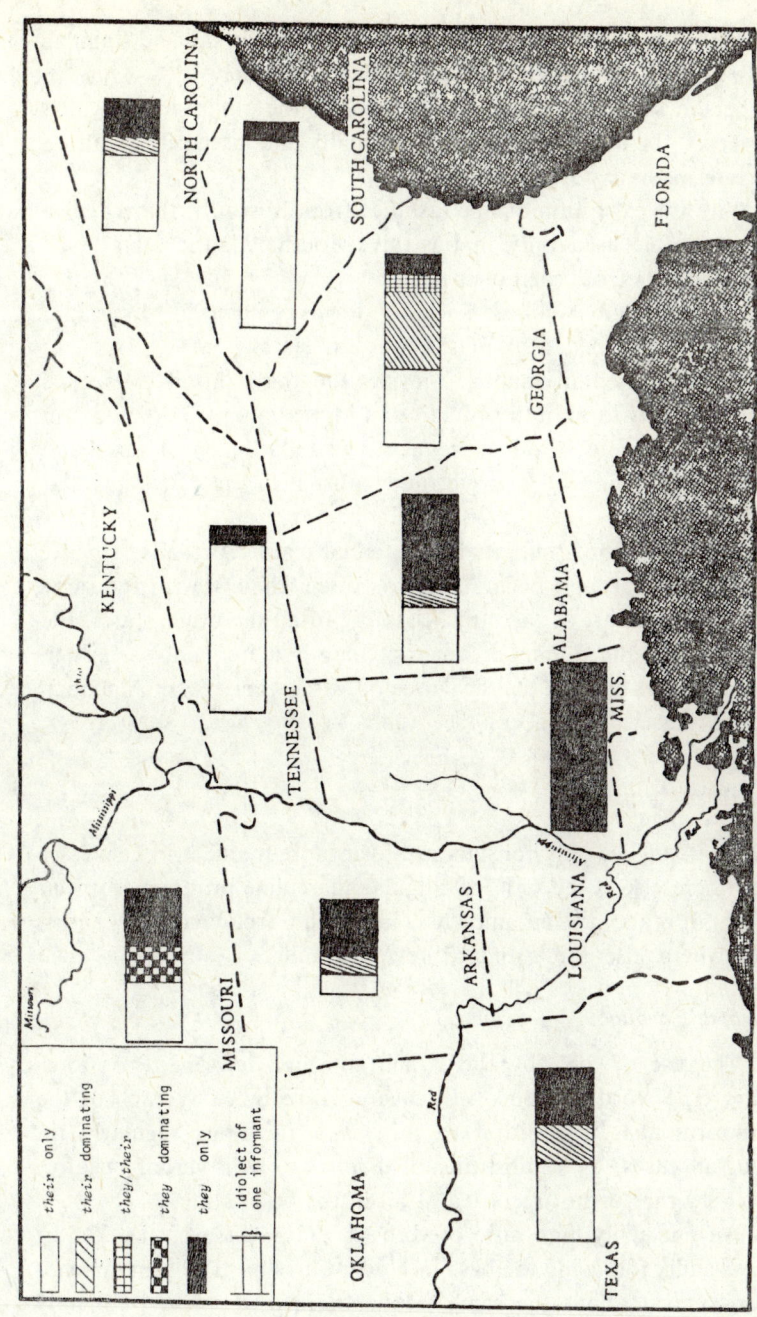

Map 2: Regional distribution of *we* and *us* as 1st person plural subject pronouns

having a high -*s*-rate in the 1st singular and a low one in the 2nd singular and 3rd plural. Interestingly enough, it has a uniquely low -*s*-rate in the 3rd person singular, as compared to all of the other states, which can be taken to be a sign of linguistic instability and insecurity resulting from its intermediate position.

2.1.3.3. With the exception of one instance from Missouri, the reflexive form *theirselves* is used only in the three South Atlantic states, viz. by two informants from each of them.

2.1.4. South-southwestern forms. These are forms centered in Mississippi but frequently recorded also in the western states.

2.1.4.1. As illustrated in map 4, *they* as the third plural possessive pronoun is the only form in this function in Mississippi, still dominant in Alabama and Arkansas, about as frequent as standard *their* in Texas and Missouri, less common in Georgia, and unusual in the Carolinas and Tennessee.

2.1.4.2. *They* as dummy subject in existential clauses prevails strongly again in Mississippi, and occurs twice as often, though with the same number of informants, as *there* in Missouri. In all the other states, the standard form is the dominant one, yet *they* is a frequent variant in the southern states close to the focal area of Mississippi, viz. in Alabama, Georgia, Arkansas and Texas (see table 1).

2.2. Northern forms

2.2.1. Tennessee. The only nonstandard form more frequent in Tennessee than anywhere else is the old 3rd singular masculine pronoun form *hit* (see map 5). It is about as common as *it* in North Carolina and Arkansas, but everywhere else the standard form prevails.

2.2.2. North Carolina.

2.2.2.1. The use of *ain't* by the North Carolina informants is idiosyncratic. The word is used on the average five times by each of the twelve informants. In addition to this, *ain't* functions regularly (in 36.7% of all cases) as a substitute of *didn't*, i.e. as a verbal negator, which is very rare or not recorded at all in the other states.

2.2.2.2. An unusually high ratio of verbs in the past tense, viz. 27.5%, have an -*s*-suffix following the base in North Carolina. The same phenomenon occurs at about the same frequency in Texas, less frequently in Missouri and only with regular verbs in Tennessee, but almost not at all in the central parts of the south (see map 6).

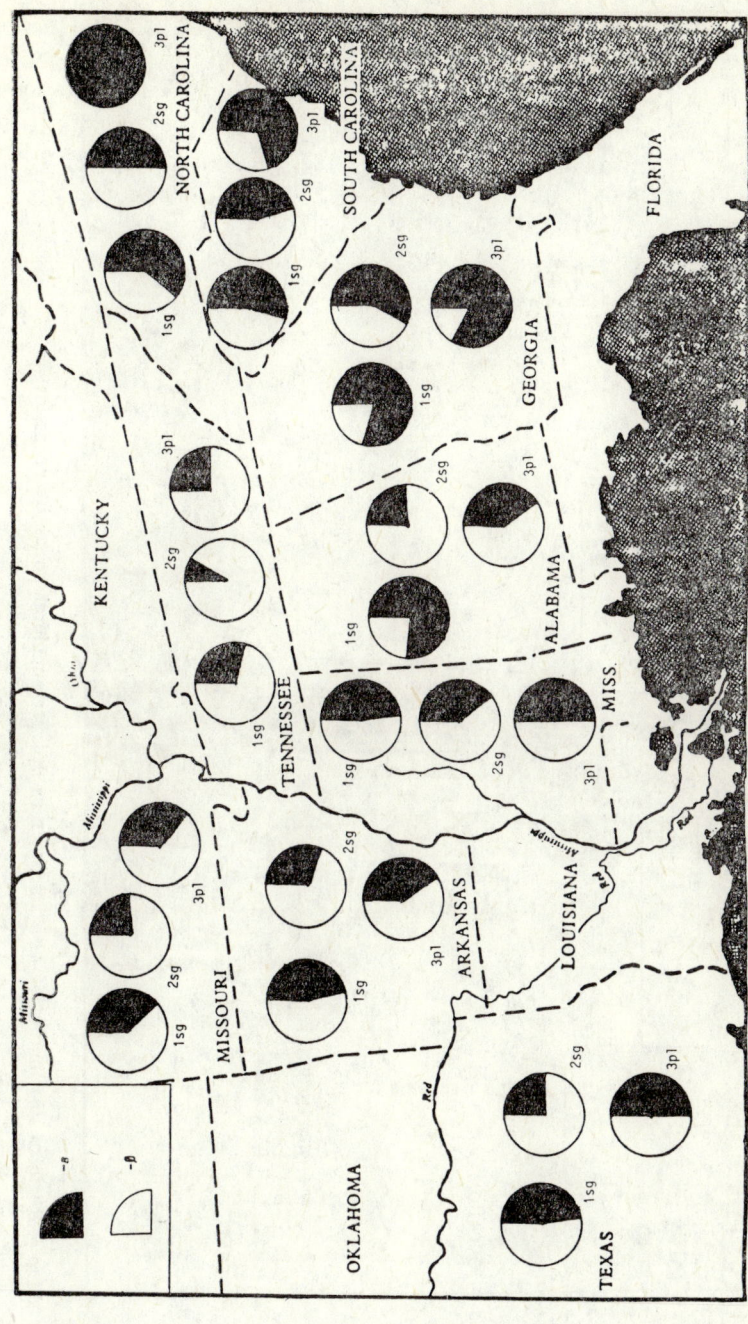

Map 3: Regional distribution of present tense verb endings -s and zero in the 1st person singular, 2nd person singular and 3rd person plural

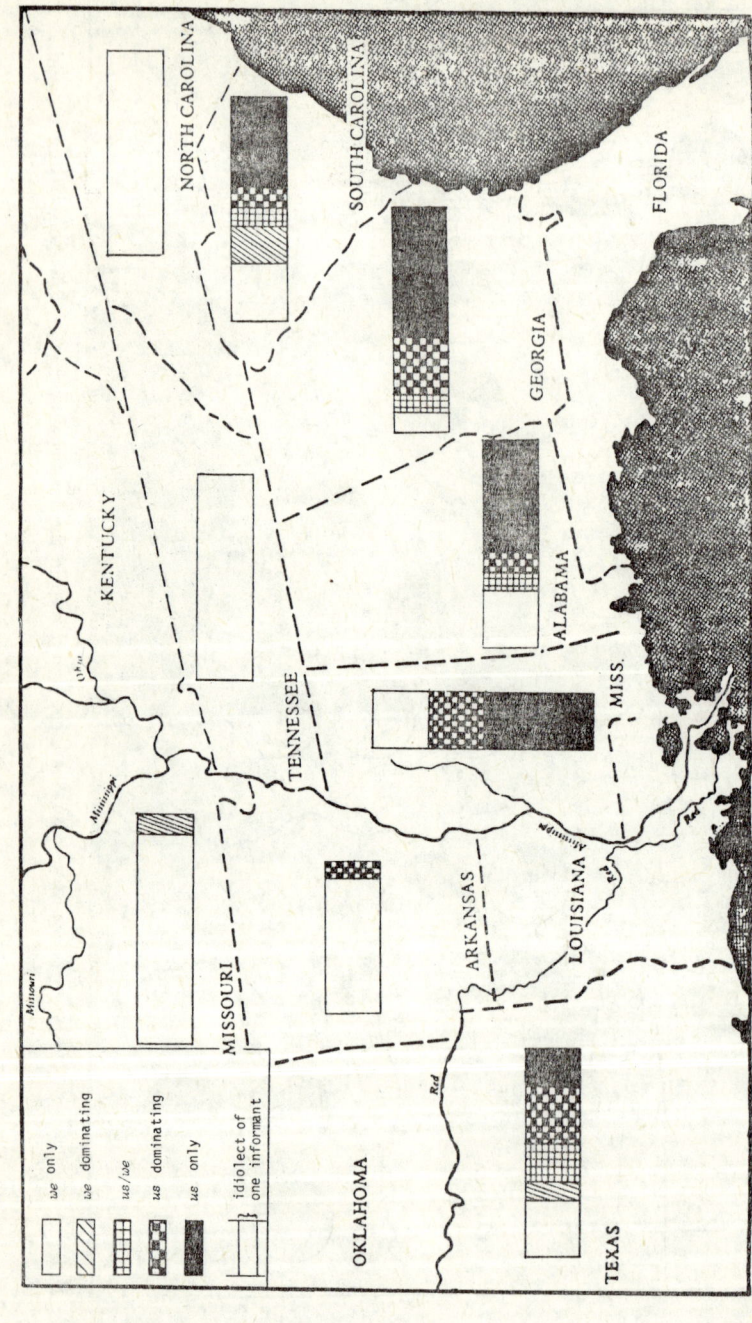

Map 4: Regional distribution of *their* and *they* as 3rd person plural possessive pronouns

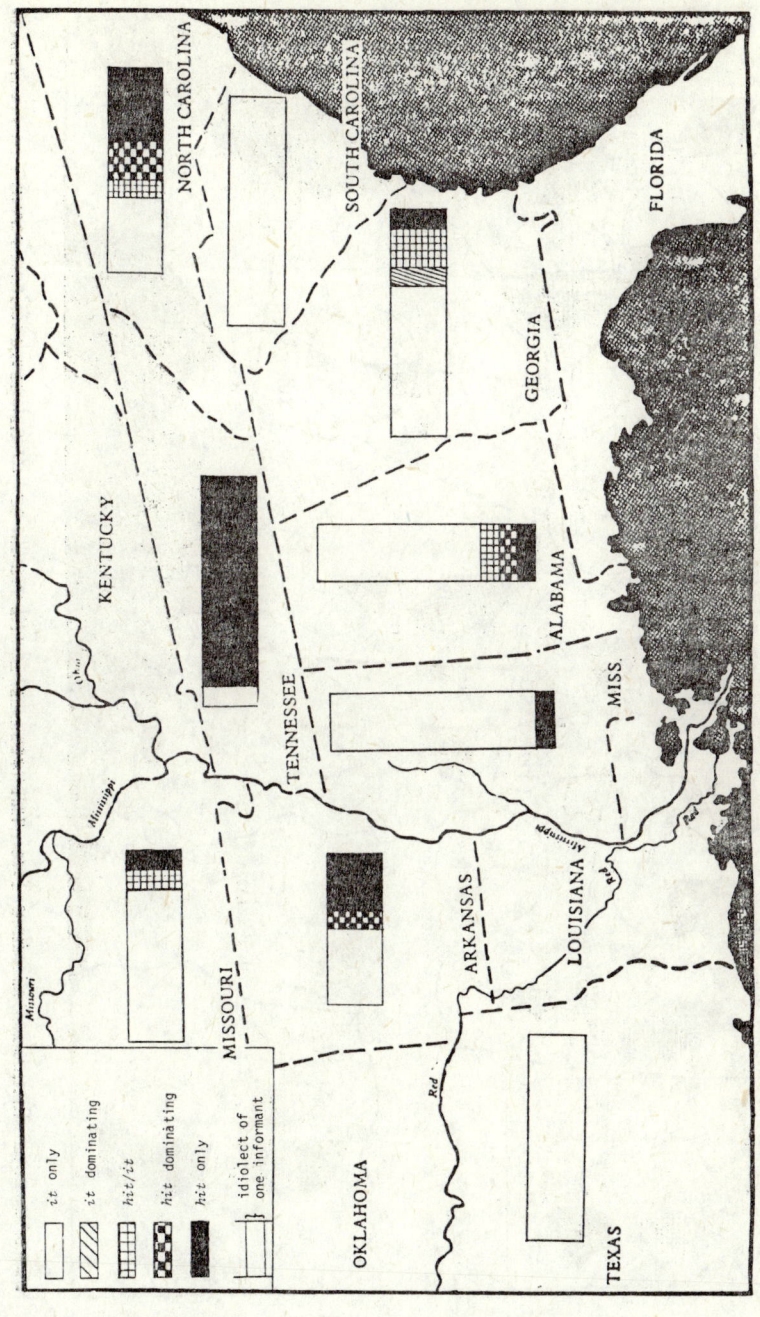

Map 5: Regional distribution of *it* and *hit* as 3rd person singular neuter pronouns

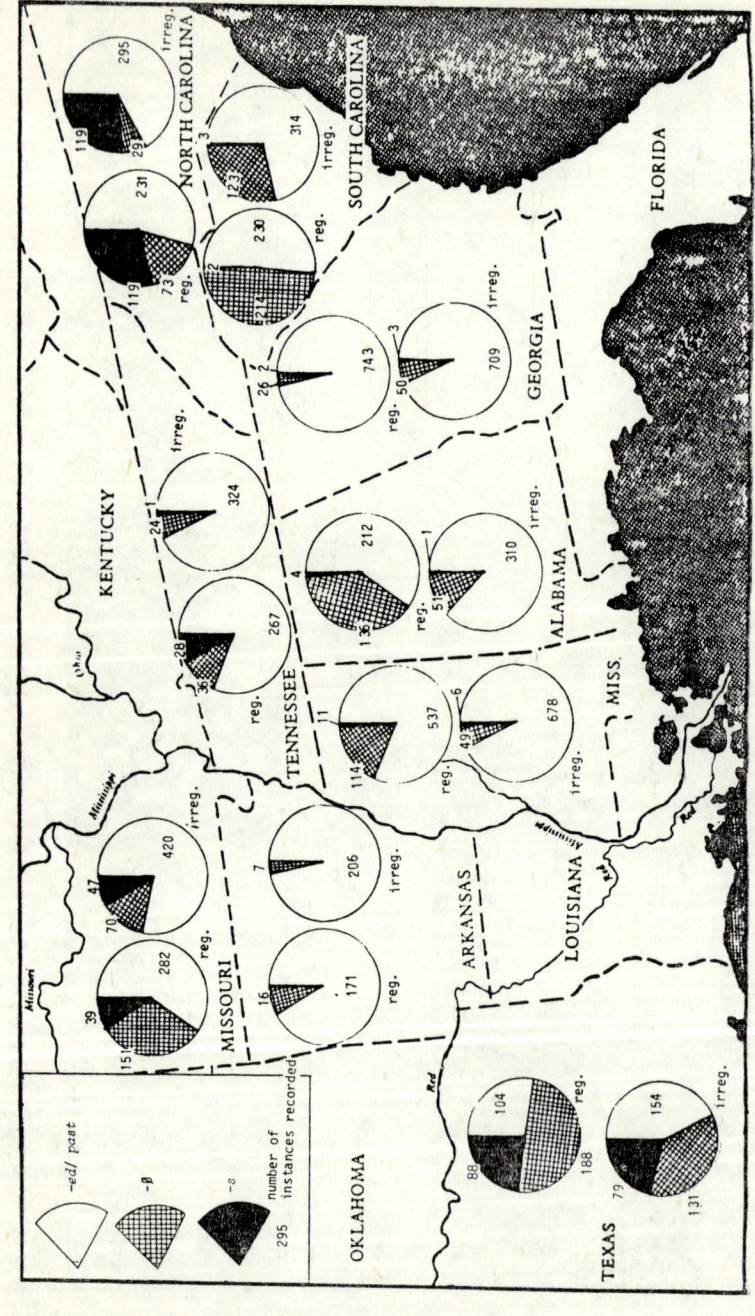

Map 6: Regional distribution of -*ed*/past-form, zero form, and -*s* with regular and irregular verbs in past contexts

2.3. Erratic and inconclusive distributions.

2.3.1. Lack of past tense marking with verbs. Map 6 shows the distribution of past forms, unmarked forms and verbs ending in *-s* of regular and irregular verbs in past contexts. Unaltered forms are generally somewhat more common with regular than with irregular verbs, because phonologically conditioned deletion of the *-ed* is added to the use of unmarked forms for grammatical or stylistic reasons, but they are not uncommon with both groups. There seems to be no regional patterning behind this use, however.

2.3.2. Morphologically irregular forms. Standard and nonstandard forms of past tense forms and past participles of verbs as well as plurals of nouns display traces of regional distribution in my materials (cf. table 2). However, the number of instances recorded is usually too low to permit conclusions. There seem to be preferences for *brought* in Tennessee as opposed to *brung* in North Carolina, Alabama and Mississippi; for *cotch(ed)* in Georgia but *caught* in Mississippi; for past tense *drunk* in Georgia, *druv* in Missouri, *give* in all states except Missouri; *run* in South Carolina, Mississippi and Tennessee; *see* in South Carolina vs. *seed* in Georgia and Tennessee and *seen* in Mississippi *tuk* in Georgia and Tennessee; for the past participles *borned* in North Carolina, *seed* in North Carolina and Georgia, and *tuk* in Tennessee; and for the plural forms *feets* in North Carolina and *mens* in North Carolina and Georgia.

3. Regional division of the area

The aim of this concluding section is to establish a summarizing division of the area under consideration on the basis of the data hitherto presented (excluding the last-mentioned verb and noun form distributions, which are too tentative). It is obvious that the traditional method of drawing heteroglosses cannot be employed in this case. It is necessary to quantify regional differences in a manner similar to the one applied by Wood (1971), who established subareas by counting the number of heteroglosses running between localities.

Map 7 presents a summary of the distributions of the nonstandard features discussed above. Linguistic nonstandard forms are represented symbolically by letters, explained in the legend, with capital letters inicating strong presence or high frequency and lower case letters. symbolizing less frequent occurrence of the same nonstandard variant. In every case, objective conditions or limits for a feature to be entered

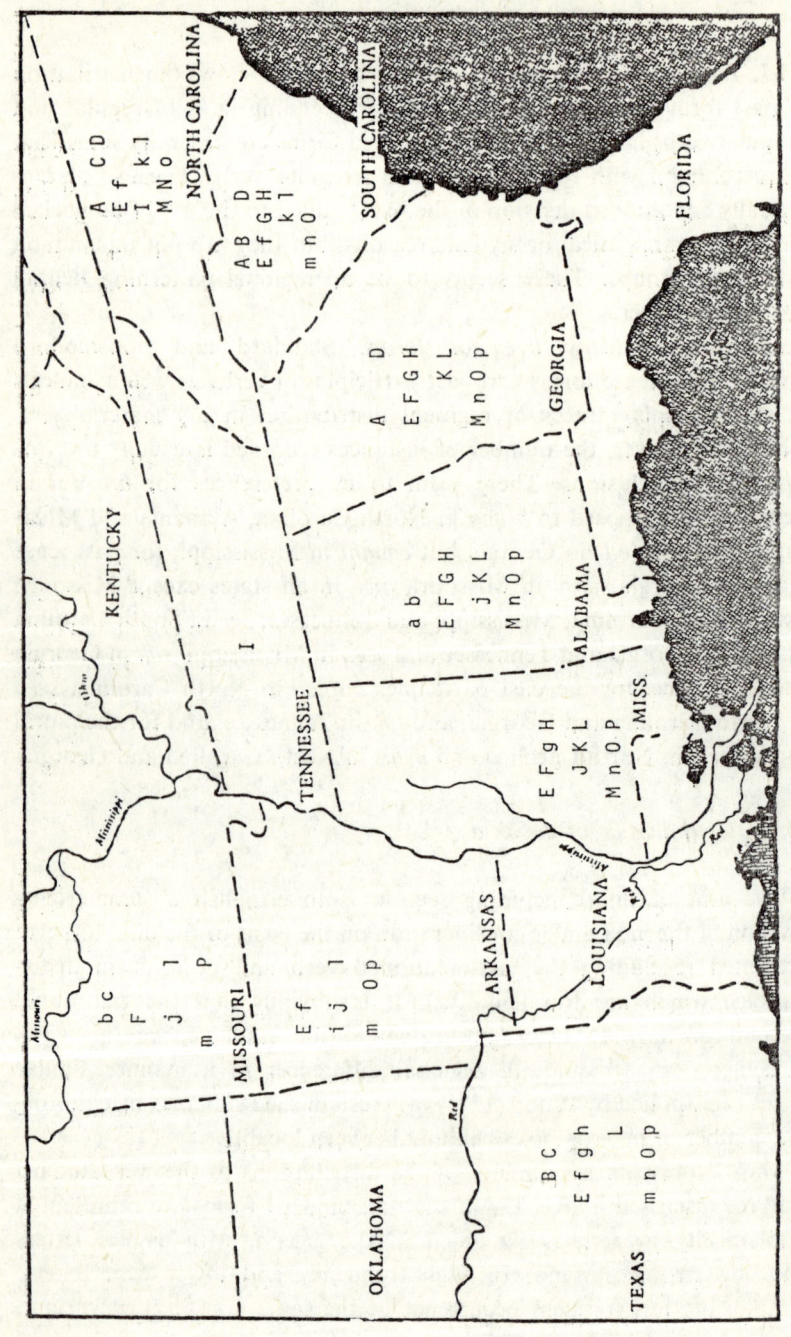

Map 7: Regional distribution of nonstandard forms

Symbol	discussed in section	Signification
A	2.1.3.2.	more than 50% -s in 2 or 3 of the 3 grammatical persons in map 3
a		more than 50% -s in 1 of the 3 grammatical persons in map 3
B	2.3.1.	more than 25% of the irregular verbs are unmarked in the past
b		more than 10% of the irregular verbs are unmarked in the past
C	2.2.2.2.	more than 20% of the irregular verbs in the past have an -s-suffix
c		more than 5% of the irregular verbs in the past have an -s-suffix
D	2.1.3.1.	is/was/had done + past participle with at least 2 informants
E	2.1.1.1.	done + past participle with at least 3 informants
F	2.1.2.4.	a-Ving with at least 50% of the informants in the state
f		a-Ving with at least 25% of the informants in the state
G	2.1.2.5.	at least 6 instances of nonstandard comparison
g		at least 3 instances of nonstandard comparison
H	2.1.2.1.	*us* dominates as personal pronoun of the 1st ps. pl.
h		*us* is about as frequent as *we*
I	2.2.1.	*hit* dominates as personal pronoun of the 3rd ps. sg. neuter
i		*hit* is about as frequent as *it*
J	2.1.4.1.	*they* is the only form of the possessive pronoun of the 3rd ps. pl.
j		*they* dominates as possessive pronoun of the 3rd ps. pl.
K	2.1.2.2.	*theyselves* dominates as reflexive pronoun of the 3rd ps. pl.
k	2.1.3.3.	if not K, *theirselves* occurs with at least 2 informants
L	2.1.1.5.	pronominal apposition with at least 5 informants
l		pronominal apposition with at least 3 informants
M	2.1.2.3.	m, + negative concord to dependent clause or negated verb after negative subject
m	2.1.1.2.	negative concord in at least 90% of the possible cases
N	2.2.2.1.	*ain't* very frequent; predominantly for *do/did* + negation
n	2.1.1.3.	*ain't* relatively frequent; rarely for *do/did* + negation
O	2.1.1.4.	relative pronoun *what* more frequent than *who/which*
o		relative pronoun *what* about as frequent as *who/which*
P	2.1.4.2.	*they* dominates as dummy subject
p		*they* less frequent than *there*, but with at least 3 informants

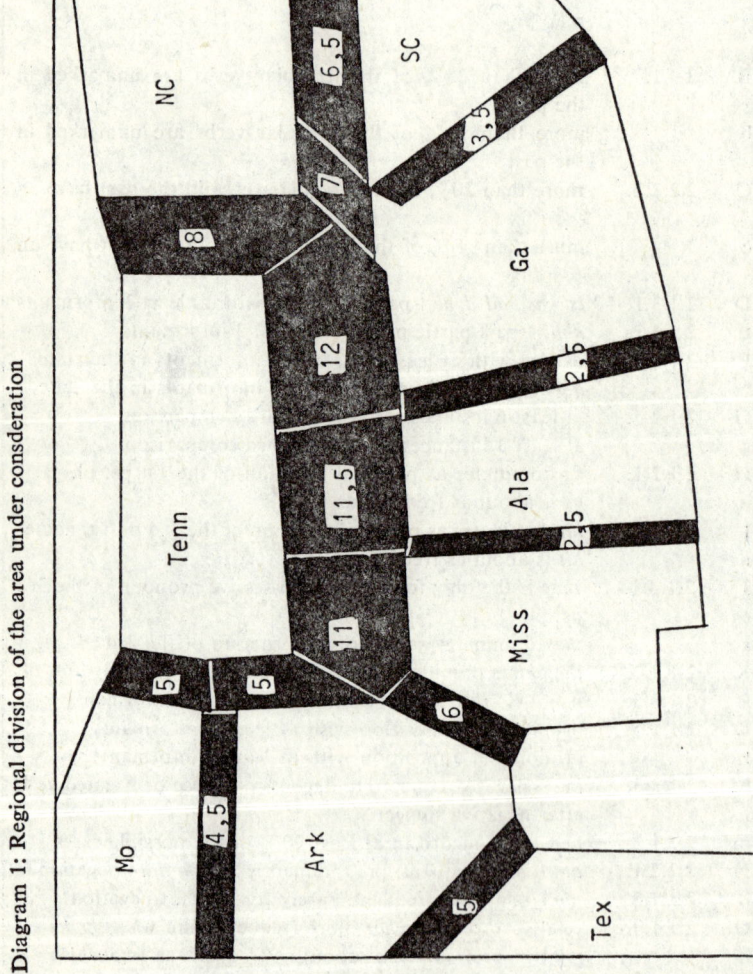

Diagram 1: Regional division of the area under consderation

Figures = number of different nonstandard features in map 7; borders are drawn in proportional size

as present or strongly present were defined. The type of conditions varies according to the nature of the linguistic feature and of the distribution recorded, to which the limits had of course to be adapted. Differences between neighbouring states were then measured by counting the difference between a strongly present and a missing feature as 1, and the one between strong and weak presence or between weak presence and absence as 1/2. The result is shown in diagram 1, which displays, visually the number of differences between neighbouring states and thus, the regional division of the whole area with respect to the linguistic features discussed.

The diagram shows that the main line of division runs between the coastal states of the lower south and the relatively northern, especially inland northern states, a separation which is very clear east of the Mississippi but becomes more diffuse west of it. The "Deep South" proper is constituted by a very homogeneous area stretching from South Carolina via Georgia and Alabama to Mississippi and extending its influence east- and westward. It is characterized generally by the frequent use of nonstandard forms, which distinguishes it most sharply from its northern neighbor Tennessee, the focus of the northern sub-area with a speech much closer to the standard grammar. The position of North Carolina is unique but not isolated. There are forms almost peculiar to this state (e.g. past tense *-s* or the use of *in't*); sometimes, it shares the northern form of Tennessee (e.g. *we*, *hit*); at other times southern features can be recorded in a weakened form (e.g. preverbal *a-*, the pleonastic pronouns), or the state joins with South Carolina and Georgia to form a distinctive South Atlantic region (see 2.1.3.). The states west of the Mississippi display a mixture of northern and southern tendencies, yet it can be observed that Missouri tends to associate more frequently with Tennessee (e.g. lack of *done*, relative *who/which*) — a union which can also include Arkansas (e.g. *twe*) —, and Texas is often closer to the range of southern states (e.g. comparison of adjectives, *us*). There are cases, however, where the southern influence extends to all the three western states (e.g. possessive *they*, preverbal *a-*, pleonastic pronouns).

A comparison of this division with the dialect areas of the South as established by Wood (1971) and — for the eastern part — Kurath (1949) reveals far-reaching parallels. We have found the same main line of division separating the lowlands of the South from the uplands and the interior, Southern proper from MidSouthern or South Midland. Both Wood's results and my own show the diffusion of this separation, the mixture of northern and southern forms, west of the Mississippi. The most prominent difference between my division based on old data and the modern one concerns Wood's distinction of a southeastern "Coastal Southern" and "Gulf Southern" west of the Chattahoochee river. It is confirmed with respect to a few old and important structures, but generally the morphosyntax of 19th c. black speech seems to have been very homogeneous from South Carolina to Mississippi.

APPENDIX

Table 1: Regional distribution of nonstandard features

			NC	SC	Ga	Ala	Miss	Tenn	Mo	Ark	Tex
2.1.1.2.:	negative concord	(A)	96.9%	94.4%	99.6%	93.4%	96.5%	61.7%	91.8%	97.8%	91.5%
2.1.1.4: relative pronouns (B/C)	wh-pronouns		16/9	6/4	3/2	6/3	1/1	5/5	8/4	—	—
	that		14/9	40/11	46/8	12/7	35/10	25/11	16/7	12/4	7/3
	zero subject		15/9	43/11	81/12	29/9	20/6	27/10	27/10	17/7	27/10
	what		17/9	12/4	83/11	14/9	49/10	1/1	2/2	16/2	24/9
	zero non-subject		2/2	5/4	5/4	2/2	1/1	1/1	—	—	1/1
	pers., poss. pron.		—	1/1	2/2	—	—	—	7/5	—	3/2
2.1.1.5:	pronominal apposition	(C)	3	3	10	5	5	1	4	3	7
2.1.2.5:	nonstandard comparison	(B)	1	7	13	6	3	—	1	—	4
2.1.4.2.: dummy subjects (B/C)	there		23/11	22/8	84/12	18/7	4/2	11/9	14/10	13/4	22/8
	they		2/1	1/1	11/6	5/3	34/9	1/1	35/10	5/3	15/6
	de		3/2	—	—	—	—	—	—	—	—
	it/'t		—	2/1	—	2/1	5/3	1/1	—	—	—
	ø		—	—	1/1	—	—	—	1/1	1/1	—

A = percentage of possible cases
B = number of instances recorded
C = number of informants using the form.

Table 2: Regional distribution of irregular verb and noun forms
(number of informants using a form)

	NC	SC	Ga	Ala	Miss	Tenn	Mo	Ark	Tex
past tense									
blew				1					
blowed			1		2	1			
brought		2	1		3	3	3	1	
brung	5		2	4	5			1	2
caught	1			1	4	1		1	
cotched			4	1	1				1
cotch			4	1		1	1		1
ketched	1	1		1		1			

Table 2 (continued)

	NC	SC	Ga	I Ala	Miss	Tenn	Mo	Ark	Tex
drank				1			1		
drunk	1	1	3	1					
drove	1	1	1						
driv		2			1				
druv				1		1	3		
fought		1		1	1		1		
fit		1	2	2	2			2	
gave			1	1			2		1
give/gib	4	5	9	5	6	5	1	2	7
gives	1						1		
gim(me)			3		2				
gived/gibd				1			1		
gin				2					
knew					1		2		
knowed	3	6	7	4	11	3	3	2	2
rode	1	2			4	2	1		1
rid	1		1		3	1			2
ran						1	3		
run	3	4	2	6	6	7	3		2
runned	1	1		4		1			
saw		2	2	1	2		3	2	
seed	9	1	8	3	1	7	7	2	3
seen		1	1	1	7		3	2	3
took	3	7	3	5	10	1	6	3	2
taken				2	1				
tooken									1
tuk			8	5	2	8	6		
tak							1		
tok							1		
past participles									
born		6	6	4	10	11	5	2	6
borned	8		7	4	1		2	1	3
birthed									1
grown		2	3	4	4	1	1	3	1
growed		2	3	1				2	1
grow		1							
seen		2		3	5	1	3	2	1
seed	4	1	7	3	1	3	5	2	1
see		2							2
taken		1	1		1		1	1	
took				1	1	2	2	1	
tuk				3	1		4		
tooken							1		

Table 2 (continued)

feet		2	2	3	3	1	4	1	1
foots		2	3	1	2			1	
footses			2						
feets	3		1	2					1
men	1	6	1	3	5	5	8	1	4
mans						2			
mens	4	1	7	2	3		1		
people		7	1	1	5	11	2	2	3
peoples	1		2	1	6	2	1		

REFERENCES

Brewer, Jeutonne P. 1973. Subject concord of *be* in Early Black English. *American Speech* 48. - 21.

— 1974. *The verb be in Early Black English: a study based on the WPA ex-slave narratives*. University of North Carolina at Chapel Hill dissertation.

— 1980 (1982). The WPA slave narratives as linguistic data. *Orbis* 29. 30 - 54.

Dillard, Joe L. 1972. *Black English. Its history and usage in the United States*. New York: Random House.

Fasold, Ralph W. 1976. One hundred years from syntax to phonology. *Papers from the parasession on diachronic syntax, April 22, 1976*, ed. by Sanford B. Steever, Carol A. Walker and Salikoko S. Mufwene, 79 - 87. Chicago: Chicago Linguistic Society.

Kurath, Hans. 1949. *A word geography of the eastern United States*. Ann Arbor: University of Michigan Press.

Labov, William. 1970. *The study of non-standard English*. Champaign, Ill.: National Council of Teachers of English.

— 1972. Negative attraction and negative concord in English grammar. *Lg.* 48. 773 - 818.

Labov W. and Paul Cohen, Clarence Robins, and John Lewis. 1968. *A study of the non-standard English of negro and Puerto Rican speakers in New York City*. 2 vols. New York: Columbia University.

Rawick, George P. (ed.). 1972. *The American slave: a composite autobiography*. 19 vols. Westport, Conn.: Greenwood Publishing Company.

Schneider, Edgar W. 1981. *Morphologische und syntaktische Variablen im amerikanischen Early Black English*. Frankfurt a. M., Bern: Peter Lang.

— 1982. On the history of Black English in the USA: some new evidence. *English World-Wide* 3. 18 - 46.

— 1983a. The diachronic development of the Black English perfective auxiliary phrase. *Journal of English Linguistics* 16. 55 - 64.

— 1983b. The origin of the verbal -s in Black English. *American Speech* 58. 99-113.

Viereck, Wolfgang. 1979. Social dialectology: a plea for more data. *Studia Anglica Posnaniensia* 11. 15 - 25.

Wise, C. M. 1933. Negro dialect. *Quarterly Journal of Speech* 19. 522 - 8. [Reprinted in *Perspectives on Black English*, ed. by J. L. Dillard, 216 - 21. Paris: Mouton.]
Wolfram, Walter A. 1969. *A sociolinguistic description of Detroit negro speech.* Washington, D. C.: Center for Applied Linguistics.
Wolfram, W. and Ralph W. Fasold. 1974. *The study of social dialects in American English.* Englewood Cliffs, N. J.: Prentice-Hall.
Wood, Gordon R. 1971. *Vocabulary change. A study of variation in regional words in eight of the southern states.* Carbondale: Southern Illinois University Press.
Yetman, Norman K. 1967. The background of the slave narrative collection. *American Quarterly* 19. 534 - 43.

RULE ORDERING AND THE DYNAMICS OF DIATOPIC LANGUAGE VARIATION

JOHAN TAELDEMAN

0. Introduction

By relating some (fairly) recent theories about rule ordering and language change to a number of cases of diatopic language variation in the dialects of Dutchspeaking Belgium (more particularly phonology and morphophonology) I arrived at a threestage hypothesis about the dynamics of the observed dialect differences. As such this hypothesis opens new perspectives for dialect geography, a discipline which is fundamentally concerned with the hows and the whys of language difference and (hence) language change.

1. Rule ordering

With regard to this topic the short but vivid history of generative phonology reveals three main points of view:

(a) Extrinsic rule ordering: Phonological rules are linearly ordered by the linguist's explicit and language specific ordering statements.

(b) Intrinsic rule ordering: The order in which phonological rules are applied does not depend on an arbitrary decision by the linguist but it is determined by the way the rules are formulated/structured (by some universal, metatheoretical principles).

(c) No rule ordering: Every phonological rule is applied automatically (as a kind of phonetic tendency) on every representation that meets its structural description.

For metatheoretical reasons (c) is fundamentally more interesting than (b) and (b) is fundamentally more interesting than (a). Yet an important argument against (c) and in a way also against (b) is my experience that structurally (very) related dialects sometimes differ from each other in that two phonological rules (x) and (y) operate in the order (x)>(y) in the one dialect, whereas in the other one they are applied in the opposite order.

All in all my position is this: there ARE universal ordering tendencies, on account of which some ordering relations between two (phonological) rules are to be considered as more common/more natural than other ones. Yet it IS possible that two (phonological) rules are ordered in a language specific (and hence uncommon/unnatural) way.

If two rules are ordered 'naturally', the grammar need not be charged with an explicit ordering statement, since the order is intrinsically determined by one or more ordering universals. Only in case of 'unnatural' ordering an extrinsic (and language specific) ordering statement must be added to the grammar.

In the literature of the past 15 years lots of ordering 'universals' have been proposed. However, confronting them with the facts — in our case the Flemish dialects — I experienced that only one really deserves that name, viz. the principle formulated by Kiparsky (1968):

'Rules tend to shift into the order which allows their fullest utilization in the grammar.'

With respect to their mutual range of application two (phonological) rules can theoretically be ordered in 6 different ways:

(1) feeding
(2) counterfeeding
(3) mutual feeding
(4) bleeding
(5) counterbleeding
(6) mutual bleeding

According to the above mentioned ordering tendency of a universal nature (Kiparsky, 1968) (1) and (5) are natural ordering relations (they are *transparent*), (2) and (4) are unnatural (or *opaque*) and (3) and (6) are undecided.

I happen to dispose of generative phonological descriptions of three Flemish dialects: Kleit (Taeldeman, 1976), Gent (De Grauwe, 1980) and Hofstade (Keymeulen, 1981). For all the ordered pairs of rules I examined in what way they are ordered. This yielded the following percentages for the three dialects together:

natural (type 1+5)	almost 78%
unnatural (type 2+4)	7%
undecided (type 3+6)	about 15%

This strongly supports Kiparsky's universal ordering tendency. At the same time however it shows that it is no more than a TENDENCY, which to some extent must leave room for less 'natural', language specific ordering relations.

2. Language change

Throughout the voluminous literature on language change we are confronted again and again with the view that natural language change (which is intrinsically connected with language acquisition mechanisms and performance mechanisms and hence is of a psycho-physiological nature) generally tends to language simplification (e.g. the Humboldtian principle: languages tend to augment formal-semantic analogy). Combining this teleological principle of natural language change to what we said about (un-)natural rule ordering in the previous section, we arrive at the following hypothesis:

If natural language change generally results in language simplification and if 'natural' rule ordering implies a simpler grammar than 'unnatural' rule ordering does *substitution of an 'unnatural' rule ordering by a 'natural' one is a very plausible type of natural language change*.

Applied to the 6 ordering relations that we enumerated in the previous section, this hypothesis can be specified as follows:

(a) Very plausible is:
- the substitution of the 'unnatural' type (2) by its 'natural' counterpart type (1);
- the substitution of the 'unnatural' type (4) by its 'natural' counterpart type (5);
- a stabilizing situation in case two rules are ordered 'naturally' (type 1 or 5).

(b) If the ordering relation is undecided (type 3 or 6), it is difficult to predict what may/will happen. Much, if not everything will depend on the socio-economical relations within the linguistic area concerned.

3. Dialect geography: the diatopic challenge

A dialect map shows *next to* each other (in space) linguistic facts/elements that must be situated *after* each other (in time). This implies that the above hypothesis must be translatable spatially (with a view to the dynamics of dialect areas).

Doing this we arrive at the following three-stage hypothesis:
(a) If we establish a 'natural' ordering relation (=type (1) feeding or (5) counterbleeding) between two rules (R1) and (R2), we may normally expect that this will be stable throughout the area where (R1) and (R2) operate. Yet if there is diatopic variation, in that the 'natural' ordering relation (1) or (5) competes with its 'unnatural' counterpart (resp. 2 and 4), we can predict that the area with ordering type (1) or (5) is expansive at the cost of the area with resp. (2) or (4).
(b) If we establish an 'unnatural' ordering relation (=type (2) counterfeeding or (4) bleeding) between two rules (R1) and (R2), we may normally expect diatopic variation, in that the area with the ordering relation (2) or (4) is rivalled by an area with the 'natural' ordering counterpart (resp. 1 and 5). In that case the area with (2) or (4) is regressive, the area with resp. (1) or (5) expansive.
(c) If we establish an 'undecided' ordering relation (=type (3) mutual feeding or type (6) mutual bleeding) between two rules (R1) and (R2), spatial variation is very likely to occur, in that one area displays the order is (R1)>(R2), whereas in the other area the order is (R2)>(R1). As for the dynamics of both areas it is impossible to make a purely linguistic prediction. In such cases much — if if not everything — will depend on the socio-economical relations within and between both areas.

As I already said, this three-stage hypothesis was confronted with lots of linguistic (phonological and morphophonological) facts taken from the Flemish dialects. This confrontation yielded no real counterevidence to the above hypothesis.

From the 10 or 15 interesting examples I select four which are quite illuminating in several respects.

3.1. The first one bears upon the first stage of our hypothesis (i.e. we may expect a stable situation throughout the area, in case two rules (R1) and (R2) are ordered 'naturally'). In our example the two rules are in a counterbleeding order (=type 5).

(R1) Voiced fricatives become voiceless after a (voiceless) obstruent:

$$\begin{bmatrix} \text{OBS.} \\ +\text{cont.} \\ +\text{voice} \end{bmatrix} \rightarrow [-\text{voice}] \Big/ \ldots \begin{bmatrix} \text{OBS.} \\ (-\text{voice}) \end{bmatrix} \# \underline{}$$

(R2) The suffix -t of the finite verb form (e.g. hij *doe+t* 'he does') is dropped if the following words begins with a consonant:

$$[t] \to \emptyset \;\Big/\; \ldots + -- \#_{\text{F.V.}} C \ldots$$

To illustrate their application we take the sentence *hij doet veel* 'he does much':

(R1) *hij doet* [f]*eel*   (R2) *hij doe* [v]*eel*
      V   V
(R2) *hij doe* [f]*eel*   (R1) —

The Flemish dialect area displays a striking stability, in that the 'unnatural' (bleeding) order (R2)>(R1) does not occur anywhere. The linguistic facts are in conformity with (the first part of) our hypothesis. It is worthwhile mentioning that the 'higher' rule is an ordinary phonological rule, whereas the 'lower' one is of a morphophonological nature. Yet in the more recent literature on rule ordering we often come across the view that morphophonological rules should be applied before phonological ones. Some authors even have no hesitation in calling this a binding principle. This and some other examples seem to point out that the *nature of the ordering relation* ('natural' versus 'unnatural') is more important than the nature of the rules themselves.

3.2. The second and the third example bear upon the second stage of our hypothesis (i.e. we may expect an area with linguistic variation, in case two rules (R1) and (R2) are ordered 'unnaturally', in that the area with the 'unnatural' rule ordering (A1) is challenged by an area with the 'natural' ordering (A2), (A1) being regressive and (A2) being expansive).

3.2.1. First we illustrate that an area (A1) with a counterfeeding rule order loses ground to an area (A2) with a feeding rule order.

(R1) Final *-n* is assimilated to the immediately following obstruent:

$$n \to \begin{bmatrix} \text{NAS.} \\ \alpha \text{ ant.} \\ \beta \text{ cor.} \\ \gamma \text{ back} \end{bmatrix} \;\Big/\; \ldots V \underline{\quad} \# \begin{bmatrix} \text{OBS.} \\ \alpha \text{ ant.} \\ \beta \text{ cor.} \\ \gamma \text{ back} \end{bmatrix} \ldots$$

This rule is applied in all Flemish dialects.

(R2) Before feminine nouns in the singular and before all nouns in plural, adjectives that end in a sonorant consonant drop the inflexional ending —ə (at least if the whole noun phrase is more or less stereotyped, cf. Taeldeman, 1980):

$$\left\langle \text{ə} \to \emptyset \;\Big/\; \ldots \begin{bmatrix} C \\ +\text{son.} \end{bmatrix} + \underline{\quad} \# A \ldots \# N \left\{ \begin{bmatrix} +\text{pl.} \\ -\text{pl.} \\ +\text{fem.} \end{bmatrix} \right\} \right\rangle [+\text{stereot.}]$$

This rule operates in the dialects of Brabant and the eastern part of East-Flanders.

To illustrate their application we take the noun phrase *een schone vrouw* 'a beautiful lady':

(A1)	(A2)
(R1) —	(R2) *een schoon vrouw*
V	V
(R2) *een schoo*[n] *vrouw*	(R1) *een schoon*[ŋ] *vrouw*

In his very accurate monograph on the dialect of Alost Colinet (1896, p. 125) amply stressed the fact that the well-known rule of -*n*-assimilation (=R1) is not to be applied to -*n* that has become final by the above mentioned deletion-rule (=R2).

Yet, an inquiry in 1978 revealed a largely different situation: most of our informants assimilated final -*n* in the example mentioned above (which means that they apply (R1) and (R2) in the 'natural' order), and some mentioned the two possibilities (with and without -*n*-assimilation), adding that the forms without assimilation are dying away. This change is predicted by (the second part of) our hypothesis: (A1) with the 'unnatural' rule order (R1)>(R2) (=counterfeeding) is regressive and it continually loses ground to (A2) with the 'natural' rule ordering (R2)>(R1) (=feeding).

3.2.2. By the next example we illustrate how an area (A1) with a bleeding rule order loses ground to an area (A2) with a counterbleeding rule order.

(R1) Attributively used adjectives in -Vd (e.g. *goed* 'good', *kwaad* 'mad', *rood* 'red', *oud* 'old') drop final -*d* if the following noun (neuter, sg.) begins with a consonant:

$$d \to \emptyset \bigg/ ...V\underline{}\#_A C......\#_N \begin{bmatrix} +\text{neut.} \\ +\text{sg.} \end{bmatrix}$$

This rule is applied in all dialects of Flanders and Brabant.

(R2) Voiced fricatives become voiceless after an obstruent:

$$\begin{bmatrix} \text{OBS.} \\ +\text{cont.} \\ +\text{voice} \end{bmatrix} \to [-\text{voice}]/...[\text{OBS}]\#\underline{}$$

This rule too operates throughout the Flemish + Brabantic dialect area.

To illustrate their application we take the noun phrase *rood zand* 'red sand':

(A1)	(A2)
(R1) roo [z]and	(R2) rood [s]and
V	V
(R2) —	(R1) roo [s]and

From a minute investigation in the transitional area between (A1) and (A2) it appeared that (A2) is expanding to the cost of (A1). Since (A2) displays a 'natural' (counterbleeding) rule order and (A1) an 'unnatural' (bleeding) one, this evolution is conformable to the second stage of our hypothesis.

Again it should be noticed that the naturalness of the ordering relation seems to be more important than the nature of the rules themselves.

3.3. The fourth example bears upon the third stage of our hypothesis (i.e. we may expect an area with linguistic variation in case two rules (R1) and (R2) are in an 'undecided' ordering relation, in that (A1) displays the order (R1)>(R2) whereas (A2) displays the reverse order. As for the dynamics of both areas much — if not everything — will depend on extra-linguistic factors, especially the socio-economical relations within and between both areas). In our example the rules are applied in a mutually bleeding order.

(R1) In the ending -ən final -n is dropped if the next word begins with a consonant (but not t-, d-, b-):

$$n \to \emptyset / \ldots + \vartheta \underline{\quad\quad} \# C$$

This rule operates in the dialects of Brabant and East-Flanders.

(R2) Schwa is deleted bwtween a coronal consonant and final -n (→ -n becomes sonantic):

$$\vartheta \to \emptyset / \ldots \begin{bmatrix} C \\ +\text{kor.} \end{bmatrix} (+) \underline{\quad\quad} n$$

This rules is applied in the dialects of Flanders and South-West-Brabant.

In East-Flanders and South-West-Brabant (R1) is in competition with (R2). In order to illustrate what may happen, we take the sequence ...zitten schrijven 'sit and write':

(A1)	(A2)
(R1) zittəøschrijven	(R2) zit[n̩] schrijven
V	V
(R2) —	(R1) —

(A1) consists of South-West-Brabant and the bigger part of East-Flanders, whereas (A2) only covers the most western parts of East-Flanders. From a microscopic sociolinguistic inquiry in the transitional area it appears that (A1) with the order (R1)>(R2) is expansive. In order to explain this expansion I can refer to the fact that deletion of final -*n* is also a common feature of the standard Dutch language and of the prestigious dialects of Brabant. In the last few decades this will not only have backed up the situation in (A1) but will also have added to the stigmatization of sonantic -[n̩] and hence to the regression of (A2).

4. Epilogue/apology

People who deal with the hows and the whys of language change, should never lose sight of the fact that language has a cognitive-communicative and a socio-cultural function. Above all things language is an *instrument* that must meet several requirements with regard to the acquisition, the concrete use (in conversation) and the social operation of that language. In this respect language change, so far as it is not caused by contact with another community, should be considered as a reaction (or an anticipation) to loss of functionality. As a consequence it is not so obvious that for the explanation of language change one should appeal to such abstract elements as the nature of the ordering relation between 2 rules, which after all looks more like a mental construct on the part of the linguist than like a functional reality of language. Hence the above hypothesis was not formulated until it had appeared — at least to me — that the observed processes cannot be explained globally in a more concrete way. Besides our hypothesis is not to be considered as a blind working mechanism but as an opinion about what is likely to happen in the situations described.

REFERENCES

Colinet, Ph. 1896. Het dialect van Aalst, eene phonetisch-historische studie. *Leuvense Bijdragen* 1. 1 - 59, 99 - 206, 223 - 309.

De Grauwe, Kathy. 1980. *Fonologische kenmerken van het Gents*. Ghent: State University of Ghent.

Keymeulen, Lutgarde. 1981. *Fonologische aspecten van het Hofstaads*. Ghent: State University of Ghent.

Kiparsky, Paul. 1968. Linguistic universals and language change. *Universals in linguistic theory*, ed. by Emmon Bach and Robert Harms, 171 - 202. New York: Holt, Rinehart and Winston.

Taeldeman, Johan. 1976. *De klankstruktuur van het Kleits dialekt*. Ghent: State University of Ghent.

—— 1977. Topics in de generatieve fonologie, belicht vanuit de Vlaamse dialekten. *Handelingen van het XXXIe Vlaamse Filologencongres*, 74 - 82.

—— 1980. Inflectional aspects of adjectives in the dialects of Dutch-speaking Belgium. *Dutch studies*. Vol. 4: *Studies in Dutch phonology*, ed. by Wim Zonneveld, Frans Van Coetsem and Orrin W. Robinson, 223 - 45. The Hague: Martinus Nijhoff.

LE DEVELOPPEMENT D'UN AUXILIAIRE MODAL EN YIDDISH: *LOZN* 'LAISSER'

MOSHÉ TAUBE

Les dialectes du moyen haut allemand se démarquent du vieil haut allemand, entre autres caractéristiques, par un affaiblissement croissant de l'opposition entre l'indicatif et le subjonctif.[1] En yiddish, ce processus aboutit, au début du XIXe siècle (exception faite de quelques textes 'germanisants'), à la disparition totale du subjonctif.[2] La décadence du subjonctif, lieé sur le plan phonétique à la réduction des désinences non-accentuées, ainsi qu'à la récession de l'opposition entre voyelles arrondies et non-arrondies, a entrainé un accroissement du poids fonctionnel assumé par les auxiliaires modaux, lesquels se sont chargés de rendre, par voie de périphrase, les diverses valeurs du subjonctif moribond. Parmi ces auxiliaires c'est le verbe *zoln* (all. *sollen* 'devoir') qui s'est procuré le plus vaste domaine, au plan de l'expression comme au plan du contenu. Sur le plan formel, cela se manifeste par une multitude de constructions dans lesquelles *zoln* avec l'infinitif remplace le subjonctif. Sur le plan sémantique, le verbe *zoln* perd de sa spécificité comme porteur de la modalité débitive pour embrasser le champ sémantique du mode subjonctif, qui comprend entre autres le jussif, l'optatif, le permissif etc.

C'est dans ces circonstances que s'annonce dès le XVIe siècle le processus que nous avons l'intention de décrire ci-dessous, à savoir la transformation du verbe *lozn* (all. *lassen* 'laisser') en auxiliaire modal, et son empiétement sur une partie du champ fonctionnel de *zoln*.

---

[1] Cf. Lockwood 1962: 128ff., Tschirch 1975: 199.

[2] Il reste bien en yiddish des expressions figées qui proviennent du subjonctif, mais qui ne sont plus reconnues comme telles, p. ex: *got helf* (formule de salutation, lit. 'Que Dieu (vous) aide!'); *bai im (ir, zei) blaib es* (formule de malédiction 'Que cela reste auprès de lui (elle, eux)'); *sai-wi-sai* 'de toute façon', lit. 'soit que soit'). Mais dans beaucoup de cas c'est l'indicatif qui remplace le subjonctif, p. ex. dans les jurons suivants:
xapt im der taiwl! 'Que le diable l'emporte!'
geit es cum taiwl! 'Que cela aille au diable!'
peigert er awek! 'Qu'il crève!'

Cette transformation commence par la désintégration syntaxique et sémantique de deux types de constructions, connus aussi en allemand, dans lesquels le verbe *lozn* se combine avec un objet personnel à l'accusatif ainsi qu'avec un infinitif.

Le premier type de construction est celui dans lequel apparaît l'impératif du verbe *lozn*, au sens de 'laisser', 'permettre'. Lorsque celui-ci conserve cette signification première, la construction subsiste sans modification jusqu'à nos jours:

(1) *di uberigen last da heimen zicen* (BA 1541: 28)
    Les autres, laissez-les à la maison.
(2) *laz mix for mein weib fregin* (MB 1602: 148 : 91)
    Permets que je demande d'abord à ma femme.
(3) *laz mix dox hin gein* (1679 II Sam. 15 : 7)
    Permets-moi d'y aller.
(4) *laz uns durx dein land cihen* (1679 Num. 20 : 71)
    Permets que nous passions par ton pays.
(5) *liber her, loz mix mit dir reizen* (MB 1703: 11 : 16)
    Cher monsieur, permettez-moi de voyager avec vous
(6) *un laz den iung mit zeini brider aheim gein* (MM 1725 Gen. 44 : 33)
    et que le jeune homme remonte avec ses frères.
(7) *loz undz soin oplebn di iorn bai di alte lompn.* (Kul. 56)
    Laisse-nous enfin terminer nos jours auprès de nos vieilles lampes.
(8) *bebeništ! loz mix lernen!* (Bash. 16)
    Ne babille pas! Laisse-moi étudier!

D'autre part, on voit agir dès le XVIe siècle les facteurs désintégrants qui conduiront à la réanalyse de ladite construction. En effet, c'est à partir de cette époque que l'emploi de notre construction devient courant (en yiddish comme en allemand [3]) avec un complément d'objet à la première personne, pour exprimer la modalité volitive ou exhortative. La comparaison de plusieurs traductions de l'ancien testament nous montre que la construction avec *lozn* remplace dans cet emploi le verbe *wellen* 'vouloir', pour rendre la première personne du cohortatif en hébreu [4]:

---

[3] Cf. Grimm *Wörterbuch*, 'lassen' col. 239 "... diese offenbare höflichkeitsformel... niederdeutschen ursprungs ist... im nhd. erst seit Luther häufig."

[4] En comparant la traduction de Luther (1545) à celle de Mentel (1466) on trouve p. ex: Gen. 19: 32 Viens, faisons boire du vin à notre père...
Mentel: *kum wir trencken (v. l. wollendt trencken) in mit wein.*
Luther: *So kom las uns unsern Vater wein zu trinken geben.*

Psaumes 51 : 15 J'enseignerai tes voies aux transgresseurs.

(9) *ix wil lernen die mistoter dein weg* (Br. 1511 Ps. 51 : 15)
(10) *loz mix lernen die zindiger dein weg* (1679 Ps. 51 : 15)

Psaumes 69 : 15 Ne permets pas que j'y reste enfonce.

(11) *un nit ix wil forzinken* (Br. 1511 Ps. 69 : 15)
(12) *un loz mix dox nit fer ziniken* (1679 Ps. 69 : 15)

Genèse 1 : 26 Puis Dieu dit: faisons l'homme à notre image.

(13) *da šprax got. mir weln maxen ein menšn in unzerm form.* (1560 Gen. 1 : 26)
(14) *da šprax got. lazt uns menšin maxen in form der unz gleix zei.* (1679 Gen. 1 : 26)

Genèse 37 : 27 Venez, vendons-le aux Ismaélites.

(15) *geit un mir wiln verkofin in den išmoelim.* (Par. XVI, Gen. 37 : 27)
(16) *kumt last unz in den išmoelim ferkofin.* (1679 Gen. 37 : 27)

Psaumes 95 : 1 Venez, chantons avec allégresse en l'honneur de l'Eternel.

(17) *geit, mir wolen zingen cu got.* (Ps. 1558 95 : 1)
(18) *geit her, last uns loben cu got.* (Ps. 1586 95 : 1)

Juges 19 : 28 Il lui dit: Lève-toi, allons-nous-en.

(19) *un er šprax cu ir štei oif un mir weln gein.* (SM 1626 Jud. 19 : 28)
(20) *un er šprax cu ir štei oif un laz uns cihin.* (1679 Jud. 19 : 28)

Le premier exemple de ce type est attesté chez Elia Levita:

(21) *kum, loz uns gein špacirn.* (BA 1541: 63)
Viens, allons nous promener.

Un autre facteur de désintégration touche au groupe nominal qui constitue le complément d'object de l'impératif. En effet, dans plusieurs formes nominales le yiddish, encore plus que l'allemand, ne distingue pas le nominatif de l'accusatif, ceci notamment lorsque le complément d'objet est un nom ou un pronom neutre ou féminin, ou bien lorsqu'il s'agit d'un pronom possessif:

(22) *nim mein zun un loz in dein eib zeigen.* (BA 1541: 9)
Prends mon fils et que ta femme l'allaite.

(23) *loz zie cu dir zein an ir štat.* (SM 1626 Jud. 15 : 2)
Prends-la donc à sa place.
(24) *un loz reidn nun dein meid in dein orin.* (SM 1626, I Sam. 25 : 24)
Permets à ta servante de parler devant toi.
(25) *laz die iungfrogue bei uns nox bleiben* (MM 1725, Gen. 24 : 55)
Que la jeune fille demeure avec nous quelque temps encore.
(26) *laz ez dir nit ibel gefalen iber den iung.* (MM 1725, Gen. 21 : 12)
N'aie point de chagrin à cause de l'enfant.

L'impact de ces deux facteurs combinés — à savoir, le fait que dans notre construction la forme verbale *loz* n'est pas toujours caractérisée comme un impératif et que le groupe nominal, lui, n'est pas toujours caractérisé comme un complément d'objet — conduit à une réanalyse de la construction (*loz*+objet+infinitif) en (*loz*+sujet+infinitif). En d'autres termes, la forme *loz*, réinterprétée, n'est plus considérée comme un impératif à la 2ème personne, mais comme la 3ème personne du singulier d'un verbe modal qui se combine avec un groupe nominal lequel n'est plus considéré comme son complément d'objet, mais comme son *sujet*.

Un facteur supplémentaire qui facilite cette transformation est l'existence, en yiddish comme en allemand, d'un autre type de construction (attesté dès le XIVe s.), dans lequel la forme *loz* se combine effectivement avec un sujet. Il s'agit de la 3ème personne du singulier du subjonctif présent de *lozn* dans sa fonction causative ou factitive, avec un sujet et un infinitif [5] :

(27) *got loz dix lange mit eiren leben* (DH 1382: 24)
Que Dieu te laisse vivre longuement avec honneur.
(28) *got los in lange im eiren leben* (DH 1382: 40)
Que Dieu le laisse vivre longuement avec honneur.
(29) *zo loz unz der šwarc muinx nit toitn* (RM XVI)
Donc que le moine noir ne nous fasse pas mourir.
(30) *got isborex-šmoi los dirs bicalin* (MB 1602: 146)
Que Dieu, béni soit son nom, t'en récompense.

---

[5] En allemand, ce tour est conservé dans l'emploi du subjonctif à la 3ème personne comme la forme de politesse pour l'impératif:

Lasz er es gut sein, Miller! (Schiller *Kabale und Liebe* 5 : 3)
Bleib er! Schweig er! (*op. cit.* 5 : 5)

(31) *un ob es iz an mir ein zind loz er mix teitn der melex.* (SM 1626, II Sam. 14 : 32)
   et s'il y a en moi quelque iniquité, qu'il me fasse mourir, le roi.

Le *Maise-Bux*, paru à Bâle en 1602, témoigne du processus de désintégration de cette construction en yiddish, suite à la récession du mode subjonctif. Ainsi trouve-t-on dans ce recueil d'histoires moralisantes, à la fin de certaines histoires parlant de la vie des justes, une formule de souhait souvent répétée: Que Dieu nous laisse profiter de leurs mérites. La forme primaire de cette formule est:

(32) *HKBH los uns ire zxus ox genisen omen.* (MB 1602 181 : 121)
   Que Dieu nous laisse aussi profiter de leurs mérites amen.
(33) *HKBH los uns ir beiden zxus genisen* (MB 1602 201 : 145)
   Que Dieu nous laisse profiter des mérites d'eux deux.

Cependant, on trouve aussi des cas ou à la forme *loz*, qui n'est plus ressentie comme exprimant la signification causative, vient s'ajouter l'infinitif de ce même verbe pour rendre cette même signification:

(34) *HKBH los uns alen zxus lozin genisen* (MB 1602 198 : 139)
   Que Dieu nous laisse tous profiter de ses mérites.

Dans un cas on trouve même l'infinitif *lozn* répété:

(35) *HKBH los uns des frumen cadik zxus ox losin genisen lozin* (MB 1602 211 : 158)
   Que Dieu nous laisse aussi profiter des mérites de ce juste pieux.

Un indice du rôle qu'assume dans cet emploi la forme fléchie *loz*, est le fait que celle-ci est substituée dans quelques cas par l'auxiliaire modal *zol*:

(36) *HKBH zol uns ir alen zxus cu aler ceit losin genisen.* (MB 1602 163 : 105)
   Que Dieu nous laisse profiter à tous temps de leurs mérites à eux tous.
(37) *got zol uns irer beider zxus genisen losn* (MB 1602 174 : 114)
   Que Dieu nous laisse profiter des mérites d'eux deux.

La forme *loz* n'est donc plus ressentie comme le subjonctif d'un auxiliaire de diathèse exprimant le causatif, mais plutôt comme l'indicatif singulier d'un auxiliaire modal, comparable et substituable à *zoln*.

C'est en effet à partir de là que l'histoire de *lozn* en yiddish prend une direction originale, inconnue des autres dialectes allemands [6].

Dès le XVIe siècle nous trouvons donc des occurrences du verbe *lozn* avec un nominatif qui lui sert de sujet, ainsi qu'avec un infinitif. Le tour sert à rendre les modalités volitive, exhortative, jussive ou optative, selon la personne du sujet.

A la 1ére personne [7] du singulier la réanalyse de notre construction s'exprime par la substitution de l'accusatif *mix* par le nominatif *ix*. Les formes verbales des deux versets cités plus haut dans les exemples 9 - 10 et 11 - 12, où l'on trouve d'abord *ix wil* puis *loz mix*, sont donc transformées en *loz ix*:

(38) *loz ix lernen die zindiger dein weg* (MM 1725 Ps. 51 : 15)
J'enseignerai tes voies aux transgresseurs.
(39) *loz ix nit farzunken wern* (MM 1725 Ps. 69 : 15)
Ne permets pas que j'y reste enfoncé.

Le premier exemple de ce type est attesté dans un manuscrit de 1511 provenant de Brescia.

(40) *los ix šterbn mit dem plištim zein* (Br. 1511 Jud. 16 : 30)
Que je périsse avec les Philistins!

Et, aux siècles suivants:

(41) *da fragt er die froie libe loz ix dix fregn* (MB 1602 1 : 2)
Alors il demanda à la femme: Ma chére, permettez-moi de vous demander...
(42) *un loz ix werdn girexnt ein rexinung eins fun meini cwei oign* (SM 1730 Jud. 16 : 28)
Que je me venge pour la perte de l'un de mes deux yeux!

---

[6] L'inclusion du verbe *lassen* dans le groupe des auxiliaires allemands, proposée par E. Krašeninnikova (1954), est rejetée par les grammairiens allemands. Cf. Brinkmann 1971: 381 "Nicht zu den Modalverben gehören *wissen* und *lassen*... Das Verbum *lassen*, bei Krasheninnikova einbezogen (102ff.), scheidet aus, weil es einen Akkusativ zulässt, der funktionales Subjekt zum Infinitum ist (*Ich lasse ihn schlafen*). Bei den Modalverben sind Subjekt des Modalverbs und des Infinitums stets identisch: ein Akkusativ kann bei ihnen nur Objekt zum Infinitum sein". La situation en yiddish est, comme nous le verrons, bien différente.

[7] Nous sommes redevables d'une bonne partie des exemples apportés dans le paragraphe suivant à l'étude de N. Prilucki, publiée dans le Ve volume de ses recherches dialectologiques du yiddish (Varsovie 1924) traitant des combinaisons de *lozn* avec la 1ère personne *lomir, lomix*.

(43) *es iz ein awle? loz ix kein greser awleništ tuhn.* (Nusb. 1885: 30)
C'est une injustice?! Puis-je ne pas en faire de plus grande que celle-ci.

La forme *loz ix* devient avec les siècles de plus en plus rare, jusqu'à disparaitre totalement de la langue moderne. Elle est évincée par une forme concurrente, attestée dès le XVIIe siècle, *lom ix*. Cette dernière forme reflète en effet la métanalyse faite par les locuteurs lorsque l'impératif *loz mix*, prononcé normalement dans certains dialects allemands et yiddish *lo mix*[8], n'est plus ressenti comme tel, et que son complément devient sujet. Les versets cités plus haut dans les exemples 9 - 12 et 38 - 39 prennent donc la forme suivante:

(44) *lom ix lernen die zindiger dein weg* (SM 1626 Ps. 51 : 15)
J'enseignerai tes voies aux transgresseurs.

(45) *lom ix nit ferzunken wern* (SM 1626 Ps. 69 : 15)
Ne permets pas que j'y reste enfoncè.

Et, dans les siècles qui suivent:

(46) *du zolst mix wašn un min wi der šnei lom ix weis wern* (Ps. 1714 51 : 9)
Lave-moi, et je serai plus blanc que la neige.

(47). *lom ex beser fun dem eisek op šnadin* (TFH 1839: 692)
Il vaudrait mieux que je me retire de cette affaire.

(48) *lozt mix, lom ix xotše on tapin di toite kale.* (Ok. 1862: 58)
Laissez-moi, que je touche au moins la fiancée morte.

A la 1ère personne du pluriel, la réanalyse de notre construction se manifeste par le remplacement de l'impératif *loz, lozt* par une forme d'indicatif au pluriel, accordée au sujet. Les versets cités plus haut dans les exemples 13 − 20 prennent donc l'aspect suivant:

(49) *lozn mir ein menš bešafen in unser form* (MM 1725 Gen. 1 : 2β)
Faisons l'homme à notre image.

---

[8] En allemend cette contraction est attestée dès le vieil-haut-allemand, p. ex:
lâ mih dine stimma vernemen (Williram LXXVII, 19) = Grimm, *Wörterb.* 'lassen', col. 214) Laisse-moi entendre ta voix.
La mich das ich gemeinsame mit dir (Mentel 1466, Gen. 38: 16)
Laisse-moi aller vers toi.
Ces formes contractées subsistent jusqu'à présent dans des dialectes bavarois, souabes et alémaniques (Grimm, *Wörterb.* 'lassen', col. 215).
En yiddish les formes contractées sont très courantes dans plusieurs dialectes (cf. Prilucki 1924: 6).

(50) *geit lozin mir in ferkafin an di išmoelim* (MM 1725 Gen. 37 : 27)
    Venez, vendons-le aux Ismaélites.
(51) *un er šprax cu ir štei oif un lozin mir gein* (MM 1725 Jud. 19 : 28)
    Il lui dit: Lève-toi, allons-nous-en.
(52) *bereit aix lozin mir cu got zingin* (1679 Ps. 95 : 1)
    Venez, chantons avec allégresse en l'honneur de l'Eternel.

La forme *lozin mir* subsiste jusqu'au XIXe siècle, quoiqu'elle devienne de moins en moins courante:

(53) *lozin mir ale gehin lerabi avrohom.* (ŠB 1817)
    Allons tous chez Rabbi Abraham.
(54) *kum, lozin mir gein abisl špacirn.* (Morg. 1895: 10)
    Viens, promenons-nous un peu.

A côté de la forme *lozn mir* on trouve aussi, quoique rarement, *loz mir*:

(55) *ruf nun cu ḥušai der arxi un las mir hern waz er wert zagen oix er* (SM 1626, IISam. 17 : 5)
    Qu'on apelle également Cusaï l'Arkite pour que nous entendions ce qu'il conseille, lui aussi.

Si dans cet exemple on peut interpréter *las mir hern* comme un impérati: 'laisse-moi entendre', il n'en est pas de même dans les cas suivantsf

(56) *loz mir zehen bei moiše rabeinu olev hašolem* (Hu. 1837: 52)
    Voyons le cas de Moïse, paix à son âme.
(57) *loz mir gein cu di cwei šutfim.* (Morg. 1985: 16)
    Allons chez les deux associés.

La forme qui se répand dès le XVIIe siècle au détriment de *lozin mir* et de *loz mir*, est la forme contractée avec assimilation du -*z* au *m*-, notamment *loh mir, lom mir* ou *lommer*, ou encore, dans son orthographe 'normalisé' qui est d'usage jusqu'a nos jours — *lomir*.

(58) *lom mir zain iber enfert in gots hent* (SM 1626, II Sam. 24 : 14)
    Tombons entre les mains de l'Eternel.
(59) *kumts un lom mir zix bukn unlom mir knien* (SM 1626, Ps. 95 : 6)
    Venez, prosternons-nous, fléchissons les genoux.
(60) *bemeile lom mir nemin ein meidlin oder ein weiblein un loh mir boideg zain* (AŠ 1708 205 : 151) (=Sh. 1979: 219)
    Prenons donc une dame ou une demoiselle et examinons-la.

(61) *šreibin mir lošn koideš lomir reidn oix lošn koideš* (Mar. 1790: 4)
Si nous écrivons dans la langue sainte, parlons donc dans cette langue également.

(62) *lommer gein aheim epis esin.* (TFH 1839: 664)
Allons à la maison manger quelque chose.

(63) *lom mir gor nit cinemin dos papir.* (Ok. 1862: 8)
Ne déplions même pas le document.

(64) *nor lom mir dos ob legen oif ein ander ceit.* (Din. 1897: 66)
Mais laissons cela pour une autre fois.

A la 3ème personne du singulier on rencontre des formes nominales au nominatif dès le début du XVIIe siècle:

(65) *iz er den ein malex azo loz er arois gein* (MB 1602 33 : 19)
S'il est vraiment un ange, qu'il sorte donc.

(66) *iber reid dein man loz er uns dos retniš zogn* (SM 1626, Jud. 14 : 15)
Persuade ton mari de nous expliquer l'énigme.

(67) *lozt cu im un loz er fluxn.* (SM 1626, II Sam. 16 : 11)
Laissez-le faire, et qu'il maudisse.

(68) *darum loz der kinig herein gein gešwint* (AŠ 1697, 3 : 48) (=Sh. 1979: 160)
Que le roi entre donc vite.

(69) *ruft im loz er mit uns brot esn* (MM 1725, Exod. 2 : 20)
Appelez-le et qu'il mange du pain.

(70) *loz er kumen der cadik cu zaine oves loz er dos beiz far zix nit zehn* (OŠ 1812)
Puisse-t-il joindre ses aïeux, le juste, puisse-t-il ne pas voir le mal sur son chemin.

Devant le pronom indéfini *men* on trouve aussi des cas d'assimilation du -z au m-, ce qui donne la forme *lom men* [9]:

(71) *lom men ankikin in moire oib men meg tuhn dos* (TFH 1839: 688)
Que l'on regarde dans le Guide (des égarés) pour voir si cela est permis.

A la 3ème personne du pluriel l'auxiliaire est accordé en nombre à son sujet, ce qui donne *lozn*:

---

[9] Cette forme est attestée dans quelques dialectes yiddish de Pologne (cf. Prilucki 1924: 47).

(72) *lozn zie feršmt un feršmaxt wern die mein leib bigern* (SM 1626, Ps. 34 : 4)
Qu'ils soient honteux et confus, ceux qui en veulent à ma vie.

(73) *lozin den die iungin leitzeligkeit gefinden in deini oigin* (1679, I Sam. 25 : 8)
Que mes jeunes gens trouvent donc grâce à tes yeux.

(74) *šik mein folk un lozn zie mix dinen* (MM 1725, Exod. 10 : 3)
Laisse aller mon peuple, afin qu'il me serve.

(75) *un lozn zi ruen oif ir geleger bešolem.* (OS 1812)
Et puissent-ils reposer en paix dans leur tombe.

(76) *lozn nor zan di werter ba dir taier wi gold.* (TFH 1839: 688)
Que ces mots te soient chers comme de l'or.

(77) *lozin andre mames zex der fin štoisin.* (Ok. 1862: 31)

(78) *lozin die cwei menšin aheim gein.* (Morg. 1895: 16)
Que d'autre mères en tirent la leçon.
Que ces deux personnes s'en aillent à la maison.

Les formes que nous venons de présenter constituent en effet un paradigme modal nouveau, consistant en la 1ère et la 3ème personnes du singulier et du pluriel, et qui entre en rapport de supplétion avec l'impératif à la 2ème personne (cf. Mark 1978: 289).

Dans la langue moderne — à partir de la fin du XIXe siècle jusqu'à nos jours — l'emploi de notre tour s'est considérablement répandu, tant par le nombre des occurrences que par la diversité des nuances modales que celui-ci s'est chargé d'exprimer.

A la 1ère personne, le tour avec *lozn* exprime les diverses nuances des modalités volitive, optative et exhortative (les exemples sont présentés dans cet ordre de nuances):

— au singulier:

(79) *git aher beide žmenies, lomix aix oisšitn dos bisl klein gelt.* (ŠA 26 : 17)
Donnez-moi vos deux mains, que je vous verse le peu de petite monnaie.

(80) *un az ix heng šoin oif ein fus, lom ix hengen oif beide.* (ŠA 1 : 53)
Et si déjà je suis pendu d'un pied, autant l'être des deux.

(81) *lom ix nit hobn oif mein gewisn di umšuld fun a šeiner iunger meidl.* (R. 7 : 245)
Je ne voudrais pas avoir sur la conscience l'innocence d'une belle jeune fille.

(82) *lom ix hobn di alofim, zog ix, wifl klecer ix hob ahincu areingefirt.* (ŠA 1 : 27)

Puissé-je posséder autant de billets de mille, dis-je, que j'ai apporté de bûches là-bas.

— au pluriel:
(83) *lomir lozn curu berekn un zix umkern cu mein fus.* (Op. 6 : 147)
Laissons Berek en paix et retournons à ma jambe.
(84) *un lomir hofn az s'wet gelingen.* (Man. 108)
Et espérons que ça réussira.
(85) — *lomir zain gezunt ...* — *trinken zei ois.* (Gub. 56)
— A notre santé... — boivent-ils.
(86) *halewai ingixn lomir esn lekex bai undz.* (MMS 1 : 128)
Plût au ciel que bientôt nous pourrions manger notre gâteau de mariage.

A la 3ème personne, notre tour exprime les diverses nuances des modalités jussive, permissive et optative (les exemples sont classés dans cet ordre):

— au singulier:
(87) *wu iz der ferwalter? loz er kumen!* (R. 7 : 36)
Où est le directeur? Qu'il vienne!
(88) *er wil hakn? loz er hakn!* (Op. 6 : 31)
Il veut couper? Qu'il coupe!
(89) *loz mir got helfn a hundert-xeilek wos ix wintš aix.* (ŠA 1 : 10)
Que Dieu m'aide ne fut-ce que d'un pourcent de ce que je vous souhaite.

— au pluriel:
(90) *lozn zei wisn wer tevie iz!* (ŠA 1 : 156)
Qu'ils sachent qui est Tevie!
(91) *dortn lozn zei undz zuxn, az zei badarfn...* (ŠA 13 : 94)
Qu'ils nous cherchent là-bas, s'ils en ont besoin...
(92) *-wos weln zei zogn?*
-gezunterheit; lozn zei zix mit im haltn. (ŠA 27 : 147)
— Que diront ils?
— A leur santé! Qu'ils restent avec lui!
(93) *lozn zei gein cu aldi šwarce ior!* (MMS 1 : 120)
Qu'ils aillent à tous les diables!

Un emploi de *lozn* qui n'est pas attesté avant l'ère moderne est celui de protase dans une proposition conditionnelle. Dans le premier exemple ci-dessous, la protase et l'apodose sont plutôt indépendentes (comme en témoigne la ponctuation faite par l'auteur), ce qui le rapproche des exemples précédents:

(94) *anu, lomix nor zen er zol mix pruwn nemen. di roite bord zaine wel ix im oisraisn.* (Man. 4)
Je veux bien voir qu'il essaye de m'attraper. Sa barbe rousse, je la lui arracherai.

Dans les autres exemples le tour avec *lozn* constitue une seule phrase avec la principale qui le suit, l'ordre des mots étant celui que l'on trouve normalement dans une proposition conditionnelle:

(95) *lomix zei waizn a finger, šlingen zei mix ain mit di kamašn.* (Pe.2 : 86)
Il suffirait que je leur cède d'un pouce pour qu'ils m'avalent tout entier avec mes bottes.

(96) *lom ix weln haint emecn fardreien dem kop, iz bai mir a meloxe?* (ŠA 25 : 52)
Et si je décidais aujourd'hui de faire tourner la tête à quelqu'un, pensez-vous que cela me serait difficile?

(97) *loz er mir nor durxgein di eršte etlexe klasn gimenazie, zog ix, max ix im xasene, mit gots hilf.* (SA 26 : 186)
Qu'il me fasse seulement ses premières classes de lycée, dis-je, après quoi je le marierai bien, avec l'aide de Dieu.

(98) *loz men nor im arainlozn ergec mit zain prošek, azoi blaibtništ ein moiz.* (SA 13 : 129)
Qu'on le laisse entrer où que ce soit avec sa poudre, et aussitôt il ne restera plus une seule souris.

(99) *loz einem zix nor daxtn epes a mindste baleidikung, iz er greit cu dergein aix di iorn.* (MMS 1 : 18)
Il suffit que les gens vous soupçonnent de la moindre offense, pour qu'ils soient prêts à vous empoisonner la vie.

(100) *di briwlex wos men šraibt zix! a tog iber a tog. a šteiger, loz nit zain azoi gix kein briw — tut zix xoišex.* (ŠA 27 : 57)
Les petites lettres qu'ils s'écrivent! Jour après jour. Si, par exemple, s'écoule un jour sans qu'il arrive de lettre — c'est le drame.

(101) *loz nor wern naxt, azoi trogn mir op di flešer cum taix.* (ŠA 13 : 124)
Attendons seulement qu'il fasse nuit, et aussitôt nous irons porter les bouteilles à la rivière.

Dans sa nouvelle forme et avec ses nouvelles fonctions, le tour avec *lozn* concurrence l'auxiliaire modal *zoln*. Cela se manifeste déjà en comparant les différentes traductions de la Bible:

Exod. 2 : 20 Appelez-le et qu'il mange du pain.
(102) *ruft cu im un er zol esn brot* (1560)
(103) *ruft in lazt inen mit uns brot esin* (1679)
(104) *ruft im loz er mit uns brot esn* (MM 1725)

Ps. 69 : 15 Ne permets pas que j'y reste enfoncé.
(105) *un nit ix zol ver zinken* (Ps. 1558)
(106) *loz mix nit far zinken* (1687)
(107) *loz ix nit far zunken wern* (MM 1725)

Notons la différence dans l'ordre des mots entre les deux auxiliaires. Le sujet qui se combine avec *loz*, historiquement son complément d'objet, ne peut que lui succéder, alors que le sujet de *zol* n'est pas soumis à une telle contrainte. Illustrons cette différence par deux exemples provenant de la traduction de 1725:

(108) *šik mein folk un zie zolen mix dinen* (MM 1725 Exod. 7 : 16)
  Laisse aller mon peuple afin qu'il me serve.
(109) *šik mein folk un lozn zie mix dinen* (MM 1725 Exod. 10 : 3)
  Laisse aller mon peuple afin qu'il me serve.

Dans la langue moderne aussi, on trouve de paires semblables, où le placement du sujet par rapport à l'auxiliaire, qui est conditionné par la structure thématique de l'énoncé, semble dominer le choix de l'une des deux formes concurrentes:

(110) *un loz dir got bacoln, zog ix, bexeifel-kiflaim.* (ŠA 1 : 133)
  Et que Dieu, dis-je, t'en rende dix fois plus.
(111) *got zol dir, zog ix, coln bexeifel-kiflaim.* (ŠA 1 : 212)
  Que Dieu, dis-je, t'en rende dix fois plus.
(112) *der nogid zol zix opšnaidn dem noz, darf nem* (!) *aix šnaidn dem noz...* (ŠA 25 : 69)
  Et si ce richard se coupe le nez, toi aussi tu devras te couper le nez...
(113) *loz zix einer opšnaidn di noz, kont ir zixer zain az af morgn hot ir dort cwei opgešnitene nezer.* (ŠA 19 : 13)
  Si quelqu'un se coupait le nez, vous pouvez être sûr que le lendemain il y aura deux nez de coupés.

Cependant, à côté de ces paires il y a bon nombre d'exemples où *loz* et *zol* se substituent sans motif apparent, qu'il soit formel ou sémantique.

a. dans des constructions impersonnelles sans sujet formel:

(114) *nu, zol zain mit glik.* (Gub. 16)
Et bien, que ce soit sous le signe du bonheur.
(115) *loz zain mit glik!* (ŠA 1 : 87)
Que ce soit sous le signe du bonheur!
(116) *zol šoin zain genug gepuct!* (Zin. 196)
Assez de ce nettoyage!
(117) *ober loz šoin zain genug geweint!* (ŠA 1 : 80)
Cesse donc enfin de pleurer!
(118) *est gezunt, zol aix woil bakumen.* (MMS 1 : 72)
Mangez à votre santé
(119) m*est gezunterheit, un loz aix woil bakumen* !(ŠA 1 : 30)
Mangez à votre santé.

b. avec un sujet indéfini:

(120) *wos šwaigt men? zol men aroisloifn nox beren!* (Kul. 7)
Que reste-t-on ~ ne rien faire? Que l'on courre chercher Bère!
(121) *wos šwaigt ir? loz men epes ton, loz men ratewen!* (Pe. 2 : 80)
Pourquoi restez-vous sans rien faire? Que l'on fasse quelque chose, que l'on aille au secours!

c. avec un sujet défini:

(122) — *krank,* — *hot di malexte xane-dvoire a plieske geton mit beide hent,* — *zoln maine sonim krank zain.* (Man. 116)
Malade! — Xane-Dvoire l'angélique se frappa les mains — Que ce soient mes ennemis qui soient malades!
(123) *lozn maine sonim, zogt zi, krenken.* (ŠA 26 : 188)
Que ce soient mes ennemis, dit-elle, qui soient malades!
(124) *nu, genug dir, sruli, far haint, un zoln zix dir gute xaloimes xolemen.* (Ni. 2 : 360)
Eh bien, ça te suffit pour aujourd'hui, Sruli, et fais de beaux rêves.
(125) *a gute naxt, un lozn zix dir xolemen gute xaloimes.* (ŠA 1 : 88)
Bonne nuit, et fais de beaux rêves.

Ces derniers exemples manifestent en effet un état de coexistence entre des variantes fonctionnellement équivalentes, reflétant peut être des différences dialectales dont nous savons trop peu.

Le processus qui a commencé au XVIe siècle se résume donc en la transformation de *lozn* en un auxiliaire modal faisant partie du paradigme supplétif de l'impératif pour les personnes autres que la 2ème (cf. Zarecki 1926: 129). Le parallelisme entre *loz* et *zol*, constaté par Mark (1978: 289) pour la 3ème personne, est valable, nous l'avons vu, aussi pour la 1ère.

Une analyse plus complète de ce parallélisme ne pourrait être fournie que dans le cadre d'une description systématique du verbe yiddish dans ses dimensions historiques, description dans laquelle les rapports sémantiques et fonctionnels entre les auxiliaires modaux constitueront sans doute un chapitre particulièrement passionant.

BIBLIOGRAPHIE

a. Sources en yiddish

1560 = Traduction du Pentateuque, Crémone 1560.
1610 = Traduction du Pentateuque, Prague 1610.
1679 = Traduction de la Bible par Jekuthiel Blitz, Amsterdam 1679.
1687 = Traduction de la Bible par Joseph Wizenhaüsen, Amsterdam 1687.
AŠ 1697 = *Ein Šein Purim Špil* Altdorf 1697. Ms. Leipzig Nr 35. Ed. Shmeruk 1979.
AŠ 1708 = *Ahašweiroš Špil* Francfort sur le Main (?) 1708. Ed. Shmeruk 1979. New York 1949.
Ba 1541 = Elia Levita Askenazi *Bovo D'antona*. Isnae 1541. Ed. Judah A. Joffe.
Bash. = I. Bashevis-Singer *Der Špigl*. Jérusalem 1975.
Br. 1511 = Traduction du livre des Juges et des Psaumes, Brescia 1511. Ms. Parma 2513, Pol. 1/5 (Juges), Pol. 1/2 (Psaumes).
DH 1382 *Dukus Horant*, Ms. Cambridge T.-S. K. 22, de 1382. Ed. L. Fuks *The oldest known literary document of Yiddish literature*. Amsterdam 1957.
Din. = I. Dinezon *Heršele*. Warszawa 1879.
Gub. = A. Gubnicki *Main Oicer*. Moscou 1973.
Hu. = Isaiah ben Abraham Hurwitz *Ec Ḥaim*. Warszawa 1837.
Kul. = M. Kulbak *Geklibene Werk*. New York 1953.
Man. = I. Manger *Dos Bux fun Gan Eidn*. Tel Aviv 1976.
Mar. = M. Markuze *Seifer Refues*. Poryck 1790.
MB 1602 = *Maise Bux*. Bâle 1602.
MB 1703 = *Maise Bux*. Francfort sur le Main 1703.
MM 1725 = *Magišei Minḥah*. Traduction de la Bible par Eliezer ben Isaac Rödelsheim Amsterdam 1725.
MMS = Mendele Moxer Sforim *Oisgeweilte Werk*. Warszawa 1953.
Morg. = I. Morgenštern *Maise Mišnei Šutfim*. Warszawa 1895.
Ni. = Der Nister *Di Mišpoxe Mašber*. IIe volume. New York 1948.
Nu. = A. Nusboim *Der Tiranišer Melamed*. Warszawa 1885.
Ok. = I. Oksenfeld *Der Eršter Jidišer Rekrut*. Leipzig 1862.
Op. = J. Opatošu *In Poiliše Welder*. = *Gezamlte Werk* vol. VI. Wilno 1928.
OŠ 1812 = *Ohev Šolem*. Appendice à la traduction du livre d'Esther, dite *Mecaḥ Aharon*. Wilno 1812.
Par. XVI = Traduction du Pentateuque, XVIe siècle. Ms. Parma 2510, Jud. Germ. 1.
Pe. = I. L. Perec *Oisgeweilte Werk*. New York 1920.

Ps. 1558 = *Psaumes*. Zurich 1558.
Ps. 1586 = *Psaumes*. Kraków. 1586.
Ps. 1714 = *Psaumes*. Francfort sur le Main 1714.
R. = A. Reizen *Ale Werk*. New York 1928.
RM XVI = *Maise Reb Meir*. Ms. du XVIe siècle, publié dans *YIVO Filologiše Šriftn* vol. 3 (1929) pp. 1 - 42.
ŠA = Šolem Aleixem *Ale Werk*. New York 1937.
ŠB 1817 = *Šivhei ha-Beš"t*. Laščov 1817.
Sh. 1979 = Chone Shmeruk *Yiddish Biblical Plays 1697 - 1750*. Jérusalem 1979.
SM 1626 = *Seifer ha-Magid*. Traduction des Prophètes et des Hagiographes, Lublin 1626.
SM 1730 = *Seifer ha-Magid*. Amsterdam 1730.
TFH 1839 = *Teiater Fun Hasidim*. Pièce anonyme de 1839, publiée dans *YIVO Historiše Šriftn* vol. 1 (1929) pp. 625 - 693.
Zin. = I. J. Zinger *Derceilungen*. New York 1928.

b. Etudes linguistiques

H. Brinkmann 1971 *Die Deutsche Sprache*^{2} Düsseldorf. (1 ère éd. 1962).
E. Krašeninnikova 1954 *Modal'nye glagoly v nemeckom jazyke*. Moscou.
W. B. Lockwood 1962 *Historical German Syntax*. Oxford.
J. Mark 1978 *Gramatik fun der jidišer klal-šprax*. New York.
N. Prilucki 1924 *Mame-Lošn*. Warszawa. (= *Jidiše Dialektiše Foršungen* vol. 5)
F. Tschirch 1975 *Geschichte der deutschen Sprache*^{2}, IIe partie. Berlin. (1 ère éd. 1969).
A. Zarecki 1926 *Praktiše jidiše gramatik*. Moscou.

CONFRONTATION AND ASSOCIATION

ELIZABETH CLOSS TRAUGOTT

Several independent studies have suggested that the set of grammatical markers used in a language to express goal-orientation, opposition and association form a semantic domain of considerable interest for historical linguistics.[1] One is Timmer (1967), in which the so-called Third Form in Arabic, the Prepositional Verb form in Swahili, and the Applied Form in Kanuri are all shown to be verb derivations which share the properties of goal-orientation, opposition or association.[2] Some examples are:

1. a) Arabic: ʕajila "to hurry", ʕājala "to hurry in order to catch up with"; kalafa "to be the successor", kālafa "to be contradictory, oppose"; maša "to pace, walk", māša "to keep pace (with someone)";
   b) Swahili: -enda "go", -endea "go to"; -nena "speak, speak of", -nenea "speak against"; -la "eat, use up", -lia "eat for, eat with";
   c) Kanuri: ŋgəarə̂mŋìn "gallop", ŋgərə́mgəskìn "gallop toward, rush into"; gə́rgâŋìn "be angry", gə́rgagə̀skín "be angry with, annoy"; kasə́skìn "run", yirkasə́skìn "run with".

Another study is Wasson (1982) which discusses the semantics of Latin verbs borrowed into English with derivative com-/con- (< Lat. cum "with"). In most cases the derivative developed, either before or after borrowing, the sense of direction or opposition. Some examples are:

2. a) compete < Lat. (com + petere "direct one's course to"; L. Lat. "make for with hostile intent"); glossed variously in sixteenth century Eng. grammars as "be suitable for" (associative), "sue for the same thing which another doth" (oppositional);

---

[1] I wish to thank Roger Wolfe for his helpful comments on an earlier draft of this paper, and Joseph H. Greenberg for drawing my attention to Timmer's work.
[2] Sometimes intensity is also involved, cf. Swahili —tazama "look at" —tazamia "look at closely". Intensity is important for the relation of the derivatives in question to transitivity and telicity, but will not be pursued further here.

b) *confront* (< Lat. *con+front+em* "together+face") "to face in hostility" (1588), "to adjoin on equal borders" (1601), "to parallel" (1641);

c) *contest* (< Lat. *con+testarī* "be a witness"); "to assert or confirm with the witness of an oath" (1579), "to dispute" (1603).

A third study is Hittle (1901) of Old English *mid* and *wid*. She discusses how the semantic domains of association and direction/opposition, originally lexicalized separately as *mid* and *wid* respectively, came to be expressed by the end of Middle English by one and the same preposition, *with* as in *fight with the enemy, go with Bill*. Other evidence for the relation between direction, opposition and association is provided by English *and*. Though the etymology is disputed, the reconstructions suggest that this term originally was directional/oppositional or at least sequential rather than strictly coordinating. The OED suggests Vedic *anti* "over against" as a cognate, and says "from the idea of opposition, juxtaposition, or antithesis, the word was used in the Teut. langs. to express the mutual relation of notions and propositions". Walde-Pokorny (1930) proposes instead that *and* is cognate with OI. *atha* "thereupon, then". In either case, *and* appears not to have meant "together with" in its earliest stages.

A number of topics worthy of study are suggested by the data in 1) and 2). For one, there is the topic of the historical relation of locative expressions to case markings (especially prepositional and postpositional markings) and to connectives, and of the constraints on possible paths of semantic transition that they evidence. Examples include the development of the English preposition *of* < OE *of* "from", and of the connective *but* < OE *be-ūtan* "on the outside" (cf. Givón 1973, Traugott 1978). Second, there is the topic of the relation of associative and "comitative" to other cases such as instrument, force, and agent on the hierarchy of control (cf. Comrie 1981, Nilsen 1973, and also the semantic spectrum manner-means-instrument-agentive-stimulus identified by Quirk et al. 1972). Although comitative itself does not exercise control, it frequently is expressed by a form that relates it directly to the instrumental (cf. *with*, Gm. *mit*, Fr. *avec*, Span. *con*, Persian *ba/amra*, Eskimo *mik*, Estonian *ga*), and even to the agentive (cf. Aymara *-mp-*, Quechua *waeng*) (Nilsen 1973).[3] Thirdly, there is the issue of the relation of

---

[3] See Schlesinger (1979) for evidence that instrumental and associative are cognitively poles on a continuum, even though they are semantically discrete. This would account for the frequency with which the two roles are expressed by the same marker.

direction/opposition and association to transitivity. Direction/opposition tends to transitivize, being connected with telicity. But association detransitivizes, as illustrated by the examples above of *They fought with the enemy* (roughly equivalent to *They fought the enemy*) vs. *John went with Bill* (roughly equivalent to intransitive *John and Bill went*). And finally there is the question of why it is that direction can so readily come to signify opposition, and that the latter can come to signify its apparent opposite, association. The present paper focusses on this last issue, with particular reference to the replacement of *mid* by *wið*, though the other topics will be touched on here and there.

In her detailed monograph on OE *mid* "associative" and *wið* "directional, confrontational", Hittle (1901) argues that *mid* (cognate with Gk μετά, Goth. *miþ*, Gm. *mit*) is prototypically "among, between" and is associated with statives.[4] *Wið*, however, is prototypically "toward, against", and is associated with directional activities.

Hittle shows how *mid* originates in a) a stative locative ("among"), becomes b) simple associative and comitative, c) a marker of manner, and d) an instrumental marker. Examples of each stage are:

3. a) Or. 274. 18. oðer waes binnan Romebyrig... oder waes *mid* Emelitum ðaem folce "one (of the emperors) was in Rome... the other was among the Emelites" (being in a city and among a people are treated as parallel) (Hittle p. 8)
   b) Or. 140. 28. se consul *mid* Romanum gefeaht wid Sabinan "the consul fought alongside the Romans against the Sabines" (Hittle p. 29)
   c) Aelfr. I 68. ða comon hi *mid* wope to ðam apostole "then they came (with) weeping to the apostle" (Hittle p. 51)
   d) C.P. 1319. geweorðode *mid* gaestlicum giefum "honored with spiritual gifts" (Hittle p. 63).

Further, she suggests that the instrumental arose from the manner preposition by extension from fundamentally stative to more action-oriented contexts, such as from *The horse was decked with a golden harness* (stative, manner) to *He bound his relative with golden chains* (action, instrumental) (p. 63). Even though the instrumental construction typi-

---

[4] Hittle does not use the term "propotypical", but her notion of "grundbedeutung" is compatible in principle with the notion of prototype semantics developed in Coleman and Kay (1981).

cally involves activity verbs, the instrumental relation itself is prototypically non-directional and associative — the actor and instrument coexist in time and space in such constructions as *He broke the window with a hammer*. Though it certainly is possible to launch a spaceship with which to explore Mars several years after the launching, nevertheless the launcher and the intended instrument are assumed to coexist at the point of launch; even if the person who conceives the project dies before any suitable spaceship is built, we nevertheless assume a definite linkage between the projector and the projectile. And it is this prototypical notion of coexistence and indeed copresence that remains to this day in the only common word to retain OE *mid*: *midwife* (*mid-day* involves the cognate noun *midd* "middle").

Like *mid*, *wið* was locative in origin. However, it was not stative but directional. From meaning essentially a) "toward" it became b) oppositional in the concrete sense of fighting with (against) someone (cf. 3.b)) and in the more abstract sense of speaking with or being angry with someone. This is the meaning preserved in e.g. *withstand*. In some contexts such as buying and selling it came to signal transaction, first marking c) the thing gained by the exchange (the goal), and then d) the price paid for the exchange (i.e. the means or instrument for the exchange). Finally it came to signal e) associative relations:

4. a) Or. 234. 10. waes eft farende *wid* daes heofones "and afterward was going toward heaven" (Hittle p. 107)
   b) Or. 72. 32. he swa grom wearð on his mode, and *wið* ða ea gebolgen "he became so furious in his spirit and so angered against the water" (Hittle p. 130)
   c) Or. 92. 21. gesealdon M punda goldes *wið* heora feore "gave a thousand pounds of gold in exchange for their lives" (Hittle p. 143)
   d) C.S. 1306. ic gean him ðaes landes... *wið* an hund mancosa goldes "I gave him the land...for a hundred mancusses of gold" (Hittle p. 144)
   e) Or. 66. 11. ðaet he his rice *wið* hiene daelan wolde "that he wanted to divide his kingdom with him" (Hittle p. 151)

In OE *mid* and *wið* were therefore fairly separate, though some overlap in the domain of exchange and finally association occurred. Hittle quotes an excellent example of an exchange in which the two prepositions are still clearly distinguished with *mid* expressing the price (instrument) and *wið* the prize (goal):

> 4. f) C.P. 449. 16. hi sellað *wið* to lytlum weorðe ðaet, ðaet hi meahton hefonrice *mid* gebycggan: sellað *wið* manna lufe "they sell for too little worth that that they could buy heaven with: they sell it for the love of men (not God)" (Hittle p. 145)

In her final chapter, Hittle notes that in the ME period *wið* rapidly replaced *mid*, and that the latter was rare except in the South West by 1400. Since the replacement started in the North, the possibility of Norse influence of *við*, which already had the associative as well as the oppositional meanings, cannot be ruled out. (Of course, if borrowing was the reason for the change in English, the question of what motivated the shift from oppositional to associative is simply pushed back to Old Norse). Hittle does not consider borrowing an important factor, because the change had already begun in the OE period. Instead, she attempts to explain the ouster on primarily internal grounds, specifically a kind of push chain and analogy. She says the directionality of *wið* was taken over by *to, toward, on, against, of, from, for*, etc.; under pressure from them, *wið* underwent "abblassung" (bleaching) (p. 171) and became associative in all but clearly adversative contexts such as fighting (though even here one can find the newer associative meaning of *wið* as in *fight with the Romans against the Gauls*). Verbal contexts such as those of exchange illustrated in 4. c, d) allowed *wið* to fall together with *mid* and to be analogically extended to *contexts* earlier restricted to *mid*.

Such an account appears to describe the facts well. But as in the case of all appeals to analogy, the interesting question remains, why one form and not the other became the target, in this case why *wið* was analogized to *mid* and not vice versa. Also, if indeed *to*, etc. caused *wið* to bleach, why was it that the set of markers for direction/opposition was so relatively large and dominant? Conversely, why was it that *mid* was replaced by a clearly smaller set, specifically *among/between, by, through, with*? To answer these questions, we need to consider not only *wið* and *mid*, but also the larger typology of markers of opposition and association, both in English and across languages. Evidence from data in 1), 2), and from *and* shows that the semantic range of *wið* during its history is not at all unusual. This suggests that the mental representations of direction, opposition, and association must be very similar, especially since the set recurs not only across languages but across case, adverbials, connectives (and indeed aspects, cf. *again* < OE *onegan* "against", cf. Traugott 1983). The further question then arises why the mental representations should be so similar. This leads us to investigate the possibility of motivations for semantic structure in perception and production, and other functional principles associated with constructing a discourse. While the arbitrariness of the linguistic sign has been central to much linguistic study since de Saussure, and arguments for the autonomy of the language faculty have dominated most thinking within the generative framework (cf. Chomsky 1980), it has for some time now become increasingly clear that arbitrariness and its close conceptual relative, autonomy, are theoretically exciting not as dogma, but only in so far as they account for precisely those aspects of language that cannot be motivated in terms of larger cognitive strategies. This means that functional motivations must be explored until they are exhausted and point to arbitrariness, not that they should be avoided as uninteresting until they are better understood. I will propose here that one of the functional motivations that can provide insight into the question why the mental representations of direction, opposition, and association should be so similar, and why the changes we have observed should be so common is iconicity, the principle by which one phenomenon is diagrammed by another (cf. Peirce 1932, Jakobson 1971, Anttila 1972, Haiman 1980, 1983).

Iconicity may diagram linguistic structure onto linguistic structure (as in the case of analogy), or nonlinguistic structure onto linguistic structure. One nonlinguistic structure that appears to be important in understanding the relation between direction and opposition that we find in the development of *wið* is the psychological perception of space. H. Clark (1973) has shown that the canonical encounter, as far as linguistic coding is concerned, is the face to face personal encounter of two speakers. This motivates spatio-temporal orientation in many languages, and can be illustrated by such deictic expressions as *Put the book in front of the vase* (the "front" is the part facing the speaker, cf. Lat. *front-* "face"). It also motivates temporal expressions such as *We must face the future with determination, I'm going to see her come Sunday* (the speaker moves toward the future which is moving toward him or her) (cf. Traugott 1978), and the slightly archaic *Put some money aside against a rainy day*. Furthermore, it motivates the spatial orientations of discourse found in the use of *this* vs. *that* in cataphoric expressions (cf. Greenberg 1983). In such canonical scenarios, moving toward a goal is viewed as moving toward a person, thing, boundary or event that is facing, hence opposing. The semantic extension of direction to opposition is therefore motivated by our physical orientation.[5]

This physical orientation is clearly asymmetric. We cannot see behind us, or even very well at the sides. Asymmetry is therefore fundamental to visual perception. In so far as it affects linguistic structure, it exemplifies the way in which extralinguistic factors can be mapped onto linguistic structure and can motivate semantic representations. Visual perception is, however, by no means the only factor which motivates the shift from directionality to opposition in language. Another, recently discussed by Haiman (1983), is the principle that "any two constituents must be conjoined in an order, and that order is asymmetrical" (cf. de Saussure's principle of the linearity of the linguistic sign; we might now prefer to call it the principle of syntactic ordering of constituents). This asymmetry motivates a number of pragmatic implicatures in language. Two sentences, A B, are interpreted as being in a narrative sequence iconic to the order of events unless otherwise marked, e.g. by transparent *at the same time* or by backgrounding elements such as progressive aspect, or by strictly anti-iconic constructions like B *after* A (E. Clark 1973). The following mini-text is therefore typically interpreted as a narrative sequence (A *and then* B), and not as describing simultaneous events (A *and at the same time* B):

5. a) Bill entered the room. Jane left.

Two clauses conjoined by *and* as in 5. b) are also interpretetd as being in narrative sequence (A *then* B); though *and* signals closer cohesion than the lack of explicit connectivity in 5. a), simultaneity is still not likely to be inferred:

5. b) Bill entered the room and Jane left.

Even the temporal connective *when*, although it allows for simultaneity, is insufficient to ensure a simultaneous reading in the absence of the progressive:

5. c) When Bill entered the room Jane left. (Contrast: Jane left when Bill was entering the room.)

---

[5] However, some languages such as Hausa maximize a different strategy, in which the speaker is conceived as the first in a line moving out to infinity; in this system, the equivalent of *the day before* (i.e. in front of) *tomorrow* is *the day behind tomorrow* (Hill 1978). Hill terms the face-to-face strategy "closed-field", and the other "open-field".

And the connective *while*, which prototypically indicates at least partial simultaneity, is interpreted as a concessive (i.e. as indicating disjoint states of affairs) wherever the tense and aspect do not prevent it:

5. d) While Bill likes country music, Jane likes acid rock.

In the case of prepositions like *mid* and *wið*, the force of asymmetry is particularly strong since Preposition is not a major category (such as Noun or Verb). It is therefore asymmetric with these major categories. Its role is to signal the differing grammatical relations between the NP's in any clause. So the extension of *mid* from contexts of plural NP's in which it means "among" (a symmetric relation) to singular NP contexts in which it means simply "along with", which Hittle calls analogy by force of the NP structure, can be seen to be motivated by the principle of asymmetry: *mid* comes to signal the subordinate relation of manner, instrument, etc. Similarly, the extension from the already asymmetric directional sense of *wið* "toward" to "against" maximizes the asymmetry. Even if fighting is a reciprocal act in some sense, fighting *wið* someone is conceived first and foremost as a directional, opposing act; the subject is dominant in agency, and therefore controls, while the object of the preposition is conceived as a goal-object without control. The maximization of asymmetry presumably also motivates the proliferation of competing directional prepositions that Hittle mentions: *to, toward, on, against, of, from*, etc. No push-chain need be posited; the principle of asymmetry is enough to drive the semantic changes.

If the canonical face to face encounter and the asymmetry of linguistic ordering motivate shifts from symmetric to asymmetric, and from directional to oppositional, what can motivate the shift from oppositional to pure associative (from *fight with* to *go with*)? The possibility that *and* used to be directional and oppositional, but is now associative semantically, and only oppositional by conversational implicature, or that *contest* could mean both *witness with/for* and *witness against* might suggest that the shifts under discussion really are arbitrary, and that functional accounts are ultimately as uninteresting as de Saussure and Chomsky have in their different ways said they are. However, to argue that the apparent contradictions in the data I have been exploring in this paper support the doctrine of arbitrariness would be to give up too soon.

There is in fact a reasonable motivation for the shift from direction/opposition to association. This is the principle of cohesion, which speakers use in an attempt to relate apparently incoherent elements in a structured discourse (cf. Halliday and Hasan 1976, Halliday 1978). The principle of asymmetry is an inevitable one—no linguistic utterance can be made without it, and constituents must occur in sequence. By contrast, the principle of cohesion is not inevitable, but something imposed by the speaker (and hearer) in the effort to construct a text. Jakobson has said that "The poetic function projects the principle of equivalence from the axis of selection into the axis of combination" (1960: 358). Certainly, the choice of symmetric-seeming cohesive patterns is most extensively evidenced in "poetic" discourse, but it can be found to a considerable extent in everyday talk as well. The very decision to use any connective at all, whether oppositional or associative, as in 5.b, c, d) points to this, as does the Gricean principle of relation that allows the two sentences in 5.a) to be understood as relevant to each other. Now opposition implies association—one cannot face something without coexisting in space, time, or at least intention. In so far as association is more neutral than opposition, it serves to mark general cohesion. In so far as it can be bolstered by other markers that force a symmetric interpretation, it can serve as a counterforce to the linearity principle (cf. *both...and*, or such structures as *Bill and Pat loved each other*, and especially *Bill entered and Pat left respectively*, which favors a simultaneous rather than sequential reading, cf. Haiman 1983). So substantial motivation can be identified for markers of opposition to become markers of association.[6]

What about *mid* and *wið*? When Hittle proposes that the entry-point of directional/oppositional *wið* into the domain of associative *mid* occurs in contexts such as *sleep with* (in the sexual sense) and transactions such buying and selling, she is pointing to precisely those contexts in which events can be viewed as either oppositional or more generally just cohesive and reciprocal. If an exchange is considered in some sense incomparable and made under duress (as in the case of ransom), the situation is one of asymmetry and confrontation, and *wið* appropriately marks only the goal (cf. 4. c, f). But if it is viewed as a fair exchange (as in the case of ordinary purchases), the transaction is more "coherent", and *wið* can be used for either the ends or the means (cf. 4. e) since they are both equal. So the shift of *wið* from opposition to goal of exchange

---

[6] Note how in English *aside from*, *besides* indicate contrast, not parallelism, despite the fact that left and right are physically (but not perceptually) symmetrical.

to instrument and ultimately comitative may be a case of "bleaching", but it is not arbitrary bleaching; it may be "analogical", but the analogy is not merely to the domain of *mid*. Rather, it is iconic with the general strategy of presenting material as cohesively related.

Once *wið* entered the domain of *mid* it was the more likely of the two prepositions to survive precisely because, owing to its history, it was potentially available to be used, at least by implicature, to express the asymmetry of linear ordering as well as cohesion (cf. also *and* in this connection [7]). As has been mentioned, a preposition expressing symmetry is relatively anomalous because of the structural function of prepositions, and therefore if one is to exist it must be marked rather specially and preferably unambiguously. *Among* was chosen to serve this purpose, while *with* was allowed to take over the asymmetric part of *mid*'s domain.

As in all cases of semantic change, the shifts in meaning did not occur by necessity — one need only note Gm. *mit* which has been retained as instrumental and comitative. But, I have argued, they were not arbitrary either. The shifts in meaning were motivated by two opposing principles. One maximizes the asymmetry necessarily attendant on saying anything. The other imposes coherence on what is said. There are many other opposing principles in language; among them are the well-known semantic principle of one-meaning-one form (the so-called Humboldtian principle) vs. the phonetic principle of reduction of contrast (*via* assimilation, contraction, etc.). All such sets of opposing principles contribute to the constant enrichment of language, and prevent it from being reduced to a system so monolithic that it could become useless. If the principle of asymmetric linear ordering were not counterbalanced, our discourses would be severely impoverished and possibly incomprehensible.

---

[7] In his discussion of the Indo-European *kue* "and" in Greek and Latin, Gonda (1975) proposes that *kue* did not originally mean "and (adding a new member to the series)"; rather, it indicated that two or more entities which might appear disparate are actually to be treated as being on a par, cf. *servi liberique* "slaves (on the one hand) and free men (on the other)". He suggests that the use of *kue* to impose cohesion is related to "primitive" and "collective thinking" (1975: 188), in which expression of complementarity predominates over expression of linear, additive relations. As the history of *with* shows, it is not necessary to assume that "primitive thinking" motivated the semantics of *kue*. However, the possibility may be worth exploring that the semantic shifts discussed in this paper may be correlated with oral, "rhapsodic" vs. linear strategies (cf. Chafe 1980, Tannen 1982).

REFERENCES

Anttila, Raimo. 1972. *An introduction to historical and comparative linguistics.* New York: Macmillan.
Chafe, Wallace L. (ed.) 1980. *The pear-stories: cognitive and linguistic aspects of narrative production.* Norwood, N. J.: Ablex.
Chomsky, Noam. 1980. *Rules and representations.* New York: Columbia University Press.
Clark, Eve V. 1973. How children describe time and order. *Studies of child language development*, ed. by Charles A. Ferguson and Dan I. Slobin, New York: Holt, Rinehart and Winston.
Clark, Herbert H. 1973. Space, time, semantics and the child. *Cognitive development and the acquisition of language*, ed. by T. E. Moore, New York: Academic Press.
Coleman, Linda and Paul Kay. 1981. Prototype semantics: the English word *lie.* Lg. 57. 26 - 44.
Feghali, Michel. 1928. *Syntaxe des parlers Arabes actuels du Liban.* Paris: Librairie Orientaliste Paul Guenthner.
Givón, Talmy. 1975. Serial verbs and syntactic cange: Niger-Congo. *Words order and word change*, ed. by Charles N. Li, Austin: University of Texa Press.
Gonda, J. 1975. The history and original function of the Indo-European particle *kue*, especially in Greek and Latin. *Selected Studies I: Indo-European.* Leiden: Brill.
Greenberg, Joseph H. 1983. Deixis and iconicity. Paper presented at the Workshop on Iconicity, Stanford University, June 1983. Forthcoming in the proceedings.
Haiman, John. 1980. The iconicity of grammar: isomorphism and motivation. *Lg.* 56. 515 - 40.
⎯⎯⎯ 1983. The iconic expression of symmetry. Paper presented at the Workshop on Iconicity, Stanford, June 1983. Forthcoming in the proceedings.
Halliday, M. A. K. 1978. *Language as social semiotic; the social interpretation of language and meaning.* London: Arnold.
Halliday, H. A. K. and Ruqaiya Hasan. 1976. *Cohesion in English.* London: Longman.
Hill, Clifford. 1978. Linguistic expression of spatial and temporal orientation. Proceedings of the Fourth Berkeley Linguistic Society Meeting.
Hittle, Erla. 1901. Zur Geschichte der altenglischen Präpositionen 'mid' und 'wið', mit Berücksichtigung ihrer beiderseitigen Bezeichnungen. *Altenglische Forschungen 2.* Heidelberg: Carl Winter.
Jakobson, Roman. 1960. Closing statement: linguistics a poetics. Style in *Lg.*, ed. by Thomas A. Sebeok. Cambridge, Mass.: MIT Press.
⎯⎯⎯ 1971. Zeichen und System der Sprache. *Selected Writings* II. The Hague: Mouton.
Nilsen, Don L. F. 1973. *The instrumental case in English: syntactic and semantic considerations.* The Hague: Mouton.
Peirce, Charles S. S. 1932. *Collected writings II: elements of logic.* Cambridge, Mass.: Harvard University Press.

Quirk, Randolph, Sidney Greenbaum, Geoffrey Leech and Jan Svartvik. 1972. *A grammar of contemporary English.* London: Longman.

Schlesinger, I. M. 1979. Cognitive structures and semantic deep structures: the case of the instrumental. *Journal of Linguistics* 15: 307 - 24.

Tannen, Deborah (ed.) 1982. *Spoken and written language: exploring orality and literacy.* Norwood, N. J.: Ablex.

Timmer, Esther H. 1967. *A semantic comparison of the third form in Arabic with the prepositional form in Swahili and the applied form in Kanuri.* Unpublished M. A. thesis, Stanford University.

Traugott, Elizabeth Closs. 1978. On the expression of spatiotemporal relations in language. *Universals of human language III: Word formation,* ed. by Joseph H. Greenberg, Charles A. Ferguson, and Edith Moravcsik. Stanford: Stanford University Press.

1979 On the spatio-temporal origins of certain logical connectives. Forthcoming in *Studies in Language.*

1983. From opposition to iteration: a study of semantic change. Forthcoming in *Studies in Language.*

Walde, Alois, rev. Julius Pokorny. 1930. *Vergleichendes Wörterbuch der indogermanischen Sprachen.* Berlin: de Gruyter.

Wasson, Richard O., J . 1982. *From comitative to adversative. Com- in English compounds derived from Latin.* Unpublished M. A. project, Standford University.

THE BIFURCATION THEORY OF THE GERMANIC AND GERMAN CONSONANT SHIFTS SYNOPSIS AND SOME FURTHER THOUGHTS*

THEO VENNEMANN

Jacob Grimm's theory for the correspondences among Indo-European (IE), Germanic (Gmc.), and High German (HG) obstruents — in short "Grimm's Law" — is determined by two fundamental assumptions which, in a modern way of speaking, may be formulated as follows:

1ST ASSUMPTION: The Proto-IE (PIE) obstruent inventory is etymologically close to those of the classical languages (Sanskrit, Greek, and Latin) and distant from those of the Gmc. languages.

2ND ASSUMPTION: The PIE obstruents, by what Grimm called the *First Sound Shift*, developed into the PGmc. obstruents which are essentially preserved in all the Gmc. languages except for the HG dialects; and the PGmc. obstruents, by the *Second Sound Shift*, developed into the Old HG (OHG) obstruents.

The essential parts of the developments, those involving the assumed PIE plosives, are summarized in (1), where capital letters are used for entire series of plosives, fricatives, and affricates, e.g. T for all voiceless fortis plosives, Þ for all voiceless fortis fricatives (except *s*), Ð for all voiceless lenis fricatives (except *z*), Tˢ for all affricates. As Grimm put it (1822: 584), except that he put it in German.: "Exactly as Old High German has, in all three grades [i.e. tenues, mediae, and aspirates, T.V.], sunk downward one step from the Gothic order [Gothic being representative of non – HG Gmc., T.V.], so Gothic itself had earlier devia-

---

* This paper is a condensed English version of Vennemann 1984, containing only few additional thoughts. It has been prepared with the idea that most linguists, even those not able to read German, are familiar with Grimm's Law and might be interested in an alternative theory for the same set of Indo-European, Germanic, and High German speech sound correspondences. Acknowledgements, further references, and a more comprehensive discussion may be found in the paper cited. For valuable suggestions specifically concerning this present paper I would like to thank Angelika Lutz, Ian Maddieson, Robert W. Murray, Edgar C. Polomé, and the students of my seminar "Probleme der Vor- und Frühgeschichte des Germanischen", University of Munich, Winter 1983 - 84.

ted downward one step from the Latin (Greek, Indic) order. Gothic relates to Latin precisely as Old High German does to Gothic." He goes on to diagram this "twofold sound shift" essentially as in (1).

(1)   Gmc. shift   HG shift
  T ⟶ þ ⟶ Đ
  D ⟶ T ⟶ Tˢ
  Dh ⟶ D ⟶ D̥

SCHEMATIC PRESENTATION OF JACOB GRIMM'S SUCCESSION THEORY

But he naturally places the representative of non-Gmc. IE at the top and OHG at the bottom, thus iconically representing his idea of the sound shifts as a kind of sinking.

Grimm's theory has been modified in various ways by a great many linguists from 1822 to the present. Some of the modifications were clear-cut improvements. Grimm's Law, as proposed by its author, was not only a very ingenious but also an extremely bold hypothesis, because the number of exceptions was of the same order of magnitude as the number of cases, and e.g. Rasmus Rask, who is sometimes granted priority over Grimm with regard to the shifts, did not care for it at all (von Raumer 1870: 514). The exceptions were collected and sorted by C. Lottner (1862), and they were subsequently taken care of brilliantly by Hermann Grassmann (1863) and Karl Verner (1875) in the Laws named for them, more than forty and fifty years after the hypothesis itself had been put forward. Some other modifications are less clearly recognizable as improvements. E.g., Grimm assumed the PIE aspirate plosives to have become mediae in PGmc., with their plosive character preserved. This idea continues to the present but only as a "minority view", as William Moulton named it (1954: 1). The "majority view", which seems to have arisen under the impression made by Verner's Law, assumes that the PIE aspirate plosives developed into voiced fricatives. Both views allow the statement of the distribution of plosives and fricatives resulting in the individual Gmc. languages and dialects. The two views are schematically represented in (2).

(2) The development of the "Mediae aspiratae"

(a) "Minority view": Dh → D ↗ D ↘ (Đ)

(b) "Majority view": Dh → Đ ↗ D ↘ (Đ)

Personality I find the philological argument in favor of the minority view, as put forward in Luick 1964: § 618.1 quite convincing. An additional, purely linguistic argument will appear later in this paper. As a matter of fact, the only argument of any force in favor of the majority view that I know of is that the Vernerian reflexes of the PIE tenues, which are usually assumed to have been voiced fricatives, completely merge with the reflexes of the PIE aspirates in all varieties of Gmc. There are, however, two ways of countering this argument. The first is to assume that the Vernerian voiced fricatives merged with the reflexes of the PIE aspirates, whatever those happened to be at that time in the various dialects. The second is to modify Verner's Law, as I will show later in this paper.

Despite the numerous modifications of these and other sorts, one essential trait of Grimm's theory has remained constant; that is what I have called the second constitutive assumption, the assumption that there was a succession of two sound shifts, the first leading from PIE to PGmc., the second leading from PGmc. to HG. This is even true of those theories that give up the first constitutive assumption, the idea that the PIE obstruents are most directly reflected in the classical languages. This move is characteristic e.g. of the so-called glottalic theories as proposed and elaborated since 1972 by Gamkrelidze and Ivanov and Paul Hopper and more recently by others as well. The idea of a succession of two sound shifts remains untouched by this modification of Grimm's theory, as has been explicity stated in Normier 1977:186f., n. 38. I therefore call all those theories *Grimmian theories*, and their constant element, the idea that there were two sound shifts, the first from IE to Gmc., the second from Gmc. to HG, I call the *succession theory* of the Gmc. and HG obstruent developments. It is this theory to which I will now present an alternative.

The usual way, started by Grimm, of reconstructing earlier obstruent inventories and obstruent developments of the Gmc. languages is to make a guess at what the PIE obstruents were and to follow these assumed elements through Gmc. in general and HG in particular. This procedure is questionable because it ties the reconstruction of one ignotum, early Gmc., to another ignotum, early IE. It has become wholly inadvisable after the recent proliferation of reconstructed PIE inventories. It is also entirely unnecessary, and I do not follow it. Rather, I reconstruct early Gmc. from the Gmc. evidence itself using non-Gmc. IE evidence only afterwards and only to reconstruct stages and develsopments prior to PGmc.

I concentrate on two extreme manifestations of Gmc. which I call Strict High Germanic and Strict Low Germanic, following an analogous terminological distinction for varieties of German, and making reference with 'High| and 'Low' to the geographical distribution of the languages at the times of their earliest written records, viz. the closeness of their speakers to the mountains (the Alps) on one hand, and to the seas (North Sea, Baltic Sea, Black Sea) on the other. Representatives of Strict HGmc. and Strict LGmc. are the southernmost Alemannian and Bavarian dialects of OHG on one hand and Old Icelandic on the other. All the other Gmc. languages and dialects assume intermediate positions between these extremes: Langobardic, the remaining Upper German dialects, and the Middle German dialects standing closer to Strict HGmc., Low German (including Low Franconian), Frisian, English, Gothic, and the remaining Norse languages closer to Strict LGmc. Their phonologies show features to various degrees that are characteristic of the opposite extreme. The extreme inventories are listed in (3).

(3) True-consonant inventories of Strict High Germanic and Strict Low Germanic at the time of the oldest records:

	Strict High Germanic			Strict Low Germanic		
1.a	p^f	t^z	k^x	p^h	t^h	k^h
b	f	z	x			
c		t				
2.a	$\overset{\circ}{b}$	$\overset{\circ}{d}$	$\overset{\circ}{g}$	$\overset{\circ}{b}$	$\overset{\circ}{d}$	$\overset{\circ}{g}$
2/3.b				v	ð	ǥ
3.a	$\overset{\circ}{v}$	$\overset{\circ}{\eth}$	h	f	þ	h
4.		ṣ			s	
5.		(r)			z	

Each speech sound is represented by a symbol suggesting its phonetic correlate in a characteristic position. Examples are given in (4), where the numbering is the same as in (3).

(4) Illustration of the correspondences in the preceding chart

1.a. #—: p^f | p^h | OHG *pfluog*, OIcel. *plógr*
t^z | t^h | OHG *zam* OIcel. *tamr*
k^x | k^h | OHG *chorn*, OIcel. *korn*
C—: p^f | p^h | OHG *werpfan*, OIcel. *verpa*
t^z | t^h | OHG *herza*, OIcel. *hjarta*
k^x | k^h | OHG *werch*, OIcel. *verk*

BIFURCATION THEORY OF THE GERMANIC AND GERMAN 531

CC: pp^f | pp^h OHG *ropfōn*, OIcel. *ruppa*
tt^z | tt^h OHG *scaz*, OIcel. *skattr*
kk^x | kk^h OHG *loc, loch*, OIcel. *lokkr*
b. V___: f(f) | p^h OHG *scaffan*, OIcel. *skapa*
OHG *hlauffan*, OIcel. *hlaupa*
OHG *scif*, OIcel. *skip*
z(z) | t^h OHG *ezzan*, OIcel. *eta*
OHG *lāzzan*, OIcel. *láta*
OHG *hwaz, wazz*, OIcel. *hvat*
x(x) | k^h OHG *sahhan*, OIcel. *saka*
OHG *buohha*, OIcel. *bók*
OHG *dah*, OIcel. *þak*
c. ___r: t | t^h OHG *trōst*, OIcel. *traust*
OHG *wintar*, OIcel. *vetr*
2.a. #___: b̥ | b̥ OHG *beran, peran*, OIcel. *bera*
d̥ | d̥ OHG *dragan, tragan*, OIcel. *draga*
g̊ | g̊ OHG *geban, kepan*, OIcel. *gefa*
N___: b | b OHG *lamb, lamp*, OIcel. *lamb*
d | d OHG *land, lant*, OIcel. *land*
g | g OHG *lang, lanc*, OIcel. *langr*
2.b. V___: b̥ | v OHG *geban, kepan*, OIcel. *gefa*
d̥ | ð OHG *beodan, piutan*, OIcel. *bjóða*
g̊ | g̊ OHG *saga, sagēn, sakēn*, OIcel. *saga*
L___: b̥ | v OHG *tharbēn*, OIcel. *þarfa*
OHG *halb, halp*, OIcel. *half*
d | ð OHG *wort*, OIcel. *orð*
g̊ | g̊ OHG *bergan, perkan*, OIcel. *bjarga*
OHG *folgēn, folkēn*, OIcel. *fylgja*
3.b. V___: v | v OHG *nefo, nevo*, OIcel. *nefi*
ð | ð OHG *brōther, bruodher*, OIcel. *bróðir*
L___: v̥ | v OHG *thurfan*, OIcel. *þurfa*
OHG *wolf*, OIcel. *úlfr*
ð | ð OHG *werthan, werdhan*, OIcel. *verða*
3.a. #___: v | f OHG *faran, varan*, OIcel. *fara*
ð | þ OHG *thrī, dhrī*, OIcel. *þrír*
h̥ | h OHG *halm*, OIcel. *halmr*
4. #___: ṣ | s OHG *smid*, OIcel. *smiðr*
V___: ṣ | s OHG *lesan*, OIcel. *lesa*
C___: ṣ | s OHG *ars*, OIcel. *ars*
OHG *wahsan*, OIcel. *vaxa*

34*

CC:	ṣṣ	ss	OHG *wissa*, OIcel. *vissa*
5. V—(V):	r	R, z	OHG *mēro*, OIcel. *meiri* (*māri), Goth. *maiza*
V—C:	r	C, z	OHG *hort*, OIcel. *hodd*, Goth. *huzd*

When reconstructing common sources for the diverse elements in the inventories of chart (3), one has to invoke certain principles of reconstruction and laws of change. Starting with position 1, one notices diversity in Strict HGmc. vs. uniformity in Strict LGmc. But the diversity is orderly, as is well known: /t/ of l.c. originally occurred only before /r/, and the fricatives of l.b. only after vowels, and only if the corresponding LGmc. form does not have a geminate stop. The principle of reconstruction to be invoked says that orderly variety points to original uniformity, rather than couversely. So one has to reconstruct uniformity for Strict HGmc. Next we have to invoke a law of change: The normal path of development is from affricates to fricatives rather than conversely. So one will reconstruct a series of affrucates, $^+/p^f\ t^z\ k^x/$, or $^+T^s$ for short, from which both the affricates and fricatives of 1 developed. Furthermore, the /t/ of l.c may be assumed originally to have been merely a positional variant of $^+/t^z/$, occurring only before $^+/r/$, where $^+/t^z/$ was excluded for good phonetic reasons, dental friction being disfavored before an alveolar trill, cf. also the intrusive *t* in words such as *stream* and *sister*. Thus we arrive at two series, $^+T^s$ for Strict HGmc. and $^+T^h$ for Strict LGmc. Again we have to invoke a law of change. The normal path of development is from stops to affricates rather than conversely. So one will have to reconstruct an earlier series of stops, say $^+T'$, from which both the HGmc. affricates $^+T^s$ and the Low Gmc. aspirates $^+T^h$ have developed. What was $^+T'$? Well, it is easy to reconstruct, over and beyond occlusiveness both voicelessness and tenseness for $^+T^s$ and $^+T^h$. Another principle of reconstruction tells us that these properties should be attributed to $^+T'$. Thus, $^+T'$ is reconstructed as a series of voiceless fortis plosives; and that is all it is wise to say at this stage of the reconstruction.

Turning to position 2 of the chart in (3), we observe a uniform series of plosives in HGmc. vs. a variety of plosives and fricatives in LGmc. The LGmc. variation is orderly, even though the order is different in the various dialects. Thus one will reconstruct uniformity. But which one? The law of change to be invoked says that frication is more normal than occlusion. Furthermore, the fricatives only occur under conditions that are known to be favorable to frication. Therefore one will reconstruct plosives, and since the major positional variant in LGmc. is easily reconstructed as lenis and not fully voiced, and the same is true for all positions in HGmc. (where in addition there is a tendency toward fortis production), one will reconstruct an earlier uniform series $^+\mathring{D}$ of lenis stops lacking full voice (at least in the major positional variants).

Turning to position 3 of the chart in (3), one again observes uniformity in HGmc. vs. orderly variety in LGmc., the LGmc. voiced fricatives of 3.b only occurring in typical voicing position. The lenis character of the HGmc. fricatives may be attributed to the co-presence of the fortis fricatives of position 1.b, invorking another law of change, the well-known push-chain idea. The odd man /h/ has positional velar and post-velar fricative variants and can be traced to a voiceless velar fricative $^+$/x/, by arguments which I would like to omit here. Thus one arrives at a uniform earlier series $^+\mathrm{þ}$ of voiceless fortis fricatives.

There is little to say about positions 4 and 5 of the chart. HGmc. /s̩/ is postalveolar owing to the development of a second voiceless dential-veolar sibilant /z/. Thus, as a common source of HGmc. /s̩/ and LGmc. /s/ one will simply posit an alveolar $^+$/s/. For LGmc. (Gothic) /z/, Runic /R/ and etymologically related /r/ one will reconstruct $^+$/z/. These two sibilants differed at least as fortis vs. lenis. Whether rhotacism of $^+$/z/, in isolation as well as in clusters with elements of $^+\mathring{D}$ (e.g. Gothic *razda, huzd*, OHG, *rarta, hort*) points to voicing of $^+$/z/ (and $^+\mathring{D}$) in addition to lenis character, I do not know. An earlier phonological identity of $^+$/s/ and $^+$/z/ may be guessed at on morphological and lexicological grounds. It cannot be arrived at on purely Germanic grounds: Verner's Law, as is well known, requires external reconstruction.

Thus we arrive at the Proto-Gmc. inventory summarized in (5).

(5) The Proto-Gmc. true consonants
    1. $^+$T′   fortis plosives
    2. $^+$D   lenis plosives
    3. $^+\mathrm{þ}$ fortis fricatives
    4. $^+$/s/   fortis fricative
    5. $^+$/z/   lenis fricative

I mention in passing that all oppositions between elements from the first three positions of (5) are neutralized after fricatives throughout the history of Gmc., a normal thing to happen considering the parallels in other languages.

In order to get beyond the inventory in (5), one has to look beyond the Germanic evidence. The PGmc. $^+$T$'$ and $^+$D̥ series have plosive counterparts in most of the other IE languages. I will speculate later about a possible common source. The same is true, however, of the fricative $^+$ƥ series, cf. Goth. OE OHG *faran*, OIcel. OFris. *fara*, but Lat *perītus*, *portāre*, Gr. περάω, πορεύομαι, OInd. *píparti*, *pāráyati*. Frication is more normal than occlusion. Therefore one will assume these series to have developed from an earlier plosive series. The voiceless plosives that show the greatest susceptibility to frication are the aspirates. Therefore I assume as a source a series of voiceless aspirate plosives, $^+$T^h. Since PGmc. $^+$/s/ and $^+$/z/ can be traced to an earlier $^+$/s/ via Verner's Law, one arrives at a Paleo-Gmc. inventory $^+$T$'$, $^+$D̥, $^+$T^h, $^+$/s/ or, changing the numbering, at (6) —

(6) The Paleo-Gmc. true consonants (arranged in a different order than in 5)

  I. $^+$T^h voiceless aspirate fortis plosives
  II. $^+$T$'$ voiceless non-aspirate fortis plosives
  III. $^+$D̥   lenis plosives
  IV. $^+$/s/   fortis fricative

an inventory not uncommon in the world's contemporary languages, Korean being perhaps the closest match.

It is well known that there are hardly any words in Gmc., perhaps none, that contain $^+$/p$'$/ and have etymological correspondences in other IE languages. Frequency counts on dictionaries of early Gmc. languages show that even in historical times the reflexes of PGmc. $^+$/p$'$/ are lexically rare. Nothing similar is true for PGmc. $^+$/p^h/ or $^+$/b̥/. Cross-language studies show that such imbalance points to a series with a higher-order mechanism than plain and aspirated plosives. As a matter of fact, a mechanism that quite commonly leaves a labial gap in series of voiceless plosives is glottalization, and, in particular, ejection. The analogous argument for PIE in general is well known, so I will not elaborate on this point. The assumption of a glottalic series $^+$T$'$ for Paleo- and PGmc. is totally in harmony with my reconstruction so far (note also that the Korean fortes are slightly glottalized); and the assumption of ejectiveness in particular may prove very valuable for a phonetic intepretation of the consonant shifts, to which I turn now. I assume the following changes between Paleo-Gmc. and the Gmc. languages:

(a) the PGmc. consonant shift: $^+$T^h > $^+$ƥ
(b) Verner's shift
(c) the accent shift

(d) the two central parts of the Inner-Gmc. consonant shift, cf. (7) below
(e) the sequels to the central parts of the Inner-Gmc. consonant shifts, viz. the HGmc. frication, cf. (8), the HGmc. fricative lenition, and the voicing and frication of the LGmc. lenis plosives in sonorant environments

(7) The Inner-Gmc. consonant shift (CS)

$$^+T' \begin{array}{l} \nearrow\ ^+T^s \quad \text{the High Gmc. CS (central part)} \\ \searrow\ ^+T^h \quad \text{the Low Gmc. CS (,,\quad ,,)} \end{array}$$

(8) The High Gmc. frication

$$^+T^s \rightarrow\ ^+TS \rightarrow\ ^+SS \quad (\rightarrow\ ^+S)$$

$\underbrace{}_{\text{after vowels}}$ $\underbrace{}_{\text{word-finally}}$

Verner's shift is usually, and certainly by Verner himself, assumed to follow what I call the PGmc. consonant shift, while naturally preceding the accent shift which eliminated one of its conditions. The disadvantage of this view is that the resulting series of voiced spirants has to be assumed to develop into plosives in HGmc., and for the dental also in Low German, Frisian, and Old English. Remembering, however, that occlusion is less normal than frication I prefer to assume Verner's shift to have preceded the PGmc. consonant shift. The Law says:

VERNER'S SHIFT: Non-initial aspirates are lnited in sonorant environment except when immediately following the accent.

Note that this formulation covers $^+/s/$, non-glottalized fortis fricatives automatically being aspirated. Assuming, however, that the fortis plosives, $^+T'$, and only they, were glottalized in addition to being fortis, the Law may be reformulated as follows:

VERNER'S SHIFT: Non-initial non-glottalized obstruents are lenited in sonorant environments except when immediately following the accent.

As a change for plosives (in addition to $^+/s/$), Verner's Shift begins to look suspiciously similar to Finnish gradation — an old thought which may have to be taken up again under the new premises developed here.

Leaving the question of Verner's Law aside, I have summarized the consonant shifts in (9).

(9) Synopsis of the consonant shifts

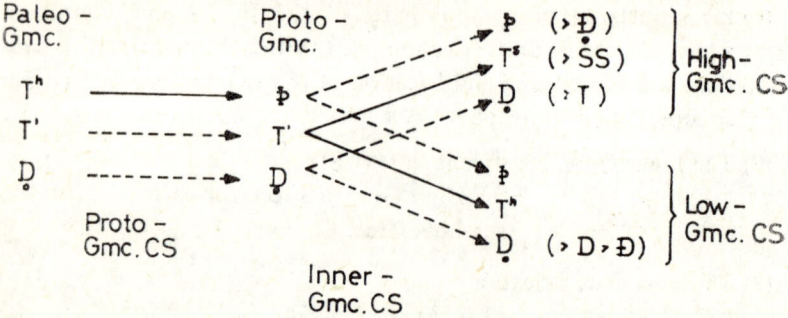

The two essential shifts, the **PGmc.** shift and the central parts of the Inner-Gmc. shift, appear there with solid lines. The portion where I deviate from all Grimmian theories is the Inner-Gmc. shift, cf. also (7). Whereas all Grimmian theories assume a succession here, whether as in (10.a)

(10) (a) The succession theory
      PIE PGmc. HGmc.
      $D \rightarrow T \rightarrow T^s$

(b) The **bifurcation theory**
    PIE **PGmc. Gmc.**
    $T' \dashrightarrow T' \begin{array}{l} \nearrow T^s \quad \text{HGmc.} \\ \searrow T^h \quad \text{LGmc.} \end{array}$

or with other phonetic mechanisms does not matter, I assume a bifurcation, in the sense in which Henning Andersen uses the term, cf. (10.b). I therefore call my theory the *bifurcation thery* of the Gmc. and German consonant shifts.

I have little to say concerning the phonetic plausibility of the bifurcation I assume. Perhaps it becomes most plausible if an ejective series $^+T'$ is assumed. According to my own subjective impression (which may, of course, be biased by my theory), ejectives sound very much like aspirates or like affricates, depending on their degree of fortisness, or "wetness". New learners of the language may thus have substituted aspirates and affricates for the unrecognized intricate glottal mechanism of ejection on the grounds of auditory similarity. Phoneticians I have asked confirmed my impression as subjectively sound but could do little beyond that that would have helped me. My hope is that comparative studies will clarify this problem, now that the question has been raised.

While this part of the theory may appear problematical, the assumed inventories seem to be entirely unproblematical. I already mentioned Korean as a close match for my Paleo-Gmc. inventory, viz. as far as the three grades are concerned. Korean has the following obstruents:

/pʰ tʰ cʰ kʰ
p'   t' c' k'
p   t   c   k
     s'
     s/

The three series of plosives, Tʰ, T', and T, are described as aspirated fortes [+tense, +aspirated], unaspirated fortes [+tense, −aspirated], and unaspirated lenes [−tense, −aspirated], respectively (Kim-Renaud 1975:5). In particular, "T" is here merely a notational variant of my "D̥". The elements of this series are voiced when surrounded by voiced segments (Kim-Renaud 1975:8). The sibilants /s'/ and /s/ are fortis and lenis, respectively, and always voiceless. The unaspirated fortis plosives are produced with a certain amount of glottal activity, though they do not seem to be ejectives (Kim-Renaud 1975:11, Park et al. 1982:659f., 669 - 671); in Maddieson 1984:070 they are labeled 'voiceless laryngealized'.

The following are some inventories which seem to contain Tʰ/T'/D̥ plosive series with ejective T' and no further plosive grades (sonorants omitted). The numbers refer to the inventory charts in Maddieson 1984, pp. 263 - 422.

Eastern Armenian (022) pʰ tʰ kʰ
                        p' t' k'
                        p   t   k

The language also has affricates tsʰ, ts', ts and tʃʰ, tʃ', tʃ, as well as fricatives v, s, z, ʃ, ʒ, x, h and a voiced nonsibilant retroflex fricative. In foreign words, also f occurs.

Quechua (819)   pʰ tʰ kʰ qʰ
                        p' t' k' q'
                        p   t   k   q

The laguage has affricates tʃʰ, tʃ', tʃ and fricatives s, ʃ, h, in foreign words also φ, β, ð, γ.

Jaqaru (820)   pʰ tʰ cʰ kʰ qʰ
                        p' t' c' k' q'
                        p   t   c   k   q

The language has affricates tsʰ, ts', ts; tʃʰ, tʃ', tʃ; t̪ʂʰ, t̪ʂ', t̪ʂ; and fricatives s, ʃ, x.

Haida (700)

p^h	t^h	c^h	k^h	k^{wh}	q^{wh}
t'	c'	k'	$k^{w\prime}$	q'	$q^{w\prime}$
p	t	c	k	k^w	q q̓

There is no p'. Also p^h is of "extremely low lexical frequency". The language has affricates $tʃ^h$, $tʃ'$, $tʃ$ as well as lateral affricates of the three grades. It has fricatives ç, x, x^w, χ, $χ^w$, h and a voiceless lateral fricative.

Navaho (702)

t^h	k^h	k^{wh}
t'	k'	
p t	k	ʔ

Here both p^h and p' are missing; k^{wh} is of "extremely low lexical frequency". There are affricates ts^h, ts', ts and $tʃ^h$, $tʃ'$, $tʃ$ as well as three lateral affricates of the same grades; and fricatives s, z, ʃ, ʒ, x, γ, h plus a voiceless lateral fricative.

PGmc., after the PGmc. consonant shift, $T^h > \textrm{þ}$, is assumed here to have had two series of plosives, T' and D̥, in addition to its fricatives and other consonants. Languages with such systems exist; the references are again to the charts in Maddieson 1984. The closest match there is Nez Perce.

Nez Perce (706)

p'	t̰'	t'	k'	q'
p	t̰	t	k	ʔ

There are, in addition, an affricate qχ and fricatives s, x, h and a voiceless lateral fricative. Also K'ekchi is rather close, the exception being that the /p'/ position is taken by a laryngealized voiced plosive.

K'ekchi (714)

ɓ	t'	k'	q'	
p̃	t	k	q	ʔ

There are, in addition, affricates ts', ts, tʃ', tʃ and s, ʃ, and x.

High Gmc., after the HGmc. consonant shift, $T' > T^s$, was left with a single series of plosives, D̥. Such systems are not rare.

Totonac (713)   p   t   k   q   ʔ

There are, in addition, affricates ts, tʃ and fricatives s, ʃ, h plus a voiceless lateral fricative.

Mixtec (728)   p   t   k k^w ʔ

There are also the affricate tʃ and fricatives β, ð, s, ʃ, ʒ, h.

Luiseño (737)   p   t̰   k k^w q q^w ʔ

There are also the affricate tf and fricatives v, $ð$, s, $ʃ$, $ʂ$, x, x^w, h.

Tonkawa (752)   p   t   k   k^w ʔ

There are also the affricate ts and fricatives s, x, x^w, h.

Maori (423)   p   t̺   k

There are two further true consonants, the fricatives f and h.

As an example of a language which has, as does the oldest Low Gmc. in my reconstruction, only aspirated and plain stops, T^h and D, I mention Wiyot, which adds to these the affricates ts^h, $tʃ^h$ and the fricatives s and $ʃ$, plus a voiceless lateral fricative.

Wiyot (753)   p^h t^h k^h k^{wh}
                  p   t   k   k^w ʔ

Ian Maddieson presents the following generalizations based on the 317 sample inventories of Maddieson 1984, selected so as to be representative of the languages of the world:

— Percentage of languages with one, two, three and four grades of plosives (p. 26)

1	2	3	4
15.8%	51.1%	24.0%	7.9%

— Percentage of languages containing unaspirated voiceless, aspirated voiceless, or ejective plosives (p. 27)

unasp. vl.	asp. vl.	eject.
91.8%	28.7%	16.4%

— Percentage of languages containing a given plosive grade, relative to the total number of plosive grades of the language (p. 28)

	1	2	3
unasp. vl.	98.0%	90.1%	89.5%
asp. vl.	0.0%	16.0%	63.2%
vl. eject. or vl. laryng.	0.0%	3.7%	42.1%

— Percentage of languages with three plosive grades having the grades given (vl: voiceless unaspirated; vd: voiced; asp: voiceless aspirated; implos: implosive including voiced laryngealized; eject: ejective including voiceless laryngealized), pp. 28f.

```
asp/vd/vl        25.0 %
implos/wd/vl     15.8 %
eject/vd/vl      17.1 %
asp/eject/vl     15.8 %
                 ─────
                 73.7 %
```

For more detailed information on glottalic consonants one may consult Greenberg 1970 and Maddieson 1984: 98 - 122.

The High Gmc. consonant shift produced affricates /p^f, t^s, k^x/ from voiceless fortis plosives /p', t', k'/. If this couldn't be verified any time by a comparison of, say, present-day English and Swiss German, I would find it hard to believe because I do not know of any parallels, the frequent change of plosives into fricatives notwithstanding. In general, while dental and alveolar affricates, as well as palato-alveolar affricates, are very common (Maddieson 1984: 221-226 lists 95 languages with /t̪s̪/ or /ts/, 33 with /t̪s̪^{h}/ or /ts^h/, 3 with /ts:/, 141 with /tʃ/, 43 with /tʃ^h/, 5 with /tʃ:/, similar affricates with special phonation or articulation types not counted), labial and velar (or postvelar) affricates seem to be fairly rare: Maddieson has three languages with labial affricates (German-Beembe, and Teke), three with velar affricates (Tavgy, Nama, Chipewyan), and three with postvelar affricates (Wolof, Nez Perce, and Karbadian). Standard German has only /pf/ and /ts/.

```
Beembe (123)    p^h   t^h   k^h
                p     t
                pf^h  ts^h
                pf    ts
                f     s     h
                v

Teke (127)      p     t     k
                b     d     g
                pf          tʃ
                bv          dʒ
                f     s           h

Tavgy (057)     p     t     c     k     ʔ
                b     d     ɟ     g
                                  kx
                      s
                ð
```

Nama (913)   p   t̠   k   ʔ
                      t̠s̠ʰ   kxʰ
                      s   x   h

Chipewyan (703)   t'   k'   kʷ'
                  p   t   k   kʷ   ʔ
                  t̠θʰ tsʰ tʃʰ   kxʰ kxʷʰ
                  t̠θ' ts' tʃ'
                  t̠θ   ts   tʃ
                  θ   s   ʃ   x   xʷ   h
                  ð   z   γ   γʷ

There are also lateral affricates of the three grades, and a velarized counterpart of *t*.

Wolof (107)   p   t   c   k   ʔ
                  b   d   ɉ
                  b: ɉ:
                                 qχ
                  f   s   χ

Karbadian (911) has the affricates

  t̠s̠, *d̠z̠*, *t̠s̠'* and *qχ*, *qχʷ*

in an elaborate Tʰ/T'/D and a somewhat reduced S/S'/Z system.

In the entire sample of 317 languages, there does not occur a single system combining labial, dental (or alveolar), and velar (or postvelar) affricates.

I turn next to the question of how my reconstruction of Paleo-Gmc. relates to PIE. Let me emphasize at the outset that my answer to that question is quite independent of my Gmc. reconstruction. One may accept the Gmc. reconstruction and reject the PIE hypothesis, or conversely; one may, of course, also accept them both or reject them both. I could assume any PIE inventory that has been proposed, e.g. the traditional T/D/Dh system, and relate it to my Paleo-Gmc. system by simply formulating a suitable "Paleo-Gmc. consonant shift" that is no more awkward than Grimm's First Sound Shift. But then: Why should I? There exists a plethora of proposals for PIE, and some of the recent ones look very similar to my Paleo-Gmc. inventory. Therefore, and since it is fashionable at present to propose new PIE inventories, I will join the game and make my own proposal. My hypothesis is: My Paleo Gmc. inventory IS the PIE inventory. Or in other words:

There was no Paleo-Gmc. consonant shift. One piece of justification for my hypothesis is that it makes Gmc. look extremely archaic sound-shiftwise, more even than the other glottalic theories proposed for PIE, a result which is in perfect harmony with the view that Gmc. is generally a very archaic, possibly the most archaic IE language, as pointed out by Edgar Polomé (1982). Another piece of justification is that the consonant shifts I have to posit for the other IE languages all make a certain amount of sense, which is more than can be claimed for Grimm's First Sound Shift. The shifts to be accounted for appear in (11).

(11) Proto-Gmc.
$$\begin{array}{l|l} T & T^h > \\ D & T' \quad T' \\ Dh & \underset{\circ}{D} \quad D \end{array}$$

Armenian
$$\begin{array}{l|l} T & T^h \quad T^h \\ D & T' > T \\ Dh & \underset{\circ}{D} > D \end{array}$$

Slav., Balt., Celt.
$$\begin{array}{l|l} T & T^h > T \\ D & T' \\ Dh & \underset{\circ}{D} \end{array} \Big\} > D$$

Sanskrit
(T^h)
$$\begin{array}{l|l} T & T^h > T \\ D & T' > D \\ Dh & \underset{\circ\circ}{D} > D \end{array}$$

Greek
$$\begin{array}{l|l} T & T^h > T \\ D & T' > D \\ Dh & \underset{\circ}{D} > T^h \end{array}$$

Latin
$$\begin{array}{l|l} T & T^h > T \\ D & T' > D \\ Dh & \underset{\circ}{D} > \text{\textit{f}} \end{array}$$

Hittite (?)
$$\begin{array}{l|l} T & T^h > T \\ D & T' \\ Dh & \underset{\circ}{D} \end{array} \Big\} > D$$

Tocharian (?)
$$\begin{array}{l|l} T & T^h \\ D & T' \\ Dh & \underset{\circ}{D} \end{array} \Big\} > T$$

The traditional and my own PIE inventory stand side by side in each table for easier orientation. In (12) I label the stages of IE obstruent development A to E.

(12)

A-IE (=PIE)	B-IE	C-IE	C1	C2		D-IE	E-IE
T | T^h	T^h		T	T	T^h	T^h	$> \text{\textit{f}}$
D | T'	T	>	D	D	T	T	T
Dh | $\underset{\circ}{D}$	D		(D)	D		D	D
				D			
Paleo-Gmc.	Armenian		Slav.,	Skt.		Gk.	Latin
			Balt.,	(Paleo-		(Proto-	
			Celt.	classic)		classic)	

A-IE is PIE and is at once reflected in Paleo-Gmc. B-IE develops from A-IE by a transformation of the fortis-lenis opposition into a voiceless-voiced opposition; it is reflected in Armenian. C-IE differs from B-IE by a shift on the aspiration-voice scale away from aspiration, whereby the old voiced plosives become "overvoiced", i.e., take on a special murmured phonation. I see the motivating factor for this shift in the development of voiceless aspirate plosives from combinations of other plosives with laryngeals as well as some other sources in the C-IE languages, i.e., a push-chain. C-IE comes in two varieties. In C1-IE, the new voiceless plosives and the new voiceless aspirates merge, as do the new and earlier sonorant plosives; it is reflected in Slavic, Baltic, and Celtic. In C2-IE, all four series are preserved. I call this stage Paleo-Classical; it is reflected in Old Indic. D-IE, or Proto-Classical, develops next by a desonoration of the murmured series preserving the breathy quality as aspiration, i.e., by merging the voiced aspirates with the voiceless aspirates; it is reflected in Classical Greek. Finally, the voiceless aspirate plosives of D-IE fricate (note the near-perfect analogy to the PGmc. consonant shift, despite the totally different source of the series affected); the result, E-IE, is reflected in Latin. — Hittite may be derived from either A-IE or B-IE; Tocharian is most easily derived from A-IE, when all three series were voiceless anyway. But do not know enough about these languages to make a clear proposal.

Reconstructions of the PIE inventory of plosives involving a glottalic series have so far not been falsified, led ad absurdum, or made implausible. As Mayrhofer (1983:152) assesses the situation: the typological arguments for such a system seem to weigh in its favor, and so far there have been objections, but no refutations.

As one example of a recent objection, I would like briefly to consider Green Ms. Green notes correctly that the PIE assimilation rules for plosives take on a new appearance in a system with a glottalic series (he compares the old T/D/Dh system to a new T/T'/Dh system). The old system has regressive voice assimilation:

$^+$werg- ~ $^+$wr̥k-to-	(*to*-Suffixation)
$^+$leg- ~ $^+$lek-to-	(,,)
$^+$ped- ~ $^+$bd-	(zero-grade)

The new system, on the other hand, seems to require a regressive glottalicness assimilation rule instead:

$^+$werk'- ~ $^+$wr̥k-to-	
$^+$lek'- ~ $^+$lek-to-	
$^+$pet'- ~ $^+$p't'-	

Green argues: ,,A rule that assimilates voicing in two stop consonants is not an unnatural one, in fact, is so *natural*, that we would not be surprised to find such a rule in any language. A glottatlization assimilation rule, on the other hand, does not seem to be a particularly natural rule, and in fact, I would claim that it is an extremely unnatural kind of rule, so much so that I have been unable to find an example of any language that has such a rule."

It seems to me that this argument arises from a too mechanical way of looking at the relations in question. Aspiration, murmur, and glottalicness are release features; they are manifest only on the second plosive of a cluster, as long as only the final plosive of a cluster is released, which is indeed the normal case. All we have to assume for the above is a rule determining that the release of a cluster is that of its plosive. In particular, the zero grade of $^+pet'$- is, under this assumption, $^+pt'$-; $^+p't'$- would merely be a "spelling variant" of $^+pt'$-. Then, as glottalic plosives gradually changed grade, their cluster would simply follow: $^+pt'$-> ^+pt-> ^+bd-. The situation is analogous to that of Bartholomae's Law in Sanskrit, except that there the idea is to preserve murmur on the cluster, e.g. -bh-t-→-bdh-. To preserve murmur means to make it manifest on the release of the final plosive; -bhdh- would again simply be a "spelling variant" of -bdh-, as I have pointed out in Vennemann 1979: 575f. and fn. 38.

I would like in closing to mention eight arguments in favor of the new theory, five for the Gmc. reconstruction, viz. the bifurcation theory, and three for the PIE hypothesis, viz. the identification of the PIE obstruent inventory with the Paleo-Gmc. T^h-T'-D inventory.

1. The new theory assumes only frications, no occlusions, whereas even the minority view of the Grimmian theories assumes occlusions.
2. The new theory has only short and straight development paths, none of the detours which are especially characteristic of the majority view. E.g., Grimm's theory, properly refined, has (D→) T→T^h→T^s, the new theory has T'→T^s and T'→T^h; and the majority view has (Dh →) Ð→Ḍ→Ḍ→T or (Dh →) Ð→D→Ḍ→T for Upper German, the new theory has D→T for Upper German, plus Ḍ→D→Ð for LGmc., but only in phonetically favorable environments.
3. According to the new theory HGmc. has *not developed from* LGmc. but constitutes a *parallel development*. This answers two questions which may trouble some linguists: First, why is OHG, which is so conservative morphologically and lexically, so progressive in its obstruent developments? Well, it isn't. Second, assuming that the HGmc. affricates developed from aspirates in a Grimmian second sound

shift, why haven't they in any of the remaining Gmc. languages in the millennium and a half that has passed? And I mean affrication of the entire series, not just of the alveolar which is known to be liable to affrication in a way that labials and velars are not.

4. In the Grimmian theories we find $T > þ$ (or $T^h > þ$) and $T > T^s$ (or $T^h > T^s$), different developments of the same series. This requires justification. The new theory has nothing to justify here as it assumes $T^h > þ$ but $T' > T^s$.

5. Most Upper German dialects do not have affrication of the velar in initial position, and the Middle German dialects do not have affrication of the labial there either. Both groups of dialects have the change (usually continued with frication) in medial and final position. If aspiration were the source of affrication, why isn't affrication most regular in the initial position where aspiration is strongest in languages with initial stress? The Grimmian theories have no answer; they fail on this account. The new theory at least has not failed yet, because nothing seems to be known of degrees of glottalization etc. according to position or in relation to stress.

6. Grimm's and Grassmann's theories combined can only take cognizance of the fact that Germanic has no trace of a Grassmannian breathiness dissimilation for the reflexes of the PIE series III (Gimm's and Grassmann's Dh), i.e. Skt. Dh ... Dh... $> D$ ... Dh ... and Gr. T^h ...T^h ... $>$ $> T$ ... T^h ... . For the new theory there is no question here: PIE and Gmc. never had a breathy series III; it only originated in C-IE, perhaps only in Paleo-Classical.

7. It is strange in the traditional theory that the oddest series, the voiced aspirates, is so extremely well represented in the PIE lexicon, even though we know that odd series commonly are not — and, by contrast, its plain voiced stops are comparatively rare and, in the case of the labial, almost non-existent. The new theory easily explains this: $\underset{\circ}{D}$ and D developed from $\underset{\circ}{D}$ and T' in post-PIE times, leaving too little time for the lexicon to adjust to the new obstruent inventory. For $\underset{\circ}{D}$ and T' the PIE lexicon shows just the distribution one would expect.

8. The traditional theory offers no explanation for the existence of the rather rare voiced aspirates, or murmured stops, in PIE. The new theory explains their existence as the result of a push chain operating *after* the PIE stage, and only in a subgroup of the IE language family.

Maybe these are sufficient reasons for considering the new theory a possible alternative to the Grimmian ones and to try and test it accordingly.

REFERENCES

Andersen, H. 1974. Towards a typology of linguistic change: Bifurcating changes and binary relations, *Historical linguistics*, ed. by J. M. Anderson and C. Jones, vol. 2, 17 - 60. Amsterdam: Benjamins.

Gamkrelidze, T. V. and V. V. Ivanov. 1972. Lingvističeskaja tipologija i rekonstrukcija sistemy indoevropejskix smyčnyx. *Working papers of the Conference on the Comparative-Historical Grammar of the Indo-European Languages, 12 - 14 December 1972*, 15 - 18. Moscow: Akademija Nauk.

—. 1973. Sprachtypologie und die Rekonstruktion der gemeinindogermanischen Verschlüsse. *Phonetica* 27. 150 - 6.

Grassmann, H. 1863. Über das ursprüngliche vorhandensein von wurzeln, deren anlaut und auslaut eine aspirate enthielt. *Zeitschrift für vergleichende Sprachforschung auf dem Gebiete des Deutschen, Griechischen und Lateinischen* 12. 110 - 38.

Green, G. M. An argument against reconstructing glottalized stops in PIE. MS.

Greenberg, J. H. 1970. Some generalizations concerning glottalic consonants, especially implosives. *International Journal of American Linguistics* 36. 123 - 45.

Grimm, J. 1822. *Deutsche Grammatik*, 1. Buch. 2nd ed. Göttingen.

Hopper, P. J. 1973. Glottalized and murmured occlusives in Indo-European. *Glossa* 7. 141 - 66.

Kim-Renaud, Y.-K. 1975. *Korean consonantal phonology*. Diss. University of Hawaii, Honolulu. Seoul: Pagoda Press.

Lottner, C. 1862. Ausnahmen der ersten Lautverschiebung. *Zeitschrift für vergleichende Sprachforschung auf dem Gebiete des Deutschen, Griechischen und Lateinischen* 11. 1161 - 205.

Luick, K. 1964. *Historische Grammatik der englischen Sprache*, 1.2. [Reprint of 1st ed. 1929 - 40]. Stuttgart: Tauchnitz.

Maddieson, I. 1984. *Patterns of sounds*. Cambridge: Cambridge University Press.

Maddieson, I. 1934. *Patterns of sounds*. Canbridge: Cambridge University Press.

Mayrhofer, M. 1983. *Sanskrit und die Sprachen Alteuropas: Zwei Jahrhunderte des Widerspieler von Entdeckungen und Irrtümein* [= Nachrichten der Akademie der Wissenschaften in Göttingen, Philol.-Hist. Klasse, 1983, No. 5]. Göttingen: Vandenhoek & Ruprecht.

Moulton, W. G. 1954. The stops and spirants of Early Germanic. *Language* 30. 1 - 42.

Normier, R. 1977. Idg. Konsonantismus, germ. 'Lautverschiebung' und Vernersches Gesetz. *Zeitschrift für vergleichende Sprachforschung* 91. 171 - 218.

Park, H. S. et al. 1982. An electromyographic study of laryngeal adjustments for the Korean stops. *Linguistics in the morning calm*, 659 - 71. Seoul: Hanshin.

Polomé, E. C. 1982. Germanic as an archaic Indo-European language. *Festschrift für Karl Schneider*, ed. by K. R. Jankowsky and E. S. Dik, 51 - 9. Amsterdam:
von Raumer, R. 1870. *Geschichte der Germanischen Philologie* [= Geschichte der Wissenschaft in Deutschland, Neuere Zeit, 9]. München: R. Oldenburg.
Vennemann, T. 1979. Grassmann's Law, Bartholomae's Law, and linguistic methodology. *Linguistic method*: *Essays in honor of Herbert Penzl*, ed. by I. Rauch and G. F. Carr, 557 - 84. The Hague: Mouton.
— 1984. Hochgermanisch und Niedergermanisch: Die Verzweigungstheorie der germanischen und deutschen Lautverschiebungen. *Beiträge zur Geschichte der deutschen Sprache und Literatur* 106. 1-45. Tübingen: Niemeyer.
Verner, K. 1877. Eine Ausnahme der ersten Lautverschiebung. *Zeitschrift für vergleichende Sprachforschung auf dem Gebiete der Indogermanischen Sprachen* 23. 97 - 130.

PROSODIC STRUCTURE AND THE DEVELOPMENT OF FRENCH SCHWA

S. PAUL VERLUYTEN

1. The present paper presents an analysis of the status of French schwa. This analysis is based on an evolution of this vowel which may be on its way at the present day, and it may lead to interesting predictions concerning the future development of the French schwa. Throughout this paper, we adopt a prosodic model inspired by recent proposals of Schane (1979a, 1979b). In various other publications we argue that Schane's model is adaptable to French, and that it accounts for many prosodic phenomena in that language. In brief, the underlying prosodic representations of French (monomorphemic) words present the following characteristics in this model:

(i) each *syllable* within the word is assigned a relative prominence marker S or W;

(ii) the prosodic representation of the word is *linear*, in the sense that no intermediate level (such as the foot) is withheld between the category of the word and the category of the syllable;

(iii) the prosodic structure of French (monomorphemic) words exhibits an underlying *alternating rhythm*, in the pattern WSWS(W). This hypothesis, which we have defended elsewhere, shall be assumed from the beginning in the present paper; the data we will adduce constitute, however, additional evidence in favor of it.

2. It is quite obvious that lexical representations which would be marked for the underlying rhythmic alternation are not redundancy-free. In fact, it is clear that the entire prosodic structure of the word can be predicted on the basis of its final syllable. So, conceivably, only the final syllable of the word could be marked for prosodic prominence in the lexicon. On the basis of, e.g., souven$\overset{s}{i}$r and étu$\overset{w}{d}$e, two simple redundancy rules ((RR1) and (RR2) below) can predict the complete prosodic representations souv$\overset{s}{e}$n$\overset{ws}{i}$r, ét$\overset{w}{u}$d$\overset{sw}{e}$, etc.:

(RR1) syllable→W/___S
(RR2) syllable→S/___W

It may seem possible to extract further redundancy from the lexical matrices. The prosodic prominence-marker of the *final* syllable is itself predictable in most cases: for all 'full' vowels (i.e., all French vowels except schwa), *the final syllable is always S*; only the vowel schwa may be W in this position. The easiest solution for writing additional redundancy rules is, of course, to represent schwa as /ə/ (in other words, to assign to it distinctive features that make it different from all other French vowels, e.g. [+back, -round, -high, -low]. However, this solution artificially introduces a distinction at the segmental level between /ə/ ('schwa') and /œ/ in most varieties of standard French, where both these vowels are *phonetically identical* (cf. Walter 1977: 50; for an overview of the question, see Fischer 1980). Let us make clear right now that everything we will say in this paper applies exclusively to this variety of French, where schwa and /œ/ are phonetically identical at the segmental level (again, this is the case for the majority of the speakers of standard French). In the solution we sketched above, diacritic use was made of a phonological feature that is without any phonetic content (we artificially distinguished schwa from /œ/ by 'making' the former, counterfactually, [+back]). Such a description is to be proscribed (Kiparsky 1973). If so-called schwa and /œ/ are identical in vowel quality, they are to be distinguished by a *diacritic* feature; for instance, the vowel that makes the final syllable of the word W (i.e. 'schwa') could be represented as /œ/, and the other, phonetically
[+D]
identical vowel, as /œ/. The use of such a diacritic marker should enable
[−D]
us to write lexical redundancy rules for the word-final syllable. However, on closer scrutiny, it appears that, in this particular position, the use of the diacritic is superfluous: the two vowels we are concerned with here (we will keep calling the [+D] vowel schwa and the other /œ/ for the sake of convenience) are in *complementary distribution* in word-final position. There is indeed a French morpheme structure condition which prohibits the occurrence of 'full' /œ/ is absolute final position (in open final syllables); in this context, only schwa may appear. The /œ/−/ö/ opposition is neutralized in favor of /ö/ in open final syllables. In closed final syllables on the other hand, only the vowel that renders this syllable S, i.e. 'full' /œ/, may appear. Compare, for example: *labeur* ('full' /œ/ in closed final syllable), *boiteux* (/ö/ in open final syllable)

s w   s w
boite, dextre ('schwa' in open final syllable). In other words, the following two redundancy rules are sufficient for our purposes:

(RR3) $/œ/ \to W/\underline{} \begin{Bmatrix} + \\ \# \end{Bmatrix}$

(RR4) $V \begin{Bmatrix} [+\text{back}] \\ [-\text{round}] \\ [-\text{low}] \end{Bmatrix} \to S/\underline{} \begin{Bmatrix} + \\ \# \end{Bmatrix}$

Given that both /œ/ vowels carry the distinctive features [−back, +round, +low], (RR4) refers to all other French vowels. An additional redundancy rule, which concerns us less here, must state that in closed final syllables all vowels are prosodically S.

3. Now of course, with the formulation of the two redundancy rules as (RR3) and (RR4), the main initial motivation for introducing the distinction between /œ/ and /œ/ no longer holds. It becomes tempting
         [+D]   [−D]
to search for an alternative analysis of the French vowel system, in which there would be only one vowel /œ/, and where the different behavior of this vowel (in particular, its effaceability vs. non-effaceability) would be due solely to its prosodic position (S or W) within the word. One of the advantages of this analysis is clear: it simplifies the phonemic inventory of the French vowels. This should make it worthwile looking at this alternative analysis in more detail. As is often the case, the simplifications it allows for in one place lead to complications in another; we shall have to determine where our preference should go. I want to argue, however, that the novel analysis leads to interesting predictions concerning the present and future evolution of the French schwa.

4. As we saw above, no particular problems arise in final open syllables of French words: whenever /œ/ occurs there, it is always W, and therefore it may be deleted, by the following rule:

(1) $/œ/ \to ø/\ \bar{W}$

(cf. also Verluyten 1982: 70 sqq. and Verluyten, to appear; rule (1) is subject to *segmental* restrictions, of which we will encounter a few examples below).

All the other French vowels are S in absolute final position; none of them are deletable. In closed final syllables, all French vowels, including /œ/, are S (and hence not effaceable): *labeur*, etc. The analysis we are developing, where the effaceability of /œ/ depends on a prosodic parameter, appears to allow for a simple and correct treatment of the effaceability in final syllables; and it may shed new light on the status of so-called schwa in French. However, it faces obvious and important difficulties in non-final syllables. Consider well-known pairs such as *genêt* – *jeunet*, where, in fact, the initial vowel is deletable in the first word, but not in the second. Under our analysis, this initial vowel is /œ/ in both cases; the initial syllable of both words also carries the same prosodic prominence-marker (W). Given that it seems impossible to differenciate the initial vowel of the two words, either segmentally or prosodically, the only possibility that is left us seems to be to mark words such as *jeunet* as *exceptions* in the lexicon, because they possess a non-deletable /œ/ in prosodic W position. Following Chomsky and Halle's proposals (1968: 172 sqq.), words like *jeunet* are then to be marked lexically [− Rule (1)].

5. Let us adopt this description for the moment, even though it may seem unattractive at first. Under the one-phoneme hypothesis we are considering here, other French words containing /œ/ may be problematic: those that have a deletable /œ/ in prosodic S position, such as *peloton* or *chenapan*. It would be conceivable to explicitly state that these words are exceptions to the lexical prosodic representation of French words, and assign them the structure WWS. In that case, however, the penultimate and the antepenultimate syllable (when it is not effaced) would go equally unstressed; this is very probably incorrect: in the trisyllabic pronunciation of *peloton*, the initial syllable is more prominent than the penultimate, evidencing an underlying SWS pattern. Making two lexical entries for words like *peloton* is equally ad hoc. Again the most honest description is to consider these words as exceptions to the generalization that /œ/ is only deletable in W position (rule (1)). If so, words such as *peloton* will carry the feature [+Minor rule of /œ/ deletion in S position] in the lexicon.

6. The question is now whether it is justifiable to consider words with non-effaceable /œ/ in W position (such as *jeunet*), or with effaceable /œ/ in S position (such as *peloton*), as exceptional. If these words are indeed exceptions, the two following general characteristics of exceptions should apply to them, and indicate the direction of future levelling:

(i) There are less exceptions than regular words. Thus, there should be relatively few words where /œ/ in W position is not effaceable, and there should be relatively few words where /œ/ in S position is effaceable;

(ii) Exceptions exhibit a tendency to become regularized. Thus, we should observe a tendency to avoid the occurrence of non-deletable /œ/ in W position (possibly by making it deletable, or through restructuring to another vowel), and of effaceable /œ/ in S position (e.g., again, through restructing toward another vowel).

Let us examine these predictions in turn. We first consider the case of /œ/ occurring in W position (mostly in penultimate syllables). There is no doubt that in this position, /œ/ is generally effaceable: *s(e)maine*, *d(e)vant*, *s(e)cret* (Fischer 1980), *saint(e)té*, *saign(e)ment*, *s(e)conde* (Martinet et Walter 1973), and so forth; hundreds of French words, presumably, behave like this. In some words, /œ/ is *always* deleted; it is therefore legitimate to say that in these cases, restructing has occurred in standard French, and the phoneme /œ/ (or schwa in the standard analysis) has been dropped from the lexical representation of the word. This happens more often, as it seems, when the /œ/ occurred *between* two Ss (SWS) than when it occurs initially (WS). Thus, the following words are always bisyllabic in standard French, and there are probably no synchronic reasons for postulating an underlying /œ/ in them: *samedi*, *médecin*, *bracelet*, *allemand*, etc. Nevertheless, there are quite a few words with a penultimate-initial /œ/ (hence in W position) that is not effaceable. Many of them, however, must not be described as exceptions to rule (1); in fact, in a large number of examples, the deletion is blocked by segmental constraints: it would create an inadmissible consonant-cluster. This explains the non-effaceability of /œ/ in words such as *bedaine*, *bedeau*, *bedon* (data from Martinet and Walter 1973), *bredouille*, *brevet*, *sevrage*, and many more. True exceptions, to be stated as such in the lexicon, are words such as *belette*, *belon*, *belote* (at least, if pronounced with /œ/; cf. below), where the initial /œ/ is not deletable although it occurs in W position and although its deletion would not lead to a violation of segmental constraints (*bl* is a possible word-initial cluster in French: cf. *bleu*, *blanc*, *bloquer*, etc.). But it is obvious that this class of words is quite small. The general characteristic stated above under (i) (there are less exceptions than regular words) certainly holds in the case at hand. Note that most of these words (those with historical schwa) are also considered as exceptions in traditional grammars: one would say that they have a non-effaceable schwa, not that they have full /œ/. The latter would be the analysis given to words like *jeunet*, of course, which are subsumed under the same class in the novel analysis presented here.

7. Let us then consider the second characteristic of exceptions,

stated above under (ii), for the words with non-deletable /œ/ in W position: do they exhibit a tendency towards restructing? Data in Martinet and Walter 1973 show that approximately half of the speakers in their inquiry have phonetic [ö] in W position rather than [œ]. For these speakers, there are no reasons for postulating an underlying /œ/ in the words we are considering. In these speakers' French, restructuring has occurred to avoid the appearance of non-deletable /œ/ in W position: the vowel has been replaced by /ö/. Martinet and Walter give the following data for the three words quoted above:

	[œ]	[ö]
belette	8	7
belon	4	10
belote	6	7

This tendency of restructuring /œ/ to /ö/ in W position, when it is non-deletable, is not restricted to words where the vowel is schwa historically. In *jeunet*, 10 speakers in the same inquiry have [ö], only 7 have [œ]; in *jeunot*, 13 [ö] vs. 4 [œ]. This lends support to the analysis we are considering here, where historical full /œ/ and historical schwa tend to merge into one phoneme. As was to be expected once we take the prosodic parameter into consideration, all speakers maintain /œ/ in *jeune*, where the vowel is in S position. It must be pointed out that in nearly all cases, the predicted restructuring takes place by replacing /œ/ here by /ö/. There are hardly any examples of the other possibility: making /œ/ deletable. The only example I came across where this second possibility may be taking place is the word *déjeuner*, which I heard pronounced as *déj'ner* [dežne] by some speakers of standard French. It may be suggested that the 'effaceability-option' is restricted to tri-syllabic words (we saw above that there are reasons to think that a W syllable may be weaker *between* two Ss than word-initially). In any case, it seems safe to conclude that the evolution of the words we are considering here is indeed correctly predicted under the one-phoneme hypothesis we are examining, where words with non-deletable /œ/ in W position are to be considered as exceptions.

8. Let us then turn to words where /œ/ occurs in prosodic S position (mostly final and antepenultimate syllables, if, for the sake of clarity, we call a W syllable that is located to the right of the rightmost S syllable 'postfinal'). In absolute final position, /œ/ can only be S in a few special configurations, such as *fais-le* (and all other imperatives of this type), *sur ce, parce que*. Notice that these cases are not to be considered as

counterexamples or exceptions to the redundancy rule (RR3): the redundancy rules only apply to *lexical* representations, and the expressions quoted above do certainly not appear as such in the lexicon. How to assign the final prosodic marker S in these cases is a question we cannot examine in this paper (for a solution, cf. Verluyten 1982: 226 sqq.); we shall simply consider that the final /œ/ is prosodically S in these cases (as is evidenced by surface stress on this syllable). There is nothing further to be said about these examples: the final vowel in S position is not deletable (*fais-lę, etc.), as is to be expected. As for effaceable /œ/ in antepenultimate S position, its occurrence is extremely rare indeed. Nearly all apparent examples are polymorphemic; it should be recalled that our hypothesis of an underlying alternating rhythm only applies to *monomorphemic* words (lexemes). Suffice it to make clear, in this paper, that examples such as *demander* (with effaceable initiail /œ/) are not to be considered as counterexamples (in Verluyten 1982: 221 sqq., they are derived from the stem, with the lexical representation *demand-*, and a suffix *-er* which is S; from there, *demander* → → *demander* through a well-established rule of weakening of one of two adjacent Ss). True monomorphemic (lexical) instances of exceptions are *chenapan* and *peloton*, already mentioned above. In fact, as far as we know, the real current pronunciation of these words has not been determined. They have not been included in Martinet and Walter's inquiry. Thus, we do not know either whether *peloton* exhibits a tendency of restructuring of the initial /œ/ to /ö/. As for the word *chenapan*, apart from its present-day evolution, it must be said that it can hardly be considered representative of French vocabulary: it is an archaic word where 'schwa' has been epenthesized to break up the initial [šn] cluster (*chenapan* comes from German *Schnapphahn*). Deletion of /œ/ may be blocked because it would create precisely this inadmissible cluster again. In any case, the first general characteristic of exceptions ((i) above) certainly holds for effaceable /œ/ in S position: it does not occur frequently.

9. We must still consider the second prediction with respect to words with /œ/ in (antepenultimate) S position: if the vowel is deletable, it tends to be restructured. In several examples found in Martinet and Walter 1973, this tendency is very clearly present. Restructuring in this case consists of replacing /œ/ by (phonetic) [e], sometimes [ɛ]. An interesting pair in this respect is *seconde* — *secundo*. Under the prosodic hypothesis we propose, the underlying prosodic structure

of these words is, respectively, *seconde* and *secundo*. This leads to the prediction that the initial vowel /œ/ is effaceable in the first of these two words, but not in the second. This prediction is borne out by the data from Martinet and Walter (1973): the initial vowel of *seconde* is deleted by five of the seventeen speakers in the inquiry; the initial vowel of *secundo* was never deleted. Another pair of the same type is *menu* — *menuet*, in our model *menu* vs. *menuet*. Here again, as expected under our hypothesis, the initial vowel is deletable in W position, in *menu* (it is deleted by two speakers in Martinet and Walter 1973), and is not deletable in *menuet*.

10. Another interesting observation is the fact that /œ/ in S position appears to be less stable in antepenultimate position than in final position, where it is under primary word-stress (for a rule to assign primary stress on the basis of the underlying prosodic representations we present here, cf. Verluyten 1982: 83). Thus, while /œ/ appears to be stable, and exhibits no tendency toward restructing in *jeune* or *fais-le*, it tends to be restructured in words such as *secundo*, etc. A tentative explanation of this phenomenon may lie in the fact that the appearance of non-deletable /œ/, mostly coming from historical schwa, in this position is a fairly recent (and still ongoing) development, caused by the introduction of the prosodic prominence parameter in the deletion rules (before this stage, supposedly, schwa was, or still is for some speakers, deletable as well in *peloton* or *secundo* as in *genêt*). Whatever the correct explanation may be, restructuring of /œ/ in antepenultimate S position is attested in several examples. However, this restructuring differs in an interesting way from the restructuring towards /ö/ in W position, of which we saw examples above. In antepenultimate S position, if /œ/ is restructured, it is toward /e/, sometimes /ɛ/. Thus, *secundo* has an initial [e] rather than [œ] for four speakers in Martinet and Walter 1973; this initial [e] does not occur in *seconde*. Other pairs of the same type are *rebelle* — *rébellion* and *devoir* — *dévoirant* (the latter being a rare word, but attested e.g. in the writings of Flora Tristan); in these instances, the restructuring toward /e/ has been registered in orthography (*e*).

11. In a few interesting examples in Martinet and Walter 1973, words with /œ/ in both the penultimate and the antepenultimate syllable have been pronounced by the subjects of the inquiry: *briqueterie*, *buffleterie*, *derechef*. In our prosodic model, the penultimate syllable is W,

                              w s w s   w s w s   s w s
the antepenultimate S: *briqueterie, buffleterie, derechef*. We thus expect
the leftmost /œ/, in S position, to be restructured, and the rightmost
/œ/, in W position, to be deletable. These predictions are to a large
extent borne out by the data from Martinet and Walter. In *briqueterie*,
all subjects delete the penultimate vowel (/œ/ in W position); ten subjects
have [ε] in the antepenultimate syllable. Similarly, in *buffleterie*, all
subjects but one delete the vowel in penultimate, W position; twelve
have [ε] in antepenultimate S position (against five with /œ/, or /ə/
distinct from /œ/ and /ö/; the latter belong to a variety of standard
French which, as we made clear, we are not considering here). In *derechef*, the vowel of the penultimate W syllable is deleted by two speakers;
the vowel of the antepenultimate syllable is not deletable, as expected;
three subjects have [ε] in this position. The difference between [e] (as
in *secundo*) and [ε], as in the examples quoted here, need not concern
us in the present paper; it has probably to do with the syllable structure
of the words after deletion, if available, of the /œ/ in W position. [ε]
occurs in closed syllables, which is the case for *briqueterie, buffleterie*
and *derechef* after deletion of the penultimate.

12. As far as we know, the hypothesis of an underlying alternating
rhythm is the only one, at the present day, which is capable of accounting
for these data. In the prosodic model we propose, two vowels that are
identical at the segmental level may be differenciated at the prosodic
level by their prominence marker; only such a differenciation can account
for the observed facts, namely, that two otherwise identical vowels
undergo a completely different evolution. It is interesting to illustrate
to what extent potential data may go unnoticed in the absence of a theoretical model that makes their observation possible. In Martinet and
Walter 1973, two words with *demi-* were included in the questionnaire
which they presented to their seventeen subjects: *demi-heure* and *demi-saison*. Their data show that the initial vowel is deletable in *demi-saison*
(it is deleted by two speakers), but not in *demi-heure*. This is, again,[1]
in agreement with the prosodic model we defend here: the vowel of
                     w s w s   s w s w
the initial syllable is W in *demi-saison*, but S in *demi-heure*. Yet al
other words with *demi-* which Martinet and Walter list in their dictionary
are given with an optional 'schwa': *d(e)mi-monde, d(e)mi-mondaine*, etc.
Very probably, the possible pronunciations as proposed by the two
authors do not correspond to real usage of the native speaker. We
strongly suspect that the prosodic parameter should be taken into

consideration. We are also convinced that the prosodic prominence marker on the vowel 'schwa' may explain so-called vowel adjustement in some verbs (such as *mener* vs. *mène, mènerai*; in our model *mener* [w s] vs. *mène, mènerai* [s w, s w s]); but the presentation of our argumentatoin would lead us far beyond the scope of the present paper (see Verluyten 1982: 76 sqq.).

13. In summary, we feel that there are strong arguments in favor of the analysis of so-called schwa we have been considering here, where the prosodic parameter of syllabic prominence plays a crucial role in the explanation of the at first glance rather erratic behavior of the vowels that are phonetically [œ] at the outset. It should be made clear that we are only claiming that the merger of 'full' /œ/ and 'schwa' into one phoneme may be an evolution which is on its way now for some speakers. We are not saying that this development is as yet generalizing in standard French, nor that it is already accomplished in some variants of French. Yet we feel that our proposals may possess some explanatory power which is lacking in previous studies. where prosodic factors play no role. Several authors would agree with us that schwa is in the process of being 'phonologized' in contemporary French (Morin 1978, Fischer 1980). According to these scholars, the phonologization of schwa may happen in one of the following ways:

(i) schwa may be reanalyzed as zero, as in *allemand, bracelet*, etc. (cf. above);
(ii) schwa may be reanalyzed as 'full' /œ/, not effaceable, and to be differentiated from unstable /œ/ by a diacritic; this reanalysis would have happened in words such as *brebis, premier, crever*, etc. (Fischer 1980), where schwa in the initial syllable is not effaceable;
(iii) schwa may be reanalyzed as 'unstable' /œ/, as in *s(e)maine, d(e)vant, s(e)cret*, etc.

In these descriptions, however, several observed facts remain unexplained. Without taking into account the prosodic parameter, it is quite mysterious why schwa tends to be reanalyzed as zero in trisyllabic words ((i) above), whereas it does not go to zero in bisyllables ((ii) and (iii)). Under the prosodic hypothesis on the other hand, it is rather natural to assume that schwa is in a weaker position *between* two more prominent syllables (SWS) than word-initially (WS). More importantly, it remains unexplained why reanalysis toward 'unstable' /œ/ occurs, according to all the examples given, in *penultimate* syllables only, and not, for instance, in antepenultimates. Again, this observation receives an explanation in the prosodically-oriented model we defend: in penultimate syllables, 'schwa' occurs in W position, where it is prone to be effaceable; this is not the case in antepenultimate syllables, where it is prosodically S. The fact that 'schwa' is often reanalyzed as /ö/ in W position, and as /e/ or /ɛ/ in S position, goes unnoticed by the authors quoted. Finally, let us point out that in the examples quoted by Fischer, where schwa is reanalyzed as 'stable' /œ/, its non-effaceability is, in our model, explained by segmental factors: in all cases, its deletion would create an inadmissible consonant-cluster (*brb*, *prmj* and *krv* respectively for *brebis*, *premier* and *crever*). Thus, these words do not constitute counterexamples to the one-phoneme hypothesis; in fact, there are no reasons to think that /œ/ in the examples of (ii) and of (iii) above is not the same phoneme.

In conclusion, we feel that the analysis of French 'schwa' which we presented in this paper may shed new light on the observed data concerning the present-day evolution of the French vowel system.

REFERENCES

Chomsky, N. and M. Halle. 1968. *The sound pattern of English*. New York: Harper and Row.
Fischer, R. 1980. La phonologisation du schwa en français. *Lingvisticae Investigationes* IV. 21 - 38.
Kiparsky, P. 1973. Phonological representations. *Three dimensions of linguistic of linguistic theory*, ed. by O. Fujimura. Tokyo: TEC.
Martinet, A. and H. Walter. 1973. *Dictionnaire de la prononciation française dans son usage réel*. Paris: France-Expansion.
Morin, Y.-C. 1978. The status of mute "e". *Studies in French linguistics* 1.2. 79 - 140.
Schane, S. 1979a. The rhythmic nature of English word accentuation. *Language* 55. 559 - 602.
    1979b. Rhythm, accent and stress in English words. *Linguistic Inquiry* 10. 483 - 502.
Verluyten, S. P. 1982. *Recherches sur la prosodie et la métrique du français*. Unpublished doctoral dissertation, University of Antwerp UIA, Belgium.
    1985. La structure prosodique des mots français: hiérarchique ou linéaire? *Linguistics in Belgium 6*, ed. by M. Dominicy et al. Univ. of Antwerp, APIL.
Walter, H. 1977. *La phonologie du français*. Paris: P. U. F.

ON THE ORIGINS AND DEVELOPMENTS OF AMERICAN ENGLISH

WOLFGANG VIERECK

With regard to the history and the present state of White, Black and Red American English, much work remains to be done.[1]

As regards Black American English the crucial question still remains open, namely, whether the offshore island English or Gullah, spoken on the Sea Islands and on parts of the Georgia and South Carolina coasts, 'is a locally creolized variety and a product of the isolation and other forces, especially demographic ones, peculiar to that one area of the South or whether Gullah represents an extreme form of creolized English that is different only in degree from varieties of speech farther inland' (Montgomery 1981: 5).

The criterion recently established by the well-known creolist and universalist Derek Bickerton (according to whom creole languages 'arose in a population where not more than 20 percent were native speakers of the dominant language and where the remaining 80 percent was composed of diverse language groups' [1981: 4]) points to the uniqueness of the Gullah area in the United States, a position always held by linguistic geographers and harshly attacked by other creolists like William Stewart and J. L. Dillard. Although Bickerton's criterion was not established in view of what is now the continental United States, it claims universal validity and may thus be applied legitimately to that area as well. However, further figures on the size of the plantations and on the black-white ratio of the people working there are no doubt necessary before the matter can be finally decided. At any rate, Wells (1975) documents convincingly with census data that the composition of the population of the northern continental colonies (with the exception of the Gullah area) was drastically different from that of the Caribbean. That this situation should have linguistic consequences is only natural.

---

[1] What I would like to say at this conference is supplementary to what I have already written on this subject; cf. Viereck 1982, 1983 and 1985.

According to Curtin (1969), the total importation of Blacks into what became the United States and Canada amounted to about 400,000. This is less than half the number shipped to Jamaica alone. But what is more important: only one eighth of the black slaves came to North America from the West Indies. The transmutation of West Indian creoles into plantation creoles, so readily alleged by creolists, is thus not substantiated by slave trade figures.

Yet even with this extralinguistic evidence pointing to the contrary, we are confronted with absolute pronouncements as the following: 'the syntax [of English-based Afro-American dialects of the New World] in its earliest form cannot be derived from English' (Alleyne 1980: 105)! It should be pointed out that Mervyn Alleyne (and others) "enriched" the picture of the origin of Black American English by advocating the Ebonics Theory. According to that theory Black American English did not develop from either a pidgin or a creole, but is a linguistic system that is a continuation of the African Hamito-Bantu language families. In Alleyne's opinion, 'To relate non-standard dialects of Black American urban communities to a pidgin would lead to the inference that there has been discontinuity, as far as the transmission of an African cultural item is concerned, and would in fact support the deficiency hypothesis' (1971: 126). Conclusive evidence to prove the validity of ebonics is, of course, still wanting (and very hard to produce, one should add).

Justification for the creolist theory of Black American English continues. Brasch 1981 proves that this is, at times, rather naive. He deliberately sets out 'to justify the creolist theory' (p. XVI) and is able to fulfil his task by simply ignoring all the evidence detrimental to his cause.[2] Brasch is so sure of the African origin of the characteristics of Black American English that in the rare instance when even he has to note a parallel from the history of English he does that with surprise, as the following example exemplifies: '... the use of the pronominal cross-reference marker, which has its roots in many West African languages, is acceptable and logical American Black English ... The pronominal cross-reference marker, *surprisingly*, is also common in Middle and Elizabethan English, as in the Biblical passage, "Thy rod

---

[2] That there are creolists who do not forget to look to England/Great Britain even when they are concerned with the Caribbean should not be overlooked here, either. Thus John Holm (1981) shows, in Figure 2, "The Provenance of British Regionalisms in Miskito Coast Creole".

and thy staff, they comfort me". ... However, we cannot simply say that in this case Middle English influenced West African languages which in turn influenced American Black English. What undoubtedly happened was a mutual, though separate, development in both Middle English and West African Pidgin English (based upon a number of West African languages)' (Brasch 1981: 293, my italics)!

It turns out that characteristics of the English spoken by minorities in the United States — whether black or red [3] — very often agree with each other. What they have in common is either a simplification (e.g. an elimination of an inflection) or an addition of redundancy (e.g. a reduplication). Thus they exhibit clear parallels with English foreigner talk, a term coined by Ferguson (cf. Ferguson 1971, 1975, 1977 [with DeBose] and 1981). Although the concept goes back to Schuchardt (1909), it has hardly received the attention it deserves.

Foreigner talk is understood here both as a simplified register of an English speaker using English to a foreign language speaker and as an interlanguage of a foreign language speaker using English to an English speaker. Tests Ferguson conducted with American students prove that the students largely agree on the characteristics of English foreigner talk. Although many are hesitant to use it, all are able to produce it. This is anything but surprising since native speakers of English (as of other languages) have several registers at their disposal and many features of English foreigner talk are attested in (earlier) cultivated and (present-day) popular British English usage.[4] For the non-native speaker of

---

[3] On the research of Red American English and its features cf. Bartelt 1981 and Bartelt, Jasper, Hoffer 1982.

[4] Only a few features can be enumerated in a footnote by way of examples: ...*myself, the boys, and servant, was at church*... (p. 21); *We was showed the house all over* (p. 36). *My wife a good deal indisposed* (p. 36); *My wife very ill all day*... *Very little trade, and she always so afflicted with illness*... *My family all at church in the afternoon* (p. 39); ... *that it is an extreme good paper* (p. 59). All examples are taken from the second edition of Turner's diary (1979). Although a Georgian shopkeeper, Turner 'certainly regards himself as an educated man..., and as a former village schoolmaster is ready to instruct' (Turner 1979: IX). Eighteenth century English grammarians criticized such sentences as *My banks they are furnished with bees; The men they were there; The king he is just*. (These examples were kindly provided by Prof. Dr. Bertil Sundby, University of Bergen, Norway, director of the project "A Dictionary of English Normative Grammar 1700—1800".) — The following examples also show cultivated usage: Alexander, Sixth Earl of Eglinton, wrote to his son, Colonel James Montgomery on July 21, 1648: ...*who is in great fear of the forces who hes approchit thair*; *The Livetenant Generall new maid*... *was evill hurt in the heid*. In a letter of Sir George Calvert to the Earl of Bristol, dated March

English, English foreigner talk is a learner's language, marking an unstable period of transition[5] where certain features may persist for a long time, for centuries even, while others disappear fairly quickly with increasing competence in English. All this depends largely on the contacts of the foreign language speakers with native speakers of English, their frequency, duration and intensity (factors which obviously have something to do with the composition of the population in the respective areas) and on the English or Englishes these native speakers used or use. It is thus quite natural to find what turns out to be present-day British English dialectal features, English foreigner talk features[6] — both often correspond and are thus reinforced —, Indianisms and Africanisms in certain types of Red and Black American English. It is likewise natural to find Indianisms and Africanisms in certain types of White American English, not to speak of present-day British English dialectalisms.

4, 1622, we find: *There be a great many of the other sorts who gett leave to go.* These examples have been taken from various *Reports of the Royal Commission on Historical Manuscripts*, published in London since 1874. To my knowledge this important source has not yet been used in linguistic research. Besides other information, these reports contain very many letters from different periods written mostly by people higher up on the social scale. Letters of, e.g., ordinary soldiers are, unfortunately, usually only summarised as are propositions made to various Indian tribes, or nations, as they are called, and their answers, if they are not just stated as facts. In these cases one would have to check the originals, which should be possible since the sources have always been indicated, e.g.: The Manuscripts of the Most Honourable the Marquis of Landsdowne, or The Manuscripts of the Earl of Egmont. It is worth noting in this connection that the above few examples prove Feagin wrong with regard to three features. She maintains: 'It must be emphasized, however, that Black English has certain features which do not occur in Southern White, British dialects, or older stages of English and which are undoubtedly grammatical remnants of Creole: (1) remote present perfect *been*; (2) lack of agreement; (3) lack of possessive -*s*; (4) *is* deletion '(1979: 263).

[5] Already Schuchardt (1888) noted variations within the English of 'his' Indian pupils without, of course, using the terms learner's language or interlanguage.

[6] English foreigner talk characteristics seem to be similar, if not identical, worldwide. In a letter written by a Chinese lady in Hong Kong, dated January 6, 1977, I note: *As you already know I still working*; ... *but he working in the Old Island School*; *I missing her very much* (deletion of the copula); *my sister she went to Canada*; *and my brother he is working in Public Work Department* (redundancy/reduplication and omission of the definite article); *no one want to marry me* (no verb inflection). In recent letters from Indian boys from a missionary school near Bombay personal pronouns are often used instead of the possessive ones. This is a wide field in which much work still remains to be done. The discovery of non-native varieties of English is very recent indeed (cf. Kachru 1982).

The problems connected with White American English and its history are also complex. What remains to be done in this field can be gathered from J. L. Dillard's 1980 revision of Albert H. Marckwardt's bestselling book *American English* (1958). Both linguists quite rightly assume that dialectal diversity was an important factor in the New World during the 17th century, but nobody has as yet sifted all the evidence contained in the numerous passenger and immigration lists, now provided by Filby 1981, with regard to the origin of the early British settlers. This would be of great importance.[7] A consideration of only some early (17th century) passenger lists has already changed considerably the traditional picture of the areas of emigration from the mother country (cf. Viereck 1975: I, 329f.).[8] Whereas Marckwardt and Dillard agree on the dialectal nature of 17th century White American English, Dillard believes that American English had become uniform in the 18th century. The uniformity of 18th century American English, however, is a myth. Undoubtedly there were factors at work leading towards a levelling of the more extreme dialectal differences, such as dialect mixture, the great number of emigrant children whose speech habits had not been firmly established and who, as modern sociolinguistic studies tell us, linguistically often follow their peers and not their parents, and the multilingual contact situation that prevailed in colonial America, but these never led to a uniformity of American English (cf. Viereck 1982 and 1983).

In the original version of *American English* (1958) Marckwardt was much more careful than Dillard in his revision of the book in presenting all available evidence. Whereas Marckwardt produced various observers reporting both on the uniformity and on the diversity of American English during the same period, which means that we cannot trust their reports, Dillard simply suppressed 19th century comments on the uniformity of American English since it did not fit into his picture.

Others are also guilty of such, at best, careless procedures. Ann L.

---

[7] We have nothing even remotely comparable to the French emigration maps to Canada where absolute numbers and percentage figures from various regions of France are given. This information has already been available since the early years of this century. It must be added, however, that as far as the British Isles are concerned, such information was not collected everywhere in the early years of emigration. '... there is no record of the places of origin of emigrants from Irish ports, because the customs authorities did not begin to compile such lists until 1803' (McCourt 1968: 79).

[8] Unfortunately, the new research results have been largely ignored. To give one example, Baugh-Cable 1978³, repr. 1980, 1981 and 1983: 377ff., only present the traditional, obsolete views on early emigration from the mother country.

Sen, in a 1982 contribution, is concerned with the loss of postvocalic and preconsonantal /r/ in Colonial America. In reviewing the literature on this subject Sen notes: 'Unfortunately Stephenson's North Carolina work [1958] provides no information on the informants' social backgrounds. Yet the variants he finds are ... probably due to social status' (1980 [1982]: 58). Only through this far-reaching assumption is it possible for Sen to maintain her conclusion that the loss of /r/ in the positions mentioned 'was a characteristic of upper class prestige speech' in Colonial America (*ibid.*: 59). In 1974: 43 Sen remarked 'Stephenson, although he examined North Carolina evidence from all ranges of the social scale — from slaves to plantation owners — unfortunately, did not include social groupings in his final analysis'. Had Sen only checked the volumes of the same journal in which her article appeared she would have found in the 1968 issue a contribution by the same Edward A. Stephenson on the same subject, i.e. the loss of postvocalic /r/, if only for North Carolina. There Stephenson is very careful in differentiating between popular and cultivated usage wherever possible and notes that 'most of them [i.e. the *r*-less spellings] come from the level of popular usage' (1968: 69)! By evaluating his evidence carefully, Stephenson is able to do justice to the complex situation and to refute for North Carolina both theories as too simplistic, namely that the change of postvocalic /r/ in Colonial America is due either to a change only in popular speech or to a change only in cultivated speech.

The largely deplorable state of the art, so-called, in the field of the origins of the American Englishes and their development can only be overcome when researchers stop to adhere to the "theory-rich and data-poor" philosophy. Data-based research is, of course, much more laborious and time-consuming. Bickerton's 'empirical plodder' (1981: 45) sadly reminds us of Lee's "dull cataloguer of data" of 1957, but as Bickerton's frequent disregard for pedestrian facts shows, it is exactly that role that must be assumed if reliable results are to be achieved.[9]

---

[9] British private libraries belong to the sources still to be checked on this side of the Atlantic. Since plantation owners also lived in England there is bound to have been a considerable amount of correspondence between both sides of the Atlantic. Overseers' letters are, moreover, of special importance also with regard to the relationship between White and Black American English, but so far very few have looked at the speech of those English and Irish men who acted as overseers on the plantations in the American South. The study even of late, i.e. 19th century, letters shows that many of these overseers wrote and spoke anything but grammar book standard English (cf. Hawkins 1982). Apart from the numerous

Furthermore, both synchronic and diachronic data must be reliable and honestly evaluated. Researchers must allow the data to change their preconceived notions rather than ignore or suppress portions of the evidence in order to keep them alive. Earlier research must be carefully reviewed and the views honestly presented. Of paramount importance is the close study of the original manuscripts and not, as a short-cut, of secondary literature. I mentioned several sources that still await exploitation. All this seems to be self-evident, but reality shows that, unfortunately, it is not. In view of the state of the research and the tasks still to fulfil it seems that we have a rather long way to go until the origins of White, Black and Red American English, their developments and interrelationships are reliably described.

REFERENCES

Alleyne, M. C. 1971. Linguistic continuity in the Caribbean. *Topics in Afro-American studies*, ed. by H. J. Richards. New York: Black Academy Press.
― 1980. *Comparative Afro-American; an historical-comparative study of English-based Afro-American dialects of the New World*. Ann Arbor: Karoma.
Bartelt, H. G. 1981. Some observations on Navajo English. Papers in linguistics. *International Journal of Human Communication* 14. 377 - 85.
Bartelt, H. G., S. Penfield Jasper and B. Hoffer, eds. 1982. *Essays in native American English*. San Antonio: Trinity University.
Baugh, A. C. and T. Cable. 1978³. Repr. 1980, 1981, 1983. *A history of the English language*. London, Boston: Routledge and Kegan Paul.
Bickerton, D. 1981. *Roots of language*. Ann Arbor: Karoma.
Brasch, W. M. 1981. *Black English and the mass media*. Amherst: University of Massachusetts Press.
Curtin, P. D. 1969. *The Atlantic slave trade; a census*. Madison, Wisc.: University of Wisconsin Press.
Feagin, C. 1979. *Variation and change in Alabama English; a sociolinguistic study of the white community*. Washington, D. C.: Georgetown University Press.
Ferguson, C. A. 1971. Absence of copula and the notion of simplicity: a study

---

volumes of the *Reports of the Royal Commission on Historical Manuscripts*, referred to in fn. 4, *A Guide to Manuscripts Relating to America in Great Britain and Ireland*, 1979, rev. ed., ed. by John W. Raimo. London: Meckler Books, Mansell Publ., is of great importance in this connection. Here, however, the originals must be examined in every case in the locations indicated. Sources on this side of the Atlantic must, of course, be supplemented by an investigation of (early) American sources. Here attention should be drawn to a project directed by Prof. Matti Rissanen at the University of Helsinki, entitled "On the study of early American English syntax". For a description of the project cf. Kytö & Rissanen 1981.

of normal speech, baby talk, foreigner talk, and pidgins. *Pidginization and creolization of languages*, ed. by D. Hymes, 141 - 50. Cambridge: Cambridge University Press.

    1975. Toward a characterization of English foreigner talk. *Anthropological Linguistics* 17. 1 - 14.

    1981. "Foreigner talk" as the name of a simplified register. *International Journal of the Sociology of Language* 28. 9 - 18.

Ferguson, C. A. and C. E. DeBose. 1977. Simplified registers, broken language, and pidginization. *Pidgin and creole linguistics*, ed. by A. Valdman, 99 - 125. Bloomington and London: Indiana University Press.

Filby, P. W. ed. 1981. *Passenger and immigration lists bibliography, 1538 - 1900. Being a guide to published lists of arrivals in the United States and Canada.* 2 vols. Detroit: Gale Research Comp.

Hawkins, O. W. 1982. *Southern linguistics variation as revealed through overseers' letters, 1829 - 1858.* Ph. D. dissertation. The University of North Carolina at Chapel Hill.

Holm, J. 1981. Sociolinguistic history and the creolist. *Historicity and variation in creole studies*, ed. by A. Highfield and A. Valdman, 40 - 51. Ann Arbor: Karoma.

Kachru, B. B., ed. 1982. *The other tongue: English across cultures*. Urbana: University of Illinois Press. [Paperback edition, 1983. Oxford: Pergamon].

Kytö, M. and M. Rissanen. 1983. The syntactic study of early American English. *Neuphilologische Mitteilungen* 84. 470 - 90.

Marckwardt, A. H. 1958. *American English*. Rev. 1980 by J. L. Dillard. New York and Oxford: Oxford University Press.

MeCourt, D. 1968. Review of R. J. Dickson, *Ulster emigration to colonial America 1718 - 1755* [1966]. Ulster Folklife 14. 79 - 81.

Montgomery, M. 1981. The study of the language of blacks and whites in the American south. Mimeographed paper presented at the biennial American Studies Association meeting in Memphis, Tennessee.

Schuchardt, H. 1888. Beiträge zur Kenntniss [sic] des englischen Kreolisch. I. *Englische Studien* 12. 470 - 4; translated into English by G. G. Gilbert 1980 as Notes on the English of American Indians: Cheyenne, Kiowa, Pawnee, Pueblo, Sioux, and Wyandot. Pidgin and creole languages. *Selected essays by Schuchardt*, ed. by G. G. Gilbert, 30 - 37. Cambridge: Cambridge University Press.

    1909. Die Lingua Franca. *Zeitschrift für Romanische Philologie* 33. 441 - 61.

Sen, A. L. 1974. Dialect variation in early American English. *Journal of English Linguistics* 8. 41 - 47.

    1980 [1982]. Some social implications of /r/ loss in American English. *Orbis* 29. 55 - 59.

Stephenson, E. A. 1958. *Early North Carolina pronunciation*. Ph. D. dissertation. The University of North Carolina.

    1968. The beginnings of the loss of post-vocalic /r/ in North Carolina. *Journal of English Linguistics* 2. 57 - 77.

Turner, T. 1979. *The diary of a Georgian shopkeeper*; a selection by R. W. Blencowe and M. A. Lower with a preface by F. M. Turner. Second edition with a new introduction by G. H. Jennings. Oxford, New York, Toronto, Melbourne: Oxford University Press.

Viereck, W. 1975. *Lexikalische und grammatische Ergebnisse des Lowman-Survey von Mittel- und Süd England.* Vol. 1. Munich: Wilhelm Fink.

—— 1982. Das amerikanische Englisch in Forschung und Lehre. *Zeitschrift für Dialektologie und Linguistik* 49. 351 - 65.

—— 1983. On the history of American English: sense and nonsense. *Eigoseinen. The Rising Generation (Tokyo)* 129/7. 329 - 31.

—— 1984. Notes on Black and Red American English. *Stockwell Festschrift,* ed. by C. Duncan-Rose, Jacek Fisiak and Theo Vennemann. Amsterdam: Benjamins.

Wells, R. V. 1975. *The population of the British colonies in America before 1776; a survey of census data.* Princeton, N.J.: Princeton University Press.

QUELQUES PROBLÈMES DES RECHERCHES ÉTYMOLOGIQUES SUR LES EMPRUNTS LEXICAUX

BOGDAN WALCZAK

Les recherches étymologiques sur les emprunts lexicaux entraînent beaucoup de difficultés et de problèmes particuliers. Certains de ces problèmes feront l'objet du présent article dont le but consiste à recueillir, développer et systématiser mes observations théoriques et méthodologiques dissipées dans des travaux consacrés aux mots empruntés en polonais.

Tout d'abord il faut attirer l'attention sur la nécessité du traitement différent, dans les recherches étymologiques, des mots empruntés d'une part et du vocabulaire hérité de la langue-mère de l'autre. Le problème se situe dans le contexte d'une controverse théorique et méthodologique entre les partisans de ce que l'on peut appeler étymologie morphosémantique et les adeptes de l'étymologie lexicale (quant aux termes étymologie morphosémantique ou morphosémantisme, étymologie lexicale ou lexicalisme — voir Weinsberg 1968).

Selon les partisans du morphosémantisme l'analyse étymologique dans tous les cas doit remonter jusqu'à l'acte de formation du mot qui lui a donné naissance. Le partisan de l'étymologie morphosémantique, en expliquant p.ex. le mot polonais *ferezja* 'sorte de vêtements de dessus faisant partie de l'ancien costume polonais' ne se contentera pas d'établir que c'est un emprunt au turc *feredže*, *feradže* 'espèce de manteau ou de pèlerine', mais en recherchant un acte de formation demandé constatera que le mot turc a été emprunté au grec *phoresía* 'vêtement' et ce n'est que là, sur le terrain de la langue grecque, il trouvera cet acte de formation: *phoresía* c'est un dérivé de *phéro* 'je porte' (cf. Sławski 1952—1982: I 226). Les représentants du point de vue morphosémantique sont, entre autres, V. Pisani (1947), G. Alessio et C. Battisti (1948), J. Corominas (1954), M. Cortelazzo et P. Zolli (1979), W. Doroszewski (1962a), J. Kuryłowicz (1953), F. Sławski (1963), en principe aussi J. Picoche (1971). L'attitude morphosémantique a été le plus profondément justifiée par J. Corominas (1954).

Par contre, les adeptes du lexicalisme réduisent le but de l'analyse étymologique à la réponse à la question suivante: comment le mot examiné s'est-il trouvé dans une langue donnée? Donc, en cas du mot *ferezja* le lexicaliste se bornerait à constater qu'il a été emprunté au turc *feredže*, *feradže*. L'attitude lexicaliste a été le plus vigoureusement formulée par A. Meillet (1975); en outre, elle est représentée, entre autres, par W. von Wartburg (1964) et P. Chantraine (1968).

Lorsqu'il s'agit de la pratique des recherches étymologiques, le problème ne se montre pas aussi clair qu'en théorie. Etant donné que les explications morphosémantiques sont, en principe, beaucoup plus "profondes", ce genre d'étymologie reste incomparablement plus difficile. Aussi les partisans eux-mêmes du morphosémantisme traitent leur attitude en tant qu'espèce d'idéal théorique qui n'est pas toujours accessible en pratique. Il en résulte qu'il existe des dictionnaires étymologiques conséquemment lexicalistes (p.ex. celui d'Ernout-Meillet (1979) ou de Bloch — Wartburg (1975)), mais, autant que je sache, il n'existe pas un seul dictionnaire qui serait conséquemment morphosémantique: dans des dictionnaires des partisans les plus acharnés du morphosémantisme on trouve de nombreuses entrées conçues de façon lexicaliste.

La controverse théorique et méthodologique entre les partisans du morphosémantisme et les adeptes de l'étymologie lexicale a été relatée par Weinsberg (1968). Son article comprend une critique détaillée des arguments en faveur de l'une et de l'autre attitude. Ici on se bornera à un seul aspect de ce problème qui n'a pas été pris en considération dans l'article de Weinsberg. Il s'agit des directives pour l'analyse étymologique résultant du caractère du mot examiné. A mon avis les emprunts lexicaux réclament un traitement étymologique à part.

Quant aux mots indigènes, les lexicalistes se bornent à constater qu'ils ont été hérités de la langue-mère. P.ex. le dictionnaire de Bloch — Wartburg explique ainsi le mot *four* : *four*, ancien français *forn*, tire son origine du latin *fornus* (cf. Bloch — Wartburg 1975: 272). D'une façon pareille le lexicaliste expliquerait p.ex. le mot polonais *stół* 'table': *stół* provient du slave commun *stălŭ* 'table'. Or, à mon avis, une telle constatation n'est aucune explication étymologique. Pour parvenir à cette conviction il suffit de se rendre compte, jusqu'au bout, de la nature du rapport qui existe entre le polonais et le slave commun. Il faut tout simplement prendre conscience du fait qu'il s'agit ici seulement des phases évolutives différentes du même système linguistique. La limite

entre le slave commun et le polonais n'est pas et ne peut pas être de
caractère linguistique: on ne peut la marquer ni la justifier qu'en tenant
compte des circonstances extralinguistiques (naissance de l'état, formation de la conscience de la communauté linguistique, etc.). C'est déjà
J. Baudouin de Courtenay qui a formulé ceci le plus vigoureusement:

"(...) należy pamiętać, że ze stanowiska naukowego, ze stanowiska
nieprzerwanej ciągłości historycznej, stosowanie nazwy "język polski"
dla danego języka zbiorowo-indywidualnego dopiero od pewnego czasu,
tj. od czasu wyodrębnienia się tego języka ze wspólnoty wszechsłowiańskiej, jest rzeczą dowolną. Obiektywnie tak zwani Słowianie czy
też Prasłowianie byli przodkami lingwistycznymi czyli językowymi
zarówno Polaków, jak i innych Słowian; język więc prasłowiański powinien być uważany za dawny język polski. Podobnie ma się rzecz ze
stanem językowym praarioeuropejskim, który w swej dostępnej dla
naszego badania, a ustanawianej drogą domysłów i odtwarzań postaci
może być również uważany za najstarożytniejszy język polski" (Baudouin
de Courtenay 1922: 12).

Si les choses vont ainsi, il est évident qu'au lieu de faire provenir le
polonais *stół* du slave commun **stǎlǔ* aussi bien on pourrait le faire
provenir de l'ancien polonais *stół* ou des formes encore plus anciennes
*stolъ, **stolь*: ou on fera provenir *stół* de la forme ancienne polonaise,
ou bien de la forme slave commune tardive, ou bien de la forme slave
commune précoce — se sera toujours une simple présentation d'une
phase évolutive plus ancienne du même mot dans le cadre de la même
langue, et non pas une explication de son origine. Le mot peut apparaître
dans la langue soit en tant que dérivé ou composé, soit en tant que
néosemantisme (sens nouveau d'un mot déjà existant dans la langue),
soit en tant qu'emprunt, soit en tant qu'onomatopée. L'héritage c'est
une persistence, une continuation — et non pas un acte de naissance du
mot. Pour éclaircir réellement l'origine du mot *stół*, il faut remonter
jusqu' à l'acte de sa formation qui lui a donné naissance, car ce mot est
un dérivé: il faut donc constater que *stół* est un postverbatif de **stěljǫ*,
stǔlāti (aujourd'hui *ścielę*, *słać* 'étendre') au sens primitif 'quelque chose
d'étendu (en tant que surface usuelle)'.

Donc, les mots indigènes doivent être expliqués étymologiquement
(en principe, car en pratique de recherches peuvent apparaître de diverses
difficultés) conformément aux exigences méthodologiques du morphosémantisme étymologique. Cette attitude seule mene à une explication
réelle du mot du point du vue étymologique, c'est-à-dire à l'explication
de son origine.

La situation est tout a fait différente en ce qui concerne les mots empruntés. Les emprunts pénètrent dans la langue de dehors, ils y passent d'un système linguistique tout distinct. De même que p.ex. le mot *stół* s'est trouvé en polonais à l'issue d'un acte de formation, le mot *ferezja* s'y est trouvé à l'issue d'un acte d'emprunt. De même qu'en cas du mot *stó* l'acte de formation marque la limite de l'analyse étymologique, en cas du mot *ferezja* c'est l'acte d'emprunt qui marque cette limite. *Ferezja* a été empruntée au turc. Et c'est tout dit. La réponse à la question d'où a apparu en turc le mot *feredže, feradže* — fait partie des tâches de l'étymologiste-turcologue. Le prolongement de l'analyse étymologique en tous les cas jusqu'à l'acte de formation, demandé par le morphosémantisme, entraîne en cas des emprunts un sui generis réductionnisme. Si le poloniste (slaviste), en expliquant le mot polonais *ferezja*, à l'issue des exigences de l'attitude admise explique nécessairement aussi le mot turc *feredže, feradže*, bah! même le mot grec *phoresía* — indépendamment de la question de la compétence, soulevée par Meillet (1975), les thèses et les constatations de l'étymologie polonaise (slave) se réduisent ici aux thèses et aux constatations du domaine de l'étymologie turque et grecque. Donc, quant aux emprunts, le type d'analyse étymologique conforme à l'attitude lexicaliste s'avère bien justifié du point de vue méthodologique.

Evidemment, en cas de certains emprunts il sera recommandé sinon nécessaire de prolonger (pour plusieurs raisons, p.ex. pour l'établissement indubitable de l'acte et de la source de l'emprunt) l'explication étymologique (entre autres jusqu'à l'acte de formation car parfois c'est lui seul qui permet d'éviter un cercle vicieux dont a écrit Corominas (1954)) — mais c'est déjà toute autre chose, de caractère pratique et non pas théorique ni méthodologique. En ces cas le prolongement de l'analyse étymologique ne serait pas une consequence inévitable du principe admis, mais aurait un caractère purement "pragmatique", supplémentaire d'une certaine façon. Pour des remarques plus détaillées à ce sujet voir Walczak (sous presse a, sous presse b).

Ayant accepté l'attitude lexicaliste et en procédant à l'analyse d'un mot particulier, on se trouve en face de différents problèmes pratiques qu'il faut résoudre pour expliquer proprement le mot donné. Tout d'abord se pose un problème de caractère philologique. Il s'agit d'établir précisément et correctement la forme du mot examiné. Bien sûr, c'est une question très importante dans chaque recherche étymologique, cependant en cas d'un mot emprunté c'est un problème d'importance toute particulière car les emprunts sont spécialement susceptibles de déformations diverses. P. ex. A. Brückner (1915: 150) cite, parmi d'autres gallicismes et sans aucun commentaire sémantique, le mot *gryalinowy* tiré de "Compendium medicum" de 1703. Le mot figure dans le dictionnaire de Linde sous l'entrée *gryglinowy*, *gryalinowy*; l'exemple illustrant la variante *gryalinowy* provient du même "Compendium medicum" (Linde 1807–1814: II 138). Sans aucun doute c'est l'expression française *gris de lin* qui est la source de notre emprunt. Il est donc évident que la forme *gryalinowy* est due à une faute d'impression dans "Compendium medicum": au lieu de *gryalinowy* devrait être *grydlinowy* (résultat de l'adaptation régulière du français *gris de lin*); la deuxième variante *gryglinowy* a apparu à l'issue du passage $dl \geq gl$, connu en polonais (cf. Taszycki 1961). Il s'ensuit que *gryalinowy* n'a jamais existé réellement dans la langue. Quant à d'autres exemples de ce genre — voir Walczak (1982a).

La forme du mot examiné correctement établie, on procède à l'explication étymologique proprement dite. W. Cienkowski a formulé six principes de l'analyse étymologique des emprunts: 1) le principe de la vraisemblance des changements et des identités phonétiques, 2) le principe du rapport du mot avec le référent et des réalités, 3) le principe de la conséquence et de la conformité chronologique, 4) le principe de la vraisemblance et de la continuité du développement sémantique du mot, 5) le principe de la vraisemblance des contacts linguistiques et 6) le principe d'examiner les mots sous toutes les faces (Cienkowski 1964).

Le sixième principe est de caractère le plus général et, pour ainsi dire, va de soi. Les autres, à la lumière de mon expérience de chercheur, demandent quelque commentaire.

Quant au premier, celui de la vraisemblance des changements et des identités phonétiques, dès le début de l'étymologie scientifique, et surtout à l'époque des néo-grammairiens, il servait de base de toutes recherches dans ce domaine. Depuis longtemps on attirait l'attention sur des régularités phonétiques dans le processus de l'assimilation des emprunts (cf., dans la littérature linguistique polonaise, Brückner 1915). Au cours des recherches étymologiques sur les emprunts français en polonais on surestimait en général le rôle de ce principe, en admettant la régularité à peu près absolue de la substitution des phonèmes dans le processus de l'adaptation phonétique des gallicismes (cf. Morawski 1928 a, Doroszewski 1934). Cependant mes propres études dans ce domaine révèlent plusieurs flottements et oscillations dans ce processus. Hors des irrégularités individuelles, concernant des gallicismes particuliers, il existe des irrégularités catégorielles, comprenant des types morphologiques entiers.

Ce sont surtout les emprunts au latin, plus anciens et déjà bien enracinés dans la langue, qui ont influencé la forme des emprunts ultérieurs au français. Soit l'exemple des mots français en —*ement* (*abonnement, appartement, département* etc.). Pénétrant en polonais, ils s'y sont stabilisés dans la forme terminée en —*ament* (*abonament, apartament, departament* etc.) ce qui est dû à l'influence des latinismes en —*ament* (*fundament, testament* etc., empruntés au latin *fundamentum, testamentum* etc.). Remarquons qu'en russe où les influences latines étaient beaucoup plus faibles et, à cette époque, à peu près exclusivement indirectes, les mots en question se terminent en -*ement* (*abonement* etc.; s'il y a egalement des mots comme *apartament, departament* — c'est à cause de l'intermédiaire du polonais ce que prouve, entre autres, la place d'accent (*apart|ament* envers *abonem|ent*).

Une influence pareille sur la forme des gallicismes a été exercée par les italianismes, eux aussi plus anciens en polonais que la plupart des emprunts français. D'où p.ex. les mots français en -*eire* : *draperie, papeterie* etc. ont été assimilés en polonais comme *draperyja* ≧ *draperia, papeteryja* ≧ *papeteria* etc., donc analogiquement aux mots italiens en -*eria* : *batteria, galleria, cavalleria* etc. (en polonais *bateryja* ≧ *bateria, galeryja* ≧ *galeria, kawaleryja* ≧ *kawaleria* etc.). Le russe qui n'a pas subi des influences italiennes directes a adapté les mots français en question comme *drapri, papetri* etc., donc d'une façon tout à fait régulière.

Il faut mentionner aussi l'influence des mots indigènes sur la forme des emprunts, surtout s'il s'agit du genre grammatical, des suffixes structuraux, des désinences flexionnelles etc. (cf. Doroszewski 1927, 1962 b, Fisiak 1963, 1975, Henke 1970, Hofman 1967, Truszkowski 1958 etc.).

Toutes ces circonstances entraînent plusieurs irrégularités dans le processus de l'adaptation des emprunts. De plus, il existe en polonais de nombreux emprunts aux langues romanes dont la source exacte ne peut être établie en tenant compte de la forme phonique du mot, p.ex. *aneks* (latin *annexus*? français *annexe*?), *wersja* (latin *versio*?, français *version*?), *balkon* (italien *balcone*? français *balcon*?), *sonet* (italien *sonetto*?, français *sonnet*?) etc.

Tout cela porte à la thèse que le principe de la vraisemblance des changements et des identités phonétiques est de caractère relatif. Bien qu'utile, même indispensable dans les recherches é'ymologiques sur les emprunts, il n'est que d'importance restreinte: son application y est incontestablement limitée (pour une étude plus détaillée de ce problème voir Walczak 1978, 1982 a).

Dans les recherches sur les mots on ne peut pas faire abstraction de leurs référents: "Każdy wyraz ze stanowiska czysto opisowego interesuje nas jako znak pewnego desygnatu, a więc w swej funkcji aktualnej skierowany ku rzeczywistości zewnętrznej" (Cienkowski 1964). D'où le principe du rapport du mot avec le référent et des réalités. Il en résulte la nécessité d'une connaissance approfondie du référent sur le fond de la spécificité civilisatrice et culturelle propre à la société des usagers de la langue — source de l'emprunt.

Il arrive souvent que le principe ci-discuté permet de résoudre un problème étymologique. P.ex., il existe en polonais un groupe d'emprunts romans dont la source exacte est très difficile à établir. Un de ces emprunts est le mot *bankiet*. Certains linguistes le considèrent comme un gallicisme, d'autres — comme un emprunt italien. Dans une telle situation le fait que le référent du mot *bankiet* était associé à des réalités italiennes ce que prouve l'expression *bankiety włoskie* ('banquets italiens'), enregistrée dans le dictionnaire du polonais du XVIe siècle (Mayenowa 1966: 303) — est un argument supplémentaire (et décisif) en faveur de la provenance italienne.

Toutefois l'ulilité de ce principe ne veut pas dire que l'application en est possible et effective toujours et partout. Au contraire, le principe est, comme le précédent, de caractère relatif et limité. Cela résulte de quelques circonstances.

Tout d'abord, le principe ci-discuté sert à établir l'ultime source étymologique du mot étudié — tandis que ce qui intéresse principalement les historiens de langue c'est la source directe de l'emprunt. Seulement l'acte même de l'emprunt est un fait historique-linguistique, un témoignage des contacts et des influences linguistiques réels et conditionnés historiquement. P.ex. ce qui est essentiel pour l'historien du polonais c'est le fait de l'emprunt au français du mot *kadryl* — tandis que d'importance tout à fait secondaire est le fait que le mot est étymologiquement espagnol ce que prouve entre autres son référent (quadrille est une danse d'origine espagnole; le français a emprunté le mot *quadrille* a l'espagnol *cuadrilla*).

Plus le référent est spécifique et caractéristique pour le pays ou la civilisation d'un peuple donné, plus vraisemblable est le fait de l'emprunt direct à la langue de ce peuple. Même s'il n'y a pas de contacts entre deux langues, un certain nombre de termes peuvent pénétrer de l'une à l'autre par la voie livresque, par l'intermédiaire des traductions des oeuvres littéraires, scientifiques etc. Dans chaque langue il existe des mots intraduisibles (tels noms d'unités monétaires, d'institutions sociales, de danses nationales, d'instruments de musique, mots comme *fjord* en norvégien ou *polder* en hollandais etc.) qui, laissés sans traduction, après un certain temps s'adaptent à leur nouveau milieu linguistique. Toutefois il faut se rendre compte que même les référents très spécifiques ne peuvent pas être pris pour un argument décisif en faveur de l'immédiateté de l'emprunt car il arrive souvent que les mots désignant des réalités les plus spécifiques sont empruntés par l'intermédiaire des autres langues. Soit, en polonais, le mot *lasso*. Il désigne un référent caractéristique pour les peuples de l'Amérique Latine, donc les dictionnaires le considèrent comme un hispanisme. Cependant le mot espagnol correspondant est *lazo* (avec une spirante interdentale) tandis que la forme polonaise par son double *s* atteste l'emprunt (graphique) à l'anglais *lasso*, au français *lasso* ou bien (ce qui est d'ailleurs moins probable) à l'allemand *Lasso*.

Pourtant il faut constater que la situation du polonais est assez singulière: à l'issue de l'absence de l'état polonais et des conditions normales de la vie et du développement du peuple polonais au XIXe siècle, la langue polonaise empruntait des termes spécifiques pour les langues exotiques par l'intermédiaire de l'anglais, du français, de l'allemand ou du russe. Les emprunts immédiats étaient très rares, à vrai dire exceptionnels. Ce n'est qu'aujourd'hui, grâce aux mass media contemporains, que les mots provenant des langues éloignées du point de vue géographique et civilisateur pénètrent immédiatement en polonais dans une plus grande mesure (p.ex. *hunwejbin* ou *tadżypao*, empruntés au chinois, ou bien *ajatollah* ou *hojatoleslam*, empruntés au persan).

Le principe du rapport du mot avec le référent ne peut pas être appliqué dans la situation où les mots d'une certaine langue pénètrent dans une autre langue par de différentes voies, conditionnées des circonstances historiques définies. Quant au polonais, c'est le cas des mots turcs (kiptchaques). Il est facile à constater que p.ex. le mot *kołpak* est d'origine turque ce qu'atteste entre autres le référent, un couvre-chef de provenance turque; mais: est-ce que le mot turc *kalpak*, nom de ce référent, est entré en polonais par l'intermédiaire de l'ukrainien (cf. Minikowska 1980: 75—76), ou immédiatement (cf. Klemensiewicz 1965: 156), ou encore par la langue hongroise (cf. Zaręba 1951: 114)? — voici le problème qui ne peut pas être résolu en tenant compte du principe en question.

Enfin, il se passe que des textes comprennent des opinions erronées au sujet de l'origine du référent. P.ex. I. Szlesiński dans son ouvrage sur la langue de Samuel Twardowski note parmi les gallicismes le mot *pasamedza*, employé par le poète dans "Przeważna legacyja": "same strony brzmiały francuskie pasamedze" (Szlesiński 1971: 180). Il n'y a pas de doute que Szlesiński a été ici induit en erreur par l'opinion de Twardowski sur l'origine française du référent ("francuskie pasamedze") et c'est pourquoi il a également admis la source française du nom bien qu'il ne l'ait pas trouvée. De fait, le mot est un emprunt à l'italien: "*passamezzo* 'danza italiana (donc l'opinion de Twardowski s'avère erronée — B.W.) del sec. XVI, di tempo ari e andamento un po'più vivace della pavana' // Da (un) pass(o) (e) mezzo" (Cusatelli 1965: 1213). L'attitude critique envers les opinions au sujet de l'origine du référent, comprises dans des textes, est donc indispensable.

Ce qui résulte des considérations présentées ci-dessus c'est que le principe du rapport du mot avec le référent, bien qu'utile, est soumis à plusieurs restrictions qui en limitent l'application dans les recherches étymologiques sur les emprunts (pour une version plus détaillée de ces remarques voir Walczak 1983 a, sous presse c).

Le principe de la conséquence et de la conformité chronologiques ne demande pas des remarques supplémentaires. Une seule restriction doit être mentionnée ici. L'application de ce principe ne peut pas contribuer à l'identification de la source de l'emprunt en deux cas: 1) lorsque l'influence d'une certaine langue dure trop longtemps pour que le facteur chronologique puisse être un trait distinctif des emprunt à cette langue et 2) lorsque les influences de deux ou plusieurs langues, les emprunts auxquelles sont difficiles à discerner, s'engrènent dans le temps, ne serait-ce que partiellement. Tous les deux cas peuvent être illustrés par les influences des langues romanes (l'italien, le latin, le français) en polonais.

Les influences italiennes échoient au XVIe et XVIIe siècles; il existe aussi des témoignages qu'encore au XVIIIe siècle l'italien était assez populaire en Pologne bien que, sûrement, non pas à tel point que dans les deux siècles précédents. Dans certains domaine (tel p.ex. vocabulaire de la musique) les influences italiennes se maintiennent encore plus tard, après le XVIIIe siècle. L'action du latin sur le polonais s'accroît dès le commencement du XVIe siècle pour atteindre son apogée au XVIIe, et surtout dans la première moitié du XVIIIe siècle; il est vrai que dès la moitié du XVIIIe siècle l'influence latine s'affaiblit assez soudain, pourtant le lexique livresque pénètre de cette langue en polonais encore au cours du XIXe siècle entier et, dans une certaine mesure, encore aujourd'hui.

Enfin, les influences françaises commencent au XVIe siècle (et sont déjà à cette époque plus fortes que l'on ne pensait jusqu'à présent (cf.

Kurkiewicz-Rzepkowa et Walczak 1983)), s'intensifient visiblement dès la moitié du XVIIe siècle, encore plus nettement dès la moitié du XVIIIe siècle (cf. Walczak 1980 a) — pour atteindre leur point culminant dans la première moitié du XIXe siècle (cf. Kurkiewicz-Rzepkowa et Walczak 1978, Walczak 1980a, 1981). Ensuite, il est vrai, elles s'affaiblissent, mais leur fin n'échoit que dans la période de la seconde guerre mondiale (et même pas tout à fait — aujourd'hui encore un certain nombre de mots français pénètrent en polonais (cf. Walczak 1982 b, sous presse d)). Ajoutons que les influences anglaises datent dès le début du XIXe siècle (cf. Walczak 1983 b), et l'action de l'allemand, particulièrement sur le polonais de l'Ouest et du Sud du pays, au moins dans certains domaines du lexique, dure presque sans cesse depuis le Moyen-Age. Dans cette situation le facteur chronologique ne peut jouer qu'un rôle très restreint dans l'identification des sources exactes des emprunts romans et, plus largement, occidentaux.

Le principe de la vraisemblance et de la continuité du développement sémantique du mot a, dans les recherches étymologiques sur les emprunts, un grand rôle à jouer, à condition qu'il soit proprement conçu. Il faut se rendre compte qu'il s'agit ici de la vraisemblance et de la continuité du développement sémantique du mot emprunté, et non pas de l'identité sémantique de l'emprunt et de sa source, comme le croyait J. Morawski qui a refusé plusieurs explications étymologiques généralement admises à cause de l'absence de l'identité sémantique (cf. Morawski 1928 b, 1929). Cependant en effet, on ne peut parler de l'identité sémantique par rapport aux emprunts que rarement, pour la plupart en cas des emprunts terminologiques (ou d'autres spéciaux), à un certain point aussi en cas des emprunts plus récents. Par contre, beaucoup plus souvent on a affaire à des changements sémantiques; indépendamment des cas singuliers du développement irrégulier (comme *granda* 'aventure', français *grande*, ou *forsa* 'argent', français *force*), c'est le rétrécissement du sens qui est un type le plus fréquent, donc régulier au sens statistique du terme, de ces changements.

Le phenomène est déjà bien connu (cf., entre autres, Fisiak 1962, Mańczak 1970 a); une étude détaillée du développement sémantique des emprunts français (et partiellement anglais) en polonais (Walczak 1980 b) a toutefois décelé des régularités plus particulières. Il s'avère que le rétrécissement du sens consiste en général en ce que l'emprunt garde seulement l'acception (les acceptions) spéciale(s) ou métaphorique(s) (p.ex. français *accompagner* 'aller de compagnie avec quelqu'un, escorter, suivre; ajouter, joindre; mus. soutenir le chant au moyen d'un accompagnement' — polonais *akompaniować* mus. 'soutenir le chant au moyen d'un accompagnement'; français *frapper* 'donner un ou plusieurs coup; blesser; donner une empreinte, fig. affliger d'un mal; estamper; atteindre par une décision juridique administrative; tomber sur; affecter d'une impression, d'une emotion; etc.' — polonais *frapować* 'intéresser beaucoup'), parfois l'une et l'autre (p.ex. français *impasse* 'voie à une seule entrée; jeux: tentative pour faire une levée avec une carte inférieure à celle que possède l'adversaire, en tablant sur la position de cette carte; fig. situation qui semble ne pas offrir d'issue favorable' — polonais *impas* 'terme de jeux, cf. ci-dessus; situation sans issue'), parfois enfin l'acception métaphorique est en même temps spéciale et inversement (p.ex. *plateau* — en polonais seulement un terme géographique 'surface peu accidentée, mais entaillée de vallées encaissées, ce qui suppose une certaine attitude au-dessus du niveau de la mer'). Il arrive aussi que le mot français donne naissance à deux mots polonais qui en partagent la signification (p.ex. français *suite* — polonais *świta* 'cortège qui accompagne quelqu'un pour lui faire honneur' et *suita* mus. 'série de pièces instrumentales écrites dans le même ton et relevant de la danse') sans d'ailleurs, dans la plupart des cas, l'épuiser.

Il s'avère donc que le développement sémantique des emprunts est beaucoup plus régulier que l'on ne le croyait auparavant (Doroszewski 1934). Néanmoins il faut avouer que les emprunts sont susceptibles des déviations diverses du sens, telle une influence sémantique des autres emprunts (à d'autres langues) à la même racine (p.ex. polonais *dywizyja* ≅ *dywizja*, empruntée au latin *divisio*, a pris son acception militaire, aujourd'hui unique, sous l'influence du français *division*; de même *partyja* ≅ *partia*, elle aussi empruntée au latin, doit certaines de ses acceptions au français *parti* et *partie*; etc. (Walczak 1982a, cf. aussi Kurkowska 1976)). A tout prendre, il faut constater que l'état où se trouve la sémantique diachronique ne permet pas de résoudre des questions particulières d'une manière bien justifiée en tous les cas. Aussi l'appréciation de la vraisemblance des changements sémantiques reste toujours encore subjective dans une certaine mesure (ce qui paraît vraisemblable à un linguiste, est considéré comme invraisemblable par un autre).

Quant au principe de la vraisemblance des contacts linguistiques, il faut constater seulement que, quoique généralement appliqué et indubitablement utile dans la pratique des recherches étymologiques sur les emprunts, il suscite certains doutes du point de vue théorique. Ce qui est tout à fait légitime c'est quand on se demande si, à la lumière de ce que l'on sait au sujet des contacts (ou de l'absence des contacts) entre deux langues (degré de la proximité de ces contacts, direction de l'influence éventuelle, son intensité etc.), les emprunts examinés dans une de ces langues peuvent être attribués à l'autre ou non. Mais il arrive que le principe en question est appliqué d'une façon un peu différente: on exclut la possibilité de l'emprunt à une certaine langue dans une langue donnée en tenant compte du fait que dans celle-ci il n'y a pas d'emprunts à celle-là. Or ici on a affaire à un cercle vicieux typique: pour constater que dans une langue donnée il n'y a pas d'emprunts à une autre langue il faudrait savoir d'avance que le mot examiné n'est pas un emprunt à cette langue.

Le dernier des principes formulés par Cienkowski, celui d'examiner les mots sous toutes les faces, va sans dire, comme on a déjà mentionné. Cependant, à mon avis, on pourrait en ajouter encore un, le septième: principe de prendre en considération des témoignages provenant de l'époque contemporaine à un emprunt étudié. P.ex. l'origine italienne du mot *towalija* (≥*tuwalnia*) est attestée par Łukasz Górnicki ("Ręczniki szerokie, iż do nas ze Włoch przyniesiono, zaraz też i przezwisko ich z nimi przyszło, bo je *towalijami* zowiemy; *tovaglia*, włoskie słowo, już u nas za polskie ujdzie "(Górnicki 1954: 85)) et l'origine française du mot *koteryja* (≥*koteria*) par Adam Kazimierz Czartoryski ("*Koteryja* jest to słowo francuskie, które oznacza społeczność z małej liczby osób osób złożoną, często schadzających się z sobą" (Czartoryski 1955: 329). Ici il s'agit des emprunts dont l'origine ne fait aucun doute — il y a toutefois des cas où un témoignage de l'époque diffère sensiblement des opinions admises au sujet de l'origine d'un mot donné. P.ex. Ignacy Włodek considère *festyn* comme un gallicisme (Włodek 1958: 475) tandis que dans la littérature linguistique prédomine la conviction que c'est un emprunt à l'italien. Ici la question est plus difficile. A mon avis, on ne peut pas négliger l'opinion de Włodek. Puisque le même mot, on le sait bien aujourd'hui, peut être — à de différentes époques, dans de divers textes, chez de différents auteurs — un emprunt à de différentes langues (cf. Bizoń 1973), on peut accepter la thèse qu'à l'époque de Włodek *festyn* était un gallicisme.

La conclusion la plus générale résultant de ce qui a été dit est la suivante: tous les principes de l'analyse étymologique des emprunts, formulés par Cienkowski, sont de caractère relatif; leur application est bornée par de différentes raisons et circonstances.

Les problèmes envisagés ici mériteraient sans doute une discussion plus détaillée mais le volume admissible du présent article rend cela impossible.

BIBLIOGRAPHIE

Alessio, G., Battisti, C. 1948. *Dizionario etimologico italiano.* Fasc. I. Firenze: G. Barbera.
Baudouin de Courtenay, J. 1922. *Zarys historii języka polskiego.* Warszawa: Biblioteka Składnicy.
Bizoń, F. 1973. Dawne *szukać* 'usiłować, próbować' — latynizm czy galicyzm? *Język Polski* LIII. 258—68.
Bloch, O., von Wartburg, W. 1975. *Dictionnaire étymologique de la langue française.* Sixième édition. Paris: Presses Universitaires de France.
Brückner, A. 1915. Wpływy języków obcych na język polski. In Łoś, J. et al. 1915. 100—53.
Bubak, J., Wilkoń, A. (réds). 1981. *O języku literatury.* Katowice: Uniwersytet Śląski.
Chantraine, P. 1968. *Dictionnaire étymologique de la langue grecque.* T. I. Paris: Editions Klincksieck.
Cienkowski, W. 1964. Ogólne założenia metodologiczne badania zapożyczeń leksykalnych. *Poradnik Językowy.* Fasc. 10. 417—29.
Corominas, J. 1954. *Diccionario crítico etimológico de la lengua castellana.* T.I. Berna: Franke.
Cortelazzo, M., Zolli, P. 1979. *Dizionario etimologico della lingua italiana.* T.I. Bologna: Zanichelli.
Cusatelli, G. (réd.). 1965. *Dizionario Garzanti della lingua italiana.* Milano: Garzanti.
Czartoryski, A. K. 1955. *Komedie.* Warszawa: Państwowy Instytut Wydawniczy.
Doroszewski, W. 1927. Polski przyrostek *-ek* w wyrazach zapożyczonych. *Prace Filologiczne* XII. 145—51.
— 1934. La langue française en Pologne. *Revue des Etudes Slaves* XIV. 36—50.
— 1962. *Studia i szkice językoznawcze.* Warszawa: Państwowe Wydawnictwo Naukowe.
— 1962 a. Kryteria słowotwórcze w etymologii. In Doroszewski, W. 1962. 227—44.
— 1962 b. O rodzaju gramatycznym wyrazów obcych w języku polskim. In Doroszewski, W. 1962. 273—75.
Ernout, A., Meillet, A. 1979. *Dictionnaire étymologique de la langue latine.* Quatrième edition. Paris: Editions Klincksieck.
Fisiak, J. 1962. *Zapożyczenia angielskie w języku polskim.* Łódź: Uniwersytet Łódzki (manuscrit dactylographié).
— 1963. Kategoria rodzaju rzeczowników zapożyczonych z języka angielskiego. *Rozprawy Komisji Językowej ŁTN* IX. 63—68.
— 1975. Some remarks concerning the noun gender assignment of loanwords. *Bulletin de la Société Polonaise de Linguistique* XXXIII. 59—63.

Górnicki, Ł. 1954. *Dworzanin polski*. Wrocław: Ossolineum.
Henke, A. 1970. *Die morphonologische Kategorisierung der "westlichen" Lehnwörter in der polnischen Sprache*. München: Forum Slavicum.
Hofman, L. 1967. *Procesy przyswajania wyrazów angielskich w języku polskim*. Londyn: Polski Uniwersytet na Obczyźnie.
Klemensiewicz, Z. 1965. *Historia języka polskiego*. Partie 2. Warszawa: Państwowe Wydawnictwo Naukowe.
Kurkiewicz-Rzepkowa, E., Walczak, B. 1978. Galicyzmy leksykalne w komedii i dramie epoki stanisławowskiej. *Studia Romanica Posnaniensia* IV. 119−35.
— 1983. Uwagi nad zapożyczeniami francuskimi w polszczyźnie XVI wieku. *Studia z Filologii Polskiej i Słowiańskiej* 21. 41−48.
Kurkowska, H. 1976. Zapożyczenia semantyczne we współczesnej polszczyźnie. In Magnuszewski, J. (réd.). 1976. 99−109.
Kuryłowicz, J. 1953. Uwagi o "Słowniku etymologicznym" F. Sławskiego. *Język Polski* XXXIII. 65−70.
Linde, S. B. 1807−1814. *Słownik języka polskiego*. T. I−VI. Warszawa.
Łoś, J. et al. 1915. *Język polski i jego historia z uwzględnieniem innych języków na ziemiach polskich*. Partie 1. Kraków: Akademia Umiejętności.
Magnuszewski, J. (réd.). *Z problemów współczesnych języków i literatur słowiańskich*. Warszawa: Wydawnictwo Uniwersytetu Warszawskiego.
Mańczak, W. 1970. *Z zagadnień językoznawstwa ogólnego*. Wrocław − Warszawa − Kraków: Ossolineum.
— 1970 a. Rozwój znaczeniowy a frekwencja. In Mańczak, W. 1970. 171−79.
Marciniak, Z. (réd.). 1963. *Wielka Encyklopedia Powszechna PWN*. T. 3. Warszawa: Państwowe Wydawnictwo Naukowe.
Mayenowa, M. R. (réd.). 1958. *Ludzie Oświecenia o języku i stylu*. T. I. Warszawa: Państwowy Instytut Wydawniczy.
— 1966. *Słownik polszczyzny XVI wieku*. T. I. Wrocław−Warszawa−Kraków: Ossolineum.
Meillet, A. 1975. Preface. In Bloch, O. Wartburg von, W. 1975. VII−XVIII.
Minikowska, T. 1980. *Wyrazy ukraińskie w polszczyźnie literackiej XVI w*. Warszawa−Poznań−Toruń: Państwowe Wydawnictwo Naukowe.
Morawski, J. 1928 a. Des mots français en polonais; voyelles finales et ə at one. *Revue des Etudes Slaves* VIII. 178−93.
— 1928 b. Polono-romanica. Uwagi romanisty na marginesie SEJP'u Brücknerowego. *Slavia Occidentalis* VII. 521−68.
— 1929. Polono-romanica. Etymologie romańsko-polskie. *Slavia Occidentalis* VIII. 420−36.
Picoche, J. 1971. *Nouveau dictionnaire étymologique du français*. Paris: Hachette-Tchou.
Pisani, V. 1947. *L'etimologia*. Torino: Eri.
Sławski, F. 1952−1982. *Słownik etymologiczny języka polskiego*. T. I.−IV. Kraków: Towarzystwo Miłośników Języka Polskiego.
— 1963. Etymologia. In Marciniak, Z. (réd.). 1963. 512−13.
Szlesiński, I. 1971. Język Samuela Twardowskiego (słownictwo). *Rozprawy Komisji Językowej ŁTN* XVII. 155−98.

Taszycki, W. 1961. *Rozprawy i studia polonistyczne.* T. II. Wrocław—Warszawa— Kraków: Ossolineum.
    1961 a. O gwarowych formach *mgleć, mgły, moglić się, moglitwa.* In Taszycki, W. 1961. 259—74.
Truszkowski, W. 1958. Hierarchizacja funkcji przyrostków wielofunkcyjnych na przykładzie przyrostka *-k-* w wyrazach zapożyczonych. *Język Polski* XXXVIII. 93—97.
Walczak, B. 1978. Adaptacja francuskich zapożyczeń leksykalnych w języku polskim i rosyjskim. *Z polskich studiów slawistycznych* 5. 315—23.
    1980 a. Wpływy francuskie w polszczyźnie epoki Oświecenia. *Sprawozdania PTPN, Wydział Filologiczno-Filozoficzny* 96. 52—56.
    1980 b. O rozwoju znaczeniowym zapożyczeń. *Język. Teoria — Dydaktyka 1980.* 159—87.
    1981. Z różnic między językiem artystycznym a potocznym w czasach stanisławowskich (Galicyzmy w poezji i korespondencji Stanisława Trembeckiego). In Bubak, J., Wilkoń, A. (réds). 1981. 289—302.
    1982 a. Z zagadnień etymologizacji zapożyczeń romańskich w języku polskim. *Język. Teoria-Dydaktyka 1982.* 172—94.
    1982 b. Galicyzmy we współczesnej polszczyźnie (Uwagi — między innymi — socjolingwistyczne). *Zeszyty Naukowe WSP w Szczecinie* 38. 327—45.
    1983 a. Rola desygnatu w badaniach nad zapożyczeniami. *Sprawozdania PTPN, Wydział Filologiczno-Filozoficzny* 97—99. 270—73.
    1983 b. The earliest borrowings from English into Polish. *Studia Anglica Posnaniensia* XVI. 121—31.
    Sous presse a. Morfosemantyzm i leksykalizm w etymologii a zapożyczenia wyrazowe. *Język. Teoria — Dydaktyka.*
    Sous presse b. W sprawie "głębokości" analizy etymologicznej. *Sprawozdania PTPN, Wydział Filologiczno-Filozoficzny.*
    Sous presse c. Rola desygnatu i realiów w badaniach etymologicznych nad zapożyczeniami. *Język. Teoria — Dydaktyka.*
    Sous presse d. Rola elementu obcojęzycznego w rozwoju leksyki współczesnej polszczyzny. *Sprawozdania PTPN, Wydział Filologiczno-Filozoficzny.*
Wartburg W. von, 1964. *Problèmes et méthodes de la linguistique.* Paris: Presses Universitaires de France.
Weinsberg, A. 1968. Etymologia słowotwórcza czy leksykalna? *Slavia Orientalis* XVII, 3. 443—47.
Włodek, I. 1958. O naukach wyzwolonych w powszechności i szczególności ksiąg dwie. In Mayenowa, M.R. (réd.). 1958. 468—93.
Zaręba, A. 1951. Węgierskie zapożyczenia w polszczyźnie. *Język Polski* XXXI. 113—25.

MORPHOLOGISCHE NATÜRLICHKEIT UND MORPHOLOGISCHER WANDEL ZUR VORHERSAGBARKEIT VON SPRACHVERÄNDERUNGEN

WOLFGANG ULLRICH WURZEL

1. Eine der interessanten Fragen der historischen Linguistik ist zweifelsohne, ob und wieweit Sprachveränderungen vorhersagbar sind. Will man diese Frage beantworten, so ist zu klären,
(a) unter welchen Bedingungen welcher Wandel eintritt oder eintreten kann,
(b) unter welchen Bedingungen welcher Wandel ausgeschlossen ist.
Die Vorhersagbarkeit von Sprachveränderungen setzt verständlicherweise deren **Nichtzufälligkeit** voraus; wenn jegliche Sprachveränderung grundsätzlich zufällig ist, dann ibt es auch keine Möglichkeit der Vorhersage. Vorhersagbarkeit erfordert also zumindest einen bestimmten Grad an **Determiniertheit**.[1]

Nun steht einerseits aufgrund des umfangreichen Faktenmaterials der historischen Sprachwissenschaft außer Frage, daß die Entwicklung einer Sprache nicht in mechanischer Weise determiniert sein kann. Mit einem gegebenen Ausgangszustand ist eben nicht eindeutig festgelegt, wie sich ein Sprachsystem innerhalb eines bestimmten Zeitraumes entwickeln wird.[2] So würde wohl niemand vorhersagen wollen, wie das Flexionssystem des Dtsch. in, sagen wir, 200 Jahren im einzelnen aussehen wird. Doch andrerseits steht es ebenso außer Frage, daß in einer Sprache mit einer bestimmten grammatischen Struktur nicht jede beliebige Sprachveränderung eintreten kann. So kann man (um eine extremes Beispiel zu wählen) wohl mit Sicherheit aus.chließen, daß im gegen-

---

[1] Zur Determinismusproblematik vgl. Hörz 1974.
[2] Wenn diese Entwicklung eindeutig festgelegt wäre, könnte es ja ohne äußeren Einfluß (Sprachkontakt) überhaupt keine Herausbildung unterschiedlicher Tochtersprachen aus einer einheitlichen Vorgängersprache geben.

wärtigen Dtsch. Veränderungen eintreten, in deren Ergebnis grammatische Kategorien anstelle durch Suffixe und 'grammatische Wörter' durch Präfixe oder gar durch Tonhöhendistinktionen ausgedrückt würden, was in anderen Sprachen ja durchaus vorkommt. Die Entwicklung einer Sprache ist also offensichtlich weder in mechanischer Weise determiniert noch absolut zufällig. Doch wieweit geht im einzelnen die Determiniertheit und damit die Vorhersagbarkeit von Sprachveränderungen?

Diese Problematik soll im folgenden anhand der Flexionsmorphologie diskutiert werden, wobei wir das Konzept der grammatischen Natürlichkeit zugrunde legen wollen.

2. Die in den natürlichen Sprachen insgesamt vorkommenden grammatischen Strukturen und Prozesse sind nicht einfach 'gleichwertig' Sie unterscheiden sich u.a. in ihrer Verbreitung, in ihrer Stellung zum Sprachwandel, im relativen Zeitpunkt ihrer Aneignung durch das Kind beim Spracherwerb, in ihrer Beeinflussung durch Sprachstörungen usw. Dieser unterschiedliche Status grammatischer Erscheinungen ist der heuristische Ausgangspunkt für das Konzept der **Natürlichekit in der Grammatik**. Grammatische Erscheinungen werden dann als **natürlich** angesehen, wenn sie

— in den verschiedenen Sprachen weit verbreitet sind,
— durch Sprachwandel häufig entstehen, aber selbst gegenüber Sprachwandel relativ resistent sind,
— bei der Sprachaneignung durch das Kind verhältnismäßig früh erworben werden,
— von Sprachstörungen in vergleichsweise geringem Maße betroffen sind usw.

Natürlichkeit ist somit ein Bewertungsprädikat für in diesem Sinne von den Sprechern bevorzugte grammatische Strukturen und Prozesse. Dabei ist wichtig, daß grammatische Erscheinungen nicht deshalb natürlich sind, weil sie sich so verhalten, sondern sie verhalten sich im Gegenteil deshalb so, weil sie natürlich sind. Der Natürlichkeitsgrad grammatischer Erscheinungen ergibt sich daraus, wieweit sie bestimmten universellen Strukturbildungsprinzipien die man am zweckmäßigsten als **Natürlichkeitsprinzipien**, bezeichnet, entsprechen. Diese legen Präferenzen der grammatischen Strukturbildung fest und beruhen (wie auch die 'strikten Universalien') auf der psychisch-physischen Ausstattung des Menschen sowie den allgemeinsten Bedingungen der sprachlichen Kommunikation. Die strukturprägende, d.h. determinierende Wirkung der Natürlichkeitsprinzipien vollzieht sich in der Sprachveränderung: Alle systematischen Sprachveränderungen, sofern sie nicht auf Sprach- und Dialektmischung, Normierung usw. beruhen, erfolgen in einer von den Natürlichkeitsprinzipien favorisierten Richtung; sie zielen auf mehr Natürlichkeit im jeweils betroffenen Bereich

3. Die gemeinsame Spezifik der morphologischen Natürlichkeitsprinzipien ergibt sich aus den Bedingungen der Produktion, Perzeption und Speicherung sowie aus der Funktion morphologischer Strukturen. Zu den morphologischen Natürlichkeitsprinzipien gehören
— das Prinzip des konstruktionellen Ikonismus,
— das Prinzip der Uniformität und Transparenz ('eine Funktion — eine Form'),
— das Prinzip des phonetischen Ikonismus
sowie einige weitere Prinzipien, deren Wirkung in der Literatur verhältnismäßig häufig diskutiert worden ist.[3] Detaillierte eigene Untersuchungen in jüngster Zeit haben jedoch gezeigt, daß zwei andere Prinzipien, die bisher fast keine Beachtung fanden, für die flexionsmorphologische Strukturbildung eine kaum zu überschätzende Bedeutung haben. Dabei handelt es sich um
— das Prinzip der typologischen Einheitlichkeit und Systematik von Flexionssystemen und
— das Prinzip der unabhängigen Motivierung von Flexionsklassen.[4]
Diese beiden Prinzipien sind allem Anschein nach die stärksten morphologischen Natürlichkeitsprinzipien überhaupt, was deutlich wird, wenn sie im konkreten Fall gegen eines der anderen Prinzipien wirken, wobei immer sie sich durchsetzen. Da also ihre Wirkung offenbar nicht von anderen morphologischen Prinzipien eingeschränkt wird, müßten durch sie bedingte Veränderungen am ehesten vorhersagbar sein. Wir wollen sie deshalb den folgenden Untersuchungen zugrunde legen.

4. Das Prinzip der typologischen Einheitlichkeit und Systematik von Flexionssystemen. Jedes Flexionssystem ist durch eine Reihe von typlogischen Parametern charakterisiert; die wichtigsten davon sind:
— ein Inventar an Kategoriengefügen und Kategorien,
— das Auftreten von Grundformflexion oder Stammflexion,

---

[3] Hier sei nur auf Mayerthaler 1981 verwiesen, wo diese Prinzipien im Zusammenhang einer natürlichen Morphologie behandelt werden.
[4] Vgl. dazu Wurzel 1984; dort werden diese beiden Prinzipien ausführlich diskutiert und in ein umfassendes Morphologiekonzept eingeordnet. Eine Skizze der Problematik findet sich in Wurzel 1983.

— die separate oder kombinierte Symbolisierung von Kategorien,
— die Anzahl und Ausprägung der formalen Distinktionen in den Paradigmen,
— die auftretenden Markertypen bezogen auf die einzelnen Kategoriengefüge,
— das Vorhandensein oder Nichtvorhandensein von Flexionsklassen.

Wir wollen dise Parameter die systemdefinierenden Struktureigenschaften nennen. Nur relative wenige Sprachen, so die streng agglutinierenden, sind bezüglich ihrer systemdefinierenden Struktureigenschaften einheitlich aufgebaut. Die flektierenden Sprachen (i.e.S.) sind dagegen in dieser Hinsicht meist uneinheitlich aufgebaut, d.h. im Flexionssystem konkurrieren verschiedene Strukturzüge wie z. B. Grundform- und Stammflexion, separate und kombinierte Symbolisierung von Kategorien und/oder Marker verschiedener Typen miteinander. Doch auch beim uneinheitlichen Aufbau von Flexionssystemen dominiert offenbar immer jeweils eine der miteinander konkurrierenden Eigenschaften deutlich, prägt das System; auch hier existieren systemdefinierende Struktureigenschaften. Die systemdefinierenden Struktureigenschaften bestimmen die Identität eines Flexionssystems.

In uneinheitlich aufgebauten Systemen entsprechen die einzelnen morphologischen Erscheinungen, d. h. Flexionsparadigmen, Flexionsformen, Marker sowie die entsprechenden Flexionsregeln, den systemdefinierenden Struktureigenschaften oder weichen von ihnen ab. Sie sind systemangemessen oder mehr oder weniger nichtsystemangemessen. Die Systemangemessenheit morphologischer Erscheinungen bemißt sich am Übereinstimmungsgrad mit den systemdefinierenden Struktureigenschaften. Die Sprecher empfinden systemangemessene morphologische Strukturen als normal, nichtsystemangemessene als mehr oder weniger unnormal.

Entscheidend für die Problematik der Vorhersagbarkeit von Sprachveränderungen ist, daß alle uneinheitlich aufgebauten Flexionssysteme eine Tendenz zur typologischen Vereinheitlichung, d. h. zum Abbau nichtsystemangemessener morphologischer Erscheinungen zeigen; das Prinzip favorisiert einheitlich aufgebaute Flexionssysteme. Wenn also in einem bestimmten Bereich der Flexionsmorphologie, in dem Erscheinungen unterschiedlicher Systemangemessenheit miteinander konkurrieren, morphologisch bedingte Veränderungen eintreten, dann immer zugunsten der jeweils systemangemessenen Erscheinungen, also in einer festgelegten und damit vorhersagbaren Richtung. Dafür einige Beispiele aus der dtsch. Substantivdeklination.

(1) **Der Abbau der Stammflexion zugunsten der Grundformflexion.** Im Nhdtsch. dominiert eindeutig die Grundformflexion gegenüber der Stammflexion: Alle großen substantivischen Flexionsklassen haben durchgängig Grundformflexion, vgl. *der Hund — des Hund-es — die Hund-e, die Frau — der Frau — die Frau-en, das Kind — des Kind-es — die Kind-er* usw. Stammflexion tritt nur bei der Pluralbildung (nicht in der Kasusflexion) einiger kleiner Teilflexionsklassen auf, vgl. *die Firm-a — die Firm-en, der Radi-us — die Radi-en, das Zentr-um — die Zentr-en* und *das Stadi-on — die Stadi-en*. Für das nhdtsch. Substantive ist also Grundformflexion systemangemessen und Stammflexion nichtsystemangemessen.[5] Demzufolge kann man entsprechend vorhersagen, daß künftig die Pluralformen mit Stammflexion abgebaut werden. Dafür gibt es bereits gegenwärtig deutliche Anzeichen Bei Wörtern des Typs *Firma* zeigen sich verschiedene Schwankungen und Übergänge, vgl. *die Konto-s* neben *die Kont-en* und *die Aroma-s* neben *die Arom-en*. Die Umgangssprache geht noch weiter, vgl. *die Junta-s* statt *die Junt-en*. Neue Plurale erscheinen partiell auch schon beim Typ *Radius*, vgl. *die Globuss-e* neben *die Glob-en*, und beim Typ *Zentrum*, vgl. *die Album-s* neben *die Alb-en*. Noch nicht begonnen hat der Prozeß beim Typ *Stadion*. Wichtig ist, daß es umgekehrte Übergänge des Typs *die Kamera-s>*die Kamer-en/die Zirkuss-e>*die Zirk-en* nicht gibt. Aufgrund der systemdefinierenden Struktureigenschaften des Dtsch. (und nicht, weil schon bestimmte Übergänge stattgefunden haben) kann man mit großer Sicherheit annehmen, daß in Zukunft bei allen Wörtern mit Stammflexion diese durch Grundformflexion ersetzt werden wird, wenigstens soweit es sich um Wörter der Allgemeinsprache handelt.[6] Es wird also einmal z.B. **die Firma-s, *die Radiuss-e, *die Zentrum-s* und auch **die Stadion-s* heißen. Damit wäre dann die dtsch. Substantivdeklination zugunsten des Flexionstyps Grundformflexion vereinheitlicht.

(2) **Der Abbau der Kasusflexive am Wort.** Eine Analyse der dtsch. Substantivdeklination hinsichtlich der vorkommenden Markertypen ergibt, daß in der Kasusflexion eindeutig der flektierte Artikel gegenüber den Flexiven am Wort selbst (Suffixen) dominiert:

---

[5] Für eine Analyse der systemdefinierenden Struktureigenschaften der nhdtsch. Substantivflexion vgl. Wurzel 1984: 93ff

[6] Das gilt nicht notwendigerweise für Wörter des Fachwortschatzes. So ist sicher kaum zu erwarten, daß z. B. einmal die Pluralform zu *Isomorphism-us*, also *Isomorphism-en*, einmal durch **Isomorphismuss-e* ersetzt werden wird.

Es kommen überhaupt nur noch drei Kasusflexive vor[7], nirgends werden im Artikel übereinstimmende Kasusformen durch Flexive disambiguiert, viele in Flexiven übereinstimmende Kasusformen werden aber durch den Artikel disambiguiert (vgl. *des/dem/den Mensch-en*) usw. Die Kasusflexive des dtsch. Substantivs sind nicht mehr systemangemessen. Aufgrund dieser Konstellation ist der völlige Abbau aller noch vorhandenen Kasusflexive am Substantiv zu erwarten, wofür es wiederum schon bestimmte Anzeichen gibt:

— Das Flexiv /n/ des D./A. Sg. 'wackelt' in der Umgangssprache speziell bei den auf Konsonant endenden Wörtern vgl. *dem/den Bär, Mensch, Kosmonaut, Präsident* usw. statt exakt *dem/den Bär-en* usw., seltener auch *dem/den Hase* statt *dem/den Hase-n* usw. Das /n/ ist des weiteren heute schon nicht mehr möglich mit Präposition ohne Artikel. Es heißt z. B. (*ein Drehorgelspieler*) *mit Affe/mit Bär*; *mit Affe-n/mit Bär-en* ist als Singular ausgeschlossen. Relativ fest ist dieses Flexiv /n/ nur noch im G. Sg.[8]

— Das Flexiv /s/ des G. Sg. wird bereits bei verschiedenen Gruppen von Wörtern völlig oder partiell weggelassen, so u. a. bei bestimmten Namen und bestimmten auf Sibilant endenden Substantiven: *des alten Goethe*,[9] *des Libanon, des* (*Ersten*) *Mai*; *des Sozialismus, des Atlas, des Thorax*. Generell fehlt auch dieses Flexiv in Verbindung mit Präposition ohne Artikel, vgl. *wegen Onkel/Vater/Otto*; *wegen Vater-s* ist nicht mehr möglich.

— Das Flexiv /n/ des D. Pl. ist zwar noch relativ fest, doch hier häufen sich charakteristische 'Fehler' im offenbar besonders förderlichen Kontext mit Präposition ohne Artikel: *ab 18 Jahre, bis zu drei Tage, außer Anlieger, Eis mit Früchte* usw.

Es läßt sich also ohne Schwierigkeiten vorhersagen, daß das Dtsch. in nicht zu ferner Zeit eine Sprache ohne Kasusflexive am Substantiv sein wird. Der Kasus wird dann konsequent durch flektierte Artikel, Pronomen und Adjektive (sowie die Satzgliedstellung) ausgedrückt werden; vgl. schon heute *die/der/der/die Frau, die/der/den/die Frau-en*.

(3) Die Einführung von Pluralflexiven am Wort. In der Numerusflexion dominiert beim nhdtsch. Substantiv die Symbolisierung am Wort selbst durch Flexiv und/oder Umlaut gegenüber der

---

[7] Das Flexiv /e/ des D. Sg. ist faktisch heute bereits abgebaut; im modernen Dtsch. heißt der D.Sg. zu *der Mann* nicht mehr *dem Mann-e*, sondern *dem Mann*.

[8] Das /n/ des G.Sg. der schwachen Maskulina wird allerdings in der Umgangssprache partiell durch /s/ ersetzt, vgl. z. B. *des Bär-s* statt korrekt *des Bär-en*.

[9] Bei Goethe selbst heißt es dagegen bekanntlich noch *des jungen Werther-s*.

Symbolisierung durch den flektierten Artikel. Symbolisierung durch den Artikel allein kommt nur bei den Maskulina und Neutra auf *-el*, *-en*, *-er*, *-chen* und *-lein* ohne Umlaut, bei Neutra des Typs *Gebirge* sowie beim Einzelwort *Käse* vor; bei den Feminina ist alleinige Kennzeichnung durch den Artikel nicht möglich, da hier in Singular und Plural die Artikelform *die* erscheint. Pluralformen ohne Marker am Substantiv selbst sind nichtsystemangemessen.

Wenn das richtig ist, müßten hier in Zukunft beim Typ *der Lehrer — die Lehrer/das Mittel — die Mittel* neue Pluralformen mit Kategoriensymbolisierung am Wort selbst gebildet werden. Bei sorgfältiger Untersuchung des einschlägigen Wortschatzes findet man auch hierfür erste Indizien; vgl. schon vom DUDEN akzeptierte neue Pluralformen auf norddtsch. /s/ bzw. mittel- und süddtsch. /n/ wie *die Kumpel-s, die Fräulein-s, die Mädel-s/Mädel-n* und *die Onkel-s/Onkel-n* sowie umgangssprachliche Formen wie *die Dackel-s/Dackel-n, die Stiefel-s/Stiefel-n* usw. Aufgrund der Struktureigenschaften der dtsch. Substantivdeklination läßt sich vorhersagen, daß im Laufe der Zeit immer mehr Substantive ohne Pluralmarker am Wort in die *s*- bzw. die *n*-Pluralklasse übertreten werden, wodurch immer mehr nichtsystemangemessene Flexionsformen verschwinden.[10]

Ziehen wir ein kurzes Fazit: In allen drei Beispielfällen determiniert das Prinzip der typologischen Einheitlichkeit und Systematik auf der Basis der systemdefinierenden Struktureigenschaften des Dtsch. langfristige Entwicklungen im Deklinationssystem der Substantive, die demzufolge auch begründet vorhersagbar sind.

5. **Das Prinzip der unabhängigen Motivierung von Flexionsklassen.** Flexionsklassen können bekanntlich außermorphologisch, d. h. phonologisch und/oder semantisch-syntaktisch definiert sein. Wenn z. B. im Russ. ein Substantiv die phonologische Eigenschaft hat, daß es im N. Sg. auf /-a/ endet, dann gehört es in die *a*- Deklination, die den G. Sg. mit /i/, den D. Sg. mit /e/ usw. bildet. In vielen Fällen können jedoch die Wörter aufgrund ihrer außermorphologischen Eigenschaften zwei oder mehreren Flexionsklassen angehören. So flektieren

---

[10] An dieser Stelle sind zwei Bemerkungen angebracht. Erstens ist festzustellen, daß die vorhergesagte Entwicklung mit Sicherheit dadurch verlangsamt wird, daß derzeit kein für den gesamten dtsch. Sprachraum geltender, einheitlicher 'sekundärer Pluralmarker' zur Verfügung steht. Zweitens zeigt dieser Beispielfall, daß es im Dtsch. keine einheitliche Entwicklung zu mehr Analytizität gibt, wie sie oft behauptet worden ist. Hinsichtlich der Pluralbildung der Substantive entwickelt sich das Dtsch. gerade in Richtung auf mehr Synthetizität!

beispielsweise die lat. Nichtneutra auf /-us/ z. T. nach der *o*-Deklination und z. T. nach der *u*-Deklination, vgl. *hortus* vs. *tribus*. Solche miteinander konkurrierenden Flexionsklassen unterscheiden sich meist deutlich in ihrer Belegung; so enthält die lat. *o*-Deklination vielfach soviel Wörter wie die *u*-Deklination. Dabei ist die jeweils größere bzw. größte Flexionsklasse **stabil**, die jeweils kleinere(n) **instabil**. Stabile Flexionsklassen nehmen Wörter auf, instabile Flexionsklassen verlieren Wörter. Für die Sprecher ist die Zugehörigkeit eines Wortes zur entsprechenden stabilen Klasse normaler als seine Zugehörigkeit zu einer der instabilen Klassen.

Aus dem Phänomen der unterschiedlichen **Stabilität von Flexionsklassen** ergeben sich wiederum wichtige Konsequenzen für die Sprachveränderung: Stabile, also quantitativ im System überwiegende Flexionsklassen tendieren zur weiteren Ausdehnung, instabile, also geringer belegte Flexionsklassen tendieren zum Abbau. Auf diese Weise entwickelt sich das Flexionssystem in Richtung auf eine strikte Kopplung der Flexionsklassenzugehörigkeit an **unabhängige außermorphologische Eigenschaften**, d. h. auf unabhängig motivierte Flexionsklassen, wobei dann die Zugehörigkeit der einzelnen Wörter zu den Flexionsklassen nicht mehr speziell erlernt werden muß. Wenn also hinsichtlich der Klassenzugehörigkeit von Wörter systematische Veränderungen eintreten, dann immer durch **Übertritt von instabilen zu den zugehörigen stabilen Klassen**, also auch hier in einer **festgelegten und damit vorhersagbaren Richtung**.[1] Auch das sei an einigen Beispielen aus der dtsch. Substantivdeklination illustriert.

(1) **Übertritte von den *n*-Maskulina zu den *e*-Maskulina**. Bei den einsilbigen Maskulina bildet aufgrund der quantitativen Verhältnisse die *e*-Pluralklasse die stabile und die *n*-Pluralklasse die zugehörige instabile Klasse.[12] Entsprechend sind bereits eine ganze Reihe solcher Substantive von der *n*- in die *e*-Klasse übergetreten, z. B. *Greis, Hahn, Mond* und *Schelm* (vgl. *die Greis-e* mit der älteren Bildung *Greis-en-alter*), dazu neuerer *Greif* und *Hagestolz*. Gegenläufige Entwicklungen des Typs die *Hund-e* > *die Hund-en kennt das moderne Dtsch. nicht.

---

[11] Das gilt allerdings nur, solange die Klassenstabilität nicht mit der Systemangemessenheit in Widerspruch gerät; vgl. Abschn. 6.

[12] Hier ist nur ein Ausschnitt einer umfassenderen konstellation behandelt. Einsilbige Maskulina können im Dtsch. auch in die *er*-Pluralklasse (*der Mann — die Männ-er*) und in die *s*-Pluralklasse (*der Park — die Park-s*) gehören.

Aufgrund der Stabilitätsverhältnisse wird sich der Übergang von der maskulinen *n-* zur *e-*Pluralklasse zweifelsohne fortsetzen und eines Tages u. a. auch Wörter wie *Held*, *Narr* und *Spatz* erfassen, die bislang noch ausschließlich *n-*Plurale haben.

(2) **Übertritte von den e-Feminina zu den n-Feminina.** Bei den einsilbigen Feminina bildet aufgrund der quantitativen Verteilung die *n-*Pluralklasse die stabile und die *e-*Pluralklasse die instabile Flexionsklasse. Schon ältere Übergänge von der instabilen in die stabile Klasse sind z. B. *Burg*, *Schrift* und *Tür*, jüngere *Flucht*, *Vollmacht* (vgl. dagegen noch *Mächte*) und *Zucht*. Auch hier kommen heute keine gegenläufigen Übergänge des Typs *die Bahn-en > *die Bähn-e* vor. Hier läßt sich ebenfalls eine Fortsetzung des Klassenwechsels prognostizieren. Wenn das richtig ist, dann werden also auch Wörter wie *Nacht* oder *Wurst* in Zukunft einmal *n-*Plurale haben.

(3) **Übertritte von der n- zur s-Pluralklasse bei vokalisch endenden Substantiven.** Die vokalisch endenden Wörter des Typs *Kino/Firma* können im Dtsch. der quantitativ stark überwiegenden stabilen *s-*Pluralklasse oder der instabilen *n-*Pluralklasse angehören, vgl. *die Kino-s — die Firm-en*, daneben auch noch (fakultativ) den instabilen 'Miniklassen' der *i-*und *ta-*Plurale, vgl. *die Kont-i*, *die Schemata*. Die Übergänge zur *s-*Pluralklasse (wie sie bereits weiter oben erwähnt wurden) stellen nicht nur Anpassungen an die systemdefinierenden Struktureigenschaften des Dtsch. dar, sondern zugleich einen Wechsel von instabilen Flexionsklassen zur zugehörigen stabilen Klasse, vgl. *Arom-en > Aroma-s*, *Kont-en/Kont-i > Konto-s*, *Schme-en/Schema-ta*[13] *> > Schema-s*. Es läßt sich vorhersagen, daß sich der Prozeß des Übergangs von Substantiven dieses Typs in die stabile *s-*Pluralklasse forsetzt.

In den diskutierten Fällen, die leicht durch viele weitere ergänzt werden könnten, sind Entwicklungen im Flexionssystem bei Voraussetzung der bestehenden Stabilitätsverhältnisse eindeutig durch das Prinzip der unabhängigen Motivierung von Flexionsklassen **determiniert** und daher auch **vorhersagbar**.

6. Die beiden diskutierten morphologischen Natürlichkeitsprinzipien können sich im konkreten Fall **widersprüchlich zueinander verhalten**, d. h. gegeneinander wirken. Wir haben oben gezeigt, daß die

---

[13] Bei der Pluralbildung des Typs *das Schema — die Schema-ta* liegt übrigens keine Stamm-, sondern Grundformflexion vor; ihre Flexion ist also hinsichtlich dieser Eigenschaft durchaus systemangemessen.

Tendenz zur Einführung von Pluralmarkern am Wort selbst wie bei *die Onkel > die Onkel-s/Onkel-n* durch das Prinzip der typologischen Einheitlichkeit und Systematik bedingt ist. Wenn man jedoch diesen Fall unter dem Gesichtspunkt der Flexionsklassenstabilität betrachtet, dann sieht man sofort, daß bei den auf *-el, -en, -er, -chen* und *-lein* endenden Maskulina und Neutra die ø-Pluralklasse des Typs *der Spiegel — die Spiegel* wesentlich stärker belegt ist als die *n*-Pluralklasse des Typs *der Bauer — die Bauer-n* bzw. die *s*-Pluralklasse. Das heißt, daß die ø-Klasse die stabile und die *n*- bzw. *s*-Klasse die zugehörige instabile Flexionsklasse darstellt. Das Prinzip der unabhängigen Motivierung von Flexionsklassen müßte also eigentlich Übergänge in gegenläufiger Richtung wie *die Bauer-n > *die Bauer* bewirken. Dem ist jedoch nicht so. Die stabile, aber nichtsystemangemessene ø-Pluralklasse nimmt zwar noch Neuwörter wie etwa *Blazer* oder *Computer*, aber keine Wörter aus der zugehörigen instabilen, aber systemangemessenen *s*- bzw. *n*-Klasse auf. Die tatsächlich stattfindenden Übergänge erfolgen von der nichtsystemangemessenen in die systemangemessene Klasse. Wenn also im gegebenen Fall die beiden diskutierten Natürlichkeitsprinzipien in gegensätzliche Richtungen weisen, dann setzt sich, wie auch andere Beispielfälle zeigen, das Prinzip der typologischen Einheitlichkeit und Systematik gegen das Prinzip der unabhängigen Motivierung von Flexionsklassen durch.[14] Auch hier bleibt die Vorhersagbarkeit erhalten.[15]

7. Wenn wir jetzt zur eingangs gestellten Frage zurückkehren, in welchem Grade Sprachveränderungen vorhersagbar sind, so läßt sich bezogen auf die Flexionsmorphologie das folgende feststellen.

Auf der Basis des (hier nur grob skizzierten) Natütlichkeitskonzepts sind — zumindest für einen beachtlichen Faktenbereich — begründete Vorhersagen darüber möglich, welche Veränderungen in einem gegebenen Flexionssystem mit seinen spezifischen Struktureigenschaften zu erwarten sind. Diese Feststellung gilt unter der Voraussetzung, daß überhaupt morphologische Veränderungen eintreten: Zwar machen

---

[14] Man beachte, daß durch die Überführung der ø-Plurale in die *s*- bzw. *n*-Pluralklasse auch hier die Entwicklung in Richtung auf eine unabhängige Motivierung der Flexionsklassenzugehörigkeit verläuft, nur wird nicht der von der Flexionsklassenstabilität favorisierte 'kürzere Weg' zu den ø-Pluralen, sondern der von der übergeordneten Systemangemessenheit favorisierte 'längere Weg' zu den *s*- bzw *n*-Pluralen gewählt.

[15] Das gilt offenbar auch für Konstellationen, in denen jeweils zwei andere der obenerwähnten Natürlichkeitsprinzipien gegeneinanderwirken. Vgl. dazu Wurzel 1984: 173ff.

bestimmte strukturelle Konstellationen Sprachveränderungen sehr wahrscheinlich, aber auch der natürlichste Sprachwandel kann sich letztendlich immer nur unter entsprechenden sozialen Bedingungen durchsetzen.[16]

Vorhersagbar sind jeweils Veränderungsprozesse im System ebenso wie das Nichteintreten von gegenläufigen Veränderungsprozessen. Die stattfindenden Veränderungsprozesse haben faktisch gesetzmäßigen Charakter; sie laufen unabhängig vom Willen des einzelnen Sprechers ab. Wie im gesamten gesellschaftlichen Bereich gibt es auch hier keine mechanische Determiniertheit für das Einzelereignis. So läßt sich eben nicht begründet prognostizieren, bis wann und mit welcher Reihenfolge von Detailveränderungen sich ein morphologischer Veränderungsprozeß vollzieht. Die Gesetzmäßigkeit kommt nicht den Einzelveränderungen zu, sondern den sich in ihnen durchsetzenden allgemeinen Entwicklungstendenzen. Vorhersagen läßt sich – wie vorgeführt – der Abbau von nichtsystemangemessenen morphologischen Erscheinungen und von instabilen Flexionsklassen,[17] nicht aber der genaue Zeitpunkt der Veränderung einer bestimmten Form oder auch der Beendigung des Gesamtprozesses sowie die Reihenfolge der Einzelveränderungen. So kann zwar vorhergesagt werden, daß es im Dtsch. einmal keine Kasusflexive am Substantiv mehr geben wird, nicht aber beispielsweise, wann genau der Marker /n/ des D./A. Sg. endgültig verschwunden sein wird oder zu welchem Zeitpunkt alle substantivischen Kasusflexive abgebaut sein werben und ebensowenig, ob zuerst das Flexiv /s/ des G. Sg. oder das Flexiv /n/ des D. Pl. beseiligt sein Abschließend müssen noch zwei wichtige die Vorhersagbarkeit wird usw. Abschließend müssen noch zwei wichtige die Vorhersagberkeit einschränkende Faktoren geflannt werden.

Ersten ist hier auf die Rolle des phonologischen Wandels zu verweisen: Bestimmte phonologische Veränderungen wirken sich auch auf das Flexionssystem aus. Durch phonologischen Wandel werden sowohl systemdefinierende Struktureigenschaften als auch die Stabilität von Flexionsklassen (oder Teilflexionsklassen) verändert, wodurch sich dann entsprechend auch die Entwicklungstendenzen des Systems ver-

---

[16] Ist allerdings ein Flexionssystem erst einmal 'in Bewegung geraten', dann kann man davon ausgehen, daß die strukturell angelegten Veränderungen auch stattfinden. Das ist die Situation in modernen Nhdtsch.

[17] Es ist möglich, daß solche Abbauerscheinungen nicht völlig konsequent zu Ende geführt werden, sondern sich bestimmte 'suppletionsverdächtige Reste' ansonsten abgebauter Erscheinungen erhalten.

ändern. Beispielsweise vollzog sich die Veränderung der ursprünglich systemangemessenen Kasusflexive am Substantiv in nicht mehr systemangemessene, d. h. zum morphologischen Abbau tendierende Marker bedingt durch phonologische Reduktionsprozesse in den unbetonten Wortausgängen. Die Maskulina auf /e/ vom Typ *Hase* bilden eine stabile Flexionsklasse; der phonologisch bedingte Verlust des /e/ bei einem Teil von ihnen wie bei *Hirte > Hirt* macht diese nun auf Konsonant endenden Wörter zu einer instabilen Klasse, deren Wörter folgerichtig zum Übergang in die stabile *e*-Pluralklasse tendieren (vgl. dazu Abschn. 4). Wenn also einschlägige phonologische Veränderungen eintreten, so werden worher abgegebene begründete Voraussagen über künftige morphologische Veränderungen gegenstandslos. Es sind dann allerdings neue begründete Voraussagen möglich.

Zweitens sind natürlich morphologische Veränderungen, die auf S p r a c h- und D i a l e k t m i s c h u n g, N o r m i e r u n g u. ä. beruhen, nicht im System angelegt und entziehen sich daher einer von den Systemeigenschaften ausgehenden Vorhersage.

8. Woher kommt es nun, daß zumindest ein großer Teil der Sprachveränderungen in eine bestimmte, vorhersagbare Richtung geht? Die natürliche Sprache stellt ein der gesellschaftlichen Kommunikation dienendes funktionales System dar, das an die psychisch-physische Ausstattung des Menschen gebunden ist. Doch nicht alle grammatischen Systeme, Teilsysteme und Strukturen sind gleichermeßen gut erlernbar und in der Kommunikation handhabbar. Sie sind für die Sprecher unterschiedlich zweckmäßig, d. h. unterschiedlich natürlich. Daraus ergibt sich das Bestreben der Sprecher, ihre Sprache zu 'optimieren'. Das ist Grund und Zweck aller durch die Struktur des Systems vorgegebenen Sprachveränderungen.

Daß eine solche 'Optimierung' immer nur lokal und oft zu Lasten anderer Bereiche des Sprachsystems erreichbar wird, liegt daran, daß es für das Sprachsystem keine einheitlichen 'Optimierungsparameter' gibt. Die verschiedenen 'Optimierungsparameter', d. h. die Natürlichkeitsprinzipien, verhalten sich widersprüchlich zueinander. So sind bekanntermaßen Morphologie und Phonologie einer Sprache nicht zugleich 'optimierbar'. Aufgrund der Widersprüchlichkeit der Natürlichkeitsprinzipien wird niemals ein 'idealer' Sprachzustand erreicht; die Sprachveränderung geht weiter, solange eine Sprache existiert.

Auch die morphologischen Veränderungen des hier behandelten Typs sind ihrem Wesen nach 'Optimierungen', genauer: S y s t e m a t i s i e r u n g e n des F l e x i o n s s y s t e m s. Sie bestehen im Abbau von nichtfunktionaler grammatischer Komplexität (nichtfunktionalen Distinktionen) im System und sind entsprechend zweckerichtet. Solche morphologischen Veränderungen — wie ein großer Teil der Sprachveränderungen überhaupt — sind deshalb nicht zufällig, sondern beruhen auf den spezifischen 'Mängeln' des Systems und den in eine bestimmte Richtung weisenden Natürlichkeitsprinzipien. Sprachveränderungen sind in hohem Maße durch schon heute bekannte Faktoren determiniert und daher weitgehend vorhersagbar, was hier am Beispiel der Flexionsmorphologie demonstriert werden sollte. Es ist ein wichtiges Anliegen der natürlichen Grammatik, die dem zugrunde liegenden Zusammenhänge künftig noch genauer und umfassender zu erfassen.

LITERATURANGABEN

Hörz, Herbert. 1974. *Der dialektische Determinismus in Natur und Gesellschaft*. Berlin: Deutscher Verlag der Wissenschaften.
Mayerthaler, Willi. 1981. *Morphologische Natürlichkeit*. Linguistische Forschungen 28. Wiesbaden: Athenaion.
Wurzel, Wolfgang Ullrich. 1982. *Flexionsmorphologie und Natürlichkeit. Ein Beitrag zur morphologischen Theoriebildung*. Studia Grammatica, XXI, Berlin: Akademieverlag.
1983. "Thesen zur morphologischen Natürlichkeit". In *Zeitschrift für Germanistik* 2/83, 196—208.

SUMMING UP

ANDERS AHLQVIST

To sum up a conference as successful as this one is no mean task.[1] This success is of course primarily due to Professor Jacek Fisiak and all his helpers, whose work has, to put it mildly, not been helped by the fact that far too many colleagues have registered but not turned up, either for genuine so-called administrative reasons or others, that it would be futile to speculate about. It is clear that they lost much by not coming: apart from the many fine papers we have heard during the week, they have also been losers in not experiencing the relaxed and tolerant atmosphere during the week. This point is worth insisting upon: we have been able to interact very well, regardless of country of origin. More significantly, however, colleagues with rather different theoretical persuasions have, here in Poznań, been willing to try to talk to each other. To be sure, there have been difficulties in this respect, not because of our use of the three congress languages, but rather (one of you has asked me to mention this here) because linguistics still remains such a fragmented branch of scholarship. Thus, we all have our own varieties, not to say idiolects, of "linguisticese", to coin a word only moderately less well-formed than the one we have in the name of our discipline. Nevertheless, the effort made here to overcome these problems has been one of the many praiseworthy features of our meeting.

In order to say something about the papers themselves, we may begin with phonology. A number of potentially fairly radical proposals have been made here, some of which may yet change the proto-shapes, so to speak, of the languages in question. This refers, in a particular way, to the papers by Fred Peng, Theo Vennemann and Michael Job, dealing

---

[1] This time, so many good abstracts had been submitted that the programme had to be organised in sections: I am most grateful to colleagues who offered valuable comments on some, but not all of the papers I could not hear myself. However, I alone must take the responsibility for all failures to mention valuable contributions, instances of excessive bias and the other deficiencies in this paper.

respectively with early Japanese, Proto-Germanic and Indo-European itself. Phenomena less remote in time have also been discussed, as for instance in Ernst Håkon Jahr's paper on Modern Norwegian. On the way from phonology to morphology, we have been privileged to hear Eugene Holman's comprehensive account of consonant gradation in Finnish and its process of grammaticalization. In this regard, it seems appropriate to mention Raymond Hickey's valuable contribution to the discussion. As he rightly pointed out, there are some functional similarities between the consonant gradation of Finnish and the initial mutations of Irish,[2] so that one may quite properly refrain from feeling so very disturbed by some of the madder looking alternations that Holman described. Another of the papers bridging phonology and morphology was that given by Wolfgang Dressler, explaining language-specific uunnatural phenomena diachronically as accidents.

Andrew Carstairs has contributed a description of the evolution of the Latin 3rd declension, which was most illuminating, not least because of his purposeful use of the evidence furnished by the ancient grammarian Varro. This reminded us that the beginning of linguistics proper cannot be dated, as some colleagues would have insisted even a couple of years back, to 1965, nor to 1957, nor even (as one used to be told by some classical philologists) to 1786. The history of linguistics has also featured otherwise during the conference. Firstly, in the way we have come to expect from him, Konrad Koerner has reminded us of the importance of de Saussure's *Mémoire*... Also, Kurt Jankowsky has dealt with Scherer's importance for the understanding of historical linguistics during the nineteenth century.

To serve as a link between morphology and syntax, we have had Eric Hamp's very interesting proposal regarding the explanation of a particularly thorny problem of Welsh etymology. This is of course not the place to judge the issue, except to stress that this paper was an example of how one may apply the well-known principle,[3] according to which yesterday's syntax is today's morphology. In a sense, this was also a theme in Martin Harris's paper, in which he gave us a lucid and commendably cautious attempt to look at some possible future changes in the word order of French. One feature he has discussed also came up in Werner Winter's lively discussion of the earliest patterns of

---

[2] As I have pointed out elsewhere (1982), the chief difference, from a structural point of view, is one of sequence.

[3] See for instance Givón 1971: 413 (and cf. n. 1); I am indebted to Martti Nyman for help with locating this reference.

word order in Indo-European, namely how a "topic" may, from its original position before the core sentence (and **not** part of it), change into an integral part of it. In such a case, the basic word order naturally also changes. In addition to this, Harris has very properly insisted on the bound nature of elements such as the unstressed subject and object pronouns in French, so that the new word order is that, not of the morphemes making up the stress group around a verb, but of major constituents, some of which originally belonged outside the core sentence. Similar developments may be observed in other languages. Modern Irish supplies a good example of how an apparent anomaly, syntactically speaking, is readily explained when looked upon in this fashion. Thus one may consider:

1) *Fuair Breandán a mhála ar ais i bPoznań aréir*
and
1a) *Fuair sé ar ais i bPoznań aréir é*

These[4] illustrate a feature of Modern Irish syntax, which may be described as follows. If the object of a sentence in Irish is a pronoun, it may follow after quite lengthy adverbials at the end of the sentence, but if the object is a noun, only a subject may be slotted in before it and after the verb. Synchronically speaking, there seems to exist no very simple way of describing this feature. The historical explanation, on the other hand, is quite simple. We need but look at a Middle Irish example like:

2) *do-s· ber diabul fo smacht **iat***

This has both the infixed pronoun (*-s·*) that is normal in Classical Old Irish and the indepedent one (*iat* = later *iad*) in the position one would expect of it nowadays. Thus one may not unreasonably infer that the final position of the object pronoun in Midle and Modern Irish is due to it originally having been used, by what Harris here has called right-dislocation, to reinforce the infixed pronoun, which itself now has disappeared from the language. Its conterpart in Modern French, on the other hand, is still with us, so that the literal translation of 2) into that language comes as no surprise:

---

[4] 1) means 'Breandán got his suitcase back in Poznań last night' and 1a) 'he (=*sé*) got it (=*é*) back...'. These two sentences I have made up myself for this presentation; although I believe them to be acceptable ones in Modern Irish, the reader may prefer to consult a fuller account of mine (1976), which supplies some possibly more genuine data with references, including that relating to 2).

2a) *Le diable les met en son pouvoir, eux*

Martin Harris has also addressed himself to another matter, which all of us here today may regard as painfully obvious, even if it unfortunately is not always so to the world at large: what practical use is historical linguistics? In his case, he has pointed to the natural implications of what he has said for the teaching of languages. This point also came up in Niedzielski's paper dealing with what he called the logical neuter in French. Here too, the importance of history emerged very clearly. Also, the reference to gender reminds me of another possible practical application for our discipline, namely to help language planners to exercise sound judgement in their to my mind quite important work. Recently, a presumably quite well-meaning but in my opinion most misguided proposal[5] was made towards removing what is seen as the androcentric bias and discriminatory nature of grammatical gender in German. According to this, one ought to re-arrange the forms existing in the language so as to use the neuter article *das* to make *das Professor* into the normal mode of expression for situations when, as is of course normally the case, the sex of the person referred to is of no importance, reserving *die Professor* and *der Professor* for cases when that peculiarity has to be made explicit. However, it seems to me that this proposal fails to take into account the long history of how gender has been grammaticalized in the Indo-European and other languages. If there is any difference between the status of women in German-speaking countries and that pertaining to English-speaking ones, it is surely not due to the use of *der*, *die* and *das* in the former as against that of mere *the* in the latter. Also, I am quite confident that no such difference of status would be observed, were one to compare Swedish-speaking parts of Finland (where speakers make a distinction between *han* 'he' and *hon* 'she' to others, in which speakers of Finnish use the pronouns *hän* and *se*[6] to refer without discrimination to persons belonging to either sex.

In any case, Harris and Winter were by no means the only speakers to deal with word order. Mirja Saari has shown us how fruitful the careful study of a large corpus of data can be. This important feature of

---

[5] This (Pusch 1980: 71) was published together with a number of other thought-provoking contributions of a similar nature.
[6] Interestingly, although this pronoun in the literary language still only means 'it', the spoken language is increasingly often using it instead of *hän* 'he, she' (cf. further Saukkonen 1967: I owe this reference to Fred Karlsson).

Saari's work is a theme that Wolfgang Viereck has mentioned, when he contrasted the importance of collecting data and that of building theories, especially ones not supported by reliable data or some other kind of real facts. I have already once referred to the amiable atmosphere at this conference: I believe that it has helped fairly substantially towards putting matters of this sort into what I personally would regard as their proper perspective. Another manifestation of the careful use of data was very evident in Witold Mańczak's presentation of the Indo-European numerals from 'sixty' upwards. He has shown convincingly that it is quite unnecessary to assume any Babylonian influence in this connexion. Like many others, his paper generated much interesting discussion, amongst other things about the origin of the vigesimal system of counting, as found in Western Europe, notably in Celtic and Danish, but also, to some extent, in English and French.[7]

If we look at the breadth of languages dealt with at the conference, it is of course natural that our organiser, who is himself such a distinguished specialist of English, should have attracted so many stimulating contributions to the study of this language, not only that of Elizabeth Closs Traugott (whose efficient running of 4. ICHL one remembers with much pleasure), but also those by Thomas Fraser, Hubert Gburek, Louis Goossens and Ruta Nagucka, in addition to which we are not at all likely to forget Suzanne Romaine's delicate treatment of word formation in English. Others, like Camiel Hamans and Johan Taeldeman, have given us food for thought about Dutch, Conradie a rare but very welcome opportunity to learn something about Afrikaans. Yet others, some of which I have already mentioned, have given us valuable contributions not only to the study of Celtic, Germanic, Italic and Indo-European generally, but also to that of Finnish, Japanese and other languages of the world. At the same time, we have been especially fortunate, as it seems to me, in getting an opportunity to learn something about the languages spoken in this part of the world, not only from distinguished Polish colleagues, such as Michał Hasiuk, Stanislas Kolbuszewski and Bogdan Walczak, but also from Jens Rasmussen of Copenhagen. Naturally enough, for an area like this one, language contact and area linguistics have featu-

---

[7] As one possible explanation for its occurence in these languages, he mentioned the possibility of a spontaneous development. A few years ago, I had the opportunity to hear something that points in this direction, from a child brought up to speak languages that normally lack this feature. Trying to count from the 20s into the 30s, my little informant proceeded as follows: *twenty, twenty-one, ..., twenty-eight, twenty-nine, twenty-ten, twenty-eleven, twenty-twelve,* etc.

red in some of the papers just mentioned, but we have also had some other treatments of these questions, notably so from Lyle Campbell, Andrei Danchev and Anna Giacalone Ramat.

One could go one, trying to summarise all that has been said here, but that is so impossible that it seems best to stop now, thus allowing the very failure of the summing up to emphasize the success of the conference itself. This success is due to two connected factors. The first is of course our friend Jacek Fisiak's long experience of organising meetings in a most professional way. The second has to do with his equally obvious skill as head of a large and very good university department, so that he has been able to get the unstinting help of numerous colleagues, students and many others. I believe that our discipline has taken a good step forward as a result of this conference. Like all other participants, I am most grateful to our Polish friends for making this possible.

REFERENCES

Ahlqvist, A. 1976. On the position of pronouns in Irish. *Éigse* 16. 171 – 76.
────── 1982. Suomen sijapäätteet ja iirin prepositiot: kontrastiivinen erittely [Finnish case-ending and Irish prepositions: a contrastive analysis]. *Acta Congressus Quinti Fenno-Ugristarum* VI, ed. by O. Ikola, K. Häkkinen, M. K. Suojanen, 345 – 9. Turku-Åbo: Suomen Kielen Seura.
Givón, T. 1971. Historical syntax and synchronic morphology: an archaeologist's field trip. *Papers from the Seventh Regional Meeting*, ed. by D. Adams et al., 394 – 415. Chicago: Linguistic Society.
Pusch, L. F. 1980. Das Deutsche als Männersprache: Diagnose und Therapievorschläge. *Linguistische Berichte* 69. 59 – 74.
Saukkonen, P. 1967. Persoonapronominien *hän*: *se, he* : *ne* distinktiivi oppositio [Die distinktive Opposition der Personalpronomina *hän* : *se, he* : *ne*]. *Virittäjä* 71. 286 – 92.

INDEX OF LANGUAGES
(LANGUAGE FAMILIES, DIALECTS)

Afrikaans 71 - 81, 605
Aquatec 381
Albanian 7, 17, 18, 44, 86, 123, 350
Alemannian 358, 530
Altaic 5, 423
American English 561 - 9
Amharic 203
Anatolian Greek 106, 107, 116, 117, 121, 124
Ancient (Classical) Greek 19, 107, 109, 111, 118, 120, 318, 319, 320
Anglian 141
Arabic 42, 47, 87, 208, 515
Araucanian 38
Armenian 41, 318, 358, 442, 443, 542
Austronesian 420, 423, 424
Avestan 208, 209, 214, 318
Aymara 38, 516

Baltic 7, 8, 9, 10, 354, 359, 360, 361, 363, 430, 443, 444, 445, 448, 449, 542, 543
Balto-Slavic 7, 8, 9, 10, 17, 338, 441 - 9
Bantu 40, 41, 255, 256, 257, 258, 259, 260
Basque 37
Bavarian 358, 530
Beembe 540
Bella Bella 390
Belorussian 8, 12, 13
Berber 6
Black English 467 - 85
Brabantic 494
Breton 44, 47
Bulgarian 13, 14, 17, 19, 84, 85, 86, 87, 88, 89, 91, 95, 100, 356
Bushman 40

Cappadocian 112, 113, 114, 118, 119, 120
Catalan 356
Caucasian 5, 41, 253
Celtic 10, 434, 445, 542, 543, 605
Chadic 6
Chemakuan 41, 47, 390
Chemakum 390, 391
Chinese 88, 578
Chinookan 47
Chipewyan 540, 541
Chuj 381
Chukchee 385, 388
Chukotko-Kamchatkan 383, 387
Coast Salish 47
Common Baltic 8
Common Bantu 41
Common Slavic 4, 8, 9, 10, 86
Copi 256, 258
Creek 45
Croatian 42
Cushitic 6, 37, 47
Czech 10, 42, 91, 356, 431

Dakhani Urdu 47
Danish 17, 203, 294, 357, 358, 605
Dravidian 5, 32, 37, 38, 43, 47, 260, 420, 423, 424
Dutch 72, 75, 186, 203, 213, 224, 225, 226, 228, 229, 232, 357, 489, 496, 605
Duwamish 41
Dyirbal 381

Early Common Slavic 5
Early Latvian 8
East Baltic 441

INDEX OF LANGUAGES

East Germanic 15, 16
East Lekhitic 12
East Nordic 16
East Pomeranian 12
East Scandinavian 17
East Slavic 11, 13, 13
Eastern Algonquian 46
Eastern Armenian 537
Eastern Cheremise 228
Eastern Pomo 41
Egyptian 6
Elamo-Dravidian 5
English 32, 45, 84, 85, 86, 87, 88, 91, 92, 99, 132, 139 - 47, 149 - 70, 202, 203, 204, 207, 208, 214, 219, 241, 245, 267, 269, 270, 272, 273, 274, 277, 292, 293, 297, 315, 351, 353, 355, 356, 357, 358, 359, 361, 365, 384, 396, 398, 399, 400, 401, 402, 404, 405, 430, 432, 434, 451 - - 65, 515, 516, 519, 523, 530, 540, 563, 564, 566, 578, 580, 605
Eskimo 393, 516
Estonian 288, 516

Faroese 16, 358
Finnish 39, 44, 45, 86, 281 - 90, 318, 535, 602, 604, 605
Finno-Ugric 351, 355
Flemish 490, 492, 493, 494
Frankish 47
Frankish 47
French 44, 47, 84, 85, 87 88, 91 99 100, 129, 131, 134, 135, 137, 235 - 47, 315, 348, 356, 357, 361, 451, 452, 453, 462, 463, 464, 516, 549 - 59, 576, 577, 578, 579, 580, 581, 582, 602, 603, 604, 505
Frisian 530, 535

German 42, 44, 84, 86, 88, 91, 100, 187, 201, 202, 203, 213, 226, 245, 269, 270, 274, 309, 355, 537, 431, 436, 452, 453, 464, 502, 505, 516, 517, 524, 547 - 46, 555, 578, 587, 593, 597, 604
Germanic 5, 10, 15, 16, 17, 92, 95, 131, 133, 142, 212, 213, 224, 260, 261, 274, 303, 308, 318, 330, 350, 357, 358, 359, 430, 534, 452, 464, 527 - 46, 605
Goiriku 40

Gothic 15, 16, 131, 318, 330, 347, 350, 356, 358, 360, 443, 444, 446, 452, 517, 527, 528, 530, 533, 534
Greco-Italic 330, 333
Greek 4, 17, 18, 19, 42, 44, 47, 91, 107, 108, 118, 119, 121, 122, 134, 315, 316, 317, 319, 320, 330, 332, 335, 336, 338, 339, 347, 349, 350, 356, 357, 360, 443, 444, 445, 446, 447, 449, 517, 524, 527, 528, 534, 542
Gullah 561
Gutnish 16
Guugu-Yimidirr 381

Haida 386, 538
Hamitic 5
Hamito-Semitic 338
Hausa 521
Hebrew 91, 99
High German 5, 351, 358, 359, 527
Hittite 7, 332, 338, 339, 444, 543
Hottentot 40, 257, 260
Hungarian 86, 94, 184, 185, 186, 379, 578

Icelandic 203, 358
Indic 528, 534
Indo-Aryan 31, 32, 37, 38, 43, 47
Indo-European 5, 6, 7, 10, 15, 17, 18, 19, 38, 131, 137, 325, 329, 332, 335, 336, 337, 338, 339, 340, 347 - 52, 356, 358, 360, 424, 430, 441 - 9, 456, 464, 524, 534, 542, 602, 603, 604, 605
Indo-Hittite 7
Indo-Iranian 5, 313, 318, 351, 443, 449
Iranian 38
Irish 267, 272, 273, 274, 602, 603
Irish English 47
Iroquoian 46, 316, 317, 381
Italian 42, 95, 171 - 80, 320, 348, 350, 356, 431, 432, 435, 576, 582
Italic 10, 445, 605
Ixil 381
Izurian 288

Japanese 355, 410, 412, 417, 418, 419, 420, 421, 422, 423, 424, 605
Jaqaru 531

INDEX OF LANGUAGES

Kabardian 540, 541
Kajkavian 187
Kalenjin 221
Kamchadal 383, 384
Kanjobal 381
Kanuri 515
Kartvelian 5
Kashubian 11, 12, 17
Kathlamet 390
K'ekchi 538
Kentish 141
Kharia 381, 382
Khmer-Nicobar 370
Khosan 257
Klamath 47
Kootenai 390
Korean 534, 535
Koryak 387, 388
Kunjen 382
Kusaiean 366, 369, 379
Kwa 356
Kwakiutl 47, 390, 391
Kwangari 40
Lakhota 369, 370, 381
Lappish 45
Late Latin 18
Late Proto-Indo-European 7, 8, 9, 10
Latin 3, 16, 19, 57 - 70, 129, 130, 131, 132, 133, 135, 136, 137, 141, 179, 274, 330, 332, 339, 347, 348, 349, 350, 351, 356, 357, 360, 361, 431, 452, 461, 462, 463, 464, 515, 524, 527, 528, 534, 542, 543, 576, 603
Latvian 354, 360, 361, 363, 441, 442, 445
Lekhiti 11, 12
Lithuanian 350, 354, 358, 360, 361, 441, 442, 443, 444, 445, 446, 447, 448, 449
Livonian 44, 285
Low Franconian 530
Low German 17, 92, 269, 351, 530, 535
Luiseno 538
Lushai 37

Macedonian 13, 14, 17, 19, 356
Maidu 47
Makah 41, 43, 390
Makua 257
Malay 356
Malayalam 45
Malayo-Polynesian 423
Mam 381
Mamean 44
Maori 192, 193, 194, 195, 539
Marathi 45
Mayan 39, 379, 381
Mbukushu 40
Melanesian 355, 356
Micronesian 366
Middle Danish 358
Middle Dutch 358
Middle English 87, 92, 94, 96, 139, 142, 143, 144, 145, 146, 158, 269, 274, 277, 358, 451, 458, 461, 462, 464, 516, 519, 562, 563
Middle Indo-Aryan 42
Middle Irish 603
Middle Low German 16, 357, 358
Middle Persian 211
Mixtec 53
Mohawk 384
Moldavian 18
Munda 379, 381, 382

Na-Dane 386
Nama 500, 541
Navaho 538
Ndebele 40, 256
Neo-Melanesian 464
Neoštokavian 188, 189, 191
Nez Perce 538, 540
Ngadha 355
Ngandi 374, 375, 376, 377, 381
Nguni 256, 257, 258, 259
Nicobarese 3*b*0
Nitinat 41, 43, 390
Nootka 41, 43, 390, 391, 393
Nordic 15
Norse 16
North Germanic 15, 16, 141
Northern Greek 106, 107, 108, 109, 110, 111, 114, 115, 116, 117, 119, 122, 124
Northern Kannada 45
Norwegian 17, 291 - 300, 351, 358, 602
Nostratic 5, 6, 337

Old Bulgarian 13

Old Church Slavic 4, 13, 350, 351, 356, 358, 443, 445, 446, 447, 448, 449

Old Danish 16, 92
Old English 94, 99, 129 - 37, 139, 142, 145, 149 - 70, 204, 267 - 79, 357, 358, 398, 402, 403, 404, 405, 451, 452, 461, 462, 464, 516, 517, 518, 519, 520, 534, 535
Old French 95, 356, 359
Old Frisian 534
Old Germanic 16, 224
Old Gotlandic 16
Old High German 92, 270, 304, 358, 443, 452, 453, 505, 527, 528, 530, 531, 532, 533, 534, 544
Old Icelandic 16, 358, 530, 531, 532, 534
Old Indic 543
Old Indo-Aryan 42
Old Iranian 208, 351
Old Irish 267 - 79, 347, 349, 350, 358, 561, 603
Old Italian 171 - 80
Old Latin 448
Old Lithuanian 446
Old Norse 131, 293, 519
Old Norwegian 16
Old Persian 208
Old Polish 12
Old Prussian 8, 360, 441, 443, 445, 447
Old Saxon 270
Old Scandinavian 16, 17, 94
Old Swedish 16
Omotic 6
Ossetic 41
Özbek 48

Patwin 41
Pawnee 385
Permian 47
Permic 47
Persian 199 - 215, 516, 578
Phrygian 7, 443, 445
Phuti 258
Pipil 45
Pitta-Pitta 381
Polish 8, 12, 13, 356, 401, 572, 573, **574**, 575, 576, 577, 578, 579, 580, 581

Polynesian 355
Pomeranian-Polabian 12
Pontic 112, 113, 119
Portuguese 348, 350, 356
Pre-Finnic 283
Pre-Indo-European 7, 338
Proto-Afroasiatic 6
Proto-Algonquian 46
Proto-Anatolian 7
Proto-Bantu 40, 257
Proto-Dravidian 43
Proto-Finnic 281, 283, 284, 285, 286, 287
Proto (Primitive)-Germanic 15, 141, 213, 303, 304, 348, 527, 528, 529, 533, 534, 536, 543, 602
Proto-Greek 444
Proto-Indo-European 6, 313 - 21, 323, 331, 332, 333, 335, 338, 340, 351, 352, 415, 446, 447, 527, 528, 529, 541, 543, 544, 545
Proto-Japanese 409 - 24
Proto-Nootkan 41
Proto-Nordic 3, 15
Proto-Slavic 5, 8, 9, 348, 448
Puqet Sound Salish 41

Quechua 38, 516, 537
Quichean 39, 44
Quileute 41, 390, 391

Red American English 561, 563, 564, 566, 567
Romance 18, 19, 95, 348, 350, 351, 355, 356, 432, 435
Romany (Gipsy) 351
Rumanian 15, 17, 18, 19, 86, 88, 91, 348, 356
Rusin 11, 12, 13, 43
Russian 12, 44, 75, 47, 84, 85, 86, 87, 88, 91, 99, 100, 351, 356, 362, 384, 576, 578, 593

Sahaptian 47
Salish 41, 47, 390, 392
Sanskrit 37, 130, 131, 315, 316, 318, 391, 323, 332, 335, 338, 350, 430, 446, 527, 542, 544, 545

INDEX OF LANGUAGES

Scandinavian 15, 16, 17, 44, 203, 213, 351, 358, 359
Scots 140, 146
Semitic 5, 6, 336, 337, 338
Serbo-Croatian 11, 13, 14, 17, 19, 91, 187, 188, 356
Shasta-Achomawi 47
Shona 254, 256, 260, 262
Shoshoni 45, 47
Sinhala 31, 32
Sinhalese 224
Sino-Tibetan 95
Slavic 4, 5, 7, 8, 9, 10, 11, 17, 38, 47, 87, 95, 109, 187, 188, 330, 355, 356, 362, 430, 431, 443, 444, 445, 446, 448, 449, 542, 543, 572, 573
Slavonian 190, 191
Slovak 10, 13, 95
Snohomish 41
Snoqualmie 41
So:ra: 365
Sotho 40, 255, 258
South Munda 379
South Slavic 10, 11, 13
Southeast Lekhitic 12
Southern Bantu 252, 253, 255, 257, 258, 259, 260, 261, 262, 263
Southern Greek 107, 108, 109, 116, 123
Southern Oriya 45
Spanish 37, 38, 39, 40, 45, 245, 348, 350, 351, 356, 516, 577, 578
Sranan 356
Stokavian 188
Swahili 356, 515
Swati 40
Swazi 256, 259
Swedish 17, 45, 86, 203, 260, 270, 358, 358
Swiss German 540

Tamil 45, 420, 423, 424
Tarascan 255
Tavgy 540
Teke 540
Telugu 45, 47
Teotepeque Pipil 45
Tewa 372, 373
Tocharian 358, 444, 445, 543

Tok Pisin 98, 464
Tonkawa 539
Torlak 17, 18, 19
Totonac 538
Tsimshian 47
Tswa 256
Tulu 45
Turkic 86, 87, 95, 100
Turkish 18, 44, 84, 86, 87, 100, 222, 223, 320, 379, 380, 578

Ukrainian 11, 12, 13, 578
Uralic 5, 43, 47
Uralo-Altaic 95
Uto-Aztecan 355, 357

Vedic 444, 446, 447, 516
Venda 256, 258, 260, 261
Vepsian 285
Vodian 288
Vulgar Latin 18, 356, 359

Wakashan 41, 390
Walmatjari 381
Wappo 41
Washo 47
Welsh 293, 356, 357, 602
West Baltic 8
West Germanic 15, 16, 141, 142, 270
West Lekhitic 12
West Nordic 16
West Saxon 141, 268
West Scandinavian 17
West Slavic 10, 11, 12
Wiyot 539
Wolof 540, 541

Xhosa 40, 255, 256

Yana 47
Yiddish 94, 499 - 513
Yir-Yoront 381
Younger Avestan 209, 210, 211, 214
Yucatec 381

Zulu 40, 254, 255, 256, 257, 258, 259, 262
Zyrian 47

INDEX OF NAMES

Acson, V. 105 - 26
Adams, D. R. 112, 117, 125, 606
Adrados, F. R. 7, 20
Ahlqvist, A. 102, 248, 438, 439, 601 - 6
Aitchison, J. 97, 98, 101
Aitken, A. J. 146, 147
Akmajian, A. 406
Alekseev, M. P. 104
Alessio, G. 571, 583
Alleyne, M. C. 562, 567
Althaus, H. P. 51
Altman, H. 245, 248
Andersen, H. 1, 20, 38, 49, 83, 84, 89, 90, 93, 101, 184, 188, 194, 196, 536, 546
Anderson, J. M. 101, 104, 147, 264, 270, 279, 546
Anderson, S. R. 299
Andriotis, N. T. 112, 113, 125
Antinucci, F. 436, 438
Antonsen, E. H. 92, 101
Anttila, R. 48, 93, 101, 118, 125, 520, 525
Aoki, H. 27, 49
Arbeitman, Y. 320, 321
Arcaini, E. 88
Ard, J. 398, 399, 406
Arlotto, A. 332, 342
Aronoff, M. 452, 453, 454, 455, 457, 465
Ashby, J. 236, 240, 241, 24*b*, 248
Auty, R. 13, 20
Awedyk, W. 92, 93, 101

Babiniotis, G. D. 118, 125
Bach, E. 497
Bailard, J. 235, 236, 237, 238, 239, 242, 243, 248
Bailey, C.-J. 249

Bailey, R. A. 258, 263, 463, 465
Baldinger, K. 457, 465
Bally, C. 328, 341, 344
Baltaxe, C. A. M. 104
Bartelt, H. G. 563, 567
Bartholomae, C. 209, 215
Bartoli, M. 25, 49
Batti*l*ti, C. 57, 1583
Baudouin de Courtenay, J. 5, 99, 573, 583
Bauer, L. 453, 455, 46*J*
Baugh, A. C. 464, 465, 565, 567
Bauman, R. 33, 55
Bech, G. 443, 450
Bechtel, F. 306, 310
Becker, H. 26, 28, 49
Bell, A. 126
Benko, L. 102, 197
Bennet, W. H. 92, 101
Benveniste, E. 7, 20, 129, 130, 339, 342
Bernstejn, S. B. 10, 20
Bertoni, G. 25, 49
Bezzenberger, A. 337
Bhat, D. N. S. 38, 41, 45, 49
Bichakjian, B. H. 95, 101
Bickerton, D. 353, 355, 363, 561, 566, 567
Bielmeier, R. 41, 49
Birnbaum, H. 1 - 24, 26, 49, 52
Bizoń, F. 582, 583
Blake, B. 205, 216, 381, 393
Bloch, O. 572, 583
Boas, F. 369, 393, 394
Boer, R. C. 223, 232
Bogoras, W. 387, 388, 389, 393
Bolinger, D. L. 353, 363
Bolozky, S. 98, 99, 101
Bomhard, A. R. 6, 7, 22, 316, 320, 321

Bonfante, G. 25, 49
Bopp, F. 6
Bosworth, J. 170
Brasch, W. M. 562, 563, 567
Braune, W. 310
van Bree, C. 224, 232
Brekle, H. E. 438
Brewer, J. P. 468, 486
Bricker, V. 381, 393
Bright, W. 27, 28, 29, 33, 48, 49, 52
Brinkmann, H. 504, 514
Broch, O. 295, 299
Brogyanyi, B. 327
Bruck, A. 180, 300
Brucke, E. 306
Brückner, A. 575, 583
Brugmann, K. 310, 311, 313, 320, 324, 329, 330, 333, 342, 350, 430
Brunner, K. 84, 99, 101, 347, 352
Bubak, J. 583
Burgschmidt, E. 139, 147
Burrow, T. 41, 42, 49, 320
Bybee, J. see Hooper, J. B.

Cable, T. 565, 567
Calaghan, C. 41, 49
Campbell, A. 142, 147, 273, 279
Campbell, L. 25 - 26, 90, 101, 429, 438, 606
Campbell, R. J. 180
Cardona, G. 450
Carstairs, A. 57 - 70, 602
Catford, J. C. 91, 101, 253, 254, 263
Chafe, W. 393, 524, 525
Chantraine, P. 572, 583
Chomsky, N. 95, 140, 147, 193, 196, 201, 203, 210, 212, 215, 278, 279, 396, 397, 398, 406, 429, 520, 522, 525, 552, 559
Chretien, C. D. 43, 50
Christea, T. 88
Christie, W. 50, 56, 406
Cienkowski, W. 575, 577, 582, 583
Cinque, G. 235, 244, 245, 246, 248
Civ'jan, T/ V. 20, 22
Clark, E. V. 521, 525
Clark, H. H. 520, 525
Clements, G. N. 223, 232

Coates, R. 69, 70
van Coetsem, F. 497
Cohen, P. 486
Cole, P. 170
Cole, R. W. 170
Coleman, L. 517, 525
Colinet, Ph. 494, 496
Collitz, H. 324
Comrie, B. 385, 393, 516
Conrad, A. 526
Conradie, C. S. 71 - 81, 605
Cooper, W. E. 248
Corominas, J. 571, 574, 583
Cortelazzo, M. 571, 583
Couvreur, W. 339
Cowgill, W. 7, 22
Crothers, J. 83, 90, 95, 96, 101, 121, 125
Culicover, P. W. 398, 406
Cuny, A. 326, 337, 338, 342
Curtin, P. D. 562, 567
Curtius, G. 327, 329
Cusatelli, G. 579, 583

Danchev, A. 83 - 101, 606
Dardano, M. 432, 438
Darnell, R. 27, 50
Dawkins, R. M. 44, 50, 112, 113, 125
Dayley, J. 379, 381, 393
DeBose, C. E. 563, 568
Decsy, G. 27, 50
De Grauwe, K. 490, 496
Delbrück, B. 310
Delorie, E. 369, 393
De Mauro, T. 433, 438
Devoto, G. 347, 352
Dezsö, L. 264
Di Paolo Healey, A. 170
Dickson, R. J. 568
Dik, E. S. 547
Dil, A. S. 51, 52
Dillard, J. L. 468, 486, 487, 561, 565
Dilthey, W. 307, 310
Dingwall, W. O. 181
Dirven, R. 149, 150, 170
Dixon, R. M. W. 379, 381, 393
Dobson, E. J. 145, 147
Doke, C. M. 254, 257, 260, 263

Donegan, P. 109, 125
Doroszewski, W. 571, 575, 576, 583
Downing, B. 205, 206, 215
Dozier, E. 372, 373, 393
Dressler, W. 50, 98, 105 - 26, 196, 300, 316, 320, 429, 431, 436, 438, 602
Driver, H. E. 35, 50
Dufriche Desgenettes, A. 333
Duličenko, A. D. 12, 22
Duncan-Rose, C. 569
Dunkel, G. 314, 320
Du Toit, H. A. 75
Dyen, I. 43

Ebeling, C. L. 190, 196
Eckman, F. 215
Eis, G. 347, 352
Ekwall, E. 277, 279
Elenski, J. 100, 101
Emeneau, M. B. 26, 27, 28, 34, 38, 41, 42, 45, 47, 50
Emonds, J. 208, 215
Endzelin, J. 441, 450
England, N. 393
Engler, R. 328, 341
Ernout, A. 59, 60, 62, 70, 572, 583

Falk, H. 357, 358, 363
Fasold, R. 468, 486
Feagin, C. 567
Felix, S. 439
Ferguson, C. 46, 54, 93, 251, 264, 525, 526, 563, 567, 568
Fick, A. 324, 327, 329, 335, 336, 337, 338, 342
Field, T. 116, 126
Filby, P. W. 565, 568
Filin, F. P. 9, 22
Filipović, R. 22, 88, 102
Fillmore, C. J. 149, 170
Fischer, O. 405, 406
Fischer, R. 550, 553, 558, 559
Fisiak, J. 22, 55, 83, 88, 89, 101, 102, 126, 127, 147, 215, 290, 439, 569, 576, 580, 583, 601, 606
Flier, M. S. 22
Fodor, J. 246, 248

Foley, J. 178, 179, 180, 192, 196, 291, 292, 293, 294, 296, 299
Fosteris, D. 112, 126
Fox, S. E. 126
Fraenkel, E. F. 448, 450
Francis, S. 39, 51
François, D. 248
Fraser, T. 129 - 38, 605
Fried, V. 148
Fujimura, O. 559

van der Gaaf, W. 403
Gair, J. 31, 32, 34, 51
Galabov, I. 86, 102
Gamkrelidze, T. 314, 320, 529, 546
Gautier, L. 344
Gburek, H. 139 - 48, 605
Georgios, C. 126
Gilbert, G. G. 568
Gilliéron, J. 25, 51
Gimson, A. C. 147
Givón, T. 253, 263, 457, 465, 516, 525, 602, 606
Gmür, R. 341, 342
Goddard, I. 46, 51
Gołąb, Z. 9, 22
Gonda, J. 524, 525
Goossens, J. 25, 51
Goossens, L. 149 - 70, 605
Gorbet, L. 34, 47, 51
Görlach, M. 147
Gornung, B. V. 22
Götz, D. 139, 147
Goyvaerts, D. 264, 300
de Grandis, R. 171 - 81
Grassmann, H. 528, 545, 546
Grayson, J. D. 71, 81
Green, G. M. 543, 546
Greenbaum, S. 406, 526
Greenberg, J. H. 43, 51, 184, 196, 215, 251, 252, 254, 263, 264, 515, 520, 525, 526, 540, 546
Greene, D. 279
Grimm, J. 301, 303, 304, 306, 307, 310, 527, 528, 529, 545, 546
Guberina, P. 22
Guilbert, L. 432, 438
Guillaume, G. 129, 130, 136, 138

INDEX OF NAMES

Gumperz, J. J. 34, 47, 51
Gundel, J. K. 238, 248
Gussmann, E. 126
Guthrie, M. 256, 264
Guxman, M. M. 103
Gvozdanović, J. 90, 102, 183 - 97

Haarmann, H. 28, 51
Haas, M. R. 27, 33, 41, 43, 45, 51, 393
Haider, H. 199 - 216
Haiman, J. 520, 521, 523, 525
Hajdu, P. 264
Hakulinen, L. 45, 52
Hall, R. A. 25, 52, 464, 465
Halle, M. 95, 140, 147, 193, 196, 217, 222, 223, 225, 226, 228, 233, 278, 279, 552, 559
Halliday, M. A. K. 523, 525
Hallowell, A. 51
Hamans, C. 87, 217 - 33, 605
Hamp, E. P. 33, 34, 43, 44, 52, 277, 279, 602
Hancock, I. 465
Hankamer, J. 395, 396, 400, 406
Harlow, R. B. 192, 197
Harms, R. T. 414, 424, 497
Harrington, J. P. 372, 373, 393
Harris, J. W. 180
Harris, M. 90, 102, 235 - 49, 435, 438, 602, 603, 604
Hart, J. 144, 147
Hasan, R. 523, 525
Hasiuk, M. 605
Hattori, S. 197
Haugen, E. 16, 17, 22, 292, 293, 294, 299
Hauptfleisch, D. C. 76, 81
Hauschild, R. 430, 439
Havet, L. 325, 327, 342, 343
Hawkins, J. 201, 215, 243, 248
Hawkins, O. W. 566, 568
Hayes, B. 228, 233
Heath, J. 374, 376, 377, 393
Heilmann, L. 22
Heinzel, R. 303, 311
Henderson, E. J. A. 26, 28, 37, 38, 41, 52
Henke, A. 576, 584
Henne, H. 51
Henry, R. 385, 394

Herbert, R. K. 251 - 65
Herzog, M. I. 104
Hesseling, D. C. 72, 81
Heusler, A. 94, 102
Hickey, R. 267 - 79, 602
Highfield, A. 568
Hill, C. 521, 525
Hill, J. H. 27, 41, 52, 437, 438
Hill, K. 437, 438
Hinnebusch, T. 255, 256, 264
Hirschbuhler, P. 235, 241, 242, 244, 248
Hirt, H. 326, 342, 347, 352
Hirtle, W. 129, 132, 138
Hittle, E. 516, 517, 518, 519, 522, 523, 525
Hjelmslev, L. 6, 331, 342
Höck, H. 38, 52
Hoel, T. 291
Hoenigswald, H. 43, 52
Hoffer, B. 563, 567
Hoffmann, K. 446, 450
Hoffory, J. 302, 303, 309, 311
Hofman, L. 576, 584
van Holk, A. G. F. 197
Holm, J. 562, 568
Holman, E. 281 - 90, 602
Holt, D. 27, 28, 33, 52
Hooper, J. B. 45, 52, 91, 93, 102, 126, 180, 184, 197
Hopper, P. 314, 315, 316, 320, 321, 379, 393, 529, 546
Horne, M. 291
Horz, H. 587, 599
Householder, F. W. 89, 102
Hrozný, B. 339, 342
Hübschmann, H. 326, 327, 342
Hudson, R. A. 69
Hufgard, J. 109, 126
van der Hulst, H. 229, 230, 231
Hütterer, C. 71, 81
Hyman, L. 47, 52, 107, 126
Hymes, D. 48, 50, 51

Ilev, S. 100, 102
Ilyish, B. A. 99, 102
Imre, S. 102, 197
Itkonen, E. 90, 102, 299, 435, 538
Itkonen, T. 44, 52

INDEX OF NAMES

Ivanov, V. V. 7, 9, 22, 314, 320, 529, 546
Ivić, P. 191, 197
Ivsić, S. 191, 197

Jaberg, K. 431, 438
Jackendoff, R. S. 79, 82, 205, 215
Jacobs, M. 30, 34, 52
Jacobsen, W. H. ,jr. 31, 32, 43, 52
Jacobsohn, H. 347, 351, 352
Jahr, E. H. 291 - 300, 602
Jakobson, R. 26, 27, 28, 29, 42, 43, 52, 93, 98, 102, 125, 264, 278, 279, 313, 321, 520, 523, 525
Jankowsky, K. R. 301 - 11, 547, 602
Janson, T. 59, 63, 70
Jasanoff, J. 444, 445, 450
Jasper, S. P. 563, 567
Jeffers, R. J. 252, 264
Jellinek, M. H. 311
Jensen, F. 172, 180
Jespersen, O. 105, 126, 184, 197, 427, 438, 452, 465
Job, M. 601
Jochelson, W. 383, 394
Joly, A. 138
Jones, C. 249, 264, 546
Jones, D. 98, 102
Jonsson, H. 334, 337, 340, 342
Joseph, B. 313 - 21
Jucker, A. 245
Juilland, A. 126, 348, 352, 453, 465

Kachru, B. B. 568
Kalman, B. 94, 102, 184, 197
Karlsson, F. 604
Kastovsky, D. 126, 438
Kats, J. 225, 226, 227, 233
Katz, H. 28, 30, 53
Kaufman, T. 27, 30, 33, 41, 42, 44, 47, 53, 55
Kay, P. 517
Kaye, J. 110, 126, 525
Kazlauskas, J. 442, 450
Keenan, E. 429
Keiler, A. R. 181
Keller, R. F. 94, 102
Keniston, H. 39, 53

Kesisoglou, I. I. 112, 113, 119, 123, 126, 127
Kettunen, L. 45, 53
Keymeulen, L. 490, 496
Kholodovič, A. A. 344
Kim-Renaud, Y. -K. 537, 546
King, R. D. 49, 94, 97, 102, 173, 174, 180
Kinkade, D. 45, 46, 53
Kiparsky, P. 173, 174, 181, 196, 197, 299, 490, 496, 550, 559
Klemensiewicz, Z. 578, 584
Klingenschmitt, G. 442, 443, 444, 450
Kluge, F. 270, 279, 310, 335, 336, 342, 358, 363
Koerner, E. F. K. 323 - 45, 602
Kolbuszewski, S. 605
Kolln, H. 441, 442, 450
Kondratjev, V. 87, 102
Korhonen, M. 44, 53
Körner, J. 302, 306, 311
Kortlandt, F. 87
Koster, J. 203, 215
Koziol, H. 463, 465
Krahe, H. 141, 147
Kraseninnikova, E. 504, 514
von Kraus, C. 311
Krauss, M. E. 386, 394
Kretschmer, P. 110, 116, 126
Kristensson, G. 88, 92, 102
Kroeber, A. L. 35, 53
Krumova, J. 88, 102
Kruszewski, M. 325, 342
Kuiper, F. B. J. 38, 41, 53
Kuliš, L. J. 98, 102
Kunene, E. C. L. 262, 264
Kurath, H. 25, 53, 483, 486
Kurkiewicz-Rzepkowa, E. 580, 584
Kurkowska, H. 581, 584
Kuryłowicz, J. 4, 22, 338, 339, 343, 571, 584
Kytö, M. 567, 568

Labov, W. 104, 110, 127, 184, 197, 224, 467, 468, 470, 486
LaBrum, R. 50
Ladefoged, P. 253, 264, 278, 279
Lakoff, G. 397, 406
Lakoff, R. 97, 102

INDEX OF NAMES

Lambrecht, K. 235, 238, 240, 241, 242, 243, 245, 248
Langdon, M. 52
Lanham, L. W. 257, 264
Lapesa, R. 38, 53
Larsen, A. B. 300
Larsson, E. 235, 237, 239, 240, 241, 342, 244, 245, 246, 248
Lass, R. 84, 95, 97, 99, 103, 140, 142, 143, 144, 145, 146, 147, 258, 260, 261, 262, 263, 264, 270, 279, 292, 293, 299, 300, 427, 428, 430, 437, 438
Lee, K. 367, 394
Leech, G. 406, 526
Lehmann, Ch. 208, 216
Lehmann, W. P. 104, 126, 200, 216, 313, 321, 330, 343
Lehnert, M. 453, 465
Lehrman, S. 353
Lejeune, M. 344, 351, 352
Lentz, W. 208, 216
Lenz, K. 99, 103
Leskien, A. 310, 332, 344
Leslau, W. 37, 47, 54
Leumann, M. 59, 70, 434, 439
Levi, J. N. 82
Lewis, G. L. 87, 95, 103, 223, 233, 379, 394
Li, C. 52, 216, 241, 244, 248, 406, 525
Liberman, M. 228, 233
Lightfoot, D. 396, 399, 403, 405, 406
Linde, S. B. 575, 584
Linell, P. 116, 121, 127
Lisker, L. 253, 264
Lockwood, W. B. 499, 514
Lorentz, O. 291, 299, 300
Łoś, J. 584
Lottner, C. 528, 546
Lötzsch, R. 11, 22
Louw, J. 41, 53
Lüdtke, H. 427, 439
Lugton, R. C. 82
Luick, K. 84, 99, 103, 529, 546
Lunt, H. 22, 51
Lutz, A. 527
Lyons, J. 129, 138, 395, 406

Macaułay, K. S. 102, 103, 104

McCormick, S. 224, 233
McCourt, D. 565, 568
Macnamara, J. 439
Maddieson, J. 537, 538, 539, 540, 546
Magnuszewski, J. 485
Maher, J. P. 102
Malikouti, A. 108, 127
Malkiel, Y. 104, 126, 432, 439
Mallinson, G. 205, 216
Malmberg, B. 37, 53, 88, 263, 270, 279
Man, E. H. 370, 371, 394
Mańczak, W. 15, 16, 23, 347 - 54, 580, 584, 605
Mandelbaum, D. 55
Marckwardt, A. 157, 565, 568
Mareš, F. V. 11, 23, 126, 196
Mark, J. 508, 513, 514
Markey, T. L. 353 - 64
Marm, J. 291, 294, 297, 300
Maroldt, K. 463, 465
Martin, L. 39, 54
Martinet, A. 31, 54, 143, 146, 147, 184, 197, 261, 428, 553, 554, 555, 556, 557, 559
Maruzeau, J. 129, 138, 442, 450
Masica, C. P. 28, 31, 38, 41, 47, 51, 54
Matejka, L. 21
Mater, E. 465
Matisoff, J. 46, 54
Matthews, P. H. 57, 70, 117, 127
Mavroxalividis, 112, 113, 119, 127
Mayenowa, M. R. 577, 584
Mayer, H. E. 9, 23
Mayerthaler, W. 105, 106, 107, 116, 119, 125, 126, 127, 429, 430, 431, 435, 439, 589, 599
Mayrhofer, W. 326, 332, 334, 337, 343, 543, 546
Meenakshisundaran, T. 43, 54
Meid, W. 23, 141, 147, 300
Meillet, A. 316, 321, 326, 338, 351, 571, 574, 583, 584
Meinhold, G. 270, 279
Meisel, J. 249, 435, 439, 465
Melchior, A. B. 92, 103
Menéndez Pidal, R. 37, 54
Menges, K. H. 47, 54
Meyer, G. 324, 343

INDEX OF NAMES

Meyer, R. M. 311
Meyer-Lübke, W. 172, 180, 181
Migliorini, B. 432, 439
Miller, W. 45, 54
Mincoff, M. 92 94, 103
Minikowska, T. 578, 584
Mithun, M. 36, 50, 316, 321, 365 - 94
Mitzka, W. 270, 279, 358, 363
Moignet, G. 129, 130, 135, 137, 138
Möller, H. 326, 335, 336, 337, 338, 339, 343
Montgomery, M. 561, 568
Moore, T. E. 525
Moortgate, M. 229, 233
Moravcsik, E. A. 47, 54, 251, 264, 526
Morawski, J. 575, 580, 584
Morin, Y. -C. 558, 559
Moulton, W. G. 528, 546
Mufwene, S. S. 406, 486
Mühlhäusler, P. 464, 465
Müllenhoff, K. 302, 303, 311
Müller-Hauser, M. -L. 235, 241, 243, 245, 246, 248
Murayama, H. 421, 422, 424
Murray, R. W. 527
Mzamane, G. I. M. 258, 264

Nadkarni, M. 34, 47, 54
Nagucka, R. 395 - 407, 605
Narten, J. 446, 450
van Nes, J. J. 229, 233
Neu, E. 23
Neue, F. 59, 70
Newman, S. 51
Newton, B. 42, 44, 47, 54, 112, 115, 127, 181
Neyt, A. 229, 233
Nida, E. A. 91, 103, 418, 425
Niedermann, M. 60, 70
Niedzielski, H. 604
Nienaber, G. S. 73, 82
Nilsen, D. L. F. 516, 525
Nixon, G. 406
Nomoto, K. 409, 425
Normier, R. 529, 546

Oeconomides, D. 112, 127

Ogura, M. 150, 151, 157, 158, 165, 166, 167, 170
Ogura, S. 409, 425
Ohala, J. 251, 264, 291, 292, 293, 294, 300
Ono, S. 420, 424, 425
Orzechowska, H. 19, 23
Osthoff, H. 310, 311, 324, 330, 343
Oswalt, R. L. 47, 54

Palmer, F. R. 103
Pam, M. D. 249
Panagl, O. 105, 106, 119, 126
Panconcelli-Calzia, G. 256, 264
Papadopoulos, A. A. 112, 127
Paraškevov, B. 103
Park, H. S. 537, 546
Parks, D. 384, 394
Patev, P. 100, 103
Paul, H. 310, 311, 323, 343
Pedersen, H. 337, 338, 339, 341
Peé, W. 228, 233
Peeters, C. 341, 321
Peirce, C. 105, 127, 520, 525
Peng, F. C. C. 409 - 25, 601
Penzl, H. 140, 147, 269, 279
Peranteau, P. M. 82
Pernot, H. 109, 127
Perveva, E. 88, 103
Peters, S. 197
Petersen, W. 343
Pfeiffer, F. 302
Pfeiffer, O. E. 50
Phares, G. C. 82
Picoche, J. 571, 584
Pieper, U. 22
Pinnow, H. -J. 379, 382, 394
Pisani, V. 347, 350, 352, 571, 584
Plotkin, V. Y. 143, 147
Pokorny, J. 317, 318, 321, 357, 363, 561, 526
Polivanov, E. 83, 84, 91, 103
Polomé, E. C. 331, 339, 340, 343, 527, 542, 547
Popowska-Taborska, H. 12, 23
Popperwell, R. G. 294, 296, 297, 298, 300
Postal, P. 397, 406

INDEX OF NAMES

Posti, L. 290
Poussa, P. 96, 103
Powell, J. 45, 46, 53
Pray, B. R. 34, 47, 54
Prilucki, N. 504, 505, 507, 514
Prince, A. 228, 233
Prins, A. A. 145, 148
Prokosch, E. 314, 321
Puhvel, J. 21, 52, 356, 364
Pullum, G. 264
Pusch, L. 604, 606
Putseys, Y. 149, 150, 170

Quirk, R. 279, 396, 400, 406, 516, 526

Raidt, E. H. 81, 82
Ramamurti, G. V. 394
Ramanujan, A. K. 28, 38, 41, 54
Ramat, A. G. 427 - 39, 606
Ramat, P. 435, 439
Rapola, M. 44, 45, 54
Rask, R. 528
Rasmussen, J. E. 441 - 50, 605
Rauch, I. 547
von Raume, R. 306, 528, 547
Rawick, G. 468, 470, 487
Redard, G. 324, 325, 327, 328, 343
Redbird, S. 369, 370, 393
Redei, K. 47, 54
Regnaud, P. 325, 326, 344
Reiter, N. 18, 21, 23
Rennison, J. R. 50
Renou, L. 446, 450
Reszkiewicz, A. 92, 103
Rhys, Sir John 324, 325, 344
Richards, H. J. 567
van Riemsdjik, H. 214, 216
Ringen, J. 42, 50, 90, 101
Risch, E. 62, 64, 65, 66, 70
Rissanen, M. 567, 568
Robertson, J. S. 379, 381, 394
Robins, R. H. 87, 103
Robinson, O. W. 497
Rodman, R. 235, 241, 244, 246, 248
Rohrer, C. 248
Romaine, S. 451 - 466, 605
Romportl, M. 126
Roques, M. 25, 51

Rosenbaum, P. 397
Rosenberg, S. 321, 442
Roenfeld, H. F. 347, 351, 352
Ross, J. R. 80, 82, 214, 216, 244, 248
Royen, G. 225, 233
Rūke-Dravina, V. 21
Ruwet, N. 248

Saari, M. 604, 605
Sadock, J. 170
Salzer, G. 82
Samilov, M. 86, 89, 103
Sanders, G. A. 93 ń
Sandoval, L. 39, 54
Sapir, E. 33, 36, 43, 45, 46, 47, 54, 55, 213, 286, 390, 391, 394
Saukkonen, P. 604, 606
Saussure, F. 323 - 45, 414, 415, 520, 521, 522
Scatton, E. A. 89, 103
Schaller, H. 2, 19, 23
Schane, S. A. 93, 97, 103, 549, 559
Scherer, W. 301 - 11
Schindler, J. 120, 127
Schleicher, A. 6, 326, 329, 332, 336, 344
Schlesinger, I. M. 516, 526
Schmid, W. P. 7, 23, 441, 442, 450
Schmidt, E. 311
Schmidt, J. 308, 311, 325, 332, 347, 350, 352
Schmitt-Brandt, R. 331, 344
Schmitz, J. 225, 233
Schneider, E. 467 - 87
Schönfeld, M. 347, 352
Schroder, E. 302, 309, 311
Schuchardt, H. 25, 55, 563, 568
Schwartz, A. 208, 216
Sebeok, T. 26, 53, 54, 263, 344, 525
Sechehaye, A. 328, 341, 344
Seckel, D. 308, 311
Sedlak, P. 95, 103
Seidel, E. 27, 55
Seiler, H.-J. 106, 118, 121, 122, 123, 127, 209, 216, 362, 364
Selinker, L. 88, 103
Selkirk,. E. O. 228, 229, 233
Selmer, E. 257, 264
Sen, A. L. 566, 568

Sezer, E. 223, 232
Shephard, S. 50
Sherzer, J. 26, 27, 28, 29, 33, 34, 35, 36, 40, 43, 46, 49, 55
Shuy, R. W. 249
Sievers, E. 139, 310
Silver, S. 52
Silverstein, M. 34, 47, 55
Simić, R. 17, 23
Šipova, E. N. 86, 103
Sjoberg, A. F. 50
Skalička, V. 95, 96, 103, 106, 119, 125, 127
Sławski, F. 571, 584
Slobin, D. 437, 439, 525
Smith, H. L. 140, 148
Smith, N. 232, 233, 291, 300
Smith-Stark, T. 48
Solta, G. R. 18, 23
Sommer, B. 382, 394
Sommer, F. 59, 70, 347, 350, 352
Sommerfelt, A. 291, 294, 297, 300
Sommerstein, A. H. 176, 181
Specht, F. 449, 450
Spešnev, N. A. 88, 103
Spier, L. 51
Spitzer, L. 25, 55
Spuler, B. 216
Stajnova, M. 87
Stampe, D. 89, 93, 96, 97, 103, 109, 125, 127
Stang, C. S. 9, 23, 354, 360, 364, 441, 442, 450
Steblin-Kamenskij, M. I. 92, 103
Steever, S. B. 406, 486
Stefanini, J. 129, 134, 138
Steiner, R. 184, 197
Stephenson, E. A. 566, 568
Stewart, W. 561
Stickel, G. 22
Stieber, Z. 12, 23
Stock, E. 270 - 279
Stockwell, R. P. 102, 103, 104, 399, 406
Stojkov, S. 89, 104
Stolz, B. 353
Streitberg, W. 326, 344
Sturtevent, E. H. 7, 23

Suárez, V. M. 55
Susuki-Jinushi, T. 419, 425
Suzman, S. M. 262, 265
Svartvik, J. 406, 526
Swadesh, M. 43, 55, 390, 391, 394
Swanson, E. 51
Swanton, J. R. 386, 394
Sweet, H. 139, 334, 335, 336, 344
Szemerényi, O. 314, 321, 333, 335, 337, 338, 340, 344, 347, 350, 352
Szlesiński, I. 578, 579, 584

Taeldeman, J. 489 - 97, 605
Tai, J. 34, 47, 55
Tannen, D. 524, 526
Taszycki, W. 575, 584
Truszkowski, W. 585
Tauke, M. 499 - 514
Tekavcić, P. 172, 181
Ternes, E. 89, 104
Thavoris, A. I. 108, 127
Thomason, S. G. 27, 30, 34, 41, 42, 44, 47, 48, 55
Thompson, S. A. 241, 244, 248, 379, 393
Thumb, A. 127, 430, 439
Thurneysen, R. 273, 279
Timmer, E. H. 515, 526
Tollemache, F. 432, 433, 439
Toller, T. N. 170
Tolstoj, N. I. 22
Topolińska, Z. 12, 23
Toporov, V. N. 9, 22
Torp, A. 357, 358, 363
Trager, G. L. 140, 148
Traugott, E C. 50, 438, 515 - 26, 605
Trautmann, R. 23, 441, 450
Traversa, V. 348, 352
Trnka, B. 140, 147, 148
Trubačev, O. N. 7, 9, 23, 445, 450
Trubetzkoy (Trubeckoj) 6, 7, 23, 26, 27, 28, 29, 33, 41, 53, 56, 88, 89, 96, 104
Trudgill, P. 434, 439
Truszkowski, W. 576
Tschirch, F. 499, 514
Tucker, A. N. 258, 265
Turunen, A. 44, 45, 56

INDEX OF NAMES

Twaddell, W. F. 92, 104

Udolph, J. 9, 24

Vachek, J. 84, 104
Valdman, A. 568
Vallini, C. 328, 345
Vassant, A. 129, 138
Velčeva, B. 95, 104
Velten, H. V. 26, 56
Venås, K. 291
Vendryes, J. 44, 47, 56
Venezky, R. L. 170
Vennemann, T. 174, 181, 199, 200, 216, 236, 249, 291, 299, 300, 527 - 47, 569, 601
Vergnaud, J. R. 217, 222, 223, 225, 226, 228, 232
Verluyten, S. P. 549 - 59
Verner, K. 528, 533, 534, 535, 547
Viereck, W. 468, 487, 561 - 9, 605
Viëtor, W. 139
Vincent, N. B. 244, 249
Vincenzi, G. C. 331, 341, 342, 344, 345
Visser, F. Th. 399, 402, 403, 406
Voegelin, C. F. 27, 56
Vogt, H. 41, 56
Voeltz, E. 256
Vogt, H. 297, 300
Vorlat, E. 149, 150, 170
Voyles, J. 92, 104
de Vries, J. 358, 364

Wagener, C. 59, 70
Wagner, H. 26, 56
Walczak, B. 571 - 85, 605
Walde, A. 516, 526
Walker, C. A. 406, 486
Walker, E. C. T. 248
Wallis, J. 87
Walter, H. 550, 553, 554, 555, 556, 557, 559
Wang, W. S.-Y. 110, 127, 172, 181
von Wartburg, W. 95, 572, 583, 585
Wasaw, T. 406
Wasson R. O. J. 515, 526
Watkins 200, 201, 216, 328, 323, 341, 345
Waugh, L. 99, 102

Weinreich, U. 2, 24, 28, 34, 42, 47, 56, 88, 89, 94, 104, 197
Weinsberg, A. 571, 572, 585
Weinstock, H. 148
Wells, R. V. 561, 569
Wełna, J. 277, 279
Weltfish, G' 385, 394
Werner, J. M. 304, 311
West, M. 149, 170
Western, A. 297, 300
Westphal, E. O. 40, 56, 257, 258, 260, 265
Wexler, K. 398, 406
Whitney, W. D. 311
Wieden, W. 98, 104
Wiegand, H. E. 51
Wiegand, N. 435, 439
Wiggen, G. 291
Wikberg, K. 291
Wilbur, T. H. 181, 300
Wilkoń, A. 583
Williams, E. 214, 216
Wilmet, M. 131, 138
Wilson, R. 34, 47, 51
Windfuhr, G. 208, 216
Winter, W. 28, 34, 56, 343, 602, 604
Wise, C. M. 467, 487
Włodek, I. 582, 585
Wode, H. 91, 104
Wolfe, P. 144, 148
Wolfe, R. 515
Wolff, H. 27, 56
Wolfram, 467, 468, 487
Wood, G. 472, 479, 483, 487
Worth, D. S. 383, 384, 394
Wrenn, C. L. 268, 279
Wurzel, W. U. 106, 107, 115, 116, 119, 125, 126, 127, 269, 281, 290, 430, 439, 587 - 99
Wyld, H. C. 344

Yaeger, M. 184, 197
Yetman, N. K. 468, 487

Zamora, V. A. 39, 56
Zaręba, A. 578, 585
Zarecki, A. 513, 514
Zeps, Vl 27, 56

Zide, N. H. 394
Ziervogel, D. 295, 265
Zimmer, H. 305, 311, 393
Zimmer, K. 380
Žirmunskij V. M. 92, 103, 104
Zinkevičius, Z. 448, 450
Zolli, P. 571, 583

Zonneveld, W. 229, 233, 497
Zubizaretta, M. L. 228, 233
Žuravlev, V. K. 5, 24
Zvelebil, K. 43, 56
Zwanziger, R. 208, 211, 215
Zwicky, A. 98, 104